RESEARCH METHODS

HOW TO CONDUCT RESEARCH IN RECREATION, PARKS, SPORT, AND TOURISM

3RD ED.

CAROL CUTLER RIDDICK

RUTH V. RUSSELL

Publishers: Joseph J. Bannon and Peter L. Bannon
Marketing Manager: Emily Wakefield
Sales Manager: Misti Gilles
Director of Development and Production: Susan M. Davis
Technology Manager: Keith Hardyman
Production Coordinator: Amy S. Dagit
Interior and Cover Designer: Julie Schechter

Library of Congress Control Number: 2015935752
ISBN print edition: 978-1-57167-718-1
ISBN ebook: 978-1-57167719-8

Printed in the United States

1807 N Federal Dr.
Urbana, IL 61801
www.sagamorepublishing.com

DEDICATION

To Dr. Betty van der Smissen, our first research methods teacher. Her commitment and enthusiastic teaching inspired us to believe objective inquiry is not only critically important for our professions, but also fascinating to study. In celebration of her life, we thank her for this as well as for the years of dedication she showed us.

CONTENTS

PREFACE

This is a third edition of the text originally titled *Evaluative Research in Recreation, Park, and Sport Settings: Searching for Useful Information* and then titled for the second edition as *How to Conduct Research in Recreation, Parks, Sport, and Tourism*. As was true with previous editions, we were guided during the revision process by feedback received from students, instructors, and practitioners.

Target Audience

The target audiences for this book are upper level undergraduates and graduate students in research methods courses, as well as professionals working in the fields of recreation, parks, sport, and tourism. Via incorporating contemporary examples, we wrote the text for those who have had little or no prior involvement in research undertakings.

We wrote this book first to share with you fundamental knowledge about what research is and the ways it can be carried out and reported. The second purpose is to equip you with the ability to critique research presented at professional meetings and in journals or study proposals. The third aim is to prepare you with the skills and understandings needed to carry out or participate in a small-scale research investigation.

Organization of the Book

We have retained the overall organization of the second edition and present the following units:

1. Overview. Presents definitions, categories of research, motives for initiating research, stakeholders interested in research, indicators for judging a "quality" research study, characteristics of a "good" researcher, and the stages and steps involved in the research process.
2. Getting Started. Covers deciding on a topic, reviewing literature, identifying theoretical roots, determining scope, and explaining significance.
3. Develop a Plan. Describes selecting a sample, choosing design, considering measurement, specifying data collection instruments, addressing ethical responsibilities, and seeking proposal approval.
4. Implementation. Reviews conducting a pilot study, preparing for data collection, and analyzing quantitative and qualitative data.
5. Reporting. Includes how-to information on creating visual aids, writing a report, and delivering a presentation.

Features

We start each chapter with an orientation outline and a relevant quote. Furthermore, as a trigger device, important words and concepts, when first introduced, are bolded and italicized. A glossary is included at the end of the book.

We kept the feature boxes introduced in the second edition and introduced additional features. In sum, you will find the following assistive devices in each chapter:

- SOMETHING TO REMEMBER! underscores an important point.
- IDEA offers straightforward, practical how-to advice.
- TEST YOURSELF (new to this edition, with answers provided at the end of the chapter) provides a quick check to assess your comprehension.
- HUMOR BOX (also new to this edition) uses a funny example to reinforce an important point.
- Your Research (new to this edition) presents an opportunity for applying chapter materials to planning your own research project.

- Review and Discussion Questions assist in determining mastery of chapter content.
- Web Exercises present computer-based activities that tie into the chapter. (*Note:* URL references were correct at the time of publication, but you may need to update them later).
- Practice Exercises contain activities that complement and expand upon chapter material that may be completed in class or assigned as homework outside of the class meeting time.
- Service Learning (another new feature) provides a template for guiding the class on designing, implementing, and reporting on a survey research study that examines a campus recreation facility or service.
- Case Studies (now found at the end of each chapter) illustrate a point made in the chapter by citing research or a real-world example.
- Glossary (also new to this edition and located at the back of the book) defines keywords that were introduced in a chapter.
- Appendices provide valuable resources for extending the educational value of this text.

Supplemental Resources

The password-protected Instructor's Manual accompanying this text has also been revised. The manual contains a new PowerPoint presentation for each chapter. With this third edition, much of the art work, figures, and special features (Case Studies, Something to Remember, Idea, and Test Yourself boxes) in each chapter have been included in the PowerPoint presentations to assist the instructor in creating customized classroom presentations. Also, the manual contains a revised test bank (suggested questions are presented in essay and multiple-choice formats) along with exam review questions and answers set up to be played by teams in a Jeopardy-style format. For more information about the Instructor's Manual, contact Sagamore Publishing LLC at www.sagamorepublishing.com or phone toll free (in North America) 800.327.5557.

Feedback

As with the previous editions of this book, we would be interested in receiving comments and suggestions from students and instructors. We are already on the lookout for new material and changes to incorporate into the next edition! Our contact information is as follows:

Carol Cutler Riddick
Gallaudet University
Department of Physical Education
and Recreation
800 Florida Ave N.E.
Washington, DC 20002
carol.riddick@gallaudet.edu

Ruth V. Russell
russellr@indiana.edu

ACKNOWLEDGEMENTS

Foremost, we want to let the world know how much we continue to value each other. Who could imagine how fortuitous it was when we began graduate studies long ago at The Pennsylvania State University!

Carol is also indebted to students, especially former student Kevin Bohlin, who shared a multitude of ideas on how to improve the content and appearance of the third edition. She also acknowledges the love and support of her family and friends throughout the revision process.

Ruth also extends appreciation to those who have directly and indirectly supported her enterprise on this book, including faculty colleagues and undergraduate and graduate students in the Department of Recreation, Park, and Tourism Studies at Indiana University, Bloomington.

Carol Cutler Riddick
Ruth V. Russell
November 2014

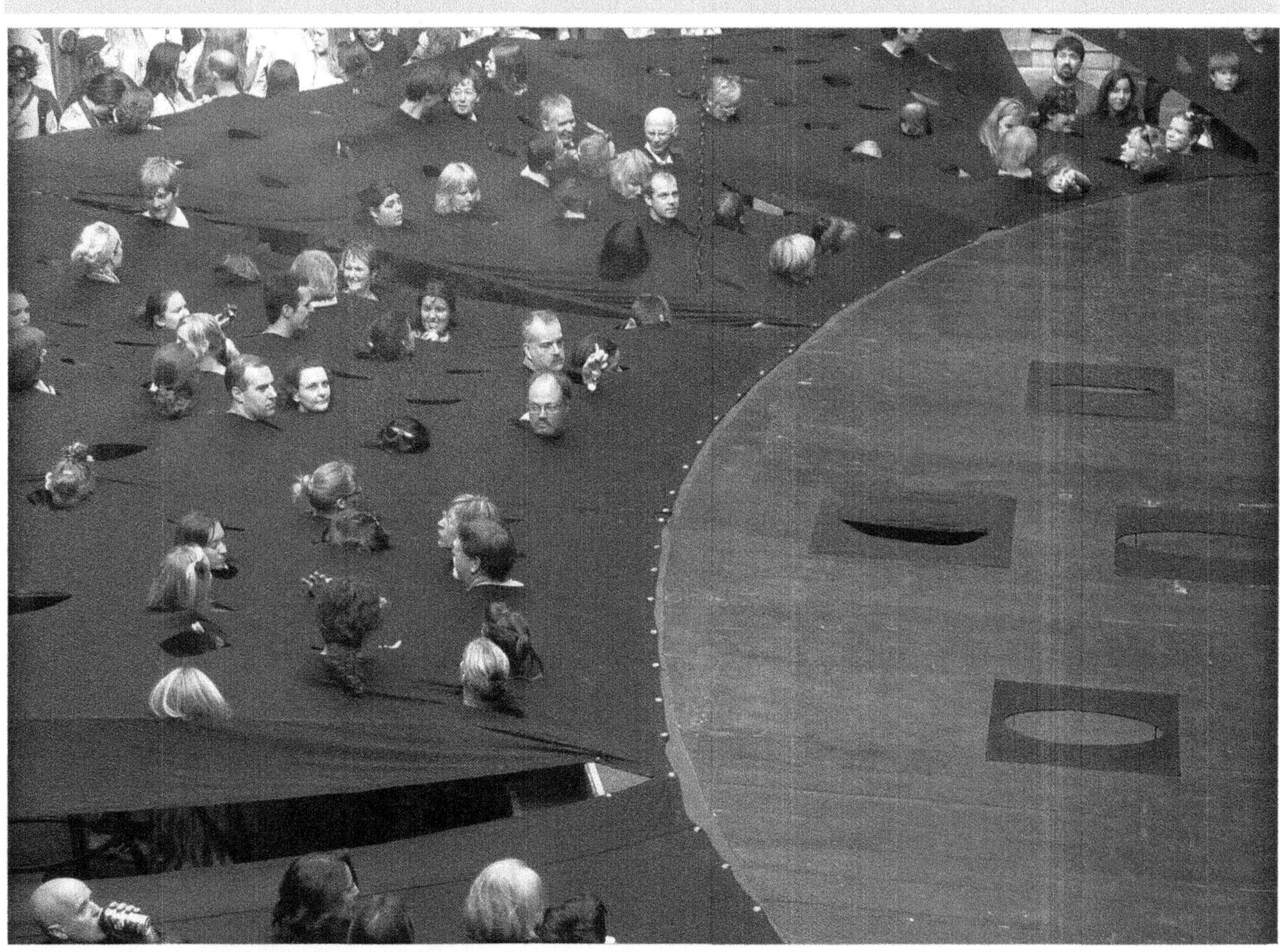

Similar to the up front "groundlings" featured in this photo, this chapter provides a research-in-the round overview, Globe Theatre, London.

PART I
OVERVIEW

WHAT WILL I LEARN IN THIS CHAPTER?

I'll be able to...

1. Provide two definitions of research.
2. Distinguish between applied and basic research.
3. Identify and explain three goals to guide the research study.
4. Describe three motives for initiating a research project.
5. Define stakeholder and recall six groups of stakeholders who may be interested in a research study.
6. Diagram and explain the four-part adaptive cycle that accounts for interactions between the researcher and stakeholders as a study is being planned.
7. Name and distinguish between primary and secondary data sources.
8. Recall and explain three indicators for judging a quality research study.
9. List characteristics of a good researcher.
10. Outline the stages for conducting a research study: getting started, planning, implementation, and reporting.

"Learning is like rowing upstream; not to advance is to drop back."

Chinese proverb

Individuals working in universities, hospitals, organizations, governments, and other think tank settings conduct research. Thus, the number and range of topics researchers choose for research investigations is staggering!

Indeed, social science researchers tend to delve into everyday as well as curious subject matter. For instance, researchers at Cornell University examined 509 million Twitter posts made by 2.4 million users living in 84 countries over 2 years (Golder & Macy, 2011). It took 50 computers working nonstop for 6 weeks to analyze the messages posted by individuals who made their tweets public when they signed up for the service. Perhaps it comes as little surprise to learn one finding of this study was that people are happier on weekends compared to weekdays!

The bottom line is, you are bombarded with research on a daily basis! Thus, the challenge confronting you is being able to discern good science from junk science. Hopefully, by the time you finish reading this text, you will be able to review studies and conduct your own research with a discerning eye and mind.

WHAT IS RESEARCH?

Research has been defined two ways:

- as a "process of collecting, analyzing, and interpreting information" (Leedy & Ormrod, 2012, p. 2) and
- as a way to "advance human knowledge...The aim is discovery" (Elias & Dunning, 1986, p. 20).

Embrace both meanings. Research encompasses how you know what you know and involves following a process to gain more knowledge about a topic.

Whether you are designing, reading, or listening to a research report, realize that you or someone else has had to answer two fundamental questions:

1. What is the focus of the research?
2. What is the goal of the research?

Research Focus

One way to categorize research is to consider the focus of the study in terms of its application, or usefulness (Figure 0.1). That is, the research is either deemed applied research or basic.

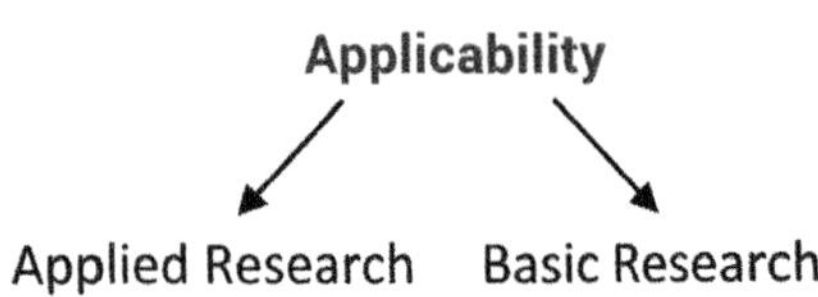

Figure 0.1. Research focus.

Applied research. You may use ***applied research***, also known as program evaluation or evaluative research, to assess or appraise a program or social intervention. The emphasis of applied research is on the practical; that is, it is used to examine service delivery.

Usually the motivation behind applied research is to determine whether a program is working or achieving its goals or to use results to improve practice or the program itself. For example, Daud and Carruthers (2008) investigated the developmental impact participating in an after-school program (that included sports, chess, music, art, drama, and dance lessons) had on youth who resided in high-risk environments.

Applied research (as will be emphasized in Step 1) is focused on real-world topics such as

- determining the need for a program;
- describing what a program offers and/or how it is funded and marketed;
- monitoring program participation levels;
- assessing program participants' reactions to a program;
- evaluating the impact a program has on participants' knowledge, attitude, skill/functional ability, and/ or aspiration change;
- examining behavior changes as a result of program participation; and/or
- investigating the effects of program participation on a social problem.

Basic research. On the other hand, you may use basic research to understand phenomena or behaviors at an abstract or theoretical level: acquiring knowledge for the sake of knowledge. This category of research arises from a person's intellectual curiosity or a desire to understand an esoteric topic rather than a topic of immediate, practical usefulness. Researchers usually use basic research to test or formulate a theory.

You may also use ***basic research*** (sometimes referred to as blue sky research) to understand conceptually aspects of aspects of a recreation- or leisure-related phenomena. For example, Palen, Caldwell, Smith, Gleeson, and Patrick (2011) examined what adolescents living near Cape Town, South Africa, do with their free time and, the motivations that influenced their free time usage (see Case 0.1).

Ideally, you gain through basic research a fundamental understanding about a topic. According to Wann (1997), "Quality basic research is the lifeblood of any scientific discipline. Without it, disciplines would stagnate, failing to advance past their current limits of understanding" (p. 17).

Interface between basic research and applied research. Sometimes basic research findings have practi-

DISTINGUISH BETWEEN APPLIED RESEARCH AND BASIC RESEARCH

Directions: For each of the following research questions, decide whether the focus exemplifies an applied or basic research topic.

Research Question	Applied research	Basic research
1. Does playing in a Grand Theft Auto tournament trigger adolescents to steal vehicles?		
2. What are people's motivations for littering?		
3. Why do some people chose to hike and others do not?		
4. What factors predict tourists' travel choices?		
5. Does participation in a noon-time, work site Zumba class affect participants' feelings of wellness?		
6. How do children like the Saturday morning public recreation program in which they participate?		

Note. Answers are provided at the end of the chapter.

cal usefulness. Dr. Roy Plunkett's basic research discovery when he was experimenting with chemical reactions to refrigerant gases led to everyday applications. A stuck cylinder valve produced a waxy solid mass with a high melting point. Eventually, this glob was named Teflon. Through the years many applications for Teflon have been found, including in cookware coating, soil and stain repellant for textiles, wire coating, and pharmaceutical production ("Inventor of the Week," 2000).

According to Lewin (as cited in Stangor, 2011), in practice, basic and applied research "inform each other" (p. 12). Basic research may provide a glimmer about ways to formulate programs or interventions. For example, Petrick, Backman, Bixler, and Norman (2001) examined study motivations for playing golf, but wound up conjecturing how their findings could enhance golf course operations.

EXAMPLE OF BASIC RESEARCH EMBEDDED IN THE CLOUDS

Two dudes riding in a hot air balloon got lost. Upon landing they realized they had no clue where they were. About this time a man walked by and one of the balloonists hollered out, "Where are we?" The walker replied, "You're in a hot air balloon." One guy in the balloon turned to his friend and commented, "I bet that man is a researcher." His traveling companion responded, "What makes you think so?" The first guy replied, "Because his answer is perfectly accurate and yet totally useless."

Adapted from Day and Gastel (2012).

Applied research may also trigger topic ideas for basic research. For instance, fitness programs are typically set up to help individuals lose weight, yet participants often do not experience a significant drop in their weight! Researchers have extended understanding of this by identifying underlying principles (e.g., the importance of a social support system) that should be incorporated into programs set up to help people lose weight.

Undoubtedly, a need exists to bridge the gap between researchers who are more interested in basic research and practitioners who depend on applied research. Some journals have attempted to provide this bridge. For instance, the *Journal of Physical Education, Recreation, and Dance* distributes applied research findings to recreation leaders, coaches, and fitness instructors via a featured column "Research Works" (http://www.aahperd.org/publications/journals/joperd/joperdissues.cfm).

Research Goal

You may also categorize research according to its goal. Are you conducting the research to describe, explain, or predict (Figure 0.2)?

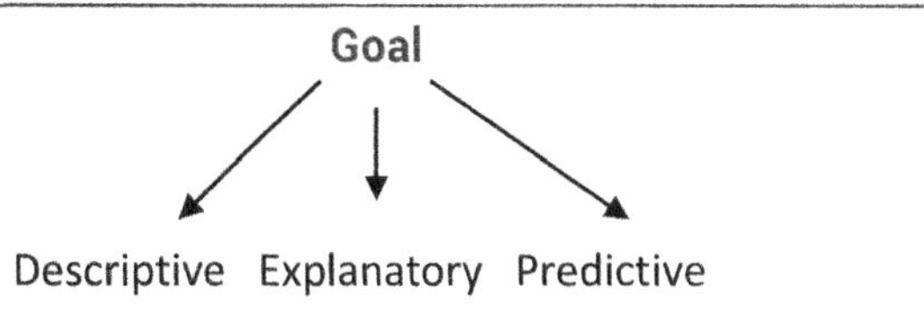

Figure 0.2. Possible goals to direct a study.

Descriptive research. Use ***descriptive research*** to understand what, where, and when. In other words, you will describe characteristics about a phenomenon rather than provide causal explanations to how or why an event occurs. For example, White, Aquino, Budruk, and Golub (2011) examined Yosemite National Park visitors' travel experiences, attitudes, and behaviors (see Case 0.2).

Explanatory research. Use ***explanatory research*** to examine examine if, why, or how something happens. In explanatory research, you will scrutinize relationships or linkages between or among social phenomena. For instance, in explanatory research, you may examine relationships within the context of a program or activity. For instance, Breunig, O'Connell, Todd, Anderson, and Young (2010) looked at how participation in a 13-day wilderness trip effected changes in college students' perceptions of sense of community (or "feeling an individual has about belonging to a group") over time (see Case 0.3).

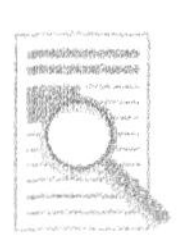

A second approach to explanatory research is to examine how two or more phenomena are related. The context of such a study is not to examine what happens within a formal program or activity, but rather to examine factors tangentially related to recreation, parks, sport, or tourism. For example, Tirone and Gooseberry (2011) studied how second-generation Canadians whose parents emigrated from South Asia negotiated among and between the cultures they knew and how those negotiations contributed to their leisure and sense of inclusion in the communities where they lived.

Predictive research. You may use ***predictive research*** to ask how factors affect future behaviors, sentiments, or events. For example, Jacobsen, Carlton, and Monroe predicted the satisfaction of persons volunteering (serving in capacities such as monitoring animal populations, teaching hunter safety, and promoting wildlife education to save endangered sea turtles) with Florida's Fish and Wildlife Conservation Commission (see Case 0.4).

Second, you may also use predictive research to estimate population values. For example, Tainsky, Salag, and Santos (2012) projected attendance at the Ultimate Fighting Championship martial arts competition.

Goals for a research study have advantages and disadvantages. These pros and cons are summarized in Table 0.1.

Table 0.1
Comparison of Three Research Goals

Research goal	Advantages	Disadvantages
Descriptive	Used to provide a snapshot of what, where, and when something is occurring.	You cannot examine relationships or linkages between or among phenomena.
Explanatory	Used to understand or explain relationships between or among phenomena.	You cannot conclude with 100% certainty that relationships exist.
Predictive	Used to estimate future events or behaviors or provide estimates of population values.	You cannot consider all the important phenomena that affect events or behaviors.

IDENTIFYING THE APPLICABILITY AND GOALS OF A RESEARCH IDEA

Directions: Read the following ideas for research. For each, decide the following:

1. Applicability... is it an example of an applied or basic research idea?
2. Goal... is its intention to be a descriptive, explanatory, or predictive study?

Topic	Applied research (record A) or basic research (record B)	Descriptive (record D), explanatory (record E), or predictive (record P)
1. Leisure time preferences of teenagers		
2. How participation in a basketball camp affects the development of offensive skills among members of a junior varsity team		
3. Expected number of visitors to Assateague National Seashore during summer 2017		
4. Favorite vacation spots of British retirees this past summer		
5. How attending Camp Mark 7 affects the self-esteem of Deaf adolescents		
6. Forecasting boredom of adults recovering from cocaine addiction		

Note. Answers are provided at the end of the chapter.

MOTIVES FOR INITIATING RESEARCH

What is the catalyst for research? Although many reasons exist for conducting a study, organization, academic, and personal motivations are the major forces.

Organization Motivation

Recreation, park, sport, and tourism organization professionals continually seek to assess program effectiveness and determine ways to improve service delivery, operations, procedures, or policy and justify expenditures. For example, Beeco, Hallo, Baldwin, and McGuire (2011) studied how managers could improve guided night hiking experiences at their parks.

Academic Motivation

Students are sometimes called upon to complete a research paper as part of an undergraduate or graduate degree requirement. Professors are frequently driven to engage in research because of professional need to contribute to the knowledge base of their discipline.

Personal Motivation

Sometimes individuals become involved in a research topic because of their personal experiences or "personal troubles" (Mills, 1959). For example, being a kayaking enthusiast could inspire a person to conduct research on the impacts of flood control projects on the sport.

STAKEHOLDERS

Stakeholders are individuals or groups who have an interest in a program or activity that is being scrutinized in a research study. The stakeholders associated with all studies are as follows:

- Policy decision makers. People who decide whether a program is to be initiated, continued, expanded, or curtailed (e.g., elected officials, funders, board of trustees).
- Program sponsors. The organization that funds the program. The funding organization may be the same entity as the policy decision makers.
- Program participants. Persons or households that receive the service, program, or intervention.
- Program managers. Persons in charge of overseeing and administering the program.
- Front-line staff. Employees and/or volunteers responsible for delivering the program or service.
- Contextual stakeholders. Individuals, organizations, groups, and other people interested or affected by the program being studied (e.g., other agencies, public officials, and/or citizens groups).

IDENTIFYING STAKEHOLDERS FOR A THESIS OR DISSERTATION

Many of you are students who need to write a senior paper, thesis, or dissertation. In tackling this, be aware of the interested and invested parties, within and outside the university, needed for your success.

The list below illustrates key players that could emerge for a study examining the effectiveness of an after-school recreation program offered by a public recreation agency. Before you peek at the examples, see whether you are able to identify the entities that belong to the six stakeholder groups.

Stakeholder group	Examples from the community	Examples from the university
Policy decision makers	• Mayor or county executive • Recreation board • Municipal park and recreation director	• Thesis committee members • Institutional review board
Program sponsors	• County council	• Small grants program
Program participants	• Participants	• Not applicable
Program managers	• After-school program director	• Thesis chair
Front-line staff	• Program staff • Maintenance staff	• Student investigator • Interviewer
Contextual stakeholders	• Other organizations that offer after-school programs (e.g., YMCA) • Local newspapers	• Student's major academic department • University as a whole • Student's parents

The point is, you will typically engage in consultative interactions with stakeholder groups during your research. Patton (2008) pointed out that working with the primary stakeholders, typically the policy decision makers, is necessary, but other stakeholders may be involved depending on the topic.

Indeed, you will interact with the users of the research at certain junctures. These interactions typically result in adapting the research plan. Figure 0.3 shows the timing and the essence of these interactions. That is, in the ***adaptive cycle for planning a study***, you need to

1. actively ask for information from the primary stakeholders, namely, their questions of interest;
2. react to these information needs by drafting a responsive proposal (see Step 11);
3. interact with the primary stakeholders to gather their feedback on the drafted preliminary proposal; and
4. based on stakeholders' feedback, adapt the proposal before implementing it.

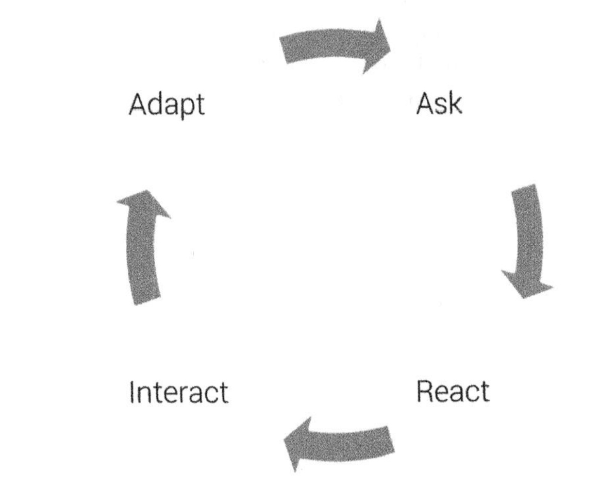

Figure 0.3. Interactions between the researcher and primary stakeholders in the adaptive cycle for planning a study. Adapted from Patton (2008).

DATA SOURCES

Data, the information collected for a study, come from primary and secondary sources. See Figure 0.4.

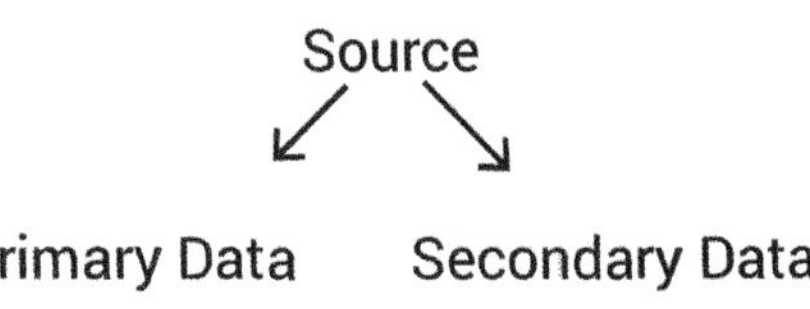

Figure 0.4. Data sources for a study.

Primary data source. If you collect your own data, you have generated a primary data source. A ***primary data*** source has not been previously published and is derived from new or original research. For example, Weybright, Datillo, and Rusch (2010) used primary data to examine how participation in Wii Sports bowling affected attention to task and positive affect (or smiling) for two older women with mild cognitive impairments. Investigators collected data over 36 monitoring sessions.

Secondary data source. Data that have been previously collected by a different person than the present researcher or have been "left behind" and then used by another person come from ***secondary data*** sources. It is thought of as being passed along to a "second set of hands." For example, Jun, Kyle, and O'Leary (2008) examined the constraints faced by people wanting to visit art museums. The authors tapped into a survey funded by the National Endowment for the Arts that had been completed years earlier.

The following are common secondary data sources:

- archived research information (e.g., surveys conducted by governmental agencies and organizations),
- official documents (e.g., census data, newspaper articles, and minutes of recreation board meetings),
- personal documents (e.g., videos, photographs, and letters), and
- physical traces (e.g., the wear in museum floor tiles or carpet, radio dial settings, and trash contents).

LOCATING SOME EXISTING SECONDARY DATA SOURCES

Several secondary data sources exist related to leisure-time recreation behaviors and similar topics:

- The Data Preservation Alliance for Social Sciences (Data-PASS) is funded by the U.S. Library of Congress (as part of the National Digital Preservation Project) and preserves digitalized social science data (http://www.data-pass.org/).
- Governmental surveys, international studies, and longitudinal databases spanning different disciplines and

themes are available to member institutions from the Economic and Social Data Service at the Universities of Sussex and Manchester (http://www.esds.ac.uk/).

- Containing quantitative and qualitative data sets, including videotape and audiotape collections and case study data, The Murray Research Centre at Harvard's Radcliff Institute for Advanced Study (http://www. murray.harvard.edu/) has data on lives over time.
- The National Opinion Research Corporation houses data sets from around the world (http://www.norc.org/ Research/DataFindings/Pages/default.aspx).
- The University of Michigan's Inter-University Consortium for Political and Social Research is a repository of over 500,000 data files of research in the social sciences worldwide. Researchers and students may purchase these computerized data sets (http://www.icpsr.umich.edu/icpsrweb/ICPSR/org).
- The University of Southern Maine's Life Story Center collects interview transcripts that record the life stories of people of diverse ages and backgrounds (http://usm.maine.edu/olli/national/lifestorycenter/).

QUALITY INDICATORS OF RESEARCH

Misconceptions about research abound. For instance, it is more than going to the library and looking up references, although this is an element in the research process. Likewise, research goes beyond asking people to answer questions, even though this step is often included in research studies as well.

Research follows a thinking process known as ***scientific inquiry***. Quality research has the following scientific inquiry characteristics (Lastrucci, 1963):

- Logical. The study topic makes sense. The stated conclusions in logical inquiries are directly supportable by the procedures used to conduct the study.
- Objective. The information collected is unbiased. In objective inquiries, empirical data are collected through formal observation or measurement. Not being objective is being subjective, or relying on divine or spiritual revelation, intuition, or personal opinion as the basis for knowledge.
- Systematic. The study is conducted in an orderly manner. Systematically conducted inquiries are also valid, meaning accurate information is recorded. In systematic inquiries, extensive documentation is provided so others can replicate or repeat the study.

IDENTIFY HOW AND WHY THE SCIENTIFIC APPROACH TO INQUIRY HAS BEEN VIOLATED

Directions: Read the following scenario and answer questions at the end.

Denise, a candidate for a master's degree, initially proposed developing and offering a leisure education program for nine adults who were developmentally disabled and mentally ill and who were living in a group home. She envisioned the program would be offered three times per week, for 1-hour sessions, for 2 weeks. Session topics would be on

- learning how to hip-hop dance,
- walking with 2-pound weights,
- sewing a teddy bear,
- setting up a personal fish aquarium,
- planting an herb garden, and
- participating in floor aerobics instruction.

Denise "just knew" that such a program would make a difference in the lives of participants! Nevertheless, her thesis advisor asked her to:

- identify what aspects of the group home residents' lives would change as a result of participating in the leisure education program;
- provide details of what would be taught at each meeting; and
- specify how she would document the benefits that are anticipated to accrue from program participation.

After thinking about it, Denise felt the goal of the leisure education program should be to enhance participants' social skills. Denise was a member of her university's dance club when she was an undergraduate, ran track in high school, and knew how to sew (thanks to her grandmother). Even though she knew nothing about fish aquariums or gardening, Denise felt she was a quick learner, and after consulting the Web and looking at videos, she concluded she could lead all six sessions herself. Ultimately, Denise thought it was a waste of time to type lesson plans for the activities since she was only introducing basic common sense material.

Denise's data collection game plan is to ask one or two of the clients she felt benefited most from the program to

- recollect the number and kinds of social interactions they had with others living in the group home the week before the leisure education program was offered and then again about a week after the formal program ended and
- reflect on whether participating in the leisure education program had improved their social life.

Questions:

1. Is the proposed study logical in terms of the chosen activities being expected to improve the study participants' social skills?

2. Is it logical to think that the proposed procedures for the study will enable Denise to make supportable conclusions at the end of the study?
3. If the study plan is executed, is it appropriate to think it will yield objective data on the participants' social skills over time?
4. Is the study set up in a systematic fashion so valid information will be recorded?
5. Does Denise's plan incorporate systematic documentation of what she will be doing at each class?

Note. Answers are provided at the end of the chapter.

When you violate these characteristics of scientific inquiry, the resulting product is ***pseudoscience*** or junk science. The by-products of studies that are not logical, objective, or systematic include findings and conclusions that may appear scientific, yet in reality lack integrity and are therefore meaningless.

In contrast, when you logically, objectively, and systematically plan and implement research, it is ***scientific research***. For word economy reasons, in this book research implies scientific research.

SOMETHING TO REMEMBER!

When designing or reading a research study, ask yourself the following questions:

- Is the study logically conceived?
- Will the procedures you use enable you to make supportable conclusions?
- What are your plans for collecting data objectively?
- Have you implemented the study in a systematic fashion so accurate information is recorded?
- Do you provide extensive documentation so others can replicate the study?

CHARACTERISTICS OF A GOOD RESEARCHER/PROGRAM EVALUATOR

According to Patton (2008), someone who is good at evaluating a program or conducting basic research has certain traits, including the following:

1. Enthusiastic. The individual should have passion for the topic of inquiry and should experience enjoyment or pleasure when undertaking and reporting on the research endeavor.
2. Open-minded. Ability to consider others' insights and learn from one's own mistakes are earmarks of an inquisitive researcher.
3. Common sense. A competent researcher uses good sense in planning and conducting the study. This means avoiding the "principle of the drunkard's search," or conducting a study by looking in the place that is easiest, rather than in the place most likely to yield results. This principle revolves around the story of the drunkard who lost his house key "and began searching for it under a street lamp even though he had dropped the key some distance away. Asked why he wasn't looking where he had dropped it, he replied, 'There's more light here'" (Rosenthal & Rosnow, 2007, p. 35).
4. Ability to be critical. The good researcher is careful in how the study is designed and executed. He or she should anticipate what the critics will fault and consequently set up and implement a study that has quality.
5. Inventive. Developing sound research questions and technical designs that are ethical are earmarks of a quality researcher. Finding solutions to problems that may arise in conducting the research project (e.g., recruiting study participants) are also signs of inventiveness.
6. Detail oriented. A good researcher takes pride in his or her work and is also organized and systematic, including proofing his or her written work.
7. Interpersonal skills. The researcher needs to be adept at working with diverse groups of stakeholders. This may entail being able to resolve conflict and possessing negotiation skills.
8. Adept at communication. The investigator must be able to write down and present details about the research in face-to-face meetings.
9. Honest. A capable researcher respects honest scholarship, meaning he or she has integrity. This extends to honorably reporting how the study was implemented and truthful reporting of results.
10. Reflective. The researcher is aware of his or her bounded knowledge and skills and hence calls upon others to assist with research endeavors. Additionally, he or she seeks out and engages in professional growth and continuing education activities to improve his or her abilities to set up or monitor research projects.

THE RESEARCH PROCESS: OVERVIEW

How you plan and execute a research study is vitally important to its success. The ***research process*** is a structured and planned approach to discovering knowledge. If there is a dramatic deviation from this process, the integrity of the study will be questioned.

Basically, the research process has four stages, two of which relate to planning the research and two that tie into the execution of the study (Figure 0.5).

In turn, you may break down the four stages of research into 17 steps (Figure 0.6). Each of these steps is featured as a separate chapter in the book; within each chapter, the details of the particular steps are addressed. It may be useful to tab down this page so it becomes a ready reference as you read the remainder of the book.

Planning ⟶		**Execution**	
Stage 1	Stage 2	Stage 3	Stage 4
Getting Started	***Develop a Plan***	***Implementation***	***Reporting***

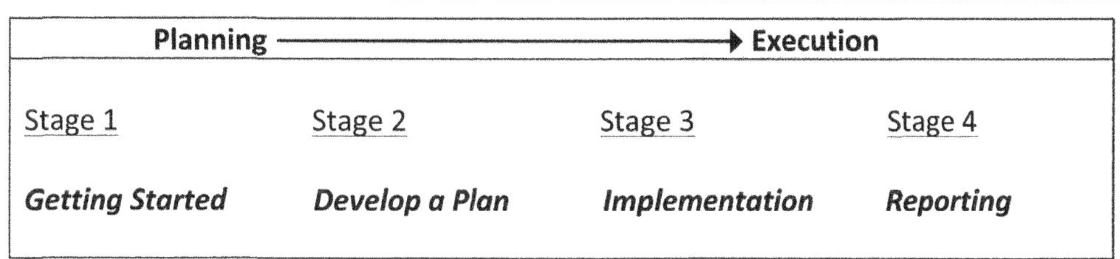

Figure 0.5. The research process. Adapted from Bickman and Rog (2009).

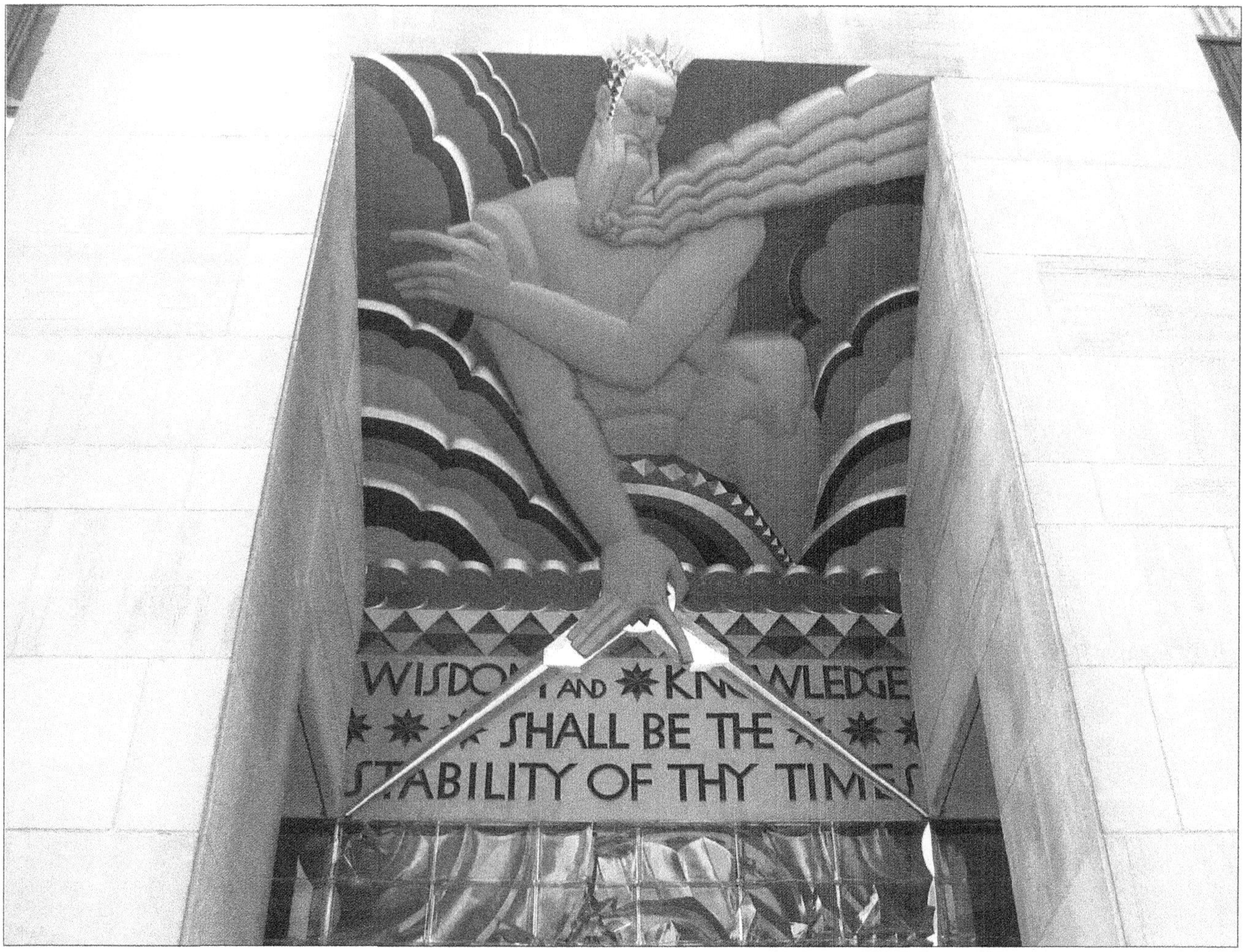

Research entails adopting a scientific inquiry process to discover knowledge and gain useful information and wisdom. General Electric Building, New York, NY. Copyright © 2015 Carol Cutler Riddick.

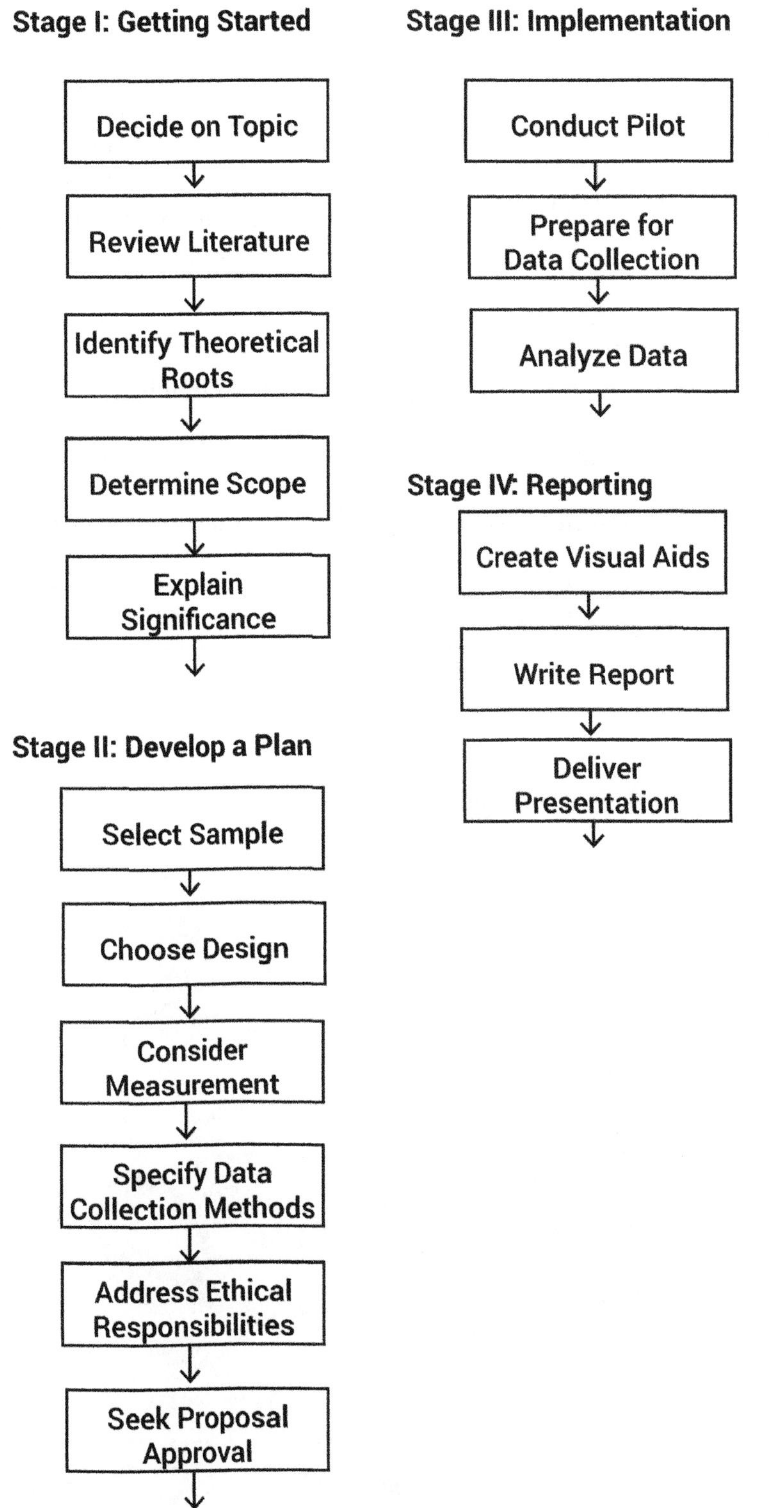

Figure 0.6. The research process. Adapted from Bickman and Rog (2009).

REVIEW AND DISCUSSION QUESTIONS

1. What are the two definitions of research?
2. What is the difference between applied and basic research?
3. Name and define the three goals behind a research investigation.
4. Summarize three motives that may trigger a research project.
5. Define stakeholder and name six groups of stakeholders that could be interested in a research study.
6. Draw, label, and explain the adaptive cycle that transpires between the researcher and primary stakeholders when planning a study.
7. What does it mean when you read that someone has used a primary data source? A secondary data source?
8. Name and explain the three indicators of a quality research investigation.
9. List characteristics of a good researcher or program evaluator.
10. What are the four stages in the research process? Which of the two stages are related to planning a study? And executing a study?

YOUR RESEARCH

1. Are you drawn to undertaking an applied or basic research project? Why?
2. Do you envision becoming involved with a descriptive, explanatory, or predictive investigation? Explain.
3. What is your primary motive for conducting the study you are considering?
4. Identify stakeholder groups you anticipate being interested in your study.
5. Drawing on the adaptive cycle, explain at which junctures you intend to work with primary stakeholders as you plan your study.
6. Do you anticipate using a primary or secondary data source? Provide a rationale for your answer.
7. Explain how your proposed study is logical, objective, and systematic.
8. What characteristics of a good researcher do you bring to planning and executing your study?
9. Outline a calendar plan of when you anticipate completing the steps involved in conducting the research process for your project.

PRACTICE EXERCISES

1. Acquire a copy of the ***abstracts*** (the summary paragraph at the beginning of an article) to the following articles (or your instructor may substitute another article):

   Tsitsos, W., & Nixon, H. (2012). The star wars arms race in college athletics: Coaches' pay and athletic program status. *Journal of Sport and Social Issues, 36*, 68–88. You may access this article at http://jss.sagepub.com/content/36/1.toc or at http://jss.sagepub.com/content/36/1/68.full.pdf+html.

   Bromley, M., Marion, J., & Hall, T. (2013). Training to teach leave no trace: Efficacy of master educator courses. *Journal of Park and Recreation Administration, 31*, 62–78. You may access this article at http://js.sagamorepub.com/jpra/article/view/2778.

   Wennberg, P., Gustafsson, P., Dunstan, D., Wennberg, M., & Hammarstrom, A. (2013). Television viewing and low leisure-time physical activity in adolescence independently predict the metabolic syndrome in mid-adulthood. *Diabetes Care, 36*, 2090–2097. You may access this article at http://care.diabetesjournals.org/content/early/2013/01/15/dc12-1948.full.pdf.

Read each abstract and classify the foci (see three questions below) of the reported research.
   a. Is it applied or basic research?
   b. Is it an example of descriptive, explanatory, or predictive research?
   c. Does it rely on a primary or secondary data source?

2. Suppose the president of your university has asked you to evaluate the school's intramurals (IM) program. The president wants to learn how the program may be improved so it better serves the overall university community.
   a. Identify the name or position belonging to each of the following stakeholder groups:

Worksheet Overview Chapter: IM Stakeholders

Stakeholder group	Names or titles of persons belonging to the stakeholder group
1. Policy decision makers	
2. Program sponsors	
3. Program participants	
4. Program managers	
5. Front-line staff	
6. Contextual stakeholders	

   b. Who do you envision being the primary stakeholder for the study? Why?
   c. Applying the adaptive cycle for planning a study, identify and briefly explain at which junctures you would interact with the primary stakeholders in planning the study.

3. Grade yourself on the 10 characteristics of a good researcher. Use one of the following ratings: *excellent*, *acceptable*, or *poor*. On which three characteristics do you need to improve? Why?

Worksheet Overview Chapter: Report Card for My Potential as a Good Researcher

How I judge myself regarding characteristics of a good researcher? Extent I am or have...	My self-rating
1. Enthusiastic	
2. Open-minded	
3. Common sense	
4. Able to be critical	
5. Innovative	
6. Detail oriented	
7. Interpersonal skills	
8. Adept at communication	
9. Honest	
10. Reflective	

WEB EXERCISES

1. Which research focus intrigues you most, applied or basic research? Are you more interested in descriptive, explanatory, or predictive research? Determine your research orientations by visiting Intute, a Web resource put together by a consortium of seven universities in England (up to July 2011): http://www.intute.ac.uk/. Click on "Social Sciences" and then under "Browse Social Sciences," choose "Sport and Leisure" or "Travel and Tourism." Browse the holdings and find a research-based report to read. How would you classify the article? That is, does it illustrate the following:
   a. Applied or basic research and
   b. Descriptive, explanatory, or predictive research?
2. Connect to the University of Michigan's Inter-University Consortium for Political and Social Research website at http://www.icpsr.umich.edu/icpsrweb/ICPSR/org. Click on "Find and Analyze Data."
   a. Search for two secondary data sets that contain leisure, recreation, park, or sport data. *Search term hints:* Leisure, Recreation, Sports, Physical Activity, Social Activities, Backpacking, Outdoors Activities, Tourists.
   b. Print out a description of the selected data sets.
   c. For each data set, identify (write in the margin of the printout) whether it is an example of the following:
      i. Applied or basic research and
      ii. Descriptive, explanatory, or predictive research.
3. Go to Bob Carroll's The Skeptic's Dictionary website at http://www.skepdic.com/.
   a. If your instructor does not assign you a topic, choose one from "Topical Indexes."
      i. Briefly state the "strange belief, amusing deception, or dangerous delusion" that is reviewed.
      ii. Using bullet points, summarize the arguments.
      iii. Which of these arguments is most convincing? Least convincing?
   b. Describe your overall reaction to this website.
4. Which of the following additional resources, for this chapter and book, do you find most useful as a novice researcher? Briefly explain why you chose one resource over the other two.
   a. Professor Saint-Germain's (University of California, Long Beach) Research Methods (PPA 696) website: http://www.csulb.edu/~msaintg/ppa696/696menu.htm. For this chapter, see "Session One: Introduction."
   b. *W.K. Kellogg Foundation Evaluation Handbook* at http://www.wkkf.org/knowledge-center/resources/2010/W-K-Kellogg-Foundation-Evaluation-Handbook.aspx. For this unit, review Chapters 2, 3, and 5 ("Planning Steps").
   c. Find the peer-reviewed electronic journal *Practical Assessment, Research, and Evaluation* at http://pareonline.net/. Click on "Articles," and under "Articles of Special Interest To," click on "Research Students" and "Evaluation Students."
5. What is pseudoscience? For an entertaining answer, check out this TED talk by Michael Shermer of *Skeptics Magazine* at http://www.ted.com/talks/michael_shermer_on_believing_strange_things.html.

SERVICE LEARNING

Background: One way to make learning about research more interesting is to find an opportunity that enables you to apply the ideas and concepts presented in the text. To this end, the service learning component of this text is set up to help the class embark on a rudimentary evaluation of a program or service offered on campus. Moreover, to coincide with the theme of the book, a university recreation or sport program should be chosen as the focus for a study by the class. For instance, depending on a program manager's support and enthusiasm, the class could design, implement, and report on a survey designed to gather feedback and ideas on how to enhance their campus intramurals program, exercise/fitness facility, natatorium, or rock climbing wall.

Hopefully, all program managers on your campus will welcome an opportunity to partner with the research class! After all, what better way to learn about students' opinions and gather ideas on how to improve the program/service. If a number of program managers are enthusiastic about partnering with your research class, the instructor may want to change each term the particular program or service that is selected as the focus for the service learning component.

Each chapter will guide the instructor and the class on how to apply the content of that chapter to conduct the service learning activity. Thus, to start (and to coincide with what is covered in this chapter) complete the following:

1. Decide on a campus recreation or sport program that will be the focus for the service learning project. The instructor should assign each student to a team and each team to a specific campus recreation or sport program. Teams will be responsible for finding a time that is convenient for all team members and the program manager to meet. The primary purpose of this meeting is to determine the manager's interest in having the class design, implement, and report on an applied research project that will consist of surveying users and nonusers of the program or facility. During the meeting with the program manager, the students should review the adaptive cycle that will be used for planning the study.
2. Use the adaptive cycle for planning a study to guide the program or service evaluation. Once the students have selected a particular program or service, the course instructor should invite the program manager to come to class and provide an overview of the program or service and identify questions to which he or she hopes the survey will provide answers. (*Note:* The timing of this guest presentation should come after Step 1 has been studied and reviewed in class.)
3. Later in the semester, as relevant chapters/steps are covered, the students will continue with the adaptive cycle of interaction with this stakeholder by drafting a survey that is intended to pose questions the manager hopes to be asked.
4. The students will interact with the instructor, program manager, and intended or actual program participants by sharing the drafted survey and soliciting their feedback.
5. Based on the feedback provided, the students will adapt the survey before implementing it.
6. At the end of the term, the students will conduct a PowerPoint presentation to the program manager and invited guests on the conducted survey. The program manager will also be provided with a written report of the research undertaking, complete with recommendations for improving program operations and policies.

TEST YOURSELF ANSWERS

Distinguish Between Applied Research and Basic Research

Questions 1, 5, and 6: Applied research; Questions 2, 3, and 4: Basic research

Identifying the Applicability and Goals of a Research Idea

1. Basic and Descriptive, 2. Applied and Explanatory, 3. Applied and Predictive, 4. Applied and Descriptive, 5. Applied and Explanatory, 6. Basic and Predictive

Identify How and Why the Scientific Approach to Inquiry Has Been Violated

1. No! It is not logical to think that the selected noncooperative activities would promote social interaction. For instance, would adults participating in the walking program, swinging 2-pound weights, really feel like chatting with each other?
2. No! Sampling only the one or two people who Denise thinks best responded to her program steps out of the bounds of proper scientific procedures. Her plan needs to be logical so some evidence collected in the final analysis indicates whether the leisure education program fostered greater social skills among all six participants.
3. No! Relying on recall to collect information from adults with developmental disabilities is questionable in terms of yielding objective data. Indeed, relying on memory is debatable, even with individuals without developmental disabilities. Realistically, are participants able to accurately recall aspects of their social life that happened weeks ago?

4. No! A better plan would be to measure the social skills, either by observation or videotaping, for the six study participants at two times. That is, to capture their social interactions (in terms of frequency and/or interactions) before they began the leisure education program and then again after they completed the leisure education program.
5. No! Written lesson plans for each session is a must. Each lesson plan should be like a cookbook! That is, session objectives (relating to ways to foster attainment of the social skills development goal) need to be identified along with providing details on the content, processes, and teaching aids used to implement each lesson.

SUPPORTING CASES FOR THIS CHAPTER

CASE 0.1. BASIC RESEARCH

Palen, L., Caldwell, L., Smith, E., Gleeson, S., & Patrick, M. (2011). A mixed-method analysis of free-time involvement and motivation among adolescents in Cape Town, South Africa. *Loisir, 35,* 227–252.

The overall purpose of the study was to understand free-time activity participation and related motivations of mixed-race adolescents living in a peri-urban area near Cape Town, South Africa. The self-determination theory was used to guide the study. Data were collected from a focus group ($N = 114$) and survey ($N = 946$).

The researchers found that the adolescents participated in several activities, with socializing, media use, sports, risk behavior, and performing arts being the most frequently mentioned. Focus group participants mentioned several motivations (intrinsic, identified, introjected, extrinsic, and amotivation) affected their use of free time. Free time involvement was strongly shaped by intrinsic motivations (competence, relatedness, and positive affect). Activities were viewed as a way to achieve outside goals. With few exceptions, multiple motivations were identified for the same activities and specific motivations were reported across multiple activity types.

The authors recommended future research of a longitudinal nature is needed. In particular, they maintain a need exists for more research linking motivational experiences to positive and negative outcomes.

CASE 0.2. DESCRIPTIVE RESEARCH

White, D., Aquino, J., Budruk, M., & Golub, A. (2011). Visitors' experiences of traditional and alternative transportation in Yosemite National Park. *Journal of Park and Recreation Administration, 29,* 38–57.

The objectives of the study were to (a) document travel mode choices for visitors entering and traveling through Yosemite, (b) identify the importance of transportation modes to visitors and their satisfaction with each mode, (c) examine visitors' perceptions of experiential dimensions of traveling via alternative and traditional transportation modes in the park, and (d) identify visitors' preferences for transportation management.

Data were collected from a random sample of adult park visitors ($N = 533$) using a self-administered questionnaire distributed on-site. The researchers found that most relied on private autos as the primary mode for travel to and through the park. Visitors rated the ability to use alternative transportation inside the park as important and were satisfied with the convenience of alternative transportation modes provided, yet private vehicles were still the most popular travel mode inside the park. The greatest level of support was for the use of hybrid or alternative fuel shuttle buses, followed by the promotion of bicycling within the park. The researchers called for additional studies that examine how stress, crowding, and other important desired experience dimensions affect travel mode choices.

CASE 0.3. EXPLANATORY RESEARCH WITHIN THE CONTEXT OF A SPECIFIC PROGRAM OR ACTIVITY

Breunig, M., O'Connell, T., Todd, S., Anderson, L., & Young, A. (2010). The impact of outdoor pursuits on college students' perceived sense of community. *Journal of Leisure Research, 42,* 551–572.

The primary aim of the study was to understand the relationship between college students' participation in an outdoor trip and changes in their perceptions of sense of community. Using a focus group, the researchers collected data from 98 primarily sophomore and junior recreation majors from a 4-year college enrolled in a 13-day Outdoor Education Practicum summer course.

Quantitative and qualitative findings revealed a significant increase in perceived sense of community as a result of participating in the outdoor trip. Factors that contributed to sense of community were group-oriented activities, preparing and eating group meals, trip challenges, debriefing activities, the feeling of "getting away from it all," meeting new people, and holding a common goal. Recommendations were made on how to foster a positive sense of community and group cohesion on an outdoor trip.

CASE 0.4. PREDICTIVE RESEARCH

Jacobsen, S., Carlton, J., & Monroe, M. (2012). Motivation and satisfaction of volunteers at a Florida natural resource agency. *Journal of Park and Recreation Administration, 30*, 51–67.

The study examined the motivations of volunteers to a fish and wildlife organization and how these motivations influenced volunteer satisfaction and commitment. A Web-based survey was sent to 569 individuals, resulting in a 59% response rate.

The strongest motivation for volunteering was helping the environment, though motivations for volunteering varied with gender and age. Strength and type of motivation as well as training and recognition activities predicted satisfaction that volunteers experienced. The researchers concluded that because motivations vary among volunteers, it is important for organizations to offer a variety of volunteer opportunities and advertise them so potential recruits may select options that best meet their needs.

PART II
GETTING STARTED

STEP 1

DECIDE ON TOPIC

STEP 2

REVIEW LITERATURE

STEP 3

IDENTIFY THEORETICAL ROOTS

STEP 4

DETERMINE SCOPE

STEP 5

EXPLAIN SIGNIFICANCE

Choosing a topic for research may come from a number of sources including studying the world around us, reflection, and soliciting advice from others. Museum of Modern Art, New York City. Copyright © 2015 Ryan Cutler Riddick.

STEP 1 STEP 2 STEP 3 STEP 4 STEP 5

DECIDE ON TOPIC

WHAT WILL I LEARN IN THIS CHAPTER?

I'll be able to...

1. Recall sources for discovering research ideas.
2. Outline how the following may influence topic choice:
   a. reductionism,
   b. paradox behind science,
   c. scientific revolution,
   d. gold reference,
   e. replication study, and
   f. extension study.
3. Explain how applied research topics related to recreation, park, sport, or tourism programs or activities may be developed using the hierarchy for program analysis model.
4. Describe two ways basic research topics related to recreation, parks, sport, or tourism typically are identified.
5. List additional considerations for appraising the "goodness" of a research topic idea.

"It is our choices...that show what we truly are, far more than our abilities."

J. K. Rowling
(British novelist, best known as the author of the Harry Potter fantasy series)

You are at the beginning of the research process. This *getting started* step in research is a challenge. This is because you need to think of useful subject matter or a topic that YOU are interested in researching. Insights typically unfold after many hours of creative contemplation. Plainly put, identifying a research topic is not easy.

To put this in context, consider that conducting research is like an hourglass (Figure 1.1). You start broadly, narrow your focus, and then broaden again. The initial step of determining a topic is a wide open enterprise. After determining the topic, narrow in by making decisions about how and when to collect the information. Finally, once you have analyzed the collected data and have the information you sought for your topic, open up your perspective again so others such as practitioners and other researchers may use your conclusions and recommendations.

1. Identify broad subject area
2. Narrow topic and focus on concepts, instruments, and design
3. Collect data
4. Analyze data and present results
5. Discuss and interpret results, state conclusions, and make recommendations

Figure 1.1. Hourglass shape of research. Adapted from Trochim (2006).

Where do ideas for research come from? If you are interested in conducting a program evaluation, what may be examined? If you want to embark on a basic research topic, how does that unfold? What should you consider when sorting through ideas to narrow them down to a manageable topic? Read on to find answers to these questions.

RESEARCH IDEAS: DISCOVERING THEM!

Research reports typically do not describe how the investigator came up with the original idea. The inspiration and perspiration that go into finding a topic may stem from almost anywhere; however, the bulk of research ideas come from real-life problems, from personal reflection, from mentors, and by reading.

Real Life

The recreation, park, sport, and tourism industries face a number of practical problems and issues. Real life provides at least three ways for discovering a research topic:

- confer with staff working within a program;
- consult professional organization websites; and
- read popular press, newspapers, and magazines and/or watch television news programs.

Ideas for research studies may be solicited from individuals who have worked in recreation, park, sport, and tourism settings. If you are not already a staff member, make an appointment with the director of an organization or program that interests you and explore ideas such as challenges that face program operations.

HOW PERSONAL EXPERIENCE SHAPES RESEARCH CAREERS

Below are special stories explaining how personal experiences affected an individual's research topic, and ultimately a research career.

Bugs and Chemical Ecology

A fascination with bugs began in boyhood for Thomas Eisner. He began by collecting caterpillars, beetles, and maggots to house in his bedroom (Brown, 2011). He noticed how insects used chemistry (e.g., liver poisons, nerve drugs, and scalding jets of toxic liquids) to interact with one another and the world at large. Dr. Eisner's early love of walking outside and observing insects steered him into studying entomology in college and to an academic career at Cornell University. The following are some of Dr. Eisner's discoveries:

- Beetles, when threatened, squirt stinky brown, caustic liquid that emerges at 26 mph and 100°C (the boiling point of water).
- Ornatrix moths trapped in spider webs persuade their captors to set them free.
- Femme fatale fireflies entice males with a mating dance, only to eat them and thus ingest a powerful, protective poison.

Tipping Behaviors

Michael Lynn worked his way through college as a waiter, thanks to tips from customers (Crawford, 2000). He went on to earn advanced degrees in psychology but never forgot about table-waiting encounters. Dr. Lynn's earlier experiences shaped his research career, which is centered on studying tipping behaviors found in hotels and restaurants around the world. (Incidentally, factors identified as likely to increase tips are the servers posture and writing phrases on a check.)

Vitamin D and Cancer

Frank and Cedric Garland were attending a seminar at Johns Hopkins University in 1974 (Maugh, 2010). The brothers were surprised when the presenter showed maps on the rates of breast and colon cancer mortality in the United States. These rates were twice as high in many northern areas compared with those in the southwest. Others had no explanation for the finding, but the brothers drew on their experience of having driven across country 2 years earlier in their convertible Mustang. Their hunch was that a beneficial effect of sunlight in the southwest was at the core of the regional differences. The brothers spent 6 years investigating vitamin D and the prevention of colon cancer. Their research ultimately was published in the *International Journal of Epidemiology*. Other studies followed, establishing the Garlands as experts on the topic of how vitamin D helps prevent colon cancer.

You may also discover research ideas that deal with the problems and issues confronting practitioners by attending state, regional, and national professional conferences. Many professional organizations support people working in recreation, park, sport, and tourism settings via conferences and workshops (see Table 1.1 for a list of these organizations).

Finally, the popular press may provide a tip for a real-life topic. News coverage may trigger your interest in a topic you had not thought much about before, such as park site graffiti, fan violence at sporting events, or synthetic "recreational" drug use. Or you may read about an issue that propels you to want to make a difference. For example, the existence of gang violence may get you involved in evaluating the impact of innovative recreation programs for this population group.

Table 1.1
Organizations That Support Recreation, Park, Sport, and Tourism Professionals

- Academy of Leisure Sciences (www.academyofleisuresciences.com)
- American Alliance for Health, Physical Education, Recreation, and Dance (www.aahperd.org)
- American Association for Health, Physical Activity, and Recreation (www.aahperd.org/aapar/)
- American Camp Association (www.acacamps.org)
- American College of Sports Medicine (www.acsm.org)
- American Psychological Association (www.apa.org) (*Note*: One section of the organization, Division 47, is devoted to exercise and sport psychology.)
- American Recreation Coalition (www.funoutdoors.com/arc)
- American Therapeutic Recreation Association (www.atra-tr.org)
- Aquatic Fitness Professional Association International (www.aquacert.org)
- Association for the Advancement of Applied Sport Psychology (www.aaasponline.org)
- Association for Experiential Education (www.aee.org)
- Association of National Park Rangers (www.anpr.org)
- Association of Outdoor Recreation and Education (www.aore.org)
- Australia and New Zealand Association for Leisure Studies (www.staff.vu.edu.au/anzals)
- British Association of Sport and Exercise Sciences (www.bases.org.uk/newsite/home.asp)
- Canadian Association for Leisure Studies (www.eas.ualberta.ca/elj/cals/home.htm)
- Canadian Parks and Recreation Association (www.cpra.ca)
- Canadian Society for Psychomotor Learning and Sport Psychology (www.scapps.org)
- European Federation of Sport Psychology (www.fepsac.org)
- IDEA Health and Fitness Association (www.ideafit.com/)
- International Festivals & Events Association (www.ifea.com)
- International Fitness Association (www.ifafitness.com)
- International Society of Sport Psychology (www.issponline.org)
- International Society of Travel and Tourism Educators (www.istte.org)
- Leisure Studies Association (www.leisure-studies-association)
- National Association of Recreation Resource Planners (ww.narrp.org)
- National Association for Sport and Physical Education (www.aahperd.org/naspe)
- National Association of State Park Directors (http://naspd.indstate.edu/index.html)
- National Dance Association (www.aahperd.org/nda)
- National Forest Recreation Association (www.nfra.org)
- National Parks Conservation Association (www.npca.com)
- National Recreation and Park Association (www.nrpa.org)
- NIRSA: Leaders in Collegiate Recreation (www.nirsa.org)
- North American Society for the Psychology of Sport and Physical Activity (www.naspspa.org)
- North American Society for the Sociology of Sport (www.nasss.org)
- Park Law Enforcement Association (www.parkranger.com)
- Resort and Commercial Recreation Association (www.r-c-r-a.org)
- The Roundtable Associates, Inc. (www.therounddtableassociates.org) (*Note*: Organization dedicated to ensure the park, recreation, and conservation profession and its practitioners serve the best interests of African American and other minority groups.)
- Travel and Tourism Research Association (www.ttra.com)
- World Leisure (www.worldleisure.org)
- World Tourism Organization (www.world-tourism.org)

Reflection

Personal experiences are often the source of a research idea. Ideally, you will want to spend time observing the phenomenon you are interested in studying and then try to recall an aspect you observed that fascinated you about it or that you found perplexing. For example, before conducting research on factors affecting exercise adoption by older persons, engage elders in an informal discussion on the topic. After going through such a sensitivity-raising experience, you should approach the getting started phase with an enlightened perspective.

Also, in your topic quest, reflect on your personal hobbies and your job, volunteer, practicum, and internship experiences. One of our graduate students, a therapeutic recreation professional who worked in a psychiatric facility was stymied about what to choose for a thesis topic. In a discussion with her thesis advisor, she revealed that she devoted much of her spare time to being an animal rescue volunteer. Ultimately, she designed, implemented, and documented how an animal-assisted therapy program affected a group of psychiatric patients.

University Faculty

When looking for a research idea, consider setting up appointments with faculty and/or university staff members. Start within your own major. Most faculty members have been or are involved in research, and many welcome an opportunity to talk about their research interests. Sometimes faculty members are looking for someone to assist them with studies.

FINDING AND WORKING WITH A RESEARCH ADVISOR

Whether you are embarking on research as a practitioner or student, consider identifying a faculty member at a local college or university who may be available to assist you. (For theses and dissertations, having a faculty ***mentor***, or an experienced and trusted advisor, is a requirement.) Identify someone whose personality and work habits are compatible with your own. This way the partnership is a win–win situation. Factors to consider include the following:

1. Enthusiasm. Is he/she open to working with research apprentices in general and with you in particular?
2. Availability. Does he/she maintain weekly office hours and routinely check e-mail messages? Will he/she be taking a ***sabbatical*** (or a paid leave to conduct research or embark on study) during the time of the study? In short, do you anticipate having reasonable access to your mentor?
3. Comfort level. Do you feel you can confide in the person regarding concerns about your research project?
4. Constructive criticism manner. Is his/her feedback understandable? Is his/her delivery style agreeable with you?

Once you have found a mentor, you may maximize your working relationship with these tips:

- Schedule weekly meetings at a fixed time. These meetings may be used to keep you on track and progressing.
- Take a laptop, iPad, diary notebook to all meetings. Date each written entry, and write out concerns you want to discuss at your next meeting. This strategy for recording your progress may be valuable.
- Take notes during your meeting. Write down any brainstorming that occurred in the meeting, issues that popped up, ideas on how to handle problems, and what you need to do or follow up on.
- Submit your study proposal several days in advance of your weekly meeting. Ask your faculty mentor how much lead-in time he/she needs to review your proposal revisions. Once you know this deadline, stick to it.
- Clarify how feedback and revisions will be submitted and handled. Also, date your revisions; you will be amazed at how many drafts/revisions you will go through!

Realize that a faculty member's academic discipline influences how he/she views the world. In technical terms, this is known as ***reductionism***, "… seeing and explaining complex phenomena in terms of a single, narrow concept or set of concepts" (Babbie, 2012, p. 103). For example, sociologists tend to study the world using a sociological "lens" (how social institutions affect individuals and groups, and vice versa), psychologists lean toward focusing on individuals (e.g., how thoughts and personality affect behavior), and economists normally focus on financial determinants (e.g., supply and demand) to explain how the world works. Thus, figuring out which discipline lens you feel most comfortable using as you embark on research is important. Then, find guidance from a mentor who shares the same outlook.

Professional Literature

Another good source for finding study topics is professional research literature. It has been said that few original ideas exist. Your idea likely has been refined and explored in the research literature a number of times already. This is good! Old research informs new research. Read the professional literature to find out what has been learned about the topic you are considering.

This is such an important source of research topics that the next step in the research process (Step 2) guides you in completing a literature review. This is a systematic search in published research and theoretical works found in professional outlets, such as journals, master's theses, doctoral dissertations, and the like, for ideas. The amount of information available from these sources is staggering.

When starting to read research, you may find the following tips useful:

- Begin browsing through journals within your major (see Appendix 1). You are more likely to understand the content and language used in your own discipline.
- Ignore articles with titles that do not "grab you." If you do not understand the title or its topic, it is not useful to you, so move on.
- Read the abstract first. If the title has captured your attention, find the article and read the abstract. The abstract is found at the beginning of the article (usually boxed in or set in a different font from the article), is about 100–200 words, and typically contains the study purpose as well as summarizes important findings and main conclusions.
- After looking at the abstract, skip to the Discussion and Conclusion sections. Typically, these include information about the limitations of the study with suggestions on how to overcome these in future research. These insights may help you pinpoint what to study.

Learn to question what you read. Being skeptical of what others have reported may lead to new knowledge, the ***paradox behind science***. According to Kahn (as cited in Rosenthal & Rosnow, 2007), "The history of science is punctuated...with revolutionary insights that have altered the way the world is perceived" (p. 5). What is believed to be true for many years may later be updated and even dispelled. As illustration, when we were graduate students, we encountered in our studies the belief that older people preferred to engage in sedentary, passive activities. This conventional wisdom later was challenged by, among other things, a landmark article that reviewed 30 years of research reports and concluded older people can and do enjoy participating in robust activities (Larson, 1978).

"Science demands that evaluators never be satisfied, always find flaws, criticize, and never permanently accept anything" (Walizer & Wienir, 2000, pp. 7–8). Therefore, when reading, remember science provides you with a tentative way of knowing. The bulk of research findings are evolutionary, producing gradual, piecemeal changes in your understanding. Every once in a while, the results of a study contribute to a major upheaval in scientific understanding of how the world works. Radical changes that overturn prevailing wisdom in a scientific field have been referred to as a ***scientific revolution*** (Kuhn, 2012).

Whether you are a novice or experienced researcher, you should try to build on the work of others. You may decide to explore contradictory or unexpected findings. If you dig around, you will come across at least one ***gold reference***, a reference with invaluable ideas (e.g., insights or a synthesis of the research that has been conducted on a topic) that you may use for the study being planned. Table 1.2 may provide you with pivotal inspiration for finding your piece of gold! Once you have found a pivotal reference, you may turn it into your research topic in several ways such as a replication study or an extension study.

A ***replication study*** may be used to confirm or disconfirm results from a previous study. Typically, the original research is repeated, using subjects whose characteristics more or less match those involved in the first study. Nevertheless, the results of one, two, or three studies will not be be definitive. In short, do not place too much confidence in the findings of a study until it has been replicated multiple times.

Contrastingly, an ***extension study*** is undertaken to embellish earlier research. You may complete an extension study in two ways. First, you may examine an additional factor or two from the original study. For instance, for many years, physical health and income were deemed paramount to the mental health of older persons. Then, additional studies were undertaken revealing additional factors (e.g., leisure satisfaction and significant others' attitudes toward leisure) also impinge on an elderly person's emotional health (cf. Riddick, 1985b; Riddick & Gonder, 1994). Second, an extension study may reconceptualize previously held simplistic views. An example is the research on the topic of barriers individuals experience when choosing leisure pursuits. Through extension studies, simplistic notions are refined and extended, resulting in the understanding that a sequential, hierarchical three-category model of intrapersonal, interpersonal, and structural constraints affects a person's leisure choices (Crawford, Jackson, & Godbey, 1991).

Table 1.2
Unusual Research That May Trigger an Idea in Your Quest to Find a Research Topic

If you are still searching for a topic, review the following articles to discover out-of-the-mainstream topics that have been published. Maybe one will trigger an idea for your topic.

Atkinson, J., & Herro, S. (2010). From the chartreuse kid to the wise old gnome of tennis: Age stereotypes as frames describing Andre Agassi at the U.S. Open. *Journal of Sport & Social Issues, 34,* 86–104.

Auster, C. (2001). Transcending potential antecedent leisure constraints: The case of women motorcycle operators. *Journal of Leisure Research, 33,* 272–298.

Berbary, L., & Johnson, C. (2012). Ethnographic screenplay: Recasting the stereotype of the dumb, blonde sorority girl. *Leisure Sciences, 36,* 243–268.

Breivik, G. (2010). Being in the void: A Heideggerian analysis of skydiving. *Journal of the Philosophy of Sport, 37,* 29–46.

Bucciard, D., Longbottom, J., Jackson, B., & Dimmock, J. (2010). Experienced golfers' perspectives on choking under pressure. *Journal of Sport & Exercise Psychology, 32,* 61–83.

Campbell, L. (2010). 'Go somewhere, do something'. How students responded to the opportunity to complete an unstructured, five-day wilderness solo in the Cantabrian Mountains, Northern Spain. *Journal of Adventure Education and Outdoor Learning, 10,* 133–149.

Cavan, S. (1966). *Liquor license: An ethnography of bar behavior.* Chicago, IL: Aldine.

Cohen, S. (2010). Personal identity (de)formation among lifestyle travelers: A double-edged sword. *Leisure Studies, 29,* 289–301.

Drew, R. (2001). *Karaoke nights: An ethnographic rhapsody.* Walnut Creek, CA: Altamira Press.

Duncan, M. (1990). Sports photographs and sexual difference: Images of women and men in the 1984 and 1988 Olympics. *Sociology of Sport Journal, 7,* 22–43.

Eccles, J., & Barber, B. (1999). Student council, volunteering, basketball, and marching band: What kind of extracurricular involvement matters. *Journal of Adolescent Research, 14,* 10–43.

Geertz, C. (1972). Deep play: Notes on Balinese cockfight. In C. Geertz, *Interpretation of cultures* (pp. 412–453). New York, NY: Basic Books.

Goffman, I. (1959). *The presentation of self in everyday life.* Garden City, NJ: Doubleday/Anchor. (*Note:* Includes observations of everyday events found in pubs and on promenades in England.)

Henderson, K., & Bedini, L. (1995). "I have a soul that dances like Tina Turner, but my body can't." *Research Quarterly for Exercise and Sport, 66,* 151–161.

Hill, A., Hall, H., Appleton, P., & Murray, J. (2010). Perfectionism and burnout in canoe polo and kayak slalom athletes: The mediating influence of validation and growth seeking. *The Sport Psychologist, 24,* 16–34.

Humphries, D. (1997). Shredheads go mainstream?: Snowboarding and alternative youth. *International Review for the Sociology of Sport, 32,* 147–160.

Jaimangal-Jones, A., Pritchard, A., & Morgan, N. (2010). Going the distance: Locating journey, liminality, and rites of passage in dance music experiences. *Leisure Studies, 29,* 253–268.

Table 1.2 (cont.)

Johnson, C. (2008). "Don't call him a cowboy": Masculinity, cowboy drag, and a costume change. *Journal of Leisure Research, 40*, 385–403.

Johnson, C., & Dunlap, R. (2011). They were not drag queens, they were playboy models and bodybuilders": Media, masculinity, and gay sexual identity. *Annals of Leisure, 14*, 209–223.

Jones, C. (2010). Playing at the queer edges. *Leisure Sciences, 29*, 253–268.

Klein, A. (1993). *Little big men: Bodybuilding subculture and gender construction*. Albany, NY: SUNY Press.

Lyng, S., & Snow, D. (1986). Vocabularies of motive and high-risk behavior: The case of skydiving. *Advances in Group Processes, 3*, 157–179.

Nixon, H. (1986). Social order in a leisure setting: The case of recreational swimmers in a pool. *Sociology of Sport Journal, 3*, 320–332.

Pearson, K. (1979). *The surfing subcultures of Australia and New Zealand*. St. Lucia, Australia: University of Queensland Press.

Roussel, P., Monaghan, L., Javerlhiac, S., & Le Yondre, F. (2010). The metamorphosis of female bodybuilders: Judging a paroxysmal body. *International Review for the Sociology of Sport, 45*, 102–109.

Ryan, J. (2000). *Little girls in pretty boxes: The making and breaking of elite gymnasts and figure skaters*. New York, NY: Warner Books.

Ryan, V. (1999). *Motivation to participate in risk sports among young adults*. Unpublished doctoral dissertation, University of Guelph, Guelph, Canada. (*Note:* Study examines factors that motivate young adults to participate in snowboarding and alpine skiing.)

Sugden, J. (1996). *Boxing and society: An international analysis*. Manchester, United Kingdom: Manchester University Press.

Thompson, H. (1972). *Fear and loathing in Las Vegas: A savage journey to the heart of the American Dream*. London, England: Picador.

Thompson, H. (1999). *Hell's angels: A strange and terrible saga*. New York, NY: Random House.

Woolsey, C., Waigandt, A., & Beck, N. (2010). Athletes and energy drinks: Reported risk-taking and consequences from the combined use of alcohol and energy drinks. *Journal of Applied Sport Psychology, 22*, 65–71.

Sometimes an earlier study may be replicated and extended. For example, a number of investigations have examined how an outdoor program affects the self-esteem of participants who can hear (for a summary of these studies see Hattie, Marsh, Neill, & Richards, 1997). A student, as part of her thesis, replicated (in terms of theory and research design) and extended (using the Rosenberg Self-Esteem Scale that had been translated into American sign language) earlier research by conducting a study that monitored how an outdoor-based program affected the self-esteem of college students who were deaf (Fisher, 2005).

NEW VOCABULARY REVIEW

Time out! Have you mastered the technical terms related to a quest to find a topic? Match each concept with its correct definition.

Term	Definition
1. Reductionism	A. Discovery of "new" knowledge that significantly and substantially changes a scientific field or discipline.
2. Gold reference	B. Knowledge evolves; what you think is "true" at one point in time later is shown to be false.
3. Replication study	C. An investigation that expands upon an earlier study either by adding another factor to the mix of variables examined to explain or understand a topic of interest or by reconceptualizing how a phenomenon is viewed.
4. Extension study	D. A study that repeats (using a different sample) an earlier investigation (in terms of topic, methods used, etc.)
5. Paradox behind science	E. A reference that contains insights on a research topic, methods that could be used for the study, and so forth.
6. Scientific revolution	F. The academic discipline "lens" that you adopt to examine and interpret the world around you.

Note. Answers are provided at the end of the chapter.

CHOOSING AN APPLIED RESEARCH TOPIC

Formally organized events, activities, or interventions may be thought of as ***programs***, and when you study programs, you are engaging in applied research. One way to choose an applied research topic is to use a ***hierarchy for program analysis*** (Bennett, 1979). Essentially, this is a model with seven ways to examine a program, with each tier or rung in the hierarchy requiring unique evidence or data (Figure 1.2).

Inputs

At the inputs level, you may consider several aspects in a research study about a program: program need, staff qualifications (e.g., competency assessment and performance appraisal), standards compliance, and resource amounts allocated to a program.

Program need. ***Program need*** is the gap between the real and the ideal, and you may assess it by identifying a problem or service need. Program need is sometimes referred to as ***needs assessment*** and essentially determines the wants, or preferences, of clients or service providers. Case 1.1 is an example.

Staff qualifications. You may evaluate staff qualifications by either competency assessment or performance appraisal.

1. ***Competency assessment*** is focused on the knowledge, skills, and characteristics needed to successfully perform a job (Hurd, 2004). Competency models have been developed for assessing roles in recreation, park, sport, and tourism professions.
2. A related idea is ***performance appraisals***, which examine a staff member's (full time, part time, seasonal, and volunteer) or organization's work performance in terms of skills, abilities, traits, and behaviors (Milkovich, Newman, & Gerhart, 2013). An example is when Taniguchi, Widmer, Duerden, and Draper (2009) asked disadvantaged youth to identify counselor attributes that made their wilderness experience beneficial.

Standards compliance. ***Standards compliance*** involves comparing how a program, facility, or organization operates against a set of norms. Standards reflect a desire to manage risks, address safety concerns, and generally reassure the public that the services are high quality. For instance, visitors to Acadia National Park were asked to identify density standards for cars and buses as well as for foot path traffic (Pettengill, Manning, Anderson, Valliere, & Reigner, 2012). Professional organizations or regulatory entities usually establish standards, which may be either elective or required by law. Examples of standards that exist for recreation, parks, sport, and tourism are identified in Table 1.3.

Resource amounts. ***Resource amounts*** include the kinds and quantities of resources used to support the program. One way to focus on resource amounts as inputs is to examine total program cost or itemize expenditures related to a program (also known as ***performance-based program budgeting***). Another way to examine resource amounts is to determine the number of full-time and part-time staff as well as volunteers involved in supporting the program or activity.

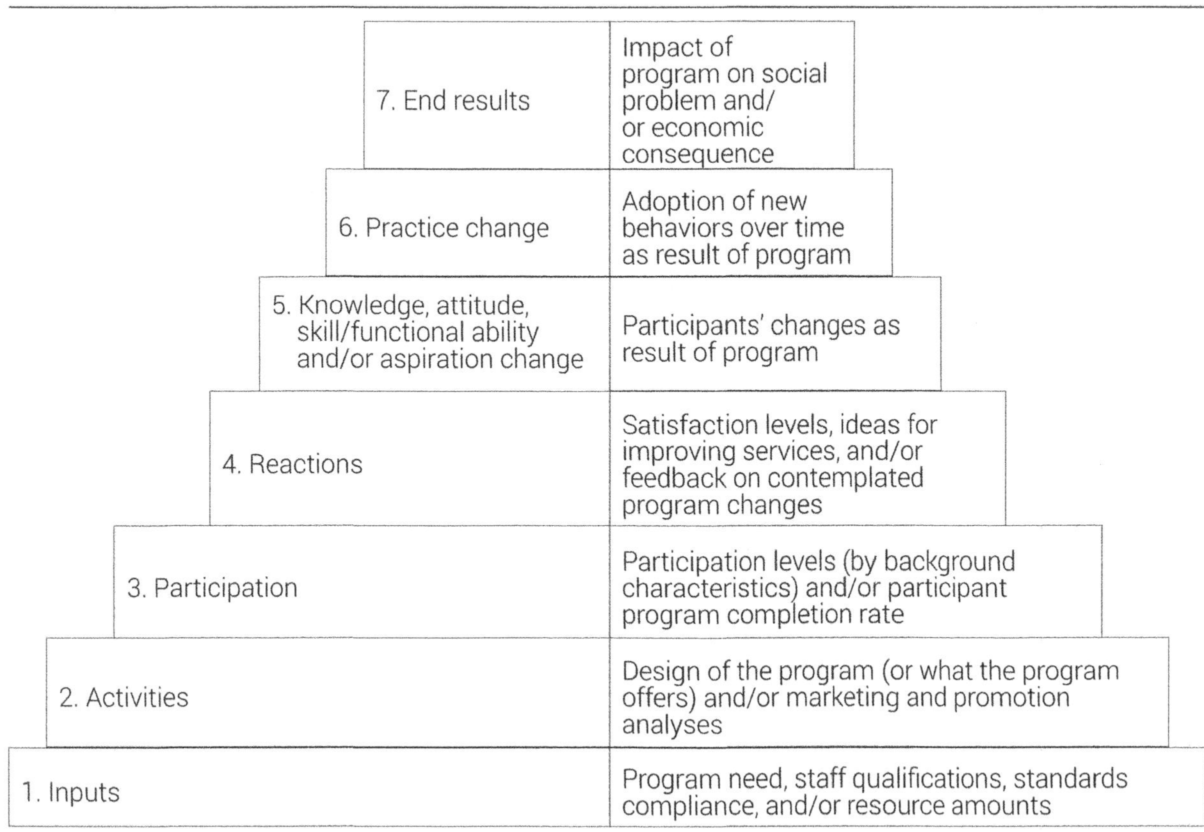

Figure 1.2. A hierarchical model for analyzing a program. Adapted from Bennett (1979).

Activities

The activities level of research and evaluation may examine process-related aspects of a program, in particular program design as well as marketing and promotion.

Program design. When studying ***program design***, you will examine its logic and organization. "Practitioners working in real-life situations may design programs based...on best practices or conventions that have evolved over time through experience" (Baldwin, Hutchinson, & Magnuson, 2004, p. 17). Studying program design, then, includes feedback questions about components, content, elements, activities (e.g., recruitment), and/or educational methods and techniques (see Borich, 2013; Slavin, 2011). For example, Furneaux (2006) examined how a training environment contributed to effective canoe and kayaking coaching.

Marketing and promotion. Determining what motivates a person to participate in or use a service is the gist of ***marketing and promotion analysis***. These studies typically focus on measuring how well advertising, public relations strategies, brochures, and/or websites accomplish what is intended. Case 1.2 presents a study on the effects of media campaigns on four benefits-based visitor market segments identified for Acadia National Park.

Participation

Another way to evaluate program process is to determine its participation. In other words, participation is the number of people involved with a program or activity. Typically, the number of program participants or users is investigated and reported. Sometimes participation is examined from the perspective of participant program completion rate. An embellishment is to break down users by their socioeconomic characteristics and/ or another classifier. An examination of variations of how race and gender affected participation in interscholastic and intramural sport programs in middle schools is an example of a participation study (Case 1.3).

Reactions

A popular approach to examining programming is to assess people's reactions, that is, to focus on their beliefs about aspects of the service delivery. This line of inquiry involves asking them to provide feedback on a number of aspects, including service satisfaction, ideas for improving service delivery, and/or reactions to contemplated program/service changes (e.g., increasing the admission price). Users, nonusers, and/or program staff may be queried. Illustrative of a reactions study is one that reported on youth's reactions to a newly opened municipal skateboard park in Canada (Case 1.4).

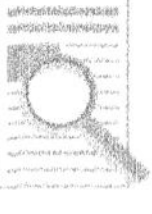

Table 1.3
Standards for Recreation, Park, Sport, and Tourism Settings

Entity	Standards regarding	For more information contact
American Camp Association	Camp operations (including site and food services, transportation, health and wellness, operational management, human resources, and program design and activities).	http://www.acacamps.org/accreditation
International Association of Amusement Parks and Attractions	Safety, general management, guest relations	http://www.iaapa.org/
Joint Commission on Accreditation of Health Care Organizations	Provision of recreation services within health care institutions	http://www.jointcommission.org/standards_information/standards.aspx
National Aquatic Management School	Management of aquatic facilities and programs	http://www.nrpa.org/Content.aspx?id=1773
National Playground Safety Institute	Certification as Playground Safety Inspector (hazard identification and risk management)	http://www.nrpa.org/playgroundsafety/
National Program for Playground Safety	Four areas of playground safety: supervision, age-appropriate design, fall surfacing, and equipment and surfacing maintenance	http://playgroundsafety.org/
Park Maintenance and Resource Management School	Maintenance management of parks and public facilities	http://www.nrpa.org/mms/
United Nations World Tourism Association	Tourism and travel industry, with an emphasis on the promotion of responsible, sustainable, and universally accessible tourism	http://www2.unwto.org/en/technical-product/quality-standards-tourism-services
United States Access Board	Compliance with the Americans With Disabilities Act and removal of architectural barriers in facilities and parks. Standards are set, for example, for amusement rides, boating facilities, fishing piers, golf courses, play areas, playground surfaces, exercise equipment and machines, bowling lanes, and swimming pools	http://www.access-board.gov/

The commercial campground company KOA uses retirees as field services representatives to travel around inspecting campgrounds for compliance with such company standards as site cleanliness, customer relations, and recreation programming. Port Huron, Michigan. Copyright © 2015 Ruth V. Russell.

Knowledge, Attitude, Skill/Functional Ability, or Aspiration Change

The impact of a program or activity service may be multifaceted. The service may affect an individual or group of participants on one or more of the following fronts (Bennett, 1979):

1. knowledge or what program participants learn in terms of subject matter, specific services available within a community, how to access services or programs, and so forth;
2. attitude or changes in participants' feelings or opinions—one research study, for instance, reported that college students' moods and anxiety levels were affected positively as a result of participating in aerobic exercise and watching a comedy videotape (Szabo, 2003);
3. skill/functional ability or changes in ability to perform a task (e.g., Farhney, Kelley, Dattilo, and Rusch, 2010, examined how an intervention resulted in increasing physical activity levels [or steps walked] among a group of females aged 64–84 years); and/or
4. aspiration regarding a future behavioral intent (e.g., expressing the desire to exercise to become healthier as well as lose weight).

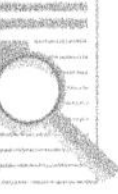

Case 1.5 demonstrates how participation in leadership development programs affected the knowledge, attitudes, skills, and aspirations of youth.

Practice Change

Sometimes researchers want to find out how long newly adopted behaviors are sustained (e.g., how long a person continues to exercise after the fitness program). ***Practice change*** is the behavior changes of individuals as a result of participating in a treatment, intervention, program, or activity.

The logic behind charting practice or behavior change, due to program or activity participation (see Figure 1.3), is focused on a starting point or baseline, goals or targets, and ending point or actual results (Patton, 2008). Also, recall that to set program goals, you should identify intended ***outcomes***, or target behaviors that are expected as a result of participating in a specific program or activity.

SOMETHING TO REMEMBER!

Identifying goals and objectives for a program is necessary yet challenging! A good refresher for learning how to write goals and objectives is the classic reference by Melcher (1999). Patton (2008) provided principles to consider when crafting objectives, including the following:

1. Identify outcomes that matter. Activities and programs should be offered that will make a difference in the lives of the participants and/or provide them with enjoyable, rewarding ways to spend their leisure time.
2. Distinguish between outcomes and activities. Outcomes are the desired impacts of the program on participants (e.g., "Individuals participating in the exercise program, over a 6-month period, will decrease their body mass index by 10%."). Contrastingly, activity statements describe how the goals will be achieved (e.g., "Participants will engage in aerobic activity three times per week.").
3. Objectives should be developed from program goals and these should be specific and understandable.* When identifying objectives for a program, remember the mnemonic "SMART":

   S = Specific
   M = Measurable
   A = Achievable
   R = Relevant
   T = Time bound

*To distinguish "goals" and "objectives," most agree "goals" are more general. That is, goals focus on overall purposes, such as "To promote the physical health of adolescents attending Sunset Recreation Center."

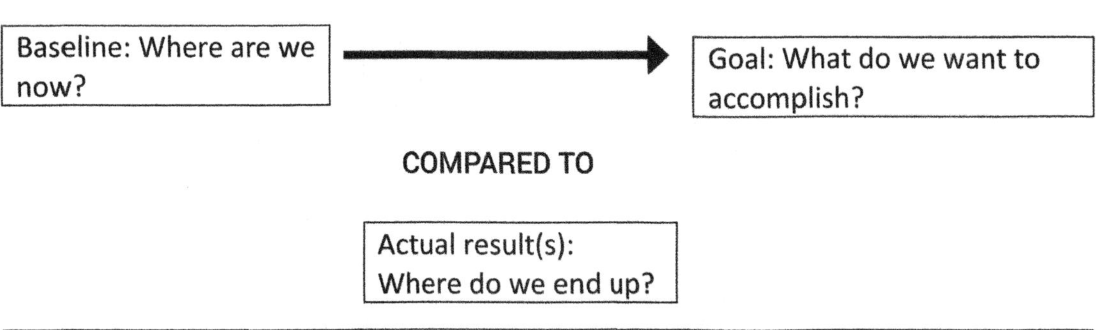

Figure 1.3. Logic behind charting impact of program participation on practice or behavior change. Adapted from Patton (2008).

A number of studies have reported on practice change. For instance, how a 3-day rock climbing trip affected the group dynamics of participants aged 10–14 was reported in an ethnographic study (Case 1.6).

End Results

End results are what happens at the community level in terms of reducing or alleviating a social problem. For example, Canadian government officials introduced an initiative to reduce obesity by providing healthy vending products in recreation facilities (Case 1.7). In end results studies, the economics of a program are commonly examined. ***Program economics*** compare program costs to program effects. This means studying cost effectiveness and cost benefit (Yates, 1996).

Cost effectiveness. In ***cost effectiveness***, program costs are compared to program outcomes. Cost effectiveness studies are used to examine the costs of two or more service alternatives relative to their effects measured in nonmonetary terms. See Figure 1.4 for an example of the information a cost effectiveness study may provide of a study that compares three program approaches (cooking class, aerobics class, and a combination cooking and aerobics class) to reduce employee weight.

Cost benefits. A ***cost-benefit study*** (sometimes referred to as an ***economic impact study***) examines the cost of the program and its benefits in dollars. That is, a cost-benefit study compares dollars spent on an activity relative to how much revenue the activity will generate directly and indirectly. For example, Siderelis, Naber, and Leung (2010) used a variation of the cost-benefit approach to determine how mountain bike site design characteristics and resource conditions influenced demand as well as the amounts people were "willing to pay" to ride on six North Carolina trails.

To summarize the hierarchy for program analysis model, Table 1.4 provides topics that you may study when evaluating a formal program or activity. Reviewing these questions may assist you in identifying a topic for your study.

Example of the Hierarchy for Program Analysis Model

Focus on more than one level of the hierarchy model during program evaluation. Evaluating a program on multiple aspects is more comprehensive than examining only one narrow aspect. Figure 1.5 illustrates how looking at components of the same program provides a more global understanding of what the program is accomplishing. At the same time, useful information about the program is generated for the program stakeholders (see Overview chapter).

CHOOSING A BASIC RESEARCH TOPIC

The curiosity you have about a topic tied to recreation, parks, sport, and tourism in general may spur a basic research project. The Overview chapter pointed out that basic research is distinguishable as being more at a "blue sky" level than applied research. Topics for basic research have no tie-in to a specific program, activity, or intervention that is formally offered. For instance, if someone were interested in why people like to travel, in general, this has the makings of a basic research topic. Contrastingly, if the research topic emerges as studying the motivations for visiting Disney World, this is an applied research topic (since the focus is on a specific program or activity).

If you desire to take up a basic research project, an idea also may come from reading about a theory. Many formal theories abound! Theories are tentative explanations of why or how something works in the social world and may guide you when choosing a research topic (see Appendix 2). How theory relates to topic selection will be covered in detail in Step 3.

Suppose three different approaches to noontime activity classes—a cooking class, aerobics class, and a combination cooking and aerobics class—are being analyzed. Cost-effectiveness data are presented below.

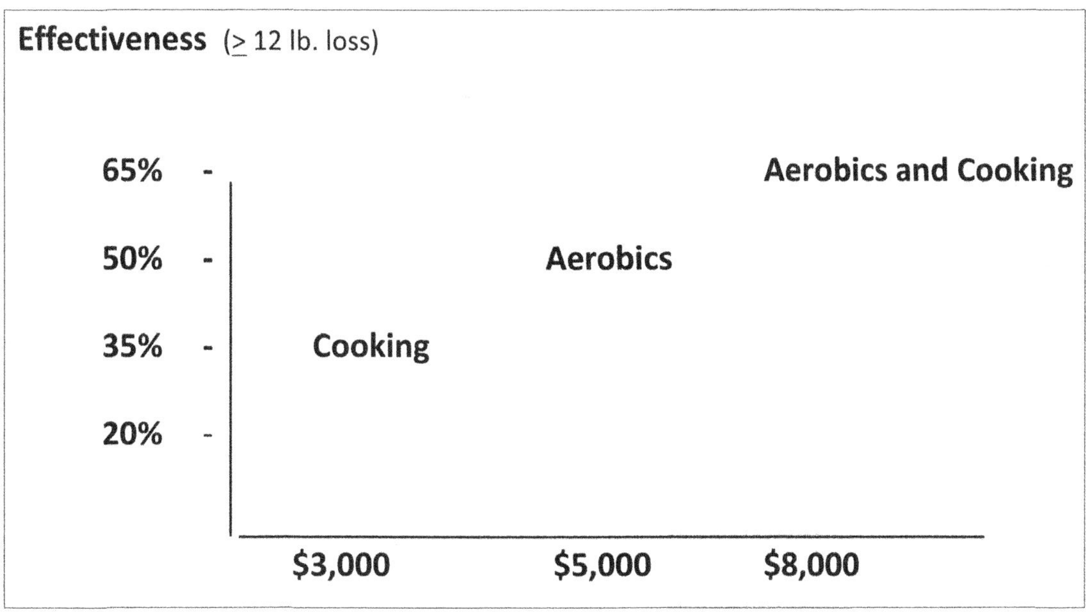

Figure 1.4. Hypothetical example of examining the cost effectiveness of three recreation programs designed to help employees lose weight. Data in this figure reveal that cooking classes were calculated as having an annual cost of $3,000/participant and were determined to be 35% effective (since 35% of enrollees lost 12 pounds or more during the year). Aerobic classes cost $5,000/participant and yielded a 50% success rate. The most expensive ($8,000/participant) yet most effective program approach to weight reduction was participating in a cooking and aerobics class. Almost two thirds of the individuals participating in a joint aerobics–cooking class experienced a significant weight loss over one year.

APPRAISING THE "GOODNESS" OF RESEARCH IDEAS

After you have come up with ideas for an applied or basic research topic, you need to narrow down the possibilities. This is more difficult than you may think! Take stock of each topic idea according to whether it is interesting, plausible, ethical, manageable, and valuable.

Interesting

Is the topic interesting to you? If not, there is little point in pursuing it. This topic will be with you for a while, so if you do not like it initially, you probably will hate it by the end of the study. You need an idea that will motivate and sustain you, especially if you are embarking on a thesis or dissertation.

Plausible

Is the idea plausible or feasible? Are data already available, or can you easily collect data on the topic? Is it too sensitive a topic? Will you have access to study participants, and will they be cooperative? Gambling habits of professional baseball players may be intriguing to you, but do you really think players will divulge this information?

Ethical

In the course of conducting your research project, do not expect other people or yourself to do anything that is morally wrong. The most compelling ethical issue at the proposal stage is ***protection of human subjects.*** This means risk of physical harm or social psychological discomfort to those involved in the research should be minimal—preferably no risk. Step 10 details ethical responsibilities and the mechanisms that are in place to ensure that you act ethically.

Table 1.4
Topics That May Be Asked Under Each Hierarchy Level for Analyzing a Recreation, Park, Sport, or Tourism Program

Hierarchy level	Question examples
Inputs	• What are the needs of the clients, citizens, or staff? • How are personnel performing (includes competencies and performance appraisals)? • Is the program operating according to standards (including risk management) or stated policies? • What resources are needed for program implementation? • What is the start-up cost of program implementation? Continuing cost?
Activities	• What programs could produce the desired changes? • How should the program be organized? • What educational and leadership techniques should be used? • How are people recruited into the program? • What marketing or promotion changes are warranted?
Participation	• Are persons in need of or desiring the program receiving it? • What is the participant program completion rate?
Reactions	• How satisfied are the program participants? • What are the perceptions of program users (e.g., what do they like and dislike)? Non-program users? Staff? • How can program operations be improved? That is, what is participant and staff feedback about program processes? What is working well? Not so well?
Knowledge, attitude, skill/functional ability, and/or aspiration change	• What changes in knowledge, attitude, skill/functional ability, and/or aspiration happen to participants by the time they complete the program? • How does the program benefit the participants? • Are some participants affected more by the program than others?
Practice change	• What behavioral changes occur because of program participation? • How long after completing the program are positive behavior changes retained?
End results	• Is the program cost reasonable relative to the magnitude of the benefits? • Would alternative programs produce equivalent benefits at less cost? • What is the economic impact of the program?

Note. Adapted from Rossi, Lipsey, and Freeman (2004).

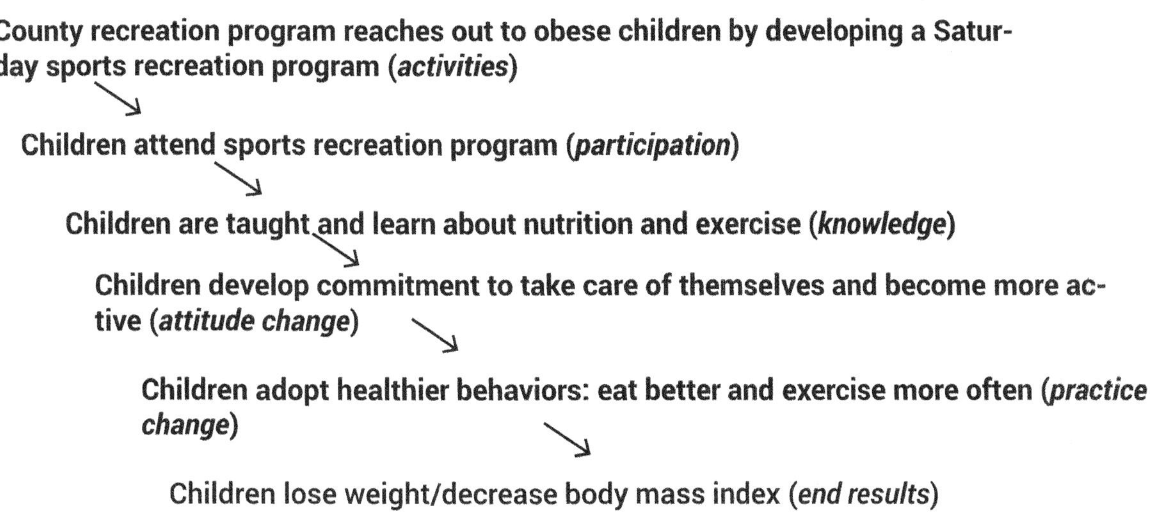

County recreation program reaches out to obese children by developing a Saturday sports recreation program (activities)
Children attend sports recreation program (participation)
Children are taught and learn about nutrition and exercise (knowledge)
Children develop commitment to take care of themselves and become more active (attitude change)
Children adopt healthier behaviors: eat better and exercise more often (practice change)
Children lose weight/decrease body mass index (end results)

Figure 1.5. Application of selected parts of the hierarchy for program analysis model: Reducing obesity in children with a community.

Manageable

When pondering a topic to pursue, give thought to the resources that will be required to conduct the study. In most research situations, planning, implementing, and completing a study take time and money.

For example, you must try to forecast how long each idea will take to study and then balance this with the reality of your situation. If you are a student, think in terms of when you want to graduate. If you are a practitioner, think about how much time you will have to devote to the research project. During a program evaluation, a certain amount of time needs to elapse as the program is conducted, yet the reality is that monitoring a program's impact over a long period of time is probably unrealistic.

You should also consider the financial resources necessary to conduct the study. What costs will be incurred? Who will be able to pay these costs? Will the the organization that serves as the setting for the research project cover the costs? If not, and you are a student, does your university have a small grants program? If so, what is the maximum amount of money you may request to cover nonpersonnel costs? If other entities are not able to support you, are you prepared to pick up the tab yourself?

Value

When selecting a research topic, consider its ultimate value (Thomas, 2004). Basically, you need to make the case for the relevance or significance (discussed more in Step 5) of a study to the knowledge base of a discipline, society, and/or professional practice. "Evaluation use is not something to be concerned about at the end of an evaluation; how the evaluation is to be used is a primary matter of concern from the very beginning of the evaluation and throughout every step of the evaluative process" (Patton, 1987, p. 73).

As mentioned in the Overview chapter, a prime consideration when you zero in on a topic for study is what will resonate with stakeholders. Research projects happen within a social and political environment. Stakeholders present in these environments define the value of a study (Cronbach, 1989). The viewpoints of stakeholder groups are diverse, sometimes resulting in disagreement or even friction. For example, the U.S. Department of Agriculture's Forest Service has had to balance the views of various groups toward controlling the number of wolves in national parks.

TIMELINE ESTIMATE FOR YOUR RESEARCH PROJECT

Creating a timeline for a research project may be useful. It helps you and those with whom you are working to know your aspirations. A timeline also enables you to assess your progress, plan personal time, and know when you will complete the project (e.g., planning your graduation). You may adapt the list of responsibilities to suit your specific situation.

Responsibility	Anticipated completion date	Actual completion date
1. Choose an advisor/mentor/research supervisor.		
2. Submit potential topic ideas to advisor/mentor/research supervisor.		
3. Narrow down and select a research topic in which you are interested that your advisor/mentor/research supervisor supports.		
4. Select thesis/dissertation/research advisory committee members (if applicable).		
5. Draft and revise proposal per suggestions of advisor/mentor/research supervisor.		
6. Seek approval of revised proposal from advisor/mentor/research supervisor.		
7. Meet with individual committee members (or others) to receive comments on distributed proposal.		
8. Review proposal comments with advisor/mentor/research supervisor.		
9. Revise proposal.		
10. Obtain approval of advisor/mentor/research supervisor for proposal changes.		
11. Distribute proposal to committee (if applicable) or others.		
12. Schedule and hold proposal meeting (if applicable).		
13. Revise proposal (if needed).		
14. If needed, seek and obtain approval from Institutional Review Board (for human subjects).		
15. Obtain final approval of proposal.		
16. Begin data collection.		
17. Analyze data and draft report.		
18. Draft and revise final report per suggestions of advisor/mentor/research supervisor.		
19. Seek final report draft approval by advisor/mentor/research supervisor.		
20. Meet with individual committee members (or others) to receive comments on final report.		
21. Review final report comments with advisor/mentor/research supervisor.		
22. Revise final report.		
23. Obtain approval of final report changes from advisor/mentor/research supervisor.		
24. Send copy of final report to committee members (if applicable).		
25. Schedule defense committee meeting (if needed).		
26. Make corrections as specified by committee members (if applicable).		
27. Obtain final approval.		
28. Distribute study results.		
29. Celebrate!		

Note. Answers are provided at the end of the chapter.

The classic and collector car hobby attracts hundreds and thousands of enthusiasts and requires even more of their financial resources. Similarly, the topic you choose to research should be one you are enthusiastic about since you will be investing a lot of your time and possibly money to carry out. Ft. Myers, Florida. Copyright © 2015 Ruth V. Russell.

SOMETHING TO REMEMBER!

Pause and take time to determine the utility of your topic. Avoid the following mistakes, often made when contemplating an applied research project, by remembering to

- select an "important" topic,
- design an evaluation that fits the context and situation, focus on intended use of findings, and
- keep stakeholders adequately informed and involved as you develop, revise, and complete the proposal.

REVIEW AND DISCUSSION QUESTIONS

1. What sources may you use to identify a topic for research related to recreation, parks, sport, or tourism?
2. What is reductionism?
3. How does the paradox behind science guide you in identifying a topic?
4. Explain what is meant by a scientific revolution.
5. What is a gold reference?
6. What is a replication study? Extension study?
7. Name and briefly explain each of the seven steps that make up the hierarchy for program analysis model.
8. Identify two sources for basic research topics.
9. What considerations can you use to appraise the "goodness" of a research idea?

YOUR RESEARCH

1. To begin to focus on your own research project,
   - identify one research topic related to recreation, parks, sport, or tourism that you have gleaned from each of the sources noted in the worksheet that follows;
   - identify whether the topic relates to applied or basic research; and
   - if it is an applied research topic, identify into which level of the hierarchy for program analysis the topic falls.

Worksheet Decide on a Topic Chapter: Research Topics Inspired by Different Sources

Source for idea	Possible topic	Topic an example of applied or basic research?	If the topic is an example of applied research, which hierarchy level to program analysis does it exemplify?
1. Real life			
2. Personal experience reflection			
3. University faculty			
4. Professional literature			

2. Now choose one of your research topic ideas recorded above. Using the report card below, grade this idea by choosing: *Definitely*, *Maybe*, or *No*.

Worksheet Decide on a Topic Chapter: Research Topics Inspired by Different Sources

Criterion	Grade
Interesting?	
Plausible?	
Ethical?	
Manageable?	
Valuable?	

PRACTICE EXERCISES

1. Make an appointment to interview one recreation practitioner (coach, intramural staff person, etc.) and one university faculty member about their ideas on points a–c below. Prepare an in-class report (as directed by the instructor) on their responses and point d.
   a. What were their college majors (for each degree earned)? What motivated them to major in what they did?
   b. What research interests do they have? How did they become interested in these research topics?
   c. Do they think their major affects how they "view the world"? *Note:* You may need to explain the notion of reductionism and see whether the person agrees with this idea.
   d. After the meetings, classify instances that an applied research topic idea cited falls within the hierarchy model for program analysis. For example, if you interviewed a coach and she said she was interested in assessing the varsity squad's feedback on the summer soccer camp she taught, then you would cite this idea as falling under "Rung 4: Reactions."

2. How may the issue of "littering at a park" be investigated by someone grounded in
   - psychology,
   - sociology, or
   - ecology/environmental science?
3. Identify a recreation, park, sport, or tourism program (real or hypothetical). If the latter, provide enough information on what the program is about and whom it serves (record answer): ______________________.
   For the program you have selected, identify an example of a research topic, linked to each level identified in the hierarchy for program analysis model.

Worksheet Decide on a Topic Chapter: Research Topic Ideas by Hierarchy Level

Criterion	Example of a research topic that could be investigated
1. Inputs	
2. Activities	
3. Participation	
4. Reactions	
5. Knowledge, attitude, skill/functional ability, aspiration change	
6. Practice change	
7. End results	

4. Acquire a copy of the following article (or your instructor may substitute another article):
   Daud, R., & Carruthers, C. (2008). Outcome study of an after-school program for youth in a high-risk environment. *Journal of Park and Recreation Administration, 26*, 95–114. You may access this article at http://js.sagamorepub.com/jpra/article/view/1324.
   Read the article and answer the following questions:
   - What is the topic of the research study?
   - Which level of program analysis was examined (refer to Figure 1.2 to assist you with identifying the ways you may evaluate a program)?

WEB EXERCISES

1. Discover the national and international organizations that exist to promote program evaluation by going to the American Evaluation Association's website at http://www.eval.org/Resources/ProfessionalGroups.asp and clicking on "National/ International Evaluation Associations" as well as examining organizations listed under "Other Associations/Organizations." Choose three organizations that interest you most. For each, briefly describe what activities/services they offer for someone wanting to learn more about research.

2. Review real-world research efforts of recreation organizations and communities by going to the California Park and Recreation Society website at http://www.cprs.org/ and clicking on, under the "Main Menu," "Resources," then "Information & Referral," and then "Needs Assessment, Measurements, Surveys, Etc." If the instructor does not give you a topic, find one example (print the page) that illustrates two levels noted in the hierarchy for program analysis model.
3. Learn something about sports/physical activity in England by going to the Sports England website and choosing one of the following reports to access. Identify one point you picked up regarding either a successful approach for meeting the sports/physical activity needs of a targeted group (gleaned from the first reference noted in point a below) or about the economic impact of sport (based on point b below).
   a. Access *Active England Final Evaluation Report 2009* at https://www.sportengland.org/media/39023/active-england-final-report-2009.pdf.
   b. Access *Economic Value of Sport in England July 2013* at http://www.sportengland.org/media/177230/economic-value-of-sport.pdf.
4. Read a study commissioned by the American Camping Association: *Directions: Youth Development Outcomes of the Camp Experience* by going to http://www.acacamps.org/sites/default/files/images/research/directions.pdf.
   a. Identify one major benefit attributed to camping that each of the groups surveyed reported: campers, parents, and staff.
   b. Classify the 10 measures of growth that were examined (see page 7 of the report) using the hierarchy for program analysis model. For instance, "self-esteem" measures an attitude and thus falls within the knowledge, attitude, skills/functional ability, aspiration change category.

SERVICE LEARNING

Following from the service learning actions in the Overview chapter, invite a program manager who is in charge of a recreation or sport program or activity on your campus to class.

1. Ask the presenter to share real-life practical problems and issues he/she faces in offering a recreation or sport program or activity on campus as well as outline what he/she would like to see covered in the survey prepared by the class.
2. Prior to the presentation, the instructor may direct you to conduct a brief review of the literature to identify current issues confronting the program or service the guest lecturer will be discussing. For instance, if the intramurals (IM) director is invited to class, then beforehand, students are to find at least one article that discusses at least one issue or problem confronting IM programs nationwide. Your instructor may set parameters for the source of this information (e.g., he/she expects the reference to be from the professional literature or to be posted on a professional organization's website) and/or when the resource was published (e.g., in the past 5 years).
3. After the presentation, reflect on the useful information the program manager desires relative to the hierarchy for program analysis presented in the chapter.
4. Finally, the class should spend time reflecting (and possibly deciding, if more than one program/service manager has been invited to present) on the research information needs of the manager. To tackle this, use the schema presented in the chapter; that is, is what the manager wants for research interesting? Plausible? Ethical? Manageable? Valuable?

TEST YOURSELF ANSWERS

New Vocabulary Review!

Questions: 1. F, 2. E, 3. D, 4. C, 5. B, 6. A

Timeline Estimate for Your Research Project

Ask someone experienced in research to review and comment on your projected timeline, in terms of whether anticipated completion dates are realistic.

SUPPORTING CASES FOR THIS CHAPTER

CASE 1.1. VISITORS' OPINIONS REGARDING SERVICE AND AMENITY NEEDS AT STATE PARKS: AN INPUTS STUDY

Kerstetter, D., Mowne, A., Trauntvein, N., Garaefe, A., Liechty, T., & Zielinski, K. (2010). Visitors' opinions of who should provide services and amenities in state parks. *Journal of Park and Recreation Administration, 28*, 21–36.

The study focused on visitors' opinions of whether the private or the public sector should operate various services within the Pennsylvania park system. On-site interviews (systematically drawn) were conducted at 13 sites, with 1,477 visitors agreeing to be interviewed.

Respondents felt state parks should be responsible for environmental education programs, park maintenance, campground operations, pool and beach staff, and outdoor recreation programs. Contrastingly, respondents believed private contractors should operate food and beverage services, watercraft rentals, and special events and festivals.

CASE 1.2. EFFECTS OF MEDIA CAMPAIGNS ON FOUR SEGMENTS OF USERS AT ACADIA NATIONAL PARK: AN ACTIVITIES (MARKETING AND PROMOTION) STUDY

Leahy, J., Shugrue, M., Daigle, J., & Daniel, H. (2009). Local and visitor physical activity through media messages: A specialized benefits-based management application at Acadia National Park. *Journal of Park and Recreation Administration, 27*, 59–77.

One purpose of this study was to investigate the effects of media campaigns on benefits-based visitor market segments. Data were collected through an on-site questionnaire (131 out of 158 people returned the questionnaire) and then again a month later (229 out of 229 people returned the questionnaire).

The effects of media campaigns had varied impacts on different market segments. Accordingly, visitors were segmented into four primary benefits-based market segments: fitness isolates, trail moderates, casual social groups, and trail enthusiasts. The media campaigns appeared to reach and influence the casual social group most, with trail moderates least influenced by the campaign. The Internet, e-mails, and television public service announcements were either not seen or not remembered by any of the visitor market segments. The study concluded that messages about the benefits of walking as a physical activity would resonate most with the casual social groups. Results were felt to be useful to park planners and managers in particular because the study demonstrated how different visitor market segments responded to media campaigns.

CASE 1.3. HOW DEMOGRAPHIC CHARACTERISTICS AFFECT SPORT PROGRAM PARTICIPATION IN MIDDLE SCHOOL: A PARTICIPATION STUDY

Edwards, M., Bocarro, J., Kanters, M., & Casper, J. (2011). Participation in interscholastic and intramural sport programs in middle schools: An exploratory investigation of race and gender. *Recreational Sports Journal, 35*, 157–173.

The purpose of the study was to compare variations, based on demographic characteristics, in how students participate in interscholastic and intramural (IM) school sport programs. The sample consisted of 582 seventh and eighth graders in two southeastern U.S. middle schools.

Gender and race differences in sport participation were found. That is, school sport participation levels were higher in IM than interscholastic sports for all studied categories of students except for white girls. The study concluded that policy and practice within school sport programs should consider cultural and structural factors that encourage or constrain student participation.

CASE 1.4. TEENS' THOUGHTS REGARDING THE OPENING OF A MUNICIPAL SKATE PARK: A REACTION STUDY

Shannon, C., & Werner, T. (2008). The opening of a municipal skate park: Exploring the influence on youth skateboarders' experiences. *Journal of Park and Recreation Administration, 26*, 39–58.

One purpose of the study was to determine youth's perceptions of and experiences with a skateboarding park that had been constructed for them in Canada. Semistructured interviews were conducted with eight skateboarders who were regular users of the facility in the first three months after it was opened.

Those interviewed reported the newly opened facility enhanced skateboarding experiences. Additionally, respondents linked their use of the new skate park to experiencing more freedom and challenge in their activity as well as improving their skateboarding skills.

CASE 1.5. EVALUATION OF HOW PARTICIPATION IN OUTDOOR LEADERSHIP PROGRAMS IMPACTED TEENS: A KNOWLEDGE, ATTITUDE, SKILL/FUNCTIONAL ABILITY, ASPIRATION CHANGE STUDY

Robers, N., & Suren, A. (2010). Through the eyes of youth: A qualitative evaluation of outdoor leadership programs. *Journal of Park and Recreation Administration, 28*, 59–80.

The intent of the study was to analyze how participation in two leadership programs, offered by the Crissy Field Center (a partnership among the National Park Service, the Golden Gate National Parks Conservancy, and the Presidio Trust), affected leadership skills, behavioral changes, and the academic and future career choices of middle and high school students. Four focus groups were conducted, involving 43 program participants and alumni.

Participants reported benefits such as gaining information to contribute to the environment, experiencing a desire to educate others, acquiring aspirations to help the environment, learning about skills that would enhance their academic work, and becoming educated about healthy lifestyles. The study concluded that the programs increased the youth's awareness or knowledge about sustainability and environmental justice as well as building social skills, self-awareness, and sense of identity. Participants felt the programs helped them make healthier choices for themselves, their families, and their communities.

CASE 1.6. ROCK CLIMBING PROGRAM EFFECTS ON GROUP DYNAMICS: A PRACTICE CHANGE STUDY

Sutherland, S., & Stroot, S. (2010). The impact of participation in an inclusive adventure education trip on group dynamics. *Journal of Leisure Research, 42*, 153–176.

The purpose of the study was to understand the impact participation in an inclusive 3-day rock climbing trip had on group dynamics. A five-stage model of group development guided this ethnographic case study. Seven participants (including an individual diagnosed with high functioning autism), aged 10–14 years, participated in the investigation.

Results noted participants bonded during the experience. The catalyst for the change in group dynamics was attributed to a team-building session conducted by the trip leaders. The study outlined recommendations on how to facilitate positive group dynamics within inclusive groups.

CASE 1.7. PROMOTION AND SALE OF HEALTHIER FOODS IN PUBLIC RECREATION FACILITIES: AN END RESULTS STUDY

Naylor, P., Wekken, S., Trill, D., & Kirbyson, A. (2010). Facilitating healthier food environments in public recreation facilities: Results of a pilot project in British Columbia, Canada. *Journal of Park and Recreation Administration, 28*, 37–58.

A British Columbia initiative explored how recreation may make environmental changes that reinforce and enable healthy choices by children and families. Government financial support enabled eight communities to participate in a pilot study. The purposes of the pilot were to implement healthy choices in vending machines that were located in communities and to see how these changes affected facility patrons' purchasing patterns, attitudes, and awareness of healthy eating initiatives.

The experiment lasted 6 months. Five of the eight communities were able to change their vending contract to increase healthy product selection during the pilot period (some facilities had contracts that were not up for renewal during the intervention period). An increase (19%) in healthy vending products offered occurred from baseline to follow-up. Recreation staff identified implementation themes including concerns about revenue loss, the time needed for changes to occur, and the importance of gaining buy-in time from decision makers, the public, and the food service industry.

Searching for useful information for a study topic can be a journey far richer than expected. Lobby of the Salvador Dali Museum in St. Petersburg, Florida. Copyright © 2015 Ruth V. Russell.

STEP 1 STEP 2 STEP 3 STEP 4 STEP 5

REVIEW LITERATURE

WHAT WILL I LEARN IN THIS CHAPTER?

I'll be able to...

1. Identify several ways a review of literature may assist with developing and writing about a research project.
2. Explain the process involved in undertaking a database literature review, beginning with using keywords to conduct the search, reviewing secondary literature sources, finding general references, and obtaining, reviewing, and analyzing primary literature sources.
3. Recall three content parts that should appear in a written literature review.
4. Conduct a literature review and locate four relevant primary sources for a chosen topic.

"I find that a great part of the information I have was acquired by looking up something and finding something else on the way."

Franklin P. Adams
(An American columnist of the 1920s and 1930s)

A ***review of literature*** is the glue that holds the research endeavor together. In conducting a literature review, you find and examine relevant information and research studies that other researchers have previously done. A literature review is not a simple string of summaries of the works of others. Instead, a literature review is a synthesis (Pan, 2008). The challenges are to interpret and evaluate individual pieces of literature and then to integrate and restate these earlier studies to support a new, coherent, and original work.

Admittedly, conducting a literature search is time consuming, but if done thoroughly, yields huge dividends. All too often, researchers (from the novice to the veteran) spend insufficient time discovering the findings and thoughts of those who have gone before them. This chapter is set up to increase your understanding of why reviewing the literature is invaluable, as well as to instruct you through the process of discovering, reviewing, and analyzing literature on a given topic.

HOW A LITERATURE REVIEW MAY HELP YOU

What are the dividends for identifying and reviewing earlier writings? Overall, a literature review may assist you with the "whats" and "hows" of your study, that is, finding a suitable topic, identifying a conceptual approach, providing rationale for the significance of your study, pinpointing data collection methods, and assisting with understanding and interpreting findings (Case 2.1 illustrates each of these points).

Find a Suitable Topic

Conducting a literature search is an important step in the research process. Not only is it useful when other authors point out something you had not previously thought about, but also a literature review may reveal gaps in knowledge, thus directly helping you frame a problem, research question, or hypothesis (see Step 4). For instance, a great deal of research literature is published each year on how outdoor experiences affect individuals. In starting a study on this topic, you would be making a mistake by not reading and synthesizing this literature to know what remains unknown about the topic. Similarly, a review of literature also may disclose that undertaking a replication or extension study would be useful (see Step 1).

Identify a Conceptual Approach

Sociologists, psychologists, and anthropologists have extensively studied individual and group behavior to produce formal theories and conceptual approaches. By discovering a theoretical approach through a literature review, you may develop a research question and hypotheses as well as a framework.

Provide Rationale for Significance of a Study

A review of literature may help you justify your study by showing how your work will address an important question. Within the literature, statistics are likely cited regarding the magnitude of the problem you are studying or that point out the need for the research you are proposing. In short, being able to state the significance of your research is important. Step 5 will address this in greater detail.

Pinpoint Methods

Earlier works also may inform your decisions about methods. Criticism of methods used in earlier studies may underscore the merit of the procedures you intend to adopt. As well, reading through previous studies may suggest new ideas for measurement tools. Another researcher's insights on what did or did not work regarding how to conduct a study may minimize your errors and lead to success.

Understand and Interpret Results

A literature review not only helps you plan a study but also serves two purposes after you have collected data. First, in discussing your results (Step 16), compare your findings to what other researchers have reported. Is there an accumulation of knowledge, or has an inconsistency been found? If your results differ from what previously has been reported, you are obligated to speculate why such findings are inconsistent. Were the differences due to design, instrumentation, and/or data collection methods?

Second, a literature review helps you to interpret your findings. Specifically, when you are preparing your report, refer back to the theoretical foundation used for the study and make inductive and/or deductive conclusions (another point discussed in Step 16). Additionally, interject ideas for future research. Other researchers before you may have suggested ideas that you now appreciate and can support.

CONDUCT THE SEARCH

Conduct the literature search using a university library rather than a public library. Public libraries do not have professional journals among their holdings. Even when using a university library, you may find the materials you need are not readily available. In these instances, take advantage of the ***interlibrary loan service***. Using this service, you will be able to obtain copies of journal articles and books from other libraries.

At this time, do not rely solely on the Internet to conduct a literature search. Even today, research on the Internet is not a substitute for library work. Information found on websites does not always undergo rigorous quality control prior to being posted. Thus, what is posted may not be valid or objective information. At best, you may find leads or background information from an Internet search, which you should cross-check with authoritative resources or references found at a library.

A literature review is best handled by beginning with a computerized ***database*** search. Information is collected and organized in a database. Online computerized databases permit you to quickly identify journal articles, books, and other references on a particular topic. As you undertake the search, either download and print the results or e-mail the findings to yourself. Libraries pay subscription fees for these computerized databases; therefore, specifics on how to conduct a database search vary by library and database. Contacting a ***reference librarian*** is another good idea. Also, many colleges at the beginning of each semester offer library research workshops.

Figure 2.1 identifies the four basic phases involved in a database literature search:

1. Think of keywords.
2. Review secondary sources.
3. Review general references.
4. Obtain primary sources.

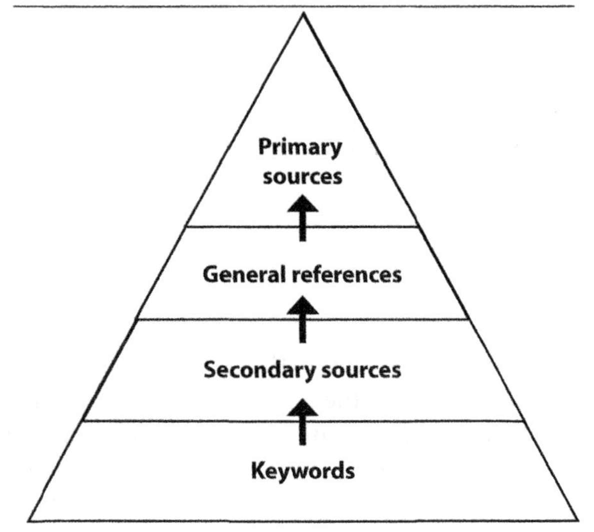

Figure 2.1. Four phases to a database literature search. Adapted from Fraenkel, Wallen, and Hyun (2011).

Begin With Keywords

In using a database for a literature search, first write a list of ***keywords***, the words or phrases that are used to search and retrieve information on a topic. Keywords are used during an online search of computerized database holdings. The goal is to use the keywords to uncover secondary sources, general references, and primary sources relevant to your topic (more on this later). In developing a keyword list, you do not want to be too narrow or too broad and end up with many useless citations.

A BOOLEAN OPERATOR

When thinking of keywords, realize most databases allow you to connect keywords together to both narrow and broaden your search. These connecting words are known as a ***Boolean operator***. Below are popular Boolean operators that are used to define relationships between words or groups of words.

Boolean operator	Meaning
AND	Narrow search and retrieve records containing all of the words it separates
OR	Broaden search and retrieve records containing any of the words it separates.
NOT	Narrow search and retrieve records that do not contain the term following it.

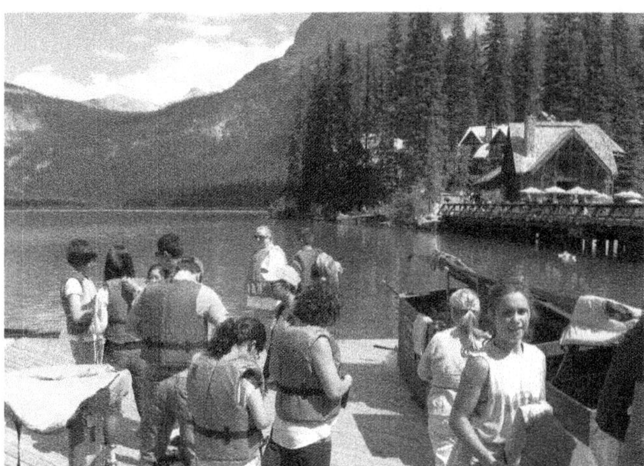

Suppose you wish to investigate the topic, "Benefits of Canoeing for Teens." Possible keywords to use in your literature search are canoeing, whitewater canoeing, and youth canoeing. Each of these keywords then could be connected (using AND) with the following keywords: *health benefits, social adjustment, emotional health,* and *appreciation of nature*. Emerald Lake, Yoho National Park, British Columbia. Copyright © 2015 Ruth V. Russell.

Sometimes journal articles contain keyword lists that apply to the topic of the reported study. Other times, a word will appear in a title of a retrieved reference, and you realize it is more useful. Pay attention to these leads, making sure you are not missing a good search term.

SEARCHING ON DATABASES FOR RESEARCH RELATED TO YOUR TOPIC

When undertaking a database search, try using the "IOP" strategy:

I = an intervention. If you are dealing with an intervention, identify the program/activity/intervention, such as aquatic therapy.

O = the outcomes. Specify the outcomes of interest, such as behavior change, attitude change, or leisure satisfaction. Try also using the words impact, effect, and evaluation.

P = the people or population of interest. The demographic characteristics (e.g., elderly women, college students, hospital patients) should be identified.

For example, a search on the PsychINFO database using the IOP strategy and the keywords Aerobic Exercise AND Body Image AND Females came up with 22 leads. In other words, with less than a minute of typing and search time, the database identified almost two dozen articles relevant to the topic.

The good news is, most online databases have two searches: "Quick" and "Advanced." The bad news is, each database has a unique operating system, so again, contact a librarian to find out nuances of the databases you plan to use. If too many leads emerge from a database search, you may want to limit your search by specifying a particular language, article type (e.g., excluding conference papers that may be difficult to acquire), and/or time frame (e.g., published since 2012).

Once you finish the keyword search in the database, read through the results by beginning with the secondary sources, following with the general references, and ending with the research articles, the primary sources. These reference sources will now be described more in depth.

Review Secondary Literature Sources

Typically, when reading about a topic with which you are not familiar, consult secondary sources first. A ***secondary literature source*** is a publication that provides introductory background information about a topic. It organizes and presents what others have written about it.

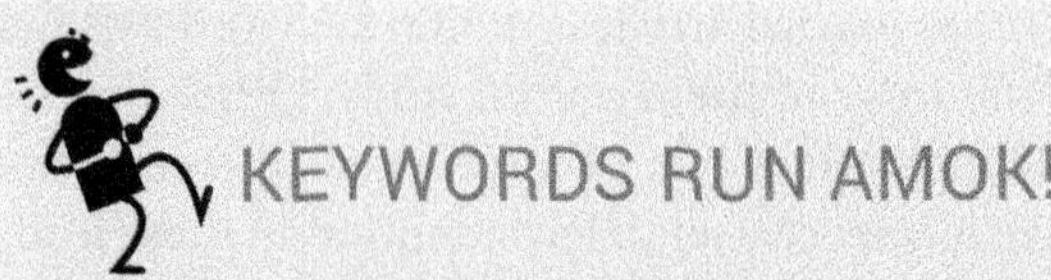

When dealing with keywords, sometimes you proceed in haste or maybe you are just dreadful spellers. Illustrating the latter, read the true story below:

A student was interested in working in military recreation. In particular, his aspiration was to land a job managing top-rated recreation programs for the Navy. Consequently, when taking a research methods class, he decided to focus an assignment trying to locate articles that had been published related to his chosen career focus. He was astounded when his database search yielded nothing! The first part of the onscreen message was, "No Results Found for Navel Recreation," but he then read on to discover being asked, "Did You Mean 'Naval' Recreation?"

Common secondary sources are textbooks, encyclopedias (see Table 2.1), and research reviews. Although textbooks and encyclopedias may provide a general overview, they usually lack depth, lack breadth, and/or are outdated. On the other hand, a ***research review*** is a focused and detailed synthesis of the literature on a particular subject matter. It synthesizes what is known about a topic by providing an integrated summary of previous investigations.

These reviews are published either as a monograph or in an existing professional journal (see Table 2.2). The topics of such reviews vary. An example of a research review is provided in Case 2.2, which basically exposes that not much is known about the topic tourism and oil! Other examples of published research reviews include

- after-school program evaluations (Aplser, 2009);
- race/ethnicity research found in leisure studies (Arai & Kivel, 2011);
- inclusive recreation best practices (Miller, Schleien, & Lausier, 2009);
- mindfulness training (meditative practices such as yoga, walking, tai chi, Pilates) effects on well-being (Carruthers & Hood, 2011);
- physical activity, health, and wellness research (Bocarro & Wells, 2009);
- physical activity/sports participation and school performance, lifelong participation, health impacts, psychological health, and community impact (Sport England maintains an online monitoring of reference sources as well as critical reviews of published research evidence on these topics at http://www.sportengland.org/research/the_value_of_sport_monitor.aspx).

A variation to traditional research reviews is the ***meta-analysis***, which serves two purposes. First, it presents an integrated literature review on a topic by summarizing the quantitative results from studies conducted on the same subject matter. Multiple databases are searched systematically to identify relevant studies (research published in journals, dissertations, etc.)

Table 2.1
Encyclopedia References

Barnard, A., & Spencer, J. (2011). *The Routledge encyclopedia of social and cultural anthropology* (2nd ed.). New York, NY: Routledge.

Kaldis, B. (Ed.). (2013). *Encyclopedia of philosophy and the social sciences*. Thousand Oaks, CA: Sage.

Loue, S., & Sajatovic, M. (2008). *Encyclopedia of aging and public health*. New York, NY: Springer.

Mizrahi, T., & Davis, L. (Eds.). (2010). *The encyclopedia of social work* (20th ed.). New York, NY: Oxford University Press.

Peterson, P., Baker, E., & McGraw, B. (Eds.). (2010). *International encyclopedia of education* (3rd ed., Vols. 1–8). Amsterdam, Netherlands: Elsevier Science.

Pizam, A. (Ed.). (2010). *International encyclopedia of hospitality management* (2nd ed.). Burlington, MA: Elsevier.

Ritzer, G., & Ryan, M. (Eds.). (2011). *The concise encyclopedia of sociology*. Hoboken, NJ: Wiley-Blackwell.

Weiner, I., & Craighead, W. (2010). *The Corsini encyclopedia of psychology* (4th ed., Vols. 1–4). Hoboken, NJ: John Wiley and Sons.

Table 2.2
Research Reviews Containing Topics Related to Recreation, Park, and Sport/Fitness Topics

American Sociological Review	*Exercise and Sport Sciences Reviews*
Annals of Leisure Research	*International Review for the Sociology of Sport*
Annals of Tourism Research	*Physiological Reviews*
Annual Review of Anthropology	*Psychological Bulletin*
Annual Review of Medicine	*Psychological Review*
Annual Review of Physiology	*Research Quarterly for Exercise and Sport*
Annual Review of Psychology	*Review of Educational Research*
Annual Review of Public Health	*Review of General Psychology*
Annual Review of Sociology	*Review of Research in Education*
Annual in Therapeutic Recreation	

on a topic. Second, the meta-analysis compares results from the studies by using a standard metric (i.e., results are converted so the same unit of measurement is used across the studies). Such a comparison allows for estimating the effect (technically referred to as ***effect size***) of either various interventions or a particular program or activity.

Dieser (2011), for example, used a meta-analysis to examine the efficacy of leisure education programs based on a 10-year review of studies reported in the professional literature. The major findings were that many of the leisure education programs had either overestimated or underestimated how participation affected individuals. That is, many of these earlier studies had overexaggerated how program participation triggered psychological change in participants or underestimated the importance of social and environmental variables in affecting behavioral change.

Excellent references exist that explain how to conduct as well as interpret a meta-analysis. To learn more, see Borenstein, Hedges, Higgins, and Rothstein (2009); Cooper, Hedges, and Valentine (2009); W. Hopkins (2004); Lipsey and Wilson (2001); and Thomas and French (1986).

Finally, be alert to a special caution. Never depend entirely on what you read in a secondary source. "Authors who write about the research or theories of others usually have different interests or backgrounds that lead them to overemphasize certain aspects and de-emphasize or leave out other aspects of the work" (Eichelberger, 1989, p. 86). If you are relying heavily on information presented in a secondary source, find the original article and confirm the findings are reported accurately.

Review General References

Once you have checked secondary sources for a better overall understanding of your topic, turn your attention to locating and reviewing general references that emerged from the keyword search or from secondary sources. ***General references*** include indices, abstracts, and bibliographies, all of which are used to identify publications that contain the reports of actual studies.

Indices are lists of research articles by subject categories, author, title, and journal publication. Many indices have been set up as online databases that access multiple journals in a search (consult Table 2.3). Alternatively, some professional organizations offer indices of research articles (e.g., National Coalition for Promoting Physical Activity at http://www.ncppa.org/resources-reports?qt-resources_reports=2#qt-resources_reports). Indices are useful in terms of being able to quickly identify reported research on a topic. Anyone undertaking a literature review would be remiss not to consult multiple indices.

In contrast to indices that only list citation information, research abstracts additionally provide a short summary. Table 2.4 identifies abstracts (most of these are available as online databases) containing holdings related to recreation, park, sport, and tourism topics.

A ***bibliography*** is considered a general reference as well. A bibliography lists books and articles relevant to a specific topic. Bibliographies may appear in two formats. First, a bibliography may appear as a feature or special article in a journal. Second, a bibliography may emerge as a freestanding publication such as *The Research and Literature on Challenge Courses: An Annotated Bibliography* (Attarian, 2005).

Some university libraries also subscribe to a ***table-of-contents service.*** With this service, libraries may access the tables of contents, identifying the titles of articles and the author names, to thousands of periodicals. One example is JournalsTOCs (http://www.journaltocs.ac.uk/).

Obtain Primary Literature Sources

Literature searches ultimately should lead to primary literature sources, with research appearing in refereed

Table 2.3
Indices With Holdings Related to Recreation, Park, Sport/Fitness, and Tourism Topics

ABI/Inform Index: Indexes articles from hundreds of business journals, covering topics including personnel issues, consumer behavior, organizational behavior, and human resource management.

British Education Index: Provides contents to hundreds of education and training journals published in the British Isles dealing with evaluation and assessment, education policy and administration, and special education needs.

Chicano Index: Contains citations of books, articles, reports, and other documents written by and about Chicanos and other Latinos in the United States.

Cumulative Index to Nursing and Allied Health Literature (CINAHL): Index to English-language and selected foreign-language journals covering health care and related journals, with a focus on evidence-based medicine.

Expanded Academic ASAP: Multidisciplinary index that abstracts articles (some available in full text) in scholarly journals related to social science, health sciences, and humanities.

Hispanic American Periodicals Index: Database of Latin American articles appearing in over 600 social sciences and the humanities journals.

Hospitality & Tourism Index: A bibliographic database indexing scholarly research relating to all areas of hospitality and tourism.

Index to Theses: Abstracts theses completed at universities in the United Kingdom and Ireland (www.theses.com).

InfoTrac: A full-text database that covers articles from thousands of scholarly periodicals (http://infotrac.thomsonlearning.com).

International Index to Black Periodicals: Cites articles on an array of topics (education, health, sociology, etc.) appearing in over a 100 international periodicals.

Physical Education Index: Subject index to literature (in coaching, dance, health education, physical education, physical fitness, recreation, sports, and sports medicine) published in hundreds of national and international journals.

Science Citation Index: Citations and abstracts to thousands of international social science and scientific journals.

Social Sciences Citation Index: Interdisciplinary citation index of thousands of social sciences journals.

Social Science Index: Indexes and abstracts articles in hundreds of periodicals as well as provides full text for some of the journal articles in the social sciences (e.g., sociology, psychology, anthropology, and environmental science).

Web of Science: Accesses three indices or *Social Science Citation Index*, *Social Sciences Citation Index*, and Arts and *Humanities Citation Index*.

Wilson Education Index: Covers a wide range of topics (e.g., dance, sports) in hundreds of education journals.

journals, theses, dissertations, and reports published by governments or private organizations.

Most scientific research is published in ***refereed journals*** (see Appendix 1 for journals that publish articles on topics related to recreation, parks, sport, and tourism). Refereed journals are primary sources that print original research after the manuscript has been reviewed and critiqued by peer researchers/academics and deemed "noteworthy" to print (see Table 2.5 for details about the peer review process that professional journals typically adopt).

Sometimes, you may access a research article via an electronic database. For instance, PsycARTICLES features full-text articles and is readily accessible (listed in Table 2.4). However, at times you will need to request a reference via your university's interlibrary loan service.

If the university library you are using does not have access to a particular reference, a number of online document delivery services exist:

- For journal articles, Infotrieve (http://www.infotrieve.com/document-delivery), ingentaconnect (http://www.ingentaconnect.com/), and The Institute for Scientific Information's ISI Document Solution (http://www.ovid.com/site/products/fieldguide/ccon/ISI_Document_Solution_%28SM%29.jsp) are reliable options.

Table 2.4
Abstracts and Databases Containing Holdings Related to Recreation, Park, Sport and Tourism Topics

I. Abstracts and Databases of Research Published in Journals

Current Contents Connect: Bibliographic information (as well as accesses table of contents and abstracts) to thousands of scholarly journals as well as relevant websites related to the social and behavioral sciences.

Cumulative Index to Nursing and Allied Health Literature (CINAHL): Bibliographic database and full-text resource for allied health literature.

Directory of Open Access Journals: Covers free, full-text, quality controlled scientific and scholarly journals. There are over 3,000 journals in the directory.

EBSCO Academic Search Complete: Multidisciplinary full-text database that includes thousands of peer-reviewed journals (e.g., *Journal of Leisure Research, Journal of Park and Recreation Administration, Leisure Sciences,* and *Leisure Studies*).

EBSCO Host Mental Measurements Yearbook With Tests in Print: Guide to thousands of tests and instruments, including those related to psychology and education.

Education Resources Information Center (ERIC): Online digital library of educational research. Provides a bibliographic and full-text database, accessing over 1 million records of journal articles, research syntheses, conference papers, dissertations, and other education-related materials. ERIC is free to all Internet users.

*E*Subscribe:* Online electronic subscription service providing full-text access to Educational Resources Information Center (ERIC) documents.

Exceptional Child Education Resources: Contains citations and abstracts (from journal articles, dissertations, books, non-print media, etc.) related to exceptional children (with disabilities and who are gifted).

Leisure Tourism Database: Provides abstracts and full-text articles to hundreds of publications in the field of travel and tourism, recreation, leisure studies, and the hospitality and culture industries.

MEDLINE: The National Library of Medicine's database of published medical and health citations and abstracts to millions of references (including indexing articles in thousands of professional journals published around the world).

OvidSP: Reviews over 1,000 health professional journals and contains over 100 bibliographic and full-text databases (including coverage of psychosocial instruments).

Proquest Educational Journals: Provides index, abstract, and full-text services to hundreds of education publications (including the *Therapeutic Recreation Journal*).

Proquest Social Science Journals: Database includes over 1,000 titles (including journals) with many of these available in full text.

PsycARTICLES: Online database containing full text articles from over 40 journals.

PsychINFO: Computer search database providing citations and abstracts to thousands of journals as well as dissertations and books dealing with psychology and behavioral sciences.

PsycLIT: Contains references and abstracts for articles from approximately over 1,000 psychological and behavioral journals as well as book chapters and books.

PubMed: Free database of biomed journal citations and abstracts set up by the U.S. National Library of Medicine.

Search ERIC: Online access of ERIC database.

Social Work Abstracts: Online database of close to 1,000 social work and human service journals.

Sociofile: Contains abstracts to approximately thousands of international sociology and related journals as well as citations to dissertations, books, book chapters, and association papers.

Sociological Abstracts: Online database provides abstracts to journal articles and citations to book reviews from thousands of serials publications.

SPORTDiscus: Online database of full-text articles appearing in sports and sports medicine journals.

Women's Studies International: Provides citations with abstracts on women's studies that appear in hundreds of sources, including journals, dissertations, theses, and proceedings.

Table 2.4 (cont.)

II. Abstracts of Research Presented at Professional Meetings

Abstracts from the Annual Meeting of the American College of Sports Medicine: Published annually as a supplement to Medicine & Science in Sports & Exercise.

Abstracts from Research Consortium Program at the Annual Meeting of the American Alliance of Health, Physical Education, Recreation, and Dance: Published annually as a supplement to the *Research Quarterly for Exercise and Sport*.

Abstracts from the Annual Meeting of the Gerontological Society of America: Published (in October) as a supplement to *The Gerontologist*.

Abstracts from the Annual Meeting of the Leisure Research Symposium: Published annually as an electronic published book of abstracts by the National Recreation and Park Association.

III. Other Abstracts

British Library Ethos (Electronic Theses Online Service): Searches over 350,000 doctoral theses from over 120 institutions in the United Kingdom.

Dissertation Abstracts International: Contains abstracts of most dissertations from North American colleges.

Proquest Dissertations and Theses: Contains abstracts and full text of dissertations and theses from hundreds of universities around the world. Students, as institutional subscribers to this database, may download free titles published from 1997 onward.

- For dissertations and theses, you may use the ProQuest Dissertation Express database (which is free if your university has an account; go to http://www.proquest.com/en-US/products/dissertations/disexpress.shtml).
- For U.S. government publications, use the information network that is operated by the Educational Resources Information Center (ERIC; http://searcheric.org/).
- For British library system holdings, consult http://www.bl.uk/reshelp/findhelpsubject/index.html.
- For research resources around the world, especially from emerging regions, go to the Center for Research Libraries (http://www.crl.edu/).
- The Internet Public Library2 (a consortium of colleges and universities that is hosted by Drexel University) contains "Resources by Subject" (once you click on this, a list of subjects is presented on the menu screen, including "Entertainment & Leisure," "Reference," and "Social Sciences"). Go to http://www.ipl.org/.

Before moving on, advice will be offered for locating primary sources and managing primary sources.

Additional hints for finding primary sources. If you find an informative research article, dissertation, or the like, review its cited references. By studying the reference section of the article, you may determine whether you have overlooked a possibly vital reference. If so, make a note to track down the lead. This snooping

RESOURCES TO HELP WITH A LITERATURE REVIEW

Directions: Match the correct definition to each tool for conducting a literature review.

Literature review tool	Definitions
1. Secondary Source	A. Research reports appearing in refereed journals, theses, and dissertations, as well as published by governmental or private organization entities.
2. General Reference	B. Identifies primary sources or publications that contain the reports of actual studies; includes indices, abstracts, and bibliographies.
3. Primary Source	C. Publication that provides introductory background information on a topic; includes encyclopedia references, research reviews, textbooks, and meta-analyses.

Note. Answers are provided at the end of the chapter.

Table 2.5
Overview of How Articles Are Published in a Refereed Journal

Do you know how to get your research published in refereed professional journals? Below is a summary of a process.

1. Refereed journals use a peer review process. ***Peer review*** means a manuscript submitted for publication consideration is reviewed and critiqued by independent experts. The purpose is to ensure the published manuscript meets the appropriate quality standards set by the journal.
2. A majority of the editors of refereed journals are members of a university faculty. An editor typically serves a 3-year term.
3. The editor appoints an editorial board, selecting educators and practitioners, based on their research expertise, interest, and availability. Members of this editorial board are known as ***associate editors***, and they also serve 3-year terms.
4. The process begins when a researcher sends a manuscript to the journal's editor. Guidelines on manuscript requirements, as well as to whom and where to send the manuscript, appear in each edition of a journal.
5. The editor then directs the submitted manuscript to an associate editor, who is responsible for identifying two external experts (outside the editorial board) who agree to review it. The submitted manuscript undergoes a ***blind review***, meaning the author(s) of the manuscript are not revealed to the three reviewers (i.e., associate editor and two external reviewers).
6. The editor considers the three reviews and makes the final decision about the manuscript. Rejection rates vary by year and by journal. The *Journal of Leisure Research*, for instance, reports that about 50% of the submitted articles are rejected outright, 20% are rejected after full review, 15% of the papers needing corrections are never revised and resubmitted, and the remaining 15% are eventually published in the journal (K. Shinew, personal communication, June 26, 2012).

around may help you discover important information for your literature review.

If you find an on-target article, find out who else has used it. The easiest way to do this is to consult the *Social Sciences Citation Index* (http://thomsonreuters.com/social-sciences-citation-index/), an index to thousands of the world's leading journals in the social sciences across 50 disciplines. For a fee (your university library already may subscribe to this service), the "Citing Reference" search feature of this index is able to identify primary sources that have referred to the same article. In other words, with this index, you may build a collection of references that are likely specific to your topic.

Managing primary sources. Maintain a written record of how the search was conducted. That is, record what databases you used, which keywords you used for each database search, the years covered in the database review, and the date you completed the database search. One reason for keeping these notes is that if you have to back up and revisit one or more of the databases you reviewed earlier, your organization will help you know where you left off.

Computer software exists to keep track of references. For example, popular commercial products are EndNote, Reference Manager (http://www.endnote.com/enabout.asp), and ProCite (http://www.procite.com/), whereas a number of reference managers are free, including Mendeley (http://www.mendeley.com/).

Gauging refereed journal quality. This section will end with a discussion on gauging the quality of a professional journal. At least two journal system ratings have emerged. For instance, the *Journal Citation Reports* publishes an impact factor listing of journals, across disciplines, each year (around June). ***Impact factor*** is a standardized measure of how often articles from a particular journal have been cited in the same journal and in other journals. A high impact factor means that articles in the particular journal are cited more often in the reference lists of articles appearing in refereed journals. In turn, impact factors (using numbers published in the *Journal Citation Reports*) for selected journals in sport, exercise science, and medicine are published (usually in July) in the online journal *Sportscience* (http://www.sportsci.org/).

To compete with the proprietary company that issues impact factors (it requires an institutional membership to access), the ***article influence score*** was developed at the University of Washington and determines the average influence of each article in a journal over the first five years after publication (meaning how often a particular journal is cited by researchers in other journals). Article influence scores are calculated using the *Journal Citation Reports* database, and these scores are available free online (http://www.eigenfactor.org/). Table 2.6 presents article influence scores of selected journals related to recreation, parks, sport, and tourism.

Table 2.6
Five-Year Article Influence Score of Selected Journals, 2012

Journal	Article influence score	Percentile in which article influence score falls
Annals of Tourism Research	.64	58
Journal of Hospitality, Leisure, Sport & Tourism Education	.06	8
Journal of Leisure Research	.32	35
Journal of Sport and Societal Issues	.59	58
Leisure Sciences	.39	41
Research Quarterly for Exercise & Sport	.52	53
Sociology of Sport Journal	.52	52
Tourism Management	.71	67

Note. Retrieved April 8, 2014, from http://www.eigenfactor.org. Scores are normalized so the mean article in *Journal Citation Reports* is set at 1.0. For ease of interpretation, the percentile in which the Article Influence Score fell is noted. The higher the percentile score is, the higher the journal's influence.

Some practitioners have criticized the use of impact factor–like ratings (Thomas, Nelson, & Silverman, 2011). One objection is these factors do not reveal whether the citation was positive or negative. Another criticism is that the impact factor could be inflated since it does not consider that authors may cite their own articles. Additionally, an article may not be cited many times if many people are not writing on the same topic. Finally, these ratings could penalize researchers who have long-term projects that result in fewer publications. Nevertheless, impact factor or article influence score may be a factor to consider when reading and mulling over a journal article.

REVIEW AND ANALYZE PRIMARY LITERATURE SOURCES

After identifying a primary literature source reference, determine its relevance to your study. Relevance of a primary or secondary source is its degree of usefulness to your study. As illustrated in Table 2.7 (and described in greater detail in Step 16), typically a primary source contains at least 11 major sections (sometimes referred to as headings). The challenge is to find a connecting link between an earlier study and the study you are contemplating. That is, your quest is to locate previous work that sheds insights or provides thoughts to you regard-

Table 2.7
Anatomy of Parts Typically Reported Within a Research Report

Most research reports contain a number of "standard" parts. The major sections or headings typically found in research studies contained in a journal, thesis or dissertation, or report are as follows:

1. Abstract or Executive Summary
2. Introduction
3. Theoretical Foundation(s)
4. Hypotheses and/or Research Question
5. Literature Review
6. Methods
7. Results
8. Discussion
9. Conclusions
10. Recommendations
11. References

ing a theoretical foundation, methods, and so forth that you could use in your own research.

Engage in ***active reading***. As you read photocopies of articles, dissertations, or short chapters (not books you have checked out of the library), highlight and make marginal notations and/or bracket (using a colored marker or ink pen) the important information. For instance, if the passage deals with theory, write "theory" in the margin or bracket the word. Likewise, if the paragraph addresses a point you may use in your introduction, write intro in the margin.

Knowledge of how to set up and implement a small-scale study (which you are learning in this book) will help you read the literature with a "skeptical yet sympathetic eye that is equipped with the ability to detect crap" (Joiner, 1972, p. 1). Do not take other people's assertions at face value. Instead, determine for yourself whether the conclusions are justified based on the research methods used. As you learn more about research methods, you will better understand and critique research proposals and reports.

WRITE THE LITERATURE REVIEW

The ultimate outcome of searching and reading, of course, is to write a literature review summary. A literature review written for a study proposal or final report uses a more technical form of writing that is unlike most of the writing researchers do (Gay, Mills, & Airasian 2012). Adopting the tone of the Review of Literature sections in your primary source articles will guide you to this form.

You may organize the literature review in different ways. A good way to organize is around introduction, body, and conclusion (Hopkins, 1999):

- Introduction. State which databases you used for the literature review, identify the keywords you used for the search, and specify the time span for the search (e.g., publications published from 2009–2013). Also note the yield or number of references you identified from the search. Then, inform the reader how the remaining Literature Review section is organized.
- Body. This section, which is the bulk of the review, presents a summary of previous research studies. One idea for organizing this section is to use subsections corresponding to the major variables (discussed in Step 4) examined in the study. For example, suppose your topic is "How an Outdoor Adventure Program Affects the Emotional Safety and Trust of Participants." The following is a possible outline for the body of the literature review:

  <u>First Subsection</u> (which could be labeled "What Is Known About How Outdoor Adventure Program Participation Affects Emotional Safety?"):
    - Paragraph 1: Summarizes studies reporting significant positive changes in emotional safety that are attributed to participation in an outdoor adventure/recreation program.
    - Paragraph 2: Summarizes studies reporting no significant changes.
    - Paragraph 3: Summarizes studies reporting significant negative effects or changes.

  <u>Second Subsection</u> (which may read, "What Is Known About How Outdoor Adventure Program Participation Affects Trust?"):
    - Paragraph 1: Summarizes studies reporting significant positive changes in trust that are attributed to participation in an outdoor adventure/recreation program.
    - Paragraph 2: Summarizes studies reporting no significant changes.
    - Paragraph 3: Summarizes studies reporting significant negative effects or changes.
- Conclusion. Identify reasons for contradictory results. For instance, highlight differences in sampling or research designs used (discussed in Steps 6 and 7), instrumentation (covered in Step 8), and data collection (reviewed in Step 9). Finish by summarizing ideas needed for future research, with special emphasis on how your research project will fill in a knowledge gap and/or be conducted in a manner that makes the proposed study unique or significant.

If you find much literature on your topic, a shorthand way to present the findings is to use a summary figure (Case 2.3). This results in presenting a lot of information in a limited amount of space. Even if this tabular approach is used, you should still present the Introduction and Conclusions sections to the literature review in full text.

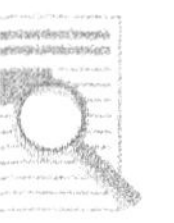

Reviewing the writings and studies of others is admittedly time consuming because it requires culling through many references. But in the end, a literature review is an investment that may be invaluable in designing, implementing, and interpreting the results of a research study. British Museum Reading Room, London, England. Copyright © 2015 Carol Cutler Riddick.

SOMETHING TO REMEMBER!

Concerning my literature review, on my honor, I pledge I have

- relied, whenever possible, on primary sources rather than secondary sources.
- incorporated relevant and up-to-date information. When I have used older references, it is because they are "classics."
- not given the impression that I read firsthand a study when I did not. In instances where I could not obtain a copy of the primary reference, I acknowledge my quoting has come from a secondary source.
- documented facts and the opinions of others.
- defined terms clearly and used them consistently.
- organized content logically, using subheadings when appropriate.
- cited contrary findings.
- avoided the temptation to include everything I found in the literature—bigger is not necessarily better! Instead, I have synthesized and interpreted what I read.
- raised methodological or problematic issues.
- followed an accepted current style manual (e.g., American Psychology Association's (2010) *Publication Manual* or the University of Chicago's (2010) *Chicago Manual of Style*.

REVIEW AND DISCUSSION QUESTIONS

1. What purposes may be served by conducting a literature review?
2. What is a keyword, and how is it used in online database searches? What keywords most relate to your own interests?
3. How do a secondary literature source, a general reference, and a primary literature source differ from each other? Cite one example of each.
4. What does it mean to say a research manuscript appears in a refereed journal? What refereed journals have you used in preparing papers for courses?
5. Identify at least five pointers for writing a literature review.

YOUR RESEARCH

1. Using the topic you have chosen (Step 1), identify at least three keywords that you may use to conduct a literature search.
2. Using at least two general reference databases, locate three primary literature sources (i.e., research articles and dissertations) on your topic. If needed, use different keywords. Print the citation and abstract of these three primary literature sources.
3. Obtain a copy of each of these primary literature references.

PRACTICE EXERCISES

1. Peruse some refereed journals to find one article related to recreation, parks, sport, or tourism that interests you. (*Note:* Your instructor may assign the topic or article.) Provide a full-text print copy of the chosen article and record marginal notations where it answers the following questions:
   a. Cited literature to identify a conceptual/theoretical approach used to conduct the research?
   b. Mentioned references to bolster the significance of the study?
   c. Identified literature to document the measures used to conduct the study?
   d. Relied on earlier writings or studies to explain and interpret results?
2. Choose a topic for a possible research study. (*Note:* Your instructor may ask to preapprove the topic before you begin this assignment).
   a. Using online databases at your university's library, locate four articles published in the past five years that report original research on your selected topic and may be downloaded as a full-text article. Three of the finds should have been published in a refereed journal, and one should be published as a thesis or dissertation. Print a citation and abstract for each of the four studies.
   b. Additionally, provide written answers to how you conducted your search:
      i. What computerized databases did you use?
      ii. What keywords did you use to conduct the literature search?
      iii. Did you use Boolean operators? If yes, which ones did you use? Was it useful to use these operators? Explain your answer.
      iv. Did you have trouble locating four research studies? If so, did you examine the references for the studies you found to help you identify additional useful literature? Did you need to use the *Social Sciences Citation Index*?
3. Choose and print one of the articles you found from Practice Exercise 2. (*Note:* Alternatively, the instructor may assign you a specific article.) Provide written responses (also noting the page number of the article that supports your answer) to the following questions:
   a. Provide background regarding how the literature review was conducted.
      i. What databases were examined?
      ii. What keywords were used?
      iii. What time span was used for the literature search?
   b. Did the article mention how the paper was organized?
   c. Did the article present a logically organized literature review section? If not, make one suggestion on how the literature review section could be improved.
   d. Did the article point out as well as try to explain why contradictory results from earlier investigations may have occurred?
   e. Did the article contain conclusions at the end of the literature review section on why or how the study would fill in some knowledge gap and/or why the study was significant?

WEB EXERCISES

1. Examine an outdoor education meta-analysis by going to the Wilderdom website (http://wilderdom.com/) and then clicking on "Outdoor Education Research and Evaluation Center." Under "Outdoor Education" click on "Research" and then click on "Meta-Analytic Research Reviews." Briefly explain in writing how this meta-analysis could be useful when conducting a research study on outdoor recreation.

2. Read the 2010 white paper *The Evidence Base for Private Therapeutic Schools, Residential Programs, and Wilderness Therapy Programs* (available at the Association for Experiential Education's website: http://www.aee.org/files/en/user/cms/NATSAP_White_Paper.pdf). Is this research review useful? Explain your answer.
3. Access the most recent article influence rating scores for journals by going to http://www.eigenfactor.org.
   a. Look up and record the percentile scores for six journals related to recreation, parks, sport, and tourism. (*Note:* Your instructor may tell you which six journals to use.) What journal in your list is most widely cited? Least cited? Give two explanations for why a journal does not have a higher rating.
   b. Identify two journals in recreation, parks, sport, or tourism that are missing from the Eigenfactor listing? *Hint:* Appendix 1 has a list of journals relevant for recreation, parks, sport, and tourism professionals.

SERVICE LEARNING PROJECT

Now that a particular campus program or service has been selected for the focus of the service learning project, collect historical or background information about it. The instructor may divide the class into teams and then assign each team the responsibility of finding references that provide answers to the following questions:

1. When did the program or service first begin?
2. Who (names and pictures) have been the program managers or directors?
3. How has the program or service changed over time (in terms of what it has or has not offered)?
4. Find pictures of students, over time, using the program, facility, or service.
5. If available, what is the estimated annual number of users during the years the program has operated?

A number of secondary and primary literature sources exist in the quest to find answers to these questions. These sources include the current program manager or director, college yearbooks, student publications (e.g., daily college newspaper), alumni newsletters or Web postings, the university archives, and faculty and staff who have worked at the institution for a long time.

TEST YOURSELF ANSWERS

Resources to Assist With a Literature Review

1. C, 2. B, 3. A

SUPPORTING CASES FOR THIS CHAPTER

CASE 2.1. TEACHING CHILDREN WITH AUTISM ROCK CLIMBING: IDEAS THAT MAY BE GLEANED FROM A PREVIOUS STUDY

Kaplan-Reimer, H., Sidener, T., Reeve, K., & Sidener, D. (2011). Using stimulus control procedures to teach indoor rock climbing to children with autism. *Behavioral Interventions, 26*, 1–22.

These researchers examined whether Green's (2001) behavioral techniques would work for teaching rock climbing to children with autism. The authors argued that their study was significant because children with autism have an abundance of free time yet may not have the skills necessary to use this time well; teaching individuals with autism to engage in leisure activities may have beneficial results, including promoting social interaction, independence, and integration into the larger community; rock climbing has the potential to promote physical health; and few studies have examined teaching exercise activities to individuals with autism.

The authors studied two children (aged 6 and 11 years) who had not participated in intensive physically engaging activities. The intervention to teach rock climbing skills consisted of multiple within-stimulus fading procedures, errorless learning procedures, positive reinforcement, error correction, and conditional discrimination.

Both children were successful in learning to climb at least 10 feet on specified routes and at least one of three routes without errors. The findings supported Green's conditional discrimination training model. The authors suggested ways to carry on this line of inquiry. For example, researchers need to tease out which behavioral approaches contributed to achieving the desired results. Likewise, they called for recording participants' enjoyment levels experienced during rock climbing and rock climbing route preferences. Finally, they speculated that the array of behavioral techniques used to teach rock climbing also may work in teaching children with autism self-help and independent living skills.

This study is illuminating for someone embarking on a research study. It may be used to identify a topic to research, pinpoint a conceptual or methodological approach to teaching, explain the significance of investigating benefits that may accrue from learning rock climbing, and/ or frame results with what has been reported previously.

CASE 2.2. A RESEARCH REVIEW

Becken, S. (2011). A critical review of tourism and oil. *Annals of Tourism Research, 38*, 359–379.

Growing scarcity of oil and increasing oil prices are highly relevant for the tourism industry. This paper provided a critical meta-analysis to assess current knowledge of "tourism and oil." The review is complex. It pointed out boundaries for the phenomenon being studied are not clear, the interpretation of facts is context dependent, and activities relevant to tourism and oil are multidimensional. The author suggested that increasing oil prices will have far-reaching impacts on tourism, including changes to people's lifestyles. Yet, it is noted our knowledge of tourism and oil is far from comprehensive and serves as a starting point for further inquiry.

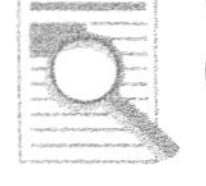

CASE 2.3. INTEGRATIVE REVIEW: EFFECTS OF SELECTED THERAPEUTIC RECREATION (TR) ACTIVITIES ON GERIATRIC PHYSICAL HEALTH

Investigator(s)	Subjects	TR Activity	Theoretical Foundations	Focus	Measure(s)	Outcome(s)
Cutler Riddick (1985)	Older residents in public subsidized housing complex with a senior center $N = 22$ (randomly assigned to one of the three groups: an aquarium group, a visitor group, a control group)	Goldfish aquariums were placed in participants' homes; nine bi-weekly visits from the researcher (from 25-35 min./visit) for six months Visitor group received 10 bi-weekly visits from the researcher (from 30-40 min./visit) for six months	None	Blood pressure	Sphygmomanometer	Significant decrease in diastolic blood pressure in aquarium group (from the pre- to posttest)
DeSchriver & Cutler Riddick (1990)	Older residents in a public subsidized housing complex $N = 27$ (randomly assigned to one of three groups: viewed a fish aquarium, viewed a fish videotape, or viewed a placebo videotape)	Viewing of the fish aquarium, fish videotape, or placebo videotape lasted eight minutes, once a week, over a three-week period	Relaxation Theory	Pulse rate Skin temperature General skeletal muscle tension	Lumiscope Digitronic I model (beats per minute) Yellow Springs Temperature Meter Bicep Electromyography (EMG)	No significant change No significant change No significant change
Gowing (1984)	Elderly home health care recipients $N = 33$ (non-equivalent control group design)	Minimal care pets (goldfish) for a six-week period	None	Blood pressure	Sphygmomanometer (assumed-not stated	No significant improvement when comparing pre- and posttest scores
Green (1989)	Elderly community residents enrolled in a community service program $N = 24$ (one-group pretest-posttest design)	Water aerobic program (two times a week for 16 months)	None	Blood pressure	Sphygmomanometer	Significant reduction in diastolic blood pressure (when comparing pre- and posttest scores)
				Resting pulse	Pulse rate	No significant improvement

Note. From Riddick & Keller (1991). Reprinted with permission of the authors.

Scaffolding is important in building and renovating facilities, as it is in research. Namely, theoretical scaffolding or a platform helps launch and frame a study from beginning to end. Shanghai, China

STEP 1 STEP 2 STEP 3 STEP 4 STEP 5

IDENTIFY THEORETICAL ROOTS

WHAT WILL I LEARN IN THIS CHAPTER?

I'll be able to...

1. Define theory and explain how theory exists informally and formally.
2. Describe how formal theories differ in terms of focus (micro-, meso- or macro-levels) and complexity (parsimonious vs. nonparsimonious).
3. Outline how theory is built and used in research by reiterating the interrelationships among concept, variable, and theory.
4. Summarize the ways theory may be used in a research project.
5. Compare and contrast three theoretical approaches (quantitative, qualitative, and mixed methods) used for conducting research, according to role of formal theory, logic, purpose, research questions, data collection methods, data analysis methods, and researcher's role.

"[Those] who love practice without theory are like the sailor who boards ship without a rudder and compass and never knows where to cast."

Leonardo di Vinci
(Italian Renaissance painter, sculptor, architect, inventor, botanist, and writer, 1452–1519)

Most people do not realize theory plays an important part of every step of the research process. Indeed, theory influences the questions that are asked, the collection of data, and the way findings are interpreted. As an evaluator and researcher, you have an obligation to be transparent about your theoretical perspectives.

In research, theories are your tools for interpreting; they provide the scaffolding by which you may understand. Simply put, a ***theory*** (sometimes referred to as a paradigm, model, or epistemology) is an explanation or assertion of why or how something works according to two meanings (D. Hopkins, 2008, p. 72). That is, a theory may be informal or formal:

1. ***Informal theory*** is a set of personal beliefs or presuppositions that you hold regarding how things work, or your individual construction of reality.
2. ***Formal theory*** is an explicit and articulated statement that attempts to explain or predict a phenomenon or concept.

Informally, your actions are grounded by your own personal assumptions about how and/or why something works. For example, if based on your own experience you believe that socialization is good for people, you will strive to design and deliver leisure programs that foster social interactions. On the other hand, formal theory comes about when someone, after observing a phenomenon, explains the phenomenon (Jasso, 2001). Formal theories differ in terms of their focus and complexity.

The focus of this chapter is on formal theory. One way to distinguish formal theories is by their focus (Neuman, 2009). They may fall within one of three categories:

THE FUN THEORY

As part of a promotion, the Volkswagen® car company developed a series of videos "testing" the fun theory. The theory maintains that you may change people's behavior through fun. Check out these studies:

- the piano stairs at http://www.youtube.com/watch?v=2lXh2n0aPyw
- the recycling bottle bin at http://www.youtube.com/watch?v=zSiHjMU-MUo

- micro-level theories or explanations limited to a small number of people;
- meso-level theories related to organizations or communities; and
- macro-level theories about large aggregates such as societies or social institutions.

The broadest macro theoretical formulation, sometimes referred to as ***grand theory***, tries to explain wide-ranging situations or behaviors. A well-known example is Csikszentmihalyi's (2008) ***flow theory***. Flow is a subjective state that is triggered by intense engagement in an activity. Moreover, flow is characterized by loss of self-consciousness, a sense of self-control, and an altered sense of time. Researchers from different disciplines have tested flow theory and in turn have examined individuals who have participated in an array of activities (including rock climbers and chess players). Study findings generally have supported the theory (R. Russell, 2012).

You may also categorize formal theories by their complexity. You may judge theory on whether or not it provides a simple explanation of complex relationships. Thus, the challenge of a formal theory is to present an explanation that has parsimony. A ***parsimonious theory*** is a concise or simple explanation of reality.

For instance, a number of theories exist for explaining sport team wins. Complex, intricate, and nonparsimonious theories abound on what factors into winning. For example, players' goal setting, imagery, self-confidence, and self-regulation have been linked to performance (cf. Tenenbaum & Eklund, 2007). However, a simple explanation for winning is set forth in sport competition anxiety theory (Martens, Vealey, & Burton, 1990). This theory is focused on how situational trait anxiety, or how a person feels right before competition, affects winning or losing the competition. That is, a person's anxiety level may either facilitate or hamper competitive performance; namely, too little or too much anxiety is deemed to have dire consequences on an athlete's performance.

The remainder of this chapter is divided into three parts: how theory is built, reasons for using theory in research, and three theoretical approaches for conducting research.

HOW TO BUILD THEORY

Although science is based on empirical observation, data are meaningless unless they are organized and interpreted. When conducting research, you are attempting to connect theory with data that you have obtained. Even though theories vary in terms of focus and complexity, they aim for precision. That is, theories achieve precision by operationally defining phenomena.

Ultimately, theory links concrete and abstract phenomena. Another label used interchangeably with phenomenon is concept. A ***concept*** (sometimes called a construct) is a label for concrete and abstract phenomena. A ***concrete concept*** is an object, trait, or behavior that you may observe in the physical environment. For example, a person's height is a concrete concept. On the other hand, an ***abstract concept*** is not visible to the naked eye; it is an intrinsic characteristic, such as a feeling or attitude.

REFLECTING ON MY ATHLETIC PERFORMANCE!

At some point, you probably have competed on an athletic or sport team (in high school, college, etc.). Reflect on your anxiety level immediately before sport competition by going to one of the following websites to gauge your sport competition anxiety level: http://www.brianmac.co.uk/scat.htm or http://www.hypnosisworks.org.uk/scat_test.pdf

What was your rating? Do you register as having high anxiety? Low anxiety? An average level of anxiety?

According to sport competition anxiety theory (Martens, Vealey, & Burton, 1990), having either high or low anxiety immediately before a competition has an adverse or negative effect on how well you compete. Yet experiencing some anxiety is beneficial, and you are more likely to compete better.

What do you think?

1. Do you agree with this parsimonious explanation of how precompetition anxiety affects your performance? Explain.
2. What factors, other than precompetition anxiety, may explain winning or losing a game?

Note. Answers are provided at the end of the chapter.

Concepts are the cornerstone of a theory. Take for instance the activity theory, which asserts that activity involvement (in domains such as voluntary organizations, friendship and kinship interactions, and hobbies) affects life satisfaction (Figure 3.1). The theory posits that the more active you are, the happier you are. Activity involvement is a concrete concept that may be observed and measured, and life satisfaction is an abstract concept because it is a feeling or attitude. Activity theory provides an explanatory bridge between activity and its effects on life satisfaction.

For you to be able to conduct research, concepts must have an operational definition. Oftentimes referred to as a ***variable***, an ***operational definition*** is the meaning of a concept expressed in terms of how it is measured (Springer, 2010, p. 543). A variable must have a minimum of two values that are mutually exclusive (Babbie, 2012). For example, the values for the variable of chronological age may range from 0 to over 100 years. Another variable is gender (with two possible values: male and female).

A concept may be defined operationally by different variables. Suppose you are interested in conducting research on how physical activity is linked to the concept of psychological health, which may be defined in a number of ways, including a few highlighted in Figure 3.2.

Suppose you are interested in determining whether first year college students participating in an outdoor recreation program grow socially. Social development is a broad abstract concept, so you need to define it operationally by identifying variables that are linked to the concept. Using Erikson's (1968) and Maslow's (1968) theories of human development, you choose to examine the variables of trust, emotional safety, and intimacy (defined by these theories as meaning commitment to affiliate with others; Figure 3.3). In your research study of determining the impacts the course has on students, you measure these variables as an indication of their social growth and development.

The basic idea in building theoretical precision is to start broadly and then become more specific by narrowing in on a concept via a corresponding variable. An analogy is the spare tire cover on the back of your Jeep® Wrangler that says, "Life is good." Why is life good? Is it because you own a Jeep®? Perhaps it has something to do with your feelings about being offered a great job when you graduate! In this case, the life-is-good concept is defined operationally by the postgraduation employment status variable.

Figure 3.1. Theory builds the bridges between conceptual relationships.

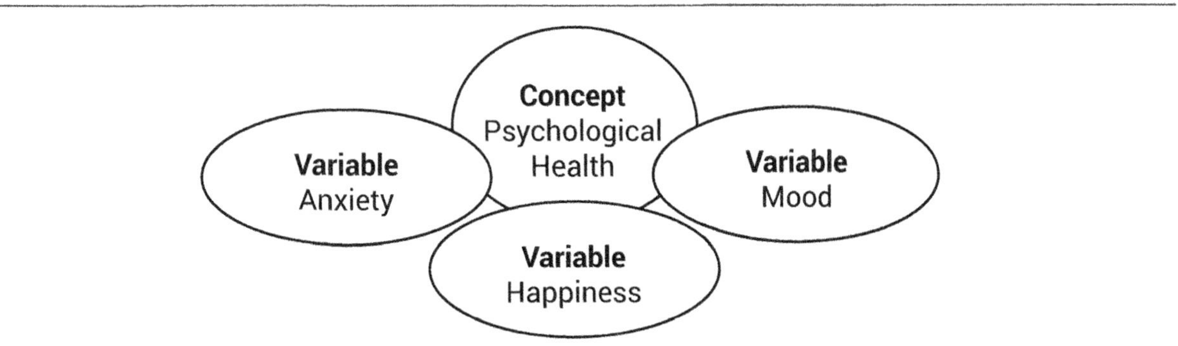

Figure 3.2. How the concept of psychological health may be operationalized.

Figure 3.3. Social development as an umbrella concept and related variables.

SOMETHING TO REMEMBER!

Theory	Identifies relationships between and among concepts to explain why or how things happen
Concept	Label to describe
	• Concrete phenomenon: an object, trait, or behavior that is found or observed in the physical environment
	• Abstract phenomenon: something not visible to the naked eye, an intrinsic trait or characteristic.
Variable	• Elaboration or operational definition of concept.
	• Characteristic or trait that describes a person or object.
	• At least two values or categories must exist.

ROLES OF THEORY IN RESEARCH

Two main reasons exist to use formal theory in research. First, theory directs research. If you select and study topics without theoretical connections, shallowness and a lack of direction and focus may result. Indeed, a theoretical framework is necessary to guide you because it is the scaffolding of your research (Basit, 2010). For example, a theoretical foundation may influence how a study is conducted in terms of

- setting the agenda for what questions the study will ask,
- establishing a rationale for answering these questions,
- directing the choice of data collection methods,
- assisting with interpreting the findings, and
- making conclusions about how well the findings relate to the real world.

Second, over time and multiple studies, theory helps you to build a body of knowledge related to recreation, parks, sport, and tourism (Burdge, 1985). A body of knowledge about leisure is important because it ultimately informs your professional practices (see Case 3.1). Research findings that have a theoretical connection may lead to improved service delivery, increased leisure functioning by individuals, and a higher quality of individual and societal life (Coyle, Kinney, Riley, & Shank, 1991; Dunn, 1996).

Even though the role of theory in research is important, the reality is many researchers choose neither to

COMING UP WITH POSSIBLE VARIABLES

Try your hand at operationally defining concepts. For each of the following concepts, brainstorm (especially fun with classmates) at least three variables each. An example is provided.

Concept	Variables
1. Enjoyment	• Self-reported fun following participation in a recreational activity • Number of times smiled while participating in the activity • Leader's rating of group's overall pleasurable experience level
2. Travel satisfaction	
3. Sport participation success	
4. Attitude toward nature	

Note. Answers are provided at the end of the chapter.

adopt nor to articulate a theoretical foundation for their studies. To demonstrate this state of affairs, a review of 700 studies appearing in professional leisure journals between 1981 and 1990 found that about one half did not address theory testing or theory development (Henderson, 1994). This common practice unfortunately has perpetuated itself, as a follow-up study of research published between 1992 and 2002 found that three fourths of the studies made no attempt to develop or test a theory (Henderson, Presley, & Bialeschki, 2004).

THEORETICAL APPROACHES FOR CONDUCTING RESEARCH

Every research project should acknowledge its theoretical indebtedness. This is not difficult because whether or not you are aware of it, you have a guiding mind-set, or philosophical worldview. A philosophical worldview (sometimes referred to as a paradigm or epistemology) is a "basic set of beliefs that guide action" (Guba, 1990, p. 17). Your worldview provides you with a general orientation about humankind and in turn influences what you research and how you conduct your research (Creswell, 2013). In short, acknowledging your mind-set is important.

FINDING A THEORETICAL BASE FOR YOUR RESEARCH

Searching for a theoretical foundation for your research? Set up a ***provenance grid*** (Jankowicz, 2004). Several ways exist to work with the grid; one strategy is to begin by identifying a topic and then searching through disciplines to locate applicable theories.

For example, suppose you want to conduct research on athletic performance. Sift through literature in a few disciplines and complete a provenance grid (see example below) identifying theories that may explain athletic performance.

Discipline	Theory
Anthropology	Anti-structure theory explains that formal rituals unique to a sport environment govern athletic performance (Turner, 2001).
Psychology	Social facilitation theory is focused on how task difficulty, skill level, and type of audience affect performance (Zajonc, 1965).
Sociology	Feminist theory is focused on the role of feelings, attitudes, and perceptions of female athletes on performance (Swigonski, 1994).
Sport psychology	Sport competition anxiety theory speculates on how player anxiety affects performance (Martens, Vealey, & Burton, 1990).

Many theoretical perspectives exist, but for ease of discussion, the following sections will focus on the ones most commonly found in research in recreation, parks, sport, and tourism: a quantitative approach, a qualitative approach, and a mixed-methods approach (Tables 3.1, 3.2, and 3.3). Which of these approaches you adopt for a study will have profound implications for the subsequent design (Step 7), data collection methods (Step 9), data interpretation (Steps 14A and 14B), and conclusions of the study (Step 16).

Quantitative Approach

A ***quantitative approach*** (also referred to as post-positivist theory, empirical science, and normative theory) is the study of the causes that influence outcomes. Its intent is to reduce big ideas into small discrete ideas to test, such as the variables contained in research questions and in hypotheses (Creswell, 2013). This approach relies on collecting numerical information on the world by focusing on and quantifying behaviors, feelings, observations, and so forth (Table 3.1). Researchers in the natural sciences (e.g., biology and physics) originally used a quantitative approach, but over time, researchers in the social science disciplines, including psychology, sociology, and leisure studies, adopted it as the basis for conducting studies.

Underlying quantitative research methods is the assumption that the world is relatively stable, uniform, and coherent and may be measured and generalized (Gay, Mills, & Airasian, 2012). Furthermore, quantitative research may be described according to many features that distinguish it from qualitative research (Table 3.1). Quantitative research differs from qualitative research by its emphasis on deductive reasoning and theory testing.

Deductive reasoning and theory testing. The quantitative approach to research relies on ***deductive reasoning***, which involves developing specific predictions based on general principles, observations, or experiences. In other words, adopting a quantitative approach in research is ***theory testing***.

Theory testing is identifying a formal theory that sheds light on how certain concepts are related (as you will learn in Step 4, speculating relationships between or among variables is known as ***hypothesis testing***). Then, data are collected to find out whether evidence exists to support the relationships that the theory speculated to exist (Figure 3.4).

Table 3.1
Features of Quantitative Research

Dimension	Answer
Role of formal theory	Theory testing/verification
Logic	Deductive reasoning; determining cause–effect relationship
Purpose(s)	To describe, explain, or predict; may infer findings from sample apply to a population
Research questions	Precise questions about relationships among phenomena (relying on hypothesis testing)
Participants	Few to many; may or may not use nonprobability or probability sampling
Data collection methods	Measurement relying on close-ended structured inquiry (interviews, questionnaires, observations, etc.)
Data analysis methods	Numerical/statistical data
Researcher role	Detached, impartial/unbiased

Idea: Gleaned from a theory

Speculation: Tests research questions or hypotheses derived from theory

Reality: Measure or observe

Figure 3.4. Deductive reasoning used in the quantitative approach.

A second way of testing theory according to the quantitative approach is by ***model development and testing***, sometimes referred to as ***conceptual mapping***. How concepts relate to each other is diagrammed. Usually a review of the research literature helps inform the "mapping," or linkages made between and among concepts. Data are then collected to determine whether support exists for the proposed model (see Case 3.2).

SOMETHING TO REMEMBER!

Two ways exist to find a theory to test. That is, research may be guided by either

- a priori theory testing or
- conceptual mapping.

One way to set up a research project is to examine relationships that existed in a previously constructed theory. Using an existing, known theory is technically referred to as ***a priori theory testing*** (see Case 3.3). Appendix 2 provides a list of sources of quantitative paradigms that you may examine in recreation, park, sport, and tourism research.

Structured inquiry. In addition to deductive reasoning and theory testing, the quantitative approach to research relies on structured inquiry. ***Structured inquiry*** involves asking specific questions or observing specific behaviors using data collection methods that use predetermined, closed-ended categories to record the answers. For instance, you could ask tourists leaving an attraction to rate their experience by choosing one answer from among the following possible responses: *excellent, good, fair,* and *poor*. In summary, deductive logic requires reasoning toward observations, so systematic collection of data must occur to determine how well a theoretical explanation holds up. This is why data are gathered using structured instruments (e.g., interviews, questionnaires, observation checklists, and record reviews; see Step 9).

Qualitative Approach

A ***qualitative approach*** (also known as social constructivism, interpretive theory, and ideological theory) gathers individuals' subjective meanings of the world in which they live. This approach recognizes these meanings are varied, multiple, and complex (Table 3.2). The approach is based on the belief that human experience varies across settings and times and therefore seeks to understand an event as participants experience it rather than in categories predetermined by the researcher (Schutt, 2011).

Anthropologists, social workers, educators, and those conducting research related to recreation, parks, sport, and tourism have embraced the qualitative approach. Even Sherlock Holmes may be considered a follower of the qualitative theoretical approach: "It is a capital mistake to theorize before one has data. Insensibly, one begins to twist facts to suit theories instead of theories to suit facts" (Doyle, 1891, p. 163).

Qualitative research has a number of unique characteristics. For instance, it relies on inductive reasoning and theory development (Table 3.2).

Inductive reasoning and theory development. The qualitative theoretical approach is based on ***inductive reasoning***, which involves developing multiple meanings based on observations of a limited number of related events or experiences. In other words, inductive reasoning moves from observation of specific circumstances toward making a general conclusion. General principles are developed from the information gathered by way of discovering a pattern that represents an order or logic among the results (Babbie, 2012). In the qualitative approach, the researcher interprets peoples' thoughts, feelings, or behaviors by identifying themes.

Table 3.2
Features of Qualitative Research

Dimension	Answer
Role of formal theory	Theory development/generation
Logic	Inductive with emphasis on understanding multiple meanings
Purpose(s)	To describe, interpret, contextualize
Research questions	Vague questions centered on "what" and "how"
Participants	Few; selected because of specific qualities
Data collection methods	Unstructured or semistructured inquiry (questionnaires, interviews, observations, record reviews, etc.) with no preset response categories
Data analysis methods	Text/image data
Researcher role	Involved and collaborative with participants

The aim of qualitative research is to develop theory. Theory emerges at the end of the study (Figure 3.5). The goal of using a qualitative framework is to develop a theoretical understanding of what has been learned at the time data were collected (see Case 3.4). Consequently, the qualitative approach is also referred to as an ***ex post facto*** explanation of concepts. A number of qualitative theoretical perspectives may be used to conduct research (see Step 7 for an introduction to some of these including critical theory and grounded theory). Appendix 2 offers a list of qualitative theory references.

Idea: A theory emerges

Interpretation: Find theme/patterns/categories

Reality: Gather information

Figure 3.5. Inductive reasoning in the qualitative approach.

Unstructured or semistructured inquiry. Another feature of qualitative research is its use of data collection methods that are centered on unstructured or semistructured inquiry. Inductive reasoning leads to theory development by way of analyzing nonnumerical data—words, pictures, and objects—that emerge from open-ended questions or observations (covered in greater detail in Step 9). This ***unstructured inquiry*** method does not rely on predetermined categories of answers (as is true of the quantitative approach), but instead it asks respondents to describe their experiences in their own words. For example, you could begin an interview by asking Elder Hostel participants, "Tell me about your impressions of your weeklong Elder Hostel experience." This unstructured, open-ended question enables the researcher to listen and learn directly from participants (Richards & Morse, 2013).

An adaptation of this is the ***semistructured inquiry*** in which open, unstructured questions are asked and followed, as needed, by preprepared structured questions. These follow-up questions are called ***probes.*** For example, a probe for the Elder Hostel participant interview cited above could be, "To what extent would you say the Elder Hostel program provided you with opportunities to feel personally challenged? Choose one answer from the following possibilities: *a lot, some,* or *not at all.*"

RECALLING FEATURES OF QUANTITATIVE AND QUALITATIVE APPROACHES TO RESEARCH

Directions: Check which feature matches which theoretical approach.

Feature	Quantitative approach	Qualitative approach
1. Deductive logic	☐	☐
2. Inductive logic	☐	☐
3. Theory testing	☐	☐
4. Theory building	☐	☐
5. Describes	☐	☐
6. Explains	☐	☐
7. Predicts	☐	☐
8. Generalizes	☐	☐
9. Focused on what and how	☐	☐
10. Structured inquiry	☐	☐
11. Unstructured or semistructured inquiry	☐	☐
12. Researcher involved and partial	☐	☐
13. Researcher detached and impartial	☐	☐

Note. Answers are provided at the end of the chapter.

Mixed-Methods Approach

A ***mixed-methods approach*** is a blend of quantitative and qualitative approaches (Table 3.3). Also referred to as ***triangulation***, this approach (Case 3.5) yields different views of complementary data (Sale, Lohfeld, & Brazil, 2002).

Whenever possible, you should adopt a mixed-methods approach. Why? Combining both approaches in a study allows you to transcend the disadvantages associated with any one approach and maximize your advantages. According to Black (1994),

> Poorly conducted quantitative studies can produce findings so trivial as to contribute little to the research literature or professional practice. On the other hand, qualitative studies can be so subjective and idiosyncratic that there is no hope of any useful contribution. (p. 3)

One way to think of striking balance in the mixed-methods approach is via an analogy with yin yang (Figure 3.6). In Chinese Taoism, the concept yin yang (sometimes referred to in the West as ***yin and yang***) shows opposing, seemingly contrary forces that are nonetheless bound together and interdependent, each giving rise to the other.

In actuality, mixed-methods studies, even though complementary, are typically conducted where one approach dominates over the other (Figure 3.7). For example, you may use a quantitative approach to confirm findings from data obtained via a qualitative approach, and vice versa. See Step 9 for more specific examples of this triangulation.

In closing, remember that deductive and inductive logic (and the quantitative and qualitative approaches they support) are useful means to constructing and/or refining theory. Ultimately, a mixed-methods approach that combines the two logics is the best to use. Research in recreation, parks, sport, and tourism is interdisciplinary, suggesting you are not directed by one single body of knowledge, academic discipline, or approach. Thus, blending the quantitative and qualitative logics provides you with a more comprehensive understanding of the concepts you are interested in studying and understanding. Appendix 2 provides sources for mixed-methods theories.

Table 3.3
Features of Mixed-Methods Research

Dimension	Answer
Role of formal theory	Theory testing/verification and theory development/generation
Logic	Deductive and inductive reasoning
Purpose(s)	To describe, explain, and/or predict; to interpret/contextualize
Research questions	Precise questions about relationships among phenomena (relying on hypothesis testing) and/or questions centered on what and how
Participants	Few to many (> 100); may or may not use nonprobability or probability sampling
Data collection methods	Predetermined and emerging methods (uses open- and close-ended questions, observation categories, etc.)
Data analysis methods	Statistical and text analyses
Researcher role	Impartial/unbiased yet assume passive to complete involvement with participants

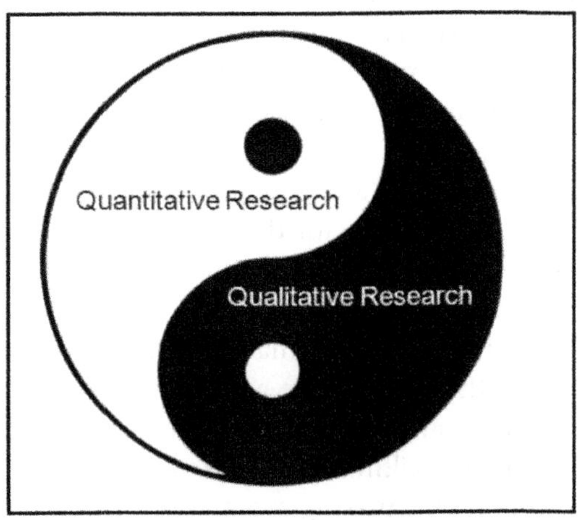

Figure 3.6. The yin yang analogy of the mixed-methods approach.

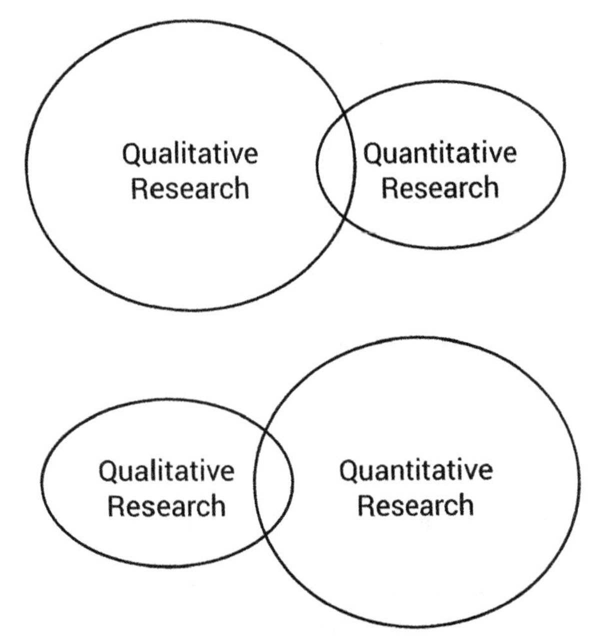

Figure 3.7. Complementary but not equal ways to conduct a mixed-methods approach.

Similar to the rope supporting this acrobat, a theory may become an invaluable lifeline in supporting a multitude of decisions made in a research project. Convent Garden, London, England. Copyright © 2015 Carol Cutler Riddick.

REVIEW AND DISCUSSION QUESTIONS

1. What is theory supposed to do? How does it do this?
2. Describe how formal theories may differ in terms of focus (micro-, meso-, or macro-levels) and complexity (parsimonious vs. nonparsimonious).
3. How is a concrete concept different from an abstract concept? Give examples of each.
4. What are the interrelationships among a theory, concept, and variable? Cite and explain a theory (e.g., the activity theory) that illustrates these interrelationships.
5. Name at least three reasons for using theory in research.
6. What three theoretical approaches discussed in the chapter do researchers typically use to conduct research?
7. For each of these theoretical approaches, describe a research situation where you could use the approach.

YOUR RESEARCH

1. Are you planning on using a quantitative or qualitative approach as the basis for your research study? Explain the rationale for your choice.
2. If you are planning to use a qualitative approach, identify and briefly summarize the theoretical perspective you could use to guide the study. *HINT:* For some leads, fast forward to Step 7 and/or consult Appendix 2.
3. If you are going to use a quantitative approach, will your study rely on theory testing or conceptual mapping? Identify and briefly explain the theory you are planning to use?
4. Have you considered a mixed-methods approach? Why is it or why is it not appropriate to use this approach for your research study? If you plan on using the mixed-methods approach, will you give the quantitative or the qualitative paradigm priority? Explain the rationale for your choice.

PRACTICE EXERCISES

1. To improve your ability to link concepts to a variable, complete the worksheet below.

Worksheet Theory Chapter: Practice Moving From a Concept to a Related Variable

Concept	Variable name	**How variable could be measured** (*Note:* Try your hand at this now as a way to be ready for Step 8)
1. Physical health	Energetic	Using a pedometer, tally the number of steps taken during a sample day
2. Mental health		
3. Competitiveness		
4. Conservation ethic		
5. Ethnocentricity		

2. Acquire a copy of the following articles (or your instructor may substitute other articles, one that represents an example of a quantitative approach and the other an example of the qualitative approach):

   Ewert, A., Gilbertson, K., Luo, Y.-C., & Voight, A. (2013). Beyond "because it's there": Motivations for pursuing adventure recreational activities. *Journal of Leisure Research, 45*, 91–111. You may access this article at http://js.sagamorepub.com/jlr/article/view/2944.

   Sharaievshka, I., Kim, J., & Stodolsky, M. (2013). Leisure and marital satisfaction in intercultural marriages. *Journal of Leisure Research, 45*, 445–465. You may access this article at http://js.sagamorepub.com/jlr/article/view/3894.

Worksheet Theory Chapter: Reading and Understanding Research Reports Using a Quantitative or Qualitative Approach

Dimension	Article 1 answer	Article 2 answer
1. Classification: Was a quantitative or qualitative approach used?		
2. Formal theory used to deduce hypotheses or research questions?		
3. Theory used was to induce or discover patterns?		
4. Study purpose(s)?		
5. Research question(s) examined?		
6. How many study participants?		
7. Data collection methods used?		
8. Data analysis methods used?		

3. Acquire a copy of the following article (or your instructor may substitute another article):

   Battenfield, F., Dzaloshinsky, B., & Todd, S. (2007). The demise of the WNBA in Florida: A mixed-method case study of newspaper coverage about women's professional basketball. Sport Journal, 10, 1–21. You may access this article at http://thesportjournal.org/article/the-demise-of-the-wnba-in-florida-a-mixedmethod-case-study-of-newspaper-coverage-about-womens-professional-basketball/.

   Read the article and answer the questions found in the following worksheet.

Worksheet Theory Chapter: Reading and Understanding a Mixed-Methods Research Report

Question	Answer
1. Which data collection methods suggest the quantitative approach?	
2. Which data collection methods suggest the qualitative approach?	
3. What was learned from the quantitative data?	
4. What was learned from the qualitative data?	
5. How did the study conclusions reflect what was learned from the quantitative approach? Qualitative approach?	

4. Acquire a copy of the following research article (or your instructor may substitute another article):

   Godbey, G., Crawford, D., & Xiangyou, S. (2010). Assessing hierarchical leisure constraints theory after two decades. *Journal of Leisure Research, 42*, 111–134.

   Read the article and answer the questions found in the following worksheet.

Worksheet Theory Chapter: Leisure Constraints Theory

Question	Answer
1. Who were the originators of the leisure constraints theory?	
2. How does this theory explain leisure behavior?	
3. In what ways has research used this theory?	
4. What issues have the research studies raised about the theory?	
5. What are recommendations for further research relevant to the theory?	
6. Which research approaches have researchers used to investigate leisure constraints?	

WEB EXERCISES

1. Think about the interface between theory and a research topic.
   a. Start by reviewing popular psychology, sociological, and social psychological theories by going to the following websites:
      - http://psychology.about.com/ od/psychology101/ u/psychology-theories.htm http://en.wikipedia.org/wiki/ Category: Psychological_ theories
      - http://en.wikipedia.org/wiki/Category:Sociological_theories
      - http://en.wikipedia.org/wiki/List_of_social_psychology_theories

   b. Identify and explain one theory that you could use as the foundation for conducting research on a topic you have identified.
2. Read more about the differences between the quantitative and qualitative approaches by visiting http://www.socialresearchmethods.net/kb/qualdeb.php, a research methods database site that discusses the "Qualitative Debate." Identify four insights you learned from this reference in a one-page paper.
3. Learn more about the mixed-methods approach by going to the website for the National Science Foundation. Find the online *User-Friendly Handbook for Mixed Method Evaluations* at http://www.nsf.gov/publications/pub_summ.jsp?ods_key=nsf97153. Read the handbook, paying particular attention to the hypothetical illustration in Chapter 2. Share with a classmate three things you learned from this reference.

SERVICE LEARNING PROJECT

Zero in on the theoretical approach for your end-of-the-term class presentation and final report. You need to either find a formal theory (Option 1 below) or rely on conceptual mapping (Option 2) to support the research project you will be undertaking on the campus program or service that has been selected to be the focus of the service learning project.

The instructor may set up teams to conduct the theoretical framework search. He or she may assign one or more teams the task of finding a formal theory that ties into the program or service being studied (Option 1). The instructor may ask another team or two to come up with a conceptual mapping schema that illustrates how program or activity participation impacts or affects student participants (Option 2).

Option 1

Identify one or more formal theories to assist with directing the service learning project. The emphasis is on locating a quantitative, qualitative, or mixed-methods approach.

To find a theoretical framework, complete the following steps:

1. Locate articles, research reviews, or theses/dissertations that have examined the same sort of program (intramurals, fitness/exercise, or whatever campus service that has been chosen) under scrutiny, with particular attention on finding studies centered on program impact evaluations (or how program participation affected participants' knowledge, attitudes, skills/functional ability, and/or aspirations; see Step 1). Examine the studies to identify one or more theories that guided the reported investigation. Summarize the theories that have served as the foundation of such studies.
2. Categorize each theory discovered as quantitative, qualitative, or mixed-methods approach.
3. Then use either Table 3.1, 3.2, or 3.3 in this chapter, to outline how you may apply the theory when conducting the service learning project.

Option 2

To answer the following questions, you will need to undertake a review of literature.

1. What benefits have been documented as accruing from participating in the particular campus recreation or sport program being studied?
2. Rename each noted benefit as a concept. For each identified concept, identify at least three related variables (use Figure 3.2 as a template for this answer).
3. Draw a conceptual map that illustrates how participation in the selected campus sport or recreation program has been found to impact participants.

TEST YOURSELF ANSWERS

Reflecting on My Athletic Performance!

1. Sport competition anxiety theory is simple and hence parsimonious.
2. Nevertheless, an array of other factors (physical condition of athlete, quality of coaching received, etc.) also may affect athletic performance.

Coming Up With Possible Variables

Concept	Variables
1. Enjoyment	• Self-reported fun following participation in a recreational activity • Number of times smiles while participating in the activity • Leader's rating of group's overall pleasurable experience level
2. Travel satisfaction	• Number of smiles in end-of-trip group photograph • Positive comments made on end-of-program evaluation form • Willingness to recommend trip to others
3. Sport participation success	• Win–loss record • Eligibility for more advanced leagues or groups • Sustained participation
4. Attitude toward nature	• Willingness to sleep overnight outdoors • Signing up for nature study workshop • Regular watching of Discovery Channel

Recalling Features of Quantitative and Qualitative Approaches to Research

Feature	Quantitative approach	Qualitative approach
1. Deductive logic	✓	
2. Inductive logic		✓
3. Theory testing	✓	
4. Theory building		✓
5. Describes	✓	✓
6. Explains	✓	
7. Predicts	✓	
8. Generalizes	✓	
9. Focused on what and how		✓
10. Structured inquiry	✓	
11. Unstructured or semistructured inquiry		✓
12. Researcher involved and partial		✓
13. Researcher detached and impartial	✓	

SUPPORTING CASES FOR THIS CHAPTER

CASE 3.1. THEORY-BASED RESEARCH GUIDES SERVICE DELIVERY

Harrolle, M., & Trail, G. (2007). Ethnic identification, acculturation and sports identification of Latinos in the United States. *International Journal of Sports Marketing and Sponsorship, 8*, 234–253.

According to researchers, sport management and marketing research has failed to study Latino fan identification as well as their sports consumption behaviors. Therefore, this study examined a theoretical model that speculated that ethnic identity (allegedly a positive influence) and acculturation (supposedly a negative influence) explain attachment to star athletes. Furthermore, attachment to star athletes was projected to influence the overall consumption of Latino-based sport products. Latinos living in the United States completed a battery of questionnaires.

Findings did not support the theoretical model. Ethic identity and acculturation had little to no influence on sports identification. This study concluded that sport marketers should not create marketing campaigns solely based on the assumption that Latinos (or any ethnic group) are necessarily fans of any particular sport (e.g., soccer).

CASE 3.2. CONCEPTUAL MAPPING THEORY TESTING

Casper, J., & Stellino, M. (2008). Demographic predictors of recreational tennis participants' sport commitment. *Journal of Park and Recreation Administration, 26*, 93–115.

The goals of this study were to (a) identify antecedents that explained amateur, adult players' tennis commitment and (b) understand how demographic characteristics (age, gender, and income) temper tennis players' sport commitment. The proposed model was adapted from the social-exchange theory of interpersonal relationships and investment theory. The following figure illustrates the model that was tested:

*Tennis Enjoyment

*Involvement Opportunities

*Personal Investments

Social Constraints

Social Support

Tennis Commitment

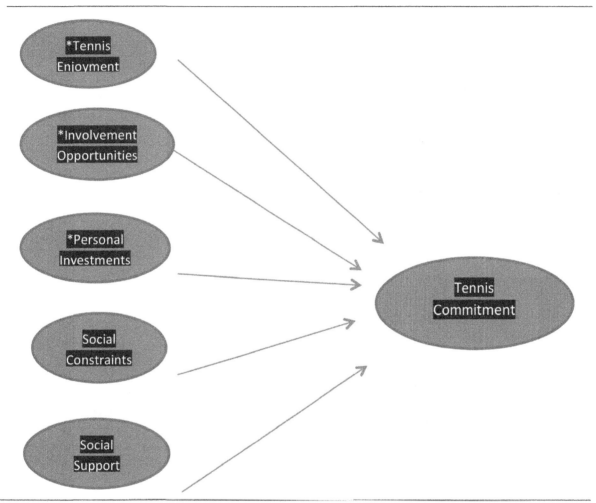

Note. Reprinted with permission of the authors.
$^*p < .05$.

Data were collected from 547 adult recreational tennis players associated with community tennis associations in the Intermountain Region of the United States. Study participants completed a Web-based questionnaire. It was found that tennis enjoyment was the strongest predictor of tennis commitment across all demographic categories. To a lesser yet significant degree involvement opportunities and personal investments also emerged as having significant impacts across all demographic groups on sport commitment.

It was concluded there are stable predictor variables of tennis commitment along with significant differences. Marketing implications of the study include providing enjoyment and involvement opportunities for tennis enthusiasts.

CASE 3.3. A PRIORI THEORY TESTING

Mulvaney, M. (2011). A study of the role of family-friendly employee benefits programs, job attitudes, and self-efficacy among public park and recreation employees. *Journal of Park and Recreation Administration, 29,* 58–79.

The effects of two family-friendly employee benefits programs—dependent care support and flexible work arrangements—were assessed for how they affected organizational commitment and job self-efficacy outcomes. Social cognitive theory (with its emphasis on the reciprocal interaction among work environment, behavior, and the person) was the basis for examining four hypotheses speculating employees, who perceive the availability of dependent care support and flexible work arrangements, will have higher job motivation and organizational commitment. Public park and recreation professionals ($N = 456$) completed an online survey.

Three of the four hypotheses were supported: dependent care positively affected job motivation and flexible work arrangements positively affected both job motivation and organizational commitment. These benefit programs are viewed as creating a strategic advantage for agencies to recruit and retain high performers within the organization as well as establishing a more productive workforce.

CASE 3.4. QUALITATIVE APPROACH USED IN RESEARCH

Misener, K., Doherty, A., & Hamm-Kerwin, S. (2010). Learning from the experiences of older adult volunteers in sport: A serious leisure perspective. *Journal of Leisure Research, 42,* 267–290.

A sample of adult volunteers aged 65 years and older in community sport organizations were interviewed. Open-ended questions were used to enable participants to share, using their own words, their experiences with volunteering.

The study found that volunteers may be described as having substantial involvement, strong identification with volunteering, and the need to persevere. The older adults viewed their volunteer experience as extremely positive; it made them feel they were making a meaningful contribution. Many benefits were associated with volunteering. The most frequently noted negative aspect of volunteering was problems centered on interpersonal relations, yet overall, this was not enough to drive participants away from this activity.

CASE 3.5. MIXED-METHODS APPROACH USED IN RESEARCH

Chareanpunsirikul, S., & Wood, R. (2002). Mintzberg, managers and methodology: Some observations from a study of hotel general managers. *Tourism Management, 25,* 551–556.

Eight general managers (seven males, one female) of luxury hotels in Thailand participated in the study. The properties they managed consisted of five city hotels and three resort hotels. Four of the managers were Thai, and four were non-Thai.

The quantitative approach initially was used for data collection. The managers were asked to complete a closed-ended questionnaire about their time allocation according to managerial roles. They were asked to estimate the amount of time they spend each day on each of 10 managerial role categories identified in Mintzberg's managerial roles theory (1973).

Then, using the qualitative approach, each manager was shadowed as they went about their daily duties to determine their actual time allocations to managerial roles. The observation period was 5 consecutive working days spent with each general manager.

Findings from each approach were triangulated. Luxury hotel managers perceived (via their questionnaire responses) that leader and entrepreneur roles were their most important and time-consuming roles. When comparing observations of how much time managers spent in these roles, however, the researchers found that managers spent little time in these roles. Most of the managers' time was spent assuming a monitoring role.

Just as the child featured in the photo is scoping out the surroundings, you need to determine exactly what information you are looking for in order to find useful information in a research study. Hollywood Studios at Walt Disney World, Orlando, Florida. Copyright © 2015 Ruth V. Russell.

STEP 1 STEP 2 STEP 3 STEP 4 STEP 5

DETERMINE SCOPE

WHAT WILL I LEARN IN THIS CHAPTER?

I'll be able to...

1. Recall what constitutes the scope of a study: unit of analysis, variable, purpose statement, and research question and/or hypothesis.
2. Explain and provide an example of independent, dependent, and intervening variables.
3. Describe and write purpose statements for a quantitative, qualitative, and mixed-methods study.
4. Explain how writing a research question is linked to testability and connectedness.
5. Write research questions for a quantitative study (a descriptive and normative question), a qualitative study (grand tour question), and mixed-methods study.
6. Describe two ways research questions may be handled in a mixed-methods study.
7. Define and write an example of a null, nondirectional and directional hypothesis.
8. Differentiate between a hypothesis that states a positive relationship and one that expresses a negative relationship.

"Somewhere, something incredible is waiting to be known."

Dr. Carl Sagan
(American astronomer, astrophysicist, cosmologist who during his lifetime published more than 600 scientific papers, books, and articles in which he advocated skeptical inquiry, including in the search for extraterrestrial intelligence, 1934–1996)

Perhaps Dr. Carl Sagan's most important contribution to the world today is that he popularized science research topics. For example, he published the book *Contact*, a science fiction thriller that centers on exchanges between human and extraterrestrial life forms. Though personally skeptical of this subject, Sagan thought scientists should study the phenomenon. The question of whether other life forms live beyond the planet earth provided Sagan (and other researchers to this day) with a "road map" for what to study. Having a road map, or setting the scope for a study, is what Step 4 is all about. To determine the scope of the study, you must define and refine an idea for a topic (Steps 1 and 2). Then, based on a theoretical foundation (Step 3), you must focus a general idea of what to study into a manageable course of action (Step 4). Accordingly, for this step, you need to determine the study elements: unit of analysis, variables, purpose, research question, and hypotheses (Figure 4.1).

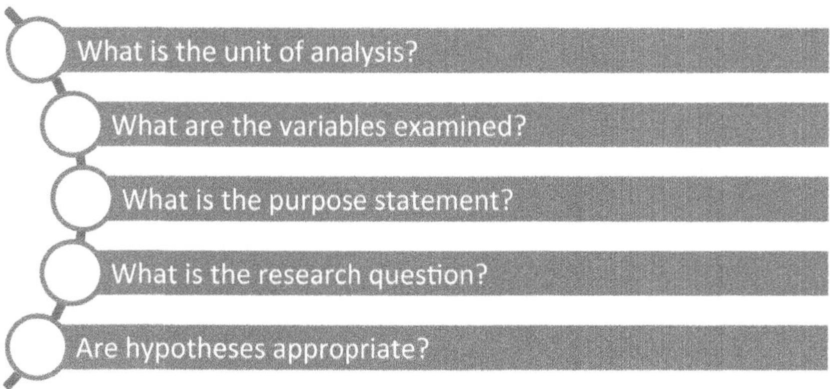

Figure 4.1. Determining the scope of a study: Following the research road map.

UNIT OF ANALYSIS

To begin, whether the study is quantitative, qualitative, or mixed methods, you need to settle on the ***unit of analysis***. The unit of analysis is specifically who or what is studied. The more common units of analysis are as follows (Miles & Huberman, 1994):

- individuals (e.g., participant, member, guest),
- groups (e.g., clubs, gangs, families),
- organizations (e.g., recreation agencies, health clubs, hospitals, resorts),
- artifacts (e.g., newspapers, meeting minutes, photos, songs),
- social interactions (e.g., at playgrounds, bars, sporting events, campgrounds).
- community (e.g., a geographical area),
- event (e.g., special activity or program held), and
- time period (e.g., from 2000 to present).

Typically, the popular units of analysis in leisure research have been groups (see Case 4.1) or individuals (Riddick, DeSchriver, & Weissinger, 1991). Meanwhile, other units of analysis, such as events, time, and lifestyles, have received less attention (Babbie, 2012) and thus possibly deserve more consideration in research related to recreation, parks, sport, and tourism.

Distinguishing the unit of analysis for a study is often tricky. For instance, are you interested in understanding

- gangs as a group or gang members as individuals,
- fitness clubs or fitness club members, or
- resort managers or the resorts themselves?

For example, suppose you want to monitor how environmental attitudes change before and after participation in a conservation program. You record the environmental attitudes of Sierra Club and National Rifle Association members before and after they complete the program. You examine aggregate scores, calculate an average environmental attitude score for Sierra Club and National Rifle Association members, and compare these averages. What is the unit of analysis for this study? In this case, it is groups because the data are compared according to the two groups.

Studying one unit of analysis and concluding the findings hold true for a different unit of analysis is not acceptable science. This extended, distorted logic is known as an ***ecological fallacy*** (Babbie, 2012). Suppose you are traveling and have a brief stopover in a country you have never visited. You had arranged to meet a tour guide, who is a native of the country, at the airport. The 4-hour tour was a disaster; the tour guide was disorganized and obnoxious! If you board the plane thinking that all persons from this country are like your tour guide, you commit an ecological fallacy. That is, you study or focus on an individual yet extend the actions of this one person to a group of people.

WHAT IS THE UNIT OF ANALYSIS?

Directions: For each noted research question, identify the unit of analysis.

Research question	What is the unit of analysis?
1. How does a college student spend his or her free time?	
2. What communication patterns do offensive versus defensive players use?	
3. How are recreation department volunteers oriented?	
4. What leisure roles for women are portrayed in Victorian novels?	
5. What will a content analysis of receptionists' check-in dialogues reveal?	
6. How did the town maintain control over strip development decisions?	
7. How have Renaissance fair participants' entertainment interests changed over the past 2 years?	
8. What destinations do Londoners visit while vacationing in the summer months?	

Note. Answers are provided at the end of the chapter.

SOMETHING TO REMEMBER!

The unit of analysis is the major entity that you analyze in a study. It is the what or who that is studied. In leisure-related research, typical units of analysis include individuals, groups, organizations, artifacts, and social interactions. Remember, a group consists of one or more individuals or individual units.

Do not confuse unit of analysis with ***unit of observation,*** which is the unit or object on which you collect information. For example, you may collect surveys from individuals residing in different neighborhoods, yet you may draw conclusions from this information to compare the neighborhoods. In this case, the unit of observation is individuals, but the unit of analysis is a group.

VARIABLES

Next, to continue to focus on the scope for a study, identify the variables. Recall from Step 3 that a variable is an elaboration of a concept. A variable is a characteristic or property that describes a unit of analysis. Therefore, what constitutes a variable will vary from study to study. Examples of variables that you may use in leisure-related studies include age, gender, recreation activity interests, leisure satisfaction, sport skills, travel behaviors, and environmental attitudes.

You must be able to observe or measure variables, and the variable must have at least two mutually exclusive values or attributes. Take age. Age is typically measured by asking respondents to reveal their age and, as such, has more than 100 values (less than 1 year of age to living 100 years or longer).

Variables are distinguished as either dependent or independent. In particular, the acting variables are independent and the reacting variables are dependent.

Dependent Variable

The ***dependent variable*** measures the concept of interest in the study. The reacting variable is the variable that is affected—sometimes referred to as the outcome or response variable. In a quantitative study, the dependent variable is examined in terms of how one or more independent variables influence it. In Figure 4.2, for example, travel destination choice is the outcome, or dependent variable, being studied.

Independent Variable

The variable you introduce into the situation, be it a treatment, program, intervention, demographic characteristic, or other causal factor, is the ***independent variable***. Thus, as the independent variable in Figure 4.2, highest education level attained is likely an acting factor in travel destination choice.

Intervening Variable

Independent variables influence dependent variables directly and indirectly. When an independent variable operates indirectly, it is an ***intervening variable***. An intervening variable mediates between another independent and dependent variable (see Case 4.2). This means the intervening variable tempers the independent variable, or makes the influence of the independent variable less clear. Thus, in Figure 4.2, the variable of income could mediate the causal relationship between attained education level and travel destination choice. Perhaps travel choices are not influenced so much by a traveler's education, but instead by the income that education may produce. Statistical tests exist that may be used to determine the amount of influence independent variables, including an intervening variable, have on the dependent variable being examined.

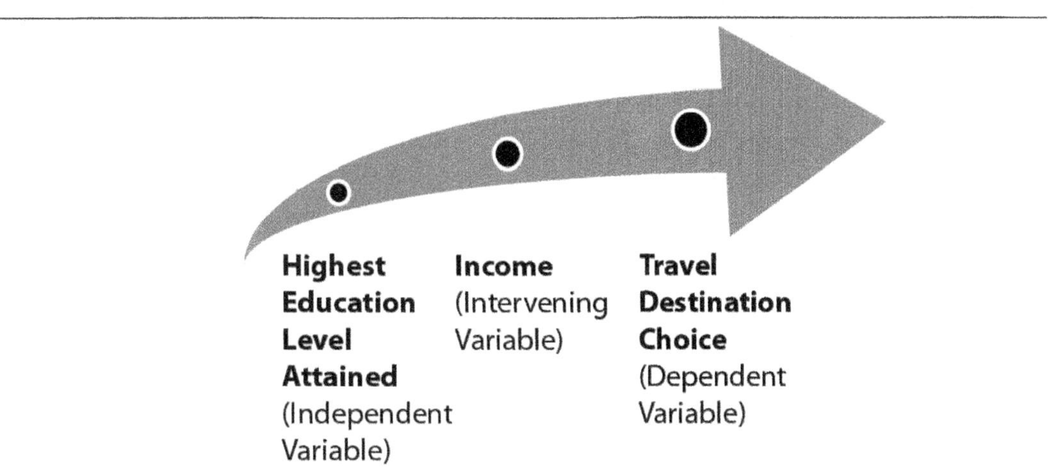

Figure 4.2. Distinguishing the dependent and independent variable.

SOMETHING TO REMEMBER!

To illustrate the difference between independent and dependent variables, think of the horse track! Suppose horse number 7 wins the race. Winning is the dependent variable. Also suppose that horse number 7's jockey is the most skilled jockey. Jockey skill is the independent variable. That is, jockey skill had something to do with horse 7 winning. Indeed, many track fans place their bets based on this independent variable! What other independent variables may be useful in hedging your bet?

What may be a plausible intervening variable between jockey skill and the winning horse? Keeneland Race Track, Lexington, Kentucky. Copyright © 2015 Ruth V. Russell.

How many variables are optimal for a research study? Researchers often debate this question. Consider examining how participation in a particular program or activity could affect an individual or a group of individuals on at least a couple of fronts. That is, consider how program participation may affect at least two or three dependent variables.

Although you should examine multiple dependent variables, avoid a shotgun approach, in which many variables are included in the study. Too many variables not only require extra work for the researcher and possibly the study participants, but also may reduce the integrity of accurate findings (Lodico, Spaulding, & Voegtle, 2010).

Contrastingly, too few dependent and independent variables in a study may result in missing important relationships or conclusions. For example, in a study on the impact of swimming on resting heart rate, you may also measure the impact of swimming on stress release because the independent variable of swimming likely benefits resting heart rate and stress release. Perhaps the best way to balance is to rely on a literature review as well as theoretical insights to provide guidance regarding what variables to examine in a study.

PURPOSE STATEMENT

In determining the research scope, you also need to declare the overall intent of the study. A well-crafted ***purpose statement*** (also referred to as the problem statement) is prepared according to specific principles (Creswell, 2013). These principles are unique according to whether you adopt a quantitative, qualitative, or mixed-methods approach. Case 4.3 illustrates this by comparing theoretical approaches and subsequent purpose statements.

IT'S TIME FOR A FEW JOKES!

Law of invisible phenomena: The absence of evidence is not evidence of absence.

In theory, there is no difference between theory and practice, but in practice there is a great deal of difference.

Raw data is like raw sewage, it requires some processing before it can be spread around. The opposite is true of theories.

Errors using inadequate data are much less than those using no data at all.

Quantitative Study Purpose Statement

For a quantitative study, the purpose statement begins with particular wording, including identifying the theoretical foundation and the independent and dependent variables (Creswell, 2013). For example, in writing a purpose statement for a quantitative study, adhere to the following principles:

- Begin with the word *purpose, aim, intent, focus, goal*, or *objective*.
- Use verbs such as describe, explain, test, or predict.
- Pinpoint the unit of analysis.
- Identify the theory or conceptual framework to be tested.
- Name the variables examined in the study by identifying first the independent variables and then the dependent variables.

DeSchriver and Riddick (1990) used these principles in their purpose statement in a study that reported on how watching aquariums affected the stress of older persons:

The *purpose* of the study was *to test* the *relaxation theory* by having elderly persons view an aquarium and determine whether *engagement in this activity* evoked a relaxation response or reduced physiological stress...or reduction in *pulse rate*, increase in *skin temperature*, and a reduction in *muscle tension* [emphasis added]. (p. 44)

Qualitative Study Purpose Statement

Likewise, you should follow certain principles when writing a purpose statement for a qualitative study (Creswell, 2013). The ingredients for a well-written purpose statement for a qualitative study are as follows:

- Begin with the word *purpose, aim, intent, focus, goal*, or *objective*.
- Use verbs such as *describe, interpret, contextualize, explore, address*, or *understand*.
- Identify the theoretical approach used in the study.

A study on Canadian curling clubs incorporates these principles (Mair, 2009):

Because curling clubs in Canada are unique sport settings, my study is *not a traditional* sport study. The insights gained from this specific endeavor enhance an *understanding* of collective leisure and sport more generally. Moreover, my approach helps *address* challenges outlined by critical sport and leisure sociologists...who argue the growing tendency to concentrate on individuals and their performance over play, community, power and access should be countered [emphasis added]. (pp. 450–451)

Mixed-Methods Study Purpose Statement

The purpose statement for a mixed-methods study conveys the intent of the study and information about its quantitative and qualitative aspects (Creswell, 2013). Guidelines for crafting a mixed-methods purpose statement include the following:

- Begin with the word *purpose, aim,* or *intent.*
- Indicate the unit of analysis (e.g., The purpose of the study is to examine tourists' reactions to...).
- Identify the mixed-methods design used (concurrent design or sequential design; see Step 7).
- Use the characteristics of a good quantitative and qualitative purpose statement (see preceding sections).
- Outline the reasons for adopting a mixed-methods approach.

For example, Mactavish and Schleien (2000) in their study on therapeutic recreation provide this purpose statement, which illustrates the guidelines for a mixed-methods study:

This research note focuses on one example of a mixed-method approach that was used to study recreation in families that included children with developmental disabilities...In particular, this note describes the dominant-less dominant mixed-method research design and its usefulness in reconciling some of the philosophical concerns...that have been expressed about mixed-method research. (p. 155)

RESEARCH QUESTION

A ***research question*** makes the theoretical assumptions in the study more explicit as it indicates what the researcher wants to know foremost. That is, the research question narrows the purpose statement. A review of literature (see Step 2) often contributes to writing a research question because what you learn from the research findings and conclusions of other studies helps you to articulate the necessary research question to answer for your study.

A research question states what is expected to be known as a result of studying the unit of analysis for a particular variable. Although advice abounds on what makes a research question good, the question may be boiled down to testability and connectedness (Springer, 2010).

Testability

Testability is being able to answer the research question. That is, you must be able to evaluate the research questions through empirical investigation. To achieve testability (Springer, 2010, p. 58), complete the following:

- Express the research question in clear and specific terms.
- Avoid value judgments (e.g., *good* and *bad*).
- Use methods for answering the questions that are feasible and ethical.

Can you detect whether a proposed research question heeds this advice for achieving testability? Which of the following research questions is more testable?

- Research Question 1: Is children's creativity increased when an arts program is leader-led?

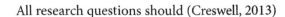

- Research Question 2: Do children describe themselves as more creative in an arts program when a leader provides positive feedback to their finished projects?

The second research question is better. It is stated in clear and specific terms, does not contain a value judgment about the variables, and contains specific language about how the variables would be measured.

Connectedness

Connectedness refers to the relationship between the research question and the theoretical and/or practical concerns that inspired the study. That is, the research question you develop for a study should have relevance. It needs to be timely and applicable. Its answer should contribute to the existing body of knowledge and/or professional practice (review Steps 1 and 2). What represents a contribution to others is a judgment call, and investigators and evaluators should not simply ask questions that are of interest only to themselves. As discussed in the Overview chapter, study results should either have a payoff to a discipline by contributing to that field's knowledge base or assist practitioners by providing insight on best practices for the profession.

To write a strong research question requires time and thought. Step away from your computer and think about what drew you to your topic. Determining a testable and connected research question is important. The following sections provide advice on writing good research questions according to whether the study framework is quantitative, qualitative, or mixed methods.

Quantitative Study Research Question

A quantitative study may set forth a research question. If you do not pose a research question, you will craft a hypothesis (which will be covered in this chapter). A research question in a quantitative study may be descriptive or normative (Hedrick, Bickman, & Rog, 1993). Case 4.4 distinguishes between these forms and provides an example of each.

As the label suggests, ***descriptive research questions*** seek answers to queries such as "What is...," "How do...," "Do...," or "Is..." (e.g., How frequently do children engage in aggressive acts on the playground?). Contrastingly, ***normative research questions*** are about discernment, such as "How serious..." or "How well..." (e.g., "How well do the community's parks meet the Americans With Disabilities Act standards?"). The topic studied is compared to a standard or norm, such as a status quo or past performance.

All research questions should (Creswell, 2013)

- be short, conceptually straightforward, and jargon-free (research questions that are too abstract or obtuse make it difficult to determine what is to be studied and accordingly what is to be answered);
- focus on the central aspect of your study rather than the variables and conditions surrounding it (although you do not want to fall into the trap of reductionism, the research question must be an unambiguous target);
- use directional verbs, such as *affect, determine,* or *relate*;
- be about the independent variables first, followed by the dependent variables;
- require more than a *yes* or *no* answer; and
- be stated in a complete sentence.

Some research situations may require multiple research questions. When this happens, organize questions hierarchically, from the primary question to subordinate questions. That is, begin by asking a central descriptive question, which is supported by several subquestions that relate variables or compare groups.

Qualitative Study Research Question

Some research topics lend themselves best to the qualitative approach. Accordingly, qualitative research questions address meaning, understanding, or interpretation of a topic. A qualitative research question explores *how* or *why* with a focus on how something feels or is experienced. As with a quantitative research question, a qualitative research question should flow from the stated purpose of the study. For example, Hebblethwaite and Norris (2010) studied intergenerational leisure and asked, "How is family leisure experienced across multiple generations?"

A qualitative research question is often referred to as a ***grand tour question*** because it is broad and stated in general terms (Spradley, 1979). A grand tour question takes the form, "Tell me about...." This could be about yourself, about camp, or about working for this organization. Typically, a study will have one grand tour research question and then branch off into subquestions, or subordinate questions (see Case 4.5).

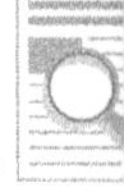

Typically, qualitative research questions explore a process (e.g., a case study), describe experiences (e.g., ethnography), or tell a story (narrative research). Therefore, these questions are more open ended than quantitative questions and, accordingly, frequently evolve and change during the study according to an emerging study design.

You should follow several principles when writing a research question for a qualitative study (Creswell, 2013):

- begin the grand tour question with the word *why, what,* or *how*;
- use exploratory verbs such as *discover, explain, seek to understand, explore,* or *describe*;
- do not use words suggesting direction, such as *affect, influence, impact, determine, cause,* or *relate*; and
- identify the specific qualitative framework used for the study, such as an ethnographic approach.

Mixed-Methods Study Research Question

Because a mixed-methods study relies on neither quantitative nor qualitative research alone, a combination of both forms of a research question provides the best approach. This means that qualitative and quantitative research questions need to be advanced in a mixed-methods study.

Creswell (2013) provided insights on mixed-methods research questions. You may write each research question separately (a qualitative research question and then a quantitative research question, or vice versa) and then present each question separately. Essentially, two studies are conducted concurrently (see Step 7).

You also may conduct a mixed-methods study sequentially, that is, either the qualitative or the quantitative research question comes first (the ordering is your decision). If the study begins with a qualitative phase, a qualitative research question leads. Later in the study, after you address the qualitative phase, you will present a quantitative research question. Likewise, you could lead the study with a quantitative phase, which would mean the quantitative question is identified first, and as the study progresses, you could pose a qualitative research question.

HYPOTHESES

Many, although not all, quantitative and mixed-methods studies rely on hypotheses. Contrastingly, qualitative studies do not use hypotheses.

A ***hypothesis*** is a conjecture or guess about relationships between or among two or more identified variables (Kerlinger & Lee, 1999). The hypothesis waits to be "tested" by data that are collected during research. Ultimately statistical analyses of the data lead to a hypothesis being supported or not supported. An example of a hypothesis is the following: "Visitors to an attraction report greater enjoyment touring the facility earlier in the day compared to later in the day when the crowd count is higher."

Where do hypotheses come from? Many hypotheses are suggested by theories and/or prior research findings. For example, Case 4.6 demonstrates the role of formal theory and previously conducted research as sources of hypotheses.

SOMETHING TO REMEMBER!

Hypotheses differ from formal theories in two ways. Theory is like a large-scale world map, representing general ideas. Theories guide observations of the whole domain. On the other hand, hypotheses are like city maps, focusing on specific ideas, or the details of the larger theoretical map (Rosenthal & Rosnow, 2007).

In addition to formal theory and prior research, hypotheses also may come from educated guesswork. These are often referred to as ***naïve hypotheses*** (Kidder & Judd, 1991). For example, the following sources may trigger a hypothesis:

- Authority. Experts and other authorities may provide insights on hypotheses to examine. For example, a university professor may claim in a lecture that leisure-oriented and work-oriented people have different attitudes toward leisure. You may develop a study to examine this claim.
- Consensus. Hypotheses driven by consensus emerge from the wisdom of colleagues or users of recreation services. For instance, to come up with a working hypothesis on how to curb graffiti on walls of a recreation center, you may consult with staff working at that site for ideas.
- Observation. Hypotheses may emerge based on your or others' observations about a situation. Perhaps you have noticed while working at a resort that fee-based activities appear to draw more participants than free activities. Thus, this formulated hypothesis becomes the focus of a study to determine whether evidence would support this hunch.

Regardless of the source for hypotheses, you must write them down. You may write hypotheses in the null, nondirectional, or directional form.

Null Hypothesis

A ***null hypothesis*** states no relationship or difference exists between two or more variables. Jones (2004) illustrated this type of hypothesis: "Being a climber or non-climber does not significantly determine whether visual preference of scenes containing evidence of rock climbing is higher than visual preference of scenes containing no evidence of rock climbing" (p. 44).

Nondirectional Hypothesis

In contrast, a ***nondirectional hypothesis*** speculates a relationship or difference exists between the variables; however, no detail about the nature of the relationship is provided. That is, a nondirectional hypothesis predicts a relationship exists between the variables, but the direction of this relationship is not specified. Anderson and Bedini (2002) used a nondirectional hypothesis: "Women and men working in therapeutic recreation have different perceptions of gender equity" (p. 267).

Directional Hypothesis

Contrastingly, a ***directional hypothesis***, also known as the alternative hypothesis, states the direction of a relationship or identifies the difference between two or more variables. For example, Buckley (2012) hypothesized that as individuals become more engaged in a particular adventure recreation activity, their motivations for participation will be become more aligned with internal motivations (e.g., challenge, achievement, control, and risk-taking) as opposed to external motivations (e.g., feeling pressured by friends or family to participate). Thus, directionality is declared by stating individuals who frequently engage in adventure activity are distinguishable by their motivations.

KEEPING THE HYPOTHESES STRAIGHT

Are you trying to keep the ways to write a hypothesis straight? If so, consider the following shorthand system:

- For a null hypothesis, use the H_0 designation: H stands for hypothesis and the *0* subscript stands for the null form. Remember *0* means the *0* part of a NO relationship.
- For a nondirectional hypothesis, use the *H* designation: NO subscript is used, indicating no directionality is stated in a nondirectional hypothesis.
- Finally, for the directional hypothesis, use the H_1 notation: The *1* subscript means a direction has been specified.

Another way to label a directional hypothesis in a quantitative or mixed-methods study is to indicate the direction of a relationship. That is, you may wish to test hypotheses about the specific nature of the relationship between the variables. Thus, when referring to the direction of a relationship between variables, specify a positive or a negative relationship. A ***positive relationship*** means that as the value of the independent variable increases, the value of the dependent variable increases. Likewise, as the value of the independent variable decreases, the value of the dependent variable decreases. That is, a positive relationship is exemplified when both variables move in the same direction.

COMING UP WITH A TITLE FOR THE RESEARCH PROJECT

You can judge a book by its cover! It is important when choosing a title for your study that all the elements of the study scope align. That is, the purpose of the study, variables, research questions, and hypotheses must be portrayed accurately in the title. For example, the study title The Effects of Hip-Hop Dance Instruction on Rhythm, Bilateral Coordination, and Balance communicates the purpose of the study is to determine the impact of hip-hop, which also matches the research question addressing what is the impact of this independent variable on the dependent variables (rhythm, coordination, and balance).

An example of a directional, positive relationship is, there is a positive relationship between the number of hours spent studying and the final grade earned in a research course. This hypothesis could be interpreted two ways. First, the more hours you study, the more likely you will earn a higher final grade in the research course. Second, if you study fewer hours, you will probably receive a lower grade in the research course.

A ***negative relationship***, sometimes called an inverse relationship, means the direction of the relationship between the variables is opposite. That is, as the value of one variable changes (increases or decreases), the value of the second variable heads in the opposite direction. Consider this sentence: There is a negative relationship between hours per week of watching television and youth sports participation. This means that as the amount of television watching increases, youth sports participation decreases. Similarly, you could interpret the same hypothesis as meaning that as the amount of television viewing decreases, participation in youth sports increases.

THUMBS UP (OR DOWN) ON THE DIRECTION OF RELATIONSHIPS!

To remember directional relationships between two variables, use the thumbs system. Use your left thumb to represent the independent variable and reserve your right thumb for the dependent variable.

Demonstration: A positive relationship between age and patience means that as age increases (thumb up) patience increases (thumb up).

Now you try it! Point your thumbs up and down according to these relationships:

1. a positive relationship between players' height and number of baskets made in a basketball game;
2. positive relationship between weight and blood pressure;
3. negative relationship between amount of litter found on a trail and hikers' satisfaction with the trail; and
4. negative relationship between physical condition and resting heart rate.

Note. Answers are provided at the end of the chapter.

Focusing in on the purpose and research question or hypothesis of a study requires thought. Lower Slaughter, England. Copyright © 2015 Carol Cutler Riddick.

REVIEW AND DISCUSSION QUESTIONS

1. In determining the scope of a study, what specifically do you need to identify?
2. What does unit of analysis mean? Which are typically used in recreation, park, sport, and tourism research?
3. Define variable, dependent variable, independent variable, and intervening variable.
4. Distinguish among the content found in a purpose statement for a quantitative, qualitative, and mixed-methods study.
5. Explain what it means to write a research question that is testable and connected.
6. What is the difference between descriptive and normative research questions used in a quantitative study?
7. What is a grand tour question? Why is it appropriate for a qualitative study, and how is it different from a research question for a quantitative study?
8. Describe the two ways you may handle research questions in a mixed-methods study.
9. What is a hypothesis? Give examples of a null, nondirectional, and directional hypothesis using the same dependent and independent variables.
10. In a directional hypothesis, what do positive relationship and negative relationship mean?

YOUR RESEARCH

1. For the topic you have selected to study, what is the dependent variable? If any, what are the independent variables?
2. What is the unit of analysis for your topic?
3. For your topic, write a purpose statement, two or three hypotheses (if your study is quantitative), and at least one research question. Is your research question testable? Characterized as having connectedness?

PRACTICE EXERCISES

1. If the free-time preferences of students enrolled in your research and evaluation class were used to make generalizations about the free-time preferences of students at your university, would an ecological fallacy be committed? Why or why not?
2. Using the worksheet below for each noted research question, identify the unit of analysis.

Worksheet Scope Chapter: Name That Unit of Analysis

Research questions	What is the unit of analysis?
1. What is the difference in problem-solving strategies used by travel agency staff the week before Christmas break versus the week before the 4th of July?	
2. What was the budget (revenue sources and expenses) for the Race for the Cure event just completed?	
3. What actions does a neighborhood citizens group take to curb graffiti in its neighborhood parks?	
4. What are the interaction patterns of the staff with each other and with the director during a staff meeting?	
5. Are editorials in the local newspapers supportive of the bond initiative for greenway expansion?	
6. What marketing strategies does the health club use to recruit new members?	
7. What motivations and benefits are derived from being part of a tour group to Alaska?	
8. What teaching technique used by the cardio-boxing instructor is most effective?	

3. Using the following worksheet for each of the following research hypotheses, name the independent and dependent variable and whether the relationship is positive or negative.

Worksheet Scope Chapter: Hypotheses, Variables, and Relationships

Hypothesis	Independent variable	Dependent variable	Positive or negative relationship?
1. Watching violence on television increases aggression in children.			
2. Alcohol drinking will decrease reaction time while driving.			
3. Wisdom improves with age.			
4. Participation in sports builds character in teenagers.			
5. As outside air temperature increases, the walking speed of pedestrians decreases.			

4. Practice the skills of hypothesis writing. For each of the statements below, specify the nature of the relationship (positive or negative) between the variables and write a directional hypothesis.

Worksheet Scope Chapter: Directional Relationships

Statement	Positive or negative relationship?	Directional hypothesis
1. Amount of unstructured playtime children experience/week and creativity		
2. Income and frequency of playing golf		
3. Stress and number of exercise events every week		
4. Amount of time adolescents play video games/week and school grades		
5. Number of swim class sessions attended and swim ability		

5. Acquire a copy of one or more of the following articles (your instructor may instruct which of the following articles you should read and/or may substitute other articles):

Spiers, A., & Walker, G. (2009). The effects of ethnicity and leisure satisfaction on happiness, peacefulness, and quality of life. *Leisure Sciences, 31*, 84–99. You may access this article at http://www.tandfonline.com/doi/pdf/10.1080/01490400802558277.

Dorwart, C., Moore, R., & Leung, Y. F. (2010). Visitors' perceptions of a trail environment and effects on experiences: A model for nature-base recreation experiences. *Leisure Sciences, 32*, 33–54. You may access this article at http://www.tandfonline.com/doi/pdf/10.1080/01490400903430863.

Tutenges, S. (2012). Nightlife tourism: A mixed methods study of young tourists at an international nightlife resort. *Tourist Studies, 12*, 131–150.

Read the article and decide whether the study is an example of a quantitative, qualitative, or mixed-methods study. Then, based on this determination, complete one of the three worksheets that follow.

Worksheet Scope Chapter: Determining the Scope for a Quantitative Study

1. What is the unit of analysis used for the study (circle one)?
   Individuals
   Groups
   Organizations
   Artifacts
   Social interactions
   Community
   Event
   Time period

2. What is the purpose of the study? Does it describe, explain, or predict something?

3. The study tested the ______________________________ theory.

4. The independent variables in the study were...

5. The dependent variables in the study were...

6. Was a research question used? If so, is it a descriptive or normative statement?

7. Was a hypothesis used? If so, is it written in a null, nondirectional, or directional format?

Worksheet Scope Chapter: Determining the Scope for a Qualitative Study

1. What is the unit of analysis used for the study (circle one)?
   Individuals
   Groups
   Organizations
   Artifacts
   Social interactions
   Community
   Event
   Time period

2. What theoretical approach was used to conduct the study?

3. What is the purpose of the study? Does it discover, explore, describe, or examine the nature of something?

4. What is the grand tour research question?

5. What are the supporting subquestions?

Worksheet Scope Chapter: Determining the Scope for a Mixed-Methods Study

1. Is this a concurrent study gathering both quantitative and qualitative data and merging or integrating them to best understand a research problem? If so, describe what transpired.

2. Is this a sequential study with the first phase being qualitative, followed by a second quantitative phase? Or is the first phase quantitative, followed by a qualitative focus, or vice versa? Describe how the study was conducted.

WEB EXERCISES

1. YouTube has many tutorials on developing the scope of a study. For example, for how to write a research question, begin with Dr. Jill Ostrow's (University of Missouri) lecture found at http://www.youtube.com/watch?v=AIJDfS33IWw. Other tutorials are available, so search and make your own discoveries.
2. To practice research purposes, questions, and hypotheses, check out Katrian A. Korb's (University of Jos-Nigeria) posting at http://korbedpsych.com/R03Purpose.html. After reading the brief tutorial, scroll down for practice activities. How did you do? What percentage of the eight questions did you correctly frame as either a research question or a hypothesis?
3. Read more about writing research questions and then practice identifying a "good" research question, meaning a statement that is neither too narrow nor too broad. To begin, read about how to write research questions by reviewing information posted on George Mason University's site: http://kehldotme.files.wordpress.com/2011/11/how-to-write-a-research-question.pdf. Once you complete the short tutorial, try to answer the questions in the following worksheet.

Worksheet Scope Chapter: Identifying a Good Research Question

Directions: There are two practice rounds. For each, identify a "good" research question from three possibilities. Select the research question you think is the best (neither too broad nor too narrow).

<u>Round One:</u>
Question 1: What marketing strategies does The Walt Disney Company currently apply?

Question 2: What is The Walt Disney Company's future marketing plan?

Question 3: What marketing strategies has The Walt Disney Company used in the past?

<u>Round Two:</u>
Question 1: Do young children who participate in free play programs start kindergarten with more developed skills?

Question 2: Do young children who participate in free play programs start kindergarten with more highly developed social skills?

Question 3: Do young children who participate in free play programs start kindergarten with more friends?

SERVICE LEARNING

Answer the following questions for the campus program or service that has been selected as the focus of the service learning project for this semester.

1. What is the unit of analysis for the study?
2. Identify three dependent variables that could be altered as a result of participating in the campus activity.
3. Write a mixed-methods purpose statement for the study. Which is envisioned: a concurrent or sequential study? Explain.
4. Compose a research question that logically flows from the study at hand. Have you used a quantitative, qualitative, or mixed-methods research question?
5. Draft three directional hypotheses (each using a different dependent variable) that relate to how participation in the program or activity are conjectured to affect participants.

TEST YOURSELF ANSWERS

What Is the Unit of Analysis?

1. Individual, 2. Group, 3. Organization, 4. Artifacts, 5. Social interactions, 6. Community, 7. Event, 8. Time period

Thumbs Up (or Down) on the Direction of Relationships!

1. Left thumb up (or down), right thumb up (or down); 2. Left thumb up (or down), right thumb up (or down); 3. Left thumb up (or down), right thumb down (or up); 4. Left thumb up (or down), right thumb down (or up).

SUPPORTING CASES FOR THIS CHAPTER

CASE 4.1. A GROUP AS UNIT OF ANALYSIS

Peguero, A. (2008). Bullying victimization and extracurricular activity. *Journal of School Violence, 7,* 71–85.

This study investigated the relationships between extracurricular activity and bullying. The hunch was that students' engagement in particular school activities increased or decreased the likelihood of being bullied while at school. Tenth grade public school students (N = 7,990) who were part of a larger longitudinal study recorded their own participation in classroom-related activities, clubs, interscholastic sports, and intramural sports. Findings suggested that students who were involved in three or more classroom-related extracurricular activities or intramural sports were likely to be a victim of bullying, whereas interscholastic athletes were less likely to be bullied.

CASE 4.2. INTERVENING VARIABLE

Van Puymbroeck, M., Payne, L., & Hsieh, P. (2007). A phase 1 feasibility study of yoga on the physical health and coping of informal caregivers. *Evidence-Based Complementary and Alternative Medicine, 4,* 519–529. You may access this article at http://www.ncbi.nlm.nih.gov/pmc/articles/PMC2176147/.

Family and friends who provide unpaid care to an individual with a disease or disability (known as informal caregivers) experience numerous threats to their physical health as a result of providing care. Hatha yoga has documented therapeutic benefits, and therefore, the purposes of this study were to (a) determine the feasibility of conducting an 8-week yoga program with informal caregivers and (b) gather pilot data on the effects of yoga on the physical fitness and coping of informal caregivers.

Informal caregivers were randomized into a yoga intervention (n = 8) or control group (n = 9). The yoga sessions were 2.5 hours per week for 8 weeks and consisted of pranayama (breathing) and asana (posture) activities. A certified yoga instructor led the classes. After the 8-week yoga program, lower body strength increased significantly for those in the yoga group. Other notable findings were yoga participants experienced improved coping skills, upper body strength, and aerobic endurance.

Caregivers in the control group experienced an unexpected increase in lower body flexibility. In this study, what are the dependent variables and the independent variables? What intervening variable do you suspect? The diagram below provides answers to these questions.

Independent Variable: 8-week yoga program

Possible Intervening Variable: a support group to talk things through with

Dependent Variable: Coping

CASE 4.3. PURPOSE STATEMENT ACCORDING TO THEORETICAL APPROACH

Quantitative approach	Qualitative approach	Mixed-methods approach
"The purpose of this study was to examine the relationship between family leisure satisfaction and satisfaction with family life." Adapted from "Family Leisure Satisfaction and Satisfaction With Family Life," by J. Agate, R. Zabriskie, S. Agate, and R. Proff, 2009, *Journal of Leisure Research, 41*, p. 205.	"The goal of this study was to explore how a community-based, non-clinical recreational center, called Gilda's Club promotes and contributes to healing and health throughout cancer survivorship." Adapted from "Dignity, Hope, and Transcendence: Gilda's Club as Complementary Care for Cancer Survivors," by D. Parry and T. Glover, 2010, *Journal of Leisure Research, 42*, p. 347.	"The aim of this thesis was to undertake an evaluation of the United Kingdom Coaching Certification (UKCC). Both quantitative and qualitative methods were employed in the form of focus groups, reflective journals and surveys." From *An Evaluation of the United Kingdom Coaching Certification in Scotland* (Unpublished doctoral thesis), by A. Bell, 2012. Retrieved from Electronic Theses Online Service. (Order No. 567687)
"The focus of this study was to determine the prevalence of different co-participants during recreational physical activity episodes, along with participants' feelings of flow and situational involvement during recreational physical activity when alone and with different co-participants." From "Social Participation, Flow, and Situational Involvement in Recreational Physical Activity," by M. Decloe, A. Kaczynski, and M. Havitz, 2009, *Journal of Leisure Research, 41*, p. 74.	"The purpose of this ethnographic case study was to understand the impact of participation in an inclusive 3-day rock climbing trip on the group dynamics of seven participants' ages 10-14 years that included a 13 year old male diagnosed with High Functioning Autism." From "The Impact of Participation in an Inclusive Adventure Education Trip on Group Dynamics," by S. Sutherland and S. Stroot, 2010, *Journal of Leisure Research, 42*, p. 153.	"A mixed-method approach was applied to explore and compare the supply-side views on the successes and failures of the event planning and organization process and to derive key success factors of the event-based approach to Integrated Rural Tourism." From "Implementing Integrated Rural Tourism: An Event-Based Approach," by E. Panyik, C. Costa, and T. Ratz, 2011, *Tourism Management, 32*, p. 1.

CASE 4.4. RESEARCH QUESTIONS FOR QUANTITATIVE STUDIES

Type of question	Example
Descriptive = Asks "What...," "How...," "Do...," and "Is..."	How do the travel preferences of tourists shape the degree to which they become suitable targets for victimization? From "Studying Tourists' Suitability as Crime Targets," by K. Boakye, 2010, *Annals of Tourism Research, 37*, p. 727.
Normative = Requires comparing against an expectation	This research compares the findings from the 2009 survey to the previous 3 decades of surveys to identify trends in therapeutic recreation education. Adapted from "Therapeutic Recreation Education: 2009 Survey," by C. Autry, S. Anderson, and S. Sklar, 2010, *Therapeutic Recreation Journal, 44*, p. 161.

Note. Adapted from Hedrick, Bickman, and Rog (1993).

CASE 4.5. PURPOSE STATEMENT, GRAND TOUR RESEARCH QUESTION, AND SUBQUESTIONS

Yuen, F. (2004). "It was fun … I liked drawing my thoughts": Using drawing as part of the focus group process with children. *Journal of Leisure Research, 36*, 461–482.

Purpose statement: Examine the extent to which participation in leisure activities directed toward effective communication and cooperation affect the development of social capital and community in children. (p. 465)

Grand tour research question: How do you feel being at camp? (p. 464)

Subquestions: Children in the study were asked to draw their responses to the following questions:

- How would you describe our camp community?
- How did you communicate with others?
- Describe the activities we did at camp and what you learned from them.
- Describe what you did during camp free time, what you learned, and why it was important to you.

CASE 4.6. EXAMPLES OF HYPOTHESES AND THEIR SOURCE

Source	Hypothesis
Formal theory–differential association theory	Funk, Beaton, and Pritchard (2011) noted, The current study tests the validity of the Psychological Continuum Model and its usefulness in understanding the progressive nature of participation in recreational golf. Attitudinal and behavioral characteristics that underpin each of the framework's four different stages of increased participation were examined...to determine if evidence supports the framework's ability to distinguish distinct stages of physically active leisure. (p. 276) From Funk, D., Beaton, A., & Pritchard, M. (2011). The stage-based development of physically active leisure: A recreational golf context. *Journal of Leisure Research, 43,* 268-289.
Prior research on avalanche-related deaths	Furman, Shooter, and Schumann (2010) stated, One explanation for why avalanche-related deaths continue to increase, despite the growth of avalanche education programs, ...is that recreational backcountry skiers fall victim to avalanche accidents by unconsciously relying on heuristics, which are "rules of thumb" that aid decision making...While, using heuristics enables decision makers to make decisions quickly...they can be misleading when assessing the stability of snowpack and making decisions to ski in avalanche terrain...The hypothesis that heuristic-based decision-making factors influence decision making warrants a closer look, and thus was the aim of this study. (p. 455) From "The Role of Heuristics, Avalanche Forecast, and Risk Propensity in the Decision Making of Backcountry Skiers," by N. Furman, W. Shooter, and S. Schumann, 2010, *Leisure Sciences, 32,* 453–469.

Leisure-related research must be judged for its significance. This attraction at Walt Disney World's Epcot stresses the reasons for taking good care of the earth's land. It would be worthwhile to find out the ways this attraction impacts tourists who view it. Orlando, Florida. Copyright © 2015 Ruth V. Russell.

STEP 1 > STEP 2 > STEP 3 > STEP 4 > STEP 5

EXPLAIN SIGNIFICANCE

WHAT WILL I LEARN IN THIS CHAPTER?

I'll be able to...

1. Describe what is meant by transformative research.
2. Argue why a study is important to conduct.
3. Defend the significance of a study in terms of
   a. improving professional practice and service delivery,
   b. solving a social problem, and
   c. adding to a scientific body of knowledge.
4. Define the concepts of prevalence, incidence, and at-risk and how they may be used to establish the significance of a study.
5. Write a significance statement for a research proposal and final report.

"Strong reasons make strong actions."

William Shakespeare
(English poet and playwright, widely regarded as the greatest writer in the English language and the world's preeminent dramatist, 1564–1616)

The last step of the getting started phase in the research process is considering the significance of the study. Making a case for the significance of the study is a crucial task because research takes time and costs money, so it must be worth it! The challenge of this step is to cogently justify why the study is needed.

Ideally, research should be transformative. ***Transformative research*** ultimately brings about change in a situation to improve people's lives (Kielhofner & Fossey, 2006). It also encompasses that findings from a research project radically advance knowledge about a topic or concept. At this juncture in the research process, the task is to make the case for the significance of the study via a significance statement.

MAKING A CASE FOR SIGNIFICANCE

In research, the term ***significance*** refers to the importance or necessity of the study or the findings of the study. Specifically, depending on its type and purpose, a study is significant for its potential to

- improve professional practice and service delivery,
- address a social problem, and
- contribute to scientific knowledge.

Improve Professional Practice and Service Delivery

A study is significant because it has the potential to help professionals learn ways to enhance what they do (see Case 5.1). Indeed, ***professional practice*** itself refers to professionals using their knowledge or formal education and training to provide a high and responsible standard of service. In recreation, park, sport, and tourism professions, for example, the rationale for undertaking a research study is often because the investigation would provide insights on improving professional conduct and the delivery of services to clients and constituents.

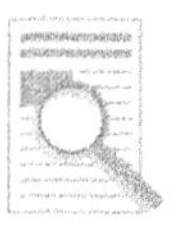

Address a Social Problem

In some situations, a study is significant because of its potential for tackling a social problem (Case 5.2). This type of research is sometimes referred to as ***action research*** (Lewin, 1946). The intent of action research—also known as participatory action research, community-based study, cooperative inquiry, and action science (cf. Leedy & Ormrod, 2012)—is to identify ways to improve conditions and practices for a particular context or situation.

IG NOBEL PRIZES

The following are research reports given awards recently at the annual ceremony of the Improbable Research organization:

"Leaning to the Left Makes the Eiffel Tower Seem Smaller"

"Shape of a Ponytail and the Statistical Physics of Hair Fiber Bundles"

"Is a Sigh 'Just a Sigh'? Sighs as Emotional Signals and Responses to a Difficult Task"

"Rollercoaster Asthma: When Positive Emotional Stress Interferes With Dyspnea Perception"

Are these studies significant? The goal of the awards given by Improbable Research is honoring research that makes people laugh and then think. See the Web Exercises, at the end of the chapter, for more of this fun.

Research that answers the question of what promotes conservation behaviors in children could be significant in alleviating the social problem of environmental pollution. Animal Kingdom, Walt Disney World, Orlando, Florida. Copyright © 2015 Ruth V. Russell.

For example, on most college campuses, some students become mired in the abuse of alcohol and other drugs. Engagement in such behaviors may be detrimental to the user's health, grades, and social relationships. A study aimed at investigating whether enhanced campus recreation and sport programs are cost effective for reducing or preventing drug abuse among students is an example of action research.

In making the case for social importance, research that is significant relies on the following number-based concepts (Rossi, Lipsey, & Freeman, 2004):

- prevalence,
- incidence, and
- at-risk.

Prevalence. ***Prevalence*** is the number of existing cases in a particular geographic area at a specified time. For example, the Centers for Disease Control and Prevention publishes the prevalence of obesity among low-income children aged 2 to 4 years (see these data at http://www.cdc.gov/obesity/data/childhood.html).

Incidence. ***Incidence*** is the number of new cases of a particular problem in a specified geographic area during a specified time. For instance, the following statement reports incidence: "In 2013, 600 new acts of vandalism were detected in our community's park system."

At-risk. Finally, an ***at-risk*** number points to a group of individuals in a specified geographic area that is in jeopardy of experiencing a condition or problem of concern. For instance, ***latchkey children*** (or children who at the end of the school day must reenter their home with a key since no adult is present) are typically considered a population-in-need. Thus, a number capturing how many individuals fall into a category may underscore the importance of a study that is set up to provide after-school recreation services.

To make claims about the significance of the study using numbers usually requires consulting secondary literature sources. Recall from Step 2 that secondary literature sources provide introductory background information about a topic. Common examples are textbooks, encyclopedias, research reviews, and organization websites.

Many secondary sources are available for confirming a social problem. Nevertheless, one challenge is to make sure secondary sources have authentic or quality information.

SOMETHING TO REMEMBER!

Believe it or not, the Web does not always contain accurate information. In fact, every once in a while, you may come across something that is not true (gasp!). To determine the quality of information found on the Web, apply the following website evaluation checklist:

1. Determine authority

___ Is it clear what organization is responsible for the information on the site?

___ Is there a link to a description of what the organization does (an "About Us" page)?

___ Is there a valid way of making sure the organization is a real place with real contact information (e-mail only is not enough)?

2. Determine accuracy

___ Are the authors and their qualifications clearly stated?

___ Are references cited for all factual claims?

___ Are there writing and spelling errors (the more errors, the more suspect)?

___ How long ago was the page updated?

3. Determine motivation

___ Is there an overwhelming bias in the information? Is the writing balanced?

___ Are the ads clearly separated from the content?

If the answers to these questions raise doubts in your mind about the site's integrity, reconsider this website as a credible source. Use common sense when considering a website as a secondary source for numbers.

SECONDARY DATA SOURCES THAT MAY MAKE A CASE FOR THE SIGNIFICANCE OF A STUDY

- Bureau of Justice Statistics (http://bjs.ojp.usdoj.gov/) provides information about crime and victims, drugs and crime, criminal offenders, the justice system in the United States, law enforcement, and prosecution.
- Centers for Disease Control and Prevention (http://www.cdc.gov/) identifies and reports (at national, state, and local levels) the prevalence of specific health behaviors, including leisure-time physical activity.
- FedStats (http://fedstats.gov/) contains links to more than 100 American government agencies as well published collections of statistics available online.
- Library of Congress Virtual Reference Shelf (http://www.loc.gov/rr/askalib/virtualref.html) is a collection of links to online resources for research topics, including encyclopedias, dictionaries, books, and reports.
- National Center for Health Statistics (http://www.cdc.gov/nchs/) contains statistics on topics of public health importance, including diseases and conditions, injuries, and life stages and populations.
- National Statistics Online (http://www.statistics.gov.uk/hub/index.html) is a gateway to UK national statistics.
- *Statistical Abstracts of the United States, State and Metropolitan Area Data Book*, and the *County and City Data Book* (http://www.census.gov/compendia/statab/) provide social, political, and economic statistics for the United States.
- Statistics Canada (http://www.statcan.gc.ca/start-debut-eng.html) produces statistics about Canada: its population, resources, economy, society, and culture.
- The World Bank (http://data.worldbank.org/) has information on social indicators around the world.
- United Nations Data (http://data.un.org/Default.aspx) contains World Health Organization data, UNICEF databases dealing with children, demographic statistics of the world, and world tourism data.
- U.S. Census Bureau (http://www.census.gov/population/international/data/idb/informationGateway.php) has demographic indicators for areas of the world.
- U.S. Department of Health and Human Services Healthy People 2010 (www.healthypeople2010.gov) is a national health promotion agenda that identifies leading disease and health-related focus areas.
- World Bank (http://data.worldbank.org/) has information on social indicators around the world.
- World Tourism Organization (http://unwto.org/en) reports national and international tourism statistics including arrival and departure and economic impact measurements of tourism worldwide.
- And many others!

Contribute to Scientific Knowledge

Curiosity is a crucial part of being a human being. It is natural to want to learn more about a topic that interests you. Why do some people choose to use their leisure time by bird-watching, whereas others prefer touring on a motorcycle? Why do more boys than girls play video games? Why are some people afraid in outdoor recreation situations? In short, the discovery of new information is exciting.

Research findings are important in terms of what they contribute, at an abstract level, to a discipline's body of knowledge. If this sounds familiar, this notion of basic research was discussed in the Overview chapter. Basic research adds to a field's knowledge base by providing insights and understanding, at an esoteric level. Thus, significance may be based, for example, on controversies or gaps in the literature including the production of "authentic" new knowledge, theory development, or theory refinement. In other words, a study may be important even though the findings have no immediate usefulness or direct application to program or service delivery (Case 5.3).

SIGNIFICANCE STATEMENT

Research and evaluation studies, in proposal and final report form, should contain a statement of the importance of the study. This is your opportunity, indeed responsibility, to point out the potential significance of the study.

The ***significance statement*** is used to establish the rationale for why the study is important. A well-written significance statement may be a challenge. It needs to convince others (some of whom may be doubters) about the merits of the study. Here is a story about one of the coauthors to illustrate: She vividly recalls trying to explain to her family what her dissertation was going to be about. After dutifully listening to a long-winded recitation, her mother offered the following advice: "Pretend you must explain the significance of your research during a phone call to me...and that long distance phone call costs you $100 per minute. So, now tell me, in terms I can understand and accept, why your study is important."

In closing, every research project needs to make the case for its importance via a written statement of significance. Since it is inevitable, the sooner it is drafted, the better. Consider it early as you prepare Steps 1 to 4 of the getting started phase.

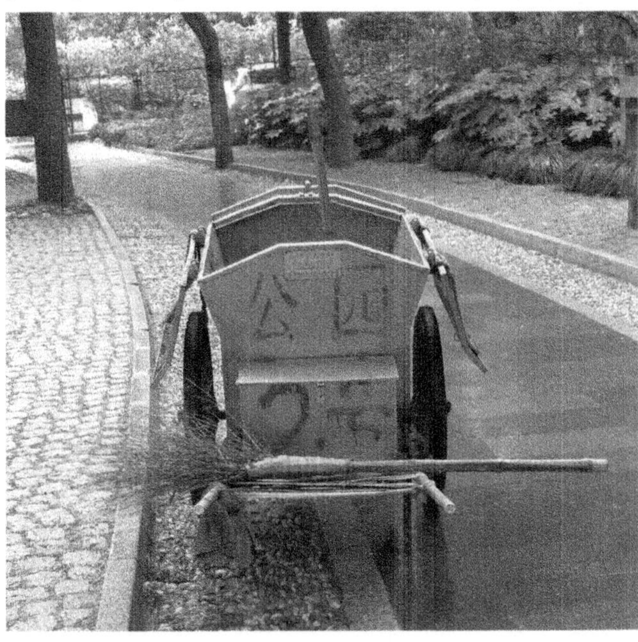

Every park around the world is challenged with cleaning up litter. A study to examine ways to reduce littering would address a social problem, contribute to scientific knowledge, and hopefully improve professional practice and service delivery. Park near the Museum of Contemporary Art, Shanghai, China. Copyright © 2015 Carol Cutler Riddick.

MAKING A CASE FOR SIGNIFICANCE

Brainstorm with classmates to identify research topics related to recreation, parks, sport, or tourism that have the potential to be transformative and significant.

The topic is significant because it...	Topic ideas
May lead to improved professional practice	1. 2. 3.
Addresses a social problem	1. 2. 3.
Will contribute to a field's scientific knowledge base	1. 2. 3.

Note. Answers are provided at the end of the chapter.

REVIEW AND DISCUSSION QUESTIONS

1. Describe the notion of transformative research.
2. Identify the three ways to make a case for the significance of a study.
3. Explain the concepts prevalence, incidence, and at-risk. How can you use these statistics to frame the significance of a study?

YOUR RESEARCH

1. In what ways is your research project important?
2. Does it have potential significance for improving professional practice and service delivery, addressing a social problem, and/or furthering scientific knowledge?
3. Write a significance statement for your research project.

PRACTICE EXERCISES

1. Complete the following worksheet.

Worksheet Significance Chapter: Making a Case for Significance

Directions: Three fictional significance statements are presented below. Indicate which one refers to the importance of

- professional practice and service delivery,
- addressing a social problem, and
- furthering scientific knowledge.

Importance to:	Significance statement
____	1. For many decades, the scientific community has claimed climate change will have critical implications for recreation policy and management. The implications of global climate change for nature-based parks and tourism have only recently begun to be assessed. This study will investigate experts opinions regarding how climate change is anticipated to affect nature-based parks and tourism.
____	2. As the attractiveness of college and professional sport becomes more prominent, winning at all costs in youth games is replacing the development as well as the respect of sportsmanship aspects of play. The aim of this study is to examine how participation in a city run sports program affects youths' attitudes surrounding sportsmanship.
____	3. The casino industry has expanded rapidly, often as a result of governmental attempts to stimulate their economies with casino-based tourism. This study combines theories of gambling and leisure behavior by focusing on the role of superstitious beliefs has on influencing customers betting habits.

2. Acquire a copy of the following article (or your instructor may substitute another article):

   Shipway, R. (2010 November). Running free: Embracing a healthy lifestyle through distance running. *Perspectives in Public Health, 130*, 270–276. You may access this article at http://www.lancashiresport.org.uk/ files/running_free_embracing_a_healthy_lifestyle_through_distance_running.pdf.

   Read the article and answer the following questions:
   a. Does the study claim to be significant in terms of improving professional practice and service delivery, addressing a social problem, or contributing to scientific knowledge?
   b. Rate (using *excellent, good, fair*, or *poor*) the research study in terms of its arguments regarding the importance of the study.

WEB EXERCISES

1. Every year people from several fields and backgrounds are awarded the Ig Nobel Prize for research accomplishments. These awards are sponsored by the *Annals of Improbable Research* and focus on "research that makes people laugh and then think." Awarded in physics, medicine, and other disciplines, the annual prize is meant to spur people's curiosity and to raise the question, how do you decide what is important and what is not?
   a. Read more about how Ig Noble awardees have shown how scientific methods may be applied to problems that are not normally thought of as being important at http://improbable.com/about/.
   b. Identify an award-winning topic you found to be humorous. Why do you think the research was significant?
2. Review consequences of abusive college drinking at the National Institute on Alcohol Abuse and Alcoholism website: http://pubs.niaaa.nih.gov/ publications/CollegeFactSheet/CollegeFactSheet.pdf.
   a. Review the statistics cited. What prevalence or incidence numbers impressed you the most?
   b. Do the cited statistics make the case for the significance of studying alcohol abuse among college students? Explain.
3. Access the article "Leisure Time Physical Activity of Moderate to Vigorous Intensity and Mortality: A Large Pooled Cohort Analysis," published November 6, 2012, in the online peer-reviewed journal *PLOS Medicine*, at http://www.plosmedicine.org/article/info%3Adoi%2F10.1371%2Fjournal.pmed.1001335. Data from six major study populations totaling more than 632,000 people are analyzed in the report. Read the article and answer the following questions:
   a. List one major finding of the study. Explain why or why you would not consider this to be transformative research.
   b. Does the study conclude it is possible to be "fat and fit"?
   c. Why is the study significant? Identify one argument for the reported significance.
   d. What is a takeaway message from this article?
4. Review the report *The Benefits of Physical Activity Provided by Park and Recreation Services: The Scientific Evidence* at www.nrpa.org/uploadedFiles/nrpa.org/Publications_and_Research/Research/Papers/Godbey-Mowen-Summary.
   a. Summarize the reasons presented in the report on why park and recreation services should contribute to leisure-time physical activity.
   b. Does the report provide a convincing argument for the significance of why public park and recreation agencies should provide physical activity opportunities? Why or why not? How would you classify the argument made for significance: as enhancing professional practice and service delivery, addressing a social problem, or furthering scientific knowledge?

5. Learn about the results of a study that tracked risk factors for heart disease and stroke in 199 countries across 28 years (1980–2008) at http://www.thelancet.com/journals/lancet/article/PIIS0140-6736%2810%2962037-5/abstract?sid=ST2011020307140.
   a. Choose the country of your own citizenship. Have changes in body mass index (BMI) and diabetes occurred over 22 years?
   b. Now, monitor changes that have transpired for another continent. Is it appropriate to conclude that obesity and diabetes are only significant problems of Western countries?

SERVICE LEARNING PROJECT

Prepare a statement regarding the significance of conducting a research study on the campus recreation/sport program/service selected as the focus for the survey. Hints: The societal significance of college students' participation in the campus service may be approached from perspectives such as reducing obesity/overweight and offsetting boredom.

TEST YOURSELF ANSWERS

Making a Case for Significance

Several topic ideas are possible to list as a result of the class brainstorming. Below are some starters:

The topic is significant because it...		Topic ideas
Can lead to improved professional practice	1.	A case study on how hotel managers respond to weather disasters.
	2.	An analysis of the causes of public park and recreation employee turnover.
Addresses a social problem	1.	Demographic distinctions between participators and nonparticipators in community wellness programs.
	2.	Factors contributing to the persistence of ethnic stereotypes by tourists visiting developing countries.
Will contribute to a field's scientific knowledge base	1.	The spiritual meaning of backcountry winter camping.
	2.	What factors motivate people to exercise as well as maintain physical activity over their lifetime?

SUPPORTING CASES FOR THIS CHAPTER

CASE 5.1. RESEARCH THAT CONTRIBUTES TO PROFESSIONAL PRACTICE

Graduate students interested in applied tourism research at the University of Illinois have been working with studies designed to inform professional practice. Enrollment in the course RST 457 Tourism Development enabled students to become involved in real-world research projects (retrieved November 17, 2012, from http://rst.illinois.edu/Graduates/Focus/ProfessionalPracticeFocus.aspx) including

- developing Web promotional technologies for the Monticello, Illinois, Chamber of Commerce;
- implementing a family reunion tourism program for the East St. Louis Park District;
- exploring the potential for agritourism on the University of Illinois' South Farms campus; and
- determining how a small outdoor recreation business in Vladimir, Russia, may expand its market share.

CASE 5.2. RESEARCH THAT HAS SOCIAL IMPORTANCE

Thapa, B., Graef, A., & Meyer, L. (2006). Specialization and marine-based environmental behaviors among SCUBA divers. *Journal of Leisure Research, 38*, 601–615.

The purpose of this study was to explore the relationship between recreation specialization (e.g., certification level) and marine-based environmental behaviors among SCUBA divers. The authors make a case for the significance of the study by pointing out the divers' behaviors have led to the degradation of underwater environments over time, thus affecting not only the natural resource, but also dive tourism.

CASE STUDY 5.3. RESEARCH THAT CONTRIBUTES TO A SCIENTIFIC KNOWLEDGE BASE

Clements, P. (2009). Cultural legitimacy or "outsider hip"? Representational ambiguity and the significance of Steely Dan. *Leisure Studies, 28*, 189–206.

Steely Dan, a rock band that has consistently produced high caliber songs but eschewed celebrity, embodies a particular idiosyncratic rock genre that contains originality, craftsmanship, and a critical attitude to art and life. In many ways, the musicians may be regarded as "intellectuals" whose songs not only offer particular individualized and self-driven "outsider" identities for the fan but also may claim cultural authority.

In this study, the ambiguous sociocultural and musical space occupied by the band in relation to rock music and the 1970s was explored. In particular, production, lyrical content, fan attachment, and the interface between individual style and cultural legitimization were examined.

PART III
DEVELOP A PLAN

STEP 6

SELECT SAMPLE

STEP 7

CHOOSE DESIGN

STEP 8

CONSIDER MEASUREMENT

STEP 9

SPECIFY DATA COLLECTION METHODS

STEP 10

ADDRESS ETHICAL RESPONSIBILITIES

STEP 11

SEEK PROPOSAL APPROVAL

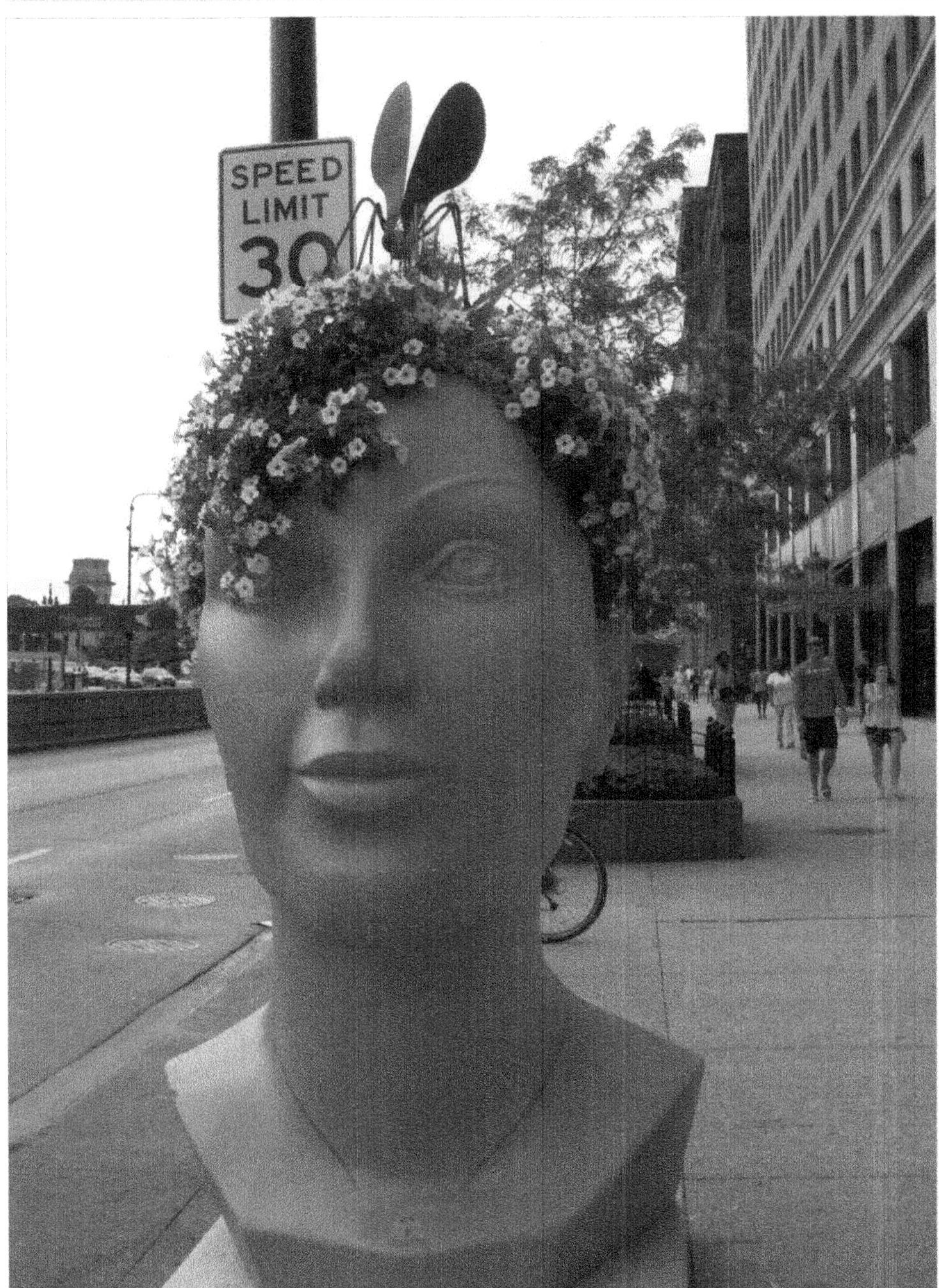

As you sample life, you may come across the unexpected...such as the art piece featured in this photo. Sampling individuals for a study also may lead to surprises in what you learn. Chicago, Illinois. Copyright © 2015 Ruth V. Russell.

STEP 6 STEP 7 STEP 8 STEP 9 STEP 10 STEP 11

SELECT SAMPLE

WHAT WILL I LEARN IN THIS CHAPTER?

I'll be able to...

1. Distinguish the difference between a population and a sample.
2. Define probability sampling as well as explain and cite an example of simple random, systematic random, stratified random, and cluster sampling.
3. Recall how to determine the appropriate sample size when the size of the population is known.
4. Explain what is meant by confidence interval.
5. Provide a definition for nonprobability sampling and distinguish among purposive, volunteer, quota, and snowball sampling.
6. Describe what is meant by a mixed-methods sampling strategy.
7. Define response rate, provide an example of how to calculate a response rate, and recall an "acceptable" response rate standard.
8. Given a research scenario, identify an appropriate sampling strategy.

"If you do not expect the unexpected, you will not find it."

Heraclitus
(Pre-Socratic Greek philosopher who had a contempt for humankind in general—called the "weeping philosopher")

The following are the steps in the research process up to this point: you have decided on a topic area for study; conducted a literature review illuminating the topic; adopted a theoretical framework; crafted a purpose statement, research question, and/or hypotheses; and set forth an argument for the significance of the study. Turn your attention now to crossing over from the *getting started* phase to the *develop a plan of action* phase. The first order of business in developing this plan is to select a sample.

On a personal level, everyone has had experience with sampling. People go through life sampling things—the expected and the unexpected! A few examples are choosing a heretofore never-visited place for a vacation destination, deciding on what pairs of running shoes to try on at the store, and making a spur-of-the-moment decision to order a different item than usual off the restaurant menu.

However, unlike most of these everyday samplings, you must conduct scientific sampling with a specific strategy. By studying this chapter, you will learn that the sampling choice made in a research project has profound implications for conclusions that ultimately and legitimately may be reached in the study.

To introduce you to sampling, this chapter is divided into five major sections: population and sample, probability sampling, nonprobability sampling, mixed-methods sampling strategy, and response rate.

POPULATION AND SAMPLE

To begin, distinguish whether you are studying a population or a sample. A ***population*** consists of the entire set of entities (individuals, objects, scores, etc.) being studied. Examples of populations are

- sport management undergraduate majors attending colleges in North America during a specified academic year;
- youth hostels located in London;
- children with documented developmental disabilities participating in Saturday recreation pro-

grams sponsored by the city of Houston during the past year; and

- music practice rooms operated by U.S. Armed Forces bases worldwide.

These examples demonstrate that populations vary by size and location.

Conducting a study of a large population, technically known as a ***census***, is often a mass undertaking and therefore typically impractical. For example, determining all college students majoring in sport management would be time consuming and expensive.

Instead, studying a sample of the population is less time consuming, less costly, and easier to manage. A ***sample*** is a subset of the population (Figure 6.1). Recall that individual cases, or entities in the sample, are referred to as units of analysis (see Step 4). A listing of units of analysis in a population is referred to as the ***sampling frame***.

You may use two approaches to select, or draw, a sample: probability sampling and nonprobability sampling. Studies based on a quantitative framework use probability sampling or nonprobability sampling. On the other hand, studies that pivot around a qualitative framework rely on nonprobability sampling.

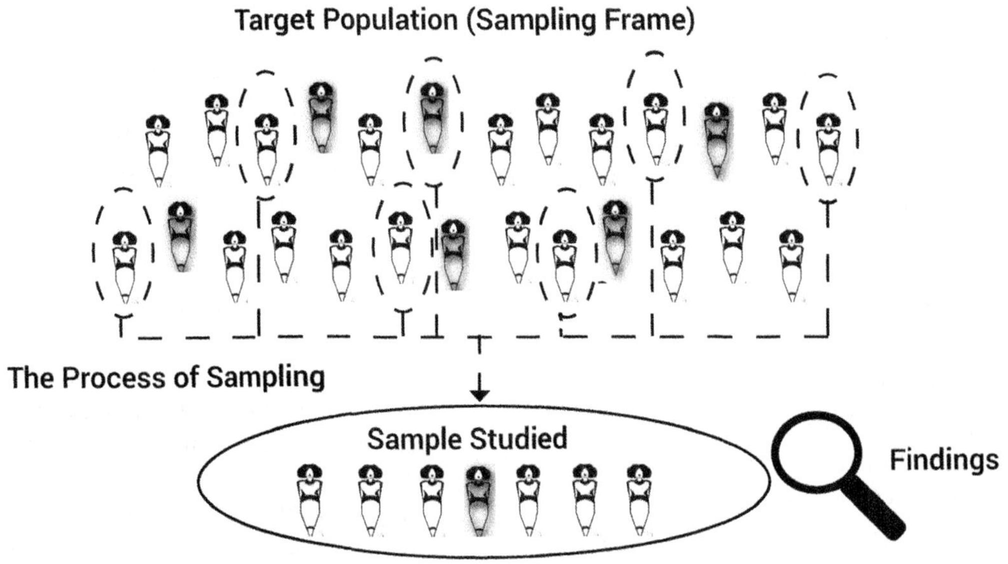

Figure 6.1. Illustration of relationship between a population and a sample.

LIKELIHOOD A POPULATION EXISTS?

Review the following sample descriptions and determine whether a corresponding population readily exists and may be easily identified and accessed. If so, place a check mark in the second column; if not, record a mark in the third column.

Sample description	Population exists	Population nonexistent or impossible to access
1. After-school programs for elementary-aged children in the United States.		
2. Adults who are deaf and interested in backpacking.		
3. Medal winners in biathlon competition at the Sochi 2014 Paralympic Games.		
4. National parks of Canada.		
5. State-level departments of tourism in the United States.		
6. Sport management professionals working in public or private settings.		

Note. Answers are provided at the end of the chapter.

PROBABILITY SAMPLING

Probability sampling is when every unit of a population has the same chance of being chosen for the sample. Stated another way, in probability sampling, every member of the population has the same chance of not being chosen for the sample. In other words, no inherent or systematic bias is used in choosing who is or is not selected to be in the study.

A sample that is selected using probability sampling is a representative, or unbiased sample. A ***representative sample*** mirrors the population from which it was selected in every way that is relevant to the study (Schutt, 2011). You may conduct probability sampling several ways. Among the more popular techniques for executing probability sampling are simple random, systematic random, stratified random, or cluster sampling.

Simple Random Sampling

In ***simple random sampling***, each member or unit of the population has an equal chance of being selected for the sample. To accomplish simple random sampling, first have the sampling frame, or list of names of individuals or units of analysis in the population being scrutinized. Examples of sampling frames include a list of

- participants in a county's youth soccer program during the season that just concluded,
- current adult members belonging to a suburban health club,
- pottery class registrants at an arts center for the past 5 years,
- newspaper articles written about a public recreation agency last year, and
- all recreational vehicle pad sites at a state park campground.

You may randomly select units from the sampling frame in many ways. If the population size is not too large, use the "pull out of the hat" or "bingo" technique. That is, record the name of each person or element in the population on a separate slip of paper, fold the slip so the name is hidden, and put into a container (e.g., hat, fishbowl, paper bag, envelope). Mix up the slips of paper (by hand or by shaking the container) and then have someone reach into the container and draw a name out of the container one at a time until you have identified the desired number of sampling units.

When a large number of units or entities exists in the population, a popular way to implement selection of a random sample is to rely on a table of random numbers (see Table 6.1). Alternatively, you may use a computer program to generate random numbers.

COMPUTER SOFTWARE TO ASSIST WITH RANDOM SELECTION

New computer software applications related to sampling unfold regularly. For example, many websites offer tools that generate random numbers or assist with selecting a random sample. One example is the Research Randomizer at http://www.randomizer.org/. To keep up with these product developments useful for sampling, consult publications such as *Social Science Computer Review*, *Byte*, *PC Week*, *PC World*, and *PC Connection*.

Regardless of the simple random selection technique you use, essentially what happens is that after assigning (in a nonbiased fashion) each unit of analysis (usually a person) a number, you will select a predetermined number of entities. Case 6.1 is an example of how to implement a randomly drawn sample using a table of random numbers.

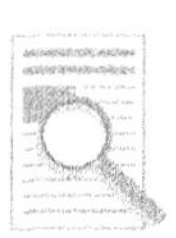

Systematic Random Sampling

Systematic random sampling is a variation of simple random sampling; that is, a particular "selection system" is applied to extend the simple random sampling technique to draw a requisite number of entities from the population. For example, after choosing the initial person or unit of analysis in a random fashion, use a logical and organized method to select the remaining sample members. In particular, a ***sampling interval*** is calculated by the following formula: Total Number of Elements in the Population ÷ Number of Elements Required for the Sample. Case 6.2 is an example of the application of systematic random sampling.

Stratified Random Sampling

A ***stratified random sample*** is randomly chosen subgroups, or categories of persons or units, represented in a population. Technically, these subgroups are known as ***strata***. Examples of strata are gender (males and females), undergraduate matriculation level (first-year, sophomores, juniors, and seniors), and place of residency (by zip code).

Subgroups within a population are examined because the dependent variables (recall Step 4) are believed to differ between or among the identified strata (*Note: Strata* is the plural of *stratum*). Thus, the dimension used to divide the population into subgroups should be relevant to the problem.

Table 6.1
Random Numbers

	Column #																	
Row #	**1**	**2**	**3**	**4**	**5**	**6**	**7**	**8**	**9**	**10**	**11**	**12**	**13**	**14**	**15**	**16**	**17**	**18**
1	2	1	0	4	9	8	0	8	8	8	0	6	9	2	4	8	2	6
2	0	7	3	0	2	9	4	8	2	7	8	9	8	9	2	9	7	1
3	4	4	9	0	0	2	8	6	2	6	7	7	7	3	1	2	5	1
4	7	3	2	1	1	2	0	0	7	6	0	3	8	3	4	7	8	1
5	3	3	2	5	8	3	1	7	0	1	4	0	7	8	9	3	7	7
6	6	1	2	0	5	7	2	4	4	0	0	6	3	0	2	8	0	7
7	7	0	9	3	3	3	7	4	0	4	8	8	9	3	5	8	0	5
8	7	5	1	9	0	9	1	5	2	6	5	0	9	0	3	5	8	8
9	3	5	6	9	6	5	0	1	9	4	6	6	7	5	6	8	3	1
10	8	5	0	3	9	4	3	4	0	6	5	1	7	4	4	6	2	7
11	0	5	9	6	8	7	4	8	1	5	5	0	5	1	7	1	5	8
12	7	6	2	2	6	9	6	1	9	7	1	1	4	7	1	6	2	0
13	3	8	4	7	8	9	8	2	2	1	6	3	8	7	0	4	6	1
14	1	9	1	8	4	5	6	1	8	1	2	4	4	4	2	7	3	4
15	1	5	3	6	7	6	1	8	4	3	1	8	8	7	7	6	0	4
16	0	5	5	3	6	0	7	1	3	8	1	4	6	7	0	4	3	5
17	2	2	3	8	6	0	9	1	9	0	4	4	7	6	8	1	5	1
18	2	3	3	2	5	5	7	6	9	4	9	7	1	3	7	9	3	8
19	8	5	5	0	5	3	7	8	5	4	5	1	6	0	4	8	9	1
20	0	6	1	1	3	4	8	6	4	3	2	9	4	3	8	7	4	1
21	9	1	1	8	2	9	0	6	9	6	9	4	2	9	9	0	6	0
22	3	7	8	0	6	3	7	1	2	6	5	2	7	6	5	6	5	1
23	5	3	0	5	1	2	1	0	9	1	3	7	5	6	1	2	5	0
24	7	2	4	8	6	7	9	3	8	7	6	0	9	1	6	5	7	8
25	0	9	1	6	7	0	3	8	0	9	1	5	4	2	3	2	4	5
26	3	8	1	4	3	7	9	2	4	5	1	2	8	7	7	4	1	3

Note. From Patten (2012). Reprinted with permission from Pyrczak Publishing.

Proportionate stratified sampling is used most commonly to rely on proportionate sampling, which ensures that the subgroups are represented in the sample in the same proportion they are found in the population. For example, if the population contains 60% females and 40% males, a proportionate stratified sample for gender would include selecting for the sample 60% who are females and 40% who are males. Case 6.3 is an example of proportionate stratified sampling.

Cluster Sampling

Cluster sampling is used when the sampling unit is not an individual but a group that "naturally" occurs in a population. In cluster sampling, a random sample of groups within a population is chosen. Examples of groups include neighborhoods (as well as cities, states, and regions), organizations, and times.

For example, you may apply cluster sampling to a geographic neighborhood. To begin, divide the target land area into mutually exclusive subareas (also known as ***clusters***) with identifiable boundaries. Then, draw a random sample of subareas, identify a list of housing units within the selected subareas, and select a random sample of listed housing units. Once you have identified the housing units, include either all people living in the selected unit in the sample or use random sampling to identify which individuals in the selected units to include in the sample.

Typically, cluster sampling is conducted in waves using a ***multistage approach*** consisting of identifying a series of samples. Begin by breaking down a large cluster into a group of smaller clusters. Within each of these smaller clusters, choose one or more subsets randomly. Case 6.4 demonstrates an application of multistage cluster sampling for conducting a survey of metro park visitors.

Each probability sampling technique has advantages and disadvantages. These have been summarized in Table 6.2.

Sample Size

Before moving on to nonprobability sampling techniques, shift your attention to a couple of remaining points relevant to probability sampling. That is, sample size and confidence interval will now be reviewed.

When conducting a study involving probability sampling, decide on the ***sample size***, or the number of units, selected for the sample. Mathematicians have issued guidelines for a desirable sample size when the population size is known. Table 6.3 identifies, for a given population size (represented by columns headed with the standard *N* notation), the sample size (represented by columns headed with the universally accepted *n* notation) that is needed.

FIGURING OUT SAMPLE SIZE

Online calculators exist for determining how many respondents are needed for a sample. To do the calculations, enter how many people are in the population group and the margin of error (also referred to as the confidence interval) you are willing to accept.

You may determine sample size using Excel (http://faq.bloglines.com/ref/Sample-Size-Calculator-Excel.html?oo=6321). Alternatively, the following online calculators are available:

- http://www.custominsight.com/articles/random-sample-calculator.asp
- http://www.surveysystem.com/sscalc.htm

WHAT KIND OF PROBABILITY SAMPLE AM I?

Suppose your university department chair has asked you to identify ways to sample for a survey of the 500 majors. For each sampling scenario below, match the name of the probability sampling technique that is most appropriate: simple random sampling, systematic random sampling, stratified random sampling, or cluster sampling.

Ways to implement the study: Identify the technique being described	Answer
1. Majors are about evenly divided into two tracks: (1) outdoor sports and (2) tourism. The names of students in each of these options are alphabetized. About 109 names from each list are randomly chosen. Each person chosen will be asked to complete a survey questionnaire.	
2. The names of all majors are alphabetized. Then someone randomly chooses (with eyes closed) one name on the typewritten list. This person becomes the first person invited to complete a survey. The person two names down from the first person chosen becomes the second person to be sent a survey. This pattern (moving down by two names) continues until 217 names have been identified.	
3. The name of each major appears on a slip of paper that has been placed into a paper bag. A volunteer reaches into the bag and removes one name/piece of paper. Removing one name at a time this continues until 217 names have been selected.	
4. Majors come from 45 states (with ~ 11 majors from each of these states). Forty states are randomly chosen, and then 5 students from each of these 40 states are randomly chosen.	

Note. Answers are provided at the end of the chapter.

Table 6.2
Advantages and Disadvantages of Probability Sampling Techniques

Sampling technique	Possible advantages	Possible disadvantages
Simple random	• Easy to implement • ***Sampling error*** (difference between the sample characteristics and population characteristics) can be calculated	• May be costly to implement • Requires first identifying all members of the population • When a large sample must be selected, it is cumbersome to randomly select by hand
Systematic random	• Convenient to use when population units are arranged sequentially • Easy to use when population list (e.g., names of registrants) is available	• If not randomly selected, ***sampling bias*** (or nonrepresentative sample) is drawn
Stratified random	• Easy to use when population can be broken down into subgroups (or strata) • Representative of population	• May be costly to implement • Requires knowing all members of the strata within the population • May require weighting and or drawing an appropriate percentage of each subgroup
Cluster	• Useful when the sampling group is spread out across a wide geographic area • Sampling error decreases as the homogeneity of cases per cluster increases	• May be costly to implement • May be difficult to identify members of chosen clusters • Sampling error increases as the number of clusters decreases

Note. Adapted from Schutt (2011).

As the population size increases, the sample size needed does not proportionally increase. This statistics principle is known as ***diminishing returns***. In general, as the size of the population increases, you will arrive at a point of diminishing returns in terms of how many persons you need to choose for a sample when the size of the population is known.

SOMETHING TO REMEMBER!

To demonstrate the diminishing returns principle in statistics determine how many persons are needed in a sample when the known population size is 500? 1,000? Use an on line calculator (for leads on such calculators, see Figure Out Sample Size Idea box). Set the margin of error at 5% and use a 95% confidence level. The correct answers are 217 (or 218 depending on which calculator you use) and 278 persons, respectively.

Did you notice that when the population increased from 500 to 1,000 the sample size did not increase that much, even though the population size doubled? This illustrates the concept of diminishing returns in sample size.

Confidence Interval

Using probability sampling allows you to generalize findings to the larger population group. That is, you may use information obtained from a sample, with some preciseness, to estimate a characteristic of the population from which the sample is drawn.

Statistical theory permits inference of a population value based on data obtained from a sample. The key to making these inferences involves a ***confidence interval***, which establishes a margin of error. Essentially, when you study a sample that is drawn from a population, result may deviate from the true population value on the variable being studied. Knowing this possibility, you need to set the level of confidence you wish to have in the findings. The norm is adopting the 95% confidence level, although you may choose a higher level (e.g., 97% or 99%).

For an example of confidence interval, suppose you read about a study of high school students attending public schools in a community. Probability sampling (in particular, cluster sampling) was used to identify students who were sent a questionnaire. Suppose a high percentage of the students returned a completed survey and the following passage appeared in the study report: "Results of the survey are accurate within ± (plus or minus) 3 percentage points, using a 95% level of confidence. The major finding is that 75% of the respondents reported playing Internet games 2 or more hours during the school week (Monday to Thursday). Thus, between 72% and 78% (±3) of high school students attending public schools in the community spend two or more hours per school week playing video games."

The range in the hypothetical example (72% to 78%) is known as the confidence interval, which means that there is 95% confidence that the "true" population value (in this instance, the amount of video game playing time) lies within this interval derived from the sample result. Alternatively put, the confidence interval also provides information about the likely amount of error (technically known as ***sampling error***, an idea that will be discussed further in Step 7). In this example, there is a 5% chance that less than 72% and/or more than 78% of the population plays 2 or more hours of video games during the school week.

NONPROBABILITY SAMPLING

The distinction between probability sampling and nonprobability sampling is how you select people/entities to be in the study. Recall that probability sampling involves randomly selecting units (usually people) from a population group.

Contrastingly, ***nonprobability sampling*** does not rely on random selection; instead, you select people or units purposively, due to convenience or accidentally. When nonprobability sampling has been used, a ***nonrepresentative***, or biased, sample has been chosen.

At first glance, using a nonrepresentative sample may seem bad. However, defensible reasons exist for using nonprobability sampling. First, in some situations, identifying all members of a population beforehand is impossible, thus dictating the use of nonprobability sampling. Second, sometimes ethical concerns (e.g., expecting chosen individuals to participate in a study) may make relying on probability sampling impossible. Third, if the intent of the research is to find whether a relationship exists between independent and dependent variables (see Step 4), with no intent to generalize results beyond the sample, using a nonprobability sample is warranted. Fourth, when a qualitative approach has been adopted for the study, nonprobability sampling is more appropriate. (Incidentally, qualitative studies may offset the criticism of using a nonrepresentative sample by using multiple sources of data to support study conclusions and/or conducting several replication studies.)

You may conduct nonprobability sampling in many ways. Common nonprobability sampling methods are purposive, volunteer, quota, and snowball.

An example of nonprobability sampling would be asking participants in this water volleyball activity, held in a retirement village, to "volunteer" for a study that examines retirement satisfaction. The resulting sample would be nonrepresentative of residents living in the entire village. That is, people who participate in water volleyball typically strive to live an active lifestyle, which probably is not the case of all residents in this community. Copyright © 2015 Ruth V. Russell.

Purposive Sampling

A ***purposive sample*** (also known as judgmental, expert, or key informant sampling) consists of using your judgment to choose individuals or units for the sample that best serve the purposes of the study. Typically, individuals with known or demonstrated expertise or experience are requested to serve as a member of the sample group.

For example, suppose declining food sales has been a reoccurring problem in a state park system. You may use purposive sampling to gain insights on how to remedy the problem. That is, invite infrequent park visitors (the "experts" or "key informants") to attend a focus group to share their ideas on how to improve concession sales within the park system.

SAMPLING VENDING MACHINES IN JAPAN

View the results of a "study" that relied on purposive sampling to discover the kinds of vending machines found in Tokyo: http://www.youtube.com/watch?v=vP43j94YtaY.

Which vending machine featured did you find to be the oddest? Funniest?

An interesting use of purposive sampling is applying it to the ***experience sampling method*** (Csikszentmihalyi, 2008; Csikszentmihalyi, Larson, & Prescott, 1977). The experience sampling method was developed to study selected individuals' time use patterns, in natural settings, as well as their feelings regarding these experiences. The method uses an alert (e.g., pager, programmed watch, or cell phone) to contact the selected, purposeful sample of individuals. The individuals are contacted numerous times over 24 hours, and usually their experiences are tracked over several days to a week. When contacted, the study participant is asked to record responses to (1) what he or she is doing at that moment in time, (2) where and with whom, and (3) their attitudes or feelings surrounding the activity and other persons present at the activity.

Volunteer Sampling

Volunteer sampling is also known as convenience, accidental, availability, or haphazard sampling. In volunteer sampling, a person is chosen to be in the sample because of expediency. That is, a person is readily available or accessible at a certain time or place in terms of agreeing to be in the study. Volunteer sampling has been referred to as the "take-them-where-you-can-find them" method of obtaining participants (Cozby, 2011).

For example, suppose a theme park wants to find out about visitors' experiences. When people purchase an admission ticket, an invitation is on their receipt to participate in an online survey. Individuals are instructed to log on to a website and complete a brief survey. Those who do so have "volunteered" to be in a study.

Quota Sampling

Quota sampling is the nonprobability equivalent of stratified sampling. You identify the subgroups of interest, set a target about the number of individuals needed for each subgroup, and then by "hook or crook" find the requisite number of people for each subgroup. In other words, in a nonrandom manner, you study people who satisfy each identified stratum, or subgroup. Case 6.5 is an example of quota sampling.

Snowball Sampling

Snowball sampling could be viewed as an adaptation of purposive sampling. In snowball sampling, you find one person who meets study criteria and then rely on that person to identify another person meeting the same criteria.

Use snowball sampling when trying to reach members of groups or subcultures who are hard to reach and no sampling frame exists. The premise is that individuals belonging to a certain group are interconnected, and your only hope is to gain access to one member of the group, who in turn will open the doors or put you in touch with other members of the group.

For example, suppose you are studying female, teenage gang members. You meet a gang member during an in-line skating contest held by the parks department. You ask the individual whether she would be willing to be interviewed later in the week. The teenager shows up at the park office and agrees to answer questions. At the conclusion of the interview, you ask her to identify another girl in the gang who may be willing to be interviewed. You interview the second person, and at the end of this interview, you ask if she would enlist a third gang member to be interviewed and so the cycle (or snowball) continues to grow.

In summary, nonprobability sampling has advantages and disadvantages. These are summarized in Table 6.3.

MIXED-METHODS SAMPLING STRATEGY

Probability and nonprobability sampling techniques tend to be used in isolation. Research endeavors in recreation, parks, sport, and tourism, however, are becoming increasingly more interconnected. More researchers are undertaking studies in which they use a combination of sampling techniques to explore the phenomenon of interest adequately.

To conduct mixed-methods sampling, use probability and nonprobability sampling (particularly purposive sampling) in the same study. As will be reviewed in Step 7, using probability sampling increases generalizability of results, whereas the reliance on nonprobability sampling bolsters trustworthiness. In conclusion, a ***mixed-methods sampling strategy***, or using probability and nonprobability sampling in the same study, increases the likelihood of gaining more insights about the topic.

WHAT KIND OF NONPROBABILITY SAMPLE AM I?

Suppose you are the director of state parks. Your boss has asked you to identify ways to gather input to learn about how to make the parks more appealing to all groups of people. Match the idea description to the correct nonprobability sampling technique being described by choosing from the answers volunteer sampling, quota sampling, purposive sampling, snowball sampling.

Ways to implement the study: Identify the technique being described	Answer
1. You set up tables outside public rest stops located on the interstate highway (that runs through the state) with the banner, "We Want Your Opinions. Please Stop to Complete a 5-Minute Survey."	
2. You form a committee of the park system's mid- and upper-level managers to come up with ideas to make the park more appealing.	
3. You think residents and nonstate residents visiting parks within a particular state differ in their opinions. As cars enter the park, you ask ~170 drivers of state and ~170 out-of-state licensed autos to complete a one-page printed survey and return it before they leave the park.	
4. Because you suspect that young adults are infrequent park users, you strike up a conversation with a young adult visiting a state park's nature center who agrees to complete the survey. Afterward, you ask him to suggest another young adult who infrequently visits state parks. You contact this person by telephone and invite her to complete a survey, too.	

Note. Answers are provided at the end of the chapter.

Table 6.3
Advantages and Disadvantages of Nonprobability Sampling Techniques

Sampling technique	Possible advantages	Possible disadvantages
Purposive sampling	• Includes units of analysis in which you are interested • Insightful if informants are knowledgeable and willing to participate	• Cannot generalize findings
Volunteer sampling	• Inexpensive • Convenient • Easy to implement	• Cannot generalize findings
Quota sampling	• Inexpensive • Potential of providing insights from different groups	• To set the correct quotas, must know the proportion of characteristics across population • Cannot generalize findings
Snowball sampling	• Useful when no sampling frame exists and members are interconnected • When sampling is repeated through several waves, the composition of the sample comes closer to being more representative	• Difficulty in identifying and/or soliciting cooperation from hard-to-reach individuals • Initial contacts may shape the entire sample or prevent access to some members of the population of interest

Note. Adapted from Schutt (2011).

RESPONSE RATE

Response rate is the percentage of people who, when solicited to participate in a study, agree to do so. It is good practice to report the response rate of individuals/entities who responded to a questionnaire or a request to be interviewed. The response rate gauges the magnitude of respondents and nonrespondents. A high rate of nonrespondents may be problematic since nonrespondents may differ from respondents in a systematic way related to the research question.

You may calculate response rate using one of two formulas:

- (Number Returned or Completed Surveys ÷ Number in the Sample) × 100
- [(Number Returned or Completed Surveys ÷ Number in the Sample) – (Noneligible or Unreachable Individuals)] × 100

Experts do not agree what constitutes an acceptable response rate. Some maintain a response rate should fall between 75% and 90% (Rossi et al., 2004).

In comparison, another authority has suggested a sliding scale to judge a response rate. In particular, the quality of a response rate may be appraised using the following standards (Babbie, 2012):

Response Rate %	Interpretation
≥ 70%	Very Good
≥ 60% to ≤ 69%	Good
≥ 50% to ≤ 59%	Adequate
≤ 49%	Unacceptable

Why do some people enjoy certain leisure pastimes and others do not? Sampling individuals may provide valuable insights to this question. For instance, why is there such a following for balloon dogs? (In November 2013, someone paid $58 million for a Koons' *Balloon Dog*, which is the highest sum ever paid for a single artwork created by a living artist.) Balloon Dog sculpture by Jeff Koons, Venice Grand Canal, Italy. Copyright © 2015 Carol Cutler Riddick.

REVIEW AND DISCUSSION QUESTIONS

1. What is the difference between a population and a sample?
2. How is probability sampling distinguished from nonprobability sampling?
3. Distinguish among the techniques that you may use for implementing probability sampling: simple random, systematic random, stratified random, and cluster.
4. How do you decide the sample size for a probability sample?
5. Describe what confidence interval means.
6. Explain each technique for implementing nonprobability sampling: purposive, volunteer, quota, and snowball.
7. What is meant by mixed-methods sampling?
8. Define response rate. What is an acceptable response rate?

YOUR RESEARCH

1. If relevant, identify the population your sample will represent.
2. Will you rely on probability, nonprobability, or mixed-methods sampling?
3. Identify the specific sampling techniques you plan to rely on to conduct your study. Explain your rationale for selecting this sampling plan.
4. How many individuals (or units of analysis) do you envision sampling? Explain the rationale for your selected number.
5. If relevant, what do you expect as your response rate?

PRACTICE EXERCISES

1. Apply some of the probability sampling approaches with this candy or dry bean selection activity.
   a. The instructor brings to class three types of jelly beans, wrapped candies (e.g., the assortment bags sold at Halloween time), or dried beans. The total count should be 180, with a 60 count of the same color/kind of candy/kind of dried bean (Three Colors Jelly Beans/Three Kinds of Candy/Three Kinds of Dried Beans × 60 Count for Each Color or Kind = 180).
   b. If feasible, divide the class into small groups (the ideal would be six or fewer per group).
   c. Give each group 180 pieces of candy or beans.
   d. One person in each group volunteers to be the recorder.
   e. Each group does preliminary tallies and records their findings using a format/worksheet similar to the following:

Worksheet Sample Chapter: Counting Jelly Beans, Candy, or Beans

Question	Answer
Simple random sampling:	
1. How many pieces from a population count of 180 should you select?	
Stratified random sampling:	
2. Using the total number of pieces that need to be chosen (see your answer above), record the number you would expect in each of the three categories.	• Expectations Candy/Bean Type 1 Count = Candy/Bean Type 2 Count = Candy/Bean Type 3 Count =
3. Randomly choose the number of pieces needed (see answer to Question 1 above) and then record the actual counts for each of the three categories/stratums.	• Reality Candy/Bean Type 1 Count = Candy/Bean Type 2 Count = Candy/Bean Type 3 Count =

2. Acquire a copy of of the following article (or your instructor may substitute another article):

   Kemeny, E., & Arnhold, R. (2012). "I can do it, you can do it": Collaborative practices for enhancing physical activity. *Therapeutic Recreation Journal, 46*, 268–283. You may access this article at http://js.sagamorepub.com/trj/article/view/2911.

   Read the article and answer the following questions:
   a. What is the study population?
   b. Was probability or nonprobability sampling used? Specify the sampling technique used.
   c. How many individuals were involved in the sample? Explain why the sample size was or was not adequate.

3. Try to construct a snowball sample of people who play paintball, pickle ball, pesäpallo (a bat and ball sport popular in Finland; for pictures of the 2012 World Cup go to http://www.pesis.com.au/), or another "uncommon" recreation activity identified by your instructor.
   a. Find someone who engages in the activity, and then ask that person to introduce you to another person who participates in the same activity.
   b. Ask the second person to introduce you to another person who participates in the same unusual activity.
   c. Continue "snowballing" until you reach an instructor-imposed time limit.
   d. Provide a report responding to the following questions:
      i. How many people were you able to identify within the imposed time limit?
      ii. Explain how using snowball sampling is easier or more difficult than you expected.

WEB EXERCISES

1. Learn more about randomization by going to the Research Randomizer website at http://www.randomizer.org/. Click on "Tutorial" and complete Lesson 1: Random Sample of 50 People…, Lesson 2: Random Assignment of 40…, and Lesson 4: Random Sampling of 100 Telephone Numbers. What did you learn from each of these tutorials?
2. Now try your hand at randomly choosing units for a study. Suppose you are asked to conduct a study dealing with the leisure pastimes of college-aged students. To do the study, you decide to rely on cluster sampling.

   a. To begin, secure an alphabetical listing of the names of the 50 states, and then number this alphabetical listing. *Hint:* Google "alphabetical list of states." One site that is identified is http://state.1keydata.com/.
   b. On the Randomizer website (http://www.radomizer.org/), click on "Randomize" and answer the questions below:
      i. "How many numbers do you want to generate?" Type in *10*.
      ii. "How many numbers per set?" Type in *10*.
      iii. "Number range?" Type in *from 1 to 50*.
      iv. "Do you wish each number in a set to remain unique?" Select "Yes."
      v. "Do you wish to sort the numbers that are generated?" Select "Yes: Least to Greatest."
      vi. "How do you wish to view your random numbers?" Select "Place Markers Off."
   c. What numbers were generated (print randomizer results)?
   d. Which states were consequently identified for inclusion in your study?

3. If you feel you need to learn more about topics reviewed in this chapter, check out information presented on the following websites. Share what you learned (the instructor may ask you to type a summary paragraph).
   a. To better understand how sampling works, go to the American Association for Public Opinion Research page at http://www.aapor.org/Why_Sampling_Works1/3712.htm.

b. The American Association for Public Opinion Research also has posted an entertaining article about how bad sampling leads to flawed results (go to http://www.aapor.org/Bad_Samples1/5051.htm).
c. To read about snowball sampling, go to the Department of Sociology, University of Surrey, *Social Research Update* website and select Issue 33, "Accessing Hidden and Hard-to-Reach Populations: Snowball Research Strategies" (http://sru.soc.surrey.ac.uk/SRU33.html).

4. Read about the largest study of camper outcomes in the United States in the report *Youth Development Outcomes of the Camp Experience*, which is available at the American Camping Association's website (http://www.acacamps.org/sites/default/files/images/research/directions.pdf).

    a. Find out about the sampling used to conduct the research by reading pages 4 and 6 of the report.
    b. Then, supply answers to the questions noted in the second and third columns of the following worksheet:

Worksheet Sample Chapter: Sampling Used in American Camping Association Report

Who surveyed?	Probability or nonprobability sampling (note page number where answer found)	Identify sampling technique used (note page number where answer found)
1. Camps		
2. Children		
3. Parents		

SERVICE LEARNING PROJECT

1. Decide how you are going to select a sample for the service learning project.
    a. First, identify whether you will rely on probability, nonprobability, or mixed-methods sampling.
    b. Second, identify the sampling technique you will use for the study.

2. Identify the sample size for the study. Justify the number chosen for the sample size.
3. Carry out the sampling technique you have chosen.

TEST YOURSELF ANSWERS

Likelihood a Population Exists?

Questions 1, 2, and 6: Population for noted sample nonexistent or impossible to access; Questions 3, 4, and 5: Population exists

What Kind of Probability Sample Am I?

Question 1: Stratified random sampling, Question 2: Systematic random sampling, Question 3: Simple random sampling, Question 4: Cluster sampling

What Kind of Nonprobability Sample Am I?

Question 1: Volunteer sampling, Question 2: Purposive sampling, Question 3: Quota sampling, Question 4: Snowball sampling

SUPPORTING CASE FOR THIS CHAPTER

CASE 6.1. USING SIMPLE RANDOM SAMPLING TO SURVEY MEMBERS OF A COUNTY SWIMMING POOL

To gather feedback on pool operations (what works and what needs to be improved), a YMCA Board of Directors has asked that a survey be conducted. About 500 individuals have paid for an annual pool membership.

Simple random sampling will be used. According to Table 6.3, 217 names need to be randomly selected. Selected individuals will receive a questionnaire to complete. The steps for selecting the 217 names follows:

1. Alphabetize (by last name) individuals who have paid for an annual pool membership. Then, assign each person in this list a unique "number name." Begin with the first person listed under the letter A. Suppose this person's name is "Alice Allison." Thus, Alice is assigned number 001.
2. Decide how to move through the table of random numbers (Table 6.1). Suppose you decide to move in a downward fashion, and once you come to the end of the column, you will move right and to the top of the next three columns, using the first three digits in a number array.
3. Begin the selection by closing your eyes, arbitrarily pointing to a number in the table of random numbers. Pretend your finger lands on Row 8, Columns 7, 8, and 9 (you need to use three columns since sample size is a three-digit number), revealing the number 152. Record the number selected.
4. Now, move downward through Table 6.1, until you identify 217 other people from the list to become part of the sample. The next few numbers that appear are 019, 340, 481, 619 (which is not a legitimate number since there are only 500 persons in the sample, so at this juncture, numbers that appear in Table 6.1 that are above 500 will be skipped), 184, 069, 109, 380, 140 (which was found when you moved to columns 10, 11, and 12).

   Note: If you encounter (a) a number that is not assigned or (b) the same number array twice, skip the number and continue until you have identified the names of 217 persons.

CASE 6.2. USING SYSTEMATIC RANDOM SAMPLING TO SELECT A SAMPLE OF MASTER'S ATHLETES

A study is being conducted on master's athletes' (people aged 35 years and older) opinions about a track and field competition. Approximately 1,200 individuals registered for the event. Consulting a table of recommended sample size (Table 6.3), you determine about 300 individuals need to be part of the systematic random sample.

The steps for conducting a survey of these individuals using systematic random sampling would be the following:

1. Number each person registered in the track and field competition. Either alphabetize and number the list of names or number names in the order of registration date. Regardless, in progressive order, assign a number to each person beginning with the number 0001 and ending with the number 1,200.

2. Calculate a sampling interval, which in this example equates to 1,200 ÷ 300 = 4. This means you need to identify every fourth individual who registered so he or she is sent a questionnaire.
3. Close your eyes and randomly choose a number from the table of random numbers (Table 6.1). This number identifies the first case, or person, to be sampled.
4. After you have chosen the first person for the sample, identify the name of every fourth person down on the registration list from the previous person selected. This step repeats itself until you have identified the desired 300 names.

CASE 6.3. SELECTING A PROPORTIONATE STRATIFIED RANDOM SAMPLE OF UNIVERSITY UNDERGRADUATES

A study is being set up on the leisure interests of university undergraduates. Previous research results have indicated that a year in college has a profound effect on students' leisure lifestyle. The following is a breakdown of the university's enrollment by matriculation year:

University's Undergraduate Student Population (N = 10,000).

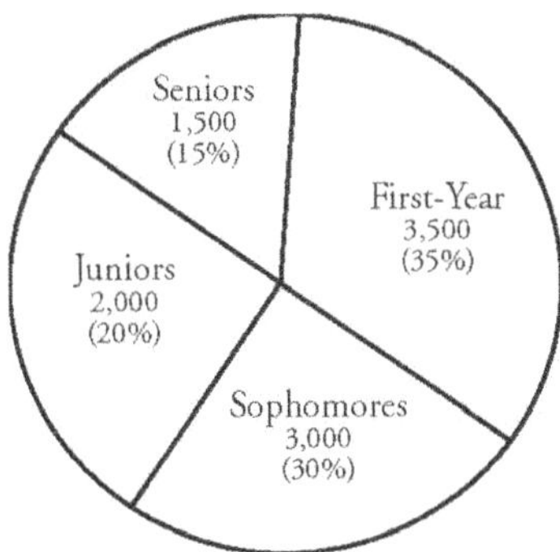

You know, by consulting a table of recommended sample size (see Table 6.3), you need a sample size of about 370. Therefore, you ask the Registrar's Office to generate (using a computerized random number generator) 370 names across the four matriculation rank strata using the same proportions found in the university's undergraduate student population. The numbers and respective percentages of those randomly selected appear in the following pie chart:

Proportionate Stratified Random Sample Selected from the Population of the University (N = 370)

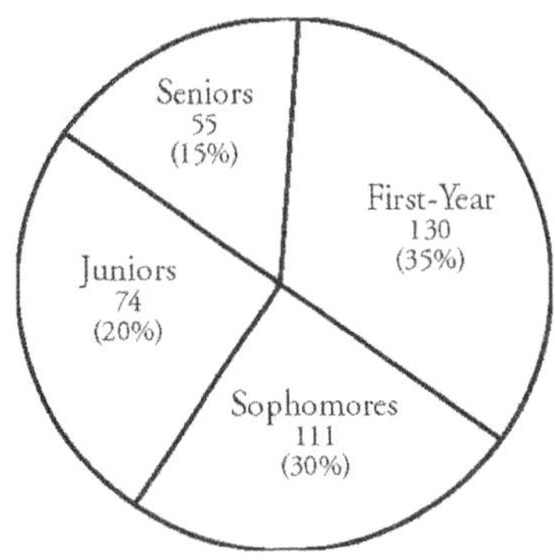

CASE 6.4. USING MULTISTAGE CLUSTER SAMPLING FOR URBAN PARK VISITORS

Suppose a study is designed to survey the opinions of people who visit parks located in American metropolitan areas. You decide to focus on parks located in geographic areas whose populations have 50,000 or more persons. Implementing cluster sampling would require you to follow the multistage approach that follows:

1. Divide the United States into five regions: East, South, Midwest, Southwest, and West.
2. Randomly select three states from each of the five regions, for a total of 15 states.
3. Randomly select two metropolitan areas from each of the 15 states selected, for a total of 30 metro areas.
4. Randomly select visitors to survey from each of the 30 metropolitan park systems.

CASE 6.5. USING QUOTA SAMPLING TO SOLICIT STUDENTS' OPINIONS ABOUT INTRAMURAL PROGRAMS

Suppose a university wants to conduct a survey about the school's intramurals (IM) program. Administrators want to learn IM users' opinions about the program as well as reasons why students do not participate in IM.

About 1,000 students are registered at the school, and records reveal that about 30% of the student body participates in the IM program. A booth is set up in the student union to recruit students to complete a short questionnaire. A quota is set. Those staffing the table are told to gather completed questionnaires from 83 students who report participating in the IM program and 195 students who say they did not participate in the IM program during the school year.

Do you follow where these numbers came from? First, per Table 6.3, the sample size should be set at 278. Second, quotas were set for the proportion of the sample that should be IM users (30% IM Participation Rate × 278 = 83 Individuals) and the proportion of the sample that should represent non-IM users (70% × 278 = 194.6, rounded equals 195).

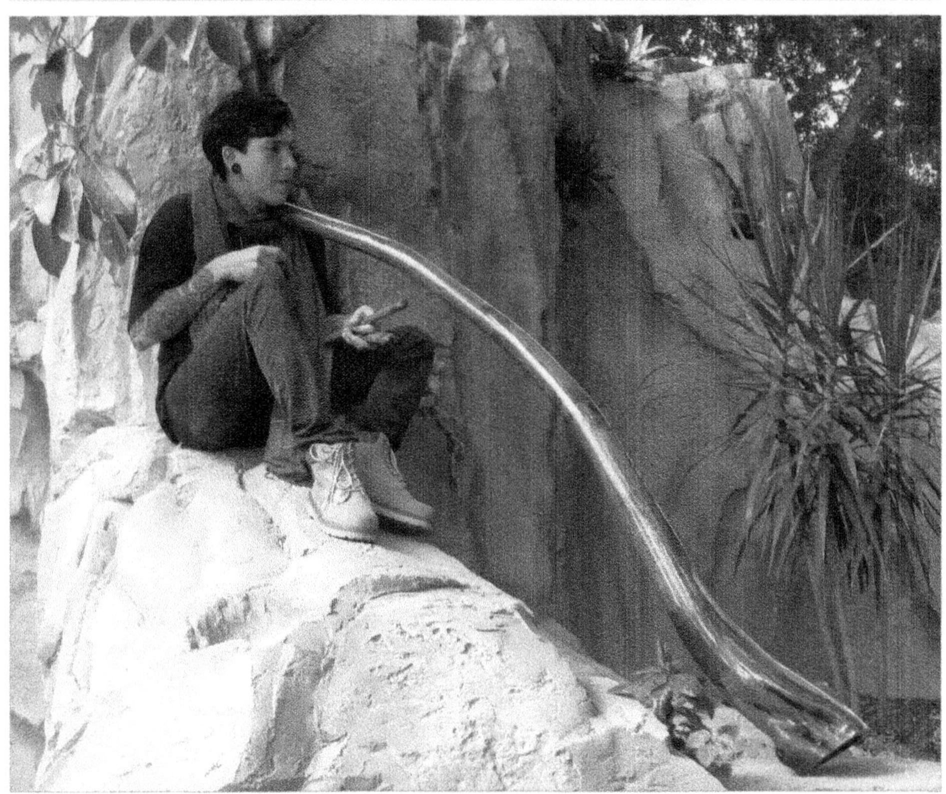

You may choose from many designs when setting up a research project, from simplistic to more complex. Likewise, in the musical world of instruments, you may find unusual designs, including the didgeridoo that showed up at a weekend rainforest program at the Selby Botanical Gardens, Sarasota, Florida. Copyright © 2015 Ruth V. Russell.

STEP 6 > STEP 7 > STEP 8 > STEP 9 > STEP 10 > STEP 11

CHOOSE DESIGN

WHAT WILL I LEARN IN THIS CHAPTER?

I'll be able to...

1. Identify and explain the six qualities of classic experimental design.
2. Diagram the popular experimental designs: pretest–posttest control group, posttest-only control group, and Solomon four-group.
3. Recall the features in nonequivalent control group pretest–posttest, single-group interrupted time-series, and control group interrupted time-series quasi-experimental designs.
4. Name characteristics normally found in preexperimental designs and diagram one-group posttest-only, one-group pretest–posttest, and static group comparison designs.
5. Describe survey and ex post facto nonexperimental designs.
6. Distinguish among ways to execute cross-sectional, longitudinal, and time-lag surveys.
7. Reiterate the guidelines for sample sizes when using experimental, quasi-experimental, preexperimental, or ex post facto designs.
8. Define criteria for choosing a quantitative design: internal validity, external validity, and sample generalizability.
9. Explain how sampling error affects sampling generalizability and list four factors that reduce sampling error.
10. Describe designs used in qualitative inquiries: case study, ethnography, critical theory, grounded theory, narrative analysis, and phenomenology.
11. Clarify the differences among criteria that are used to judge rigor of qualitative designs: truthfulness, applicability, and consistency.
12. Distinguish between concurrent and sequential design mixed-methods approaches.

> **"Would you tell me, please, which way I ought to go from here?' 'That depends a good deal on where you want to get to,' said the cat. 'I don't much care where ---,' said Alice. 'Then it doesn't matter which way you go,' said the cat."**
>
> Lewis Carroll
> (English writer, mathematician, logician, author of *Alice in Wonderland*, 1832–1898)

As previously discussed, your world view, as represented in the theoretical approach that is adopted for the study (Step 3), has a ripple effect on the design you use to conduct the study. In other words, unlike Alice's meanderings, the theoretical lens that you have identified brings into sharp focus the design options available to structure the study (Table 7.1).

The challenge is choosing a way to design or structure the theoretical framework guiding the study. This is labeled a ***research design***, and choosing it depends on several factors (Weiss, 1972, p. 4):

- research purpose and question, information needs of the stakeholders,
- constraints the program or sponsoring organization imposes, and
- protection of human subjects.

To introduce you to your design choices, the chapter is divided into three parts. The first section deals with quantitative design options, guidelines for sample size, and criteria for choosing a quantitative design. The second part reviews popular ways to structure a qualitative inquiry, traditions behind qualitative designs, and criteria for assessing the rigor of a qualitative design. The third section covers mixed-methods designs.

Table 7.1
Overview of Design Options

Theoretical framework adopted		
Quantitative designs	**Qualitative designs**	**Mixed-methods designs**
• Classic experimental • Quasi-experimental • Preexperimental • Nonexperimental	• Case Study • Ethnography • Critical theory • Grounded theory • Narrative analysis • Phenomenology	• Concurrent • Sequential

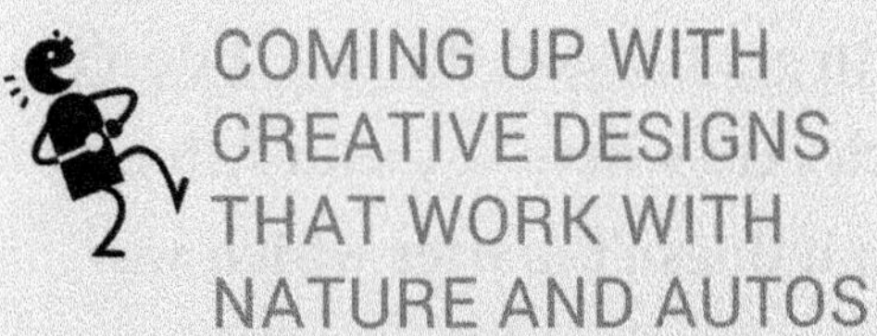

COMING UP WITH CREATIVE DESIGNS THAT WORK WITH NATURE AND AUTOS

Review how nature and human designs have affected people at the following websites:

- http://www.snotr.com/video/7331/The_Living_Bridge
- http://www.youtube.com/embed/auSo1My-
- Wf8g?rel=0
- http://www.flixxy.com/volkswagen-levitating-car.htm#.UCf0raDAETA

QUANTITATIVE DESIGNS

Designs related to a quantitative framework have been labeled ***fixed designs*** (Robson, 2011) and may be divided into four categories:

- classic experimental,
- quasi-experimental,
- preexperimental, and
- nonexperimental.

Fixed designs vary in practicality, cost, and level of technical skill required to implement (Rossi, Lipsey, & Freeman, 2004). This is why choice of design is dependent on the realities of the research situation, including the focus of the research question (Step 4). For example, with one exception, fixed designs are used to measure the impact of an intervention, treatment, or program. The exclusion, ***nonexperimental design***, is used when the focus is on surveying individuals or groups.

Classic Experimental Design

Before you review the quantitative designs frequently used in recreation, park, sport, and tourism research, historical perspective is in order. In the 1800s, the physical sciences developed the ***classic experimental design***. This design was considered the "perfect" or "true" design when conducting medical research involving lab rats! Classic experimental design has six distinguishing qualities: random selection, experimental group, control group, random assignment, pretest, and posttest.

Table 7.2 highlights the scientific notation typically used for each experimental element. This notation system should be useful when reading about the designs.

Ultimately, modifications to the classic experimental design were needed since random selection and random assignment in particular are difficult to accomplish when studying human beings in social contexts. For example, some people will refuse an invitation to participate in a study. Others refuse to be randomly assigned to a control group, even if they are promised that the treatment or intervention will be offered to them once the experiment is over. Thus, in identifying a design for research in recreation, parks, sport, or tourism, one or more of the distinguishing qualities of classic experimental design likely will be dropped.

Nonetheless, experimental designs attempt to control the environment and measure the effects of "manipulated change." More commonly used experimental designs are the pretest–posttest control group, the posttest-only control group, and Solomon four-group. Each of these designs is explained in Table 7.3.

Quasi-Experimental Designs

Compared to experimental designs, ***quasi-experimental designs*** are more practical. In quasi-experimental designs, study participants are not randomly selected to be involved in the study, and if a control group is featured, individuals are not randomly assigned to one group or the other (i.e., the experimental or control group). Quasi-experimental design is often used because of ethical difficulties with implementing the random selection and random assignment features of experimental designs.

Table 7.2

Qualities and Notations of the Classic Experimental Design

Quality	Notation
Random selection uses probability sampling to choose from a study population (see Step 6) a unit of analysis (usually a person) to be included in the study	**RS** = random selection
Experimental group (the group offered or exposed to the treatment, program, intervention, or activity) and the ***control group*** (the group not participating in the treatment, intervention, program, or activity but is part of the research design)	The experimental group is recorded on the line with the **X** designation, whereas the control group appears on the line without the **X** notation
Random assignment to the experimental group or the control group; relies on probability selection to make the assignment	**RA** = random assignment
Pretest, or baseline data collected on groups before the treatment, intervention, program, or activity is introduced or experienced	**OX**, with **O** = observation or measurement; since **O** comes before, or is to the left of **X**, this indicates the pretest is occurring before **X** is introduced or experienced
Posttest, or data collected on groups after the treatment, intervention, program, or activity is completed by the experimental group	**XO**, with **O** = observation or measurement; since **O** follows, or is to the right of the **X**, this indicates the posttest is occurring after **X** is introduced or experienced

Note. This notation system was developed by Campbell and Stanley (1963).

Table 7.3

Popular Classic Experimental Designs

Design name	Schematic	Summary	Comment
Pretest–posttest control group	RA O---X---O RA O-------O	• Participants randomly assigned to experimental or control group • Both groups receive a pretest and posttest • Treatment, program, intervention, or activity is only experienced by the experimental group	• Able to determine whether two groups are equivalent (did not differ in any systematic way) on dependent variables at the beginning of the experiment
Posttest-only control group	RA X---O RA ---O	• Participants randomly assigned to one of two groups • Treatment, intervention, or program only given to experimental group • Both groups receive a posttest	• Assumes at the beginning of the experiment the two groups were equivalent • Appropriate to use this design when pretesting is impractical
Solomon four-group	RA O---X---O RA O--------O RA X---O RA O	• Random assignment to one of four-groups • Some groups receive pretest and/or treatment, intervention, or program • All groups receive posttest	• Relative to other experimental designs, requires more research participants • Logistical work required since four-groups need to be set up

Note. RA = random assignment; O = observation; X = experimental group.

Many quasi-experimental designs exist. The most commonly used are nonequivalent control group pretest–posttest, single-group interrupted time-series, and control group interrupted time-series designs. These designs are detailed in Table 7.4.

More discussion of the first quasi-experimental design listed in Table 7.4, nonequivalent control group design, is helpful because this design relies on matching to select a comparison group. ***Matching*** is pairing persons in the experiment and control groups on the basis of age, gender, or other relevant characteristic. Matching essentially is an attempt to equate important characteristics of individuals in the experimental group to those possessed by the control group (Schutt, 2011). As outlined in Case 7.1, matching may occur by intact group matching, individual matching, or aggregate matching.

Originally, matching emerged as an alternative technique to random selection. In reality, you may perform matching only when individuals are alike on one or two characteristics. Thus, matching is a poor alternative to random selection because other characteristics that were unmatched may influence outcomes.

Preexperimental Designs

Simply put, ***preexperimental designs*** lack the rigor found in experimental and quasi-experimental designs. In other words, preexperimental designs do not feature random selection, random assignment, pretest, and/or a control group. Interpreting results and drawing conclusions becomes problematic when these designs have been used. Three of the most popular preexperimental designs are introduced in Table 7.5.

Experts (Patten, 2012) have advised that preexperimental designs are best suited for a pilot study (discussed in greater detail in Step 12). Nevertheless, many people opt to use a preexperimental design, even with their known disadvantages, when conducting a program evaluation because these designs are easier to implement relative to more rigorous designs.

Nonexperimental Designs

In studies that use a nonexperimental design, a treatment, intervention, or program is not the focus of the study. Instead, individuals or groups are studied as they are. Survey and ex post facto designs are examples of nonexperimental designs.

A ***survey design***, typically implemented by using probability sampling and a questionnaire, examines individuals' self-reported attitudes, beliefs, preferences, and/or behaviors. In the past, survey research has been the most popular design used in studies published in recreation and leisure journals (Bedini & Wu, 1994; Rid-

Table 7.4
Popular Quasi-Experimental Designs

Design name	Schematic	Summary	Comment
Nonequivalent control group pretest–posttest	O---X---O O--------O	• Both groups are selected without using random selection and random assignment • Both groups take pre- and posttests • Only the experimental group receives treatment, intervention, or program	• Used when random assignment to the two groups is impossible • To address equivalency of the two groups at the pretest phase, matching on important characteristics should be considered
Single-group interrupted time-series	O-O-O-X-O-O-O	• Individuals not randomly selected • Only one group, the experimental group • Multiple pretests and posttests	• Number of pre- and posttests may vary • Pretest trend score (or "average") is estimated and compared to posttest "trend" score
Control group interrupted time-series	O-O-O-X-O-O-O O-O-O- O-O-O	• Two groups, not randomly selected or assigned • Treatment, program, or intervention is received only by experimental group • Multiple pre- and posttests	• Number of pre- and posttests may vary • Pretest trend score is estimated and compared to posttest trend score

Note. O = observation; X = experimental group.

Table 7.5
Popular Preexperimental Designs

Design name	Schematic	Summary	Comment
One-group posttest-only	X---O	• Experimental group receives treatment, intervention, or program followed by a posttest	• Provides no documented information regarding changes study participants experienced
One-group pretest–posttest	O---X---O	• One group, the experimental group, receives pre- and posttest	• Noted changes from pre- to posttest do not necessarily stem from the intervention
Static group comparison	X---O O	• Both experimental and control groups receive a posttest	• No assurance that the two groups were equivalent at the beginning of the experiment

Note. O = observation; X = experimental group.

dick, DeSchriver, & Weissinger, 1991). Such reliance on survey design has likely been driven by either the topic being studied or the ease of using this design.

You may use surveys to study people at one or several points in time. Surveys may be used to monitor age differences, age changes, or both. If using age as the basis for selecting groups, administer a one-time questionnaire, also known as a ***cross-sectional survey***, to show how age groups may differ, at one time, in terms of the dependent variables.

If surveying the same age group at different times, however, use a ***longitudinal survey*** (or panel study). A longitudinal survey is designed to monitor how people change as they age. For example, you could follow the same group of adults over time to record changes in their leisure-time pursuits. You could query these individuals three times, such as in 3-year intervals.

Moreover, several age groups studied over time but with different persons being used to represent each age group at the different data collection points is known as a ***time-lag survey***. A time-lag survey investigates age differences and age changes. For instance, you may set up a study to determine age differences and age-related changes that occur over the life cycle related to preferred tourist or holiday destinations. An excellent reference explaining these survey designs is Hooyman and Kiyak (2010).

The ***ex post facto design***, also known as a correlational design, is a variation of the survey design. Ex post facto design is used to determine whether one or more variables are linked to the dependent variable. This design does not involve focusing on a specific treatment, intervention, program, or activity; indeed, the study occurs "after the fact."

For example, one study used ex post facto design to examine the relationship between hot temperatures and baseball pitchers' aggressive acts during Major League Baseball games (Reifman, Larick, & Fein, 1991). If you guessed that batters had a greater chance of being hit by pitchers in warmer (≥ 90 °F) rather than cooler weather, your scientific intuition is good!

Sample Size Guidelines

For studies using classic experimental, quasi-experimental, and preexperimental designs, experts have suggested a minimum of 10 to 15 individuals are needed for each experimental group and each control group (Kerlinger & Lee, 1999). This is only a guideline, however.

Many other considerations that are beyond the scope of this book (e.g., effect size, levels of power, and alpha level) may come into play; thus, consulting a statistician or statistical reference (e.g., Hedrik, Bickman, & Rog, 1993; Henry, 1990) is advisable. The sample size for a survey research design, when the size of the population is known, was reviewed in Step 6. For ex post facto designs, statisticians have provided guidance on the desirable sample size as well. That is, approximately 35 individuals are needed for each independent variable in the study (Kerlinger & Lee, 1999).

Criteria for Choosing a Quantitative Design

Paramount in choosing the "best" design to use for a study is how the findings will be used. The chosen design has profound ramifications for how much "integrity" is behind the study. The ***integrity of a design*** is the internal validity of the study, the external validity of the study, or the sampling generalization. Internal and external validity affect experimental designs, quasi-experimental designs, and preexperimental designs. On the

IDENTIFY A SUITABLE QUANTITATIVE DESIGN

For each scenario, identify which quantitative design category and specific design would work for the situation: experimental, quasi-experimental, preexperimental, or nonexperimental.

Design categories	Specific designs that fall within the category
Classic experimental	• Pretest–posttest control group • Posttest-only control group • Solomon four-group
Quasi-experimental	• Nonequivalent control group pretest–posttest • Single-group interrupted time-series • Control group interrupted time-series
Preexperimental	• One-group posttest-only • One-group pretest–posttest • Static group comparison • Alternative treatment posttest-only with nonequivalent groups
Nonexperimental	• Survey • Ex post facto

Scenario	Category and specific design?
1. Find out whether participation in a 10 -week aerobics class affects body image.	
2. Assess tourists' impressions of a guided Grand Canyon mule trip.	
3. Determine how daily participation in a soccer class, held during a 7-day camp, affects kicking and defensive skills.	
4. Does participation in the intramurals program affect first-year students' stress levels?	
5. Evaluate the effectiveness of a swim instruction program for 5-year-olds.	
6. Identify factors affecting hiking satisfaction.	
7. Evaluate how participation in a 2-week wilderness course affects 400 teenagers attending a 4-week camp. Before arrival to camp, individuals will be assigned to one of four-groups. During the first two weeks of camp, two groups will experience the wilderness program and two groups will not. Data will be collected on all four-groups.	
8. What benefits do senior center attendees participating in a tai chi class experience? Two senior centers will be involved in the study. Initially, attendees of the first center will be offered the class and attendees of the second center will not. After the initial 2 months, the class then will be offered to attendees of the second senior center.	

Note. Answers are provided at the end of the chapter

other hand, sampling generalization becomes relevant when dealing with nonexperimental designs.

Internal validity. Most research in recreation, park, sport, and tourism professions centers on the concern for ***internal validity***, or determining whether a specific treatment, intervention, program, or activity works or positively impacted the participants. Internal validity is also known as causal validity or causal effect.

If changes are due to aspects other than the program or intervention, the internal validity of the study is "threatened." A threat to internal validity is "a mislabeling of the cause of an effect" (Reichardt & Mark, 1998, p. 196). ***Threats to internal validity*** are also called alternative explanations, meaning an aspect other than the treatment, intervention, program, or activity could be responsible for the noted effect. (See Table 7.6 for major threats to internal validity.) You cannot control all threats to the internal validity of a study. Thus, acknowledge the threats to internal validity in any written or group presentation about a study you have conducted (Step 16).

Threats to internal validity may be divided into two categories. The first is threats associated with the study participants, for example, maturation changes. ***Maturation*** threats are related to natural changes or processes that occur over time with study participants. Suppose you are studying how physical education classes affect the fitness levels of children as they move through their elementary school years. A confounding factor is the natural developmental changes that occur with children as they age (e.g., older children typically run faster and smoother). Thus, maturation may become a threat to your ability to draw meaningful conclusions about the merit of physical education instruction.

A second category of threats to internal validity is the procedure used to implement the research, for instance, ***repeated testing***. Repeated testing centers on the notion that the first pretest may educate or sensitize people; in essence, the act of testing itself becomes the change agent.

Suppose a group of park professionals are involved in a 1-day workshop on cultural sensitivity. Administering a pretest centered on cultural attitudes to the workshop attendees may be more responsible for triggering greater sensitivity than the workshop they attended.

Which designs are strong and which are weak when examining threats to internal validity? Figure 7.1 catalogs how the quantitative designs stack up to these threats. In general, designs that feature random assignment to an experimental or control group maximize internal validity (Schutt, 2011). When you are concerned with particular threats to internal validity, choose the strongest design given these realities. For example, if you are particularly concerned with maturation and history threats to internal validity, the pretest–posttest control group or Solomon four-group designs are likely your best choice.

SOMETHING TO REMEMBER!

Research designs have been ranked according to their ability to maximize internal validity. Therefore, if internal validity is an important consideration, work through the following list (in descending order) when deciding on a design. If any design appearing high up in the list is not possible, work your way down the list until you find a design that will work in your situation.

1. Classic experimental design (random selection, random assignment to one of two groups, pretest and posttest).
2. Pretest–posttest control group design.
3. Classic experimental design, with no pretests (this amounts to having random selection, random assignment to the experimental or control group, and a posttest).
4. Posttest-only control group design.
5. Solomon four-group design.
6. Nonequivalent control group pretest–posttest design.
7. Quasi-experimental design with pre- and posttests but no control group (i.e., a design that uses random selection to an experimental group, pretest and posttest).
8. One-group pretest–posttest design.
9. Static group comparison design.
10. One-group posttest-only design.

Note. Adapted from Green (1976).

External validity. Every so often, individuals are concerned with conducting an evaluation of a treatment, intervention, program, or activity that emphasizes ***external validity***, the ability to generalize study findings beyond the sample to the population that the sample represents. An emphasis on external validity becomes critical when

- study results will be used to decide whether an expensive (in terms of monetary costs) treatment, intervention, or program will be duplicated (or set up in other locations);
- the treatment, intervention, program, or activity being evaluated is controversial in nature; and
- the treatment, intervention, program, or activity being evaluated has been set up to remedy or manage a serious situation or condition (e.g., a recreation program intended to stem the number of crimes juveniles commit).

Table 7.6
Threats to Internal Validity

Source of threat	Threat	Explanation	Example
Study participants	***Maturation***	Refers to changes or processes that occur over time with study participants; people change due to natural development (e.g., grow stronger or wiser with age).	Was participation in a yearlong after-school arts program or naturally occurring developmental changes responsible for improved fine motor skills of 9-year-olds?
	History	An event, other than the treatment or intervention, occurred between the pre- and posttest and caused change in the outcomes of interest.	Do teenage athletes' attitudes toward drug use change due to participating in an antidrug education program or because a young and promising athlete died from a cocaine overdose?
	Regression to the mean	Individuals with extreme high or low scores on the pretest tend to have scores closer to the mean on the second test.	Athletes are chosen to be on the cover of *Sports Illustrated* because of their exceptional sport performance. The statistical principle of regression toward the mean predicts exceptional performance is likely to deteriorate. Guess what? Many athletes, shortly after their picture appears on the cover, go into a "slump" (Cozby & Bates, 2011). The question is, does the exposure trigger the downfall or is what is occurring an example of regression to the mean?
	Experimental mortality	Also known as attrition or drop out. Experimental mortality happens for many reasons. People do not complete a posttest for reasons such as they exerted their right to quit the study, moved away, became ill, or died.	Do dropouts from a research project skew results? The nagging question is, are noted changes due to the treatment, intervention, program, or activity or the result of experimental mortality?
	Selection bias	Does not rely on random selection of study participants; instead, "intact" groups or volunteers possess unique attitudes and inherent characteristics (e.g., age) that may be responsible for noted changes.	Do recreation majors completing a leisure attitudes survey accurately reflect the sentiments of all undergraduates on campus?
	Selection bias interaction	Selection bias interacts with another threat.	Counselors at Camp A, the experimental group, are returning staff and have previously taken the environment awareness inventory test; counselors at Camp B, the control group, are first-time counselors (an interaction between selection bias and history)

Table 7.6 (cont.)

Source of threat	Threat	Explanation	Example
Procedures	***Repeated testing***	The first testing educates or sensitizes people; thus, the initial pretest or observation becomes the change agent.	Prior to participating in a friendly companion program, a group of "temporarily able-bodied" teenagers completes a pretest designed to measure on prejudice toward individuals with a physical disability. Did the pretest sensitize or trigger these individuals to recognize the negative stereotypes they hold and therefore motivate them to change their ways of thinking?
	Instrumentation	Between pre-and post-testing, a change occurs in the way observations or testing is defined or recorded.	The definition of "acceptable aerobic activity" is changed between the pretest to the posttest (from "participating > 30 minutes at least 3 times/week" to "participating > 45 minutes at least 3 times/week").

Design	Threat to internal validity							
	Maturation	History	Repeated testing	Instrumentation	Regression to the mean	Experimental mortality	Selection bias	Interaction
Pretest–posttest control group	+	+	?	?	+	+	+	+
Solomon four-group	+	+	?	?	+	+	–	+
Nonequilvalent control group	+	?	?	?	?	+	–	–
One-group pretest–posttest	–	–	?	?	?	–	–	–
Static group comparison	–	–	+		?	+	–	–
One-time posttest	–	–	+		?	+	–	–

Figure 7.1. Report card on the threats to internal validity of selected research designs. Adapted from Van Dalen (1979). Plus sign (+) denotes the factor is not a threat to the design; minus sign (–) designates the design fails to control for the threat; question mark (?) indicates the factor could be a threat; a blank symbolizes the factor is not relevant.

ASSESS THE INTEGRITY, LIMITATIONS, INTERNAL VALIDITY, AND EXTERNAL VALIDITY OF A STUDY

Directions: Read the following scenario and answer the questions.

Scenario: Dr. Doolittle set up a new noontime exercise program at one office of a major, international corporation. She decides, after having offered the program for 2 months, to investigate the physical health benefits participants derive from the program. Records reveal that 30 people have used the program, on average, at least three times per week. She decides to ask five people, who have faithfully exercised on a regular basis, to agree to be interviewed for the study. These individuals report that they have benefited from the program. Dr. Doolittle concludes that the program should be offered at all of the 200 company's offices.

1. Identify two limitations associated with how the study was implemented?
2. If you have a problem in accepting Dr. Doolittle's contention that the noontime program is beneficial to participants' physical health, you are questioning the ____________ of the study.
3. If you have a problem in accepting Dr. Doolittle's advice to offer this program at all 200 offices of the company, you are questioning the ____________ of the study.

Note. Answers are provided at the end of the chapter.

Threats to external validity are factors that stand in the way of being able to extend study results to other individuals, such as those outside the group that have been involved in the research project. In other words, threats are the obstacles that preclude having conclusions extended or generalized to other contexts. Table 7.7 details the threats that may emerge to challenge the external validity of a study, and Figure 7.2 highlights threats to external validity specifically for the quantitative designs frequently used in recreation, park, sport, and tourism research.

You may use two strategies to boost the external validity of a research project: rely on a representative sample (Green, 1976) and replicate a study several times. If similar studies are done in different contexts, and if the same findings and conclusions are reached, at least an indirect case exists for external validity.

When all is said and done, which quantitative designs are best in terms of maximizing external validity? Generally speaking, designs that feature random selection maximize generalizability (Schutt, 2011).

SOMETHING TO REMEMBER!

Research designs have been ranked in descending order according to their ability to maximize external validity. If any design appearing at the top of the following list is impractical, work your way down through the list until you find a design that will work in your situation.

1. Classic experimental design (random selection, random assignment to one of two groups, pre- and posttest).
2. Modified classic experimental design (random selection, random assignment to one of two groups, posttest but no pretest).
3. Nonequivalent control group pretest–posttest design.
4. Randomly selected individuals who experience treatment, intervention, program, or activity and pre- and posttest.
5. Randomly selected individuals who experience treatment, intervention, program, or activity and posttest.
6. Choices 1, 2, 4, and 5 but with no random selection.

Note. Adapted from Green (1976).

Sample generalizability. If you are using a nonexperimental design (i.e., survey or ex post facto) and want to generalize from the sample to its population, you are engaged in ***sample generalizability***. Recall the rationale behind using probability sampling is to be able to generalize. That is, you want to assert that findings from the sample apply to the population from which the sample was selected.

Thus for nonexperimental designs, the ability to generalize hinges on ***sampling error***. The difference between the sample and population values is the sampling error. Sampling error relates to the quality of the sample (Case 7.2). Samples with larger sampling error have less quality. This means, "the larger the sampling error, the less representative the sample and thus the less generalizable the findings" (Schutt, 2006, p. 136).

Table 7.7
Threats to External Validity

Threat	Explanation	Example
Selection bias	See Table 7.6.	See Table 7.6.
Reactive effects of experiment	Observations or responses recorded in an artificial environment/lab do not indicate what happens in a natural setting.	Ability to hit the ball inside a batting cage is not going to predict the ability to hit the ball during a game of softball.
Repeated testing	See Table 7.6.	See Table 7.6.
Multiple treatment interference	Study participants are exposed to several treatments, interventions, or programs, making it difficult to "tease" out how each unique treatment, intervention, or program has affected them.	Adjudicated youth participate in a 1-month high adventure camp. Which of the program offerings (bungee jumping, survival camping, white-water rafting, etc.) is responsible for notable changes in mental and social health?
Instrumentation	The instrument used to measure the variable is no good (inadequately measures the variable under scrutiny).	Sport management majors are asked on a paper-and-pencil test, "Do you aspire for a white-collar or blue-collar job upon graduation?" Respondents have no idea what the question means but nevertheless record a "guessed" answer.
Hawthorne effect	People consciously and subconsciously react to being tested. The act of being measured affects outcome, the so-called ***guinea pig effect*** (Webb, Campbell, Schwartz, & Sechrest, 1981).	Some employees opt to participate in a stress reduction seminar. All employees at the agency take a pre- and posttest measuring their perceived stress. Stress reduction seminar participants and nonparticipants (due to perhaps repeated testing) experience decreased stress levels over 3 months.
Selection interaction	Selection interacts with another threat (e.g., with reactive effects of the experiment, multiple treatment interference).	A study is undertaken to measure the effectiveness of a new lifeguard training program. If the people volunteering for the program change, is the change due to self-selection into the study, knowledge that he or she will be observed during work hours, or because of what was learned in the course (an example of an interaction between selection and Hawthorne effect)?

Design	Threat to external validity					
	Selection bias	Reactive effects	Repeated testing	Instrumentation	Hawthorne effect	Selection interaction
Pretest–posttest control group	+	?	?	?	?	+
Solomon four-group	-	?	?	?	?	?
Nonequivalent control group	-	?	?	?	?	?
One-group pretest–posttest	-	?	?	?	?	-
Static group comparison	-	?	+	?	?	-
One-time posttest	-	?	+	?	?	-

Figure 7.2. Report card on the threats to the external validity of selected research designs. Adapted from Van Dalen (1979). Plus sign (+) denotes the factor is not a threat to the design; minus sign (–) designates the design fails to control for the threat; question mark (?) indicates the factor could be a threat; a blank symbolizes the factor is not relevant.

So what affects sampling error? As a rule, sampling error is reduced when

1. the population from which the sample was selected is known (if the population cannot be defined, the possibility of sampling error becomes astronomical);
2. the population is homogeneous, or is alike regarding key characteristics (confidence regarding the representativeness of the sample decreases when variation exists in the population for the variables examined);
3. probability sampling has been used; and
4. the size of the sample increases (as the sample size increases, confidence that the sample represents the population also increases).

QUALITATIVE DESIGNS

Many designs used in real-world studies, sometimes referred to as ***flexible designs*** (Robson, 2011), are available for qualitative inquiries as well. As with a quantitative design, a qualitative design initially will depend on the adopted theoretical framework (Step 3) and unit of analysis (Step 4). Six of the more popular qualitative designs, by unit of analysis, are outlined in Figure 7.3. Examples of how these designs have been used are cited in Case 7.3. A summary of each of these designs then follows.

Case Study

A ***case study*** is an extensive, descriptive study of a specific unit of analysis to explain why occurrences happened as they did (Yin, 2014). Thus, case studies may become in-depth descriptions of individuals, groups, organizations, artifacts, social interactions, communities, events, or times. Most case studies, however, interpret what has been experienced at an individual or group level.

Studying a single unit of analysis (e.g., a program participant, an activity program, an organization, or a community) typically is done when a new phenomenon is of interest. For example, a case study of the experiences of tourists on a European tour the first time a company offers it would determine whether itinerary and hospitality sites and attractions need adjusted for future tours.

For case studies, the independent variable is not experimentally manipulated, rather the goal is to report comprehensively about the case as it is. You may study a case using quantitative and qualitative data collection. For example, to study the phenomenon of camp counseling, you may conduct a case study of a single coun-

Unit of analysis	Design option					
	Case study	Ethnography	Critical theory	Grounded theory	Narrative analysis	Phenomenology
Individuals	☑		☑	☑	☑	
Group	☑	☑	☑	☑	☑	☑
Organization	☑	☑	☑	☑	☑	☑
Artifacts	☑		☑		☑	
Social interactions	☑	☑	☑	☑	☑	☑
Community	☑	☑	☑	☑	☑	☑
Event	☑	☑	☑	☑	☑	☑
Time	☑		☑	☑	☑	☑

Figure 7.3. Popular options for qualitative designs by unit of analysis. Adapted from Cozby and Bates (2011) and Creswell (2013).

selor or a team of counselors by collecting demographic information from questionnaires, attitude and values data from rating scales, daily diary entries, and situational interviews and observations.

Ethnographic Study

A case study is focused on a specific case, whereas an ***ethnographic study*** is an in-depth study of a group, culture, situation, or institution by a researcher who is immersed into its natural setting for an extended period, usually a year or more (Fetterman, 2009; Le Compte & Schensul, 2010; Wolcott, 1999). In the literal sense, it is "walking a mile in someone else's shoes." The emphasis is on portraying the regular, everyday experiences of the group or situation by observing extensively and/or interviewing intensely over a sustained time (Miles & Huberman, 1994).

Researchers use an ethnographic approach to comprehend as much of what is occurring as they can, that is, to appreciate the "whole picture" of a recreation, park, sport, or tourism situation (Fraenkel, Wallen, & Hyun, 2011). Insider and outsider views combine to provide deeper insights than would be possible by a single researcher alone. For example, Scounten and Alexander (1995) used an ethnographic study to study the "new" biker culture that has emerged in the United States.

Ethnographic studies have two unique features (Miles & Huberman, 1994):

1. Discovery process. The evaluator observes and/or interviews for a time, then develops initial conclusions that lead to additional observations and/or interviews, winds up observing/interviewing again, and so on.
2. Descriptive enterprise. Reaching across the multiple sources of information to uncover what is typical about the setting or situation studied. The emphasis is on depicting "how things are."

IF YOU ARE SEARCHING FOR AN ETHNOGRAPHIC DATABASE

Are you considering an ethnographic study? Try Yale University's electronic collection of world culture. These cross-cultural studies contain anthropologists' descriptions organized by culture and subject classification. Access is available through institutional (universities, colleges, public libraries, museums, high schools, etc.) or individual membership. For more information, go to http://www.yale.edu/hraf/or phone 203.764.9402.

Critical Theory

Critical theory also incorporates a subjective and interpretative view of social reality through meanings and individuals' interpretations (Matchua, 1996). Going beyond the focus of an ethnographic study, however, the critical theory design seeks to empower research participants by examining reality through their self-reflections and insights. Understanding gained from the study may be used to provide a vision of how social institutions and/or public policies may be improved (Tyson, 2006).

Feminist theory is a popular subset of critical theory (Kinloch, 1977). As originally articulated, the feminist theory approach asserts that women occupy an inferior status in capitalist and patriarchal societies, meaning that women's experiences are shaped by social, economic, and political forces or inequities rather than individual choices. Over time, feminist theory has become more expansive, and today, this design examines experiences from gender, race, and social class interpretative perspectives.

For example, photography has been used as a data collection tool for critical theory. Here, study participants are given a camera and asked to take pictures of their surroundings or activities. The idea is to experience the world through the viewpoint of a group of people, sometimes referred to as ***photovoice*** (cf. Walton, Schleien, Brake, Trovato, & Oakes, 2012). The participants essentially become part of the research team since they capture their social world and then explain what they saw and interpret the meanings of their recorded experiences.

Illustrative of this design approach is a study conducted by Burns (2007). In this project, as part of a university's personal discovery course, each student was given a camera and asked to take pictures that would memorialize a camping trip to a wilderness area. Later, the investigator met with students to hear the meanings attached to their favorite pictures.

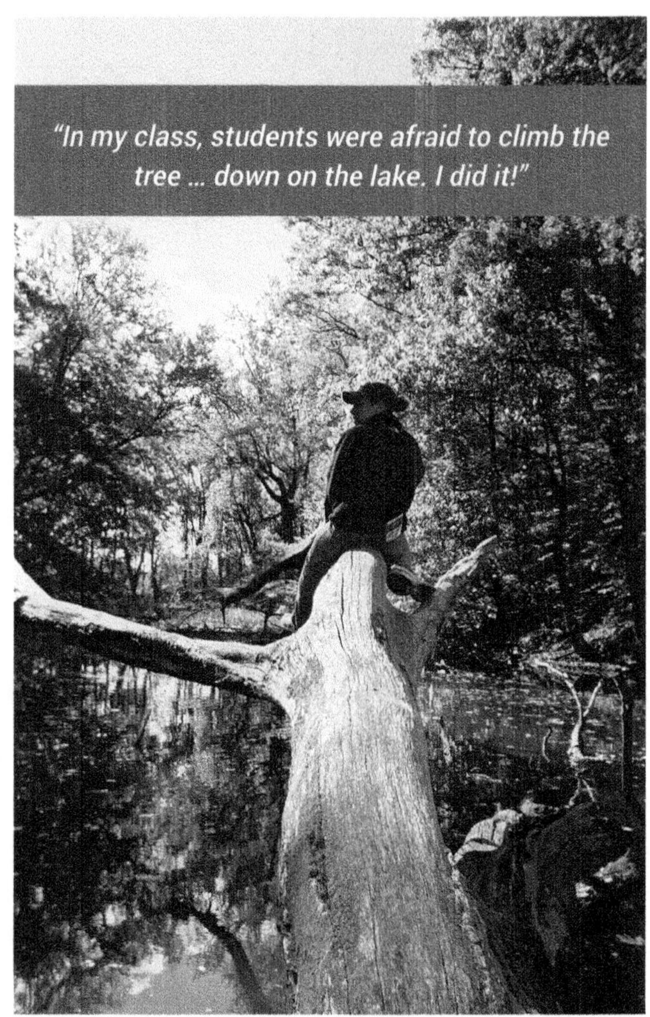

"In my class, students were afraid to climb the tree ... down on the lake. I did it!"

Critical theory is a qualitative design that may use photovoice as a way to collect data. A university student who was asked to record the meanings and memories a class-sponsored weekend camping trip had for him took this picture. The student interpreted the picture as capturing the sense of accomplishment he felt when being able to climb to the end of the fallen tree. Wye Island Natural Resources Management Area, Queenstown, Maryland. Copyright © 2015 Justen Burns.

Grounded Theory

Grounded theory is an approach designed to construct theory from the words and actions of individuals (Glaser & Strauss, 1967). The term *grounded* refers to the aim of having theory emerge from the data collected. The theory that is developed is thus a generalization inducted (introduced in Step 3) and constructed from data that have been collected. Thus, the term *grounded theory* refers to a method of inquiry and to the product of inquiry (Charmaz, 2011).

Grounded theory is context specific (cf. study of museum visitors by Goulding, 2000). The process unfolds following defined procedures for repeated data collection and analyses that are without a priori direction from existing theories (Charmaz, 2014; Corbin & Strauss, 2008a).

You may use several data collection tools in grounded theory, the most common being in-depth interviews and observations that describe situations, record events, note feelings, and keep track of ideas. In the first wave, use open-ended questions to generate insights. Then, reflect upon responses to identify emerging categories. Study these categories collectively to induce a theory or explain the phenomenon. Challenge the drafted theory through another round or two of data collection that involves other groups of individuals and then ultimately refine the theory using data analysis (Corbin & Strauss, 2008a).

In the long run, the successive refinements "... ensure the theory is grounded within the data" (Gratton & Jones, 2010, p. 99). This process is referred to as ***constant comparison***, in which you compare each new piece of information (attitude, behavior, opinion, etc.) to each other piece of data as you gather it.

Although a grounded theory design undoubtedly may be informative, at least one disadvantage exists. As you may surmise, the major challenge is the design usually takes a long time to complete. Illustrative of the time commitment involved in using a grounded theory approach is Moe's (2012) study of belly dancers (see Case 7.3).

Narrative Analysis

Narrative analysis is the use of interviews (and sometimes documents and observations) to put together stories about events and experiences as participants understand them (Clandinin & Connelly, 2004). By reading the stories and using a coding strategy to classify what you read and identify general patterns, you will discover "... how respondents impose order on the flow of experience in their lives and make sense of events and actions in which they have participated" (Schutt, 2006, p. 376).

Although research is an attempt to understand the "story" of a phenomenon, narrative analysis is distinguished as a qualitative design that takes as its object the investigation of the story. What is the structure of the story, and why was it told that way? The following distinct narrative types have emerged:

1. Personal stories or autobiographical accounts of an individual's own personal history (Reissman, 1993). For example, Smith, Santucci, Xu, Cox, and Henderson (2012) used the personal stories approach to study the career development of women working in park or recreation programs.
2. Dominant cultural narratives or stories about persons, places, or things that contain consistent storylines and thematic content. These narratives are transmitted through social institutions (e.g., mass media) and in conversation (Richardson, 1990). For instance, a study of the lyrics and tone of a rap song could reveal the context of urban life for young residents.
3. Community narratives or descriptive and historical accounts that represent the collective knowledge and experience of a specific group. Consistent themes that emerge from the personal stories are studied (Rappaport, 2000). The stories parents pass on to their children and grandchildren, for instance, provide an understanding of the nature of family life for a particular ethnic group.

Phenomenology

Phenomenology originates out of philosophy and is "both a way of doing research (method) and a way of questioning and conceptualizing thought (philosophy)" (Luborsky & Lysack, 2006, p. 335). This makes for a complex and multifaceted endeavor, but at its most basic level, phenomenology is focused on everyday life and the prime attention to the ordinary that people experience and express (Moustakas, 1994). The goal is to deepen understanding of human experiences by engaging in a crucial reflection of conscious experience. Examples of phenomenology-based research include studies of compulsive shoppers (O'Guinn & Faber, 1989) and rave dance culture in Britain (Goulding, Shankar, & Elliott, 2002).

Phenomenological research studies a small number of persons through extensive interviews to discover meanings and patterns. Phenomenology is unique from other qualitative research approaches in that it regards the "lived experiences" and meanings that study respondents provide as paramount. Only those who share an experience are thought to be fully knowledgeable about the experience.

In this qualitative approach, as with the narrative analysis, do not apply many analyses to the data. Rather, present the findings in the form in which they are originally expressed, by identifying themes or patterns, based on the "...essence of lived human experiences about a phenomena as described by participants" (Creswell, 2013, p. 13).

Traditions Behind Qualitative Designs

Many of the qualitative designs just reviewed may seem difficult to distinguish. Though they share the "core" definition of the qualitative theoretical approach (see Step 3), they are used according to their particular research tradition: interpretivism, social anthropology, or collaborative social research (Miles & Huberman, 1994).

Interpretivism has a long intellectual history in which human activity is seen as "text"—as a collection of symbols expressing layers of meaning. In phenomenology, for example, meaning is interpreted by the research subjects and the researcher.

IDENTIFY A SUITABLE QUALITATIVE DESIGN

For each scenario, identify which qualitative design would work for the research situation: case study, critical theory, ethnography, grounded theory, narrative analysis, or phenomenology.

Scenario	Category and specific design?
1. Interview women who are homeless regarding how they overcome constraints related to engaging in leisure pastimes.	
2. Over many months, observe and record the play choices children living in a third world country make.	
3. Interview adults with asthma regarding their opinions about running and walking opportunities offered in their local parks.	
4. Study diary entries of older women who are learning to windsurf.	
5. Undertake a descriptive study of three first-time fathers involved in a 1-week sport camp with their son.	
6. Interview a group of adults about their expectations for going on a cruise for the first time. Based on these initial discoveries, develop a tentative theory explaining amenities first-time cruisers seek. Then check to see if the drafted theory is supported as more interviews are conducted with a new group of first-time adult cruisers.	

Note. Answers are provided at the end of the chapter.

In the tradition of social anthropology, on the other hand, the methods stay close to what is studied via description only, without interpretation. Grounded theory and narrative studies stem from this tradition.

Finally, in ***collaborative social research***, an element of "action" is applied. The researcher is a protagonist for using the process and conclusions from a study as a change strategy. Examples of collaborative social research are instances where the researcher, with various stakeholders, helps design studies resulting in everything from changing the therapeutic recreation offerings in a rehabilitation center, to redesigning gender equity in the staffing of a camp. The design of critical theory would fit this tradition.

Rigor in Qualitative Designs

Regardless of the qualitative design you choose, the findings should be accurate (Creswell, 2013). That is, the descriptions and interpretations of the findings are defensible and not so subjective that they cannot be trusted. This notion of rigor is obviously important. Sometimes ***rigor*** is referred to as trustworthiness.

Trustworthiness requires that designs possess the following criteria (Lincoln, Lynham, & Guba, 2011):

1. Truthfulness. Refers to the truth value of the results from the study. Truthfulness is somewhat parallel to the internal validity of quantitative designs.
2. Applicability. Denotes how useful the evaluation findings are to other situations. Applicability is parallel to the external validity of quantitative designs.
3. Consistency. Sometimes referred to as dependability, which means the findings from the study are reliable (an idea that will be reviewed in Step 8).

STRATEGIES FOR MAXIMIZING THE TRUSTWORTHINESS OF QUALITATIVE DESIGNS

1. Truthfulness = Aspire for truthfulness by checking for the accuracy of the findings via the following procedures:
   - ***Triangulation.*** Rely on multiple data sources. That way converging sources of information should build a coherent justification for the themes that emerge.
   - ***Prolonged engagement.*** Engage in lengthy and intensive contact with respondents or phenomena in the field. That way in-depth understanding occurs so distortions of reality (that may emerge from too brief an engagement) are avoided.
   - ***Member checks.*** Conduct follow-up interviews with study participants by asking them to identify errors you may have made in either under-

standing what they said initially and to comment on the findings or conclusions reached.

- ***Peer debriefing.*** While the study is in process, obtain an objective assessment by sharing information about procedures, findings, and tentative conclusions with a disinterested professional peer. This peer review is done so questions are asked about the study that provide an account that will resonate with people other than the researcher.

2. Applicability = Achieve applicability by using ***thick descriptions*** to convey the findings. This means the written report is richly developed, with the context and descriptions thoroughly presented so judgments about the "fit" or transferability of the findings to another situation may be judged.
3. Consistency = At the end of the study, confirm consistency by conducting an external audit of the final product. In an ***external audit***, a competent "outside" person examines the process used to collect data and cross-checks the results of the study to confirm your interpretations. To have an external audit, leave an ***audit trail***, or the notes and materials that help the auditor trace how the evaluator arrived at the conclusions.

Note. Adapted from Creswell (2013).

MIXED-METHODS DESIGNS

As mentioned in Step 3, researchers increasingly are using mixed-method designs for implementing their studies. Again, mixed methods refer to integrating elements of qualitative and quantitative designs so the strengths of each may be maximized.

Mixed-methods designs run on a continuum. A study design may be primarily quantitative with a smaller part that is qualitative. In contrast, the study design may be primarily qualitative with a small quantitative component.

Then again, the study may be more or less an even split, relying on qualitative and quantitative approaches equally. Regardless of the mix or blend, you may execute a mixed-methods design by concurrent design or sequential design.

Concurrent Design

The ***concurrent*** (sometimes referred to as parallel) ***mixed-methods design*** involves collecting qualitative and quantitative data to provide a "comprehensive analysis" of the research problem. Both approaches are conducted simultaneously yet are independent of each other. Results of the approaches then are merged or integrated when interpreting the findings. Case 7.4 reviews how this design was used when examining the motives

and meanings older women reported for participating in yoga.

Sequential Design

The ***sequential mixed-methods design*** consists of conducting the study in two waves to elaborate or expand upon initial findings. The topic may influence whether a qualitative or quantitative approach is used in the first wave (Case 7.5).

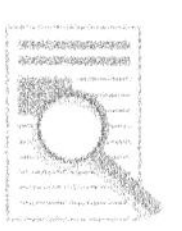

For example, the first study may be an exploratory study, using qualitative methods, with a small number of participants. The insights learned from individuals in the first study then would form the basis of a follow-up study, using quantitative methods with a large number of participants.

Alternatively, the topic of the research may dictate using a quantitative design for the first wave. Suppose you are investigating how participation in college-sponsored physical activity programs (e.g., spin classes, Zumba, aerobics) influences the physical health of college students. You also want to learn about obstacles students face when trying to adopt a more active lifestyle.

The first wave of the study could be quantitative by conducting physiological assessments and tracking health changes over time that may occur as a result of participating in an exercise class. The second phase of this hypothetical study of college physical activity programs could be qualitative by conducting unstructured interviews (which will be reviewed in Step 8). You may talk to a few of the study participants involved in the first wave of the study again to obtain a richer and fuller understanding of the obstacles college students encounter in exercise as well as solicit feedback on how the exercise programs are structured and delivered.

Walkers and runners may face challenges navigating the terrain near St. Paul's Cathedral, which includes walkways, a piazza, office space, and restaurants. Choices also abound when it comes to designing a study. Paternoster Square, London, England. Copyright © 2015 Carol Cutler Riddick.

REVIEW AND DISCUSSION QUESTIONS

1. Identify the six elements of the classic experimental design. Which are more difficult to execute in recreation, park, sport, and tourism research?
2. Summarize pretest–posttest control group, posttest-only control group, and Solomon four-group experimental designs.
3. Diagram nonequivalent control group pretest–posttest, single-group interrupted time-series, and control group interrupted time-series quasi-experimental designs.
4. Give a hypothetical example of one-group posttest-only, one-group pretest–posttest, and static group comparison preexperimental designs.
5. Contrast survey and ex post facto nonexperimental designs used in recreation, park, sport, and tourism research.
6. Distinguish ways to execute a cross-sectional survey, a longitudinal survey, and a time-lag survey.
7. Explain the guidelines for sample size when experimental, quasi-experimental, preexperimental, or ex post facto designs are used.
8. Delineate how internal and external validity influence quantitative design choice.
9. How does sampling error affect sample generalizability? What four factors reduce sampling error?
10. Compare and contrast the following qualitative designs: case study, ethnography, critical theory, grounded theory, narrative analysis, and phenomenology.
11. List three strategies for increasing rigor or trustworthiness in qualitative designs.
12. What is the difference between a concurrent and sequential mixed-methods design?

YOUR RESEARCH

1. Think of a research project you would be interested in undertaking. Recalling Step 4, or the Scope chapter, write a purpose statement. Then, to figure out which design you are inclined to adopt for the research, answer the following questions (Gratton & Jones, 2010):
   a. Is what I am interested in something that can be measured numerically?
   b. Am I mostly concerned with measuring "facts"?
   c. Am I mostly concerned about individuals' explanations, rather than a societal perspective, of what is happening?
   d. Do I think that "truth" varies by individual?

   If you answered *yes* to the first two questions and no to the last two questions, you are likely to choose a quantitative design. If you answered *no* to the first two questions and *yes* to the last two questions, you are likely to adopt a qualitative design. Finally, if you answered *yes* to all four questions, you are headed toward a mixed-methods design.
2. Accordingly, identify the research design you are planning to adopt for your study.
3. About how many persons/units do you anticipate having in your study? Provide a rationale for this number.
4. Is your study focused on internal validity? External validity? Sample generalizability? What are the threats or limitations associated with the design you have chosen?
5. Or have you elected to conduct a qualitative study and hence need to focus on rigor? If so, what strategies could you use to increase truthfulness, applicability, and consistency?

PRACTICE EXERCISES

1. Acquire a copy of the following article (or your instructor may substitute another article):

   Dawson, S., Knapp, D., & Farmer, J. (2012). Camp war buddies: Exploring the therapeutic benefits of social comparison in a pediatric oncology camp. *Therapeutic Recreation Journal, 46*, 313–325. You may access this article at http://js.sagamorepub.com/trj/article/view/2914.

   Read the article and answer the following questions:
   a. Was a quantitative, qualitative, or mixed-methods design used for the study?
   b. If quantitative design was used, identify threats to the internal and external validity of the study. How confident are you the findings have internal validity and external validity?
   c. If qualitative design was used, what efforts were directed at ensuring truthfulness? Applicability? Consistency?
   d. If a mixed-methods design was used, did it rely on a concurrent or sequential design? Answer questions noted in 1b and 1c.

2. Quasi-experimental designs lend themselves to certain research questions but not to others. Identify three research questions that you could investigate using a quasi-experimental design.
3. Try your hand at undertaking abbreviated qualitative studies using the designs and scenarios in the following worksheet. *Note:* The instructor may assign each student one or more of the following exercises.

Worksheet Design Chapter: Practicing the Use of Qualitative Designs

Directions: For the design you choose or are assigned to, follow the directions that have been provided.

Qualitative design	What to do
Case study: Conduct a ~20-minute interview (you may be asked to tape or video record the interview) with a college senior regarding his or her favorite recreation activity.	Ask the following questions of the person you interview: 1. What was your favorite recreational activity in high school? 2. Did your favorite activity change while you were in college? 3. Explain why you liked your favorite activity in high school? In college? (*Note*: Explore with the person the physical, social, and/or psychological benefits and emotions with taking up the particular recreation activity.) 4. Submit a typed paper of the (a) answers you recorded to the questions asked during the interview and (b) your reactions/impressions related to undertaking a case study.
Ethnographic study: Attend a sport/recreation activity wearing the "lens" of an ethnographer. Conduct a ~20-minute observation of what occurs at the event/ activity.	1. Take field notes that include a description of the setting, event, people, and what you observed (including nonverbal interactions). 2. In a one-page typed paper (a) interpret and provide personal impressions of what you observed (remember to attach your field notes to the paper) and (b) describe your reactions to undertaking an ethnographic study.

Qualitative design	What to do
Critical theory: Conduct a photovoice study by taking ~20 photos (on a cell phone or digital camera) of what you do with your leisure time over the weekend (please do not record anything that violates your privacy).	1. Choose and print 10 photos that have the most meaning to you. 2. Type a paragraph about (a) what the experience captured in each photo means to you and (b) your feelings and thoughts using photography as the medium to implement a small-scale study based on critical theory.
Narrative analysis: Find two individuals who have an "unusual" hobby and are willing to be interviewed for ~10 minutes. Conduct a tape- or video-recorded interview asking the individual to tell you the "story" behind how she or he was introduced to the leisure-time activity.	Provide typewritten responses to the following: 1. Provide the script or story captured in the recorded interview. 2. Identify the themes that emerged from the two interviews? 3. What are your feelings and thoughts about conducting a narrative study?

4. Suppose you were asked to identify a means to test the research question, "How do teenagers use their leisure time?" Provide a written outline for how you could conduct the study using a mixed-methods design.

WEB EXERCISES

1. Read about the American Camp Association's research study *Directions: Youth Development Outcomes of the Camp* at http://www.acacamps.org/sites/default/files/images/research/directions.pdf.
   a. What research design was used for the camper survey? Parent survey? Staff observation?
   b. Do findings have internal validity? What are two threats to the internal validity of the study?
   c. Do findings have external validity? What are two threats to the external validity of the study?
2. Find out whether you understand threats to internal validity by going to a tutorial written by Drs. Polson, Ng, Grant, and Mah at Athabasca University at http://psych.athabascau.ca/html/Validity/. If need be, review the threats to internal validity presented in Part I of this tutorial. Then, go to Part II and decide whether each of the 36 hypothetical experiments has internal validity, and if it does not, decide what threat exists to compromise the noted findings.
3. Participate in an online social psychology experiment at http://www.socialpsychology.org/expts.htm/.
   a. Review and consider volunteering to participate in one of the social psychology research studies listed under "Category of Interest."
   b. Was a quantitative, qualitative, or mixed-methods approach used to conduct the study in which you elected to participate?
      i. If a quantitative approach was used, what was the research design?
      ii. If a qualitative approach was used, how was the study structured?
      iii. What sampling technique was used to conduct the study?
      iv. From what you surmised about how the study was conducted, would you argue the findings have internal validity? External validity? Why or why not?

4. If you feel you need or want to learn more about the topics reviewed in this chapter, check out information presented on the following websites:
   a. Another reference on design is William Trochim's web page for Research Methods Knowledge Base at http://www.socialresearchmethods.net/kb/. Click on "Design."
   b. For experimental designs, quasi-experimental designs, preexperimental designs, and sources of invalidity (Sessions 4–7), go to Professor Germain's (California State University Long Beach) web page at http://www.csulb.edu/~msaintg/ppa696/696menu.htm.
   c. For case study, ethnography, and grounded theory, consult Dr. Graham Gibbs' (University of Huddersfield) lectures on these topics at http://www.youtube.com/watch?v=b5CYZRyOlys, http://www.youtube.com/watch?v=V8doV3P0us4, and http://www.youtube.com/watch?v=4SZDTp3_New.d.
   d. For narrative analysis and phenomenology, consult Dr. Jason J. Campbell's lectures. The first of several presentations on narrative analysis may be found at http://www.youtube.com/watch?v=4SZDTp3_New. For the phenomenology lecture, consult http://www.youtube.com/watch?v=LLjKdvVzKXM.

SERVICE LEARNING PROJECT

1. Decide on a research design for the service learning project:
   a. If you are using a quantitative approach, name the design that will be used.
   b. Now determine whether you are going to incorporate a qualitative approach into the study. If so, identify the flexible design that will guide the study.
   c. If you plan to use mixed-methods design, identify whether you will rely on a concurrent or sequential mixed-methods design. Outline how you intend to conduct this part of the study.
2. If using a qualitative design, elaborate on the strategies you will use to increase the rigor or trustworthiness of this part of the study.

Test Yourself Answers

Identify a Suitable Quantitative Design

1. Preexperimental: One-group pretest–posttest, 2. Nonexperimental: Survey, 3. Preexperimental: One-group pretest–posttest, 4. Preexperimental: One-group pretest–posttest or static group comparison, 5. Preexperimental design: One-group posttest-only, 6. Nonexperimental: Ex post facto, 7. Quasi-experimental: Solomon four-group, 8. Quasi-experimental: Nonequivalent control group pretest–posttest

Assess the Integrity, Limitations, Internal Validity, and External Validity of a Study

1. Selection bias (how the sample of five was chosen), small sample size, no pretest, instrumentation (reliance on self-report); 2. Internal validity; 3. External validity

Identify a Suitable Qualitative Design

1. Critical theory, 2. Ethnography, 3. Phenomenology, 4. Narrative analysis, 5. Case study, 6. Grounded theory

CASE 7.1. MATCHING OF EXPERIMENTAL AND CONTROL GROUP MEMBERS IN STUDY ON THE IMPACTS OF VIDEO GAME PLAY ON NURSING HOME RESIDENTS?

Suppose you've decided to introduce a novel activity to nursing home residents: video game play. You want to adopt a nonequivalent control group design to conduct the study. Your challenge is how to identify two groups, the experimental and control, for the study. Below are your options for matching individuals belonging to the two groups.

Approach to matching	Application
1. Intact group matching. Locate a second group, usually in a different geographic location, whose demographic characteristics and/or pretest scores are anticipated to resemble the experimental group.	Choose to implement the study in two nursing homes owned by the same chain in the same town.
2. Individual matching. Each control group member is selected because he or she is a close or perfect match in terms of having the same pretest score on the independent variable (or variable that is strongly related to the dependent variable) as his or her corresponding experimental group member. Individual matching may be time consuming and, if many variables are matched, difficult to implement.	If length of time living in the nursing home is considered an important matching variable, each person in the control group would be an equivalent match to an experimental group member. For instance, if an experimental group member had lived in the facility for 5 years, the control group equivalent would have lived in a nursing home for 5 years.
3. Aggregate matching. The overall "average" on important pretest variable scores for experimental and control groups are matched. Aggregate matching is deemed less desirable to use than individual matching.	If age is an important matching variable, the control group would be constituted so that their "average" age matched the experimental group, though the range of ages in the groups would vary. For instance, suppose the age of experimental group members spanned between 70 and 80 years, whereas control group members' age spread was from 74 to 76 years. Although both groups' mean age emerged as 75, one group relative to the other group had much younger and older members.

CASE 7.2. DO THE EXPERIENCES OF GRAND CANYON VISITORS REPRESENT THOSE OF VISITORS TO OTHER NATIONAL PARKS?

Often at the beginning stages of defining your population, you are faced with having to delimit the population base. This means you define the population more narrowly than initially planned.

For instance, a population for a study may have started out as being defined as anyone visiting a U.S. national park during the current calendar year. When you realize that it would be difficult, if not impossible, to secure the names of the millions of people visiting all the national parks, you may redefine the population to apply to a particular park, say Grand Canyon visitors.

The problem with delimiting the population is that you lose the ability to generalize, to conclude what you find in one population group extends to other population groups. In other words, a probability sample of Grand Canyon visitors has sampling error. You should not conclude Grand Canyon users' impressions apply or pertain to users of other parks in the national system. Indeed, it would be premature to conclude that satisfaction levels found at the Grand Canyon mirror what is occurring at other national park sites because the visitors to specific parks may have unique demographic and experiential characteristics.

CASE 7.3. DESIGNS FOR THE QUALITATIVE APPROACH

Structural designs available for qualitative research	Example of published research using the design
Case study	Beames, S., & Ross, H. (2010). Journeys outside the classroom. *Journal of Adventure Education and Outdoor Learning, 10*, 95–109. This is a case study of 33 participants, aged 8 to 11 years, living in Edinburgh, who participated in an outdoor learning program.
Ethnography	Magnussen, L. (2012). Play—the making of outdoor experiences. *Journal of Adventure Education & Outdoor Learning, 12*, 25–39. Describes findings from two years of ethnographic fieldwork conducted in a kayak community. Meanings produced by kayakers are shared.
Critical theory	Trussell, D., & Mair, H. (2010). Seeking judgment free spaces: poverty, leisure and social inclusion. *Journal of Leisure Research, 42*, 513–533. This study explored the experiences and meanings of leisure for individuals living in poverty who are homeless or at risk of becoming homeless.
Grounded theory	Moe, A. (2012). Beyond the belly: An appraisal of middle Eastern dance (aka belly dance) as leisure. *Journal of Leisure Research, 44*, 201–233. This study involved three distinct rounds of data collection. First, 1,000 hours of observation field notes were recorded from 2003 to 2010. Second, journal entries made by 20 persons involved in belly dancing were collected over 2 years. Third, online statements from women in two belly dancing discussion boards were monitored.
Narrative analysis	Rupprecht, P., & Matkin, G. (2012). Finishing the race: Exploring the meaning of marathons for women who run multiple races. *Journal of Leisure Research, 44*, 301–331.
Phenomenology	Shannon, C. (2013). Bullying in recreation and sport settings: Exploring risk factors, prevention efforts, and intervention strategies. *Journal of Park and Recreation Administration, 31*, 15–33.

CASE 7.4. CONCURRENT MIXED-METHODS DESIGN

Riddick, C., & Humberstone, B. (2010). Practising yoga later in life: A mixed-methods study of English women. In B. Humberstone (Ed.), *Third age and leisure research: Principles and practice* (LSA Publication No. 108, pp. 117–130). Eastbourne, England: Leisure Studies Association.

The purpose of the study was to examine how practicing yoga later in life may impact older women's well-being and health. The study represents a coming-together of the differing epistemological positions the two authors hold, together with their diverse professional and physical experiences. Feminist and self-determination theories guided the investigation.

Questionnaires completed by a group of 21 yoga participants provide data concerned with competence, self-determination, and intrinsic and extrinsic motivations associated with older women practicing yoga. Due to time constraints, open-ended interviews between the researchers and six of the 21 participants were conducted to explore in greater depth the experiences of women, providing qualitative data.

Quantitative inquiry found partial support for the posited model. Intrinsic and extrinsic motivations appear to regulate positive emotional benefits older women derive from yoga. Additionally, yoga instructor's style of teaching spills over to whether older women experience earmarks of tranquility (or a sense of calmness, peacefulness, and relaxation). Furthermore, self-perceived yoga competency appears to play a pivotal role in how much pleasure (an extrinsic motivation) older women experience from practicing yoga. Qualitative methods unveiled insights regarding why the interviewed women began yoga, how yoga has influenced their lives, and the physical and mental benefits they experienced from yoga.

Further in-depth interpretative, narrative analysis, that accounts for the social-cultural contexts of older yoga participants and considers the ways in which "aging bodies" are theorized is advocated. Such research may highlight the ways in which older people resist contemporary discourses on aging through physical activity and hence would add considerably to knowledge and praxis around aging.

CASE 7.5. SEQUENTIAL MIXED-METHODS DESIGN

Shim, C., Santos, C., & Choi, M. (2013). Malling as a leisure activity in South Korea. *Journal of Leisure Research, 45*, 367–392.

The purpose of the study was to explore Korean fascination with shopping malls and "malling" as a leisure activity/experience. Using a mixed-methods approach, Phase 1 consisted of conducting a quantitative mall visitor survey to learn why people were motivated to visit the mall. In the second stage, a qualitative content analysis of blog posts was conducted to discover what specific aspects of the mall appeal to visitors.

The quantitative approach found three main motivations behind mall visits: recreational, purchase related, and meeting related. Content analysis of blog posts generated 16 themes for why study participants visit the mall. Implications for future research are outlined, including further conceptualization of the nexus between leisure and consumption in the urban context particularly applied to shopping malls as being viewed as leisurescapes.

A simple and valid way to test the range of motion in the shoulder joints is the shoulder stretch flexibility test. Most people will notice that one shoulder is more dominant in flexibility than the other. Shoulder flexibility is important to performing in activities such as swimming, racket sports, or sports involving throwing and catching. Judge the shoulder flexibility of the individuals featured in the photo by using the following criteria: overlapping opposing fingers as excellent; touching fingers as good; fingers less than 2 inches apart as average; and fingers 2 inches or more apart as poor. Copyright © 2015 Haiwen Ding.

STEP 6 > STEP 7 > STEP 8 > STEP 9 > STEP 10 > STEP 11

CONSIDER MEASUREMENT

WHAT WILL I LEARN IN THIS CHAPTER?

I'll be able to...

1. Diagram and explain the four parts of the logic of measurement.
2. Summarize three categories that may be used to classify measuring instruments: reactive, nonreactive, and psychophysiological measures.
3. Explain the merit of using multiple-variable measures of the same concept.
4. Provide an example of a concept and three companion variables that could be used to investigate the given concept.
5. Differentiate between single- and multiple-item measures and be able to identify which approach is better to adopt when selecting a measure.
6. Differentiate between an index and a scale.
7. Distinguish between instrument validity and instrument reliability and explain how these concepts are important to consider when measuring a variable.
8. Provide a definition for these ways of establishing validity for an instrument: face validity, content validity, concurrent validity, predictive validity, convergent validity, and discriminant validity.
9. Describe ways to establish the reliability for an instrument: interrater reliability, test–retest reliability, split-half reliability, and interitem reliability.
10. State the minimum reliability coefficient value that suggests acceptability for interrater reliability, test–retest reliability, split-half reliability, and interitem consistency.
11. Define what it means when normative data exist for an instrument.
12. Identify two resources for locating a good instrument.

"Even with the best maps and instruments, we can never fully chart our journeys."

Gail Pool
(Professor of anthropology,
University of New Brunswick)

Knowing the basics of measurement is a must for today's recreation, park, sport, and tourism professionals. This holds true regardless of whether you are a practitioner conducting a program evaluation; a student completing an honors paper, thesis, or dissertation; a full-time researcher; or the judge at a flamingo race. A fundamental understanding of measurement basics "... is not only a prerequisite to providing appropriate interventions to the clients that we serve, but is an integral part of dictating the efficacy of services" (Zabriskie, 2003, p. 330).

The initial stages of a study, as introduced in Steps 3 and 4, entail identifying concepts and variables. This is just the beginning of a sequence of actions that has been dubbed the ***logic of measurement*** (Bouma & Atkinson, 1996), which consists of specifying the following (Figure 8.1):

1. Identify each concept or construct. Remember, you may find these concepts or constructs in the research question, objective, or hypothesis.
2. Select a variable that reflects each concept's working definition, officially known as the ***nominal definition***.
3. Choose or devise a measuring instrument, technically known as the ***operational definition***, for each variable.
4. Specify ***units of measurement*** for each variable in the instrument. In other words, you must adopt or devise a system for categorizing answers.

Logically planning a study—identifying a concept in the purpose statement, selecting a variable to signify the

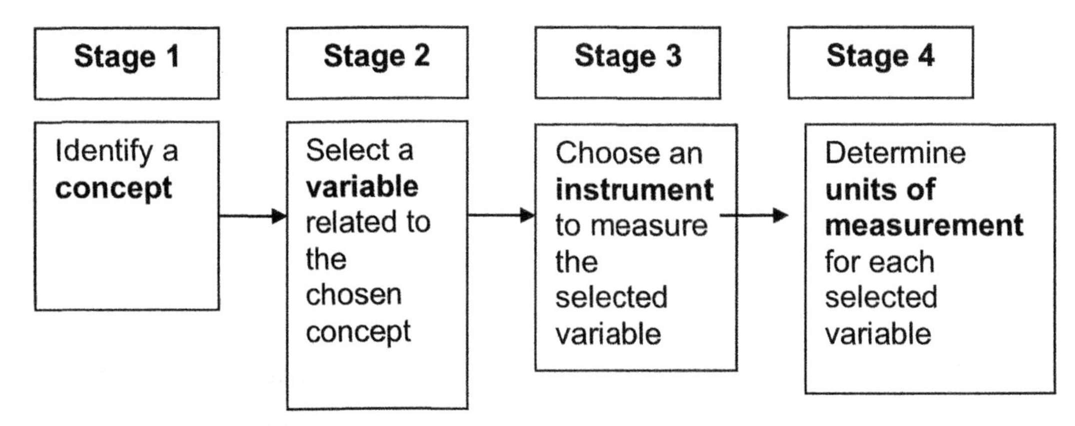

Figure 8.1. Logic of measurement.

concept, choosing an instrument to measure and categorize each variable, and finally determining the units of measurement—is often referred to as ***operationalization***. Crucial to the logic of measurement, then, is the extent the concept has been encapsulated by the variable, instrument, and units of measurement.

INTERCHANGEABLE WORDS

Some words are used interchangeably in research reports. For example, the words *measurement, measures, instruments, instrumentation*, or even *operationalization* refer to the measuring instruments that were used in the study.

To illustrate, research reports are organized by conventional labeling rules (introduced in Step 11 and covered in more detail in Step 16). That is, usually the measuring instruments used to collect information for a study are described as a subsection in the Methods section of a report. This subsection may be titled several ways, including Measures, Measurement, or Instruments.

Incidentally, note that the Methods section should never be called Methodology. This is taboo because methodology is the study of methods and not the methods themselves.

The ideal is to attain a high level "goodness-of-fit" (Grosof & Sardy, 1985) between the concept and the operationalized variable. Review Table 8.1 for goodness-of-fit between the concepts and corresponding measurement instruments highlighted.

Searching for a measuring instrument is analogous to shopping at the grocery store. At the concept level, you have decided to buy a beverage to drink, but after a few

Table 8.1
Examples of Goodness-of-Fit?

Concept	Variable	Measurement instrument	Units of measurement
Mental ability	Intelligence	College grade point average	0 to 4.0
Social support network	Best friends	Self-reported count	0 to hundreds!
Body composition	Body density	Underwater or hydrostatic weighing	Lean fat ratio
Good life	Quality of life	Time devoted to walking, hiking, playing outdoors, and engaging in sports	Minutes

Note. Adapted from Scitovsky (1992).

minutes, you realize you have a hankering for fruit juice, the variable of choice (Figure 8.2). You enter the store, walk to the aisle containing juice drinks, and search for the shelves storing the juice brands. Now, you must ponder on what to purchase and drink. You narrow your choice between a 32-ounce container of the store brand or a 12-ounce concentrate made by Welch's. The instrument of choice for satiating your thirst and taste preferences ends up being the brand name concentrate.

Figure 8.2. Linkage for concept, variable, and instrument: Grocery shopping analogy.

You may choose an instrument to measure a variable by adopting an already existing instrument or by creating your own. To teach you more about this, the remainder of the chapter is broken into an overview of points to consider when choosing an instrument and resources for finding good instruments.

POINTS TO CONSIDER WHEN CHOOSING AN INSTRUMENT

Many instruments may exist for the variable you are considering measuring. Indeed, you will want to choose a "good" one, but you may feel overwhelmed choosing one instrument from among those available or wonder whether you should create your own measurement instrument. To alleviate this anxiety, consider the following when choosing an instrument: measure, multiple-variable measures of the same concept, single- versus multiple-item measure, instrument validity, instrument reliability, and existence of normative data.

Measure

One way to classify measuring instruments is to label them as a reactive, nonreactive, or psychophysiological measure. Each measure provides unique information, yet each has its own limitations. Ultimately, you must decide to adopt one or more of these measures.

Reactive measures. Instruments that create and measure responses are ***reactive measures*** (Webb, Campbell, Schwartz, & Sechrest, 2000). For example, when you ask people questions on a questionnaire that require self-report, you may make them aware that you are studying them. When people know their words are being measured, they may not always respond normally or truthfully. In other words, they may portray behaviors, attitudes, preferences, beliefs, or behaviors in ways that are socially acceptable.

Reactive measures operate the same as taking people's photo. People know their picture is being taken so they pose for the camera. Mascot and fans at a Michigan State University women's basketball game. 2005 NCAA Final Four championship, Indianapolis, Indiana. Copyright © 2015 Ruth V. Russell.

Nonreactive measures. On the other hand, ***nonreactive measures*** are used to examine "naturally" occurring information (Webb et al., 2000, p. vii). A nonreactive measure is anything that does not tamper with the nature of the measured response. Physical traces and documents/records are nonreactive measures (Webb et al., 2000).

1. ***Physical tracing*** is finding and recording visible evidence or traces of behavior that are not specifically produced for the research project, but they are nonetheless available to measure. Physical traces are inconspicuous and anonymous; those who left them behind have no knowledge of their potential for use in a study. Erosion and accretion are broad classes of physical traces (Webb et al., 2000).

- ***Erosion physical traces*** are the degree of selective physical wear on objects or the environment. Such measures may be an index to popularity. Erosion physical traces may be the wear patterns on floor tiles in front of museum exhibits or shortcut paths in the grass that deviate from paved sidewalks in a park.
- ***Accretion physical traces*** involve the deposit or accumulation of material. Accretion physical traces may be the amount of garbage found on a beach (as a measure of the level of compliance with the city's no litter policy) or the number of alcohol containers left in the stadium after a football game (as a measure of compliance with a no alcohol policy).

2. ***Documents/records***, also known as archival data, may be categorized as public records or personal documents (Table 8.2). ***Public records*** are materials created to provide unrestricted information or accounting (Step 9 reviews public document or record review in greater detail). Public records may determine an organization's priorities and concerns, financial resources, values (e.g., commitment to diversity), operating processes (e.g., evaluation of staff), and consistency of policies (Neuendorf, 2001).

   The second type of document is a personal document (Table 8.2). ***Personal documents*** are first-person accounts of events or personal experiences (Merriam, 2009). People keep various personal documents, and by examining these documents, you may begin to understand how the person views his or her experiences.

Table 8.2
Examples of Documents/Records

Documents	Examples
Public Records	• Advertisements • Annual reports • Books • Bulletin board postings on the Internet • Census data • Class or activity registration records • Meeting minutes • Mission statements • Newspaper articles/ editorials • Organization and program budgets • Policy manuals • Promotional literature/ videos • Songs • Speeches • Strategic plans • Television shows or programs • Visitor and convention bureau records • Web pages
Personal Documents	• Appointment calendars • Children's drawings • Diaries • E-mail messages • Personal letters • Photographs • Scrapbooks

Psychophysiological measures. ***Psychophysiological measures*** are used to assess the physiological functioning of the central nervous system and autonomic and somatic nervous systems (Cacioppo, Tassinary, & Berntson, 2013). Instruments that have been used as proxy indicators of psychophysiological concepts include blood pressure, heart rate, skin temperature, respiration rate, and muscle tension. These measures are used almost exclusively in sport studies, though a few exceptions have occurred in the recreation literature (cf. DeSchriver & Riddick, 1990; Riddick, 1985a).

Multiple-Variable Measures of the Same Concept

Another important point to remember in choosing measuring instrumentation is to select multiple variables for each concept. At best, you may view each measure of the same concept as only a partial glimpse of what is happening, but together the measures provide a "truer" whole picture. Each variable contributes a different perspective of what is studied—each is a unique nominal definition of a concept. This is often accomplished by measuring multiple dependent variables.

To illustrate, suppose you want to measure how participation in physical fitness training affects people's emotions. The concept of emotions could encompass variables such as depression, anxiety, and happiness (see Figure 8.3).

Single- Versus Multiple-Item Measures

In addition to examining multiple variables for each concept, consider using multiple items to measure the variable. The following is an example of the single versus

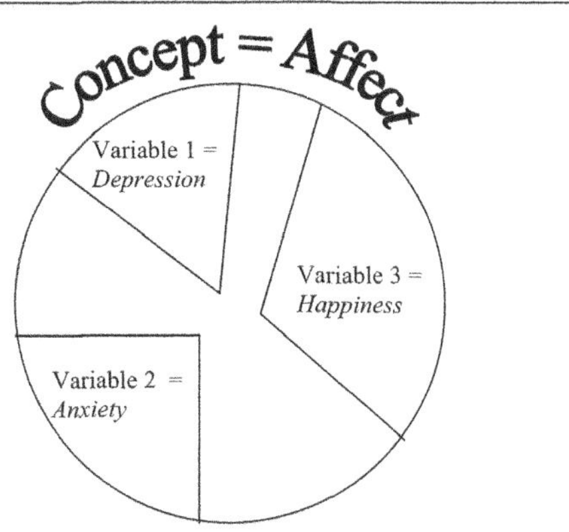

Figure 8.3. The psychological effects of physical fitness training: Example of multiple-variable measures of the same concept. Adapted from Folkins and Sime (1981).

multiple item debate. A single question is often popular when measuring demographic variables. For example, the variable of age can easily be measured with the question, what is your age? Variables that are complex, on the other hand, need to use a multiple-item instrument. For instance, how many different perspectives should be considered when measuring the variable of happiness? The challenge is to find or develop an instrument that delivers the comprehensive information you need in as short a time as possible. There are essentially two types of multiple-item measures. These are an index and a scale.

Index. An ***index*** is created when you use several questions to measure one variable. The responses then are tallied to obtain a sum or average (Case 8.1). Generally, an index provides a more complete measure of a variable than any single question.

Creating an index is difficult to do well. The goal is for each question to measure the same item but from a different angle. If you have succeeded in measuring one variable with several questions, people's responses to the questions should show consistency. A special statistic, called an ***internal consistency reliability*** statistic, is available to determine whether the questions comprising the index are "holding together" to measure the same variable.

Occasionally, an index is created containing questions that may be broken down into "clusters" that measure different aspects of the variable. Technically, this is known as a ***multidimensional index***. For instance, the Competitive State Anxiety Inventory-2 is a 27-item self-report test designed to measure overall competitive state anxiety and three independent competitive states in high school and college athletes: cognitive state anxiety, somatic state anxiety, and confidence (Martens, Vealey, & Burton, 1990).

Scale. Sometimes responses to questions in an index are given different weights before an average score is calculated. Responses to one or more questions may be counted in the calculation of the overall scale score as worth twice (or higher) as much as responses to another item. Technically, ***weighting*** answers in an array of questions is referred to as a ***scale*** (Case 8.2). Normally, extensive testing is used to assign the weighting.

Instrument Validity

Instrument validity is the accuracy of a measuring instrument. In other words, does the instrument capture its intended variable (Monette, Sullivan, & DeJong, 2008)? A logical relationship must exist between the way a variable is defined nominally and the way it is operationalized. For instance, if you propose to measure intelligence based on hair color, you most assuredly would have an invalid measure of intelligence.

To establish the validity of an instrument, use a construct validity or criterion validity approach. You may implement each approach in more than one way.

Construct validity. Because it is the easiest way to address validity, ***construct validity*** is used frequently to establish validity of an instrument. In construct validity, you make a subjective judgment regarding the adequacy of the instrument. You may use face validity and content validity to establish construct validity.

Face validity is a subjective judgment that the instrument appears to be an adequate measure of the variable. One person, usually the researcher or primary investigator, has decided that the variable (or nominal definition of the concept) has been captured in the operational definition provided by the instrument. In other words, the instrument appears to measure what it is supposed to measure.

Suppose you are trying to figure out how to measure leisure attitude. Items to measure this variable initially include "I often feel nervous when faced with what to do in my free time" and "I learned how to tie my shoes when I was 5." Because the first item appears to be more closely related to leisure attitude, you choose to use it in the instrument designed to measure leisure attitude. In other words, the item is deemed to have face validity.

However, face validity alone is not able to demonstrate the validity of an instrument. Indeed, appearance is not a good indicator of accuracy or meaningfulness (Cozby & Bates, 2011). Nonetheless, face validity is a good place to start when you are trying to create items for an instrument, but once the instrument is completed, you should pursue other ways of determining its validity as well.

Content validity may be used to examine the content of an instrument to determine whether it represents the content, elements, or instances of what is being measured (Monette et al., 2008, p. 114). For instance, if you want to create a new leisure satisfaction measure, a review of literature would reveal that satisfaction derived from leisure may affect components of a person's life, including psychological, social, and physical satisfaction. Therefore, if the statements used in the instrument to measure leisure satisfaction dealt with only psychological satisfaction, this instrument would not demonstrate content validity because it did not include the other aspects of leisure satisfaction according to the literature.

Content validity is established by a jury. ***Jury opinion*** consists of asking a group or panel of knowledgeable experts or persons (which could include members of the studied population) to review and verify that the selected items measure the concept. Jury opinion, though subjective, is considered superior to an individual researcher's declaration that an instrument has face or content validity.

Criterion validity. In ***criterion validity***, the newly developed instrument and objective evidence, such as a preselected standard that is known or believed to measure the variable accurately, are compared. Unlike content validity approaches, criterion validity involves collecting information that substantiates the validity of an instrument. You may establish criterion validity through concurrent, predictive, convergent, and discriminant validity.

Watch the video at http://www.youtube.com/watch?v=BUJl9Umkm2k. You be the judge... Do the selected maneuvers serve as good measures for fitness ability? For both entities featured?

Over time, many unusual units of measurement have evolved. View the following video and identify which two measures intrigued you most and why: http://www.youtube.com/watch?v=Q8qQ-olqkTU0.

The criterion for establishing ***concurrent validity*** is determining whether two or more groups of people score differently on a concept in expected ways (Cozby & Bates, 2011). Suppose you have developed an Appreciation of Nature Scale. You expect that people active in the outdoors will score higher on the scale than those who report no involvement in the outdoors. If this is found to be the case, you have established concurrent validity for the newly developed instrument.

Predictive validity is the ability of a measure to predict or foretell. For example, the Scholastic Assessment Test's (SAT) validity was established by determining its ability to predict graduation from college. Similarly, predictive validity for Zuckerman's (1980) Sensation Seeking Scale was authenticated when it was determined that people who scored high on the scale behaved differently from individuals who scored low on the scale. High sensation seekers, relative to low sensation seekers, were found to engage in dangerous activities (e.g., driving over the speed limit).

Convergent validity occurs when a new measure is found to be related to a previously validated instrument that was designed to measure the same concept (see Figure 8.4). If the new and old comparable instruments are administered to a group of individuals, both tests basically should yield the same results: People who score high on one measure should score high on the second measure and, likewise, people who score low on one measure should score low on the second measure. Many consider ***correlation statistics*** (a statistic that basically compares test scores) in the range of .40 to provide evidence of convergent validity (Stangor, 2011).

Suppose you thought of a new way to measure perceived leisure functioning. You ask a group of 100 persons to complete the new test and Witt and Ellis' (1985) Leisure Diagnostic Battery (LDB), a previously validated test that measures perceived leisure functioning. Convergent validity would be documented if test scores coincided. That is, respondents who scored high on the LDB would also attain a high leisure functioning score on the new test. Likewise, individuals who received a low leisure functioning score on the LDB would receive a similar low rating on the recently developed test.

Discriminant validity is established when the new measure is found not to be related to another instrument that has been documented as validly measuring a different concept. The new measure should discriminate between the construct being measured and other unrelated constructs (Cozby & Bates, 2011). For instance, individuals who scored high on a previously documented valid test of aggressiveness would be expected to have different scores (i.e., low scores) on a newly developed measure of passiveness. If this happens, then the new test is deemed to have discriminant validity.

Finally, sometimes efforts are made to document how older and newer instruments measuring the same variables stack up. This sort of study, sometimes referred to as a ***multitrait-multimethod study***, requires identifying two variables and two tests intended to measure each variable. Figure 8.4 illustrates this notion of convergent discriminant validity by comparing and contrasting the administration of the four instruments, two of which are designed to measure extrovert personality and two of which focus on introvert personality.

VALIDITY

Directions: Decide whether the statement is *true* or *false*. If *false* briefly explain why.

Check yourself	And the answer is...
1. Face validity is considered an excellent measure of validity.	
2. Content validity is essentially the same as face validity.	
3. Concurrent validity requires documenting two or more groups of people who score differently on a concept in expected ways.	
4. Comparing the results summer camp applicants received on "Suitability for the Job" ratings versus final ratings their supervisors gave at the end of camp is an example of predictive validity.	
5. If a group of park rangers who scored high on a previously documented valid test for assertiveness have low scores on a newly developed measure for shyness, the new test has convergent validity.	

Note. Answers are provided at the end of the chapter.

Instrument Reliability

Another goal of research is to use measurement instruments that are reliable. ***Instrument reliability*** is the repeatability, constancy, and/or stability of responses of or within an instrument (Stangor, 2011). Several factors may result in unreliable data (Creswell, 2005, p. 162):

- Questions are ambiguous and unclear.
- Administration procedures for the instrument are inconsistent.
- Respondents are tired, are anxious, and/or misinterpret or guess at questions.

One way to determine the ***reliability*** of a measured variable is to conduct the measurement a second time. For example, using your bathroom scale, weigh yourself two times in a row. If the weight recorded both times is the same, the scale is reliable. Contrastingly, if the scale records different weights seconds apart, the scale is unreliable.

SOMETHING TO REMEMBER!

Here is a summary of the approaches to assessing the validity of an instrument.

Type of validity	Description
I. Contruct validity	A subjective judgment is made that the instrument is adequate
Face validity	Individual decides measure is good
Content validity	A determination by a jury or group of knowledgeable experts has been made that the instrument contains a representation of content, elements, or instances of what is being measured
II. Criterion validity	Correlates with objective evidence (or preselected standard)
Concurrent validity	Groups of people score differently on the construct in expected ways
Predictive validity	Foretells a future outcome or event
Convergent validity	New measure is correlated to a previously validated instrument that was designed to measure the same variable
Discriminant validity	New measure does not correlate with a previously validated instrument designed to measure different variable

Reliability coefficient is a numerical value that measures the consistency of a measuring instrument. The coefficient may range from 0.0 to 1.0. A reliability coefficient of 1.0 indicates perfect reliability with no error. If your instrument has a reliability coefficient of .90 or higher (written as $\geq .90$), 90% of the differences that are measured are true for the variable, and the likelihood of making an error in determining reliability is only 10%. A reliability coefficient of .90 means the instrument is reliable.

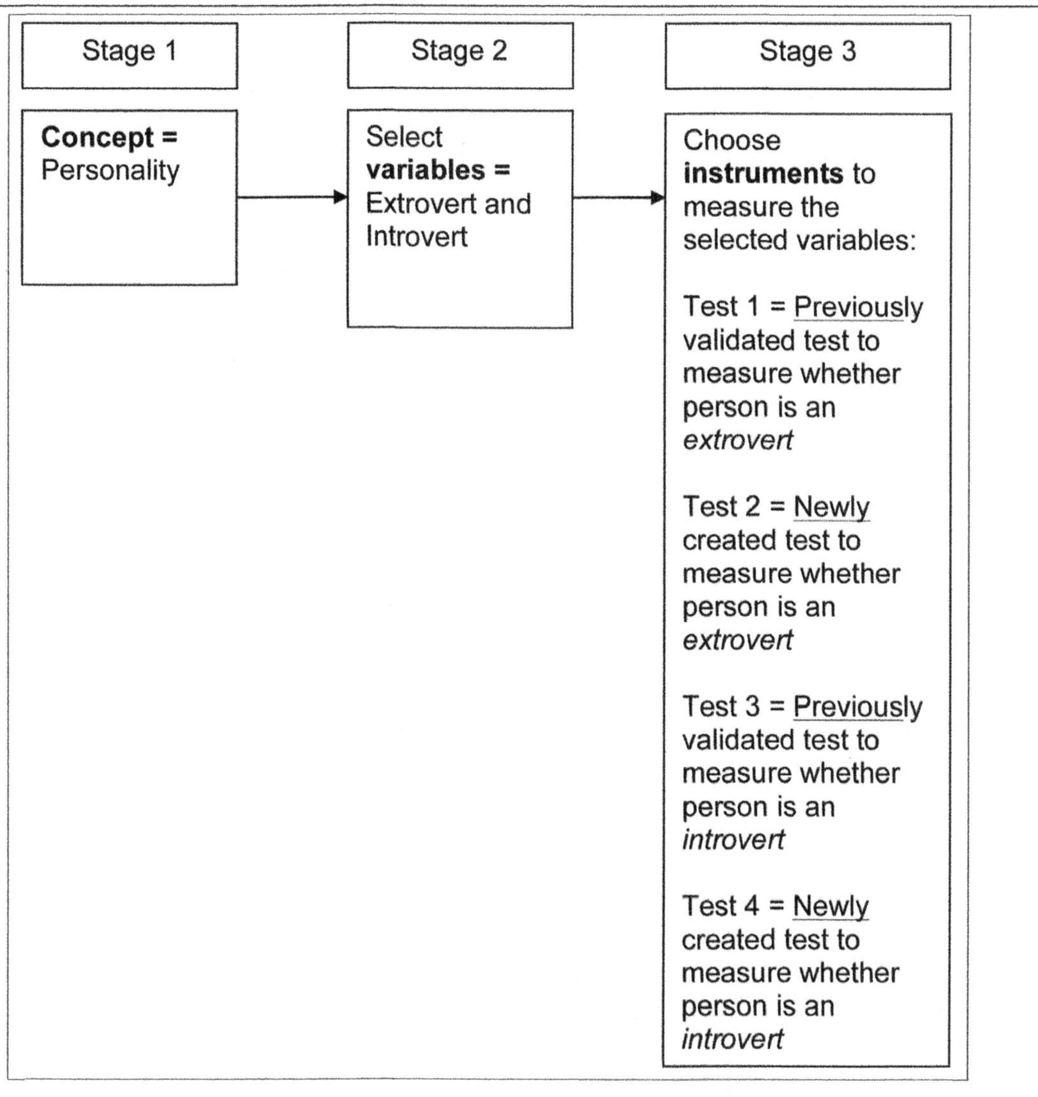
Stage 1
Stage 2
Stage 3
Concept = Personality
Select variables = Extrovert and Introvert
Choose instruments to measure the selected variables:
Test 1 = Previously validated test to measure whether person is an extrovert
Test 2 = Newly created test to measure whether person is an extrovert
Test 3 = Previously validated test to measure whether person is an introvert
Test 4 = Newly created test to measure whether person is an introvert

Expectation	Tests used	Results
People who score high extrovert (i.e., their personality is characterized as very outgoing) using previously validated (or old) instrument will also score as high extrovert using newly established test (i.e., the two test results converge)	Administer Test 1 and 2 to the same group of individuals	People who scored high on Test 1 also scored high on Test 2
People who score high introvert (i.e., personality is viewed as as inward and quiet) using previously validated (or old) instrument will also score as high introvert using newly established test (i.e., the two test results converge)	Administer Test 3 and Test 4 to the same group of individuals	People who scored high on Test 3 also scored high on Test 4
People who have high extrovert scores also will have low introvert scores (i.e., the tests will be able to discriminate between extroverts and introverts)	Administer Tests 1, 2, 3, and 4 to the same group of individuals	People who scored high on Tests 1 and 2 scored low on Tests 3 and 4; likewise, people who scored high on Tests 3 and 4 scored low on Tests 1 and 2

Figure 8.4. Convergent discriminant validity. Hypothetical example involving extrovert versus introvert personality. This is only a partial illustration (Stage 4 is not covered) of the logic of measurement outlined in Figure 8.1.

SOMETHING TO REMEMBER!

Did you notice in the preceding paragraph (covering instrument reliability) the ≥ sign was used? Many people confuse the < and > mathematical notations. Here's the key:

< = less than
> = more than

To remember this, think about writing numbers across the page, moving from left to right, beginning with 0, 1, 2, 3, 4, and so on. Imposing < on this line of numbers points to numbers that are going down in value. Likewise, placing the > on this line points to numbers that are going up in value.

A spin-off of the notations above are as follows:

≤ = equal to or less than
≥ = equal to or more than

The addition of the straight line below the arrow equates to "equal to."

A number of approaches can be used to document an instrument's reliability. These are interrater reliability, test-retest reliability, parallel-forms reliability, and internal consistency.

Interrater reliability. ***Interrater reliability***, also known as interobserver reliability, involves two or more observers independently rating phenomena at the same time. These ratings, typically centered on assessing behavior, are compared to determine the degree of agreement. If the raters' ratings are relatively consistent or in agreement, interrater reliability has been established.

One way to determine reliability among raters is to calculate an interrater reliability coefficient. Suppose you ask two swimming experts to independently judge whether 30 individuals achieved proficient swimmer status at a the culmination of a course. For 25 individuals in the class, the two judges are in complete agreement (i.e., their ratings for each individual are the same), and for the remaining five, the two judges are not in unison. This means that the interrater reliability correlation coefficient is .83, or $(25 \div 30) \times 100 = 83\%$ (or .83) agreement. An ***interrater reliability coefficient*** should be at least .60 (Patten, 2012).

Test–retest reliability. To measure ***test–retest reliability***, measure a phenomenon with the same instrument two times and then compare these results. For example, Yang (2004) wanted to know the reliability of the smiley face assessment test. The test was administered to children with disabilities attending Camp Koinonia. The same children took the same test twice, 1 day apart. Test–retest reliability then was checked to determine whether the campers were consistent in their use of smiley faces to rate their camp experience. A ***test–retest reliability coefficient*** of .80 and greater suggests the instrument is stable over time (Fisher & Corcoran, 2007).

Split-half reliability. In ***split-half reliability***, also known as alternate-forms reliability, two versions of the same instrument are compared. Each version is designed to be interchangeable with the other. The same content supposedly is covered in both forms, even though the questions are different. For instance, suppose you want to compare the long and short form of the Leisure Diagnostic Battery on a group of people. You administer the long form of the test to a sample, and the same sample takes the second form, or short version, a few days later. Thus, each respondent will have two scores, and you compare these scores to determine the split-half reliability. ***Split-half reliability coefficients*** above .80 are needed to consider the equivalent forms as consistent (Patten, 2012).

Interitem reliability. When multiple items are used to measure a single construct, determine whether the items are indeed measuring the same construct. ***Interitem reliability***, or internal consistency, verifies that items used in an index belong together. The answer provided to one item is paired successively to answers provided on remaining questions. If items are a consistent measure of the same construct, the items should be highly and positively correlated. The stronger the relationship or association between each pair of items, the higher the interitem reliability.

Cronbach's alpha coefficient is the statistic commonly used to measure interitem reliability. It determines the extent to which each item used in the instrument measures the same concept and should be > .80 (Fisher & Corcoran, 2007). Items that do not belong in the index are identified when interitem correlations are < .50 or when negative interitem correlations are found (Shannon & Davenport, 2001).

Suppose you measure socioeconomic status (SES) using the traditional approach of asking about the respondent's educational attainment, occupation, and income. The Cronbach's alpha for this index likely would be higher than .80 since previous research repeatedly has indicated responses to these three questions are highly interrelated. That is, people with higher levels of educational attainment typically hold more prestigious jobs and subsequently earn higher incomes. If you decide to measure SES by asking about a respondent's education, occupation, and height, the Cronbach's alpha for this index likely would fall below .80 because the three questions are not measuring the same construct. Indeed, it is ludicrous to envision height as having any bearing on SES, unless you are tall enough to play at the National Basketball Association level!

SOMETHING TO REMEMBER!

There are several ways to document the reliability of an instrument. These approaches and acceptable levels of reliability are summarized below

Approach	Description	Look for a reliability correlation of...
Interrater reliability	Measure of agreement or extent ratings, made by two or more judges, are consistent	≥ .60[a]
Test–Retest reliability	Extent scores on the same instrument, administered at two times, are comparable with each other	> .80[b]
Split-Halves reliability	Degree scores on two similar instruments, administered at two times, correlate with each other	> .80[a]
Interitem consistency	Measures how well mulitple items/questions, used in an index, are measuring the same concept	> .80[c]

[a]Patten (2012). [b]Fisher (2005). [c]Shannon and Davenport (2001).

In review, knowing a measuring instrument's reliability and validity is important. Actually, measurement reliability is a prerequisite for measurement validity (Figure 8.5). An instrument cannot have measurement validity if it does not have measurement reliability. An instrument may be (a) reliable but invalid, (b) unreliable and invalid, or (c) valid and reliable.

You cannot assume that if an instrument has been documented as reliable, it is automatically valid as well. Reliability alone is insufficient for selecting an instrument. For instance, an inaccurate bathroom scale consistently may report your weight as being 10 pounds lighter than your true body weight. This inaccurately calibrated scale could be described as consistently reliable but invalid. Remember, for an instrument to be useful, it must be valid and reliable. Because reliability is easier to establish, many instruments used in recreation, park, sport, and tourism research have documented reliability but no documented validity.

Normative Data

Finally, a good instrument ideally has ***normative data***; that is, data produced from a study that characterize what is usual in a defined population. This is technically known as ***standardization***. That is, the instrument has been administered under controlled circumstances to a well-defined large group, and this group's average performance has been recorded (Case 8.3). For example, normal body mass index has been determined given a person's gender and height.

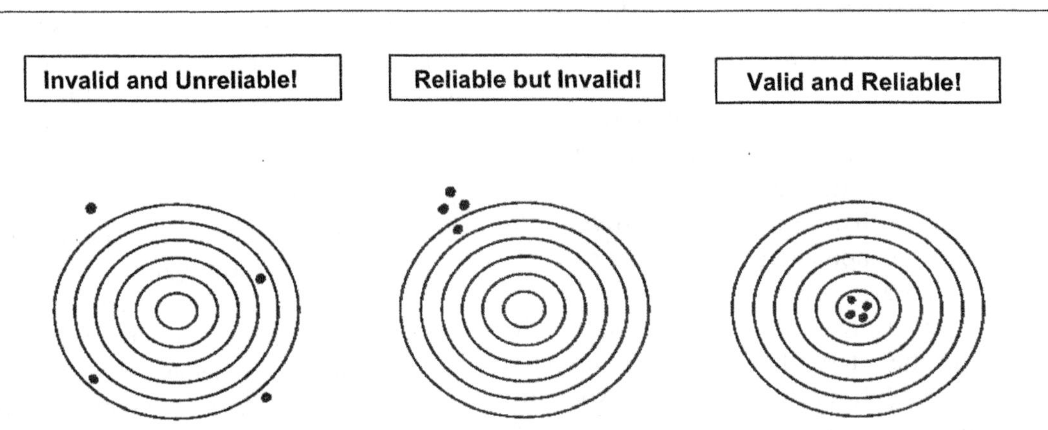

Figure 8.5. Think of instrument validity and reliability as marksmanship ability.

RELIABILITY

Directions: Decide whether the statement is *true* or *false*. If *false*, briefly explain why.

Check yourself	And the answer is...
1. Two people observe whether kids share during playtime. They observe 250 children during play, and the two raters disagree 63 times. The interrater reliability is 75% or .75.	
2. An interrater reliability correlation coefficient of .70 or higher is considered good.	
3. You invented a new test to measure the agility of children. Initially, you test a group of children. You may wait a year to administer the retest.	
4. A split-half reliability coefficient of .60 is acceptable.	
5. Suppose the concept of intelligence was going to be judged using answers to the following questions: grade point average in major, SAT score, and aggressiveness rating score (ranges from 0–100). You would expect a high (> .80) interitem reliability coefficient using answers to these questions.	

Note. Answers are provided at the end of the chapter.

If you use an instrument that has established normative data, you are able to compare a group for which you have collected information to the norms that have been reported for the measure. Such a comparison may establish the relative need for a recreation program or the relative effectiveness of one program against another. Unfortunately, few standardized instruments have yet to be developed to assist recreation, park, sport, and tourism professionals.

RESOURCES FOR LOCATING A GOOD INSTRUMENT

Multitudes of instruments to measure variables have been developed by other researchers. When sifting through what is available, be mindful of the measure, multiple-variable measures, single- versus multiple-item measures, instrument validity, instrument reliability, and availability of normative data.

Yet, locating tests, surveys, or scales may be challenging and time consuming. Sometimes, you must purchase a published instrument directly from its publisher. In instances where part or an entire instrument is published within a research article, contact the author to contact the author(s) to secure inspection copies of the instrument and/or seek permission to use their test.

Several sources exist for locating instruments you may use when conducting research related to recreation, parks, sport, and tourism. Secondary print sources for finding measuring instruments are cited in Appendix 3.

FINDING AN INSTRUMENT RELATED TO YOUR TOPIC

Finding instruments appropriate to use for a study takes time. The following are a few tips:

- Focusing on the concept you plan to use in the study, undertake a literature review (see Step 2) to unearth instruments designed to measure the concept.
- When you find an article on the same topic you are interested in studying, pay particular attention to the Instrumentation section of the report. You may find information on the chosen instrument's validity and reliability; consequently, you may be able to rule out or zero in on possibilities.

Additionally, a review of the major leisure science journals (*Journal of Leisure Research, Sport and Exercise Psychology, Therapeutic Recreation Journal*) during the years 2008–2013 uncovered newly created instruments measuring leisure-related phenomena (see Table 8.3). Also, other excellent sources for identifying measurement instruments include articles or books published in other disciplines and abstracts of professional conferences and symposia. Many excellent Internet resources for locating tests, surveys, or other research instruments are available as well. Examples of these appear in Table 8.4.

Table 8.3
Selected Articles Reporting on the Development of Instruments Related to Leisure Phenomena Appearing in Journals 2008–2013

Budrik, M. (2010). Cross-language measurement equivalence of the place attachment scale: A multigroup confirmatory factor analysis approach. *Journal of Leisure Research, 42,* 25–42.

Chiang, L., Casebolt, K., Tan, J., Lankford, S., & Wilson, J. (2011). A pilot study of an instrument measuring leisure satisfaction and life satisfaction in an outpatient leisure activity program. *Therapeutic Recreation Journal, 45,* 234–255.

Cleghorn, S., Kucharewski, R., Olsson, R. H., Jr., Leiras, C., Crockett, C. A., Gill, J. R., . . . Friedlmeier, M. (2013). The reliability and validity of the reality comprehension clock test (RCCT) with a Hispanic population. *Therapeutic Recreation Journal, 47,* 109–121.

Eys, M., Loughead, T., Bray, S., & Carron, A. (2009). Original research development of a cohesion questionnaire for youth: The youth sport environment questionnaire. *Journal of Sport & Exercise Psychology, 31,* 390–408.

Gould, J., Moore, D., McGuire, F., & Stebbins, R. (2008). Development of the serious leisure inventory and measure. *Journal of Leisure Research, 40,* 47–68.

Kavussanu, M., & Boardley, I. (2009). Original research: The prosocial and antisocial behavior in sport scale. *Journal of Sport & Exercise Psychology, 31,* 97–117.

Marsh, H., Martin, A., & Jackson, S. (2011). Introducing a short version of the physical self-description questionnaire: New strategies, short-form evaluative criteria, and applications of factor analyses. *Journal of Sport & Exercise Psychology, 32,* 438–482.

McLean, K., Mallett, C., & Newcombe, P. (2012). Assessing coach motivation: The development of the coach motivation questionnaire (CMQ). *Journal of Sport & Exercise Psychology, 34,* 184–207.

Myers, N., Feltz, D., Guillen, F., & Dithuribe, L. (2012). Development of, and initial validity evidence for, the referee self-efficacy scale: A multistudy report. *Journal of Sport & Exercise Psychology, 34,* 737–765.

Sithorp, J., Bialeschki, M., Morgan, C., & Browne, L. (2013). Validating, norming, and utility of a youth outcomes battery for recreation programs and camps. *Journal of Leisure Research, 45,* 514–536.

Tsaur, S., Liang, Y., & Lin, W. (2012). Conceptualization and measurement of the recreationist–environment fit. *Journal of Leisure Research, 44,* 110–130.

Vagias, W., Powell, R., Moore, D., & Wright, B. (2012). Development, psychometric qualities, and cross-validation of the leave no trace attitudinal inventory and measure (LNT AIM). *Journal of Leisure Research, 44,* 234–256.

Williams, S., & Cumming, J. (2011). Measuring athlete imagery ability: The sport imagery ability questionnaire. *Journal of Sport & Exercise Psychology, 33,* 416–440.

Williams, S., Cumming, J., Ntoumanis, N., Nordin-Bates, S., Ramsey, R., & Hall, C. (2012). Further validation and development of the movement imagery questionnaire. *Journal of Sport & Exercise Psychology, 34,* 621–646.

Table 8.4
Web-Based Instrument Sources

EBSCOHost *Mental Measurements Yearbook with Tests in Prints*: Guide to over 3,000 tests and instruments, including those relating to psychology and education.

ERIC/AE Test Locator (go to http://www.ericdigests.org/1996-1/test.htm): The Clearinghouse on Assessment and Evaluation, the Educational Testing Service, the Buros Institute of Mental Measurements, Region III Comprehensive Center at George Washington University, and Pro-Ed Publishers have collaborated to produce a comprehensive test locator service. The Test Locator service contains free tests and instruments, several searchable testing databases, and test selection tips.

Performance Evaluations and Performance Appraisal for Management Employees: Available at the California Park and Recreation Society's website: http://www.cprs.org/. Click on "Resources," then click on "Information and Referral," and go down to "Creating Community: VIP Planning Tools" and look at "Performance Appraisal Evaluation for Management Employees" and "Performance Evaluation."

Tests and Measures in Social Sciences. Through the use of 100 resources, over 12,000 tests have been identified and made available at the University of Texas: http://libraries.uta.edu/helen/test&meas/testmainframe.htm.

Measurement is critical in instruments used in research as well as for the Eagle Scout candidate building this accessible area to a butterfly garden. Brookside Nature Center at Wheaton Regional Park, Wheaton, Maryland. Copyright © 2015 Carol Cutler Riddick.

REVIEW AND DISCUSSION QUESTIONS

1. Recall the four steps associated with the logic of measurement. Cite a recreation, park, sport, or tourism example using these steps.
2. Define and differentiate among reactive, nonreactive, and psychophysiological measures.
3. Why is it important to use multiple-variable measures of the same concept?
4. Why is it important to consider multiple-item measures and not a single-item measure?
5. Identify how an index differs from a scale.
6. Provide a brief definition of instrument validity, and then illustrate the concept by drawing a representation of validity and lack of validity on an archery target.
7. Explain how you may use face validity and content validity to establish construct validity.
8. Describe how you may use concurrent validity, predictive validity, convergent validity, and discriminant validity to determine criterion validity.
9. Define instrument reliability, and then illustrate the concept by drawing a representation of reliability and lack of reliability on an archery target.
10. Explain how you may document interrater, test–retest, split-half, and interitem reliability.
11. Recall the minimum reliability coefficient value that suggests acceptability for interrater reliability, test–retest reliability, split-half reliability, and interitem consistency.
12. What is normative data?
13. Identify two resources for locating a good instrument.

YOUR RESEARCH

1. Have you chosen reactive, nonreactive, and/or psychophysiological measures for your study?
2. Do you plan on using multiple-variable measures?
3. Will you be using single- or multiple-item measures?
4. For each measure you have chosen, provide documentation regarding its validity and reliability.
5. Do normative data exist for any of your chosen instruments? If so, provide a brief profile of the group that was used to establish the normative data.

PRACTICE EXERCISES

1. Acquire a copy of the following article (or your instructor may substitute another article):

   Allsop, J., Negley, S., & Sibthorp, J. (2013). Assessing the social effect of therapeutic recreation summer camp for adolescents with chronic illness. *Therapeutic Recreation Journal, 47*, 36–46. You may access this article at http://js.sagamorepub.com/trj/article/view/2631.

   Read the article and answer the following questions:
   a. What logic of measurement was used in the study? Identify each concept examined and corresponding variables and instruments.
   b. What measures were used: reactive, nonreactive, and/or psychophysiological instruments?
   c. Were multiple measures used to examine each concept?
   d. Were single- or multiple-item measures used?
   e. Did the article address validity of the instrument? If *yes*, what was stated?
   f. Did the article address reliability of the instrument? If *yes*, what was stated?

g. What were the strengths and weaknesses of the instruments selected?
h. Did the article cite norms for any variable? What were they?

2. Practice calculating and interpreting an interrater reliability score centering on a basketball skill assessment. This exercise will require a calculator to complete.

   a. Depending on the class size and time available, the instructor may have everyone, or a few volunteers, demonstrate a basketball skill. The skill could be dribbling alone or around a few other students or shooting the basketball from three or four designated places on the half court.
   b. Other members of the class will complete a rating on the person demonstrating the skill (see the worksheet below).
   c. Then, the class calculates the interrater reliability score for each student demonstrator. If the class or number of demonstrators is large, the class may be broken down into smaller groups and each group assigned to calculate the interrater reliability score for a few of their classmates (if this option is used, the instructor should distribute several rating sheets to each student so each student is recoding the same set of names as on the first form).
   d. What were the results? By and large, were ratings consistent for each student judged? If not, discuss what could have caused variation in the judges' ratings?
   e. What did the class think of this exercise? Did it, for example, make it clearer what interrater reliability is all about and how it is calculated?

Worksheet Measurement Chapter: Calculating the Interrater Reliability Ratings for Basketball Skills

Rater's Name: ____________________

Calculate interitem reliability by identifying the rating category that received most votes. That is, use the number of votes cast in this top vote category and calculate % of agreement that existed within this category. For instance, suppose 10 persons voted on Sammy's skills: Five judged the skill shown as *excellent-good*, three rated his performance as *fair*, and two rated the skill set *poor*. Since *excellent-good* received highest number of votes, the percentage of agreement is 50% (5 ÷ 10) or .5.

Name of student competitor	Rating			% of agreement
	Excellent/Good	Fair	Poor	

WEB EXERCISES

1. Read about tools and measures used in research to prevent childhood obesity and create active living communities at the Active Living Research website: http://activelivingresearch.org/toolsandresources/toolsand-measures. If your instructor does not assign you specific tools and measures to examine, find one tool or measure listed for (a) observational tools to assess the environment, (b) observational tools to assess physical activity, and (c) surveys to assess perceptions of the environment. Your instructor may ask you to provide a paragraph summary of each tool you located or to give a brief in-class presentation on your choices.
2. For more information about instrumentation, consult the resources noted below. Your instructor may give you instructions regarding which website to visit and/or ask you type a summary of what you learned from each website.
   a. William Trochim's website at http://www.socialresearchmethods.net/kb/measure.php. Click and read about "Measurement," "Construct Validity," Reliability," "Levels of Measurement," "Qualitative Validity" that appears under "Qualitative Measures," and "Unobtrusive Measures."
   b. Learn more about instruments that evaluate the impacts of psychosocial training and intervention programs (e.g., in outdoor education) by consulting the following Wilderdom links:
      i. Review a list of available instruments (set up in categories such as youth-at-risk outcomes, psychological and behavioral health measures) at http://www.wilderdom.com/tools/ToolsIndex.html
      ii. For an in-depth description of instruments, go to http://www.wilderdom.com/tools/ToolsSummaries.html
3. The University of Surrey presents (on a quarterly basis) *Social Research Update* (http://sru.soc.surrey.ac.uk/SRU33.html). Some of the topics relate to documents and records, including the following:

   - Issue 2: "Using Diaries in Social Research"
   - Issue 11: "Visual Research Methods"
   - Issue 40: "Photo-Interviewing for Research"
   - Issue 53: "In-Depth Interviewing by Instant Messaging"
   - Issue 61: "Internet Research and Unobtrusive Methods"
   - Issue 63: "Humor Analysis and Qualitative Research"

   a. The instructor may assign you one of these bulletins to read and report on. If not, choose one to read.
   b. Provide a typed reply to the following points/questions:
      i. Provide a definition for the measurement device featured in the article.
      ii. Summarize three important points you learned about the measurement tool.
      iii. Provide one example of how the measurement tool could be used in a recreation, park, sport, or tourism setting.

SERVICE LEARNING PROJECT

Decide on instruments you will use for the service learning project by providing answers to the following questions:

1. First, decide on the measures you will select: reactive measures (e.g., interviews, questionnaires, observations)? Nonreactive measures (e.g., erosion physical traces or accretion physical traces)? Documents/records?
2. Identify the concepts on which the study will be focused; then, identify at least two variables that you will use to measure each concept.
3. Identify one instrument you plan to use for each variable in the study. Are single or multiple items used for each instrument? If a measure is chosen that only includes one item, identify one limitation of this choice.

4. Outline the instrument validity and instrument reliability that exists or that you will establish for each instrument.
5. Does normative data exist for any of the instruments?

TEST YOURSELF ANSWERS

Validity

1. False: Face validity is the weakest form of establishing validity for an instrument (only one person, usually the investigator, simply proclaims the developed measure is valid) and is focused on whether a test "looks" valid, not whether it truly is valid; 2. False: Content validity requires a panel or group of individuals (whereas face validity requires only one person) to deem the developed instrument measures multiple facets or aspects of the concept; 3. True; 4. True; 5. False: Definition cited is for discriminant validity.

Reliability

1. True (250 − 63 = 187 and 187 ÷ 250 = 75% [or 74.8, rounded up to 75] or .75 agreement, which exceeds the ≥ . 60 minimum threshold needed); 2. True; 3. False: Too much time has elapsed, and waiting 1 year to retest agility would confound results (due to age changes/maturation, etc.); 4. False: Need split-half reliability coefficient > .80; 5. False: The third variable is "odd man out." That is, it is difficult to imagine aggressiveness belongs as part of the package to tie together with grade point average and SAT score as a way to examine intelligence. Thus, Cronbach's alpha for this index would be expected to fall below the > .80 threshold needed to document interitem reliability.

SUPPORTING CASES FOR THIS CHAPTER

CASE 8.1. FITNESS LEADER INDEX

Suppose you are a supervisor who wants to ask members of a fitness class to rate their instructor. You feel that a good leader (the concept) should exhibit three attributes (the variables) equally: prepared, able to communicate, and able to maintain a safe environment. Consequently, you ask class members to complete the following form.

Please rate your leader on the following three qualities (draw an arrow to each of your answers):

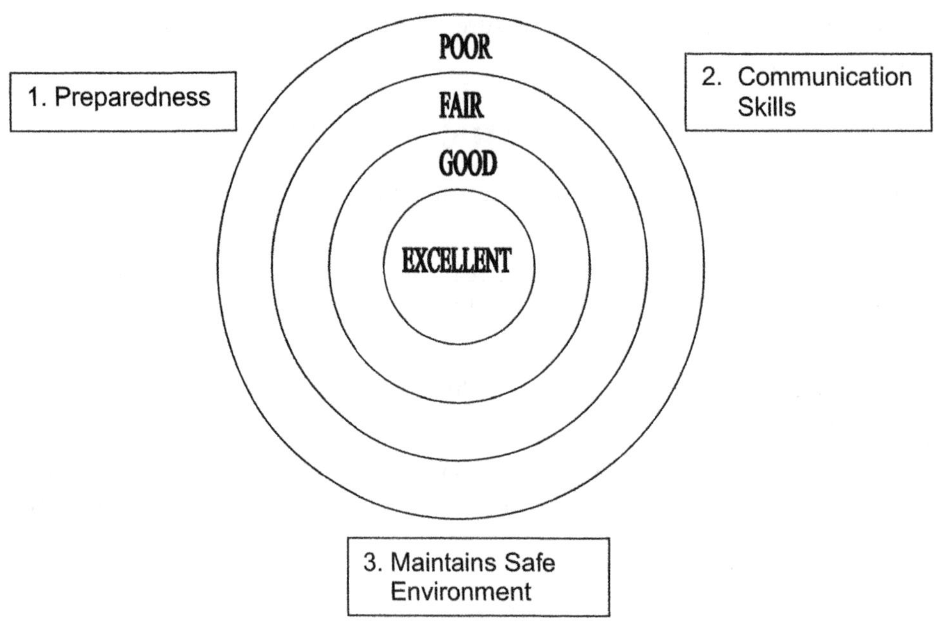

Treat answers to each question equally. That is, regardless of the question, the following numerical values would be assigned for the answers recorded: *excellent* = 4 points, *good* = 3 points, *fair* = 2 points, and *poor* = 1 point.

Given the scoring system, the range of scores for the Fitness Leader Index could be 3–12 points. (Remember, each answer is converted to a number, or 1, 2, 3, or 4 points). A good instructor will receive a higher number of points than a marginal instructor.

CASE 8.2. FITNESS LEADER SCALE

Remember Case 8.1? Suppose the supervisor revisits how to assess a fitness leader. Because of a rash of accidents that have happened during classes, the supervisor wants to double-weigh or count environment safety.

Suppose Ms. Lily assigns her fitness instructor the following scores:

Attribute	Rating
Preparedness	EXCELLENT
Communication skills	EXCELLENT
Maintains safe environment	FAIR

Converting Ms. Lily's answers would result in her instructor receiving 12 out of 16 points. Given that the range of scores could be between 4 and 16 points, a score of 12 is not awful, but it is not great either! This one score suggests the instructor has room for improvement.

Do you follow how this scale was calculated? In other words, one attribute, safe environment, received double points. That is, the initial rating was multiplied by 2, due to its weighted importance.

		Points		
Attribute	Rating	Assigned	Weighting	Subtotal
Preparedness	EXCELLENT	4	1	4
Communication skills	EXCELLENT	4	1	4
Maintains safe environment	FAIR	2	2	4

CASE 8.3. LEISURE DIAGNOSTIC BATTERY'S NORMATIVE DATA

Witt, P., & Widmer, M. (2008). *LDB computer software and users' manual.* State College, PA: Venture.

The Leisure Diagnostic Battery (LDB) assesses leisure functioning and consists of two parts. The first part examines perceived freedom in leisure. The second part examines recreation activity preferences, recreation activity style preferences, and barriers to recreation participation.

The LDB is available in four forms: a short and long form for children and a short and long form for adults. Documentation is available on the LDB's validity (content, predictive, convergent, and discriminant) and reliability (Cronbach's alpha coefficient).

Extensive testing of the long form versions of the LDB with hundreds of individuals has resulted in normative data for groups including junior high students; university students in a rehabilitation/therapeutic recreation class; university students voluntarily participating in physical education activity classes; hospitalized asthmatic adolescents; adolescents who have been hospitalized for emotional disturbances; veterans who have been hospitalized for drug dependency; individuals with physical disabilities; individuals who are emotionally disturbed; people with mental illnesses; and high school students attending regular or special education classes who have been classified as educable mentally retarded, learning disabled, emotionally disturbed, or nondisabled.

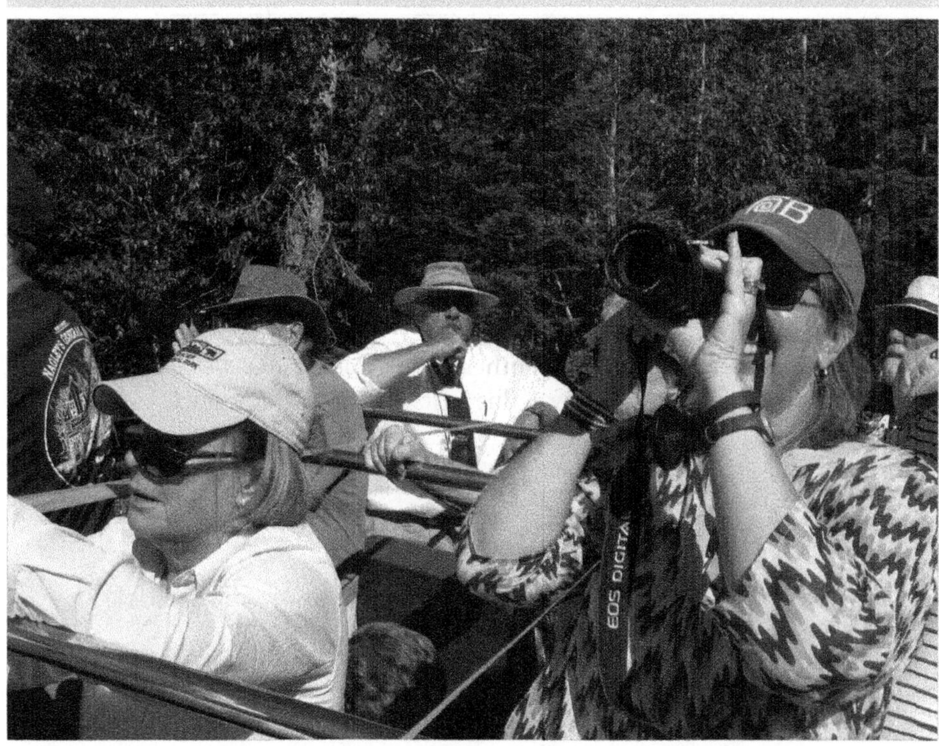

Collecting data in research often means looking for the answers you seek and being open to the unexpected. This is similar to the experience of these visitors who are on a guided wildlife tour. Glacier National Park, Montana. Copyright © 2015 Ruth V. Russell.

SPECIFY DATA COLLECTION METHODS

WHAT WILL I LEARN IN THIS CHAPTER?

I'll be able to...

1. Distinguish among these quantitative data collection tools: structured questionnaires, structured observations, and tests and scales.
2. Draft questions for a questionnaire using different response options.
3. Identify how observational guides may be prepared to record structured observations.
4. Give an example of a test or scale used in leisure studies.
5. Distinguish among these qualitative data collection tools: unstructured in-depth interview, focus group, participant observation, projective method, and document/record review.
6. Contrast unstructured in-depth interview methods: descriptive information interview, discovery interview, and problem-solving interview.
7. Describe the purposes of a focus group.
8. Explain the participant observation continuum.
9. Give an example of a projective data collection method.
10. Share an example of a document/record review.
11. Explain the function of triangulation in collecting information for research.

"There is nothing like looking, if you want to find something. You certainly usually find something, if you look, but it is not always quite the something you were after."

J.R.R. Tolkien
(English writer best known for his classic fantasy works *The Hobbit* and *Lord of the Rings*, 1892–1973)

Ultimately, research comes down to making decisions about exactly how you will collect the information needed to answer the research question. Finding this information is a matter of selecting and implementing the best data collection tools.

Suppose you want to evaluate a beach program for the children of resort guests. You could ask multiple research questions to determine the program's effectiveness, and thus you could use multiple methods to obtain the answers. Perhaps you want to know parents' perceptions of how their children benefited from the program and thus conduct open-ended interviews with them.

Then again, maybe resort management would like you to confirm the marketing power of the program, so you analyze online comments guests have made about the children's program. Alternatively, if you want to determine the children's enthusiasm for participating in the programmed events, you could observe them in the program for 1 hour on 2 days, recording reactions such as laughing, smiling, and sharing. Any of these data collection tools (open-ended interviews, document analysis, and participant observation) are appropriate depending on the research question.

In this chapter, a few of the many data collection methods are cataloged. First, specific methods appropriate to quantitative studies are highlighted, followed by those useful in qualitative studies. Then, data collection triangulation, that is, employing more than one method in the same study, is explained.

DATA COLLECTION TOOLS FOR QUANTITATIVE STUDIES

Several data collection tools exist for conducting quantitative studies, including structured questionnaires, structured observations, and tests and scales. The one you choose depends on your research questions and setting.

Structured Questionnaire

A popular tool for collecting data in the leisure services fields is the ***questionnaire***, which is also known as a ***survey***. (The label *survey* reflects that it is an instrument used to collect data. Do not confuse survey with survey design; the latter was covered in Step 7.)

Examples of questionnaire use are plentiful in everyday life (see Figure 9.1). Computerized kiosks in public places request input from service users. Your restaurant server presents you with a short customer satisfaction questionnaire with your check. You are asked to complete a short pop-up list of questions when you visit a website.

PART II: The following questions ask about the reasons you work out.

Do you work out to (circle answer):

1. Improve physical health ....YES NO
2. Lose/maintain weight ....YES NO
3. Gain strength .... YES NO
4. Improve performance .... YES NO
5. Challenge self .... YES NO
6. Improve appearance .... YES NO
7. Have social experience .... YES NO
8. Have fun .... YES NO
9. Other reason (specify):______________________

Figure 9.1. Example of a questionnaire. Excerpt from questionnaire prepared and administered by students in the Measurement and Evaluation class (PER 400) at Gallaudet University in fall 2013. The purpose of the project was to assess undergraduate students' experiences and thoughts about changes needed for working out in the campus Field House. Reprinted with permission of the author.

Typically, a questionnaire is simply a set of questions. It is ***structured*** because you will identify beforehand the questions to be asked and also the response options from which a respondent may choose. Structured questionnaires have strict administration and scoring rules. For example, in collecting data using a structured questionnaire, ask the same questions of all the study participants and do not deviate from the preplanned questions. This seeming rigidity will enable you to statistically analyze the information.

Questionnaire types. Questionnaires are distinguished by how they are administered. These include structured interviews delivered face-to-face or over the telephone and structured self-administered questionnaires distributed through the mail or Internet. Table 9.1 offers points of comparison for these questionnaire types.

1. During a ***face-to-face structured interview***, you need to be present physically as you pose questions to a respondent. Face-to-face interviews typically, relative to other questionnaires, enable you to collect more information (see Case 9.1) Also, a face-to-face delivered interview using a questionnaire is less boring because the interviewer is able to establish rapport with the respondent. This also means you may ask more complex questions. One possible problem with face-to-face interviews, as well as all questionnaires, is the ***halo effect***. This occurs when a respondent feels pressure to provide answers that are socially acceptable, especially if their anonymity has been lost.

2. Almost everyone is familiar with the ***telephone structured interview***. Most major public opinion polls that are reported in the news are this type. You may administer telephone interviews with automated random dialing methods and automatic data collection and recording (e.g., computer-assisted personal interviewing). The telephone interview enables you to gather information rapidly, but it offers limited personal contact with respondents. Another caution is that some people do not have telephones or publicly listed telephone numbers, which may introduce sampling bias into the results. Also, people often do not like the intrusion of a call. This means that the questionnaire used must be relatively short. Nonetheless, studies directly comparing face-to-face with telephone structured interviewing tend to conclude that telephone interviews produce data at least comparable in quality (Sturges & Hanrahan, 2004). Thus, determining which questionnaire types to use depends mostly on administration logistics (summarized in Table 9.1).

Table 9.1
Comparison of Structured Questionnaire Types

Type	Description	Advantages	Disadvantages
Face-to-face interview	Preprepared questions, orally asked of a respondent by a researcher in person	• Suitable for longer and more complex questionnaires • Because researcher records answers, likely higher quality of data • Lower response bias	• Higher administrative costs ($100–$300/respondent) • Lengthier data collection period • Lower response rate • Smaller sample size
Telephone interview	Preprepared questions, orally asked of an individual subject by a researcher over the telephone	• Shorter data collection period • Subjects may be in wider geographic area • May be medium-long in length • Handles sensitive topics fairly well • Because researcher records answers, likely higher quality of data • Lower response bias	• Higher administrative costs • Cannot be complex • Fair response rate • Smaller sample size
Mail survey	Preprepared questions, written in paper format and mailed to and from individual subjects	• Lower administrative costs • Larger sample size • Subjects may be in wider geographic area • Handles sensitive topics well • Fair to good data quality • More anonymity	• 4- to 10-week data collection period • Must be fairly short in length • Must be moderately simple • Likely poorer response rate • Medium response bias
Internet survey	Preprepared questions, written in an Internet-based format and answered by individual subjects over the Internet	• Lower administrative costs • 1- to 2-week data collection period • Larger sample size • Subjects may be in wider geographic area • Fair to good data quality • More anonymity	• Must be short in length • Must be moderately simple • Handles sensitive topics poorly • Likely poorer response rate • Medium response bias

Note. Adapted from Czaga and Blair (2005); Lodico, Spaulding, and Voegtle (2010); and Rea and Parker (2005).

3. Many people typically think of a ***self-administered structured questionnaire*** when using the term *questionnaire*. As the label suggests, these use written questions and answer options, and you may administer them via the mail or Internet (more about these later). You also may hand deliver the questionnaire to the respondents, who fill it out and return it directly to you.

   Self-administered questionnaires are a relatively inexpensive means of obtaining information. For example, in most countries bulk postage is cheap. However, using the mail introduces the possibility of long time delays in receiving returned questionnaires. Internet questionnaires are also relatively easy to distribute and may render prompter responses. Although mailed and Internet questionnaires allow respondents to answer at their own convenience, the opportunity for respondents to seek clarification of questions may be burdensome. You may overcome these disadvantages by administering the written questionnaire to individuals in a group setting.

4. Within the past decade, and first introduced by market researchers, ***online self-administered structured questionnaires*** have become widely used in research. With Web survey software (e.g., Survey Monkey), these questionnaires are big business. Companies spend billions of dollars

each year soliciting potential customer input by using the time and expense saving power of the Internet. Also, the data received may be read and reported automatically using statistical analysis software.

Online surveys are conducted in e-mail, social networking sites, and other evolving electronic forms. This suggests that samples are likely to be skewed toward a younger population group. In spite of the many advantages, honesty of responses also may be an issue. Also, if the questionnaire is not password protected, users may manipulate it and complete it multiple times, thus invalidating the results. These disadvantages may be partially improved by using ***online panels***, in which selected respondents have agreed beforehand to complete a questionnaire.

Question response options. All forms of questionnaires (face-to-face and telephone structured interviews, as well as mail and Internet self-administered questionnaires) are based on the same structure, or a posed question followed by a response option. Responses may be structured using closed-ended (for examples of this format, see Table 9.2) or open-ended questions.

1. A popular form of questionnaire questioning is ***closed-ended questions*** that offer fixed-choice answers from which to choose. This format has advantages and disadvantages. For example, the questions are easy and quick to answer, and you may assign numerical scores or codes to each answer. On the other hand, you cannot anticipate all answers, and thus the responses may be inaccurate or misleading. An additional criticism is that respondents cannot qualify their answers, thus preventing additional information from being provided. One adjustment to this limitation is using a ***combination closed-ended question***, which asks a question and then provides possible answers along with an option to provide another answer. For an example, see the last question in Figure 9.1.

   When deciding which question and response format to use, stay alert to the intended purpose of the question, the theory related to the constructs being measured, and the sample to which you will administer the questionnaire. For example, using the smiley face continuum (Table 9.2) is more appropriate for preliterate children, where you may assume that feelings may be reduced to two basic emotions.

2. Sometimes questionnaires include a few unstructured, or open-ended, questions. ***Open-ended questions*** consist of asking a question and then not providing answer choices. Respondents provide an answer in their own words. An example of an open-ended question is, "Please explain why you signed up for this trip."

   A few open-ended questions typically are included in a structured questionnaire for good reason. Adding them as a follow-up to a closed-ended question may clarify responses. They also may be more efficient for obtaining certain information. For instance, suppose the question is, "Where were you born?" From a space perspective, asking this as an open-ended question rather than trying to list every city or state or nation in the world makes sense. However, the more open-ended questions included in a questionnaire, the more time consuming it is to analyze and interpret the responses.

CHECK THOSE QUESTIONNAIRES!

Checking questionnaires that respondents had just filled in, a researcher was amazed to note that one of them contained the numbers 125 and 127 in answer to "Age of Mother, If Living" and "Age of Father, If Living." "Surely your parents can't be as old as this?" asked the incredulous researcher. "Well no," the respondent answered. "But they would be if they were living!"

Where do questions for a questionnaire come from?

1. From an already existing published instrument (review Step 8).
2. Created specifically for the study.
3. Blended questions, meaning some questions were developed by others and others are newly written.

Questionnaire mechanics. A common misperception about developing a questionnaire is that it is easy. However, to secure honest, useful, and meaningful information, you must plan and pilot questionnaires carefully. What do you do when preparing and using a structured questionnaire? The following instructions will maximize the quantity of responses you receive and the quality of information in these responses.

Table 9.2
Closed-Ended Question and Response Options

Question type and response option	Example
Dichotomous: Question offers two response choices	Did you work out in the university's exercise room yesterday (circle one answer)? YES NO
Multiple-choice: Question offers more than two choices	What weekend days do you typically exercise (check all that apply)? FRIDAY __ SATURDAY __ SUNDAY __ NONE __
Likert scale: Respondent is asked to indicate the amount of agreement or disagreement with a statement	Generally speaking, after working out, I feel better about my body (circle the extent you agree with this statement): STRONGLY AGREE AGREE NEITHER AGREE NOR DISAGREE DISAGREE STRONGLY DISAGREE
Semantic differential: A continuum is set up between bipolar words and the respondent selects the point that represents the direction and intensity of his or her feelings	Place a check mark in the space on each line below to show your opinion of the quality of the food served at the snack bar. EXPENSIVE __:__:__:__:__INEXPENSIVE GOOD __:__:__:__: __ BAD FRESH __:__:__:__: __ OLD
Forced ranking: Asking respondent to place options in a designated order	Indicate, in rank order, the times you prefer the exercise room to open on the weekends by placing 1 next to your most preferred opening time through 4 for your least preferred opening time. 5 a.m. __ 6 a.m. __ 7 a.m. __ 8 a.m. __ Other (specify) __
Adjective checklist: Asks respondents to rate or judge something	Put a check mark in the space next to the word that best describes your opinion of your personal trainer (check all that apply): PLEASANT __ DEMANDING __ REASONABLE __
Smiley face continuum: The continuum is expressed	Respondent is asked to identify one emotion from an array provided ARCHERY CANOEING CRAFTS

First, the principles for writing questions will be discussed. You should know the reason behind asking each question. That is, each question should be directly responsible for answering each research question and hypothesis in your study.

Table 9.3 highlights important principles for writing questions for structured interviews and self-administered questionnaires. Review this table, and then identify problems with drafted questions and answers presented in Troubleshooting Questionnaire Questions.

TROUBLESHOOTING QUESTIONNAIRE QUESTIONS

Identify what is wrong in the following questionnaire questions. Suggest why each question will result in incomplete and/or inaccurate responses.

1. What is your age (circle one answer)?
   0–10
   10–20
   20–30
   > 30

2. How often do you use the exercise room in your residence hall (check one answer)?
   NEVER __
   RARELY __
   FREQUENTLY __

3. On a scale of 1 to 10, how would you rate the services of our gold medal award-winning Parks and Recreation Department?

4. What do you recommend for improving the fairness and efficiency of the Colesville YMCA's aquatics program? ____________________

Note. Answers are provided at the end of the chapter.

Additional pointers for preparing questionnaires evolve around piloting. You may be tempted to proceed too quickly and skip obtaining feedback on the drafted questionnaire (this is conducting a pilot, see Step 12). Ask others to review and critique the questionnaire before administering it. Seek feedback on question content, order, and amount of questions. Spend sufficient time and effort on the cover letter, or introductory statement (Figure 9.2).

Response rate to the questionnaire (Step 6) is likely to increase if the cover letter includes these points (Dillman, Smyth, & Christian, 2008; Lodico, Spaulding, & Voegtle, 2010):

- name of the organization and researcher conducting the study;
- the study purpose;
- why the study is important, including to the study respondents;
- a promise of confidentiality or anonymity (Step 10);
- statement that completing the questionnaire is voluntary;
- information about whom to contact and how if questions arise;
- instructions on how and by when to return the answered questionnaire; and
- an expression of thanks for the individual's cooperation in completing the questionnaire.

In addition to a well-crafted cover letter, other factors may affect the response rate (Solomon, 2001; Veal, 2011):

- questionnaire length;
- questionnaire design;
- reward for responding (e.g., a lottery drawing for prizes);
- provision of a postage-paid envelope (for mailed questionnaires); and
- number and timing of follow-up reminders.

For mail and Internet questionnaires, using a ***tailored design strategy*** has been found to improve response rate (Dillman et al., 2008). This requires using at least three follow-up reminder phases. For example, 1 week after the initial mailing/sending, send a postcard reminder to everyone. Then, 3 weeks later, send a replacement questionnaire to nonrespondents. Seven weeks after the initial mailing, send nonrespondents a certified mail questionnaire replacement.

For face-to-face structured interviews, many factors have an influence on whether the questionnaire successfully gathers the information needed for the study. For example, you should have characteristics similar to those you are interviewing, such as gender, race, ethnicity, age, dress, and language patterns (Bailey, 1994). Above all, be yourself and use a communication style that feels natural (Lodico et al., 2010).

What else can you do to increase the likelihood that interviews and questionnaires will be successful? Check the following ideas presented in Table 9.3.

Table 9.3
Principles for Writing Questions for Structured Interviews and Self-Administered Questionnaires

1. Use simple language. Use wording appropriate to the educational and cultural background of the respondents. To illustrate, the second example uses simpler language than the first:
   "Now, can you tell me how often you used parks within the borders of our state?"
   "Did you visit a state park in Maryland during summer 2013?"
2. Avoid jargon. Questions should not use acronyms. If they do, make sure they are spelled out when first used. For instance, the second example clearly defines the acronym used:
   "Do you have a SOB background?"
   "Do you usually experience shortness of breath (SOB)?"
3. Do not use leading questions. A leading question sets an expectation that becomes socially difficult to rebut. For example, compare the following:
   "Why should the city raise use fees for the swimming pools?
   "Are you in favor of raising fees for the city-sponsored swimming pools?"
4. Avoid using words that are ambiguous or open to multiple interpretations. For example, response options such as *a lot* and *frequently* cause confusion since respondents differ on what they mean. Compare the following:
   "How often do you participate in sports?"
   "How often did you play any of the following sports during the past month?"
5. Only ask for information respondents possess. Be sure the specificity called for in the question is answerable by the respondent. For example, compare how best to ask a parent about the leisure of their adolescent children:
   "What does your teen do in his or her free time?"
   "Do you feel comfortable about your teen's leisure expressions?"
6. Steer clear of double-barreled questions. A double-barreled question contains two or more questions. For example, compare the following:
   "Do you agree that video games are a bad influence on today's youth and thus should be banned from municipal recreation centers?"
   "Do you agree that video games should not be included in recreation center services?"
7. Avoid using double negatives.
   "Do you agree that it is not good practice for youth sport coaches to not meet the recreational needs of players?"
8. Make sure response options do not overlap.
   "What is your annual income level?"
   __ $0–$10,000
   __ $10,000–$30,000
   __ $30,000–$40,000
   Those who have incomes of $10,000 and $30,000 may respond in two categories.
9. Include all response options. In the above example, those who have incomes of more than $40,000 do not have a response option.
10. Demographic questions should be useful for the research questions and not as a shotgun approach to gathering information. Too many demographic questions may frustrate respondents and affect their desire to complete the questionnaire.
11. Demographic questions may go at the beginning or end of the questionnaire depending on their purpose. Most questionnaires place these questions at the end since they often are perceived as a turn off or boring, but in some situations, it may be more relevant to the research questions to place them at the beginning.
12. Make sure each question gathers data directly needed to answer research questions. The questions (sometimes called ***items***) must be relevant to why the study is being conducted.
13. List these questions in descending order of importance and usefulness. Place questions the respondents are likely to see as useful first and less useful last.
14. Put related questions together and use transitions between sections of questions. Group questions of similar content. When shifting between groups of related questions, use a one- or two-sentence transitional statement to prepare respondents for the change.
15. Use branching questions. ***Branching questions*** provide filters that determine whether succeeding questions apply. If the question does not apply, ask the respondent to skip the question and move to another part of the questionnaire. The following is a branching question:
   "Have you participated in the Personal Discovery Program before (circle answer)?"
   YES → go to Question 2
   NO → go to Question 3

GALLAUDET G UNIVERSITY

DEPARTMENT OF PHYSICAL EDUCATION AND RECREATION

KENDALL GREEN
800 FLORIDA AVE. NE
WASHINGTON, DC 20002-3695

February 15, 2014

Dear Gallaudet Student,

As a student at Gallaudet University, one of the services offered to you is the Intramurals (IM) Program. Some people participate in IM, while others do not.

You are one of a small number of students being asked to provide insights into barriers you may be confronting in using the IM program. Your name was randomly drawn from the list of full-time spring 2014 students. In order that the results of the study truly represent the thinking of students, it is important you consider participating in this study. The questionnaire will take about 10-15 minutes to complete. As an incentive, each person completing the survey will receive $5.

The study has been approved by Gallaudet's Institutional Review Board (IRB). If you are interested in participating, please complete and return the attached informed consent form. Once we receive that, you will be sent the questionnaire.

You may be assured of complete confidentiality. The questionnaire will have an identification number for mailing purposes only. This is so we may check your name off the mailing list when your questionnaire is returned. Your name will never be placed on the questionnaire itself.

We would be happy to answer any questions you may have about this study. If you are not interested in participating in this study, please email me at Joseph.Kolcun@gallaudet.edu

Thank you very much for your assistance.

Joseph Kolcun, Gallaudet University's IM Coordinator

Carol Riddick, Ph.D. & Professor

Figure 9.2. Sample cover letter. Reprinted with permission of the authors.

POINTERS FOR CONDUCTING STRUCTURED INTERVIEWS

1. In advance, confirm with respondents the date, time, and location of the interview.
2. Prepare questions and know them well enough so you are able to maintain eye contact with the respondent while asking them.
3. Initially, introduce yourself, explain the purpose of the study, remind the participant of the confidentiality of his or her responses, and outline how the interview will proceed.
4. Ask the same questions and give the same response options for every interviewee.
5. The interviewer should listen, record the responses, say as little as possible, avoid interrupting, and not engage in debate.
6. Avoid suggesting answers, such as "Is your reason for not using parks because they are located too far away."
7. Use attending and responding behaviors. When vague, one-word, or unclear answers are given, use probes (e.g., "What do you mean?") or feedback phrases (e.g., "I want to make sure I heard you right" and then repeat the answer).
8. Do not be afraid of silence, giving people time to think.

POINTERS FOR DEVELOPING SELF-ADMINISTERED MAILED QUESTIONNAIRES

1. Using 16-pound paper, print the questionnaire in a booklet format with an interesting cover and use of front and back pages so that length is downplayed.
2. Choose paper color with care; an off-white (yellow or beige) color prevents the questionnaire from getting lost on desks and is not viewed as an obnoxious color.
3. Use first-class mailing along with a personalized address label.
4. Include a preaddressed, postage-paid return envelope.
5. In timing the mailing, mail on a Monday or Tuesday so they arrive before the weekend and avoid the month of December.

Note. Adapted from Bailey (1994) and Dillman, Smyth, and Christian (2008).

POINTERS FOR DEVELOPING INTERNET QUESTIONNAIRES

1. Investigate the availability of free or purchased software packages to create a Web-based survey.
2. Consider carefully what you choose to put on the subject line.
3. Use a prenotification that the Web-based survey is coming.
4. Provide prospective respondents with a password permitting them exclusive access to the questionnaire.
5. Include personalized e-mail cover letters.
6. Adopt simple layout formats.
7. Use at least a 13-point font and limit the display line length to approximately 70 characters.
8. Use colored headings and small graphics when appropriate.
9. Use multiple items on each screen as opposed to a single item.
10. Place open-ended questions as optional at the end of the questionnaire.
11. When respondents click the "submit" icon, make sure a brief thank-you note pops up onto their screens.

Note. Adapted from Couper, Traugott, and Lamias (2001).

Structured Observations

Perhaps the most basic way to gather information is to simply observe. In fact, you likely do it all the time! No equipment is needed other than your ability to perceive and record what you learn. ***Observation*** is gathering firsthand information by watching people or events. Typically, you will study the behaviors and actions deemed important to understanding a particular phenomenon. Observation is highly flexible as it accommodates data that are lengthy, highly creative, or seemingly irrelevant. The data collection method is receptive to the information the study participants reveal.

You may use observation techniques in quantitative and qualitative studies. ***Structured observation*** (compared to unstructured participant observation) is a useful form of observing in the quantitative approach. *Structured* means that you will not try to observe all aspects, but you will observe specifically what you decide in advance to watch. When using this method, try not to influence the environment you are observing.

In recreation, park, sport, and tourism research, observation may be the appropriate means of collecting data in several situations (Taylor & Kielhofner, 2006; Veal, 2011). For example, recreation program participants' behaviors typically are measured by observing specific actions such as parental aggressive acts during a youth sport season, number of positive comments psychiatric patients make to each other during art therapy sessions, and ritualized reverence when tourists visit a particular sacred site. M. Russell (2012) used structured observation to determine what passengers do with their time while using public transportation. Moreover, the spatial use of recreation sites provides research questions for which observation methods are useful as well. For instance, you could measure boater patterns on a lake by aerial time-lapse photography.

Observation mechanics. Conducting good observational research, in spite of its simplicity and flexibility, takes time and practice. Before beginning, carefully prepare by reviewing the research questions of your study to be sure you are clear on the behaviors and actions to observe. Practicing ahead of time is also useful (see Step 12) because you will learn ways to fine-tune protocols and the observational guide to more directly focus your observing attention.

The location for the observations is an important protocol decision. Do you need to post yourself at a park, playground, coffee shop, the beach, or the back of a boat? Plan carefully so the site for the observation is appropriate to the research questions. Similarly, make sure the nature of what is being observed fulfills the ethical responsibilities expected of researchers (Step 10). For instance, you may need to obtain informed consent to observe minors.

In determining when to conduct observations, you have three choices (Lofland, Snow, Anderson, & Lofland, 2006; Veal, 2011). Using ***continuous observation***, you watch for any and all behaviors during a lengthy time (e.g., every day for 7 days). ***Intermittent observations*** occur at specific and set times and/or days, such as the hour before and the hour after a facility opens on a Friday and then on a Tuesday. You also may adopt ***random observation*** involving different times and different days.

Another protocol of structured observation requiring preparation is how what is observed will be recorded. Many options exist, including photography and videography, with the most commonly used record-keeping mode being taking notes by hand. For this, you may develop a structured ***observational guide***, a pre-structured and preprinted form that provides specific ways to record what is seen or heard. These guides include checklists, rating scales, or structured note-taking fields. Case 9.2 illustrates a structured observational guide adapted from a study on the social behaviors of deaf adults during therapeutic recreation programs.

STRUCTURED OBSERVATION POINTERS

- Keep observations brief at first, working up to longer observing sessions as your skills improve.
- Observe from different vantage points if possible to gather information from various perspectives.
- Remain consistent in using continuous, intermittent, or random observations.
- Concentrate on specifics of behavior and/or actions rather than global impressions.
- Remain as unobtrusive as possible to avoid changing the activities and behaviors of those you are observing.
- Use an observational guide to keep notes.

Note. Adapted from Lofland, Snow, Anderson, and Lofland (2006) and Veal (2011).

Tests and Scales

In some quantitative research situations you will want to choose a particular questionnaire. Tests and scales are questionnaires that other researchers have developed and piloted and determined to be useful to measure a particular phenomenon for a variety of respondents. They contain fixed questions and strict instructions for administering and scoring, and the responses often may be compared to a referent such as a group norm, criterion, or professional standard.

Tests and scales are usually developed over many years using multiple researchers' effort, time, and expertise and are subjected to continuous refinement to ensure their accuracy and reliability. As well, controversy with their use typically exists, especially when social policy decisions are made based on results. For example, in the area of public education, using state-mandated tests to determine teacher salary and tenure, school district funding, and who graduates from high school continue to be hotly debated.

In general, tests and scales are used to measure five broad areas (Lodico et al., 2010):

1. ***Achievement tests*** are typically used to measure information learned (e.g., content knowledge such as facts, principles, and skills). For example, achievement tests often are used in studies focused on acquiring sport skills.
2. ***Aptitude tests***, unlike achievement tests, are not focused on what is known but rather the potential for knowing. Intelligence and career tests are aptitude tests.
3. ***Personality tests*** are used to measure self-perception or personal characteristics (see Case 9.3).
4. ***Attitude or interest scales*** are used to examine a respondents' self-reported disposition on a particular topic or issue. As noted in Step 8, a popular example of an attitude-interest scale is the Leisure Diagnostic Battery, which is used to measure topics such as leisure preferences, knowledge of leisure opportunities, and barriers to leisure experiences.
5. ***Behavior rating scales*** are used to quantify observations of behaviors, often to assist in diagnosing problems.

For more guidance on the mechanics of working with tests and scales in data collection, see DeVellis (2011).

SOMETHING TO REMEMBER!

Data collection methods in quantitative studies rely on structured instruments that fit responses into predetermined categories. They produce results that are easy to summarize, compare, and generalize.

DATA COLLECTION TOOLS FOR QUALITATIVE STUDIES

What data collection tools are available for qualitative studies? The next section of the chapter presents popular data collection instruments typically associated with this approach, including unstructured in-depth interview, focus groups, participant observation, projective methods, and document/record review. Instructions for how to use each tool are highlighted as well.

Unstructured In-Depth Interview

Interviewing respondents often involves a face-to-face meeting between the researcher and the study participant. When used with a quantitative approach, the interview data collection method is an orally delivered structured questionnaire. In contrast, when used with a qualitative approach, interviewing involves open-ended questions asked in an unstructured conversational manner.

Because of the open-ended questions, you may use the unstructured in-depth interview format to delve more deeply and thoroughly into a particular event, issue, or situation. Although the unstructured in-depth interview may require a lot of time to conduct, it nevertheless has the greatest flexibility compared to other interview methods. The conversation is usually tape recorded, and a verbatim transcript is prepared from the recording. Also, a s***emistructured interview*** contains formally structured questions and response options as well as open-ended conversational questions.

Unstructured in-depth interview types. Unstructured in-depth interviews, depending on the research question, are divided into descriptive information, discovery, and problem-solving interviews (Cunningham, 1993).

1. You may use a ***descriptive information interview*** to collect information about the following:
    - attributes (e.g., "What is the highest karate level you have achieved?"),
    - preferences (e.g., "Which of our recreation center programs offered have you enjoyed the most?"),
    - beliefs (e.g., "How might the hospital arts therapy program be changed to better meet your needs?"),
    - experiences (e.g., "During the past week, in what camp programs have you participated?"), and
    - reactions to hypothetical situations (e.g., "If you directed the fitness center, what would be your operating philosophy?").

2. You may use the ***discovery interview*** to identify impressions, concerns, suggestions, and/or ideas with respondents (see Case 9.4). For example, suppose a municipal recreation department is interested in learning about current users' thoughts on the county's bike trail system. You may ask interviewees about their experiences when using the trails, their favorite aspects of the current system, the problems they encounter using existing trails, and their ideas about goals for the municipality's bike trails.
3. The ***problem-solving interview*** responds to the mutual interests of the interviewer and interviewee, with a focus on a specific problem to be solved or goal to be set. Problem-solving interviews most commonly are used in personnel situations to help employees and/or volunteers identify ways to improve performance. For example, during a job review, a supervisor could ask an employee who continuously fails to meet deadlines questions such as "What effect do you think your failure to meet report deadlines has on other staff?" and "How could I, as your supervisor, help you do a better job of meeting deadlines?"

Unstructured in-depth interview mechanics. This qualitative form of interviewing is conversation-like. The interviewer has a general idea of the direction of the discussion, but the interviewee determines the pace and content. The conversation begins with a couple of open-ended questions that the interviewer has decided on beforehand. Then depending on the nature of the interviewee's responses, the interviewer asks additional questions to probe for more details or redirect the flow of the conversation to areas that have not been discussed.

This protocol may sound easy, but unstructured in-depth interviews that produce useful information demand high levels of skill from the interviewer. For example, the interviewer requires a high level of skill and practice with ***active listening***. This means putting aside his or her own presuppositions and listening carefully for the meanings being expressed by another. A good interviewer listens attentively and makes interviewees feel their responses are important (this will be reviewed further in Step 13).

One of the first preparations in an unstructured in-depth interview is carefully crafting the opening question. It should be a broad question inviting the interviewee to talk in a general way about the topic. This interview-initiating question is often referred to as a ***grand tour question***; it asks interviewees to share about themselves or their situation (Spradley, 1979). Its goal is to stimulate the informant's recall and thinking without suggesting that particular responses are desired. For example, you may ask the following:

- "Tell me about a typical day at camp."
- "How would you describe this yoga program to someone who has never participated?"

Following the opening grand tour question, ask additional open-ended subquestions, some of which are preplanned to ensure that all areas of the topic are fully addressed (see Table 9.4 for an example of a grand tour question and subquestions). For grand tour questions and subquestions, those that lead to a *yes* or *no* response are inappropriate because they fail to encourage rich and detailed responses. That is, instead of beginning a question with "Do you...," begin with "Tell me more about..."

As well, you may use additional questions that are not preplanned to fulfill the goals of the interview. These are ***probes***, or follow-up questions asked to clarify a response or seek elaboration or more detail from a response. Probes are used when interviewees give responses that are too brief or unclear and to avoid making assumptions about what the interviewee meant. Table 9.4 provides examples of grand tour questions, subquestions, and probe questions (Merriam, 2009; Weisberg, Krosnick, & Bowen, 1996).

You also may accomplish probing in nonverbal ways, including quietly listening, nodding to acknowledge responses, allowing periods of silence for interviewees to think, and taking and reviewing notes. These techniques, however, require special care to use well. Avoid actions that may change or bias what the interviewee says. For example, if you nod when the interviewee is complimentary of the adventure trip and not when the response is critical, you are not likely to hear the more negative comments about the trip.

POINTERS FOR CONDUCTING UNSTRUCTURED INTERVIEWS

- Match interviewer characteristics (gender, age, race/ethnicity, dress, and speech patterns) with those of interviewees as much as possible.
- Precheck the interview location to be sure it is quiet and private enough to enable the respondent to feel comfortable and relaxed.
- Confirm the date, time, and location of the interview a week in advance.
- Begin the interview with prescripted introductory remarks, including reintroducing yourself.
- Remind the interviewee of the confidentiality of his or her responses.
- Obtain general descriptive information according to the focus of the research question.
- Begin with a grand tour question, and then order questions from least sensitive to more sensitive.
- Strive for neutrality throughout the interview; avoid suggesting answers.
- Do not be afraid of silence.
- Record the interview (check your equipment in advance) for later transcribing (see Step 14B).

Table 9.4
Examples of Unstructured Interview Questions for an Adventure Travel Trip Evaluation

Type of question	Example
Grand tour question	Tell me about the trip in general. What would a tourist considering signing up for this trip need to know?
Subquestions	
Example question	Give me an example of something you liked or did not like particularly about the trip.
Language question	What do the trip participants call a tour leader who allows for a lot of independent exploration?
Hypothetical question	Suppose it is your last day of a trip. How would you like to experience it?
Devil's advocate question	Some people would say trips that keep travelers busy throughout the day and evening are overscheduled. What would you say to them?
Ideal position question	What would your ideal day of sightseeing be like?
Interpretive question	What do you think are the strengths and weaknesses of this trip?
Probes	
For vague or one-word answers	What do you mean? Tell me a little more about...?
For clarification	Let's see if I understand what you mean. To summarize what I think I heard you say...
For providing feedback	That's interesting. That's useful information. Remember, there are no right or wrong answers.

Focus Groups

Whereas unstructured in-depth interviews are conducted one at a time with an individual interviewee, ***focus groups*** consist of a group of two or more people being asked about their beliefs, attitudes, perceptions, and/or opinions. Focus groups require a great deal of preplanning and interviewer skill and practice, the goal—as the name implies—is to focus on one or more purpose and capture spontaneity and synergism from the group.

Focus groups are only one of several interview techniques you may use with groups. For example, you also may choose among the nominal group or Delphi techniques or brainstorming sessions and leaderless discussion groups (Steward & Shamdasani, 2014). Sometimes several of these techniques are combined. For example, in one study, the Delphi technique was combined with focus groups to explore constraints experienced by African American and Latino visitors and nonvisitors to U.S. national parks (Roberts, 2003).

Specifically, you may use the focus group data collection method to collect information about a specific topic from multiple participants at once and observe and record their interactions and group dynamics. The interactions and group dynamics also may help participants build on each other's comments, producing ideas or details that would not occur in individual interviews. To prepare for a successful focus group meeting, study the questions in Table 9.5, which are useful to securing responses.

Purposes. You may use focus groups for many purposes. For example, depending on your research question, you may wish to

- obtain general background information about a topic;
- tap into many perspectives to generate new service ideas, ones that may not have been thought of previously;
- provide insights on how to structure a new program or make changes to an existing program;
- troubleshoot specific problem areas in an existing program or service;
- receive reactions to a new product or service;
- confirm results collected by another data collection method (i.e., provide a triangulation of data collection tools); and
- generate hypotheses, and then test these with additional research using a quantitative approach.

Focus groups mechanics. A focus group generally has six to 12 members, who discuss a particular topic under the guidance of a facilitator (Stewart & Shamdasani, 2014). Group members may or may not know each other. Most of the time only one focus group is convened, and the session lasts 1 to 2 hours; however, when the research question is complex, you may assemble three to four focus groups to provide broader insights about the issue or topic. Typically, focus group discussions are audio or video recorded, and then a written summary is prepared for later analysis.

As already mentioned, the interviewer's role in a focus group is as a facilitator. The facilitating role is to guide the discussion, making sure all aspects of the topic are covered and ensuring that everyone in the group contributes to the discussion and no one monopolizes the conversation. Therefore, the interviewer needs to be well trained in group dynamics and practiced in interviewing skills.

The facilitator is chosen carefully for personality characteristics, such as for being articulate and animated, having a sense of humor, and being empathetic and genuinely interested in people. The facilitator also needs to be able to shift among several roles during the meeting, from being supportive, to directive, participative, and achievement oriented.

POINTERS FOR CONVENING A FOCUS GROUP

- Develop a focus group interview guide that clearly identifies the topic of interest and the relevant population.
- Develop the interview guide in collaboration with parties interested in the results.
- Choose an accessible, convenient location for the meeting.
- Schedule the meeting toward the end of the workday or early evening on a Tuesday, Wednesday, or Thursday.
- Take care in recruiting focus group members (usually via convenience sampling) so they are both more and less representative of the population of interest.
- Use a multistep method to recruit focus group members; make initial contact by mail, e-mail, or telephone or in person, and if they show interest in the topic, confirm their participation with the specifics of where and when, and then remind them of the meeting the day before.

Note. Adapted from Stewart and Shamdasani (2014).

Participant Observation

As discussed in the previous section of the chapter, people's actions are often of interest to researchers. Consequently, one way to learn about behaviors is to observe! Unlike observations in quantitative studies,

Table 9.5
Examples of Questions to Use With a Focus Group

Type of question	Purpose	Example
Grand tour question	Broadly focused on the topic or issue studied in the main research question.	The topic today is to explore how you feel about the services provided at our newly opened aquatic center.
Starter question	Get the group talking and comfortable.	Take the index card in front of you and write down one idea that comes to mind about how the aquatic center services could be improved.
Leading question	Carry the discussion to deeper meanings.	Why do you say that?
Testing question	Find the limits of an issue and then pose an extreme yet tentative question.	Are you saying that the food in the aquatic center snack bar is not very nutritious?
Steering question	Nudge the group back onto the main grand tour, or research, question.	Well, to return again to overall reactions to the aquatic center, tell us some more.
Obtuse question	Help the group go into territory it may find uncomfortable by asking an abstract question.	What do you think a first-time guest would think of the aquatic center employees?
Factual question	Requires a factual answer that can be answered easily.	Let's go around the circle and each person tell me about how many times you have used the aquatic center in the past month.
Silence	Sometimes the best question is no question.	Simply wait and allow group members time to respond.

observations in qualitative studies are unstructured and referred to as ***participant observation***, a systematic way of recording information by meaningfully interacting with the individuals being observed (Springer, 2010). In other words, it consists of logically watching the naturally occurring actions of people. Depending on the nature of the research question, this may occur in a single event over a brief time or may be done long term with repeat observations (see Case 9.5).

Participant observation continuum. The advantages and disadvantages of participant observation stem from the same source: interactions with people. You may be able to obtain more information, but this may change participants' behaviors. Therefore, adjust the nature of your interaction with those being observed according to the research question and situation. This requires increasing or decreasing your degree of participation. Think of this as a continuum. As illustrated in Figure 9.3, interaction ranges from minimal, or passive, to complete.

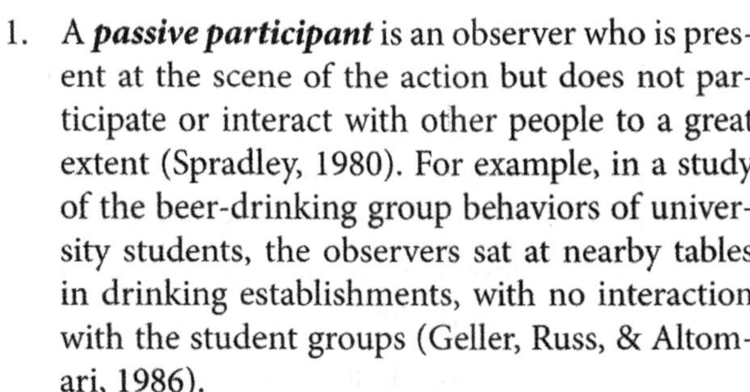

1. A ***passive participant*** is an observer who is present at the scene of the action but does not participate or interact with other people to a great extent (Spradley, 1980). For example, in a study of the beer-drinking group behaviors of university students, the observers sat at nearby tables in drinking establishments, with no interaction with the student groups (Geller, Russ, & Altomari, 1986).
2. The ***marginal participant*** adopts the role of a peripheral, though completely accepted, participant (Spradley, 1980). The observer assumes limited or cursory interactions and involvement with the persons observed. For instance, in a study about the strategies women use in singles bars and nightclubs to fend off unwanted male advances (Snow, Robinson, & McCall, 1991), the observer stood or sat where she could hear, see, and chat with the women.
3. The ***complete participant*** becomes a full member of the group being studied (Spradley, 1980).

Furthermore, the observer may be in an overt or a covert role. The ***overt complete participant's*** role as a researcher is fully disclosed, whereas the ***covert complete participant's*** intentions are not disclosed to the people being observed.

For ethical reasons, take special care when the observation is covert. For example, Robins, Sanders, and Cahill (1991) examined how pet dogs facilitate the development of relationships among previously unacquainted people in public places. The observer visited the same park for 3 months with his puppy and presented himself as "just another dog owner." Since the actions observed occurred in a public location and were equally observable by anyone, the study did not put the subjects at risk of undue harm because of the researcher's covert role.

IS IT PASSIVE, MARGINAL, OR COMPLETE PARTICIPANT OBSERVATION?

Indicate whether the following situations are examples of passive, marginal, or complete participant observation.

________ 1. Shopping along with others at the community farmer's market on Saturday, observing children's attentiveness to the fruits and vegetables.

________ 2. Standing in front of a controversial painting at an art museum, listening to viewers' comments and critiques about the painting.

________ 3. Playing first base on the adult softball team, and then after the game recording the circumstances that elicited aggressive behaviors observed during the game.

Note. Answers are provided at the end of the chapter.

Participant observation mechanics. Participant observation places considerable responsibility on the observer because the data produced through this tool are interpretations of what is observed. Therefore, an observer needs special training and mentored practice to do it well. Furthermore, although participant observation is unstructured in terms of an absence of required rules and protocols, systematic approaches may be taken to guide data collection.

For example, you must take great care in selecting the observation site. Evaluate potential sites in terms of their (Lofland et al., 2006)

- appropriateness: a good fit is crucial between the research question and the setting;
- access: the observation post must be natural and legitimate; and
- physical and emotional risks: the risks associated with the site must be minimal and fair to the observer and those observed.

Also, an observation recording sheet is worthwhile for capturing information during the participant observation session. Such handwritten material often is referred to as ***field notes***. In contrast to observational guides for structured observations, field notes are a running description of the setting, events, people, things heard, and interactions observed. The following are the important components of field notes (Lofland et al., 2006):

- an explanation of the setting;
- a description of the participants in the setting;
- date and time of the observation;
- who the observer is and other needed identification information;
- restatement of the research question and subquestions as they are determined;
- detailed descriptions of what people do and how they interact;
- verbatim conversations and direct quotes; and
- subjective comments about what was observed.

Following the observation session, rewrite field notes to fill in more material and initiate interpretive ideas. Getting a full record of what was observed may take as long as the original observation! In a qualitative study, this process is part of data analysis (see Step 14B for more information).

Passive Participant	***Marginal Participant***	***Complete Participant***
Lowest amount of participation ←	→	Highest amount of participation

Figure 9.3. The participant observation continuum. Adapted from Spradley (1980).

PARTICIPANT OBSERVATION POINTERS

- Initially, keep observations brief and then extend the time according to your time sampling plan as the setting becomes more familiar to you.
- Conduct your initial observations without recording data to get a feel for what happens in general in the setting and to confirm that what needs to be observed to answer the research questions is indeed present at the observation site.
- Alternate between observing the broad picture of what is happening and focusing on specific individuals and activities.
- As well, concentrate on recording examples of everything observed.
- Remain as unobtrusive as possible to avoid changing the actions and behaviors of those observed; even if you have chosen to be an overt complete participant observer, you still want to observe natural processes and activities at the site rather than initiating or leading them.

Note. Adapted from Lodico, Spaulding, and Voegtle (2010).

Projective Methods

When direct questioning and observing is inappropriate, you may use ***projective methods*** for indirectly measuring people's attitudes, beliefs, and perceptions (Bailey, 1994). A projective data collection method gathers responses to ambiguous stimuli, such as abstract patterns or incomplete sentences. These methods also may use photographs, word associations, cartoons, and drawings—or anything that provides indistinct provocations for people to interpret. You are perhaps familiar with an example of projective methods, the Rorschach inkblot test, in which people are asked to describe what they see in inkblot images.

Although not widely used in leisure research situations, projective methods are found when collecting information from preliterate children, from persons with communication challenges, or where study participants cannot know the true purpose of the study. For example, Lashua (2010) studied two films, Crossing the Line and Crossing the Line: Northern Exposure, produced by young people to address issues of violence in neighborhoods. Another study analyzed tourist-created drawings and short stories to measure trip experiences (Figure 9.4).

You may implement projective methods using the following techniques (Linzey, 1959):

- associative: a particular stimulus is used to elicit the first thing that occurs to a respondent;
- completion: the respondent completes sentences or drawings;
- constructive: the respondent creates a drawing, sculpture, or story;
- choice/ordering: the respondent chooses from a group of or orders a group of pictures, sentences, etc.; and
- expressive: the respondent organizes and incorporates a particular stimulus into a self-expressive process, such as role-playing and dance.

For more guidance on the mechanics of working with projective methods in data collection, see Soley and Smith (2008).

Document/Record Review

The last data collection technique typically associated with the qualitative research approach does not require access to people. Instead, document or record review deduces people's feelings and behaviors through observation of the artifacts they make (Neuendorf, 2001), such as written records, art expressions, photographs, or videotapes. This process also is known as ***content analysis***.

The decision to use documents is driven by the research questions of your study. Examples include studies that examined Disney movies (Rojek, 1993), heavy metal rock music (Straw, 1999), newspaper coverage of women's sport (Rowe & Brown, 1994), Wimbledon television coverage (Fishwick & Leach, 1998), tourist postcards (Cohen, 1993), personal photo albums (Walker & Rosalind, 1989), and video game characters in top-selling gaming magazines (Dill & Thill, 2007).

As with other qualitative data collection methods, even though unstructured, document review requires a systematic approach. This may include counting specific content found in the document. For example, suppose you are interested in predicting the outcome of a new recreation bond initiative in an upcoming election. You may rely on the numerical counts of particular words in campaign speeches and advertisements as evidence of the support for the ballot measure, as well as your own interpretation of the meaning of the words according to their context in the speeches and advertisements.

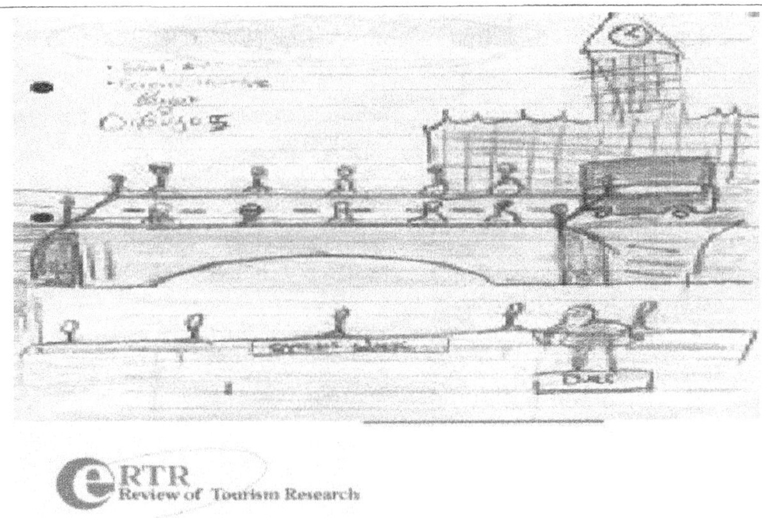

The drawing reflects order. Pictorially, he drew himself in the bottom of the sheet as a sign of subordination to a status-quo that gives to him a symbolic refuge. The sun also symbolizes his need of centrality and power subordinating his own opinion. The drawing can be examined in the following manner: a) the trace denotes a certain aggressiveness and perseverance against obstacles; b) the horizontal and vertical lines lead us to the idea of planning and rationality, and c) the lack of intensity in colors reflects a great psychological dependence on others. (p. 97)

Figure 9.4. Drawing of a 26-year-old male's experience vacationing in London. Researcher's analysis is from Korstanje (2010). Reproduced with permission.

Document/record review is focused on manifest and latent content. ***Manifest content*** is the visible surface content in the document, and ***latent content*** is the underlying meaning of the document content (Babbie, 2012). To record manifest content, category codes are usually developed to enable the placement of each unit of analysis (words, images) into an organized system. That way patterns emerge that then may be analyzed. Such codes may be taken from existing theory or created according to the research question.

DOCUMENT/RECORD REVIEW POINTERS

- Identify the population of documents: all documents of a certain time?
- Pinpoint the unit of analysis: the entire document or certain parts (e.g., if focusing on a newspaper, do you look only at columns? Paragraphs? Lines?).
- Select a sample of units from the document population, such as random or stratified.
- Develop a data recording sheet to record manifest and latent content.

Note. Adapted from Babbie (2012), Flick (2006), Gratton and Jones (2010), and Schutt (2011).

SOMETHING TO REMEMBER!

Data collection methods in qualitative studies rely on unstructured techniques that do not fit responses in predetermined categories. They produce results that describe and interpret meanings.

TRIANGULATION

In triangulation, you may use more than one data collection tool in the same study and then compare the results obtained. In making the case for data collection triangulation, Denzin and Lincoln (2011) suggested that using multiple methods secures "an in-depth understanding of the phenomenon in question" (p. 5).

Triangulation adds thoroughness and richness of understanding to the study (Lodico et al., 2010) because it relies on more than one source of information to establish a fact (Bogdan & Biklen, 2006). Although research may never fully capture objective reality, triangulation will help you get closer. Data collection triangulation is worth the effort because you will be able to better understand a phenomenon by considering it from multiple perspectives and looking more broadly to find the expected and unexpected answers to a research question.

You may accomplish data collection triangulation within and between theoretical approaches. As noted in Step 3, triangulation across theoretical approaches paradigms is referred to as mixed-methods research. For example, you could evaluate a resort's children's beach program by asking parents unstructured, open-ended questions and by asking beach program staff to complete a questionnaire.

Thus, when possible, conduct your studies using data collection triangulation to (Greene, Caracelli, & Graham, 1989)

- facilitate convergence of results when different data collection tools yield the same results;
- identify unique and contradictory facets of the same phenomenon;
- discover information from one approach that assists with directing what data are collected using a second approach; and
- add breadth to the study.

Appendix 4 presents supplemental readings on data collection tools used for quantitative, qualitative, and mixed-methods research.

Peter Rabbit and his friend are busy being passive observers, a data collection method used by humans, too! The World of Beatrix Potter™ Attraction, Bowness-on-Windermere, England. Copyright © 2015 Carol Cutler Riddick.

REVIEW AND DISCUSSION QUESTIONS

1. Name and distinguish three data collection tools used in quantitative studies. Explain the nature of the data rendered from each.
2. What is the difference between closed-ended and open-ended questions? Invent an example of each.
3. Write questions that illustrate the following response options: dichotomous, Likert scale, semantic differential, forced ranking, adjective checklist, multiple choice, and smiley face continuum.
4. Define structured observation and identify three techniques that may be used to record such observations.
5. Describe a research situation of interest to you whereby a published scale or test would be useful.
6. Name and distinguish five data collection tools used in qualitative studies. Explain the nature of the data rendered from each.
7. Distinguish among descriptive information, discovery, and problem-solving unstructured interviews.
8. What is the participant observation continuum? Distinguish the three observer roles.
9. Describe a research situation of interest to you whereby a projective method would be useful.
10. Identify examples of document review.
11. What is data collection triangulation? Why is it used?

YOUR RESEARCH

1. If your approach is quantitative, what data collection tools are you using?
2. If your approach is qualitative, what data collection tools are you using?
3. Review your research questions and then determine whether you need to use data collection triangulation for conducting your study. If not, why not?
4. For each of the data collection tools you have chosen, make a detailed list of how to prepare and conduct data collection using this tool. If the tools require coding or recording sheets, prepared questions, or cover letters, and so forth, prepare these materials according to the instructions provided under the relevant sections in the chapter.

PRACTICE EXERCISES

1. For each item in the list below, identify (a) what data collection tool you would use to collect the information and (b) the rationale behind your choice. Conduct this exercise in small group discussions.

Worksheet Data Collection Chapter: Choosing a Data Collection Tool

Variable	Data collection	Rationale for selection
1. Children's impressions of a trip to a museum.		
2. College students' free-time choices.		
3. Ideas for reducing crowding at a local state park.		
4. Reasons why children have not learned how to swim.		
5. Media coverage of the Deaf Olympics.		
6. Stair climber machine usage at a health club.		
7. How 10K participants in the local YMCA run compare to 10K participants nationwide.		

2. Different questions produce different information—an important rule to remember when selecting data collection tools. To demonstrate, try this activity comparing structured and unstructured interviewing.
   a. Select a classmate to interview. Use the questions below to conduct a structured interview. Record the answers provided.

Worksheet Data Collection Chapter: Conducting a Structured Interview

Questions
1. Have you ever been a leader (circle one answer)? YES NO
2. Do you consider your leadership to have been successful (circle one answer)? YES NO
3. Where has your leadership experience been at (choose as many as apply)? RECREATION SETTING WORK SETTING SCHOOL SETTING
4. What do you think are the most important qualities of good leadership (choose as many as apply)? INTELLIGENCE CREATIVITY COMMUNICATION SKILLS GROUP MANAGEMENT

b. Now, interview the same student, only this time use a more unstructured interview approach. That is, ask the following questions and then write down the answers that are provided.

Worksheet Data Collection Chapter: Conducting an Unstructured Interview

Question	Answer
1. Please tell me about a specific situation when you were a leader.	
2. In what ways would you describe this as successful leadership?	
3. In what types of situations do you most often exhibit leadership?	
4. What do you consider to be the most important qualities of good leadership?	

c. Discuss with your classmate the differences in the two interview experiences. Identify the differences in the information received from the two approaches. Did you or your classmate prefer the structured or unstructured interview experience? Why? What may be implications for analyzing the answers from the two interview experiences? Write your conclusions in one paragraph.

3. This exercise demonstrates how the focus group method may provide useful information. Your task is to design a focus group that measure's people's attitudes or beliefs about a particular issue. Begin by thinking of an issue of interest to you that involves controversy (e.g., allowing the use of all-terrain vehicles in state parks or selling beer at city-owned park concession stands).
   a. By hand, draft several questions about your chosen issue and determine specific closed-ended responses to each.
   b. Now, convene a small group of classmates or friends and ask each of your prepared questions to them as a group, without offering the response options you also developed. Take notes on their responses.
   c. After you have asked the questions and the group has offered no more responses, compare the group's answers with your prepared closed-ended responses. How well do they match?
   d. Share your prepared responses with the group and ask them how well your expectations for answers captured their opinions.
   e. What did you learn from this exercise?

4. Practice passive participant observation by using a camera to record five examples of neglect, damage, and/or litter to a recreational site. If the site is not identified by your course instructor, choose your own.
   a. Write a one page summary of what you found and attach the five photographs you took.
   b. What were the advantages and disadvantages of this data collection method?

WEB EXERCISES

1. Consider a special technique of participant observation: experimental phenomenology. Scrolling down the table of contents for Dr. George Boeree's *Qualitative Methods Workbook* for PSY 405 (http://www.ship.edu/~cgboeree/qualmeth.html), select the Observation section (Part 3). Then scroll down to Chapter 13. Read the chapter and describe an example of how you could use this data collection technique in a leisure research situation of interest to you.
2. To become more adept at recognizing data collection techniques in studies, go to the "Data and Statistics" page of the website for the Centers for Disease Control and Prevention at http://www.cdc.gov/datastatistics/. Select a topic, such as alcohol or physical inactivity, and then either read the statistics presented for that topic or, in some cases, select a specific subcategory of statistics and read about them. What data collection methods do you surmise were used to collect the information for these statistics? What clues let you know this?
3. Conduct a document/record review.
   a. Acquire from your community park and recreation department a copy of the booklet for program offerings. Sometimes these are available on their website.
   b. If not otherwise directed by your instructor, choose two or three categories and corresponding levels that you may use to analyze the document. For example, some of the categories and corresponding levels that can be considered are as follows:

Category	Levels
Program location	Indoors, outdoors
Program type	Art, dance, fitness, music, sport, nature, etc.
Time of day for program	Weekday, weekend, holiday
Participants' gender	Males, females, coed
Participants' age group	Toddler, children, teens, young adults, middle adults, seniors
Cost of program	Free, less than $25, $26–$50, $51 or more
Program length	Half day or less, full day, 1 week, 2 months, 3 months or longer
Program frequency	Once only, once a week, twice a week, three times or more a week
Participant ability level	All ability levels, beginners only, intermediates only, advanced only

   c. Set up a form that helps you tally the number of programs that fit in each category level.
   d. Fill in the form by counting the programs offered by the department according to the category levels.
   e. Examine the findings on the form. What are the tendencies for each category? What do you conclude?

SERVICE LEARNING

For the campus program or service that has been selected as the focus of the service learning project for this semester, consider the following:

1. Review the decisions and choices made up to this step in the research process.

2. To measure the variables chosen and answer the research question designated, will you need to choose a quantitative or qualitative data collection tool? Or is a data collection triangulation preferable. Why?
3. Determine exactly which tools you will use, and outline the actions you need to take to prepare them for data collection.
4. Present your chosen tools to your instructor as well as to the director of the campus program or service with whom you are working. What is their reaction and advice? Make adjustments to the data collection tools accordingly.
5. If the tools require coding or recording sheets, prepared questions, cover letters, and so forth, prepare these materials according to the instructions provided under the relevant sections in the chapter.

TEST YOURSELF ANSWERS

Troubleshooting Questionnaire Questions

1. Response options are not mutually exclusive, 2. Ambiguous options, 3. Leading question and not clear what values are for the number answers provided, and 4. Double-barreled question

Is It Passive, Marginal, or Complete Participant Observer?

1. Marginal, 2. Passive, 3. Complete

SUPPORTING CASES FOR THIS CHAPTER

CASE 9.1. FACE-TO-FACE STRUCTURED INTERVIEW

Shannon, C., Robertson, B., Morrison, K., & Werner, T. (2009). Understanding constraints younger youth face in engaging as volunteers. *Journal of Park & Recreation Administration, 27*, 17–37.

Many nonprofit organizations need volunteers but struggle to find those who will provide the hours of support their programs, services, and events need. Although youth volunteer, little is known about the experiences they have. The purpose of this study was to explore constraints younger volunteers face and ways in which these constraints are negotiated. Using structured, face-to-face interviews, data were collected from 73 youth volunteers (31 males, 42 females) aged 8 to 12 and seven executive directors from Boys & Girls Clubs (BGC) in Atlantic Canada. The findings indicated that attitudes of adults in the community toward younger youth may (a) limit the volunteer opportunities that are welcoming for this age group, (b) affect younger youths' perception of their abilities, and (c) influence youths' enjoyment of the volunteer experience.

CASE 9.2. STRUCTURED OBSERVATION GUIDE

Riddick, C., & Baron-Leonard, R. (2003). *Affiliate social behaviors scale for deaf adults.* Unpublished manuscript, Gallaudet University, Washington, DC.

Guide for Observing and Recording Receptive Skills

Directions: Mark the number of times each behavior is exhibited by the patient during the activity session.

Patient # ____________

1. Alertness:
   Paying attention ____________
   Sleeping ____________
   Uninterested ____________

2. Eye Contact:
   Eyes open & maintain eye contact with group leader ____________
   Eyes open but no eye contact with group leader ____________
   Eyes closed ____________

3. Facial Expressions:
   Smiling ____________
   Unexpressive or flat ____________

4. Attentive Listening:
   Oh-I-see sign ________________
   Nodding of head up and down in agreement with person talking ____________
   Nodding of head sideways in disagreement with person talking ____________
   Twitching of nose signifying agreement with person talking ________________
   If not clear, follows up or asks for clarification ________________________________
   Summarizes from time-to-time ____________ ________________________________

Note. Reprinted with permission of the authors.

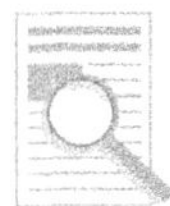

CASE 9.3. COLLECTING DATA WITH A SCALE

Devine, M., & Dawson, S. (2010). The effect of a residential camp experience on self-esteem and social acceptance of youth with craniofacial differences. *Therapeutic Recreation Journal, 44*, 105–121.

Children and adolescents with significant disabilities often have been at greater risk for lower self-esteem than their peers with mild to moderate disabilities or without disabilities. This study explored the impact of a week-long summer camp specifically for children and adolescents with craniofacial differences on their self-esteem. A standardized scale, the Rosenberg Self-Esteem Scale, and a single-item indicator of social acceptance were administered to 31 youth prior to, at the conclusion of, and 6 to 8 weeks after a 5-day residential camping experience. Results indicated that the campers demonstrated significant gains in self-esteem and social acceptance by the end of the week, but the gains for both variables had dissipated 6 to 8 weeks later.

CASE 9.4. DISCOVERY IN-DEPTH INTERVIEW IN EXTREME SPORTS

Brymer, E., & Gray, T. (2009). Dancing with nature: Rhythm and harmony in extreme sport participation. *Journal of Adventure Education & Outdoor Learning, 9*, 135–156.

Research on extreme sports has downplayed the importance of the athletes' connection to nature and the environment. This study involved conducting open-ended interviews with 15 individuals who participated in BASE jumping, big-wave surfing, extreme skiing, waterfall kayaking, extreme mountaineering, and solo rope-free climbing. Participants spoke extensively about developing a deep relationship with the natural world akin to an intimate "dance" between actively engaged partners. The experience-based analysis found that for veteran adventure athletes, nature and the environment act as facilitators to a deeper, more positive understanding of self and place in the environment.

CASE 9.5. PARTICIPANT OBSERVATION IN STUDYING A MUSIC FESTIVAL

Mackellar, J. (2009). Dabblers, fans and fanatics: Exploring behavioural segmentation at a special-interest event. *Journal of Vacation Marketing, 15*, 5–25.

This paper explored the behavioral segments of the audience at the Elvis Revival Festival in Parkes, Australia. Audiences were observed traveling to and participating in this 2-day event, which celebrated the life and music of Elvis Presley. The study highlighted differences in fan behavior, resulting in four behavioral audience segments: social, dabbler, fan, and fanatic. It was concluded that differences in marketing and management strategies should be created to cater to the different needs and expectations of visitors and local communities.

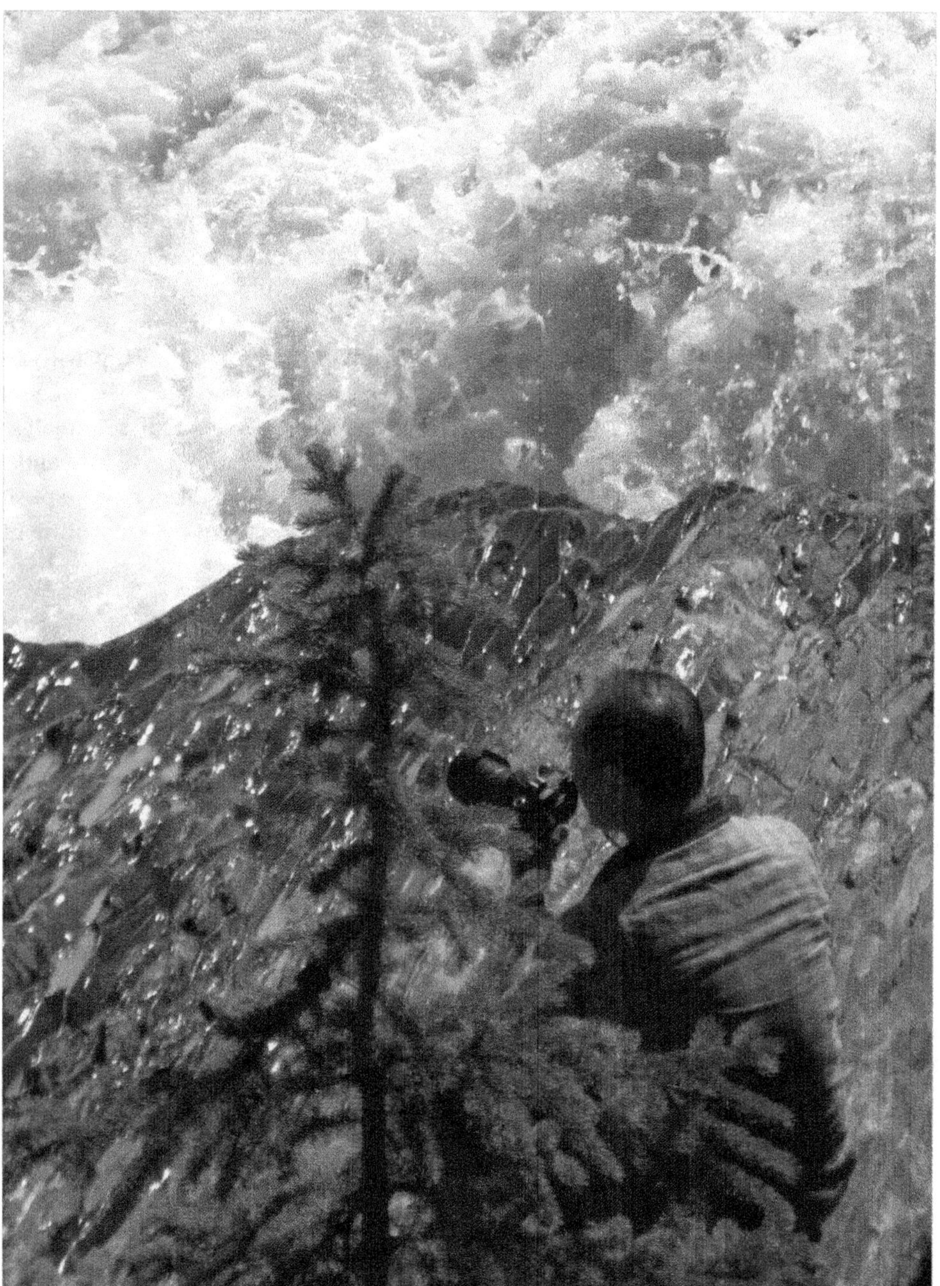

To begin this chapter, take a philosophical pause and consider "aesthetic ethics," which refers to the idea that human conduct ought to be governed by that which is beautiful and attractive. This unity of aesthetics and ethics in fact is reflected in your understanding of behavior being "fair"—meaning both appealing and morally acceptable. Glacier National Park, Montana. Copyright © 2015 Ruth V. Russell.

ADDRESS ETHICAL RESPONSIBILITIES

WHAT WILL I LEARN IN THIS CHAPTER?

I'll be able to...

1. Provide definitions for ethics and a professional code of ethics.
2. Identify when an institutional review board (IRB) must be established and its primary function.
3. Define research ethics and distinguish among the following principles of research ethics:
   - nonmaleficence (including the four potential risks facing study participants);
   - beneficence (and three categories of benefits that may be offered to study participants);
   - respect and how an informed consent form reinforces the principle of respect;
   - honesty and aspects of honesty including data falsification, misrepresentation, plagiarism, data sharing, and authorship credit;
   - justice; and
   - competence.

"Rather fail with honor than succeed by fraud."

Sophocles
(an ancient Greek playwright whose plays have survived, most famous today are the tragedies *Oedipus* and *Antigone*, 497–406 BC)

Research may be "messed up" in many ways, such as violating expected ethical research behaviors. To review the topic of ethics, this chapter has been divided into three sections. First, definitions for ethics and a professional code of ethics are reviewed. Second, research ethics and the institutional review board are discussed. Third, ethical principles that should guide research are covered.

WHAT ARE ETHICS AND A PROFESSIONAL CODE OF ETHICS?

Ethics are moral duties and obligations of proper and improper behavior (Reese & Fremouw, 1984). Ethics operate on two levels. First, you have your own personal ethics, or principles of right and wrong. Second, you have professional ethics, principles of right and wrong applying to your specialized training, experience, and knowledge. When joining a profession, you will face the challenge of blending your personal and professional ethics.

In fact, most professions have a ***professional code of ethics*** (Stumbo, 1985), that is, norms, values, and principles that govern professional conduct and relationships with clients, colleagues, and society (Kornblau & Burkhardt, 2012; Strike & Ternasky, 1993). According to Sylvester (2002),

> Professions are moral institutions because their policies and practices are intended to contribute to a good society. The quintessential element of professionalization, then, is ethics, which guides professional practice in the right spirit toward the right ends using the right means. (p. 315)

Ethical behavior applies to all aspects of how a profession operates. For example, therapeutic recreation professionals are encouraged to embrace and practice virtue, feminist, and communicative ethics (Sylvester, 2002; Velasquez, Shanks, & Meyer, 2013).

- ***Virtue ethics*** strive toward ideals related to humanity and moral character and thus include character traits such as courage, compassion, generosity, and self-control.
- ***Feminist ethics*** create environments for clients that are inclusive and incorporate the experiences of individuals whose concerns have been marginalized in the past (e.g., women).
- ***Communicative ethics*** entail professionally appropriate listening and conversational skills.

RESEARCH ETHICS AND INSTITUTIONAL REVIEW BOARD

Ethical behavior also extends to research activities. ***Research ethics*** are the ethical principles that are expected when designing, conducting, and reporting research. In large part, society's confidence in and support of research requires trusting the integrity and ethics of researchers. Indeed, people involved in research must conduct studies responsibly; in fact, their actions must be beyond reproach.

Program administrators and researchers are confronted frequently with ethical research issues. Suppose a teen respondent mentions during an interview that she uses drugs at the recreation center. Should the police be notified? Would it be fair when testing the effectiveness of a new aquatics treatment program in your rehabilitation center that control group clients are denied access to the program? What if evaluation results reveal a stress reduction program for your corporation's employees has failed? Do you need to shut down the program immediately and report these results to the company CEO?

To navigate through research ethics, visit the Resources for Research Ethics Education website: http://research-ethics.net/. Likewise, professional organizations, in an attempt to standardize and regulate actions, have identified acceptable and unacceptable ethical research practices. These codes alert researchers to the ethical expectations of their work (Case 10.1).

In the United States and Canada, government regulations require organizations that receive federal funding such as universities and hospitals to establish review systems that oversee research dealing with human subjects. These are known as ***institutional review boards*** (IRB) and essentially act as an ethics committee. The overall responsibility of IRBs is to determine whether a researcher will be treating study participants ethically. Consequently, a researcher must seek and obtain IRB approval before he or she may proceed with a study (this review process is described further in Step 11).

ETHICAL PRINCIPLES TO GUIDE RESEARCH

Researchers must responsibly design, implement, and report on their studies. Ethical behavior in research is determined by adherence to the following fundamental principles that are the foundation to all human service codes of ethics (McCrone, 2002):

- nonmaleficence,
- beneficence,
- respect,
- honesty,
- justice, and
- competence.

Nonmaleficence

Nonmaleficence is related to the doctrine of "do no harm" (McCrone, 2002). A study is expected to be executed in a way that causes no unnecessary harm to participants. You must anticipate and avoid risks that are likely to result from your research. The potential risks to study participants include physical harm, psychological harm, loss of privacy, and loss of confidentiality.

Physical harm. Avoid study procedures that could cause physical harm to participants. For instance, asking people to ski down a slope as fast as they can to measure the quality of snow produced by new snow-making equipment would be unacceptable and negligent.

Psychological harm. Although you may be able to predict and easily guard against physical harm, psychological or emotional harm may occur without your awareness. For example, asking people about unpleasant events in their lives could cause stress for some.

Loss of privacy. This means people are reasonably shielded from public view. Individuals involved in a research study have the right to determine when, how, and to what extent information about them is communicated to others. You may observe public acts that

HUMOROUS PSYCHOLOGY EXPERIMENTS?

To review the 25 most intriguing psychology experiments of all time, go to http://list25.com/25-intriguing-psychology-experiments/. Some of the featured experiments are funny (Free Hugs, Carlsberg Social Experiment, Candid Camera Elevator Experiment—you may also view the latter at http://www.brainpickings.org/index.php/2012/01/13/asch-elevator-experiment/). However, some of the experiments are not funny but instead underscore questionable, if not unethical, research behaviors.

Which experiment did you like most, and why? For your choice, what ethical issues could come into question or perhaps be argued as being violated?

others would normally view (e.g., a baseball game). Yet, observing activity that is personal or sensitive is an invasion of privacy.

This principle sounds clear enough, but it is easy to violate. For example, asking people about their attitudes or opinions may conflict with their right to privacy. To be ethical, consider how sensitive the questions posed or behaviors observed are to the individuals or groups you are studying. Many people perceive information such as body weight and annual personal income to be too private in nature to be asked, let alone answered!

If you observe the drinking behaviors of these boaters for a study, will their right to privacy be violated? Lake Michigan, South Haven, Michigan. Copyright © 2015 Ruth V. Russell.

Loss of confidentiality. ***Confidentiality*** occurs when you can identify a response or observation as belonging to a particular person but promise not to do so. Many persons confuse confidentiality with anonymity. ***Anonymous*** means that any given response cannot be connected with a specific respondent. That is, no information (e.g., name, phone number, address, social security number) is asked or recorded that could be used to identify an individual study participant.

In research, confidentiality is an extension of the right to privacy. Privacy refers to persons, whereas confidentiality refers to information. Once you have collected information for a study, you have an ethical responsibility to protect it.

If you have recorded identifiers, such as names, home addresses, e-mail addresses, or phone numbers of study participants, remove these from the interviews, questionnaires, and observation forms (Fowler, 2014). To apply this rule, record the name or other identifying information at the end of the form. That way, you may readily separate the identifiers from survey responses or observational data. In short, not even the evaluator or researcher should be able to link the data to a specific individual.

Likewise, assure study participants you will hold information collected from or about them in strict confidence. This also means never revealing a study participant's identity in written reports, staff and professional meetings, and/or social situations.

HOW TO HANDLE CONFIDENTIALITY AND ANONYMITY

To ensure confidentiality in survey research that involves follow-up or in research that requires individuals to be studied on multiple occasions over time, use a unique code number to identify each interview or questionnaire. The code could be an assigned number but not any sequential numbers related to a person's social security number, last name alphabetical order, and so forth.

Commercial numbering machines are available that repeat the same number multiple times before advancing. For instance, you can successively number a master list of address labels and the front of a questionnaire. One number will be assigned to one person's name appearing on the master list and then the same number will be stamped on the front of the questionnaire. The numbering machine's tumbler then will advance to a new number. Keep the name assigned to each number as well as completed pretests, posttests, or survey results under lock and key.

To ensure anonymity when using a questionnaire in a group setting, have respondents place their completed questionnaire, without identifying information, inside an envelope and then seal the envelope. These envelopes may be dropped into a collection box.

Beneficence

The ethical principle of ***beneficence*** is the welfare or the benefits individuals involved in research receive (McCrone, 2002). A study that applies beneficence is conducted in a manner that study participants receive some advantage from their involvement. The benefits extended to people for participating in research may be direct, material, or "less tangible" (Table 10.1).

Respect

When you have respect for others, you recognize their autonomy in making their own choices (McCrone, 2002). In research, you must accept the right of individuals to decide about whether, and to what extent, they want to participate in a study (Case 10.2). You are ethically expected to inform potential study participants about the purpose of the study, the risks and benefits of participation, and their right to refuse or cease participation in the study at any time without retribution. Procedures that limit an individual's freedom to consent voluntarily are coercive.

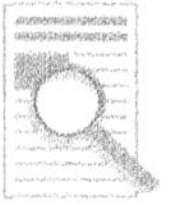

NONMALEFICENCE

Directions: Identify which ethical principle of nonmaleficence is being violated in the following research situations: physical harm, loss of privacy, psychological harm, or loss of confidentiality.

Situation	Ethical principles of nonmaleficence being violated
1. To gather data, a horseback riding program offered at a regional park requires individuals to record their name on an after-class customer satisfaction survey and leave it at the desk as they exit.	
2. A university ropes course instructor wants to document for a conference presentation the gains students make in her course. After 3 hours of instruction, she demands the students attempt a demanding maneuver.	
3. A health club offers beginning swim lessons to adults. Two classes are taught by different instructors, and both classes are offered when open swim is occurring. The pool manager wants data collected to determine which instructor does a better job teaching.	
4. As part of a thesis research project, a student is teaching adults who are blind how to sail. Wearing harnesses while in the boat is not required.	

Note. Answers are provided at the end of the chapter.

Table 10.1
Possible Benefits of Participating in Research

Benefits	Examples
Direct	• Learning a new skill • Treatment of a "problem"
Material	• Money • Nonmonetary gift or prize
Less tangible	• Satisfaction or enjoyment in being part of a scientific investigation • Contribute to a profession's body of knowledge • Potential to improve future practices

As an acknowledgement of a potential study participants' autonomy, informed consent has become common practice (see Table 10.2). By using ***informed consent***, you are making an ethical commitment to ensure that a potential study participant has enough information about the study to make a sound decision about participating. Typically the form is printed for the participant to read and sign (Case 10.3); therefore, the individual reading the form must understand the information being presented.

CONSENT FORM RESOURCES

At least two resources are available to help you develop an informed consent form. To begin, check out the University of Minnesota's "Web-Based Instruction on Informed Consent" at http://www.research.umn.edu/consent/orientation.html. Complete the first three modules. Another resource for phone and written consent forms is the American Association for Public Opinion Research (http://www.aapor.org/Consent_Form_Examples1/3965.htm).

Informed consent procedures become more complex when the research involves members of special populations, such as minors. When dealing with minors, two consent forms are necessary: a written consent form signed by a parent or guardian and an agreement to participate in the study signed by the minor.

Likewise, permission to involve patients residing in a public psychiatric hospital in research requires different levels of permission. For instance, before proceeding, you must obtain approval from the IRBs of the hospital and state agency responsible for regulating the psychiatric facility. Moreover, informed consent by the patient, if deemed capable by the hospital or their advocate/guardian, is also required.

Table 10.2
Components of an Informed Consent Form

In the United States, federal guidelines (45 C.F.R. 46) specify the critical information that must appear on an informed consent form:

1. The identity of the researcher and the name of the organization that is conducting or sponsoring the research.
2. A statement that says the study involves "research," the purposes of the research, and the expected duration of the participation as well as experimental procedures that will be used in the study.
3. A description of reasonably foreseeable risks or discomforts to the participant.
4. A description of benefits to the participant or to others that reasonably may be expected from the research.
5. A disclosure of appropriate alternative procedures or courses of treatment, if any, that may be advantageous to the participant.
6. A statement describing the extent, if any, to which confidentiality of records identifying the participant will be maintained.
7. For research involving more than minimal risk, an explanation as to whether compensation is to be made and an explanation as to whether medical treatments are available if injury occurs and, if so, what the treatments consist of or where further information may be obtained.
8. An explanation of whom to contact for answers to questions about the research, research participants' rights, and research-related injury to the participant.
9. A statement that states, "Participation is voluntary; refusal to participate will involve no negative consequences, including penalty or loss of benefits to which the participant is otherwise entitled; and the participant may discontinue participation, without need to cite reasons at any time without penalty or loss of benefits to which the participant is otherwise entitled."
10. Assurance that the respondent can skip questions he or she does not want to answer.

Note. Protection of Human Subjects (2009).

Consent forms should be written in simple, straightforward language that is devoid of jargon. The consent form for adults should be composed at a sixth to eighth grade reading level; that is, the writing may easily be checked under the "grammar check" feature of text editing software (Cozby & Bates, 2011). The reading bar is at this level because the respondents must clearly understand what they have consented to do; otherwise, the consent is not legally binding (Berg & Latin, 2008).

Honesty

Honesty, or ***fidelity***, is establishing a relationship of trust between the researcher and the study participant. In research, the major caution associated with honesty is deceptive practices. ***Deception*** is the misrepresentation of information. Deceptive practices amount to ***scientific fraud***, the "...deliberate falsification, misrepresentation, or plagiarizing of data, findings, or the ideas of others. This includes embellishing research reports, reporting research that has not been conducted, or manipulating data in a deceptive way" (Monette, Sullivan, & DeJong, 2008, p. 62). Thus, honesty has many aspects: data falsification, misrepresentation, plagiarism, data sharing, and authorship credit.

Data falsification. You are expected to complete data collection procedures, analyses, and reporting truthfully and are obligated to make known shortcomings or failures experienced in data collection. Additionally, you are expected to not commit unintentional mistakes in data collection, let alone falsify data. One of the most infamous examples is Andrew Wakefield's research linking vaccines with autism. Wakefield deliberately altered facts and falsified data trying to convince parents that vaccines are dangerous (to read more about this, go to http://www.bmj.com/content/342/bmj.c7452). The *British Medical Journal* and *Lancet* ultimately publicly retracted the dishonest research by Wakefield they had published.

Misrepresentation. Another way deception may creep into a study is misrepresenting to potential and actual study participants the purpose or nature of the study (Case 10.4). For example, Moeller, Mescher, More, and Shafer (1980a) compared campers' attitudes toward

pricing using formal and informal interviews (the latter were conducted using incognito interviewers who posed as campers). Guess what? Different answers were provided depending on whether the person was interviewed by an official interviewer or a supposed fellow camper. The deception used in this study was subsequently questioned (Christensen, 1980), and an ensuing controversy erupted (Moeller, Mescher, More, & Shafer, 1980b).

Some code of ethics, for instance, the American Psychological Association's, allow for such deceptive practices as concealed observation, when it is "necessary" for the research. For example, some social psychologists and psychologists maintain deception is needed when studying phenomena such as stereotyping and aggression. If participants in these situations are informed ahead of time about the true nature of the study, they will change their behavior and not act naturally. When deception is used, the expectation is study participants will be debriefed about the true nature of the research after the research study has been completed (Rosenthal & Rosnow, 2007).

Our position is that in the recreation, park, sport, and tourism fields deceiving people about the real purpose of the study is unacceptable. First, it is morally wrong to mislead people. Second, deceptive practices harm the reputation of reputable researchers and research in general.

Plagiarism. The most common mistake novice researchers make is failing to give proper credit for ideas or statements found in their research proposal or final report. The hallmark of research is building on the works of previous studies and the thoughts of others, but it is important to give credit where credit is due. In other words, avoid ***plagiarism*** (which incidentally comes from the Latin word meaning kidnapper), or intentionally or accidentally stealing another person's ideas or work and passing these as your own. Cite sources for any ideas or thoughts that are used.

> To appropriate the thoughts, ideas, or words of another—even if you paraphrase the borrowed ideas in your own language—without acknowledgement is unethical and highly circumspect. Honest researchers do not hesitate to acknowledge their indebtedness to others. (Leedy & Ormrod, 2012, p. 102)

Data sharing. Another ethical practice you should be cognizant of is ***data sharing***, or making data that has emerged from a study available, under certain conditions, to other investigators. Data sharing is an example of how the honesty principle is applied to research since it accentuates research being open and transparent, which are earmarks of scientific inquiry (see the Overview chapter).

Some organizations that fund research projects require data sharing. For example, the National Institutes of Health (see http://grants1.nih.gov/grants/policy/data_sharing/) and the National Science Foundation (http://www.nsf.gov/pubs/2001/gc101/gc101rev1.pdf, see Article 38) require that data from a study they fund be archived and made available to other scientists. When data are stored for this purpose, all identifiers must be removed.

Data sharing has become a global phenomenon. For instance, the Austrian government advocates that data generated from government-funded research be available for "sustained open access" (http://www.fwf.ac.at/en/public_relations/oai/index.html). In addition, the United Kingdom has set up a portal where researchers may deposit their data.

SOMETHING TO REMEMBER!

The UK Data Archive has been designated the Place of Deposit by the National Archives. Thus, it acquires, curates, and provides access to over 5,000 digital data collections covering social and economic topics. For more information, go to http://www.data-archive.ac.uk/home.

Likewise, individuals involved in gerontological research may deposit their findings with the National Archive of Computerized Data on Aging (http://www.icpsr.umich.edu/icpsrweb/NACDA/). This is the largest library of electronic data on aging in the United States.

Journal editors and colleagues may expect data sharing as well. For example, data sharing requests may emerge as part of the manuscript review process or years after publication of a study. Indeed, some journals and publishers, such as *The American Naturalist* and Royal Society of Publishing, expect authors to deposit their data into data deposit archive systems that have been set up for the soon-to-be published author. Incidentally, at this point, no refereed recreation, park, sport, or tourism journal has such a policy.

Likewise, colleagues may ask for a copy of a data set to review, confirm, or build upon the findings of the study. For instance, the National Science Foundation encourages data sharing to better support meta-analysis (Step 2). Nevertheless, at least one medical sociologist has questioned whether an initially obtained respondent consent counts as an ongoing "one-and-for-all" and extends to secondary data analysis (Grinyer, 2009).

Despite the existence of data sharing policies and expectations, data withholding happens. An author may fail to archive some or all of the data he or she collected. At other times, an investigator may simply refuse to share. Such refusals inevitably make you wonder whether the ethical principle of honesty has been breached or the person simply does not embrace the collegiality principle that often is found in professional codes of ethics.

Authorship credit. Finally, there is the matter of ***authorship credit***, or the designation of whose names go on the final research report or article. The stance of professional codes of conduct that address this point is to name someone as a coauthor who has significantly contributed to the write-up of the study. Individuals who assisted with data collection and/or data entry should be acknowledged in a footnote or acknowledgements section.

Related to authorship credit, avoid ghost authors or gift authors (Creswell, 2013). A ***ghost author*** is an individual who has made significant contributions to the research but has been omitted from the list of authors. For instance, sometimes graduate research assistants toil away on a project, only to be "forgotten" when the authors are listed in a manuscript or report. For a fascinating read about a ghost author, consult Peter Pringle's (2012) *Experiment Eleven*. The book recounts how streptomycin, the first antibiotic effective against tuberculosis, was discovered by a lab assistant, yet the lab director took full credit for the discovery even though he did not participate in the experiments that discovered the drug at all!

Likewise, do not practice gift authorship. A ***gift author*** is listing as an author a person who did not contribute to the research. For example, sometimes a new faculty member who is conducting a research project feels subtle pressure to list a senior faculty person who has not contributed to the research project on the final report.

SOMETHING TO REMEMBER!

According to the Institute of Medicine National Research Council (2002), the integrity of an individual research scientist embodies above all else a commitment to intellectual honesty and personal responsibility for his or her actions. Practices that define individual integrity include

- protection of human subjects in the conduct of research;
- intellectual honesty in proposing, performing, and reporting research;
- accuracy in representing contributions to research proposals and reports;
- fairness in peer review; and
- collegiality in scientific interactions, including communications and sharing of resources.

Justice

The ethics principle of ***justice*** has been defined as addressing fairness in receiving the benefits of research and accepting the risks (Cozby & Bates, 2011), or the fair, equitable, and appropriate treatment relative to what is owed to people (Sylvester, Voelkl, & Ellis, 2001). Justice comes into play when selecting study participants. In particular, equity must prevail, meaning any decisions to exclude or include certain people from a research study must be based on scientific merit. Therefore, if you use gender, age, ethnicity, sexual orientation, disability, social status, or any other characteristic to select or not select participants, you must have a legitimate scientific reason (Case 10.5).

Good research practice frequently requires adopting a design involving one or more control groups. But what happens when a program or treatment emerges as being beneficial to the experimental group members? Should people assigned to the no-treatment control group have equal access to the service or intervention offered to the experimental group (Case 10.6)? Legally, the answer hinges on whether a treatment is being offered for a life-threatening situation. In these situations, once data reveal that lives are being saved or even improved by the treatment, you must move control group members into the treatment group.

Competence

Finally, you are expected to be competent. ***Research competence*** means that an individual is qualified by training, qualifications, and experience to conduct the research study. Know your limitations, engage in continuous education activities, and seek assistance when necessary.

For instance, if your knowledge of statistics is restricted, as you design your research and develop a data management plan, consult with others who have expertise in this area. Likewise, if you plan to use measurement instruments that require special credentials (e.g., degree or license, certification, specialized training), attain these prerequisites or seek assistance from people who have these qualifications.

ETHICAL PRINCIPLES

Directions: Identify which ethical principle is being violated in each situation: beneficence, respect, honesty, justice, or competence.

Situation	Ethical principles violated
1. A camp director wants to determine how exercise affects the behavior of children attending his camp. The study is done without the parents' or children's' knowledge.	
2. As part of an experiment, children attending a camp are offered the opportunity to participate in novel yet physically demanding evening activities (e.g., hip-hop dance, Zumba classes). Only campers who are at the high end of normal weight are selected for these special night programs.	
3. During a focus group, feedback is given about the quality of hiking trails in a national park. The researcher feels some sentiments shared are biased and consequently omits them from her reporting.	
4. A college student is hired one summer to drop in unannounced at city pools and evaluate the performance of lifeguards as well as the cleanliness of operations.	
5. A faculty member asks students to answer 300 questions dealing with any recreation activities they may have ever tried. No known advantages for why students should complete the survey are made known to them.	

Note. Answers are provided at the end of the chapter.

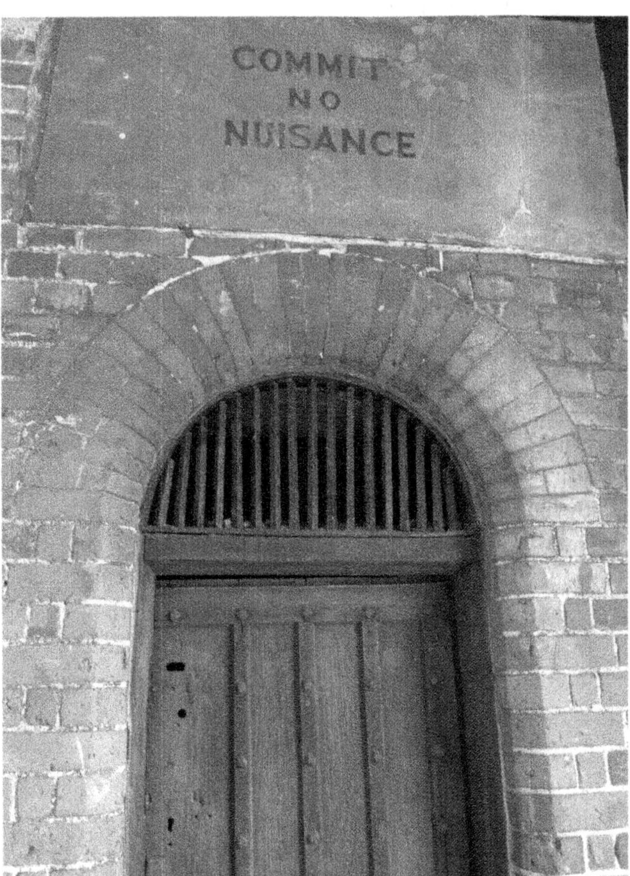

The photograph features a street from a town whose key industry in the 17th and 18th centuries was brewing. Perhaps the chiseled message was an effort to remind the citizenry of their moral duty and obligation? Amersham, England. Copyright © 2015 Carol Cutler Riddick.

REVIEW AND DISCUSSION QUESTIONS

1. Provide definitions for ethics, professional code of ethics, and research ethics.
2. Describe when an institutional review board needs to be established, and what its primary function is.
3. What is nonmaleficence? Identify four categories of maleficence risks you should minimize when conducting a study.
4. Distinguish between confidentiality and anonymity.
5. Explain beneficence. What are three types of beneficence that can be used in a study?
6. What does the ethical principal of respect encompass?
7. Identify three or more points that should be addressed in an informed consent form.
8. Define honesty and explain data falsification, misrepresentation, plagiarism, data sharing, and authorship.

9. Do you support deceiving study participants about the real purpose behind a research project? If so, what do you think are the allowable limits of deception? If not, why not?
10. Characterize how justice should prevail in a research study?
11. How do you define competence as it relates to individuals involved in conducting research?

YOUR RESEARCH

1. What are the ethical issues involved in your research project?
2. How will you ensure your research project will not violate the six ethical principles?
3. Draft a consent form for your research study. Before doing this, review "Tips on Informed Consent" at http://www.socialpsychology.org/consent.htm/. *Note:* The "United States Government Guidelines" offered in the first set of tips relate primarily to biomedical research, and the second set of tips is by the American Psychological Association (APA). The APA site also provides tips on developing a consent form for a Web-based study. Click on "Sample Consent Form" to view an example.

PRACTICE EXERCISES

1. Acquire a copy of the following article (or your instructor may substitute another article):

   Dattilo, J., Martire, L., & Proctor, D. (2012). B-Active: An interdisciplinary approach to healthy aging. *Therapeutic Recreation Journal, 6*, 191–201. You may access this article at http://js.sagamorepub.com/trj/article/view/2799.
   a. Which of the ethical principles—nonmaleficence, beneficence, respect, honesty, justice, competence—are not issues in this study?
   b. Which of the ethical principles appear to be an issue or problematic for this study?
   c. What actions did the investigators take to ensure that the ethical principles were not violated?
2. Search for research ethics in the news. Over a week or two, keep a scrapbook of newspaper clippings, magazine articles, research presentations, and television reports that deal with a research example of an ethical principle either upheld or breached. Organize the scrapbook according to the ethical principles outlined in this chapter. Use a selection of your scrapbook contents to contribute to class discussions.
3. For each of the following scenarios, decide whether the research is ethical. Identify the ethical principles that were violated. Discuss your decisions with classmates.

Worksheet Ethics Chapter: Which Ethical Principle Was Violated?

Scenario	Ethic principles violated?
1. Suppose you are interested in learning about conflict resolution strategies used when children play. You could obtain accurate information on this topic by hiding a video camera in a trashcan centrally located on the playground.	
2. Interviews on how boredom relates to drug use and abuse were conducted with a college class of 20 students. A detailed report on the findings was published. Even though fictitious names were used in the report, a majority of the 20 original study participants could read the report and identify to whom the report referred.	
3. A study was set up to identify what types of people were most likely to give money to a stranger at a jogging park. People at a public park were asked for money by an individual who said she had just lost her purse. No one was told that he or she was part of a research project.	
4. Suppose a beginning tennis instructor will give her students extra credit to be in a study. They are told the purpose of the study is to examine how well they serve and return a tennis ball throughout the semester. In truth, the students will be observed for frequency and intensity of losing their temper while playing tennis.	
5. As part of his thesis research, a graduate student was approved to survey students at his college. Random sampling was used to identify 200 individuals, who subsequently were invited to participate in the study. Over 3 days, the contacted individuals were supposed to stop by a table set up in the student union and complete a consent form and a 10-minute questionnaire. On the third day, only 35 students had completed the survey and the graduate student panicked. He walked around the student union pleading with people he saw to participate in the study. In the end, he wound up adding 40 volunteers to the database (or people he picked up walking through the student union).	
6. A recent recreation major graduate begins a new job at a health club. She has a black belt in karate. She proposes to her boss that she evaluate students in the beginning martial arts class she is teaching. She thinks class members will be willing to help her when informed she is undertaking a scientific study. She plans on providing each person with group results at the conclusion of the study. Her idea is to measure range of motion and hamstring flexibility. Through her reading, she found a way to measure each of these dependent variables using tests with which she was not familiar but appeared easy to administer.	
7. An in-home leisure education program is offered to older adults who had difficulty adjusting psychologically after a stroke. A randomized clinical trial design is used to conduct the study. That is, participants were assigned to either a 10-week experimental leisure education group or a 10-week placebo "friendly visit" group. Five weeks into the study, the first posttest was conducted, and it revealed that those receiving the leisure education program experienced a substantive and significant reduction in depression. The decision is made to continue the study for another 5 weeks.	

WEB EXERCISES

1. Visit the websites of two professional recreation, park, sport, or tourism organizations that have their code of ethics available online (for a listing of many of these organizations, see Table 1.1 in Step 1). Summarize one important point made at each site regarding research ethics.
2. Review the code of ethics for the following organizations serving professionals involved with research and evaluation. For each organization, identify one ethical behavior you find interesting.
   - The Canadian Evaluation Society: www.evaluationcanada.ca/site.cgi?s=5&ss=4&_lang=en.
   - The Australasian Evaluation Society: http://www.aes.asn.au/join-the-aes/membership-ethical-guidelines/7-aes-codes-of-behaviour-ethics.html and click on "Guidelines for the Ethical Conduct of Evaluations"
3. Review 10 scientific misbehaviors found in the following article:
   Martinson, B., Anderson, M., Crain, L., & De Vries, R. (2006). Scientists' perceptions of organizational justice and self-reported misbehavior. *Journal of Empirical Research on Human Research Ethics, 1*, 51–66. You may access this article at http://www.ncbi.nlm.nih.gov/pmc/articles/PMC1483900/.
   a. Based on your value system, identify the two worst misbehaviors committed by early and mid-career scientists.
   b. Identify two suggestions highlighted at the end of the article (in the Educational Implications section) you found most appealing for combating organizational injustices that foster ethical misbehaviors.
4. Read more about ethical issues by downloading N. Steneck's ORI Introduction to the *Responsible Conduct of Research* at http://ori.dhhs.gov/ori-intro (Office of Research Integrity, U.S. Department of Health and Human Services). Read the following parts and answer the posed question:
   a. Part III, Chapter 6, Data Management Issues: Identify two data management issues.
   b. Part III, Mentor and Trainee Responsibilities: Identify two mentor and trainee responsibilities.
   c. Part IV, Reporting and Reviewing Research: What are two things you learned?
5. Learn more about ethics of data handling and data ownership by consulting online tutorials offered on these topics by Northern Illinois University at http://ori.dhhs.gov/education/products/n_illinois_u/datamanagement/dmmain.html.

SERVICE LEARNING PROJECT

1. Do you anticipate needing IRB approval for the project? Visit your university/organization's website to learn when the IRB meets and the timelines for submitting materials for IRB review.
2. Does what you are proposing or contemplating comply with the doctrine of nonmaleficence? That is, minimal or no physical harm and/or psychological harm to study participants is expected? Loss of privacy? Loss of confidentiality?
3. Which categories of beneficence will you offer to study participants?
4. Do you need to develop an informed consent form? If so, draft one.
5. Are you mindful of ways you need to be honest, including avoiding plagiarism in the write-up of your proposal and/or final report?
6. Have you designed the project so justice prevails in terms of who is and who is not invited or tapped to become a study participant?
7. Do you possess the competencies to conduct the proposed service learning project, including having the requisite skills to collect, analyze, interpret data, and write and present the project and findings?

TEST YOURSELF ANSWERS

Nonmaleficence

1. Loss of confidentiality, 2. Physical harm and psychological harm, 3. Loss of privacy, 4. Physical harm and psychological harm

Ethical Principles

1. Respect, 2. Justice, 3. Honesty (data falsification), 4. Competency, 5. Beneficence (less tangible benefit)

SUPPORTING CASES FOR THIS CHAPTER

CASE 10.1. WHAT SOME PROFESSIONAL CODES OF ETHICS SAY ABOUT RESEARCH

American Anthropological Association

In obtaining informed consent and necessary permissions, "researchers must present to research participants the possible impacts of participation, and make clear that despite their best efforts, confidentiality may be compromised or outcomes may differ from those anticipated. These expectations apply to all field data, regardless of medium. Visual media in particular, because of their nature, must be carefully used, referenced, and contextualized" (Retrieved July 27, 2013, from http://www.aaanet.org/profdev/ethics/upload/Statement-on-Ethics-Principles-of-Professional-Responsibility.pdf).

American Association for Public Opinion Research

"We shall recommend and employ only those tools and methods of analysis that, in our professional judgment, are well suited to the research problem at hand... We shall not knowingly make interpretations of research results that are inconsistent with the data available... We shall not knowingly imply that interpretations should be accorded greater confidence than the data actually warrant." (Retrieved July 27, 2013, from http://www.aapor.org/AM/Template.cfm?Section=AAPOR_Code_of_Ethics&Template=/CM/ContentDisplay.cfm&ContentID=3142).

American Psychological Association

Regarding the principle of integrity, the American Psychological Association seeks "to promote accuracy, honesty and truthfulness...psychologists do not... cheat or engage in fraud, subterfuge or intentional misrepresentation of fact...In situations in which deception may be ethically justifiable to maximize benefits and minimize harm, psychologists have a serious obligation to consider the need for, the possible consequences of, and their responsibility to correct any resulting mistrust or other harmful effects that arise from the use of such techniques." (Retrieved July 27, 2013, from http://www.apa.org/ethics/code/index.aspx?item=3).

American Sociological Association

Regarding the principle of social responsibility, sociologists "are aware of their professional and scientific responsibility to the communities and societies in which they live and work ... When undertaking research, they strive to advance the science of sociology and to serve the public good." (Retrieved July 27, 2013, from http://www.asanet.org/about/ethics.cfm).

Association for Applied and Clinical Sociology

Regarding the principle of responsibility, "as scientists, sociological practitioners accept the ultimate responsibility for selecting appropriate topics and methods of research. We plan our research in ways to minimize the possibility that our findings will be misleading. We provide thorough discussion of the limitations of our data and alternative explanations, especially where our work touches on social policy" (Retrieved July 27, 2013, from http://sandy.canvasdreams.com/~aacsnefp/wp-content/uploads/2011/08/code-of-ethics-association-for-applied-and-clinical-sociology.pdf).

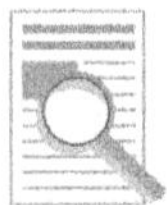

CASE 10.2. A CASE OF RESPECT?

Several years ago a state tourism agency mounted a television marketing campaign. Paddlers on scenic state waterways were filmed and aired as public service announcements. One clip showed a male and female adult paddling joyfully down a stream. The problem that arose was that the filmed couple was married but not to each other! Did the actions of the state tourism agency demonstrate respect to those who were clandestinely filmed?

CASE 10.3. SAMPLE INFORMED CONSENT FORM

Project Title: Effects of Animal-Assisted Therapy
Principal Investigator: Randi Baron-Leonard, CTRS
Address:
Phone:
Email:
Faculty Sponsor: Dr. Carol Cutler Riddick
Gallaudet University's Department of Physical Education and Recreation

I am a Masters' Candidate in the Department of Physical Education and Recreation at Gallaudet University. As part of my thesis, I'm evaluating an Animal-Assisted Therapy (AAT) program. I am a Deaf, Certified Therapeutic Recreation Specialist, who has advanced signing skills. I would like you to consider volunteering to be a study participant for this research project. You will be asked to:

1. Participate in eight AAT sessions, each lasting about one hour. During these organized recreational therapy programs you will be interacting with a dog. These sessions will be offered two or three times a week over a three to four week period.
2. Complete a questionnaire two times, once before the AAT program begins and again at the end of the eight sessions. The questionnaires ask about your experiences with pets, mood, and feedback about the AAT program. If needed, Randi Baron-Leonard will provide verbal instructions related to the questions appearing on the questionnaire. It should take about 15 minutes to complete each questionnaire.
3. Be videotaped at two of the AAT sessions. The videotapes will be used to record what happens during the group session. The videotape will be viewed by two raters and then the tape will be destroyed.

There is no more than low risk to individuals who participate in this study.

Please note that the answers you give on the questionnaires as well as the videotapes will be handled with confidentiality. If your data are used in a publication or presentation, your name, picture, or other identifying information will not be used. Once the questionnaires and videotapes have been analyzed, they will be destroyed.

Possible benefits from participating in this study include improved mood and improved social skills. You also would be contributing to our knowledge about the effectiveness of using AAT with individuals who are Deaf and have been hospitalized for a mental disorder.

Staff will also be asked to provide diagnoses for each person consenting to be in the research study. This information will only be used to describe the medical background of the study group.

Your participation in this study is voluntary. You will not receive any payment for participating in this study. You may withdraw from this study at any time, for any reason and without penalty. If you decide not to participate in the study or to withdraw from the study, it will not change your relationship to Gallaudet University or the Hospital.

Questions about the risk of participation in this study may be addressed to the researcher named at the top of this form or the Chairperson of the Gallaudet University's Institutional Review Board for the Protection of Human Subjects (phone 202.651.5400 [v/tty] or email irb@gallaudet.edu). If you should have any questions regarding your rights, contact Gay xxx at the Maryland Department of Mental Hygiene (phone 410.767.xxxx).

I have read the Informed Consent Form and agree to participate in the study Effects of Animal-Assisted Therapy by Randi Baron-Leonard.

Your Printed Name: ______________________________
Your Signature: ______________________________
Printed Name of Staff Witness: ______________________________
Signature of Staff Witness: ______________________________
Date: ______________________________

Note. As cited in Baron-Leonard (2004). To qualify for the study, the head of each patient's medical team had to attest the individual had no known allergies to dogs, was not fearful of dogs, and had no history of animal abuse. The animal used for the treatment was a certified therapy dog. Reprinted with permission of the authors.

CASE 10.4. A DECEPTIVE EXPERIMENT

Milgram, S. (1963). Behavioral study of obedience. *Journal of Abnormal and Social Psychology, 67*, 371–378.

The impetus for this and other related experiments was whether Nazi war criminals were just following orders. Milgram subsequently designed an experiment to find out whether people would be obedient to an authority figure in a lab setting. The subjects of the experiment were recruited to become "teachers" in a study that supposedly focused on learning.

The experiment consisted of three persons. Two of the persons were accomplices in the experiment: the primary investigator (a man in a white lab coat) and a "learner." The third person in the experiment was the "teacher," again, the real subject of the experiment. Forty men were recruited to participate in a "scientific study of memory and learning" that was being conducted at Yale University. These individuals were paid $4.50 to be in the experiment.

The "teacher" saw the "learner" being strapped into a chair that supposedly was set up to be able to deliver jolts of electricity. The experiment was really designed to test how far the "teacher" subject reacted to instructions from an authority figure (the "researcher" in the white lab coat) to administer seemingly increasing volts of electricity to the "learner" whenever he delivered wrong answers. The "researcher" sat in the same room as the "teacher." If the "teacher" objected, the "researcher" reminded him that he the "researcher" was in charge and they (the "teacher") should do as they were told. The "student" actor would react in audible signs of distress (that were prerecorded) and eventually bang on the wall complaining to stop the experiment and/or announce he was experiencing heart problems.

About two thirds (25 out of the 40 subjects tested) of the study participants complied with the authority figure. That is, they followed the "researcher's" instructions and administered what they thought was ever-increasing electric jolts, including beyond the clearly labeled *Danger Severe 420 Volts* up to the final *XXX 450 Volts* mark.

This study has been repeated many times in many countries, yielding essentially the same result, which is about two thirds of study participants comply with instructions from an authority figure. The experiment is controversial. Many feel the study was conducted in an unethical manner since "teacher" study participants were subjected or experienced physical and psychological abuse.

For footage of this original experiment go to http://www.youtube.com/watch?v=fCVlI-_4GZQ. To view a modern day replication study of this basic experiment, view one televised on ABC News *Primetime* at http://www.youtube.com/watch?v=HwqNP9HRy7Y.

CASE 10.5. A REPREHENSIBLE EXAMPLE OF INJUSTICE DONE IN THE NAME OF RESEARCH

Jones, J. (1993). *Bad blood: The Tuskegee syphilis experiment.* New York, NY: Free Press.

In 1932, 399 African Americans who had been imprisoned in Tuskegee, Alabama, were singled out and infected with syphilis. To track the long-term effects of the disease, medical treatment was withheld from these individuals for 40 years. The outrage that ensued over public exposure of this horrific experiment resulted in an overhaul of ethical regulations in medical and behavioral research.

CASE 10.6. YOU BE THE ETHICAL JUDGE

Riddick, C., Spector, S., & Drogin, E. (1986). The effects of video game play on the emotional states and affiliative behavior of nursing home residents. *Activities, Adaptation and Aging, 8*, 95–107.

In the following description of a study, what ethical principle has been violated?

Researchers examined whether video game play would improve, among other things, the affiliative behavior of nursing home residents. The research experiment was structured so two nursing homes were involved in the study. Ten volunteers from one nursing home (the experimental group) played PacMan three times a week for up to 3 hours per session for 6 weeks. Twelve volunteers from a second nursing home (the control group) were not offered any opportunity to play video games.

By comparing changes in the pre- and posttest scores of the two groups, the study found that the video game players experienced a significant positive change in their affiliative behaviors. Apparently, the stimulation of playing PacMan triggered social interaction. For example, several players were overheard saying, "Help! That pink critter is out to get me. What can I do?" (p. 105).

Did the researchers acted fairly by withholding the treatment from the control group? If you think not, you've earned an *A*.

In actuality, the researchers were sensitive to upholding the ethical principle of justice. In fact, nursing home residents were recruited with the promise all study participants eventually would be offered the opportunity to learn how to play a video game (which is technically known as a ***wait-list control group***). At the conclusion of the study, as originally promised, the video game equipment was made available to residents in the second home, the control group, for 6 weeks.

Every day, an average of more than 86,000 passengers ride more than 300 Amtrak trains in the U.S. To offer this service, the company has to secure elaborate permission arrangements with freight railway companies to travel on 21,300 miles of route. Normally, seeking permission to conduct a research project is not as complicated as what Amtrak encounters (thank goodness)! Copyright © 2015 Ruth V. Russell.

SEEK PROPOSAL APPROVAL

WHAT WILL I LEARN IN THIS CHAPTER?

I'll be able to...

1. Define what a proposal is and provide examples of entities that may need to be involved in a proving a proposal.
2. Distinguish between an expedited review and a nonexpedited review completed by an institutional review board.
3. Explain the difference between proposal writing styles: objective style, informal style, technical jargon style, and blended style.
4. Identify three writing and grammar mistakes frequently made when writing a proposal.
5. Recall headings typically appearing in a written proposal.
6. Describe how the three major categories that appear in a line-item budget are calculated: personnel (including explaining full-time equivalent and fringe benefits), other direct costs, and indirect costs.

"You create your opportunities by asking for them."

Patty Hansen
(American author and contributor to *Chicken Soup for the Soul* and other books)

Research projects require permission before you may conduct them. This usually requires preparing a ***proposal***, a preliminary plan that contains information on what you will study, why the selected topic is important to study, and how you will conduct the study. Think of it as a road map to the research process that others could follow to conduct the project themselves.

A written proposal serves as an agreement between you—the researcher—and other invested and interested parties. For example, proposals signal your intentions to agency staff, committees, review boards, and external funding groups. Using the proposal, these gatekeepers judge the adequacy and usefulness of the planned study. These checks and balances promote implementation of useful scientific research and ensure study participants will not be harmed. Seeking and attaining these approvals is good for recreation, park, sport, and tourism professions.

To assist you with learning more about how to secure approval for a research proposal, this chapter is divided into four parts. Read on to learn about approval entities, proposal language and writing styles, proposal content, and a checklist for judging the worthiness of a proposal.

APPROVAL ENTITIES

In seeking approval for a study, first identify whose permission is required. Even though recreation, park, sport, and tourism enterprises often are public, you should seek and acquire approval to conduct research in these areas from the relevant authorities. In fact, never collect data without permission from them, even if you are sure it is forthcoming at any moment (Case 11.1).

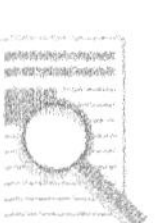

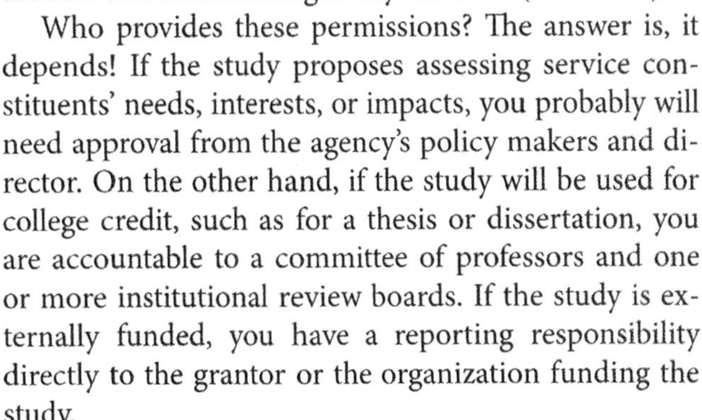

Who provides these permissions? The answer is, it depends! If the study proposes assessing service constituents' needs, interests, or impacts, you probably will need approval from the agency's policy makers and director. On the other hand, if the study will be used for college credit, such as for a thesis or dissertation, you are accountable to a committee of professors and one or more institutional review boards. If the study is externally funded, you have a reporting responsibility directly to the grantor or the organization funding the study.

Study Site

Even if your study will assess a program for an organization for which you work, you still need to clear data collection methods and procedures with your supervisors. If you will conduct the study in an organization other than your own, contact the appropriate officials for permission as early as possible. If the research is being conducted in a public place, obtain approval from the appropriate government agencies. For instance, if you are surveying visitors to a public garden, obtain prior approval from the organization that manages the garden. If you are doing an observation study, especially on public property (e.g., a park), inform the police who have jurisdiction in the area. That way, if someone contacts them about you or your study, these entities already know what is happening.

Thesis or Dissertation Committee

Most universities require a faculty member to supervise student research. For example, if you are conducting a study as part of a course requirement, the course instructor likely will be your supervisor. On the other hand, if a study fulfills a degree requirement for a master's or doctoral degree, you decide who serves on your committee.

To begin, identify a faculty member to serve as chair of the thesis or dissertation committee. The ***chair*** serves as a ***mentor*** or study advisor and is "...a person of competence who instructs a less experienced person in an area of mutual interest" (Mauch & Park, 2003, p. 43). You will work closely with your chair throughout the research process.

Therefore, identify a chair who can provide the skills and knowledge needed to support your research project. In choosing this person, remember that the chair serves the following roles (Polonsky & Waller, 2010):

1. Information source. Your chair should have research experiences and skills to assist you in completing your project. Essentially this individual is instructing you as you learn how to plan and conduct research.
2. Sounding board. You should be able to use your chair as a reviewer who helps you to think and write more clearly. This person evaluates your research and provides timely and useful feedback, keeping you on track.
3. Motivator. Your chair should inspire you to complete the project. Take notes when you meet with your chair, complete with dates, issues discussed, and tasks you have agreed to complete. This log will help you see your progress and keep you motivated.
4. Approval authority. Your chair tells you when you are ready to convene a proposal meeting. He or she also is responsible for issuing a grade for your research project and authorizing your graduation. In some universities, before a grade will be issued, student-conducted research projects also must be examined by people external to the university, such as field professionals.

Besides the committee chair, three to five other professors serve on a thesis or dissertation committee. The purpose of the committee is to further guide the student researcher. Approval of the proposal is also discussed at a proposal meeting.

Before collecting data, hold a formal ***proposal meeting*** with the chair and committee to discuss the merits of the proposal and seek permission to execute the study in the manner outlined in the proposal. At a proposal meeting, members of a thesis or dissertation committee usually determine the following points (Mauch & Park, 2003):

- Is the study topic suitable?
- Is the study appropriate for the student's major?
- Will the study contribute to the literature and/or professional practice?
- Does the student have the capabilities to complete the study?
- Is the study manageable in terms of how much time the student has to complete the work?

Tables 11.1 and 11.2 have tips for experiencing a successful proposal meeting.

Institutional Review Board

In the United States, Canada, and other countries, governmental regulations require universities, hospitals, and other organizations receiving federal funding to establish review boards for research involving human subjects. These ***institutional review boards*** (IRB) are another common approval authority for studies.

The overall responsibility of IRBs is to determine whether the researcher is treating study participants ethically. The criteria used by IRBs in reviewing research proposals seek to determine that

- risks to research study participants are minimal,
- benefits of participating in the study are greater than the risks,
- vulnerable populations (e.g., children, institutionalized individuals) are selected and dealt with sensitively, and
- participants are extended the right to informed consent.

The timeliness of submitting a proposal to an IRB is important. For example, you should learn how far in advance a proposal needs to be received to be considered at an upcoming IRB meeting. Also, depending on the nature of the study, the approval of more than one IRB may be required. For example, Baron-Leonard

Table 11.1
Tips for Preparing for a Proposal Meeting

1. Allow for plenty of lead-in time before a proposal meeting. Check with your committee members on how much time they need to read your proposal. This may vary; some members may request receiving the proposal 3 days in advance of the meeting and others may insist on a 1-month lead time.
2. If permissible, sit in on another person's proposal meeting beforehand. If this is possible, you will gain firsthand experience of what transpires at these meetings. Hopefully, you will become reassured that these meetings are not a "David meeting Goliath" encounter.
3. Conduct a rehearsal. Reread your proposal, making sure you understand every word and sentence you wrote. Anticipate the most difficult questions you can imagine, and make sure you can deliver a brief and clear answer.
4. During the meeting, take notes of requested changes. At the end of the meeting, to make sure no misunderstandings have occurred, summarize the suggested changes.
5. Understand how proposal committee meetings are conducted. Meetings usually begin with a summary presentation, followed by questions from the committee for you to answer. When committee members have finished questioning, you will be excused. Then, each committee member is polled about the proposal and asked to reject, approve with conditions, or approve unconditionally. Do not be surprised if changes are suggested. This is the norm! Once the committee has made a decision, you will be called back into the room, and the chair will report the committee's decision. You will meet with the chair afterward to review revisions suggested in the meeting.
6. Finally, sleep well the night before the meeting. You have worked hard, so do not worry. Be confident yet humble.

Table 11.2
Handling Questions at a Proposal Meeting

When presenting a proposal, you may experience perplexing questions. The secret to success? Think before you respond. Organize your thoughts and answer questions as directly and simply as possible. If the questioner is long-winded, take notes on what is being asked. You also may find the following strategies for replying helpful:

- Responding to a question you do not understand: "I'm sorry. I don't get what you're asking. Would you mind restating your question or point?"
- Responding to a question when you do not know the answer: "I've never thought about this point. What do you think?" or "I'm sorry. I don't know the answer to the question." or "I don't know the answer. Will someone help me out?"
- Handling a disagreement among those in attendance: "I'm lost now. I hear different advice. I'd appreciate it if we could spend a few minutes trying to reach an agreement about what I'm being asked to do or change."
- Responding to biting criticism: "I did what I thought was best or warranted. Now I understand what I did was wrong, and I appreciate you correcting me."
- Wrapping up the proposal meeting: "Thank you all for taking the time to read and respond to the proposal. You've given me good constructive criticism. I'd appreciate receiving the written comments you made on my proposal, and I will earnestly try to address every concern raised."

(2004) needed months to obtain approval from a university IRB, a state hospital IRB (that hosted the intervention designed for the study), and a state department of mental health that governed the hospital involved in the study.

IRB reviews may be expedited and nonexpedited. The IRB chair determines whether the research proposal qualifies as an expedited or nonexpedited review.

Expedited review. An ***expedited review*** occurs when the proposed study does not present more than minimal risk to human subjects and does not involve vulnerable populations or novel or controversial interventions or data collection techniques. Studies using educational tests, surveys, interviews, or observation of public behavior typically are expedited reviews and require only written approval from the IRB chair.

Nonexpedited review. A ***nonexpedited review*** occurs when vulnerable subjects or controversial interventions or data collection techniques are proposed. A study involving institutionalized individuals automatically triggers a nonexpedited review and requires a full IRB meeting with a quorum of members present. A majority of those members present at the meeting must approve the proposal.

Funding Sponsors

Often individual researchers and leisure service organizations cannot afford to pay for an evaluation project from their own budgets. The expenses associated with conducting a study may necessitate finding a funding sponsor (Case 11.2).

Many universities have a small grants program supporting student research. Additional funding sources for studies in recreation, parks, sport, and tourism include foundations, government agencies, and corporations.

Grant support may range from a few hundred dollars, to thousands of dollars, to hundreds of thousands of dollars. To be eligible for support, be sure to follow guidelines issued by the funding sources regarding the content and timing of submission.

SOMETHING TO REMEMBER!

Many foundations use a two-stage grant application process. The first stage involves sending a ***prospectus***, essentially a preproposal, usually no more than three pages, that provides an overview of the proposed study.

Make sure you adhere to submission requirements, to the letter. Foundations, and for that matter federal government agencies, receive hundreds if not thousands of prospectus submissions. An easy way for reviewers to narrow the list is to reject those that do not follow submission directions and guidelines.

If the foundation is interested in your idea contained in the prospectus, you will be invited to submit a full-fledged, detailed proposal. This is the second stage. In most cases, if you have been invited to submit a full-fledged proposal, you may have a short time to turn materials in, anywhere from 1 to 2 months.

Often, multiple external funding sources are used to fund a research study. For example, the After School Alliance Organization (2011) reviewed evaluations that have been completed on after-school programs and found these programs have been funded by the federal government, state governments, and private foundations (e.g., the Charles Stewart Mott Foundation, the William T. Grant Foundation, and the Wallace Foundation).

FINDING A FUNDING SOURCE

To find research funding sources, ask other professionals or a university grants office for leads. Also, in the United States, you may read government-issued ***requests for proposals*** (often referred to as RFPs) in the *Federal Register*, consult foundation directory references available in libraries, and read the acknowledgements in a research report or journal article. Additionally, commercial services exist, including Community of Science (http://pivot.cos.com/), that track federal, foundation, private, and other funding opportunities.

Specialized funding sources also are available. For example, the Robert Wood Johnson Foundation supports promising new ideas that are designed to reduce childhood obesity. Additionally, it promotes active living research aimed at identifying environmental factors and policies that may increase levels of physical activity, especially among children and families in low-income areas. For details, visit http://www.rwjf.org/.

If you are interested in outdoor recreation research, check out Mazamas (http://mazamas.org/index.php/resources/research-grants/). Mazamas (a Native American term for mountain goat) is a nonprofit mountaineering organization that provides research grants relating to wilderness and the mountain environment (including research promoting the enjoyment and safety of outdoor recreation). The Graduate Student Grant program awards master's and doctoral candidates up to $2,000 for field studies, whereas faculty research is funded up to $3,500.

Still, another research funding source (up to $500) for professionals and students in the field of outdoor recreation and education is sponsored by the Association of Outdoor Recreation and Education. Research grant monies may be used to conduct empirical studies, analyze secondary data sources, and develop new theories. For more information, visit http://www.aore.org/assets/association%20of%20outdoor%20recreation%20and%20education_final.pdf.

PROPOSAL LANGUAGE AND WRITING STYLE

The following language and writing styles are appropriate for the research proposal (Gratton & Jones, 2010):

1. Objective style. The writing has a business or scientific-like tone, devoid of humor and personal pronouns.
2. Informal style. The writing tone conveys information in an unpretentious manner.
3. Technical jargon style. The information is presented in a detailed and exhaustive format using academic language.
4. Blended style. The writing style is a mix objective and informal.

The style you use depends upon the audience for the research proposal. If the project is needed to satisfy a degree requirement, the convention is to use objective and/or technical jargon language typically adhering to the American Psychological Association's (2010) *Publication Manual.* Conversely, if the proposal is for laypeople, such as a recreation board of directors, a style that reflects a blend of objective and informal writing is more desirable.

SOMETHING TO REMEMBER!

One popular style manual adopted by many professional journals and universities is the American Psychological Association's (APA, 2010) *Publication Manual.* Frequently asked questions related to APA style are available at http://www.apa.org/ (select "APA Style" and then "Quick Answers-References," "Quick Answers-Formatting," and "Most Popular-The Basics of APA Style" and "APA Style: Learning APA Style").

You also may find the following APA style resources helpful: the abbreviated version of the *Publication Manual, Concise Rules of APA Style* (http://www.apastyle.org/products/4210004.aspx); the University of Wisconsin–Madison's *The Writer's Handbook* (that covers, among other topics, improving writing style, grammar and punctuation, and citing references; http://writing.wisc.edu/Handbook/); and Perrla APA software (http://www.perrla.com/APADetails.aspx?gclid=CNaOxo_f3bgCFcie4AodvUUA-g), which details entering references using APA style guidelines within the body and the reference section of a paper, thesis, or dissertation.

SOMETHING TO REMEMBER!

The following blunders are frequently made when writing a proposal. (*Note:* For some of these rules, an APA, 2010, reference marker has been noted parenthetically.)

1. Writing a one-sentence paragraph. A paragraph must, at a minimum, contain at least two sentences.
2. Failure to seek copyright permission. Permission must be secured to use quotations of 50 or more words and for tables and figures that someone else developed. Permission often requires paying the copyright source a fee.
3. Not knowing the difference between the Latin abbreviations *i.e.* and *e.g.* The former means *that is*, and the latter means *for example*. A period follows each letter and a comma appears after the second period. (Chapter 4)
4. Not knowing when to spell out a number or record it numerically. Numbers less than 10 are spelled out and numbers 10 and higher are written numerically. The following sentence is an example: There were 25 study participants, all of whom were eighth grade students. (Chapter 4)
5. References used in the text do not show up in the References section, and vice versa. Sit down and go page by page through your proposal, checking off references as they are encountered in the References section. Also, make sure the spelling of reference names in the text corresponds to what appears in the References section. Ditto with the year of the cited publication. The year in text should match the year in the References section.
6. Not knowing when to use an ampersand (&) in a reference. The rule is, if two or more authors are cited in the ***running text*** or narrative (body of the text), you need to join the authors by the word *and*. If the authors are cited parenthetically in the text (inside parentheses), connect authors' names with the ampersand. In the References section, two or more authors are joined together by an ampersand. (Chapter 6)

PROPOSAL CONTENT

Writing a research proposal is a time-consuming and difficult task. To assess your readiness to write a proposal, ask yourself these questions:

- Have I read extensively on my topic?
- Do I understand what I must include to obtain approval for the proposed study?
- Have I set time aside on a daily, or almost daily, basis to work on the proposal?
- Am I motivated to complete the research study?

GETTING THE MOST OUT OF YOUR WRITING SESSIONS

1. Begin writing sooner rather than later. Many proposal writers find it helpful to start with the Purpose Statement section, followed by the Introduction and Literature Review sections.
2. Keep a research diary. Record ideas and questions you have about the proposal as soon as you have them. As you review these notes later, the answers may become evident, or you will be prepared to ask for your advisor's or chair's advice.
3. Recognize your writing habits. What time of day and in what location do you prefer to write? How can you minimize distractions? Do you need to turn off Instant Messenger and post a sign on your door that says "DO NOT Disturb. Writer at Work!"?
4. Follow a routine. Know your getting started rituals: rearranging your desk, sharpening your pencils, pouring yourself a cup of tea, or whatever. If you need these prewriting rituals, allow for them.
5. If you are stalled and have been working for a while, take a break. Before the break, jot a note to yourself about what you are getting hung up on, and if you are still stalled after the break, discuss the issue with someone whose advice you value.
6. Cover the basics and then go back and tighten up. Analogous to putting a new grill together, you first need to have everything in place before you tighten things down. When you think the content is okay, edit and edit some more.
7. Proofread your work. Use the spelling and grammar check tool on your computer software with caution. For example, one student wrote a proposal for a study on pheasant hunting. The trouble was that the writer mistakenly used the word *pheasant* throughout, and since peasant appeared in the word processing dictionary, the student submitted a proposal about peasant hunting for review.
8. Plan on many revisions. A good proposal will not be written after one, two, or three efforts. A novice researcher may write 10 or more proposal drafts, so allow plenty of time for writing and revising. As well, to save frustration in the long run, date each revision.
9. Always have three updated backups of your text file. Two of the proposal backups should be on separate hard drives. At least one copy should be on a portable device, such as a flash drive, CD, or floppy disk.
10. Set up achievement milestones, and reward yourself for accomplishing them. If you feel you have made significant gains in the writing, such as completing the first draft to the Introduction section, celebrate! Go on a hike, invite friends over for a potluck dinner, or participate in a recreational activity you find gratifying.

Proposals often have common ingredients. Research proposals, however, differ from final research reports in that some information you expect in a final report is not initially presented in the proposal (see Table 11.3).

Table 11.3
Outline of Typical Headings in a Proposal

Heading	Contained in proposal
Title page	√
Abstract/executive summary	
Acknowledgements	
Table of contents	√
List of figures, tables, and appendices	√
Introduction	√
Theoretical foundations	√
Research question and/or hypothesis	√
Literature review	√
Methods	√
Results	
Discussion	
Conclusions	
Recommendations	
References	√
Appendices	√

Note. The final research report contains information on all points of this table.

Regardless of how you organize the proposal content, clearly delineate the sections. Table 11.4 displays the format for headings and subheadings per the APA (2010) *Publication Manual.*

The content and organization of the proposal may be dictated by the group or organization receiving or sponsoring the research. For instance, foundations and government agencies typically require a proposal to contain a line-item budget and vitae of the primary investigators. Thus, prior to writing, find out the requirements for content and presentation style.

Table 11.4
Headings and Subheadings for a Research Proposals/Reports According to the American Psychological Association (2010)

Level of heading	Format
1	**Centered, Boldface, Uppercase and Lowercase Heading**
2	**Flush Left, Boldface, Uppercase and Lowercase Heading**
3	**Indented, boldface, lowercase paragraph heading ending with a period.**
4	***Indented, boldface, italicized, lowercase paragraph heading ending with a period.***
5	*Indented, italicized, lowercase paragraph heading ending with a period.*

Title Page

The title page should contain certain information. Listed in order of appearance, the following information is placed on a title page:

- Descriptive title. The title should identify the major variables examined by the study and the study population. The trick is to use a title that is concise yet informative (Case 11.3).

- Name of ***principal investigator*** (PI) or person who will be leading the research project or team.
- Organizational affiliation of the PI.
- Date proposal was submitted or distributed.

Table of Contents

This section is an overview of how the proposal is organized. List the major headings and subheadings used in the proposal along with the respective page numbers. Having a table of contents may immensely help a reader who wants to revisit a particular section.

Lists of Figures, Tables, and Appendices

Incorporate figures and tables into your proposal. Why? They provide mental relief to reading only narrative and provide a quick way to present or summarize information. Following the table of contents, create lists for figures, tables, and appendices. Note page numbers for each figure, table, and appendix.

Introduction

Introductory paragraphs should provide background on the topic of the study. Although all parts of the proposal are important, the introduction sets the stage and tone of the study for the reader. Open with a statement about real people as opposed to referring to the work of others or statements dealing with past research. Also, the introduction provides a logical transition into the study itself. Include the following information in the introduction:

- background about the problem being investigated,
- definitions of key concepts and variables,
- purpose statement (Step 4), and
- explanation of the significance of the study (Step 5).

Theoretical Foundation

Include information about the theoretical bases of the study (Step 3) in the proposal. Identify how the theoretical foundation relates to the concepts and the data collection methods.

Purpose Statement, Research Questions, and/or Hypotheses

Write a purpose statement (sometimes referred to as a problem statement) for every research proposal. Likewise, include a research question for every research proposal. If you adopt a quantitative approach, you can either identify a research question(s) and/or hypotheses. If you use a qualitative approach or triangulation, state the research questions guiding the study.

Literature Review

As discussed in Step 2, this section presents a review and appraisal of previously completed studies that relate to your topic. At this proposal stage, the literature review is brief (e.g., three to four pages). When readers finish reading the review of literature, they should see a logical link between the literature presented and the objectives of your study.

Methods

The Methods section details how you will conduct the study. To help the reader follow the discussion, and as demonstrated in the following discussion, use subheadings for the subcomponents.

Research design and study participants. This subsection identifies the research design that you will use for the study and the study participants expected (Steps 6 and 7). If you are conducting a survey, present the sampling that you will use to identify potential respondents, the number of persons that you will contact, and the rationale for how you identified your desired sample size.

EASILY CONFUSED WORDS AND COMMON GRAMMAR "MISTEAKS"

Good writing requires practice. All of you have committed writing mistakes, some of which in retrospect you now can laugh about! Below are common "misteaks."

Term or phrase to avoid	Why you should not use
Bad, Good, Ideal	Judgments should not be stated in formal writing.
Perfect	Nothing is!
Today	Today is tomorrow's yesterday!
Soon	A relative term ... tomorrow, next year, in 5 years?
He was surprised to learn ...	To be understood, a pronoun (such as *he* or *she*) must refer clearly to a single nearby antecedent; otherwise, the reader does not understand to whom the word *he* or *she* refers
Seems or Seemingly	It does not matter how something appears!
Kind of, Lots, Lots of	Vague and colloquialisms
A number of...	Vague
Obviously or Clearly	Really, obvious and clear to everyone?
Must or Always	Absolute terms.
Few or Most	Be precise, these are relative terms!
Can or May	Don't confuse these words. *Can* denotes ability, whereas *may* is used when seeking permission.

Note. Adapted from "How to Write," n.d.

For qualitative studies, another point to be made in this section is to acknowledge how the investigator's biases might affect the study. This is known as ***reflectivity*** (Case 11.4).

Intervention. This subsection appears only if you are involved with evaluative research or a program evaluation study. If so, provide a program description or information on program objectives, the content of the program, programming process, and length of each program session and the entire program.

Instrumentation. For a quantitative study, this subsection of the Methods section identifies every instrument to be used to measure each independent and dependent variable. If adopting an existing instrument, name and reference the tool and identify the number of items. If you are measuring any of the variables by an instrument you are devising, explain how you developed the instrument and provide a copy in the appendix. In either case, provide information on the validity and reliability of the instrument, coding of responses, and theoretical range of scores.

The details provided for the Instrumentation section of a qualitative study will depend on the data collection tool used. The main goal is to write a description detailing the open-ended questions you will use in the unstructured interview, the research questions you will pose to the focus group, the observation recording sheet you will use in the observation, and/or how you will perform the content analysis for a record review.

Data collection. This subsection begins, if relevant, with a statement of intent to apply for IRB approval. A copy of the informed consent you plan to use should appear in the appendix.

You also need to outline details on the content and timing of communications with potential study recruits, with copies of the exact wording you plan to use in these contacts appearing in the appendix. If you are conducting survey research and are using a variation of the total design method (reviewed in Step 9), identify the intended dates of your follow-ups and provide copies of the appeals in the appendix.

Additionally, present information on your data collection procedures (e.g., the questionnaire will be distributed in a group setting, through postal mail, or over the Web) and when data will be collected (e.g., playground observations will be made the first workday week in October, during the hours of 9 a.m. to 3 p.m.; see Step 9). Include forms that you will use for data collection purposes in the appendix.

Data analyses. Present information on the statistical analysis tools that will examine each research question and hypothesis used in a quantitative study and/or the data analysis schema for interpreting each research question in a qualitative study. Advance planning is important because if you give little or no thought to data analysis until after the information is gathered, you may discover that analyzing it in the way you wish is impossible.

Limitations. Shortcomings in research are sometimes identified in the proposal stage as a subsection of the Methods section. ***Limitations*** may affect the study adversely (Mauch & Park, 2003) and may stem from sources such as the theoretical approach, sampling, research design, instrumentation, data collection, and/or data analyses of the study (see Steps 3, 6–9, and 14).

Time budget. Sometimes inclusion of a ***time budget*** in the proposal may be beneficial, especially when the proposed study is going to be executed by other professional staff within an organization. A time budget projects clock and calendar time needed to complete specified tasks for conducting a study. You may create a time budget by using a person-loading chart and a Gantt chart (see Step 13).

Financial budget. If a budget is needed for a study, you may prepare a ***line-item budget***. Figure 11.1 illustrates a line-item budget used by a student to solicit extra funding from a university to support his thesis. Funding organizations, such as the federal government, may require a ***narrative budget***, which describes how you will spend the funds requested for each line item and how you determined the amount.

Typically, direct costs and indirect costs are the major parts to a research budget. ***Direct costs*** may be broken down into personnel and nonpersonnel expenses. When personnel costs are identified in a budget as a direct cost, the norm is to list the base salary of each person needed in the project and then identify the percentage of time or effort that individual will devote to the project, or the ***full-time equivalency*** (FTE). FTEs are noted in decimal form. For instance, if .25 is the FTE for the principal investigator, he or she is expected to devote 25% (or 10 hours per week) of full-time effort toward the research project.

Another important component of personnel costs is fringe benefits, the collection of benefits other than wages or a salary provided by an employer. ***Fringe benefits*** cover items such as health insurance, social security, workers' compensation, disability insurance, group term life insurance, retirement or pension fund (e.g., 401[k] plan), and other benefits provided to employees. The U.S. Office of Management and Budget, Circular A-21, *Cost Principles for Educational Institutions*, identifies allowable direct cost categories (http://www.whitehouse.gov/omb/circulars_a021_2004).

A percentage of a person's salary is used to calculate fringe benefits. The applicable fringe benefit rate is negotiated between each university or organization and the federal government. The rate varies among institutions. For example, the negotiated rate for Gallaudet University is in line with what other institutions use (A. Foster, personal communication, August 1, 2013). That is, the rate used for calculating the fringe benefits depends on whether the faculty or staff member is working part time or full time. The fringe benefit rates for part-time and full-time workers are 23.59% and 28.5%, respectively. Unless prohibited by the sponsor, anticipate that fringe benefits are normally projected to increase at a rate between 0.5% and 1.0% each project year.

Budgets submitted for funding consideration by other organizations also include facilities and administration costs. These ***indirect costs*** are overhead expenses such as building maintenance (e.g., custodial services), utilities, and miscellaneous supplies purchased in bulk (e.g., paper, pens).

The indirect cost rate used by a university or organization also is negotiated with the federal government. Federally negotiated indirect cost rates, used for research conducted at most institutions of higher education, hospitals, and research centers, is about 44% of the salaries and wages for personnel involved in the research project (cf. Circular A-21). Most nonprofit organizations, such as foundations, do not reimburse direct and indirect costs at federally negotiated rates.

References

References, or citations appearing in the proposal, must be alphabetized in the References section. The way in which cited references are formatted will depend on the style manual you have adopted. As well, your instructor or organization may provide examples of a preferred reference list format.

Appendices

Appendices are used to present information dealing with technical details, such as informed consent forms; copies of correspondence; and copies of interview schedules, questionnaire or observation instruments, and directions to interviewers. Cite appendices you include at the end of the proposal in the text.

CALCULATING A RESEARCH BUDGET

Directions: Suppose your university president has asked that your upper level research class design, implement, and then report on students' impressions and ideas on how to improve the recreational sport program. The research class will design, pilot, and then send a survey to students via their university e-mail account. Information you need to know to prepare the budget is presented below. Complete the budget using the template provided.

Budget period: From month/day/year to month/day/year
Grant period: From month/day/year to month/day/year
PROJECT YEAR 1 2 3 4 5 (Circle)

	Base salary	FTE	Total
I. PERSONNEL			
Principal investigator	______	______	______
Project staff	______	______	______
Administrative staff	______	______	______
Other staff	______	______	______
Fringe Benefits (@ ___%)			______
SUBTOTAL			______
II. OTHER DIRECT NONPERSONNEL COSTS			
Office operations (phone, supplies, etc.)			______
Communications/ marketing			______
Equipment			______
Travel expenses			______
Other			______
SUBTOTAL			______
III. INDIRECT COSTS (@ _____%)			______
GRAND TOTAL			______

Figure 11.1. Sample line-item budget for an evaluation project.

Background

The instructor for the research methods class will serve as principal investigator (PI). She earns $100,000 per year (or $10,000 per month since she is on a 10-month appointment). The PI projects needing to devote 10% of her time over 16 weeks to supervise the research project.

The instructor will hire one student to be a research assistant. This student serves as a program liaison to the recreational sport program and the class. The person hired will work on the project 8 hours per week for 15 weeks and will be paid $12 per hour.

Given a known student body size of 10,000, 370 students will be randomly selected to receive a Web-based survey. As an incentive, 40 students from among those responding to the survey will be selected randomly to receive a $10 gift card that they may use at the university's bookstore.

Template

I. PERSONNEL	Base salary	FTE	Total
Position			
PI	____	____	____
Research assistant	____	____	____
Fringe benefits (@ 23.5%)	____	____	____
SUBTOTAL			____
II. OTHER DIRECT NONPERSONNEL COSTS			
Gift Card			____
SUBTOTAL			____
III. INDIRECT COSTS (@ 44% rate)			____
GRAND TOTAL			____

Note. Answers are provided at the end of the chapter.

JUDGING THE PROPOSAL

A written research proposal should be used to gather constructive feedback on the adequacy of a study. In addition to the required approving entities who will judge your study via the proposal, you may determine the strengths and weaknesses of the proposal yourself.

Review Table 11.5 prior to submitting your proposal. You also could ask mentoring colleagues to use this checklist for providing feedback on a proposal draft. Remember, every study has its shortcomings; the concern is whether fatal flaws exist that will call into question the credibility and usefulness of study findings.

Approval is a part of daily life. For example, these marchers seek wage and pension reforms from the British Parliament. Researchers also have to secure approval for their studies from entities such as overseersof a study site, an institutional review board, and/or a funding authority. Theatre District, London, England. Copyright © 2015 Carol Cutler Riddick.

Table 11.5
Checklist for Judging a Proposal

INTRODUCTION

[ ] Beginning paragraphs provide a logical transition to the study.
[ ] Study purpose is clearly stated.
[ ] Purpose or problem is researchable.
[ ] Key concepts and variables have been defined.
[ ] Study population is identified.
[ ] What is being proposed is reasonable.
[ ] Study is significant; results will (a) be used by practitioners, (b) address a social problem, and/or (c) contribute to a body of knowledge.

THEORETICAL FOUNDATION

[ ] Acknowledgement of the theoretical approach of the study.
[ ] Mixed-methods approach adopted is described if applicable.
[ ] Theoretical framework is identified.

Table 11.5 (cont.)

PURPOSE STATEMENT, RESEARCH QUESTION, and/or HYPOTHESES

[ ] Unit of analyses is stated.
[ ] Problem statement is included.
[ ] Research question is focused and testable.
[ ] Hypotheses deductively flow from the theoretical framework.
[ ] Hypotheses state expected relationships or differences.
[ ] Hypotheses are unambiguous, testable, and concise.

LITERATURE REVIEW

[ ] Important previous studies have been included.
[ ] Literature review is comprehensive, relevant to study purpose or problem, addresses the independent and/or dependent variables of the study.
[ ] Problems or flaws with earlier studies have been noted.
[ ] When possible, primary sources have been used.
[ ] The review of literature is up to date.

METHODS

[ ] Overall, methodology is appropriate to the purpose of the study.
[ ] Sufficient documentation is provided so the study may be replicated.
[ ] The principal investigator and research team has the necessary training, skill, and attitude to conduct the study.
[ ] Limitations are not so major that the proposed study should not be done.

Research Design and Study Participants

[ ] A research design is identified for the study.
[ ] The number of groups that will be involved in the study is acknowledged.
[ ] Sampling strategy used to identify study participants and/or assignment to groups is stated.[a]
[ ] Fairness prevails in terms of how study participants are selected and assigned to groups.
[ ] Study will not be harmful to study participants.
[ ] Study participants have not been unnecessarily misled about the study's purpose
[ ] Study participants will benefit from the study.
[ ] An adequate number of study participants are available.
[ ] Study participants will be able to provide credible answers to the research questions.
[ ] Threats to the truthfulness or internal validity of the study are estimated.
[ ] Threats to the applicability or external validity of the study are estimated.

Intervention

[ ] An adequate description of the intervention has been provided in terms of program content and process.

Instrumentation

[ ] Instruments are appropriate in terms of the purpose or scope of the study and study participants.
[ ] Information on the validity and reliability of instruments is provided and supports using these instruments.
[ ] The coding of possible answers has been spelled out and the theoretical range of scores provided.
[ ] The adopted instruments have sensitivity.
[ ] Whether normative data exist for the selected instruments is mentioned.

Table 11.5 (cont.)

Data Collection

[ ] Whether IRB approval is needed.
[ ] Whether informed consent is an issue.
[ ] Details about the procedures for collecting data are described.
[ ] The chosen data collection method provides enough quality data for sufficient analyses.
[ ] If used, interviewers/observers are adequately trained.
[ ] If confidential information is being collected, provisions that will be made to keep the responses or observations secure are thought through.

Data Analysis

[ ] The proposed data analyses provide meaningful understanding.
[ ] A statistical and/or qualitative analysis plan to answer the research question and hypothesis are included.
[ ] The proposed statistics or data management plans are appropriate.
[ ] How missing data will be handled is described.
[ ] The adopted level of significance is appropriate.

BUDGET

[ ] The time budget is sensible.
[ ] The financial costs are reasonable.

MECHANICS POSTSCRIPT

[ ] The author has not plagiarized.
[ ] The language and writing style is acceptable.

[a]Ultimately, the response rate must be reported. Then, the pressing questions are, (a) "Is the rate acceptable?" and (b) "Are nonrespondents markedly different from those who responded?"

REVIEW AND DISCUSSION QUESTIONS

1. Why should a proposal be drafted and then used to seek prior approval for the study?
2. Identify at least two approval entities with which a researcher must work.
3. Explain what functions a thesis or dissertation committee serves.
4. Distinguish between an expedited and nonexpedited institutional review board (IRB) review?
5. Identify and contrast four writing styles that you may use in drafting a proposal.
6. Review three common writing/language mistakes that often appear in a proposal.
7. List the major headings found in a proposal.
8. Explain how the following are calculated when appearing in a research line-item budget, and explain the noted terms associated with these categories: personnel (full-time equivalent and fringe benefits), other direct costs, and indirect costs.

YOUR RESEARCH

1. Prepare a proposal on your research topic. Then, using a copy of Table 11.5, review and judge your proposal by completing the checklist. If time is available, ask someone who has a background in research to read and evaluate your draft using the checklist.
2. If appropriate, draft an IRB application for your proposal. If you are a university student, complete the forms issued by your institution's IRB.
3. If your university or agency has a small grants application program, complete an application to support your proposed study. If asked to do so, include a line-item budget.

PRACTICE EXERCISES

1. Find answers to the following questions regarding your institution's IRB. If your instructor does not invite a guest speaker to come to class to discuss your institution's IRB, visit your school's website to find the answers.
   a. How are IRB openings publicized? How long does a person serve on the IRB once appointed?
   b. How are persons chosen to serve on the IRB? What factors are considered in extending an invitation to become an IRB member?
   c. What common mistakes are found in IRB applications?
   d. After a proposal has been approved, what oversight responsibilities does the IRB have?
2. Review a research proposal. This may be a proposal you have written, one distributed to you by your instructor, or one a graduate student working on a thesis or dissertation is willing to share with you.
   a. Identify which of the four writing styles the proposal used.
   b. Rate the content of the proposal. Unless instructed otherwise by your teacher, use Table 11.5 to judge the proposal. Identify the three weakest points, in your opinion, that need the most work, and recommend how to strengthen these.

WEB EXERCISES

1. Review confused words and common grammar mistakes by visiting http://www.grammar-monster.com/easily_confused_words.htm and clicking on "List of Confused Words" and "List of Common Mistakes." Identify two words you confuse and two grammar mistakes you often commit.
   - Additional resources for improving your writing are Oxford Dictionaries' "Grammar and Usage" page. Click on the units under "Grammar," "Spelling," "Punctuation," "Writing Help," "Usage," and "Abbreviations" (http://oxforddictionaries.com/words/better-writing); Purdue University's Online Writing Lab (http://owl.english.purdue.edu/owl/); and Jane Straus' *The Blue Book of Grammar and Punctuation* (http://www.grammarbook.com/).
   - Finally, lest you think you are the only one who struggles, view the Plain Language Report Card that has been issued for United States federal agencies at http://centerforplainlanguage.org/report-cards/.
2. Read more about how to write and present a thesis or dissertation proposal. After visiting the following sites, identify three useful points you learned about writing a proposal that you could share with your classmates.
   a. S. Joseph Levine's (Michigan State University) thesis/dissertation guide, *Writing and Presenting Your Thesis or Dissertation*. In particular, read Stage 2 - Preparing the Proposal at http://www.learningace.com/doc/4301793/78e76133f390d16db6e79616083bd8ae/dissguid.
   b. Listen to the Massey University lecture that includes points on how to organize and write a thesis or dissertation proposal at http://www.youtube.com/watch?v=zJ8Vfx4721M.

3. Learn more about writing. Review the following tutorials and indicate which you found most useful and why.
   a. American Psychological Association (APA) *Basics of APA Style* tutorial (http://www.apastyle.org/learn/tutorials/basics-tutorial.aspx).
   b. Visit the University of Toronto's website with advice on planning and organizing at http://www.writing.utoronto.ca/advice/planning-and-organizing. Review "Developing Coherent Paragraphs" and "Using Topic Sentences."
4. Discover who funds some of the research that is done related to Healthy Kids. Visit the W.K. Kellogg Foundation website at http://www.wkkf.org/grants/grants-database.aspx. Click on "Focus Areas" and then "Healthy Kids." You should see results of entities that have funded research related to promoting the health of children for the given year. Click on a few of the grant recipients to read about their funded research. Identify and briefly summarize two studies you found interesting.

SERVICE LEARNING PROJECT

1. What entities or persons need to approve your service learning project? What is the timeline for obtaining these approvals?
2. What writing style will you adopt for the proposal and final report?
3. Who or which team will be responsible for which parts of the formal proposal?
4. Is a budget needed to conduct the service learning project? If so, develop a line-item budget.
5. Seek necessary approvals. What feedback was shared with these approvals? What changes, if any, are necessary, and who will be responsible for addressing shortcomings?

TEST YOURSELF ANSWERS

Calculating a Research Budget

I. PERSONNEL	Base Salary	FTE	Total
Position			
PI	$100,000	.10	$4,000[a]
Research Assistant	$12/hour	.20[b]	$1,440[c]
Fringe Benefits (@ 23.5%)			$1,278[d]
SUBTOTAL			$6,718
II. OTHER DIRECT COSTS			
Gift Card			$400
SUBTOTAL			$400
III. OTHER DIRECT NONPERSONNEL COSTS			
(@ 44% rate)			$2,956[e]
GRAND TOTAL			$10,074

[a]10% of $10,000 per month salary = $1,000 per month × 4 months (16 weeks) = $4,000.
[b]Person will work 8 hours per week: 40 ÷ 8 = 20% or .20 FTE.
[c](8 hours per week × 15 weeks) × $12 per hour = $1,440.
[d]$4,000 (Salary of PI) + $1,440 (Salary of Research Assistant) = $5,540 × 23.5% (Fringe Benefit) = $1,278.
[e]Indirect costs are calculated on the total cost of salaries: $6,718 × 44% = $2,955.92, which was rounded to $2,956.

SUPPORTING CASES FOR THIS CHAPTER

CASE 11.1. FAST OUT OF THE GATE YET SLOW TO THE FINISH!

Phil is a hardworking guy. In the first semester of his 2-year master's program, he took a research methods course. Inspired, during the second semester, he began working on a thesis idea. He wanted to evaluate a softball skills clinic for adolescent girls. During the semester, he had several meetings with his advisor to discuss revisions to his proposal. His thesis advisor told him he had a gem of an idea.

The semester ended and Phil accepted a job at a summer softball skills camp. Phil thought he would get ahead in his graduate program collecting data for his thesis while at camp. At the end of the semester, he was rushed: finishing final exams, packing, driving to camp, and greeting the first group of campers. So without prior approval, he collected data from the campers.

When he returned to campus in the fall, he met with his thesis advisor and told her what he had done. Guess what? He was informed that the data he collected could not be used for his thesis because he had never obtained approval for data collection from the camp, his thesis committee, or the IRB. He was crushed.

CASE 11.2. NONMONETARY SOURCES FOR LEISURE RESEARCH.

People often limit themselves by soliciting only money to fund their research. If appropriate, think of how nonmonetary donations may help in getting your project off the ground.

For instance, to conduct a research project on video game play, Riddick, Drogin, and Spector (1987) approached the American Amusement Machine Association. As a way of showing support for the study, the organization loaned arcade games for several months. The regional supplier delivered and picked up the equipment at the senior center involved in the study. The supplier appreciated acknowledgement in the presentations and papers written on the study.

Another time, a student was interested in studying the exercise behaviors of pregnant women. In exchange for completing three surveys throughout their pregnancies, study participants were given baby care products donated by a pharmaceutical company. In this instance, the company asked their name not be identified publicly identified.

CASE 11.3. TITLE POSSIBILITIES

You are planning a study to examine the impacts of an outdoor education course on college students. The dependent variables of the study are self-esteem, problem solving, and nature appreciation. What are the possibilities for the title of the study?

Title possibility[a]	Critique
Evaluation of an Outdoor Education Course	If written for laypeople, the title is short and simple, yet more specificity would be in order (e.g., who the target audience was for the course). If written for a university requirement or professional publication, the title falls short. Final Grade: C, a so-so title!
Impacts of an Outdoor Education Course on Social Psychological Health	An improvement from the first title in that the reader is now learning which independent and dependent variables will be examined. Nevertheless, the title is vague, especially in the sense of not knowing who was involved in the study. Final grade: B-, better than first title!
How Participation in an Outdoor Education Course Affected the Self-Esteem, Problem-Solving Skills and Nature Appreciation of Collegians	The most descriptive title yet. A reader would learn from this title which variables were examined and the sampling frame used for the study. Final grade: A-, best descriptive title out of the three possibilities but admittedly long. The APA (2010) recommends a title be no more than 12 words!

[a]Notice each title is set up using APA Style (2010) or inverted triangle appearance (first line is longer than second line, second line longer than third line, and so forth).

CASE 11.4. REFLECTIVITY OR ACKNOWLEDGING POSSIBLE BIASES IN A QUALITATIVE STUDY

Burns, J. (2007). *A photo-elicitation study on the meanings Gallaudet University students derived from a weekend camping trip* (Unpublished master's thesis). Gallaudet University, Washington, DC.

A qualitative study was conducted on how an outdoor camping trip affected college students. Study participants were given cameras and asked to record memories of the 3-day experience. Each camper was asked to select six photographs and describe, during an interview using probes, the meanings each photo held for them.

Study participants involved in this research had either experienced congenital or adventitious deafness. The student conducting the thesis research acknowledged and reflected on how his background could have affected study findings. "The principal investigator is a male in his early thirties, was born with congenital deafness and grew up in Canada...He attended a mainstreamed school from 5-years-old to 18-years-old" (p. 14).

PART IV
IMPLEMENTATION

STEP 12

CONDUCT PILOT TEST

STEP 13

PREPARE FOR DATA COLLECTION

STEP 14A

ANALYZE QUANTITATIVE DATA

STEP 14B

ANALYZE QUALITATIVE DATA

Prior practices, such as dress rehearsals, are important for many services sponsored by recreation, park, sport, and tourism agencies. This importance is certainly illustrated at this studio back lot tour attraction. Likewise, dress rehearsals are necessary for research studies. In this case, they are called pilot studies. Disney World's Hollywood Studios, Orlando, Florida. Copyright © 2015 Ruth V. Russell.

STEP 12 STEP 13 STEP 14 STEP 15

CONDUCT PILOT TEST

WHAT WILL I LEARN IN THIS CHAPTER?

I'll be able to...

1. Define and describe the purposes of pilot testing.
2. Explain how mixed methods may be used in pilot testing.
3. Recall general principles that should be adhered to when pilot testing.
4. Identify specific pilot testing guidelines for an interview, questionnaire, and observation.

"Anything that can go wrong, will—at the worst possible moment."

Finagle's Law of Dynamic Negatives
(A folk version of Murphy's Law)

Isn't it time to collect data for the study yet? After all, you have accomplished many steps in the research process. For example, you have

- decided on a topic,
- reviewed the literature,
- identified a theoretical approach,
- determined the study scope,
- explained the significance of the study,
- selected a sample,
- chosen a design,
- considered measurement,
- specified data collection tools,
- addressed ethical responsibilities, and
- sought proposal approval.

Whee! Seemingly, all bases have been covered, yet one important task remains: pilot testing. This chapter begins with the purposes of pilot testing, then discusses using mixed methods in pilot testing, and ends with guidelines for conducting a pilot test for interviews, questionnaires, and observations.

PURPOSES OF PILOT TESTING

Pilot testing is a small-scale preliminary study to test the design and methods (instruments, data collection, etc.) tentatively identified for use in a full-fledged study. Think of a pilot test as a mini version of the full-scale study: a trial run, dress rehearsal, shakedown cruise, or a last chance to work out the kinks. Although the pilot test serves many purposes, essentially it checks the feasibility of your study as proposed. That is, you need to (Basit, 2010; Stangor, 2011; Van Teijlingen & Hundley, 2001)

- establish whether the sampling technique is effective;
- test data collection method validity and reliability as well as workability of administration protocol (see Case 12.1);

- test question wording;
- test question sequencing;
- estimate time needed to complete the questions;
- estimate response rate;
- find out whether resources (staff, funding, equipment, etc.) set aside for the study are adequate;
- improve the data collection skills of the research staff;
- test planned data analysis methods; and
- identify the politics that may affect the research process.

Pilot testing is a crucial step in the research process because it saves time and money. "Unfortunately, pilot studies are in general under-discussed, underused and under-reported" (Prescott & Soeken, 1989, p. 60). Beginner and experienced researchers may be overconfident about how many subjects they can recruit and/ or how much usable data they can obtain. Therefore, interviewing and observing even a few individuals will reveal whether the main study is workable. Pilot test results give advanced warnings about flaws in implementing the research plan, allowing you to correct them.

However, completing a pilot study successfully is not a guarantee of the success of the full-scale study. How could this happen? For instance, although pilot study findings may indicate the likely size of the response rate, no guarantee exists that participants in the full-fledged study will cooperate as the participants in the pilot study did.

SOMETHING TO REMEMBER!

A pilot test is a preparatory investigation that does not test the research question, but rather the research plan. Although it does not guarantee success for the larger study, undertaking a study without at least some piloting is risky.

USING MIXED METHODS IN PILOT TESTING

Pilot testing is conducted for studies using quantitative and qualitative approaches. Typically, the goal is to imitate the main study circumstances; thus, you test the same data collection methods for the main study and the pilot study.

In a pilot test, however, you may use one data collection method that will be used to support another data collection method in the main study. For example, suppose you use in-depth unstructured interviews (a qualitative approach) in a pilot study. You could use points of view that emerge from the pilot to prepare a questionnaire (a quantitative approach) for the main study. As another example, you could use a questionnaire with a pilot group and then use the most popular responses as indicators of the questions to be posed in open-ended unstructured interviews for the main study.

PILOT TESTING GUIDELINES

Practice the following general guidelines during a pilot study regardless of which data collection methods you use:

- Secure permission. Seek and secure permission to conduct the pilot from your ethical review board and the pilot study site (see Step 11).
- Use a convenience sample. You do not need to randomly select pilot respondents from the population group even if the main study requires this. Rather, you choose pilot participants based on their availability.
- Choose pilot respondents who match those in the main study. In spite of using a convenience sample, match individuals selected for the pilot with the same social and cultural characteristics of respondents for the main study.
- Use a small sample size. For a questionnaire, include 15 to 20 individuals in the pilot test (Fowler, 2009). You may use fewer respondents when piloting interviews and observations.
- Imitate everything about the main study in the pilot. Pilot test every question, the sequence of questions, the instructions, the observation and interview schedule, and so forth.
- Do not use pilot respondents again in the main study. These individuals will have already experienced the study instruments and protocol, which contaminates the results.
- Do not merge pilot data into the main data. Do not use the data collected from a pilot to test a hypothesis in the full-fledged study.
- Acknowledge pilot testing in study reports. Include information in the final report about the pilot testing. Identify and defend the changes made in the directions, questions, observation and response categories, and/or data collection procedures so lessons learned are shared with future researchers.

Piloting an Interview

Structured and unstructured interviews may benefit from being pilot tested. Practicing the questions will ensure the questions can and will be answered.

When conducting a pilot interview, begin by reminding respondents of the purpose of the pilot. That is, specify that you are not interested in learning about their answers to the questions, but instead you seek their advice on how you may improve the directions, questions, and possible answers.

You may solicit feedback from a pilot interview by asking one question and then soliciting feedback on that question. Repeat this cycle until you ask all the questions appearing on the interview schedule. Alternatively, you may ask pilot respondents to complete a rating form after all the questions have been asked.

TIPS FOR PILOTING AN INTERVIEW

Method 1: Pilot respondents critique one question at a time.

1. Pose one interview question.
2. Allow the respondent to answer the question and record the answer.
3. Ask the respondent what was going through his or her mind during the questioning.
4. Ask the respondent to paraphrase his or her understanding of the question.
5. Ask the second interview question and repeat Steps 2, 3, and 4 above.
6. Continue this cycle until you have asked all questions.
7. After you have asked all questions, inquire whether the sequencing of questions was logical and the directions and transitions were clear.
8. Finally, invite the pilot respondent to share other thoughts on how the interview experience could be improved, including the interview introduction and directions.

Method 2: Rate questions after they have been asked based on whether

- it was easy to understand as worded,
- the question and/or possible answers (when provided in a closed-ended interview) need clarification,
- the respondent felt capable of answering the question, and
- the respondent felt willing to answer the question.

Note. Adapted from Forsyth and Kviz (2006) and Fowler (2014).

Ideally, and if acceptable to the participants, pilot interviews should be video-recorded or at least audio-recorded (Fowler, 2014). Studying these recordings afterward will help you determine changes or corrections necessary in the interview process and/or your interviewing skills. For example, you may review the recordings to determine the following:

- Was the interviewer's body language appropriate?
- Did the interviewer ask the planned questions?
- Did the interviewer frequently interrupt?
- Did the interviewer use prompts, probes, and silence effectively (see Step 9)?
- Was the interviewer capable in handling the recording equipment?
- For which questions (and possible answers if provided) did interviewees ask for clarification or seem to have trouble identifying what you wanted.

WHICH IS A PILOT TEST?

Directions: If the cited example exemplifies a way to pilot test, write *yes*; if not, write *no*.

___ 1. You ask an expert who knows about this topic (e.g., a faculty member) to provide feedback on what he or she thinks of your research design.

___ 2. You ask some participants who are like your potential sample to take your survey; then you could ask them which parts were confusing or need revising.

___ 3. You have potential participants explain to you what they think your questions mean to see whether they are interpreting them as you intended or you need to make questions clearer.

Note. Answers are provided at the end of the chapter.

You should also assess the utility of the interview form and/or recording guide. Were the answers easy to record? Was there enough memory or tape to record responses to all questions posed during the interview?

Piloting a Questionnaire

Questionnaire construction is an imprecise science; therefore, pilot testing drafts is a must. Pilot tests not only identify flaws in the questionnaire instrument, but also increase response rates, reduce the possibility of missing data, and increase the possibility of obtaining more valid responses on the final version (Schwab, 2005). For example, in Case 12.2, the pilot test revealed only minor changes to wording that made huge differences in respondents' comprehension.

When pilot testing, check whether set responses occur during a questionnaire. ***Set responses*** are typical responses to questions from a particular perspective or direction, usually due to social desirability. For example, if you ask young campers how often they practice a list of desirable health habits while at camp (brushing teeth, washing hands before meals, etc.), they likely will tell you what they think you want to hear rather than the truth!

Also, conducting a second pilot test may be useful. If the first pilot reveals that substantial changes are needed in the questionnaire and/or methods used to collect questionnaire data, you should conduct a second pilot study. This is particularly warranted when findings from the first pilot reveal the collected data do not address the purpose of the study or research questions (Neutens &

Rubinson, 2013). These tests take time, of course, and should be built into the timeline of the study.

TIPS FOR PILOTING A QUESTIONNAIRE

1. Administer the questionnaire under the same circumstances as the main study, including mailing it with a cover letter and stamped, self-addressed return envelope if it is a mail questionnaire.
2. For Internet questionnaires, be sure pilot respondents can log on to a secure website and retrieve the survey.
3. Ask respondents to provide feedback on clarity of directions, questions and response categories, questioning sequences, and design and layout.
4. Check that all questions are answered. If not, find out why the individual did not answer the question. Also, pay attention to the frequency with which people indicated "Don't Know" or skipped or did not answer questions.
5. Ask respondents whether the amount of time needed to answer the questionnaire was adequate. If not, shorten it (e.g., by reducing the number of open-ended questions).
6. Analyze the data collected from the questionnaire and determine whether the data analysis plan for the main study is adequate.

Note. Adapted from Couper (2004), Gratton and Jones (2010), and Peat, Mellis, Williams, and Xuan (2002).

Piloting an Observation Plan

If you will use structured or participant observations to collect information, conduct a pilot test. Foremost, thoroughly check the ethical care given to the observation situation (Step 10). Was it difficult to gain access to the observation site? Did the pilot observation subjects behave in their customary way? Were observations able to be recorded as planned? Will the degree of observers' participation need adjusted?

In a pilot, for example, it was revealed that adjustments were needed in an observation study of a coffee klatch program in a Florida recreational vehicle resort. The investigator (one of the coauthors of this text) originally intended to use marginal participant observation in the full study. The pilot revealed, however, that the coffee klatch participants would not allow for this, insisting that the researcher become a bona fide member of the coffee hour. Thus, this intended protocol was changed for the main study as well (i.e., the researcher adopted a complete participant observation role).

Success in learning Chinese yo-yo requires practice, practice, and more practice. Having someone teach you who is skilled in this art helps immensely. Rehearsing or pilot testing is equally important before fully implementing a research study. Jingshan Park, Beijing, China. Copyright © 2015 Carol Cutler Riddick.

WOULD PILOT TESTING HAVE MADE A DIFFERENCE?

In the field of canine behavior and cognition research, dog participation does not always go as planned! The following underscore Finagle's Law of Dynamic Negatives:

- Dogs were excluded from one study due to "interference from a squirrel," "excessive activity," and "food aggressiveness" (Kundey et al., 2010).
- In another study dogs were required to "give a paw" to an experimenter numerous times. A pair of dogs "was excluded because one of them (a border collie) tried to herd the partner dog instead of concentrating on the task" (Range, Horn, Viranyi, & Huber, 2009).

REVIEW AND DISCUSSION QUESTIONS

1. What is a pilot test?
2. Name at least three purposes for a pilot test.
3. Explain how you may use mixed methods in a pilot study.
4. Identify principles that you should adopt when pilot testing.
5. Give at least two tips each for piloting an interview, questionnaire, and observation.

YOUR RESEARCH

1. Now that your research study or project is planned, will you conduct a pilot test of your data collection tools, procedures, and planned data analysis methods? If not, why not?
2. If you will be conducting a pilot study, what specifically will you check? That is, what do you want to know before conducting the main study?
3. When and how will you conduct the pilot test?
4. Do you anticipate changes as a result of the pilot test? How will you implement these?

PRACTICE EXERCISES

1. The purpose of this exercise is to demonstrate what you may learn from conducting a pilot study of an unstructured interview schedule. Specifically, this is an opportunity to practice Method 1 in Tips for Piloting an Interview.
   a. Pair up with a classmate. One of you will be the interviewer and the other the pilot respondent.
   b. Using the interview schedule below, the interviewer follows Method 1, that is, seeks feedback about each question after each is asked and answered. The interviewer also takes notes on the pilot respondent's answers to the questions and critique about the questions.

Worksheet Pilot Chapter: Respondent's Pilot Study Feedback for a Drafted Interview Schedule

Question	Feedback
1. Are you looking forward to winter/spring break this year?	
2. If you were to go to Cancún, Mexico, this year with a group of friends, what would you look forward to doing there?	
3. What do you think you might do for your winter/spring break this year?	
4. How important is it to you to experience winter/spring break with friends? With family? Alone?	

   c. Afterward, discuss with your partner how the interview went, including what changes you would recommend making to the interview question content and order, the skill of the interviewer, and so forth.

2. The purpose of this exercise is to practice the steps for conducting a pilot study of a questionnaire.
   a. Complete the pilot study questionnaire below in class.
   b. Form into discussion groups of no more than six people. Within each group, compare individual responses to the questionnaire and discuss the experience of taking the questionnaire. Specifically, discuss the following:
      - the clarity of directions,
      - ambiguities or difficult questions or response categories,
      - question transitions and questioning sequences,
      - design and layout,
      - whether all questions were answered (if not, why not),
      - whether set response patterns are evident, and
      - whether the amount of time needed to complete it is acceptable.
   c. Discuss how your group would change the questionnaire, accordingly.

Worksheet Pilot Chapter: Respondent's Pilot Study Feedback on Draft to Questionnaire

Question	Feedback
1. Are you a male ____ or female ____?	
2. Are you between ages 18 and 25?	
3. What would you say is your favorite leisure pursuit?	
4. Do you participate in this pursuit frequently? ____ YES ____ NO	
5. What keeps you from pursuing your favorite leisure pursuit more frequently? ____ no time ____ no money ____ no one to do it with	
6. What is your annual income? ____ Is it below $10,000 ____ Is it between $10,000 and $20,000 ____ Is it more than $20,000	
7. What other sports do you enjoy?	
8. Why don't you participate in them more frequently? ____ no time ____ no money ____ no one to do it with	
9. Are the recreational facilities on campus good? ____ YES ____ NO	

3. The point of this exercise is to practice pilot testing your observation and field note-taking skills and to demonstrate the difference perspective may make in what is "seen" when using the observation data collection method (Janesick, 2003).
   a. Arrange yourselves in a large circle (may be several layers deep) so enough room is available for a small table in the center. The teacher places four to six objects on the table (e.g., a vase of flowers, a framed picture, a stack of magazines, a coffee mug).
   b. From your seated vantage point, observe and record information about the objects on the table. Use descriptive terms to describe what you see, such as color, size, and shape.
   c. After 5 minutes, everyone changes seats, moving as far away from their original location as possible. Repeat the observation for 5 more minutes, again taking field notes on your observations.
   d. Engage in a class-wide discussion of the differences in observation notes. Were these differences a result of vantage point? What does this activity demonstrate about the importance of pilot testing an observation procedure?

WEB EXERCISES

1. Read the paper at http://www.biomedcentral.com/content/pdf/1471-2288-10-1.pdf and then answer the following questions:
   a. Should the pilot study be published? Why or why not?
   b. What do the authors advise about combining the data from the pilot with that of the main study? How and why does this differ from the advice in this chapter?
   c. What is the recommended sample size for a pilot study?
2. Explore SurveyMonkey, the online free survey data collection tool by visiting https://www.surveymonkey.com/. Click on "How it Works," "Examples," and "Survey Services" as part of your exploration. Finally, check out the pilot testing option with the SurveyMonkey help center at http://help.surveymonkey.com/articles/en_US/kb/Pilot-Test-Tips-How-to-verify-the-design-and-settings. Try preparing a brief questionnaire, and pilot test it using SurveyMonkey.

SERVICE LEARNING

For the campus program or service that has been selected as the focus of the service learning project for this semester, complete the following:

1. Plan a pilot test of your data collection tools, procedures, and planned data analysis methods.
   - What specifically will you check?
   - What do you want to know before conducting the full study?
   - When and how will the pilot test be conducted?
2. Share your pilot testing plan with classmates. What else do they recommend?
3. Conduct your pilot testing plan. What protocol changes are needed? What changes are needed to the data collection instrument?

TEST YOURSELF ANSWERS

Which Is a Pilot Test?

For all questions, the answer is *yes* (all situations are examples of pilot testing).

SUPPORTING CASES FOR THIS CHAPTER

CASE 12.1. PILOT TESTING A DATA COLLECTION METHOD

Myllykangas, S. (2005). *Meaning of leisure: A case study of older women with HIV/AIDS and their female caregivers* (Unpublished doctoral dissertation). Indiana University, Bloomington.

To collect information about the meaning of leisure for older women diagnosed with HIV or AIDS, study participants were going to be asked to take photographs of the nature of their leisure before and after diagnosis. To be sure this method of collecting data worked, the researcher first conducted a pilot test. She gave disposable cameras with automatic flash to a small sample of older men with HIV or AIDS. (Men were chosen for the pilot because the entire population of older women with HIV or AIDS in the community was to be included in the main study.)

After the photos were taken, debriefing interviews with the men revealed that the photo-taking instructions for the study needed to be modified. Thus, the instructions were altered for the full study by making the definition of leisure clearer. Also, the pilot revealed that respondents needed many more cameras than originally thought. Consequently, in the full study, each participant was given 16 cameras, that is, one camera for each research question.

CASE 12.2. A QUESTIONNAIRE PILOT TEST

Chan, P. C. (2005). *Relevant attributes in assessment for design features of indoor games hall: The application of importance-performance analysis* (Unpublished doctoral dissertation). Indiana University, Bloomington.

The purpose of the study was to evaluate the design features needed for a successful indoor games hall in Hong Kong, China. Prior to administering the questionnaire, the researcher conducted a pilot study. Several participants of the Kowloon Park Indoor Games Hall were asked to complete the questionnaire draft under similar conditions that would be implemented for the main study.

As a result of the pilot test, the questionnaire was determined to be reliable and feasible. The pilot, however, also revealed that the questionnaire needed changes: make a better distinction between the terms *importance* and *performance*, add squash and tennis to the list of recreational sports from which to choose, and add a question about the respondent's profession.

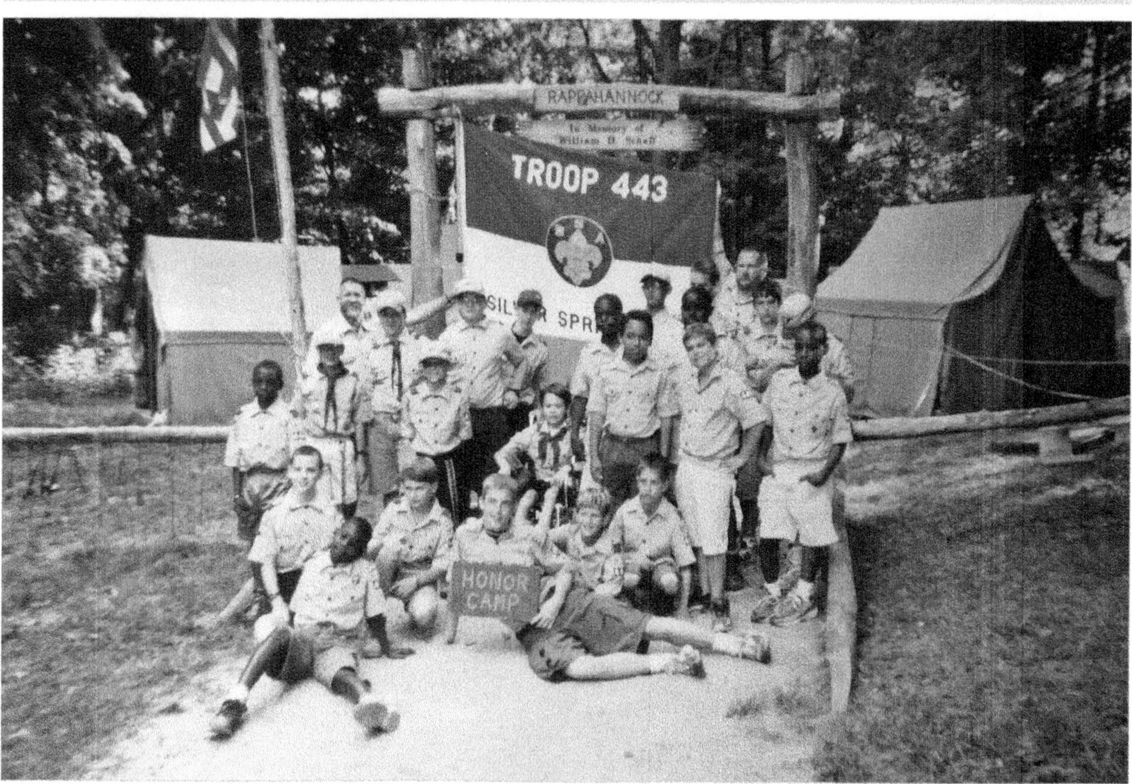

Lack of preparation may mess you up. "Be prepared" is the motto of the Scouts, a good piece of advice that should be heeded when preparing for the data collection stage of the research project. Rappahannock Scout Camp, Jamaica, Virginia. Copyright © 2015 Carol Cutler Riddick.

STEP 12 STEP 13 STEP 14 STEP 15

PREPARE FOR DATA COLLECTION

WHAT WILL I LEARN IN THIS CHAPTER?

I'll be able to...

1. Recall materials, supplies, and equipment that may be needed for collecting data.
2. Identify two techniques for avoiding proofreading mistakes.
3. Explain why hiring indigenous field staff to collect data is useful.
4. Distinguish between expressive and receptive skills development for interviewers.
5. Define data verification and outline two ways it may be accomplished.
6. List the typical key players on a research team.
7. Differentiate between a person-loading chart and a Gantt chart.

"Be prepared."

Scout motto
(Shared by millions of Boy and Girl Scouts/ Guides around the world since 1907)

The previous chapter advised that before you may collect data for a study, you need to complete pilot testing. One more step remains before data collection begins, namely, preparing for data collection! Preparing for data collection requires devoting time to taking stock of materials, supplies, and equipment needed to conduct the study; recruiting, hiring, and training staff; and making plans for managing and supervising the research team.

TAKE STOCK

Regardless of the nature of your study, make sure the materials, supplies, and equipment needed to collect data are available and in working order. For example, if special equipment is necessary to collect data, (e.g., video cameras, audio-recording devices, and laptops), take time to check out the equipment. Does the needed equipment work? Are attachments and accessories (e.g., microphones, spare batteries, connecting cables) in place and working? Are blank videos or audio cassettes in the supply cabinet? Are the people assigned to use equipment proficient in their operation? Has equipment been reserved for training purposes and for data collection times?

HEAVY-DUTY NOTEBOOK PERSONAL COMPUTER (PC)

If you are conducting face-to-face interviews and using a laptop to enter answers, consider investing in a notebook PC that is rugged or designed for road warriors (e.g., individuals involved in law enforcement, utility work, and emergency response). These PCs are wireless; have shock-mounted hard drives; are built with anti-reflective, outdoor-readable liquid crystal display (LCD) screens and backlit keyboards; and are housed in a heavy-duty case that can withstand dropping. Several manufacturers make these notebook PCs, so shop around.

LUCILLE BALL AND VIVIAN VANCE, UNPREPARED FOR THEIR "FIRSTDAY WORKING AS CANDY WRAPPERS"

Sometimes people are vaulted into a new position without receiving preparation on how to do their job. Watch this classic clip at http://milkandcookies.com/link/224416.

If you will collect data through phone interviews, you likely will need extra phone lines or cell phones. If so, allow sufficient lead time so additional telephone lines may be installed. If you will mail questionnaires, purchase postage. If you will have to travel to data collection sites, arrange for car rentals, lodging and meal reimbursements, and other travel-related costs.

As well, special computer software may be required to set up online surveys, record interviews, or analyze data. The learning curve on mastering these programs ranges from easy to steep. To master the software, you may need to register for special workshops or tutoring. Regardless, make sure enough time has been allocated to master the software that you will use to conduct the study.

Taking stock of the data collection materials includes allowing enough time to have necessary printed materials (new staff orientation materials, release forms/informed consent, interview schedules, questionnaires, observation forms, cover letters, follow-up letters, etc.) prepared, proofread, and reproduced. Commercial printing companies usually are busy from Thanksgiving to New Year's (with holiday greeting cards and social invitations) and again in the spring (with wedding announcements). If printing will be in-house, check how much lead time is needed for you to obtain your printed material. Proofread your work prior to turning it over for duplication and again when you pick it up from the printer.

HOW TO AVOID PROOFREADING MISTAKES

The following are ideas for proofreading the final copy of forms used for data collection (or anything else for that matter):

- Allow adequate time to proofread. Write one day, and proofread the next. Better yet, have someone else read your draft.
- Proof it on paper. If you think the copy is ready for mass or commercial printing, print and proof a paper version before sending it to the printer.
- Have adequate reference materials available. This includes a dictionary and a stylebook. Computer software cannot be trusted to check spelling.
- Look for one type of error at a time. Check first for grammar, then for punctuation, sentence structure, and spelling.

Finally, prepping for data collection includes preparing space needs. For example, is a quiet space for testing available? Does the basketball court need to be reserved for collecting data? Will cloud storage be needed to manage completed questionnaires? Adequate space is important, especially where interviews and group questionnaires are administered, to ensure confidentiality of respondents and maintain optimal conditions for their participation.

RECRUIT, HIRE, AND TRAIN STAFF

Some research projects are simple enough for a single person to conduct without the assistance of additional staff. At other times, research studies require recruiting, hiring, and training staff.

Recruiting and Hiring

You may need to hire research assistants, or ***field staff***, to conduct interviews, distribute questionnaires, or observe a study. Occasionally, individuals are hired to assist part time or full time with data entry into a computer or interview transcription.

If you hire individuals to assist with a research project, contact your agency's human resources unit. In particular, ask about regulations governing advertising position openings; payment schedules; and supervision and evaluation of hourly, part-time, temporary, and full-time employees and volunteers. To promote cooperation and lower refusal rate, sociologists and social psychologists advise hiring ***indigenous field staff*** who share similar social characteristics (age, gender, ethnicity, etc.), to the group being interviewed (Case 13.1).

Training

No one template fits research staff training. The content and delivery method, as well as the amount of time that will be needed, will vary depending on aspects such as data being collected, how the data are being collected, and the organization's resources. Sometimes, training happens before data collection; sometimes continuous retraining occurs throughout the research project.

The content of training is either general information or information specific to the study (Fowler, 2014). For topics that may be covered in these content areas see Table 13.1.

If you are hiring interviewers, they will need in-service training to ensure their communication skills are at an acceptable level to the data collection task. Specifically, they will need training in expressive and receptive communication skills.

Expressive skills (also known as conversational language) are related to a person's ability to communicate a message to others. Expressive skills also encompass nonverbal language, such as body language. A ***closed***

Table 13.1
Suggested Content for Study-Specific Information for Field Worker Orientation

- Provide an overview of the research project: its sponsor, purpose, significance, methods, and anticipated uses of the findings.
- Distribute the interview, questionnaire, and/or observation forms that will be used.
- Discuss the importance of following interview, questionnaire, or observation instructions.
- Provide overview on sampling used to select potential respondents, as well as steps that will be taken to safeguard their confidentiality or anonymity.
- Present tips for conducting and recording successful interviews, group questionnaires, and observations. For interviews and questionnaires, this includes how to greet and terminate contact with respondents.
- Suggest other conventions to be used with the measurement instrument (wording of questions, "skip" instructions, probing inadequate or incomplete answers, etc.).
- Suggest procedures for recording answers or observations.
- Offer guidelines for handling the interpersonal aspects of the interview or contact.
- Emphasize the need for legibility.
- Demonstrate and practice administering interviews, questionnaires, and/or observations. Questions should be asked exactly as written, with no wording changes. Videotaping practice sessions will be useful for those being trained.
- Review policies for submission of collected data.
- Discuss data verification procedures and consequences of falsifying data.
- Address dress and behavior codes.
- If the organization is providing transportation, announce policies and procedures for reserving motor pool vehicles.
- Outline procedures for submitting worked hours and travel-related expenses (mileage, per diem lodging, meal expenses, etc.).
- Disseminate emergency contact information (for emergency situations that happen while in the field).

Note. Adapted from Alreck and Settle (2004), Fowler (2009), and Veal (2011).

body posture (e.g., having your arms folded in front of you or your legs crossed) does not convey a warmth or desire to interact with the other person. Contrastingly, an ***open body posture*** (e.g., no folded arms or crossed legs and with a slight lean by the interviewer toward the interviewee) is receptive and welcoming.

Receptive skills are related to a person's ability to understand or comprehend language heard or read or being expressed (Baker, 1981). An example of a receptive skill is ***probing***, that is, asking for clarification. For instance, the interviewer may state, "I'm not sure what you mean. Are you saying that it is difficult to answer this question with a yes or no answer?"

The delivery methods and length of training are also important. You may use several techniques to teach members of the research team, including lectures and presentations, written materials, planned exercises, role-playing, and computer-based tutorials. Furthermore, the time devoted to training research staff should be at least a full day (Fowler, 2014).

SOMETHING TO REMEMBER!

To improve your expressive and receptive skills, have someone observe you and issue a report card that identifies your strengths and weaknesses related to your communication practices.

Regarding desirable expressive and receptive skills, when interacting with someone do I

1. demonstrate open posture (no crossed legs or arms),
2. lean forward and maintain eye contact,
3. make sure I understood correctly by summarizing a comment the other person made or their answer to an open-ended question,
4. clarify when necessary (e.g., "I'm not sure what you mean," "I want to make sure I understand you. I think you are stating...," "Would you mind explaining that answer more?"),
5. give positive feedback ("Oh, I see," "Uh-huh," or nod head up and down), and

6. maintain the pace of the conversation/interview—not too fast or not too slow?

Regarding undesirable expressive skills and receptive skills, when interacting with someone do I

1. maintain a crossed arm or leg position,
2. not hold eye contact with the person with whom I am interacting (e.g., look around, seem uninterested in what the other person is expressing, look at my watch or clock),
3. cut off the other person (do not let him or her complete the answer or thought),
4. incorrectly summarize what the other person has expressed,
5. appear "flat" or show no emotion, and
6. read the survey questions too fast or too slow?

MANAGE AND SUPERVISE A RESEARCH TEAM

In addition to recruiting, hiring, and training field workers to help with data collection, other people may help with the study. In large research studies, you may be working with a team of people who have different research-related skills and who make different contributions to the process. Table 13.2 summarizes key players on a research team and their roles and responsibilities.

Quality Control

When managing field staff, control the quality of the research data collected. For example, when dealing with open-ended questions (Step 9), instruct field staff to record all responses verbatim. In other words, they should not summarize or paraphrase a response or reply.

SOMETHING TO REMEMBER!

Field staff who conduct face-to-face interviews or observations should make sure they carry with them their identity badge and a letter of introduction.

The field staff should wear the identity badge around the neck or attached prominently on the left side (since it is easier to read in this location) of their chest. The badge should contain the following:

- name of sponsoring organization (and logo if available),
- a picture identification of the field worker, and
- the name and signature of the field worker.

The letter of introduction for field staff should be laminated (to reduce wear and tear) and made available to the prospective study participant. The letter of introduction specifies the following:

- identity of the sponsoring organization,
- purpose of the study, and
- name and phone number of a contact person at the organization in case a question arises about the legitimacy of the project.

Another quality control measure for paper-and-pencil instruments is ***sight editing***, a standard procedure to check for completion that is conducted by someone other than the person who conducted the interview or survey (Alreck & Settle, 2004). This ensures all questions are answered, unless the respondent refused to answer the question or the answer did not apply to the respondent.

Additionally, completed interviews and questionnaires are normally subjected to ***data verification***, which consists of contacting a proportion of those reported as completing interviews or questionnaires. Verification protects the data against the event of an interview or questionnaire being completed by a field staff member instead of the respondent (Alreck & Settle, 2004). Fowler (2009) suggested two methods to conduct data verification. First, you may mail respondents a brief follow-up note asking them to verify they were interviewed. Second, you or an interview supervisor may contact the individuals to confirm they were interviewed.

Time Management Tools

When a study is conducted using a team of staff, you must coordinate everyone's efforts. Regardless of the size of a research project, designate one person within the organization as the point person. This individual should be well versed on activities of the research endeavor and able to field questions related to the project. Also, keep your thesis or dissertation chair current about developments related to data collection efforts, as well as staff working in your academic department (in case that person needs to handle phone calls dealing with aspects of the program evaluation). To manage these and other persons related to the research project, you may use a person-loading chart or a Gantt chart.

A ***person-loading chart*** itemizes the individual assigned to each task and the estimated number of hours or clock time needed to complete the task (Figure 13.1). A Gantt chart illustrates the calendar time projected for each task and the timing among the identified project activities (Figure 13.2). The ***Gantt chart***, once adopted, becomes a management tool or reminder of the tasks that are supposed to be completed during a certain time.

Table 13.2
Typical Members of a Research Team

Title	Typical roles and responsibilities
Principal investigator (PI)	Responsible for all steps in the research process
Project coordinator	Working closely with the PI, the project coordinator coordinates steps in the research process
Research assistants/field workers	Primary data collectors
Statistician	Advises on data management and analysis
Data entry specialists	Converts raw data into electronic format
Administrative assistant	Provides management assistance and clerical support

	Personnel				
Task and activity	Director	Youth sports coordinator	Business manager	Lifeguard	Consultant
Choose or design instrument					
1. Specify data needs	10	5	2		20
2. Review existing instrument					
2.1 Locate instruments					30
2.2 Evaluate instruments	20	5		2	20
3. Modify existing instruments and/or develop new instruments					
3.1 Develop interview schedule	4	4		2	20
3.2 Pilot interview schedule		4		4	4
3.3. Analyze and revise interview schedule	2	2			10
TOTAL	36	20	2	8	104

Figure 13.1. Person-loading chart (in hours) for developing an interview schedule for evaluation of a hypothetical YMCA youth swim program.

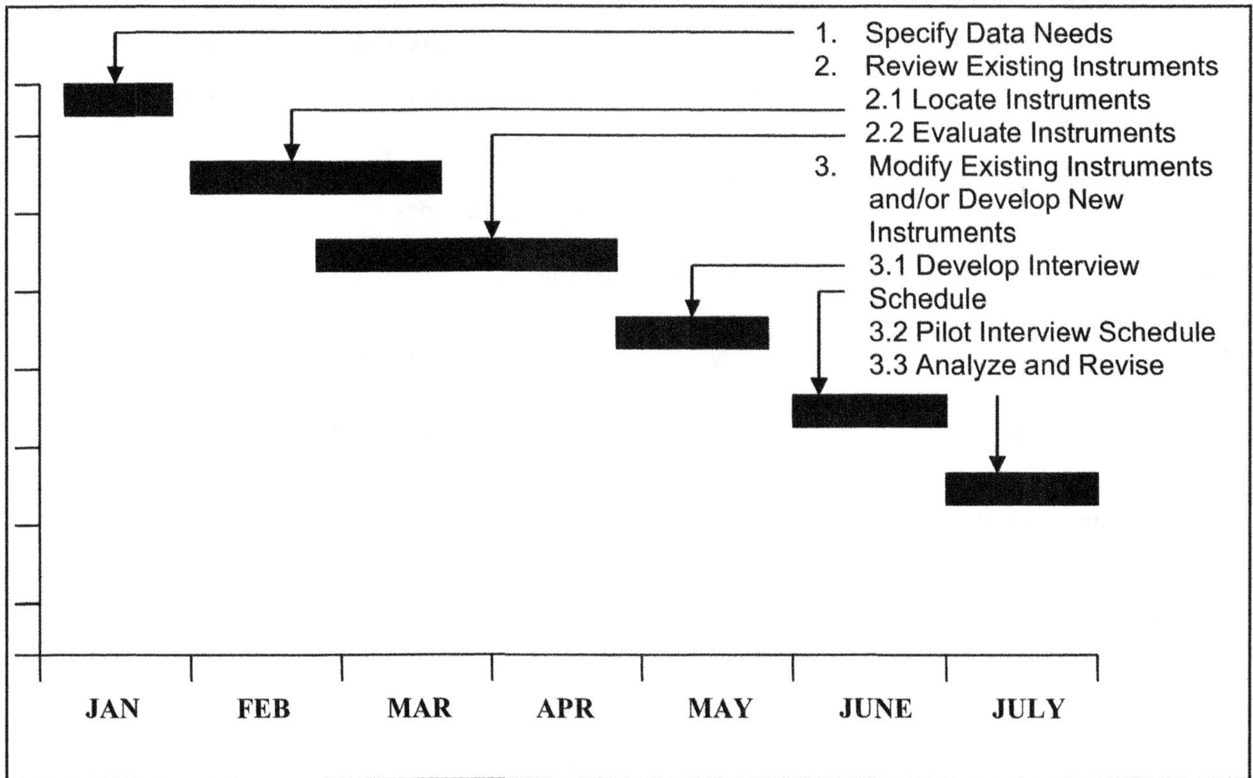

Figure 13.2. Gantt chart for developing interview schedule for evaluation of a hypothetical YMCA swim program.

PERSON-LOADING CHART QUIZ

Check your understanding of a person-loading chart by answering the statements as *true* or *false*.

A person-loading chart ...

____ 1. May be used as a visual representation for tasks to be completed for a research project.

____ 2. May be used to record estimated time needed to complete a specific research-related task using full-time equivalent measurement.

____ 3. May be used to assign a task to be completed to a specific research team member.

Note. Answers are provided at the end of the chapter.

PREPARE A GANTT CHART

Directions: For the course that is using this text, think of what remaining responsibilities you have to complete. Set up a Gantt chart identifying the tasks that remain to be accomplished until the end of the semester, along with a projection of how much time and when the activities will be accomplished.

Note. Answers are provided at the end of the chapter.

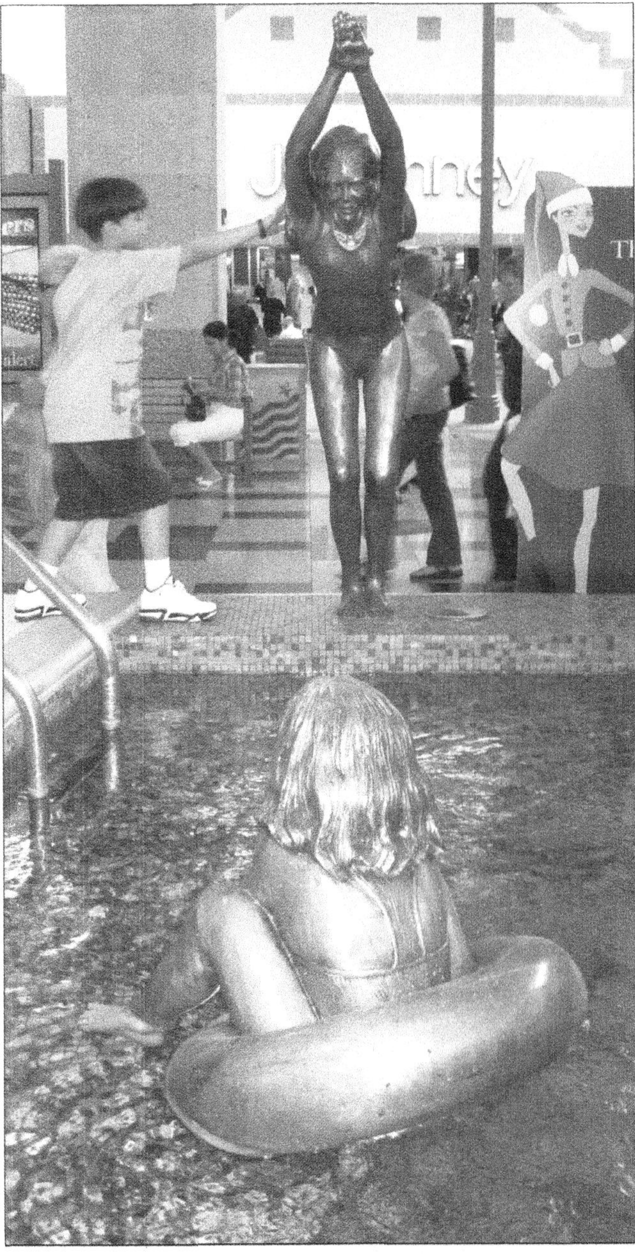

These days shopping malls give us what we expect (shopping) and what we do not expect (public art). Tampa, Florida. Copyright © 2015 Ruth V. Russell.

REVIEW AND DISCUSSION QUESTIONS

1. Recall materials, supplies, and equipment that are often used in data collection.
2. Name at least two tips for avoiding proofreading mistakes.
3. Why is hiring indigenous field staff to collect data useful?
4. Describe and differentiate between the two skills that need to be developed in interview training: expressive skills and receptive skills.
5. Explain data verification.
6. Who are the typical key players on a research team?
7. What is the difference between a person-loading chart and a Gantt chart?

YOUR RESEARCH

1. Make a comprehensive list of the equipment (cameras, laptops, phones, software, etc.) and supplies (printed materials, etc.) you will need to conduct your study. Prepare a checklist.
2. Will travel arrangements need to be made to conduct your study?
3. Who will be on your research team? What are their individual responsibilities?
4. Will you need to hire data collection field workers? If so, how will you recruit and train these field workers? To what, if any, organizational requirements will you need to adhere in hiring extra research staff?
5. If more than one person will implement your study, prepare a person-loading chart for each team member. Likewise, draft a Gantt chart for each major task associated with your research project.

PRACTICE EXERCISES

1. To experience a field staff training endeavor, set up a role-playing exercise that has each student rotating through two parts, or assuming the role of an interviewer and then acting as the interviewee. If possible, videotape the role-playing. *Note:* The instructor may ask the interviewee to assume behaviors such as the following:

- refusing to cooperate or take part in the study,
- being vague,
- making no sense or giving an inappropriate answer to the question,
- refusing to answer a question,
- giving a long-winded answer, or
- stopping the interview.

a. Use an interview schedule distributed by the instructor or one that was developed for the service learning project.
b. If you are observing the role-play, complete a modified version of the first Something to Remember section presented in this chapter (add a last column that is labeled Number of Times Demonstrated for each interviewer). Score each time the interviewer demonstrates a noted behavior during the role-play. These forms will be anonymous, and the instructor will share them at the end of the class with each interviewer.
c. Following the role-play, discuss with classmates your thoughts regarding how the interviewer could improve in future interviews.
d. If the mock interviews are taped, watch yourself and type a paragraph on your strengths and weaknesses.

2. To demonstrate field staff training, play the role of an interviewer trying to enlist the cooperation of a potential respondent for a survey with a few classmates. Other students in class observe this scene and at the end share what you did correctly, in their opinion, as well as provide tips or strategies on how to better approach prospective interviewees.

WEB EXERCISES

1. Go to the American Association for Public Opinion Research's "Best Practices" website at http://www.aapor.org/Best_Practices1/4081.htm. Unless your instructor advises you otherwise, read about the following topics listed on this page and provide typed answers to the noted questions.
   a. "Train Interviewers Carefully on Interviewing Techniques and the Subject Matter of the Survey." What three topics should be covered in interview training?
   b. "Maximize Cooperation or Response Rates Within the Limits of Ethical Treatment of Human Subjects."
      i. Identify three procedures that may be used to encourage cooperation or participation in an inter view.
      ii. Identify three strategies to deal with non-respondents and refusals. Do you agree with these strategies, why or why not?
2. Take a proofreading test, created by Trevor Horwood, a freelance proofreader and copyeditor, at http://www.copyediting.co.uk/test.htm. Print the test and then see whether you can identify the 30 errors in the passage. When you finish proofing, click on the answers at the end of the test. How did you do? Are you an ace proofreader?
3. Visit the American Association for Public Opinion Research's website at http://www.aapor.org/AM/Template.cfm?Section=For_Researchers&Template=/CM/ContentDisplay.cfm&ContentID=3194 to read the article "Interviewer Falsification in Survey Research: Current Best Methods for Prevention, Detection and Repair of its Effects." Unless instructed otherwise, type brief answers to the following questions:
   a. What is interviewer falsification? Is there a continuum of severity of falsification?
   b. Identify five ways organizations can prevent or reduce interviewer falsification.
   c. What are five effective ways of detecting falsification?
   d. What are two effective actions to take when evidence of falsification exists?

SERVICE LEARNING PROJECT

1. Take stock. Prepare a checklist of supplies (e.g., printer toner and paper for printed questionnaires if this is how the survey will be administered) and equipment (e.g., computers and printers) you need to have to conduct the project. Are the designated computer workstations for data entry in working order (users can log on successfully, computer interfaces properly with designated printer, etc.)?
2. Where will the completed interviews/questionnaires be stored so students in the research class have access to code and perform data entry into the computer? Is the place secure? Has a system been set up to ensure the confidentiality (Step 10) of individuals participating in the study?
3. Have student interviewers been properly oriented (refer to the Training section) regarding how to conduct a survey?
4. Is data verification needed for the study? If so, who will decide which respondents to contact and how these individuals will be contacted?
5. Develop a Gantt chart recording the various steps of the research project and time estimate when each step is expected to transpire.

TEST YOURSELF ANSWERS

Person-Loading Chart Quiz

1. True, 2. False (uses hours as the time measurement), 3. True

Prepare a Gantt Chart

The "answer" for this exercise is unique to each course. Among other points, the following should appear on the students' lists:

- Study time needed to read remaining assigned chapters in the text.
- Study time needed for remaining exams (including the final exam) for the course.
- Completing outstanding homework assignments for the course.
- Completing the service learning project for the course.

SUPPORTING CASE FOR THIS CHAPTER

CASE 13.1. HIRE INDIGENOUS FIELD STAFF

If you are in a position to hire research assistants, be expansive in your thinking about their qualifications. Often, the educational prerequisites for a job are addressed more than the human dimensions of hiring.

Whenever possible, hire indigenous people who have similar demographic characteristics as the group being sampled to conduct interviews, distribute questionnaires to groups, or make observations.

For example, during a university project that was funded by a state agency on aging, graduate students were hired to conduct door-to-door structured interviews in an inner city neighborhood from 9 a.m. to 5 p.m. on weekdays. The graduate students canvassed the neighborhood, dressed up (ties worn by the males, females in dresses) and carried briefcases containing their interview forms. Not one of the interviewers was a person of color. Most of the time door knocks met with no doors opening! The few instances when someone opened the door and the student began speaking the door suddenly closed.

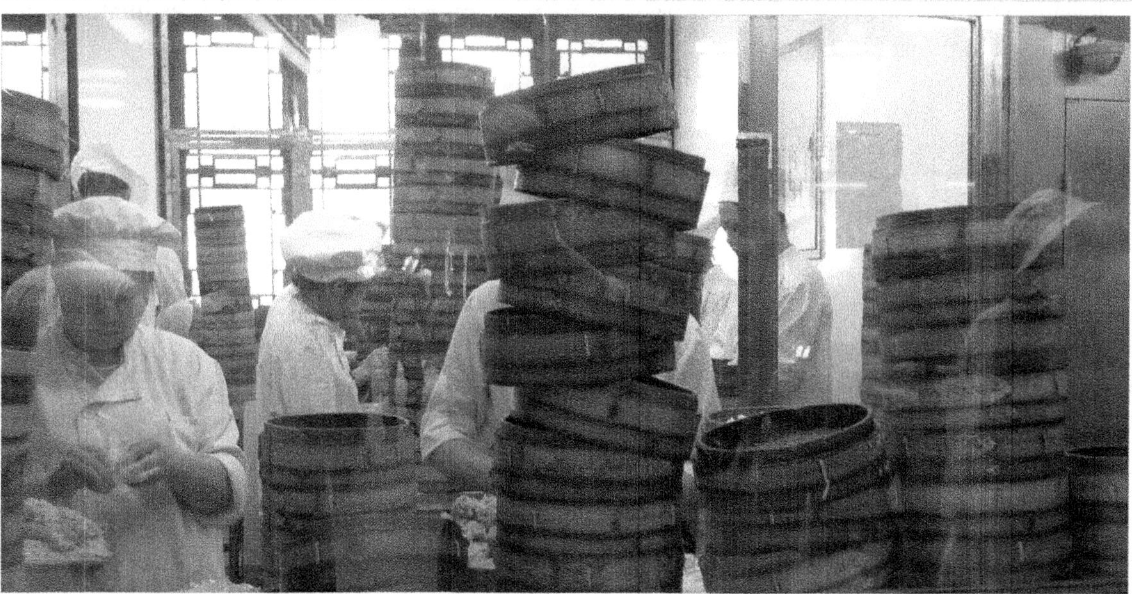

Analyzing quantitative data is a task that nonresearchers and researchers alike take on. Likewise, the owner of a popular dim sum restaurant needs to organize his cooked dishes into an understandable form that easily represents which steamed dishes are available. Notice how the bamboo steamers form a frequency distribution of sorts? Shanghai, China. Copyright © 2015 Carol Cutler Riddick.

STEP 12 › STEP 13 › STEP 14A › STEP 14B

ANALYZE QUANTITATIVE DATA

WHAT WILL I LEARN IN THIS CHAPTER?

I'll be able to...

1. Distinguish among the levels of numerical measurement: nominal, ordinal, interval, and ratio.
2. Define descriptive statistics.
3. Describe and prepare a frequency distribution.
4. Calculate relative comparisons: rates, ratios, proportions, and percentages.
5. Differentiate and calculate measures of central tendency: mean, median, and mode.
6. Define and calculate measures of variability: range and standard deviation.
7. Explain the difference between univariate and bivariate statistics.
8. Define and interpret correlation coefficient and coefficient of determination values.
9. Outline the focus of inferential statistics.

"Facts are stubborn, but statistics are more pliable."

Mark Twain
(Samuel Clemens, better known by his pen name Mark Twain, an American author and humorist, most noted for *The Adventures of Tom Sawyer*, 1876, and its sequel, *The Adventures of Huckleberry Finn*, 1885, 1835–1910)

Thinking about how to conduct the data analysis is integral to planning the research project. Indeed, many think the meat of the study is analyzing collected information in order to be able to recommend professional practices and/or further research (O'Toole & Beckett, 2014).

Yet, generally speaking, raw data do not speak for themselves. Analyzing data requires organizing the information that has been gathered from interviews, questionnaires, case study notes, field observation journals, rating forms, and the like so they are understandable. The information you collect in research is either numerical—information presented as numbers—or nonnumerical—information in text form. Examples of ***numerical data*** are

- number of participants in an adult fitness program,
- percentage of the black diamond ski trail users who prefer longer operating hours, and
- participants' accuracy of shot scores following a basketball clinic.

Illustrations of ***nonnumerical data*** include

- adjectives used by aquatics supervisors to describe lifeguards' performance,
- ideas for new services voiced by infrequent health club users, and
- handwritten notes of observations made of an outdoor adventure leader's actions during a mountain climbing expedition.

This chapter is focused on making sense of numerical data using quantitative analysis (the next chapter examines how to handle nonnumerical data, or qualitative analysis). Many quantitative data analysis tools exist. These tools are referred to as ***statistics***, a set of procedures for describing, synthesizing, analyzing, and interpreting numerical data (Pyrczak, 2009). You may sort statistics by classifying them as

- descriptive statistics,
- correlational statistics, or
- inferential statistics.

This chapter will introduce only a small selection of the statistical analysis tools available. Thus, you should take a course in statistics for your professional preparation and/or ask for help from a consultant when analyzing data from your studies. Also, keep in mind that "statistics" are not "sadistics." Despite what you may have heard, statistics is easy. To calculate the statistics in this chapter, you need to know only how to add, subtract, multiple, and divide.

STATISTICS ONE-LINERS

- 80% of statistics quoted to prove a point are made up on the spot.
- According to recent surveys, 51% of the people are in the majority.
- The Lipton company is big on statistics, especially *t* tests.
- The allegation that statisticians are mean is not true. They are your standard normal deviates.

Retrieved November 18, 2013, from http://www.ahajokes.com/m027.html.

LEVELS OF NUMERICAL MEASUREMENT

The level of measurement is the first aspect you should consider in selecting appropriate descriptive, correlational, or inferential statistical tools. That is, whenever a variable is measured, nominal, ordinal, interval, and ratio are the possible ***levels of measurement***. As shown in Table 14A.1, you may order these levels in a hierarchy according to the amount of specificity of the measurement. If you read from top to bottom in the table, you will see the precision of the measurement increases when moving from nominal to ratio levels.

Nominal Data

The ***nominal level of measurement*** is used to measure a variable using labels or categories that are mutually exclusive. Examples of nominal variables are gender as measured as being male or female; park location defined as rural, suburban, or urban; and club membership measured as members and nonmembers.

Often, numbers are used as labels for the nominally scaled categories. For instance, gender may be coded as 1 for males and 2 for females. However, these number labels cannot be analyzed mathematically. The numbers simply identify two groups; they have no mathematical value. That is, to value females as higher than males would be terribly inappropriate!

Ordinal Data

The ***ordinal measurement level*** ranks categorical information by size or magnitude. As the word implies, data are arranged in rank order. For example, you may measure the variable college class standing as first year, sophomore, junior, and senior. Likewise, you may record finishes for the swim club as first place, second place, and third place. Additionally, a supervisor may rate playground leaders' creativity as *high*, *medium*, or *low*.

Table 14A.1
Levels of Measurement for Variables

Level of measurement	Defined	Example	Amount of precision
Nominal	Categorical	Vacation homeowners, non-vacation homeowners	Least precise; no math may be applied.
Ordinal	Nominal with rank order	First, second, and third place finishers in a track meet	More precise than nominal, yet no math may be applied.
Interval	Ordinal with equal distances between measurement units	Water temperature	More precise than ordinal; math may be applied, yet because of a meaningless zero, ratios cannot be calculated.
Ratio	Interval with meaningful zero	Amount of money paid for a tour to China	More precise than interval, math may be applied, and because of a meaningful zero, ratios can be calculated.

Like with nominal data, with ordinal data, you may use numbers as codes, but these cannot be manipulated mathematically. The number represents relative magnitude, meaning something is more or less than something else. That is, the fastest swimmer at the meet is certainly the number one finisher. This mathematical limitation for nominal and ordinal data is overcome when variables are measured at the interval and ratio levels.

Interval Data

Interval data have the rank order characteristic of ordinal data yet go one step beyond. For the ***interval level of measurement***, the distance between the numbers is equal. What does this mean? Look at a thermometer in Fahrenheit. The difference between 60 and 70 degrees is the same as the difference between 70 and 80 degrees, that is, 10 degrees. But, also notice on the thermometer that 0 does not mean there is an absence of temperature; that is, the 0 point is arbitrary. This suggests that for the interval level of measurement you may work with the numbers mathematically, but the 0 in the scale is not meaningful. That is, a ratio cannot be determined with interval data.

To be truthful, sometimes researchers use data collection tools requesting responses measured in an ordinal level yet for statistical analyses treat these data as interval. For example, suppose respondents were asked their opinion on a public pool admission fee increase. These answer categories are used: *strongly agree, agree, neither agree nor disagree, disagree*, and *strongly disagree*. Although the categories represent an ordinal level of measurement, many researchers will treat these data as an interval level of measurement because more precise statistical tools are available for interval data.

Ratio Data

The ***ratio level of measurement*** is the most precise because ratio data have a rank order, with equal units of measurement, and an absolute zero. Think of ratio level data as interval data but with a meaningful zero.

Salary is a common example of ratio data. The difference between an annual salary of $35,000 and $45,000 is the same as the difference between $70,000 and $80,000. Furthermore, a salary of $0 is truly an absence of salary. For information collected as ratio data, you may apply mathematical operations that include calculating a ratio; for example, a person making $80,000 a year is earning twice as much as someone making $40,000. Other examples of ratio-scaled data include height, weight, age, and scores on a statistics test!

Knowing the level of measurement for numerical information is more than a textbook discussion. It matters in research because level of measurement has implications for, among other aspects, testing hypotheses with statistics, preparing tables and graphs, and interpreting conclusions. Most studies examine several variables, typically with different levels of measurement being used in the same study (see Case 14A.1).

DESCRIPTIVE STATISTICS

Once you understand the level of measurement used for study variables, you may decide the best ways to describe or characterize the collected data. In some studies, the data analysis process will consist solely of calculating and interpreting descriptive statistics. ***Descriptive*** or ***univariate statistics*** are used to summarize one variable at a time (Pyrczak, 2009). An arsenal of descriptive statistics is available, including frequency distributions,

LEVELS OF MEASUREMENT

For each scenario indicate the level of measurement: nominal, ordinal, interval, or ratio.

1. A hotel manager wants to know which room type patrons most prefer. She counts the number of reservations according to standard, queen, and king beds.
2. To be placed in a league, children in a sports program are evaluated from 1 to 10, with 1 = *least ability* and 10 = *most ability*.
3. A naturalist wants to develop a wildlife plan for a park. He divides the acreage into categories according to use: hunting, fishing, and education.
4. You want to measure run times for the gold, silver, and bronze medalists in the four-man bobsled event at the Winter Olympics.

Note. Answers are provided at the end of the chapter.

relative comparisons, measures of central tendency, and measures of variability.

Frequency Distributions

In quantitative studies, you usually have large amounts of numerical information. Therefore, the immediate analysis task often is to organize these numbers into an understandable form so you may easily detect trends in the data. The first descriptive statistical analysis tool, frequency distribution, gives a broad and general overview of the collected data.

Specifically, a ***frequency distribution*** describes how data are distributed; it organizes the values of a variable. A frequency distribution lists the variable and the number of responses or scores that correspond to it. A frequency distribution also shows the location of an individual response relative to the others in the data set.

Table 14A.2 is a hypothetical frequency distribution. Hopefully, once you organize the data, it becomes easier to draw conclusions. For example, do you notice that the female campers and those with mild asthma conditions seem to be more frequent attendees of the camp? Often, frequency distributions are summarized visually in tables (as is Table 14A.2) or graphs (see Step 15).

Relative Comparisons

Another descriptive statistic is ***relative comparison***. Rates, ratios, proportions, and percentages are the most typical relative comparisons used to describe collected quantitative information in a research study.

Rate

A ***rate*** is the frequency of occurrence of an outcome. You may calculate rates by dividing the number of actual occurrences by the number of possible occurrences, and then this answer usually is multiplied by a base.

Suppose that for your college, the number of graduating student-athletes this year was 64. This is the number of actual occurrences. Also, suppose the number of student-athletes who started at the college 4 years ago was 97. This is the number of possible occurrences (i.e., 97 could have graduated after 4 years). To calculate the graduation rate for student-athletes, the actual occurrence is divided by the possible occurrence, or $64 \div 97 = .66$. This means that .66th of a student-athlete graduated. Since this is hard to visualize, the answer is usually multiplied by a base, for example, 10. Continuing the calculation using this base would result in $.66 \times 10 = 6.6$. This means the graduation rate is 6.6 per 10 student-athletes.

Another relative comparison often used to describe numerical information is a ***ratio***, which compares the frequency of one response with another. That is, the elements in one response set (A) are compared to the elements in another response set (B) by dividing A by B.

Suppose a comparison is needed between reasons people miss outpatient activity therapy. Reviewing the records, you learn that 23 individuals missed therapy sessions last month because of not being able to get off work (A), whereas 10 participants missed sessions because they simply forgot (B). The ratio of the one excuse to the other is $23 \div 10 = 2.3$. Thus, the ratio of missing

Table 14A.2

Hypothetical Example of a Frequency Distribution of Campers' Characteristics (N = 10)

Camper number	Age	Gender	Number of seasons attending camp	Severity of asthmatic condition
1	12	Female	4	Mild
2	13	Female	5	Moderately severe
3	10	Female	5	Moderately severe
4	10	Female	4	Mild
5	9	Male	3	Mild
6	13	Male	4	Moderately severe
7	12	Male	2	Severe
8	12	Male	2	Severe
9	9	Male	1	Moderately severe
10	12	Male	2	Moderately severe

outpatient activity therapy due to work versus forgetting is 2.3. This means that for every patient who missed the sessions because he or she forgot, 2.3 patients missed because they could not get off work.

A ***proportion*** is a ratio of the total. You may use proportions to compare the frequency of a response with the total frequency. Suppose you want to determine the proportion of playground injuries due to falls from play equipment. Pretend the number of playground injuries last year was 68, with 41 of these due to falls from the play apparatus. To determine the proportion of injuries due to falls from the equipment, divide 41 by 68, which equals .60.

If a proportion is multiplied by 100, it is converted into a ***percentage***, the most commonly reported proportion. To continue with the playground injury example, if you multiply .60 by 100, the result is 60%. Thus, you could conclude that regarding playground injuries, 60% were caused by falls from play equipment.

SOMETHING TO REMEMBER!

Rate = (Number of Actual Occurrences ÷ Number of Possible Occurrences) × Base Number.

Ratio of A to B = A ÷ B.

Proportion = A ÷ (A + B).

Percentage = [A ÷ (A + B)] × 100.

Measures of Central Tendency

Another way to describe numerical data is to determine its center. These statistical tools are called ***measures of central tendency***, meaning you may describe a frequency distribution's center with a single number. That number represents the average or typical score of a sample. The most commonly used tools for describing the center of data are mean, median, and mode.

Mean. Actually, there are many different types of means, but the arithmetic mean is the most popular. The ***mean*** is the arithmetic average of the scores and is only appropriate for interval- and ratio-scaled data. You may calculate it by adding all the scores in the distribution and dividing the answer by the number of scores (see Case 14A.2).

Suppose four participants in the personal training program jog 3, 7, 4, and 6 miles, respectively, in 1 week. The mean, then, is the number of miles jogged by all individuals divided by the total number of joggers:

$$3 + 7 + 4 + 6 = 20 \text{ and then } 20 \div 4 = 5$$

Thus, the mean miles the personal training program participants jogged per week is 5.

Median. The ***median*** is another descriptive tool for determining the centrality of information. It requires ordinal, interval, or ratio data. The median is the score that divides a set of scores into equal halves (Pyrczak, 2009) and is sometimes referred to as the middle value.

If the distribution has an odd number of scores, to determine the median, first arrange the data into ascending or descending order and then identify the value at the middle location. For example, suppose the annual staff performance scores given by a YMCA supervisor range from 0 to 25, with 25 representing perfect performance. To determine the median staff performance score for this year, all 11 scores are arranged in ascending order (you could also arrange in descending order):

5 7 8 8 8 9 12 15 17 19 23

By studying this ordered list of scores, you see that the middle score is 9. That is, the median of 9 leaves the same number of values (five) to the left as to the right. This means that one half of the staff had scores worse than 9 and one half of the staff had scores better than 9.

If the distribution has an even number of scores, the median position is the arithmetic mean of the middle two scores. Suppose you have the following staff performance scores, which are organized in descending order (again, you need to first arrange data):

23 19 17 15 12 11 9 8 8 8 7 5

To calculate the median for this distribution of scores, you would complete the following steps:

- Step 1: Determine the number of scores: 12.
- Step 2: Add 1 to the number of scores: 12 + 1 = 13.
- Step 3: Divide the answer derived in Step 2 by 2: 13 ÷ 2 = 6.5. The median score is 6.5, that is, the halfway point between 11 and 9.
- Step 4: Calculate the mean of the scores revealed by Step 3. Applied to this example, (11 + 9) ÷ 2 = 10.

Thus, the median of this distribution of staff performance scores is 10, the point that divides the distribution in half (even though no staff member had this score).

Mode. Finally, the ***mode*** is the most frequently occurring response category. Think of the mode as a popularity contest. The value that shows up the most often in the distribution is the mode. The mode of the staff performance scores in the above example is 8 since this score occurs more frequently than the other scores.

SOMETHING TO REMEMBER!

Mean = arithmetic average; Sum of X ÷ *N*.

Median = middle score in an ordered distribution.

Mode = most common or popular response.

CALCULATING MEASURES OF CENTRAL TENDENCY

The following is a distribution of players' ages at a midnight basketball program:

Players' age	Number of players
17	1
18	5
19	1
20	4
21	1
22	1

1. What is the mean age of players?
2. What is the median age of players?
3. What is the mode age of players?
4. Which average would be the most appropriate to cite in a report? (*Hint:* Read on, and consult Table 14A.3)

Note. Answers are provided at the end of the chapter.

Measures of Variability

Although measures of central tendency are useful for describing a data set, they are not always sufficient. Oftentimes, a summary of the diversity of the data is helpful. These ***measures of variability*** summarize with one number the dispersion or spread of the individual responses in the data set. In other words, they provide a description of the degree that responses are close to or far from each other. Range and standard deviation are popular forms of variability (see Case 14A.3).

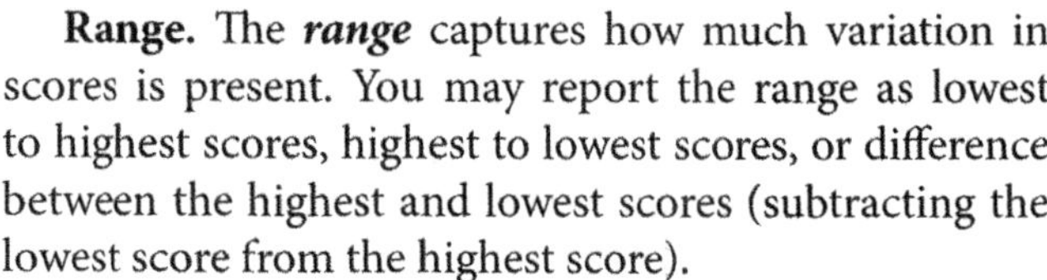

Range. The ***range*** captures how much variation in scores is present. You may report the range as lowest to highest scores, highest to lowest scores, or difference between the highest and lowest scores (subtracting the lowest score from the highest score).

For example, calculate the range for the staff performance scores noted earlier:

5 7 8 8 8 8 11 12 15 17 19 23

The range of these scores could be reported as either 5 to 23, 23 to 5, or 18 (i.e., 23 – 5).

Because of its simplicity, the range may be problematic. Although it depicts the distance between the two most extreme values in the distribution, it ignores the values in between. For example, suppose a new supervisor performed an evaluation of the same 12 staff and recorded the following results:

5 6 6 6 7 7 7 7 8 8 8 23

No matter how it is reported (5 to 23, 23 to 5, or 18), the range of new supervisor's answers is the same as the first supervisor's ratings, yet the values between these numbers in the distribution are spread differently. This is where the statistical tool standard deviation is useful.

Standard deviation. To account for the dispersion of scores in a distribution, you may calculate a ***standard deviation***, which uses the mean of the distribution as a reference point and measures the spread between each score and the mean point. Think of the standard deviation as the average distance from the mean. When the standard deviation equals 0, there is no spread of scores (i.e., the scores are the same). As the spread of scores around the mean increases, the size of the standard deviation increases.

While most calculators have a function for determining standard deviation, the following steps demonstrate how to hand-calculate a standard deviation for a frequency distribution (also see Figure 14A.1):

- Step 1: Calculate the mean.
- Step 2: Subtract the mean value from each score. These are called ***deviation scores***.
- Step 3: Square each of these deviation scores.
- Step 4: Add up these squared deviation scores.
- Step 5: Divide this sum by $N - 1$ (where N represents the number of responses).
- Step 6: Calculate the square root of the answer found in Step 5.

SOMETHING TO REMEMBER!

Range = X (Highest Score) - X (Lowest Score), or X (Lowest Score) - X (Highest Score), or Highest Score - Lowest Score

Standard Deviation = Square Root of the Sum of Squared Deviation Scores ÷ (N - 1)

What does the standard deviation of 2.9 from Figure 14A.1 represent? Think of the standard deviation value as describing the typical distance of each night's stayed value from the mean of the distribution. That is, the average difference between individual guest values and the average for the sample is almost 3 nights.

STANDARD DEVIATION

Now you try it. Calculate the standard deviation for a distribution of the number of people over a 5-day period that stopped at a petting zoo exhibit, using the following data:

1 2 2 3 3 4

Note. Answers are provided at the end of the chapter.

Selecting the Best Descriptive Statistics

Now that you understand ways of describing numerical data, how do you decide which to use? One answer is according to the objective the descriptive statistic will serve. Do you want to know the percentage for a variable? Do you want to analyze the center of the distribution? A second consideration is the level of measure-

A sample of guests stayed the following number of nights at a resort: 1, 3, 5, 5, 7, 7, 10.

To calculate the standard deviation of these data, complete the following steps:

- Step 1: Calculate the mean: (1 + 3 + 5 + 5 + 7 + 7 + 10) ÷ 7 = 38 ÷ 7 = 5.42, rounded to 5.4 nights.
- Step 2: Calculate the deviation score (see this calculation in the third column).

Guest's name	Number of nights stayed	Deviation score	Square of deviation score
Johnson	1	1 - 5.4 = -4.4	19.4
Allen	3	3 - 5.4 = -2.4	5.8
Cutler	5	5 - 5.4 = -0.4	0.2
Ramos	5	5 - 5.4 = -0.4	0.2
Oliver	7	7 - 5.4 = 1.6	2.6
Smith	7	7 - 5.4 = 1.6	2.6
Martin	10	10 - 5.4 = 4.6	21.2

- Step 3: Square each deviation score (see the last column).
- Step 4: Sum the squared deviation scores: 19.4 + 5.8 + .2 + .2 + 2.6 + 2.6 + 21.2 = 52.
- Step 5: Divide the sum of the squared deviation scores by N – 1: 52 ÷ (7 - 1) = 8.66, rounded to 8.7.
- Step 6: Calculate the square root of the answer to Step 5. Thus, the square root of 8.7 = 2.9.

Consequently, the standard deviation for nights stayed at the resort is 2.9.

Figure 14A.1. Example of a standard deviation calculation.

ment used to collect the data. Finally, decision making will be influenced by extreme scores in the distribution and the sample size. Accordingly, Table 14A.3 has advice for choosing the best descriptive statistic.

Correlational Statistics

Up to this point, every descriptive statistic has applied only to one variable at a time. Again, this is known as univariate statistics. You also may examine the relationships between two variables, also known as ***bivariate statistics***.

The ***correlation coefficient*** is a bivariate statistic that describes the relationship between two variables. A correlation coefficient is a numerical index that reflects the degree of relationship between the scores for two variables (Pyrczak, 2009). That is, it captures how fluctuation in one variable links to the fluctuation in another variable. If one variable increases in value, does the other variable increase or decrease?

You may calculate several correlation coefficient statistics depending on, among other aspects, the level of measurement of the data. One is the ***Pearson product-moment correlation coefficient*** (Pearson's *r*). Pearson's *r* is used with interval and ratio data. Its calculation produces an index that ranges between −1 and +1.

For example, as reported in Case 14A.4, Pearson's *r* for the relationship between leisure-time physical activity and physical function was +.28, which is a positive correlation. Thus, in this study, the correlation coefficient indicates that as leisure-time physical activity increased so did physical functioning.

Table 14A.3
Choosing the Best Descriptive Statistic

Descriptive statistic	Describes	Level of measurement	Comments
Rate, ratio, proportion, percentage	Relative comparisons	Interval or ratio	Typically understood by nonresearchers
Mean	Distribution's center as an average of all values	Interval or ratio	Most precise measure of centrality; not useful when distribution has extreme scores
Median	Distribution's center as the middle value	Ordinal, interval, or ratio	Less precise than the mean, more precise than mode; useful when distribution in a smaller sample has extreme scores
Mode	Distribution's center as the most frequently occurring value	Nominal, ordinal, interval, or ratio	Least precise, yet only choice for nominal data; useful when distribution in larger sample has extreme scores
Range	Spread of a distribution between the highest and lowest values	Ordinal, interval, or ratio	A simple indicator, yet not precise
Standard deviation	Spread of a distribution as the average distance of every value from the mean	Interval or ratio	Most precise, yet not useful when distribution has extreme scores

This interpretation of an $r = +.28$ is focused on the direction of the relationship. That is, the signs attached to the index (+ or −) indicate whether the variables change in the same or opposite directions. A ***positive*** (or direct) ***correlation*** means that the two variables change in the same direction and is depicted with a plus sign (+).

Variables also may change in opposite directions, which is called an ***inverse*** or ***negative correlation***, and is depicted with a minus sign (−). Suppose Pearson's r in Case 14A.4 was reported as −.28. This negative correlation means that as leisure-time physical activity increased, physical functioning decreased (thank goodness a negative relationship was not found in the study!). This characteristic of direction for correlation coefficients is summarized in Table 14A.4.

The correlation coefficient also shows the ***strength*** (or magnitude) ***of the relationship***. The larger the correlation coefficient value is, the stronger the relationship. That is, the closer the value is to 1.00 (considered a perfect relationship), the stronger the association between the variables. Thus, a correlation of .70 is stronger than a correlation of .50 because .70 is closer to 1.00. Now, how close to 1.00 does the value of the coefficient need to be in order to be a strong relationship?

Opinions on what constitutes a strong relationship vary. Salkind (2013) recommended a fairly conservative approach:

- 0.8 to 1.0 = Very strong relationship
- 0.6 to 0.8 = Strong relationship
- 0.4 to 0.6 = Moderate relationship
- 0.2 to 0.4 = Weak relationship
- 0.0 to 0.2 = Nonexistent relationship

A mistake made frequently with interpreting correlation coefficients is confusing the direction of the relationship with the strength of the relationship. The rule is, when interpreting the direction of the relationship depicted in the coefficient value, pay attention to whether a plus or minus sign is recorded and ignore the actual number. Conversely, when evaluating the strength of the relationship, pay attention to the number and ignore the plus or minus sign.

Does competition relate to skill development in outdoor recreation pu suits? That is, does having more opportunities to compete in kayaking increase river paddling skills? Calculating a correlation coefficient will help answer this research question. Copyright © 2015 Ruth V. Russell.

Table 14A.4
Illustrating the Direction of Correlation Coefficients

Relationship between variables	Example	Direction of correlation
As one variable increases, second variable increases	The more you practice, the more you win	Positive
As one variable decreases, second variable decreases	The less you practice, the less you win	Positive
As one variable increases, second variable decreases	The more you exercise, the lower your resting heart rate	Negative
As one variable decreases, second variable increases	The less you exercise, the higher your resting heart rate	Negative

To more precisely interpret the strength of a correlation, you may compute the ***coefficient of determination***, which is calculated as a percentage and tells the amount of change in one variable that is accounted for by the change in the other variable. Compute it by squaring the correlation coefficient. For example, if the correlation coefficient between basketball practice and winning games is .73 (a strong positive relationship), you would calculate the coefficient of determination as the square of .73:

$$.73 \times .73 = .53$$

This means 53% of the games won may be explained by practicing a lot. Of course, this also means that 47% of the losses are explained by something other than practicing. You do not know how other factors (e.g., players' natural abilities and coaching style) are influencing a team's win–loss record.

INFERENTIAL STATISTICS

Inferential statistics are a family of analysis tools that tell you how much confidence you have when generalizing from a sample to a population (Pyrczak, 2009). With the help of these analysis approaches, you are able to make inferences about a population from a sample's data (see Steps 6 and 7).

Suppose you selected stratified random samples of male and female undergraduates attending a university that had an enrollment of 25,000 students. Students' physical fitness levels were measured using a standardized test. The results suggested that male students in the sample had higher levels of fitness than the female students in the sample. But do they really? Could the differences have been due to sampling errors? Could the population mean for undergraduate males and the population mean for undergraduate females be identical, and the difference between the means for the two samples be only because of chance errors associated with random sampling? You may use inferential tests to guide you in concluding whether the study results are applied to the entire university's undergraduate male and female populations.

Thus, inferential statistics allow decisions about populations based on information about samples. That is, inferential statistics are quantitative data analysis techniques for determining the likelihood that results obtained from a sample are the same results that would be obtained for the entire population.

Many inferential statistical tools are available, including the *t* test, analysis of variance (ANOVA), and chi-square. At this point, learning what inferential statistics to apply requires completing basic and intermediate statistics courses and/or consulting someone knowledgeable in statistics.

INTERPRETING DIRECTION AND STRENGTH OF CORRELATION COEFFICIENTS

For each coefficient value, identify its direction and strength and how you would interpret it in terms of the variables.

Coefficient value	Direction	Strength	Interpretation
.35 between leisure-time physical activity and physical functioning			
-.78 between amount of television watched and number of best friends			

Note. Answers are provided at the end of the chapter.

STATISTICAL SOFTWARE

Statistical software packages are readily available to analyze quantitative data. One of the most popular statistical software packages used in many colleges and universities is the Statistical Package for the Social Sciences (SPSS). SPSS is widely used in quantitative research and is relatively easy to learn. A free software alternative to the proprietary SPSS is PSPP (https://www.gnu.org/software/pspp/).

Other statistical software options include SAS, SYSTAT, and Minitab. Microsoft Excel also has statistical functions. As well, several statistical software sites are available on the Internet. There are Web-based stat programs (no download), no cost, and incredibly easy to use. One such site is VassarStats (http://vassarstats.net/) and another is StatCrunch (http://www.statcrunch.com).

Because these statistical software packages make the calculations easy to use, a final caution is necessary. What is not easy is choosing which statistical analyses button to push!

In the bicycle world, one-, two-, and three-wheeler bikes are used. Likewise, analyzing quantitative data entails using univariate, bivariate, or multivariate statistics. Wooden bicycle, Ljubljana, Slovenia. Copyright © 2015 Carol Cutler Riddick.

REVIEW AND DISCUSSION QUESTIONS

1. Name and define the four levels of numerical measurement.
2. Define descriptive statistics.
3. What is a frequency distribution? How does it help describe numerical information?
4. What comparisons do rates, ratios, proportions, and percentages make?
5. How are the descriptions from calculating rates, ratios, proportions, and percentages different?
6. What do measures of central tendency describe?
7. How are the descriptions from calculating means, medians, and modes different?
8. What do measures of variability describe?
9. How are ranges and standard deviations calculated?
10. What is the difference between univariate and bivariate statistics?
11. What does the correlation coefficient describe? Likewise, what does the coefficient of determination reveal?
12. What is the focus of inferential statistics?

YOUR RESEARCH

1. Make a list of the variables in your study about which you have collected quantitative information.
2. For each variable in your list, determine the level of measurement. Are the data nominal, ordinal, interval, and/or ratio?
3. What descriptive story would you like to tell about your variables?

4. What descriptive statistics should you use to tell these stories? For each quantitatively measured variable, complete the following:
   a. Create a frequency distribution.
   b. Calculate a rate, ratio, proportion, and/or percentage as appropriate.
   c. Calculate a measure of central tendency.
   d. Calculate a measure of variability.

5. What relationships and/or differences may be interesting to determine for your data? What statistics will help you determine these?

PRACTICE EXERCISES

1. The following are data from 572 persons who completed a camper satisfaction survey conducted by a commercial nationwide campground chain.

Worksheet Analyzing Quantitative Data Chapter: Relative Comparisons

Responses by question regarding campground experience	Frequencies (N = 572)
Overall experience was excellent	135
Would definitely return	151
Good value for the price	369
Appealing recreational activities	421

   a. What is the *overall experience was excellent* rate? Interpret the answer.
   b. What is the ratio of *would definitely return* to *appealing recreational activities*? Interpret the answer.
   c. What percentage of respondents considers the campground to be *good value for the price*?

2. The following are made-up data about the number of shore excursions a sample of passengers on a ship cruising the Panama Canal took during a 2-week cruise:

   2, 1, 0, 3, 3, 3, 3, 3, 5, 2, 7, 4, 3, 2, 1, 1, 0, 6, 10

   a. Organize the data by creating a frequency distribution.
   b. Calculate the mean, median, and mode for this distribution. Why are the answers to these measures of central tendency different or the same? Which measure is more truthful about the center of these data?
   c. What is the range for these data?
   d. Calculate the standard deviation for these data.
   e. Write a statement that describes the data overall.

3. The following are possible correlation coefficients. For each example, describe the direction and strength of the relationships. What are the coefficients of determination for each? Write a summary about each relationship.

Worksheet Analyzing Quantitative Data Chapter:
Explaining and Interpreting Pearson's *r*

Pearson *r*	Direction	Strength	Coefficient of determination	Intepretation
1. Number of years on the pro circuit and Masters golf tournament score in the year, *r* = .35				
2. Body mass index score and self-esteem score, *r* = −.65				
3. Amount community annually spends on public recreation services and the community's quality of life index score, *r* = .89				
4. Number of years participating in Girl Scouts and number of truancy days in high school, *r* = −.92				

WEB EXERCISES

1. Learn more about the measures of variability by going to the website for Dr. Linda Woolf 's statistics course at Webster College: http://www.webster.edu/~woolflm/variability.html. Work on one of the four variability problems. Calculate the range and the standard deviation (ignore the variance). Check your answers by clicking on "Answer."
2. Suppose you have data (see below) on two variables for a sample (number of tennis players in the family and price willing to pay to join a private tennis club). Using either VassarStats (http://vassarstats.net/) or StatCrunch (http://www.statcrunch.com) online statistics software, calculate and record (a) Pearson's *r* for these data and (b) the coefficient of determination. What do you conclude?

Worksheet Analyzing Quantitative Data Chapter:
Calculating and Interpreting Pearson's *r* and Coefficient of Determination

Respondent number	Number of tennis players in family (X)	Price willing to pay to join a private tennis club (Y)	Pearson's *r*	Coefficient of determination	Conclusion
1	1	$50			
2	2	$100			
3	4	$450			

Respondent number	Number of tennis players in family (X)	Price willing to pay to join a private tennis club (Y)	Pearson's *r*	Coefficient of determination	Conclusion
4	0	$50			
5	3	$250			
6	3	$500			
7	1	$150			
8	2	$250			
9	1	$100			
10	0	$0			
11	4	$600			
12	5	$350			
13	2	$100			
14	0	$50			

3. Acquire a copy of the following article (or your instructor may substitute another article):

   Wolff, K., & Larsen, S. (2014). Can terrorism make us feel safer? Risk perceptions and worries before and after the July 22nd attacks. *Annals of Tourism Research, 44*, 200–209. You may access this article at http://www.sciencedirect.com/science/article/pii/S0160738313001345.

   Find the section of the article that reports the research results. By answering the following questions you should learn something about yourself. Even though you may not feel you have mastered the quantitative analysis tools discussed in this chapter, you will probably be impressed that you can at least recognize them!

   a. In the Results section of the article, mark the statistical procedures used to organize and analyze the data. How many of them can you identify?
   b. Was a mean and/or standard deviation reported?
   c. Was an inferential statistic used in the study? If used, name the specific statistic used.

SERVICE LEARNING

For the campus program or service that has been selected as the focus of the service learning project for this semester, complete the following:

1. What descriptive statistics would be appropriate to use in reporting characteristics of the sample? Set up a grid identifying each variable and specific descriptive statistic that you plan to use in presenting this data.
2. What descriptive or bivariate statistics would be appropriate to use in reporting results? Set up a grid identifying each variable and the specific descriptive or bivariate statistic that you plan to use in presenting this data.
3. Present your ideas for statistic presentation and analyses to your instructor. What is his or her reaction and advice? Adjust the chosen statistical analysis plan accordingly.

4. Finally, calculate the statistics designated in your plan.

TEST YOURSELF ANSWERS

Levels of Measurement

1. Ordinal, 2. Ordinal, 3. Nominal, 4. Ratio

Calculating Measures of Central Tendency

1. Mean = 19.2, 2. Median = 19, 3. Mode = 18, 4. Mean, since only 13 players and the distribution is not spread out (age range is from 17 to 22 years)

Standard Deviation

1.048

Interpreting Direction and Strength of Correlation Coefficients

Coefficient value	Direction	Strength	Interpretation
.35 between leisure-time physical activity and physical functioning	Positive	Weak	There is a weak positive relationship between physical activity and physical functioning. That is, as we increase our physical activity in leisure, our physical functioning also increases slightly.
-.78 between amount of television watched and number of best friends	Negative	Strong	There is a strong negative relationship between watching television and having friends. That is, those who watch a lot of television, tend to have fewer friends.

SUPPORTING CASES FOR THIS CHAPTER

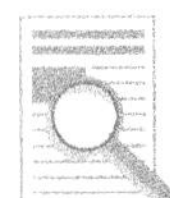

CASE 14A.1. USING MULTIPLE LEVELS OF MEASUREMENT IN A STUDY

Larsen, S., Ogaard, T., & Brun, W. (2011). Backpackers and mainstreamers: Realities and myths. *Annals of Tourism Research, 28*, 690–707.

This study compared the budget traveler to mainstream tourists in terms of travel motivations, subjective judgments of risk, tourist worries, and tourists' self-identifications. The variables in the study (and the level of measurement noted parenthetically for each) were as follows:

- tourist type was measured as being self-declared either a budget or mainstream traveler (thus, a nominal scale was used);
- length of current trip was determined as number of days spent traveling (ratio scale); and
- travel motivations was broken down into categories (e.g., relaxation, knowledge, cultural awareness, and escape), and each was measured using a 7-point scale ranging from *not important* to *very important* (depending on the question, either an ordinal or interval scale was used).

Few differences were found between groups. Budget travelers, however, were less motivated by needs for luxury and relaxation; as well, they judged travel-related hazards to be less risky. For example, budget travelers worried less about food, terror, and foreign cultures. Budget travelers also perceived themselves to be less typical tourists than mainstream tourists.

CASE 14A.2. MEASURES OF CENTRAL TENDENCY

Furman, N., Shooter, W., & Schumann, S. (2010). The roles of heuristics, avalanche forecast, and risk propensity in the decision making of backcountry skiers. *Leisure Sciences, 32*, 453–469.

Backcountry winter recreation accidents and deaths due to avalanches have grown considerably in recent decades. To better understand how individuals make decisions in avalanche terrain, this study examined the decision-making factors that are believed to be complicit in avalanche accidents. As part of the analysis of data, descriptive statistics were calculated for the sample.

Respondents were queried about the likelihood they would ski under varying conditions. Likelihood to ski was measured by responses to several questions. Scores ranged from 1 to 7 (7 = *very likely*). When the avalanche forecast was low, the mean was 5.9 for likelihood to ski a slope. When it was moderate, the mean was 4.7 for likelihood to ski a slope. When it was considerable, the mean was 3.7 for likelihood to ski a slope. When the avalanche hazard was high, the mean was 2.8 for likelihood to ski a slope.

CASE 14A.3. MEASURES OF VARIABILITY

Breunig, M., O'Connell, T., Todd, S., Anderson, L., & Young, A. (2010). The impact of outdoor pursuits on college students' perceived sense of community. *Journal of Leisure Research, 42*, 551–572.

A primary purpose of outdoor pursuits is developing positive interpersonal relationships and group experiences that lead to enhanced sense of community. The aim of this study was to understand the relationship between college students' participation in outdoor pursuit trips and changes in their perceptions of sense of community over time. Findings indicated a significant increase in sense of community as a result of participation in outdoor pursuit trips. For example, on Day 3 of the trip, the mean was 3.6 for sense of community (SD = .71), whereas on Day 13 of the trip it was 4.2 (SD = .64).

CASE 14A.4. PEARSON'S *r* CORRELATION COEFFICIENT

Paxton, R., Jones, L., Rosoff, P., Boner, M., Ater, J., & Demark-Wahnefried, W. (2010). Associations between leisure-time physical activity and health-related quality of life among adolescent and adult survivors of childhood cancers. *Psycho-Oncology, 19*, 997–1003.

Survivors of childhood cancer are at an increased risk for reduced quality of life. However, few studies have explored factors associated with improving the quality of life of adolescents and adult cancer survivors. Adolescent and adult survivors of childhood lymphoma, leukemia, and central nervous system cancers (N = 215) completed mailed surveys. Pearson's r was calculated.

The study found in the adolescent sample a modest association (r = .27) between the variables of leisure-time physical activity and health-related quality of life measures. Specifically, leisure-time physical activity of adolescent cancer survivors was positively associated with cancer worry reduction (r = .36), physical function (r = .28), cognitive function (r = .32), body appearance (r = .29), and social function (r = .27) in adolescence.

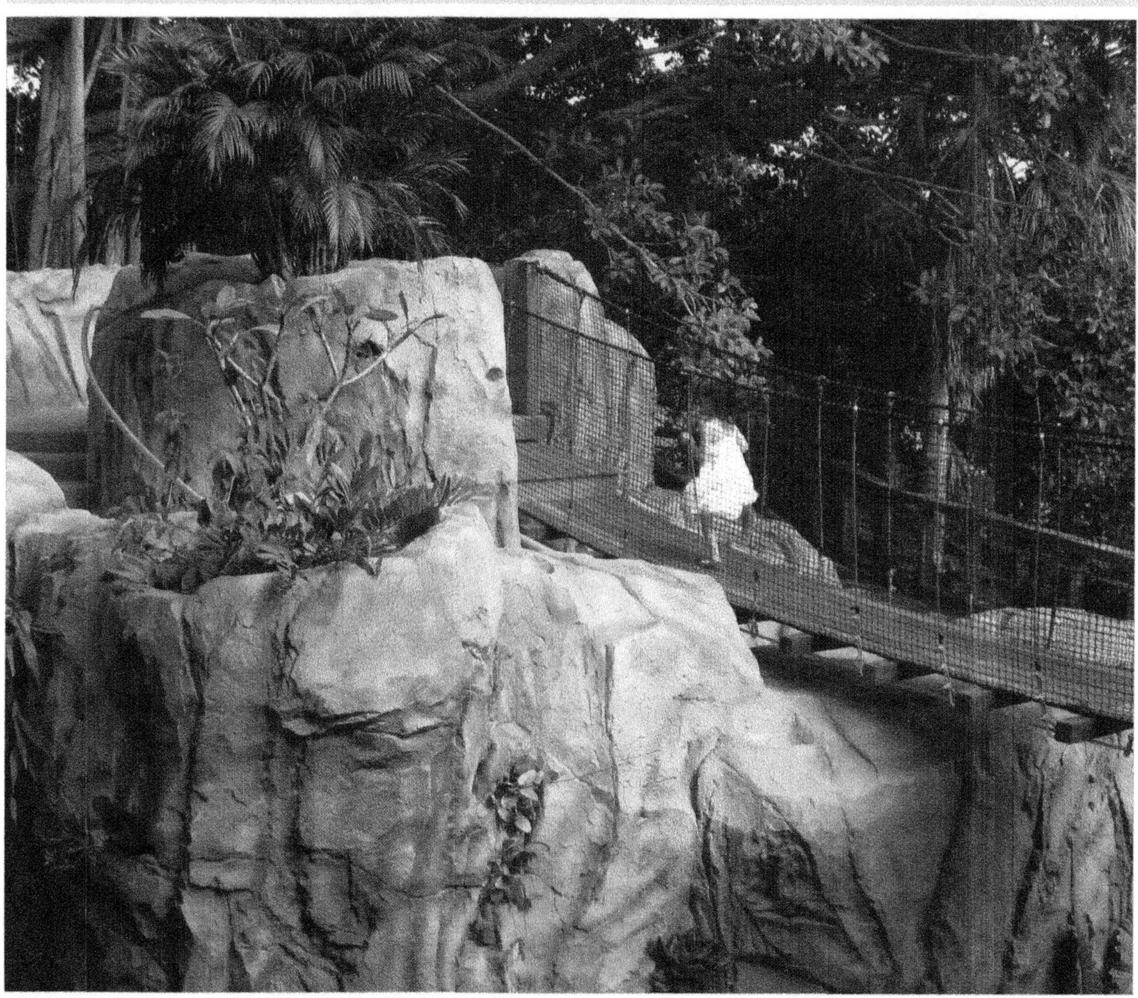

In qualitative data analysis, you must use your skills of looking and understanding, just as children are encouraged to do at the Ann Goldstein Children's Rainforest Garden at the Marie Selby Botanical Gardens, Sarasota, Florida.

STEP 12 > STEP 13 > STEP 14A > STEP 14B

ANALYZE QUALITATIVE DATA

WHAT WILL I LEARN IN THIS CHAPTER?

I'll be able to...

1. Define qualitative data analysis.
2. Distinguish between the inductive process and the cyclical process.
3. Clarify ways of organizing qualitative data, including condensed and expanded accounts, memos, coding into categories, and data displays.
4. Draft two data displays: matrices and networks.
5. Summarize what is entailed in making tentative conclusions from qualitative data analysis.
6. Outline strategies for making tentative conclusions, including clustering, subsuming particulars into the general, counting, seeing plausibility, and making metaphors.
7. Describe what it means to verify conclusions in qualitative data analysis and how checking for data quality and testing explanations can do this.
8. Explain how to check data quality by examining representativeness and researcher effects.
9. Provide details regarding testing explanations through replication of findings and rival explanations.

"Research is to see what everybody else has seen, and to think what nobody else has thought."

Albert Szent-Gyorghi
(Hungarian physiologist who won the Nobel Prize in Physiology/Medicine in 1937, credited with discovering vitamin C, 1893–1986)

As previously pointed out, information gathered in research is either numbers or words. Ways of analyzing numerical information were discussed in Step 14A. This chapter discusses analyzing qualitative data and is arranged into four parts. To begin, qualitative data analysis will be defined and explained. Then, ideas on how to organize and prepare qualitative data will be provided, followed by insights on how to make and verify tentative conclusions.

QUALITATIVE DATA ANALYSIS DEFINED

At its essence, ***qualitative data analysis*** is making sense of text from interviews transcripts, notes from participant observation sessions, written words and thoughts found in public or private documents (e.g., minutes of meetings, marketing materials, journals, diaries, or letters), and images found in audio-visual materials (e.g., photographs, videotapes; Schutt, 2011). Analyzing qualitative data has been described as "... organizing, abstracting, integrating, and synthesizing, which ultimately permit researchers to report what they have seen or heard" (Thomas, Nelson, & Silverman, 2011, p. 360). As the name suggests, qualitative data analysis is focused on qualities more than quantities. You may use it to seek themes or patterns by extracting meaning from rich, complex sources of narratives or images (Suter, 2011). Schutt (2011) said, "Qualitative data analysts seek to describe their textual data in ways that capture the setting or people who produced this text on their own terms rather than in terms of predefined measures and hypotheses"(p. 358).

You may analyze qualitative data in many ways. However, inductive and cyclical processes govern all of the approaches.

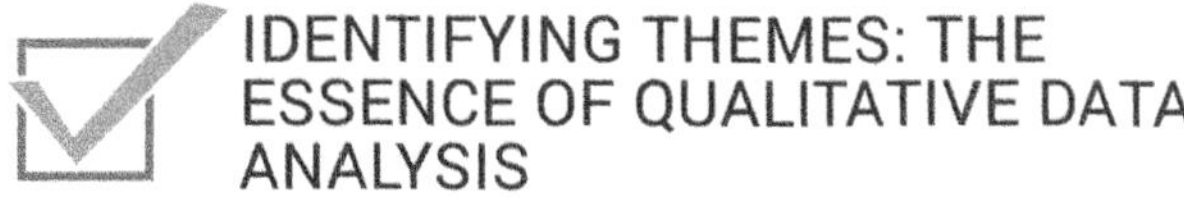

IDENTIFYING THEMES: THE ESSENCE OF QUALITATIVE DATA ANALYSIS

Before you read the rest of the chapter, assess your skills as a qualitative analyst! Identify the themes in a study of young female gang members. In-depth unstructured interviews about roles and meanings were conducted with women aged 13 to 18 years who claimed affiliation with youth gangs. The following are excerpts taken from the interview transcripts:

- "Well, I didn't get any respect at home. I wanted to get some love and respect from somebody somewhere else." (p. 107)
- "I didn't have no family...I had nothin' else." (p. 107)
- "Some of 'em are like me, don't have, don't really have a basic home or steady home to go to, you know, and they don't have as much love and respect in the home so they want to get it elsewhere." (p. 108)
- "[We] play cards, smoke bud, play dominoes, play video games. That's basically all we do is play. You would be surprised. This is a bunch of big kids." (p. 109)

Note. Adapted from Miller and Glassner (1997). Answers are provided at the end of the chapter.

Inductive Process

Qualitative data analysis is based on inductive reasoning (introduced in Step 3). With inductive thinking, patterns and relationships emerge from the data. In other words, insights evolve from data collected in the study, not from preconceived notions stemming from directives or ideas from existing theories. Contrastingly, quantitative data analysis relies on deductive thinking, where patterns and relationships are established before the study is executed and collected data are then analyzed to determine whether these hunches may be supported.

The distinction between inductive and deductive thinking plays out in multiple ways in how qualitative and quantitative data are analyzed. Table 14B.1 compares the ramifications of these approaches for data analysis.

Cyclical Process

In addition to being inductive, the qualitative data analysis process is a series of cyclical phases that moves among four areas (Figure 14B.1): (a) collecting data, (b) organizing data, (c) casting tentative conclusions, and (d) verifying conclusions. Gradually, more advanced levels of synthesis are achieved after each cycle. Creswell (2012) noted, "It is an ongoing process involving continual reflection about the data, asking analytic questions, and writing memos throughout the study...that qualitative data analysis is conducted concurrently with gathering data, making interpretations, and writing reports" (p. 184).

This means that you begin the inductive and cyclical processes with an analysis when you have collected the earliest data. Proceed by organizing and dividing the data into relevant chunks, or pieces, of information. Organize these into categories. Sorting ideas is an ongoing task requiring checking and rechecking, or comparing and contrasting, new information as you continue to collect it.

Table 14B.1
Differences Between Qualitative and Quantitative Data Analysis

Comparison points	Qualitative data analysis, or reliance on inductive thinking	Quantitative data analysis, or reliance on deductive thinking
Data source	Narrative and visual	Numerical
Timing of data analysis	Begins during data collection	Occurs at the end of data collection
Treatment of raw data	Abstract concepts emerge from words and images, often to explain or illustrate	Numbers manipulated, often to test hypotheses
Order of analysis	Circular, iterative	Linear
Point of analysis	"Paint a picture"	"Crunch numbers"

Note. Adapted from Gratton and Jones (2010).

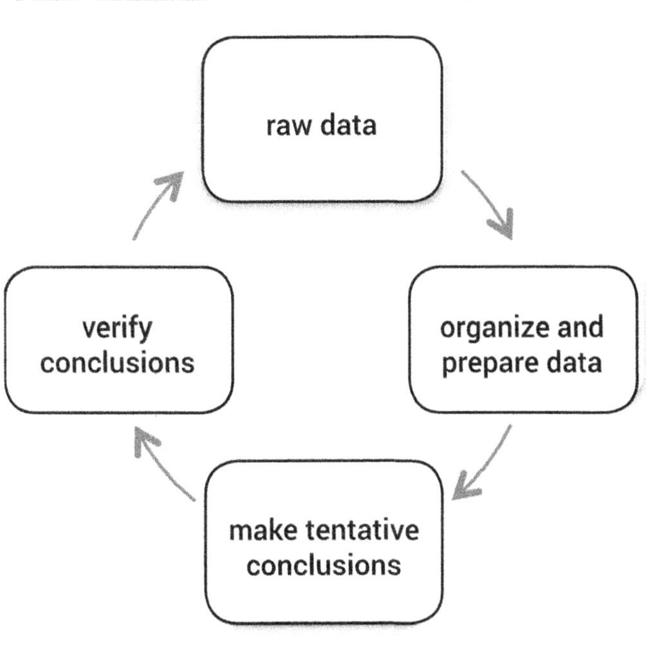

Figure 14B.1. The cyclical qualitative data analysis process.

After you check and recheck category groups, a tentative organization system will emerge. As necessary, re-form and shore up the categories with the new information collected. The initial and emerging categories are preliminary and tentative and remain as flexible working tools rather than rigid findings. Recheck the tentative themes or patterns that have been identified, and if they seem meaningful and clear, they become the verifiable conclusions of the study.

SOMETHING TO REMEMBER!

Inductive thinking: Working from the specific raw data to broader generalizations; bottom-up approach to research.

Deductive thinking: Working from an assertion or speculation, such as that advanced by a theory, to the specific; top-down approach to research.

Qualitative data analysis is based on an inductive thinking process, whereas quantitative data analysis is based on a deductive thinking process.

Since Steps 9 and 13 reviewed data collection, the remainder of this chapter is focused on what happens after you have begun to collect the initial raw data. In particular, the following will be reviewed: organizing and preparing data, making tentative conclusions, and verifying the conclusions.

ORGANIZE AND PREPARE DATA

Organizing qualitative data requires managing ***raw data*** (i.e., originally collected words or images) so you may categorize insights or observations. Organizing data is similar to working a puzzle. People working a jigsaw puzzle usually use one of two approaches for putting the puzzle together. Some sort through the pieces, dividing them into discrete piles that correspond with images or parts of the puzzle (e.g., all blue sky pieces are set in one mound, all people pieces are put into another pile). Others begin by finding and separating into one pile the border pieces. With either puzzle strategy, once the puzzle pieces are sorted and categorized, they may be fitted together. Some puzzlers begin by putting the border together, and others assemble the sky and people in the picture first.

As is true with puzzles, no single approach is correct for organizing qualitative data. When organizing the words and images of raw data, you are conducting a ***meta-analysis*** (Peacock & Paul-Ward, 2006) and creating ***meta-data***. That is, new words and/or graphic products are created to represent key themes and relationships emerging from the data. Common meta-data are

- condensed and expanded accounts,
- memos,
- category codes, and
- data displays.

Condensed and Expanded Accounts

Most qualitative data begin as words on a page because the most common sources of data collected in qualitative research are ***transcripts***, a written record or printed version of material originally presented in another medium (e.g., recorded interviews, field notes from observations, and reviews of documents; Creswell, 2013). In most cases, the qualitative data is raw data and a ***condensed account***, meaning phrases, single words, and unconnected sentences (Spradley, 1980). Condensed accounts do not record everything that occurred or was said, yet they have enormous value because they were recorded in the field and are therefore rich in information (see Table 14B.2).

After acquiring a condensed account, you need to enlarge it into an ***expanded account*** (Spradley, 1980). In an expanded account, you fill in the details from the condensed account (see Table 14B.2). For example, an expanded account may emerge from observations or a transcript from a taped interview.

Table 14B.2
Example of Condensed and Expanded Accounts

Condensed account of observation at a local park	Expanded account of same observation at a local park
• D & M guitars • D asked to play • Others looking on • Young male kid watching • More kids approach • Nervous, cautious, drawn in	Doris and Michelle brought their guitars to the park. Doris was asked to play. Doris began to play and sing with Michelle accompanying her, both playing guitar and singing. I was sitting on top of a picnic table a few feet away, and Tim sat beside me. From where I sat, I could see not only Doris and Doreen, Bill, Shereen, and Jess, but also the many kids in the background who had noticed us and were curiously looking on. Finally, one brave soul (a young man who appeared 10 years old) approached the corner of the area and unobtrusively watched. He appeared almost mesmerized by the whole scene. After this first young man had ventured into "our territory," more children began to approach. Those who were younger held expressions of curiosity, fear and intensity.

Note. Adapted from Kielhofner and Takata (1980).

As the expanded account notes begin to grow, make a decision about note management. More specifically, you need to develop a filing system to keep expanded accounts organized so you are able to cross-reference linked information and locate it as the analysis proceeds.

MANAGING EXPANDED ACCOUNTS

The following are ways to keep your expanded account notes organized. Choose the ones best suited to you and your data.

- Cut field notes up and put in theme folders. Create a manila folder for each possible category of information. Cut the paper version of your expanded accounts apart and file them in the appropriate folder according to tentative themes. Write a circled number on each expanded account piece of paper and keep a running directory of what notes are in what folder according to the numbering system (Bogdan and Biklen, 2006).
- Use a file card system to retrieve relevant notes. Number each line on the expanded account transcripts consecutively. Record on each file card (e.g., 3 × 5 inch) the relevant and corresponding phrase across the top of the card appearing in the original condensed accounts and the corresponding relevant lines found in the expanded accounts (Bogdan and Biklen, 2006).
- Order notes in terms of sequence. Write dates (month, day, year) on expanded account notes and then sequence them with label notes according to type (e.g., field notes, interview transcripts) (Bogdan and Biklen, 2006).
- Later in this chapter computer software that can assist in qualitative data analysis is discussed. However, at this initial phase of organizing data, most programs have proven unsatisfactory. One exception is FileMaker Pro (2007; now in version 9), which with practice can serve as a true relational database (Johnson, Dunlap, & Benoit, 2010).

Memos

After creating and organizing expanded accounts, add ***memos***, or notes suggesting explanations for the expanded account content. It is a reflective action whereby you (the fieldworker and/or analyst) record what is being learned from the data as you are analyzing it. The resulting memos become aids that assist with moving more easily from raw data to building an understanding of the information you recorded, heard, or observed.

No rules exist for memoing; however, each memo should contain one idea and should be dated and referenced (Given, 2008). Also, you may write initial memos in the interview transcript margins or in observation notes or underline sections within the transcript or observation notes. Later, when you are deeper into the analysis, you may find that many of these early impressions are useful. Regardless, many researchers think memo writing provides "conceptual epiphanies" (Miles & Huberman, 1994, p. 74).

Essentially, memoing requires you to stop and think about the data. You will use memos when the first information comes in and continue to use them until you write the final report.

Identify Category Codes

Qualitative data analysis is a process of breaking down data into smaller units, determining importance, and putting the pertinent units together in a more general, analytical form (Gay, Mills, & Airasian, 2006). Breaking down data typically occurs through the process of ***coding***, or classifying data into themes (see Case 14B.1). This involves taking text data or images gathered during data collection and segmenting sentences, paragraphs, or images into categories and labeling those categories with a term (Creswell, 2012).

You may create category codes in a couple of ways. For example, you could adopt the term used in the language of the research participant or you could adopt codes proposed by others, such as those reported in other studies. Perhaps more germane is to create category codes according to your problem statement, research questions, or key variables. This could be your start list of codes (Miles & Huberman, 1994). For example, if the research question is, "What do people do when they take a break from work?" a start list of codes may be *stay at or near home* and *go away for more than a day*.

Remember, this is only your start list, as a coding scheme is developed on an ongoing basis. As you gather new raw data, constantly compare them to the existing codes. Sometimes, these new data easily fit into existing codes, and at other times, the data trigger the necessity of initiating new code categories or merging old code categories. For example, as you acquire more data, it may become obvious that a what-the-person-is-doing component (e.g., start a new hobby, go for a hike, and work out at the gym) and a relationship dimension (who one goes with when taking a break, such as family, close friends, work friends, sport friends) exist. Hence, you need to add new code categories to process the raw data.

CONSTANT COMPARISON

For a creative presentation of how the constant comparison approach can be used in everyday living, go to http://www.youtube.com/watch?v=nxIErzX3aQQ.

To track the category codes you prepare, create a ***code book***. As demonstrated in Case 14B.2, a code book is a list of the codes assigned to transcript material (like listings in a telephone book). As you code subsequent expanded accounts, this code book will remind you of the meanings of the codes and help you to see patterns in the data.

Obviously, the way you code your data will play a large role in determining the nature of the results. Therefore, danger exists in approaching your data with preconceived categories and assumptions. If you adopt this stance, you will likely begin analyzing your data by coding the expanded account according to what you expect to find.

SELF-QUIZ ON CODING

Directions: Label the statements *true* or *false*.

___ 1. Coding of expanded accounts categorizes emerging patterns.

___ 2. The term used for the code label could be based in the language of the research participant.

___ 3. A code book is a list of all codes created.

Note. Answers are provided at the end of the chapter.

CODING TIPS

When thinking of codes, use codes that

- capture or encompass what others outside the study would expect to find;
- you did not anticipate at the beginning of the study;
- are unusual, yet are, in and of themselves, of conceptual interest; and
- address a larger theoretical perspective found or noted in the literature.

Note. Adapted from Creswell (2012, p. 186).

How do you code? These steps are recommended:

1. Begin by carefully rereading all the expanded accounts. Identify statements/or images relating to the research question.
2. For each statement or image, ask yourself, "What is this about?"
3. Accordingly, assign a code representing a theme to each identified statement or image. Organize every relevant statement or image thereafter under the theme that best describes it.
4. Reread the expanded accounts again to be sure the assigned codes capture all the themes, and make changes as needed.
5. Begin to cluster together similar themes. For example, ask yourself,
   a. "Can I combine certain coded themes together under a more generic one?"
   b. "Can I organize the coded themes in a meaningful sequence?"
   c. "Can I identify causal relationships among the themes?"

6. Consult your memos for descriptive wording, organizing scheme, and new code possibilities.
7. Restudy the coding analysis that you have done to this point and begin drawing preliminary conclusions.

Create Data Displays

In qualitative data analysis, you are continuously collecting data, converting your condensed accounts into expanded accounts, writing interpretive ideas as memos, and coding expanded accounts. However, early in the analysis, information typically leaps out as an answer or insight to the research questions. Conclusions appear to be in sight. Be careful, though, because initial conclusions are just that: premature. Resist the temptation to feel finished too early.

After creating category codes, develop a ***data display*** to continue qualitative data analysis. A data display is a visual chart that systematically presents information that you have collected. It is a narrowed view of the data, meaning you are able to see the full data set in a single format. Ultimately, a data display is the next step to developing conclusions.

Many data display types exist; the most popular are the matrix and network (Verdnell & Scagnoli, 2013). Which you use depends on what you are trying to understand.

Matrices. A ***matrix display*** is helpful for understanding connections among information by offering "exploratory eyeballing" or a "thumbnail sketch" (Miles & Huberman, 1994, p. 93). A matrix is essentially the intersection of two lists set up as rows and columns. The column list is referred to as the ***domain list*** and presents types of some quality. The row lists the characteristics of each type in the domain list. This is also called the ***attribute list***.

For instance, you could develop a matrix display for a study on television watching by preparing a domain list according to types of television programs: news, comedy, talk, reality, sport, and so forth. These would be listed down the left column. Furthermore, you could distinguish television shows by attributes, such as length of program (30 minutes, 1 hour, 2 hours, etc.), accompanying commercial messages, and expected viewer reaction. These distinguishing characteristics are then highlighted in a list of attributes. The attributes list is placed across the top row of the matrix display.

Thus, a matrix display compares domain and attribute lists. Table 14B.3 has the steps to building a matrix display. Case 14B.3 is an example of a matrix display.

Networks. A ***network data display*** is a collection of nodes or points connected by lines that display streams of participant actions, events, and processes (Miles, Huberman, & Saldana, 2013). You may use a network to focus on the sequential order of what is being studied. Also, a network is useful when you want to examine multiple events simultaneously. Case 14B.4 is an example of a network display for a made-up study on the interactions of weight lifters and their trainers in a weight room. Notice, you are able to display and contrast what those involved in the workout (lifter and trainer) are doing in terms of frequency, duration, and intensity along a timeline.

In the network display, the points are the events and the line connecting the events have the meaning "is followed by." From studying a network display, you should be able to detect patterns about why situations happen as they do. For example, in Case 14B.4, the personal trainer's involvement with the lifter is an inverted *U*. That is, it rises to a peak in the middle of the lifting program, meaning lifters use trainers less before and after this point.

In essence, formatting data into displays is a decision-making tool. You are making choices about how to separate the data. Where do you get ideas for a matrix or network? Through inductive thinking, the ideas are a translation of the coded expanded accounts and memos. How many displays do you need? Prepare as many networks and matrices as you need to understand your findings. See Table 14B.4 for steps to building a network display.

SOMETHING TO REMEMBER!

Distinction	Matrix display	Network display
Is the intent descriptive or explanatory?	Use when trying to describe data organization.	Use when you want to generate explanations about why situations happen as they do.
Do you need partial or complete order?	Use when data in rows and columns represent descriptive categories, not order.	Use when ordering the categories in a specific way, such as time, influence, intensity, and procedures.
Are you focusing on two domains or more than two domains?	Use when comparing and contrasting two domains.	Use when comparing and contrasting three or more domains.

Table 14B.3
Steps to Building a Matrix Display

1. Identify a domain. Study the coded categories for a domain that has emerged from data collection. For example, in Case 14B.3 the domain is type of hotel lobby waiters. This idea first appeared in the researcher's memos. The researcher did not begin the study with the purpose of analyzing waiting behavior, but during the memo process the researcher found that waiting was the most common use of hotel lobbies. The domains were drawn from the coded categories of the expanded accounts. You will find that a domain with less than 10 types makes the process more manageable; however, the actual number does not matter.
2. Identify attributes of the chosen domain. Inventory the expanded accounts, memos, and coded categories for ideas to contrast the domains. The domains should be distinguishable by these characteristic contrasts or attributes.
3. Prepare a matrix worksheet and begin to fill it in. Create the worksheet so it contains the list of the domains in the subheadings on the left and the list of attributes as the column spanner across the top. Leave enough room in the cells to write a short phrase of information. Now, complete the matrix by referring to the expanded accounts, memos, and coded categories.
4. For information missing from the cells, prepare a list of contrast questions and then conduct additional data collection. Notice in Case 14B.3 several cells are blank. This is normal. That is, one of the biggest benefits of a matrix display is that it quickly reveals the information you need to collect next. Every blank space in the worksheet suggests the observations or interviews you still need to do.
5. Complete the matrix. The final matrix is an approximate outline for the final report, but it may not be the only outline. You may prepare a data display matrix for as many domains as possible or limit your study to one or only a few.

Note. Adapted from Spradley (1980).

Table 14B.4
Steps to Building a Network Display

1. Identify major event patterns. Determine an ordered pattern of events that has emerged from the data. For example, in Case 14B.4, the events are ordered on a weight room use timeline. In reviewing the coded expanded accounts, the researcher notices each participant goes through an ordered series of ways of using the weight room (e.g., the initial orientation, development of a personal workout regime). This pattern of events becomes the horizontal axis of the display.
2. Identify qualities of the event pattern. Inventory your data and the coded expanded accounts for how you may contrast the events. For example, in Case 14B.4, the weight room use timeline may be contrasted according to amount of weight lifter–trainer contact. Levels of this quality become the vertical axis of the display.
3. Prepare the network display. Draw a graph with the major event pattern and quality labels installed on the axes.
4. Use dots to represent the relationship between the events and the qualities. For example, in Case 14B.4, the dot for the event of the weight lifters' introduction to the club corresponds to the quality moderate amount of involvement with a trainer.
5. Connect the dots. Link the events with the qualities.

Note. Adapted from Spradley (1980).

MAKE TENTATIVE CONCLUSIONS

The procedures in qualitative data analysis—expanded accounts, memos, category codes, data displays—are tools for finding meaning in the information gathered. These first and provisional meaning statements are ***tentative conclusions***. Producing tentative conclusions, however, is not as difficult as you may think because you naturally tend to seek meaning. You try to make sense of things around you daily. When applying this human skill to qualitative data analysis, you are reflecting on the following (Rubin & Rubin, 2011):

- What am I going to call this meaning?
- How am I going to define the nuances and variations of this meaning?
- Why does this meaning matter?
- How well does this meaning answer the research questions?

Strategies

You may make tentative conclusions in many ways. Try one or a combination of the following strategies: clustering, subsuming particulars into the general, counting, seeking plausibility, and making metaphors (Miles & Huberman, 1994).

Clustering. Data display tools (matrix and network) enable you to cluster information into patterns or themes. By ***clustering*** the information in these displays, patterns of similarities or differences emerge. Via inductive thinking, clustering involves combining the matrices or networks you have already constructed into a more integrative diagram (McMillan & Schumacker, 2009). Suppose for the matrix display of a hotel lobby in Case 14B.3 you combine the waiting intensity attribute column with a timeline of movement around the lobby for solos and groups. You would have a unique picture of how waiting intensity changes across time.

Subsuming particulars into the general. Clustering involves clumping information that goes together and giving it a common label, whereas ***subsuming*** determines whether information is part of a more general category. Subsuming is the process of drawing a conclusion by moving up a step on the abstraction ladder. According to Glaser (1978), this is a matter of looking for basic social processes that are more general in description than the specific variables being analyzed. Suppose the following behaviors of children were observed in a playground program: bullying, aggression, rule infractions, and defiance of authority. You could subsume these behavior themes into a more general social process called "antisocial behavior."

Counting. Counting may also be useful in drawing conclusions for qualitative data analyses. When you have noted information several times, it as a ***pattern***. When you say a pattern is important, you have come to that conclusion, in part at least, by counting its occurrence. Suppose that 70% of the interviewees mentioned lack of child care as their reason for irregular participation in a fitness program. The frequency of this response provides a useful idea for a study conclusion and recommendation; that is, offering child care at the fitness program site may boost attendance.

Seeing plausibility. Tentative conclusions are also derived from the act of determining what makes good sense or what intuitively emerges. This is the ***plausibility*** basis for conclusions, or "it just feels right." This should not be the sole tactic for drawing a tentative conclusion, but many scientific discoveries at least initially appeared to their inventors this way.

Making metaphors. You may also use metaphors to draw conclusions. ***Metaphors*** are literary devices that involve comparing two aspects via their similarities and ignoring their differences. For example, the idea of the empty nest phase of a parent's life is a common metaphor for children growing up and leaving home. A metaphor from a study of what happens in the hotel lobby example may be, "the lobby is the stage for a series of one-act plays, complete with entrances and exits...with the drama or comedy varying in terms of plot and performance" (Russell, 1991).

Holistic Understanding

The strategies for drawing tentative conclusions involve intellectually shuttling back and forth among the coded expanded accounts, memos, and category codes in the data displays. Ultimately, making tentative conclusions requires putting this discrete information together to achieve a holistic understanding. ***Holistic understanding*** signifies the findings of the study must be tied to overarching explanations, meaning the broader application of the patterns on which you have focused.

These broader applications are constructs. Ask yourself, "Do any broader constructs put these patterns together the way I am putting them together?" Your greatest ally in this will be your understanding of the research literature you studied in Step 2. What constructs from theories or models from the work of other researchers fit your patterns?

You may now think of the tentative conclusions you made about the qualitative data as possible answers to the research questions. In applied research circumstances, these answers will become solutions or recommendations for how a recreation, park, sport, or tourism organization changes or improves policies or service delivery practices. In basic research situations, the conclusions will be further developed into theory, such as grounded theory.

SHAKESPEARE'S *HAMLET* AND QUALITATIVE DATA ANALYSIS

The following is an excerpt from William Shakespeare's *Hamlet* (Act 3, Scene 2). Think broadly and holistically and explain how it captures the essence of drawing conclusions in qualitative data analysis.

Hamlet: Do you see yonder cloud that's almost in shape of a camel?

Polonius: By the mass, and 'tis like a camel, indeed.

Hamlet: Methink it is like a weasel.

Polonius: It is backed like a weasel.

Hamlet: Or like a whale?

Polonius: Very like a whale.

Note. Answer is provided at the end of the chapter.

Computer Assistance

Increasingly, computer software is being used to assist with qualitative data analysis. The key word in this statement, however, is *assist* because no software will actually do the analysis for you. In fact, this is a highlight of qualitative data analysis: Your own intellect is the primary analysis tool.

Even though you may complete every step in this chapter by hand (and many researchers prefer this), computers are useful and extremely fast labeling and retrieval tools for every step. For example, coding is a laborious and time-consuming task. For this reason, you may choose to work with software computer programs, such as MAXQDA, Atlas.ti, HyperResearch, Ethnograph, Nudist, and Nvivo.

To decide whether to locate and learn a qualitative data analysis software package, consider the following factors that may affect your decision (Gay et al., 2006, p. 476):

- Are you analyzing large amounts of data (e.g., more than 500 pages of field notes and transcripts)?
- Do you have the resources to purchase the software, or do you have access to the software through a research university?
- Are you, or other research staff working on the project, adequately trained in using the programs?

All computer software that assists with qualitative data analysis begins with a preparatory step of ***data conversion***. That is, after you have recorded field notes, condensed accounts, expanded accounts, memos, and data displays, you will still need to convert these text-based materials into digital form for the software to perform the data management tasks.

VERIFY CONCLUSIONS

The final step in qualitative data analysis is to confront the issue of soundness of conclusions. According to Miles and Huberman (1994), "qualitative analyses (like quantitative analyses) can be evocative, illuminating, masterful—and wrong" (p. 262). Therefore, you must confirm tentative conclusions. To verify tentative conclusions, check for data quality and test explanations.

Check for Data Quality

Checking for data quality means determining whether the information upon which tentative conclusions are based is "good." You may do this by examining representativeness and researcher effects.

Representativeness. ***Representativeness*** entails determining whether the gathered information is typical of the people, organization, or events that are being studied. For example, if only those people who can be contacted easily are interviewed, conclusions are likely to be based on nonrepresentative information, which is not good. If you suspect that the data are not representative, what can you do?

First, you may purposively sample more interviews, observations, or document reviews to see whether the findings from these match the conclusions. Second, you may randomly select two or three people from the study and ask them to judge the typicality of the conclusions. This is called ***member checking***. That is, you ask members of the observed or interviewed group to read the tentative conclusions and to assess how closely their worlds have been captured and whether or not they agree with the conclusions (Thomas et al., 2011).

Researcher effects. You may also check for data quality by determining whether ***researcher effects*** exist. This means ascertaining whether you influenced the data collected and/or analyzed. You may alter the usual status quo; your interactions with individuals create behaviors in those studied that would not ordinarily have occurred. As well, the situation studied may affect you. For example, you may form biased conclusions because information in the data personally struck you. Avoiding researcher effects on conclusions requires keeping research questions firmly in mind and thinking conceptually and not sentimentally (see Case 14B.5).

Testing Explanations

Finally, verifying conclusions entails testing explanations. You may do this by replicating the findings and checking rival explanations.

Replication of findings. Findings are more dependable when other research studies are able to confirm them. This duplication of results is known as ***replication*** (Miles & Huberman, 1994). You may accomplish replication in several ways. At the most basic level, throughout the study, you are replicating as you collect new information from new respondents or new events.

At a more rigorous level, you may replicate conclusions by studying different respondents, cases, or situations to see whether the conclusions are repeated. Suppose the local authority for tourism development in a rural tourist site has been studied. To check conclusions made about one town, the study could be repeated in another town. The purpose of doing this is to look for matching patterns or a replication of the findings.

Rival explanations. One last way you may confirm the quality of tentative conclusions is checking ***rival explanations*** (Miles & Huberman, 1994), conclusions that are opposite or different from the ones you determined from the study. Anyone who has spent weeks or months coming up with one explanation of the study topic will have difficulty becoming seriously involved with identifying an alternative explanation, so you may want to involve someone who is not attached to the study, who has "cognitive distance" (Miles & Huberman, 1994, p. 275) to the tentative conclusion you have derived from analyzing the data. You may ask them, "Here's how I see it, but can you think of another way to look at it?"

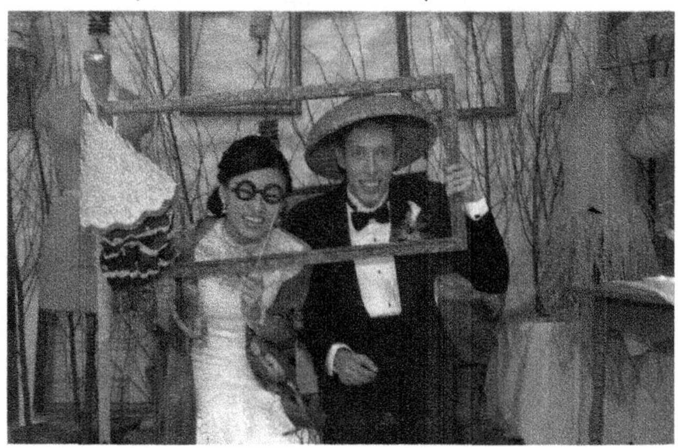

Viewing the world through the lens of the persons of interest unveils unique perspectives. You need to organize and prepare data emerging from this qualitative approach to arrive at tentative conclusions. You must then verify and confirm the soundness of these tentative conclusions. Wedding celebrants, Belhaven, North Carolina. Copyright © 2015 Xiaoyun Liul.

REVIEW AND DISCUSSION QUESTIONS

1. How does qualitative data analysis rely on inductive thinking? Give an example of inductive thinking from your daily life?
2. Qualitative data analysis is a cyclical process. What does this mean?
3. What are meta-data? What are the four common meta-data? What experiences have you had with these?
4. What is the difference between a condensed account and an expanded account?
5. What is memoing? What is category coding? What ultimately happens to memos and codes in analyzing qualitative data?
6. What is a data display? What are two types of data displays, and how are they different? Which one best matches your natural inductive thinking skills?
7. Identify the five strategies you may use to make tentative conclusions. Can you adopt more than one for a single study? Why or why not?
8. What are four techniques that you may use to verify conclusions?

YOUR RESEARCH

1. Have you collected qualitative data in your study? That is, do you have written, verbal, or pictorial text data from interviews, focus groups, observations, or documents?
2. If so, how will you go from condensed accounts of these data to expanded accounts?

3. How will you provide memos for the expanded accounts?
4. What category codes will you tentatively use?
5. Will you use a matrix or network data display? Why?
6. What strategies will you use to make tentative conclusions?
7. Is there a computer software program available to you for analyzing your qualitative data? If yes, how will you use it?
8. What steps will you take to verify conclusions?

PRACTICE EXERCISES

1. Use the following questions to conduct a self-analysis about your skills and interests in qualitative data analysis.
   a. In what ways do you apply qualitative data analysis in your daily life?
   b. When you read the Results section of a research journal article using qualitative data analysis, what is your usual response? Why?
   c. What can you do today to make progress in developing expertise in qualitative data analysis procedures for your future professional work?
   d. What can you do next semester to make progress in developing expertise in qualitative data analysis procedures for your future professional work?
2. Conduct a 30-minute open-ended interview with someone you know who enjoys playing a sport. Why do they enjoy it? What would it be like for them if they had to give it up?
   a. Record condensed notes during the interview.
   b. Create an expanded account from your condensed account field notes.
   c. Now, develop category codes for the expanded account.
   d. Can you see tentative conclusions from your coding? What are they?
3. Review the steps in preparing a matrix form of data display, and then create one using your experience with the subject of favorite spring break destinations.
   a. Make a list of the types of spring break destinations (e.g., beaches, ski resorts, other countries). Types of spring break destinations become the items on the the domain list of the matrix.
   b. Although the domains are types of spring break destinations, they have their own attributes. What are the attributes for beaches? In what ways are these different from the attributes of ski resorts? These and other attributes of the types of spring break destinations become part of the attributes list. Now, make a list of other attributes.
   c. Using these domains and attributes to form the two lists of a matrix, sketch one and fill it in from your experience in choosing spring break locales.
   d. What tentative conclusions about spring break destinations can you make from studying your matrix?

WEB EXERCISES

1. Use your favorite Web search engine and investigate the possible software packages applicable to qualitative data analysis.
   a. Begin by checking up on the latest on MAXQDA, ATLAS.ti, HyperResearch, Ethnograph, Nudist, and NVIVO. Read user critiques of them as well.
   b. Discuss these software packages with university researchers who are using them. What are the pros and cons of using these from their perspective?

2. Learn more about memo writing, identifying themes and codes, and developing a coding list by checking out an excellent tutorial, *Online Data Analysis*, from the UK Economic & Social Research Council–funded website: http://onlineqda.hud.ac.uk/Intro_QDA/how_what_to_code.php. With this brilliant yet down-to-earth resource, you may read more explanations, watch short videos, and participate in interactive exercises.
3. The following are additional Web-based resources for further study and practice with qualitative data analysis:
    a. How to code text for qualitative analysis using Microsoft Word, follow the link to Greg Fulkerson's excellent tutorial at http://www.youtube.com/watch?v=FX9R6Y6fyfk.
    b. Step-by-step guide for qualitative analysis of interview data, visit Kent Löfgren's posting at http://www.youtube.com/watch?v=DRL4PF2u9XA.
    c. Overview of qualitative data analysis, consult Dr. Khaiie's (University of Utaha Malaysia) presentation at http://www.youtube.com/watch?v=B-aIq_36MAQ.

SERVICE LEARNING PROJECT

Complete the following for the campus program or service that has been selected as the focus of the service learning project for this semester:

1. If you will be conducting a qualitative research project, following the outline for this chapter, make a list of the steps that would be appropriate to follow to analyze the textual data you have collected and answer the research questions. For example, how will you create expanded accounts, memos, data displays, and tentative conclusions and how will you verify conclusions?
2. For this analysis plan, determine how each action will progress you and your team to answer the research questions. That is, why have you chosen to do what you have planned?
3. Present your chosen analysis ideas to your instructor. What is his or her reaction and advice? Adjust the chosen qualitative analysis plan accordingly.
4. Finally, carry out your plan and come up with tentative conclusions. Following the discussion in this chapter, confirm the soundness of your tentative conclusions.

TEST YOURSELF ANSWERS

Identifying Themes: The Essence of Qualitative Data Analysis

If you identified that the two meanings emerging from the data presented were *gangs provide family* and *gang members like to play*, you have done a terrific job at your first practice run in qualitative data analysis.

Self-Quiz on Coding

All are true.

Shakespeare's *Hamlet* and Qualitative Data Analysis

The point being made by the bard, which is analogous to what is occurring when drawing conclusions as part of qualitative data analysis, is that humans seek patterns to help understand the world around them.

SUPPORTING CASES FOR THIS CHAPTER

CASE 14B.1. CATEGORY CODES IN QUALITATIVE DATA ANALYSIS

Smith, C. (2010). *The beliefs and motivations that impact travel and leisure of millennial generation students* (Unpublished senior project). California Polytechnic State University, San Luis Obispo.

The purpose of this study was to explore the beliefs, motivations, and attitudes of college students about travel. Essays on travel and leisure written by students in a course were read and scanned, by hand, for word usage and phrases. Then, these data were placed into categories. The most frequent phrases and common word usage on the spreadsheets led the researcher back to the raw data to analyze the context in which the phrases were used. The results indicated that the major beliefs, motivations, and attitudes college students had about travel fell into the following themes: the whole experience, education, freedom, and personal growth.

CASE 14B.2. A CODE BOOK

A study was conducted on how hotel lobbies are used. Using passive participant observation, data were recorded into field notes (condensed accounts), data were expanded, and a code book was devised for assigning categories to the information collected.

Code Book	
Lobby Users	Code
Tourists	tour
Local business people	bus
Local people using the lobby as part of a recreation activity	rec
Amount of Time	
10 minutes and so on	10 min
Lobby Activity	
Meeting others for another purpose	meet
For processing hotel check-in procedures	check in
To relax or rest between activities	rest

Coding the Expanded Account

Tour	Man and woman couple approaches the end of the couch. They are dressed as tourists though conservatively. Woman sits down; man stands and studies tourist brochure. Woman rises after about 20 seconds to look at tourist map on wall. Hotel staff member (in yellow bellman-type jacket) approaches and exchanges some words (I can't hear). Both tourists sit
10 min	down on the couch and resume study of brochure. After 10 minutes young man approaches (not in hotel uniform) and inquires, "Mr. and Mrs. …?" while fingering folded sheet of paper. Couple affirms and gets up and follows
meet	man out front door.

Note. Adapted from R. Russell (1991, 2004).

CASE 14B.3. A MATRIX DISPLAY FOR HOTEL LOBBY OBSERVATIONS

Domain: Type of hotel lobby waiters	Attributes of waiting		
Solos	**Waiting intensity**	**Posture**	**Emotion**
Watchers	Most intense; focused on waiting; can be distracted; increases with time	Often inert; lots of micro-flow; pacing; narrow range of emotion	Anticipation; can be impatient
Workers	Usually focus is not on waiting but on work; rarely distracted		Patient; studious; contemplative
Players	Not focused on waiting; occasionally distracted	Relaxed	Usually patient; preoccupied
Groups			
Socials	Varies	Often seated opposite or at right angles to others	Lighthearted; often animated
Ad hoc committees	Casual	Highly animated	

Note. Adapted from R. Russell (1991, 2004).

CASE 14B.4. NETWORK DISPLAY FOR WEIGHT LIFTER–TRAINER CONTACT AND WEIGHT ROOM USE

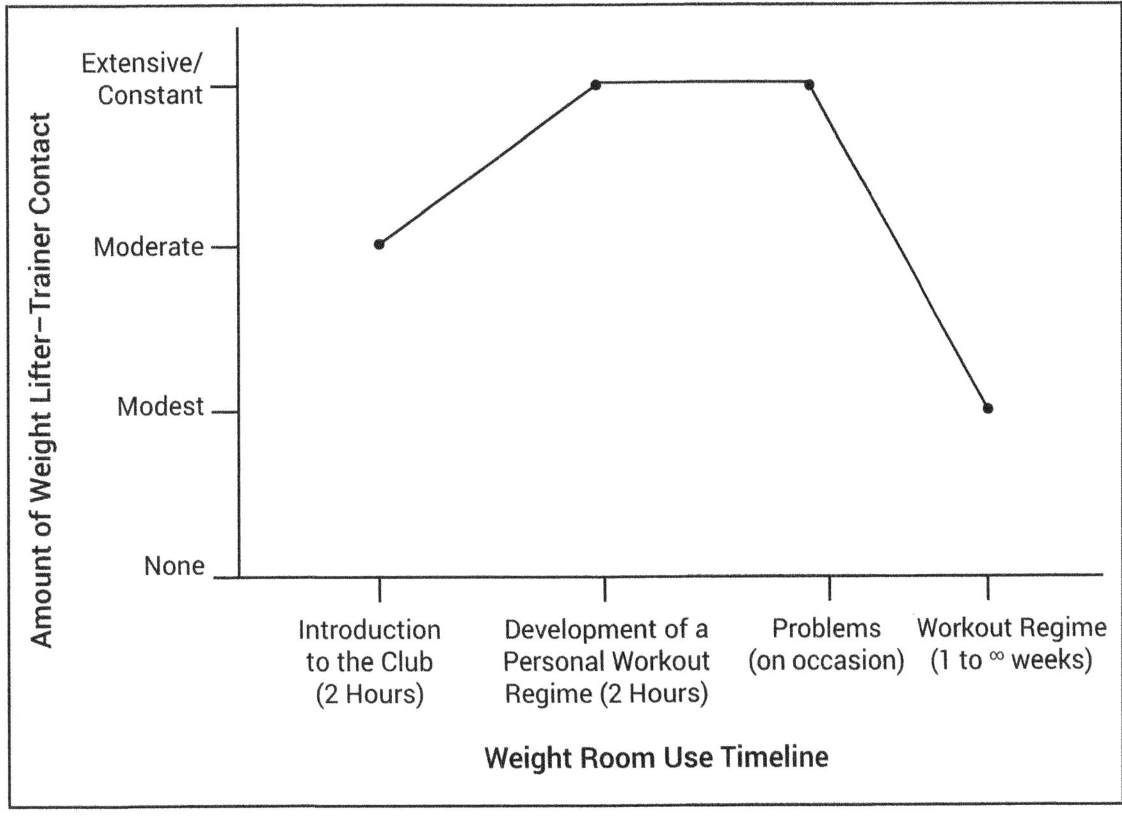

CASE 14B.5. CONTROLLING FOR RESEARCHER EFFECT

Becker, A. (2009). It's not what they do, it's how they do it: Athlete experiences of great coaching. *International Journal of Sports Science & Coaching, 4*, 93–119.

The purpose of this study was to explore athlete experiences of "great coaching." Eighteen in-depth interviews were conducted with elite-level athletes (nine female, nine male) representing several sports (baseball, basketball, football, soccer, softball, volleyball, and water polo). Analyses of the transcripts revealed 1,553 units of discrete information, which were further grouped into subthemes and general themes. This led to the development of a final thematic structure revealing these dimensions of coaching: coach's attributes, the environment, relationships, the system, coaching actions, and influences. To avoid the researcher's own biases in the analysis, a ***bracketing interview*** (or a discussion in which the researcher identifies and owns up to his or her biases on a topic) with an expert in qualitative methods was used. This allowed the researcher to examine the phenomenon studied more openly and attempt to control for researcher effect.

PART V
REPORTING THE RESEARCH

STEP 15

CREATE VISUAL AIDS

STEP 16

WRITE REPORT

STEP 17

DELIVER A PRESENTATION

Visually reporting the results of a study speaks volumes. This photo is of the start of the weigh-in for a White Marlin Open Tournament. The crowd is paying rapt attention to the "data" being displayed on the scale. By the time the measurement of the fish's weight was finished, the angler of this 78.5-pound fish took home a whopping $1.6 million in prize money. Ocean City, Maryland. Copyright © 2015 Ruth V. Russell.

STEP 15 STEP 16 STEP 17

CREATE VISUAL AIDS

WHAT WILL I LEARN IN THIS CHAPTER?

I'll be able to...

1. Define a numerical table and a frequency distribution.
2. Provide an illustration of ungrouped data and grouped data found in a numerical table.
3. Describe the contents of a word table.
4. Explain collapsing data.
5. Recall a definition for missing data, and explain how a valid percent is calculated when responses are missing.
6. Sketch a representation and explain the differences among pie graphs, bar graphs, histograms, line graphs, and charts.

"If I can't picture it, I can't understand it."

Albert Einstein
(German-born theoretical physicist who developed the general theory of relativity, one of the two pillars of modern physics, 1879–1955)

After collecting and analyzing data, you will summarize the results. For instance, if 100 people answer 20 questions each, 2,000 responses are available. Your challenge now is to summarize these responses clearly and accurately so others can understand them. You may do this through visual aids, in particular tables and figures.

When developing a table or figure, you should have a clear vision about the purpose each visual aid is to serve. What are you trying to convey? Visual aids should communicate important information. This means a table or figure should complement rather than replace text. In other words, never display a table or figure without discussing and referring to it within the body of the report or presentation.

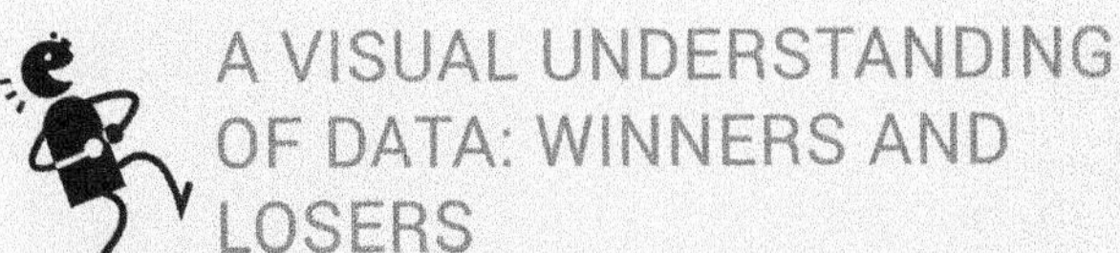

A VISUAL UNDERSTANDING OF DATA: WINNERS AND LOSERS

Michael Friendly (York University) has put together a humorous website, "The Best and Worst of Statistical Graphics." Visit http://www.datavis.ca/gallery/ to learn about visual aids that have landed on the Laurels and Darts awards lists.

This chapter provides guidelines for developing tables and figures. Researchers in recreation, park, sport, and tourism professions have typically adopted the standards and styles of the American Psychological Association (APA). Nicol and Pexman (2010a, 2010b) wrote excellent APA references that deal with figures and tables. Nevertheless, guidelines for setting up tables and figures vary, and you should check with the publisher or organization to which you will submit your work.

TABLES

You may use numerical tables and word tables to display your data. The following sections describe different tables and offer useful tips on creating them.

Numerical Tables

A ***numerical table*** is the most basic way to illustrate data, meaning data are presented as a ***frequency distribution***, which involves tallying and presenting how often scores occur. Table 15.1 is an example of a frequency distribution.

A frequency distribution may involve ungrouped data, grouped data, or a combination of ungrouped and grouped data. A frequency distribution that uses ***ungrouped data*** reports each score for the variable (e.g., living situation in Table 15.1); that is, the frequencies for each category of the variable are reported.

In instances where many answers appear for the measured variable, adjacent values are combined into a category and the number of responses in each category, or ***grouped data***, are then reported. For example, in Table 15.1, age is reported by grouping possible responses into 18–21, 22–25, and 26–29 categories.

Table 15.1
Example of a Frequency Distribution

Table 1
Demographic Characteristics of Study Participants, Spring 2014 (N = 187)

Characteristic	*N*	%
Gender		
Male	80	43
Female	107	57
Age		
18–21	63	34
22–25	53	28
26–29	71	38
Year in college		
First-year	22	12
Sophomore	37	20
Junior	25	13
Senior	59	32
Graduate	44	23
Living situation		
On campus	109	59
Off campus	78	41

Incidentally, usually the first numerical table encountered in a research report is a frequency distribution of the demographic or social characteristics of the study sample (cf. Table 15.1). Typically, this table of background information contains reported frequencies using ungrouped data (e.g., gender) and grouped data (e.g., age categories).

Guidelines for setting up frequency distribution tables, include the following (Nicol & Pexman, 2010b; Salkind, 2013; Torres, Preskill, & Piontek, 2005):

1. For a grouped frequency distribution, use between three and eight categories. If a table has too many categories, it defeats the purpose of summarizing the data. Conversely, if the table has fewer than three groups, it will not communicate much about how the data are distributed.
2. Use mutually exclusive categories. A score should appear only in one grouping. For instance, if you have established one category as ranging in age from 18–21 years and the second from 21–24 years, you have violated this rule because responses of age 21 would go in two categories. Age 21 should appear only in one grouping.
3. Minimize table junk. You do not have to use every function, every graph, and every feature a computer has to make your visual aid. Less is more. Simple is best.
4. Numbering and insertion. Assign numbers to tables, number tables consecutively, and insert tables sequentially into the body of the report.
5. Title. Place the title immediately above the table. Title the table so it briefly conveys what information is being focused on, the data collection date, and total sample size. Regarding total sample size, the convention is to note this parenthetically using the standard ($N =$) with the appropriate sample size number inserted to the right of the equals sign.
6. Horizontal lines. Use horizontal lines to mark sections of the table.
7. Headings. Each row and column should have identifiable subject headings.
8. Limit the number of words. You must label everything so misunderstandings do not occur, but too many words may detract from the visual message.
9. Continuing a table to another page. If a table spills over to a second or multiple pages, repeat the table number and the row and column headings on the continuing pages.
10. Totals. Totals should be shown, usually using whole numbers.

Word Tables

Word tables are used to summarize and present descriptive text or qualitative information (Nicol & Pexman, 2010b). You may use word tables to describe referenced studies (Table 15.2) and present definitions of variables.

Table Pointers

Creating a numerical or word table as a visual aid may be challenging, especially in building a manageable table and handling missing data. Sometimes, a variable has a broad range of scores (covered in Step 14A). Thus, to make it manageable, you may compress, condense, or group data into categories, sometimes referred to as ***collapsing data***. Suppose students are asked the primary reason they use the university's swimming pool. The first five respondents out of 30 students interviewed reported the following answers:

Table 15.2
Example of a Word Table

Table 2
Reported Translational Research Focusing on Older Adults, With a Leisure/Recreation Component

Citation	Intervention and target audience	Design	Major findings
Dorgo, Robinson, & Bader (2009)	14-week physical fitness intervention, with peer support, for older (60 years) American adults	Pretest–posttest	Perceived improvement in physical and mental well-being, social functioning, enhanced ability to carry out physical and emotional roles, general health, and vitality level
Hughes et al. (2006)	Fit and Strong Program combined flexibility, aerobic walking, and resistance training with education, group problem solving (to enhance self-efficacy for exercise and maintenance of physical activity), and individualized long-term maintenance plans, for older (50 years or older) American adults with osteoarthritis	Randomized control trial	Relative to control group, treatment participants experienced significant improvements in minutes of exercise per week and lower extremity stiffness, reduced pain, and an increase in self-efficacy for arthritis pain management

Note. Adapted from Riddick (2010).

- "Tone up."
- "To chill or relax."
- "Lose weight."
- "Reduce stress."
- "Help my aching back."

Since a word table will be used to present the findings, and since you know that you need to limit reasons to three to eight categories of answers, collapse similar answers together. Thus, a category titled "Improve Physical Health" makes sense, and in that category, answers such as "Tone up," "Lose weight," and "Help my aching back" should be included.

COLLAPSING DATA

Are you trying to figure out how to turn interval or ratio scores into nominal group categories? Consider using a proportionate distribution to guide you in setting up the scores used for grouping or collapsing data into categories.

For instance, if you know you want to use four groups of scores, examine the frequency distribution of individual scores to determine logical groupings. Using this principle for age, you may discover that about one fourth of the sample was between ages 18 and 21 years, one fourth fell between 22 and 25 years, one fourth fell in the 26 to 29 range, and the remaining one fourth reported being 30 years or older. Applying this reasoning, you have saved space by successfully converting individual scores into rational groupings.

For many reasons, a data set may be incomplete, which is sometimes referred to as ***missing data***. That is, some people did not answer one or more questions. The interviewer may have overlooked a question, the respondent may have forgotten to answer a question, or the person completing the survey or interview may have chosen not to respond to a particular question (e.g., they thought the question was too personal, did not know what the question was asking, could not find an answer that applied to him or her).

Missing data may pose a dilemma. Sometimes, you may decide to toss or omit the person for whom data are missing from the entire data set (the person is not included in any of the statistical analyses). Other times, you may exclude the person from analyses dealing with the particular variable for which data or an answer is missing.

HANDLING MISSING DATA WHEN CONSTRUCTING A TABLE

To construct a table that includes missing data, use percentages. You may calculate the following percentages for a variable:

- Percent: Based on percentage of responses in a particular category relative to other response categories, including missing or skipped answers.
- Valid percent: Calculates percentage after dropping missing or skipped answers.
- Cumulative percent: Running tally of valid percentages.

You will often see these three percentages calculated by statistical software. For instance, the Statistical Package for Social Sciences printout (presented below) reports the number of intramural (IM) activities college students, at an imaginary college, participated in during the 2013–2014 academic year ranged from zero to six. Additionally, the printout reveals that an answer to this question was missing for some students; in particular, 20 people (4.7%) skipped or did not answer the question.

Do you understand how the numbers appearing in the cumulative percent column were derived? Some students, 102 persons to be exact (25.2% of the respondents), reported not participating in IM. However, a majority of students, 266 (65.7% of the sample), reported participating in one IM activity during the school year. These two percentages together, 25.2% + 65.7%, result in a cumulative percentage of 90.9% of the sample reporting participating either in no IM activity or in one IM activity during the school year.

Score	Frequency	Percent	Valid percent	Cumulative percent
0	102	24.0	25.2	25.2
1	266	62.6	65.7	90.9
2	15	3.5	3.7	94.6
3	7	1.6	1.7	96.3
4	6	1.4	1.5	97.8
5	4	1.0	1.0	98.8
6	5	1.2	1.2	100.0
Missing	20	4.7		
Total	425	100.0		

Note. If no data were missing, the values recorded in the percent and valid percent columns would be the same.

Which percentage should you use in the table you are constructing? The rule of thumb is that unless a majority of the responses are missing, you should report numbers from the *valid percent column*.

DRAFTING A TABLE AFTER SORTING THROUGH MISSING DATA

You have been asked to develop a table reporting on the age distribution of students at College West who participated in a study on their feelings about their school's swimming facilities. The study occurred in spring 2014. Look at the results below regarding the age distribution of the 425 people who participated in the study.

1. Decide how to collapse data to form age groups. What is your rationale for these age categories?
2. Draft a table with the results. Remember to include a title.

Age of respondent (in years)	Frequency	Percent	Valid percent	Cumulative percent
18	35	8.2	8.6	8.63
19	32	7.5	7.9	16.5
20	30	7.1	7.4	23.9
21	34	8.0	8.4	32.4
22	45	10.6	11.1	43.4
23	43	10.1	10.7	54.1
24	43	10.1	10.7	64.8
25	36	8.5	8.9	73.7
26	33	7.8	8.2	81.9
29	21	4.9	5.2	87.1
31	22	5.2	5.4	92.5
36	10	2.4	2.5	95.0
40	10	2.4	2.5	97.5
44	10	2.4	2.5	100.0
Total	404	95.0	100.0	
Missing	21	5.0		
Total	425	100.0		

Note. Answers are provided at the end of the chapter.

FIGURES

A ***figure*** is any graphic illustration other than a table (Leedy & Ormrod, 2012). Figures, like tables, graphically summarize data from a frequency distribution. Figures take many forms including the popular pie graphs, bar graphs, histograms, line graphs, and charts.

Many people consider figures a visually more meaningful way to view results than tables. However, figures must be carefully constructed so as to not distort data findings. To create clear figures, adhere to the following principles (Nicol & Pexman, 2010b; Salkind, 2013; Torres et al., 2005):

1. One idea, one figure. A figure should communicate only one idea. If you have more than one idea, use more figures.
2. Numbering. In a report, number each figure consecutively.
3. Title. Place the title immediately below the figure. The figure title briefly conveys the information content, the dates data were collected, and the sample size. The figure title (sometimes referred to as ***figure caption***) should match the font used in the text.
4. Font style and size. All figures use the same font style (Arial or Helvetica), and the font size within a figure should range from 8 to 14 points.
5. Legend or key guide. If a ***legend*** or key guide is used, the first letter of the first word and all major words are capitalized.
6. Insertion. In the report, locate the figure as the next "paragraph" following where it is first mentioned.

SOMETHING TO REMEMBER!

Rules for creating pie charts:

1. Use five or fewer slices to present the findings.
2. Arrange the slices in descending order of magnitude. The largest percentage should be placed at the 12 o'clock position. The second largest percentage should be next and so on, moving clockwise.
3. Use different shading, contrasting patterns, or color for each slice. Generally, color is used for live presentations (e.g., poster sessions and group presentations). Due to the cost of color production, shading often is used for print versions of articles and reports.
4. Report whole percentages (using decimal points provides too much detail and makes the visual too busy), and percentages should total 100%.
5. Place the percentage value inside the pie slice or outside the slice if the segment is proportionately small.
6. Label the pie slices inside the slice itself or provide a legend next to the pie.
7. The legend should have the first letter of the first word and major words capitalized.

Note. Adapted from Nicol and Pexman (2010b) and Torres, Preskill, and Piontek (2005).

Pie Graph

A ***pie graph*** (also known as a pie chart) presents a circle or pie divided into sections that represent relative percentages in a frequency distribution (Figure 15.1). Pie graphs are used to depict the nominal categories of a variable (see Step 14A).

Bar Graph

A ***bar graph***, also called a column graph, uses columns that do not touch to show the nominal or ordinal data categories for a variable, compare variables, or emphasize changes in groups over time (Figure 15.2).

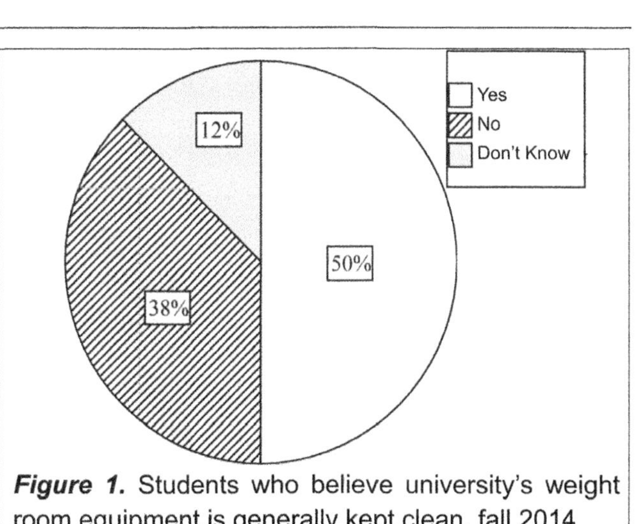

Figure 1. Students who believe university's weight room equipment is generally kept clean, fall 2014 (*N* = 186).

Figure 15.1. Example of a pie graph.

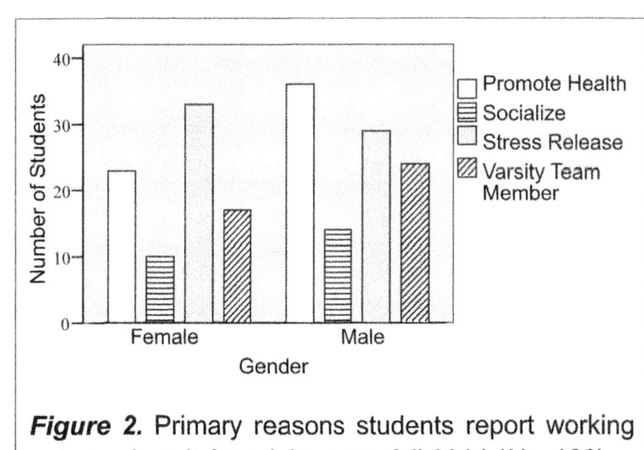

Figure 2. Primary reasons students report working out at university's weight room, fall 2014 (*N* = 186).

Figure 15.2. Example of a bar graph.

SOMETHING TO REMEMBER!

Important standards to follow when creating bar graphs:

1. The vertical axis (y-axis) is labeled and represents from bottom to top lower to higher frequency counts.
2. The horizontal axis (x-axis) is labeled with categorical groupings of the variable.
3. One grouping should have no more than six bars.
4. Bars should be the same width.
5. The entire bar graph is constructed so its height (y-axis) is approximately two thirds to three quarters the length of its width (x-axis). Failure to follow this rule will provide a distorted picture of the data.
6. The y- and x-axis labels should have the first letter of the first word and major words capitalized.

Note. Adapted from Nicol and Pexman (2010b) and Torres, Preskill, and Piontek (2005).

Histogram

A bar graph illustrates data that are in a nominal and/or ordinal scale, whereas a ***histogram*** illustrates a frequency distribution of interval and/or ratio data. Adjacent columns in the histogram (unlike a bar graph) touch (Figure 15.3).

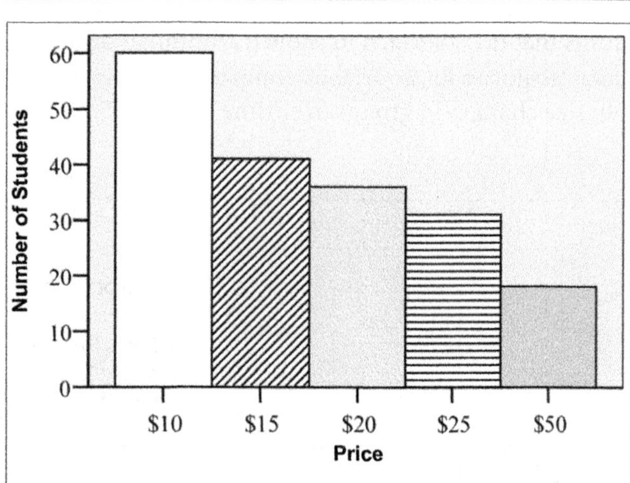

Figure 3. Hourly rate students are willing to pay for a personal trainer, fall 2014 (N = 186).

Figure 15.3. Example of a histogram.

SOMETHING TO REMEMBER!

Principles for setting up a histogram:

1. The horizontal axis depicts the variable scores/values.
2. The height of the bar (y-axis) denotes the frequency (or count) of the variable, and the values should increase when moving from bottom to top.
3. Bars are the same width and touch each other in the x-axis.
4. The entire graph is constructed so its height is approximately two thirds to three quarters the length of its width.
5. The y- and x-axis labels should have the first letter of the first word and major words capitalized.

Note. Adapted from Nicol and Pexman (2010b) and Torres, Preskill, and Piontek (2005).

Line Graph

Line graphs use a continuous line to connect data points over time (Figure 15.4). They are commonly used to examine rates of change and how fluctuations in an independent variable affect a dependent variable (see Step 4).

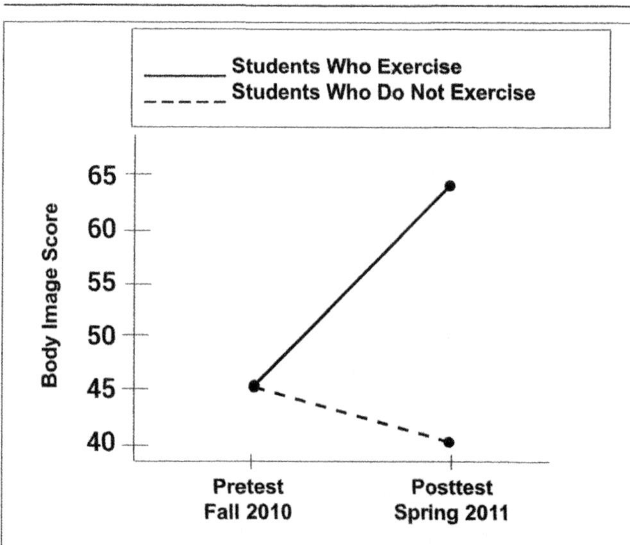

Figure 4. Body image scores of college students who routinely exercise versus those who do not exercise, fall 2014 (N = 186).

Figure 15.4. Example of a line graph.

SOMETHING TO REMEMBER!

Rules for creating line graphs:

1. The y-axis represents the dependent variable and the x-axis represents the independent variable.
2. A line graph figure must have at least three data points.
3. If printing in black and white, use a different shape or texture for each line. If using color, use a different color for each line, reserving the brightest color for the most important line.
4. The entire line graph is constructed so its height is approximately two thirds to three quarters the length of its width.
5. The y- and x-axis labels and legend should have the first letter of the first word and major words capitalized.

Note. Adapted from Nicol and Pexman (2010b) and Torres, Preskill, and Piontek (2005).

Chart

You may use a ***chart*** to present theoretical and conceptual models (Figure 15.5) or multivariate statistical model results. A chart is made up of enclosed boxes, circles, and/or squares that are connected with lines or arrows (Nicol & Pexman, 2010a).

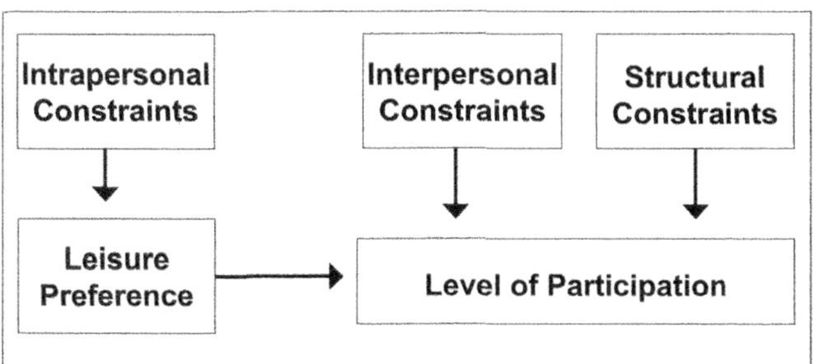

Figure 5. Model for explaining how constraints affect leisure preferences and level of intramurals participation. Adapted from Kolcun (2005, p. 5).

Figure 15.5. Example of a chart.

SOMETHING TO REMEMBER!

Tips for creating charts:

1. Charts should be set up to read from top to bottom and left to right.
2. For each variable identified within the chart, only the first letter of the first word is capitalized.

Note. Adapted from Nicol and Pexman (2010a).

WHAT FIGURE WORKS FOR THE GIVEN SITUATION?

You have been hired to provide advice on what visual aid to adopt in presenting data from a study on students registered in a weight lifting class offered at their university. Possible answers are pie graph, bar graph, histogram, line graph, or chart.

1. Present a diagram that identifies a theoretical model for explaining reasons college students work out.
2. Portray the primary reason students report working out (respondents were asked to choose one answer from four reasons).
3. Analyze by matriculation year (first-year, sophomore, junior, or senior) the primary reasons for working out.
4. Examine by matriculation year (first-year, sophomore, junior, or senior) how many hours on average a student works out per week.
5. Look at self-reported stress levels of students the first day of class and then again the last day of class.

Note. Answers are provided at the end of the chapter.

In summarizing findings, visual aids are useful to bring home a point in written and oral reports as well as in other venues. For instance, the wall art visual aid presented in this poignant photo displays a sample of garbage found floating in the waterway. "Little Venice" waterway, London, England. Copyright © 2015 Carol Cutler Riddick.

REVIEW AND DISCUSSION QUESTIONS

1. Define a numerical table and a frequency distribution.
2. Distinguish between ungrouped data and grouped data in a frequency distribution.
3. Identify two best practices for developing the grouped data categories for a table.
4. Recall five rules for setting up a frequency distribution table.
5. Describe the contents of a word table.
6. Explain what is meant by collapsing data.
7. Define missing data and describe how a valid percent is calculated when responses are missing.
8. List two rules each for setting up a pie graph, bar graph, histogram, line graph, and chart.

YOUR RESEARCH

1. What numerical tables do you anticipate developing when reporting your research study? Why? Draft titles for each table you envision appearing in your study.
2. What is your plan for dealing with missing data when putting together your tables?
3. What figures do you think you will be inserting into your study report? Why? Draft titles for each figure and indicate whether the figure will be a pie graph, bar graph, histogram, line graph, or another figure.

PRACTICE EXERCISES

1. Present the scores reported below by creating a frequency distribution table, a pie graph, and a histogram. You may use Microsoft Word to type the frequency distribution table. You may create the pie graph and histogram using commercial software programs (e.g., SPSS, Excel, Quattro Pro, or Access), or your instructor may request you sketch these by hand.

a. The following data are the final exam scores for a research methods course: 92, 100, 65, 20, 90, 87, 86, 80, 88, 75, 75, 60, 65, 64, 92, 100, 0, 70, 80, 95, 91, 86, 71, 70, 88, 80, 88, 85, 98, 97, 76, 70, 85.
b. Hints:
   - For the frequency table, report group data using the following score groups: 91–100, 81–90, 71–80, 61–70, and ≤ 60.
   - For the pie graph, convert scores to grouped data using the following grading scheme: 90–100 = A, 80–89 = B, 70–79 = C, 60–69 = D, and < 60 = F.
   - For the histogram, use the listed absolute scores.

2. Refer to the Handling Missing Data When Constructing a Table text presented in this chapter.
   a. Draft a typed numerical table (complete with title) that presents the IM participation rates of students at this imaginary college.
   b. Draw a pie graph that approximates the noted results.
3. Acquire a copy of the following article (or your instructor may substitute another article):

   Reid, C., Landy, A., & Leon, P. (2013). Using community-based research to explore common language and shared identity in the therapeutic recreation profession in British Columbia, Canada. *Therapeutic Recreation Journal, 47*, 69–88. You may access this article at http://js.sagamorepub.com/ trj/article/view/2623.

   Read the article and answer the following questions:
   a. Were tables (numerical table, word table) and/or figures (pie graphs, bar graphs, histograms, line graphs, charts) used?
   b. Were any of the visual aid guidelines identified in this chapter violated? If so, did these violations result in a distracting or misleading table or figure? How could the tables or figures in question be improved?

WEB EXERCISES

1. Consult the Common Sense Media research study *Social Media, Social Life: How Teens View Their Digital Lives* at https://www.commonsensemedia.org/research/social-media-social-life-how-teens-view-their-digital-lives.
   a. What visual techniques were used to present the results?
   b. Did the tables and figures conform to content and appearance considerations pointed out in this chapter? If so, what were the deviations?
   c. What did you like and dislike about the way results were presented?
   d. Incidentally, did any of the key findings surprise you? If so, which ones, and why?
2. Identify three pointers you learned about presenting numbers in tables or graphs by reviewing the University of Leicester's posting at http://www2.le.ac.uk/offices/ld/resources/numeracy/numerical-data.
3. Try creating tables and graphs using Excel. One resource for helping you with this task is http://www.slideshare.net/giordepasamba/creating-tables-and-graphs-excel-2011-2012.
4. Identify two tips related to creating tables and figures by consulting APA blog posts on these topics at http://blog.apastyle.org/apastyle/2009/11/table-tips.html and http://blog.apastyle.org/apastyle/2009/12/figureconstruction-resisting-the-urge-to-obscure.html.

SERVICE LEARNING PROJECT

1. Review the data collected for your class study. Decide the format for presenting data. That is, should data results on a particular variable be presented in a table? Pie graph? Bar graph? Histogram? Line graph? Chart?

2. To decide which visual aid tool you will use to present the findings, develop a grid with the following:
    - *Variables* being the name of the first column (also called a stubhead), with each variable name listed on a separate row (also known as a stub or stub column).
    - The names of ways to present the data spread across the remaining columns/width of the page (column heads will be labeled as *Table, Pie graph, Bar graph,* etc.).
    - Then, for purposes of data presentation in a final written report and/or presentation, check the visual medium (table, pie graph, etc.) you will use to present data results on the particular variable.

TEST YOURSELF ANSWERS

Drafting a Table After Sorting Through Missing Data

Table 1

Age of Study Participants Surveyed Regarding Their Opinions of College West's Swimming Facilities, Spring 2014 (N = 404)

Age category	*N*	%
18–21	131	32.4
22–24	131	32.4
25–44	142	35.2

What Figure Works for the Given Situation?

1. Chart, 2. Pie graph, 3. Bar graph, 4. Histogram, 5. Line graph.

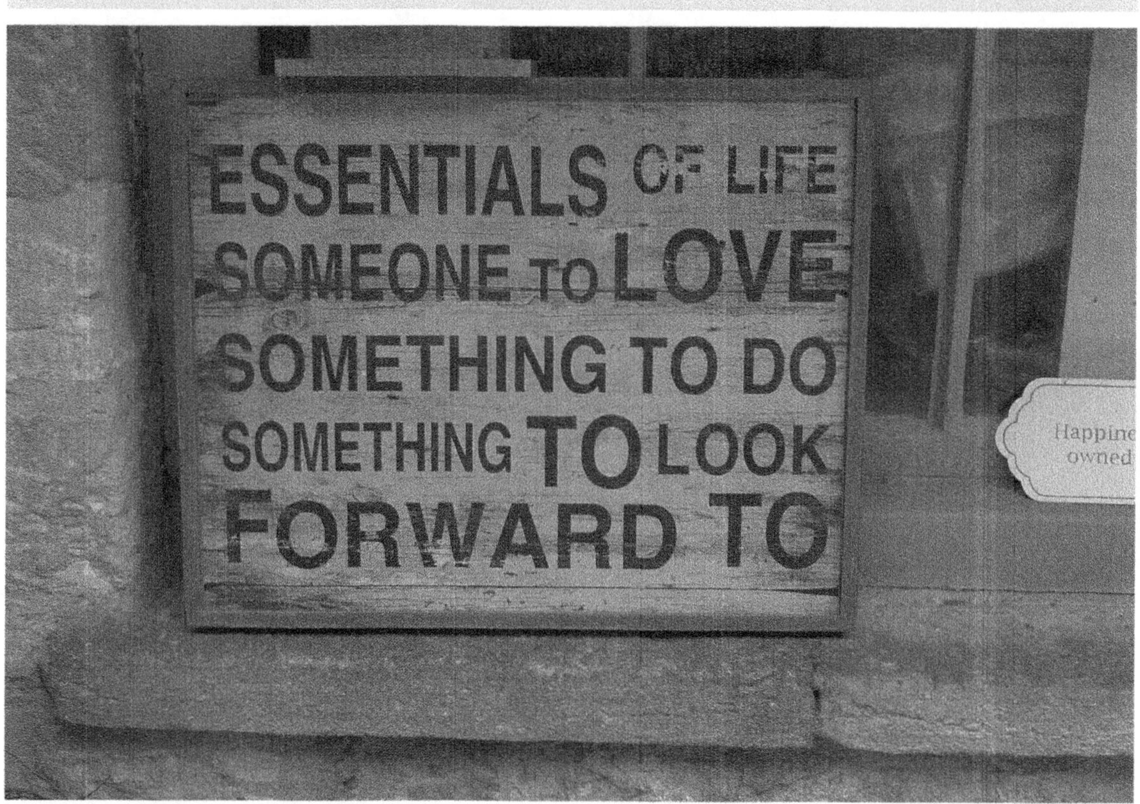

The content and the style of writing you adopt for the final written research report are important considerations. Choice and presentation of words have profound effects on the reader, whether that person is reading a report or signage. Burford, England. Copyright © 2015 Carol Cutler Riddick.

WRITE REPORT

WHAT WILL I LEARN IN THIS CHAPTER?

I'll be able to...

1. Explain the distinction between what is found in an academic report and a business report.
2. Distinguish among what typically is written in the Results section of a study report using a quantitative approach, a qualitative approach, and a mixed-methods approach.
3. Describe what should be in the Discussion section.
4. Recall what is stated in the Conclusions section of a report, including guidelines for how much certainty should be used when making statements about conclusions.
5. Contrast Recommendations for Professional Practice and Policy and Recommendations for Future Research sections in a final report.
6. Outline ideas on how to gather constructive feedback to draft a final research report.
7. Summarize ways a final report may be disseminated.

"For me, words are a form of action, capable of influencing change."

Ingrid Bengis
(American author, best known for essays on love, hate, and sexuality, 1944–)

You have come a long way in the research cycle by developing and implementing a plan that has enabled you to collect, analyze, and interpret information to gain new knowledge about your study topic. You now have arrived at the point of having answers. But until your research has been recorded in written and/or presentation form, it remains hidden and, thus, is completely useless! Indeed, if research reports are not written, "... professional knowledge cannot be advanced, nor can implications for practice and theory be put into effect" (Corbin & Strauss, 2008b, p. 276).

Preparing a useful report, whether it is written or delivered orally, takes time and work. This chapter focuses on preparing the written final report first by contrasting academic and business reports, then by reviewing the subsections typically found in a written report, by sharing ideas on how to acquire constructive criticism on a draft of the report, and by providing tips on report dissemination.

WRITTEN REPORTS

The basic types of research reports are academic and business (Polonsky & Waller, 2010). They differ in terms of the audience for whom they are intended; thus, they also differ by language, writing style, and structure detail.

Academic Report

An ***academic report*** is used to present research to leisure scholars and managerial level professionals. You may present academic reports in many formats including a written thesis or dissertation, an article appearing in a research journal, a report for discussion at an agency staff meeting, or a presentation at a professional conference (covered in Step 17).

The audience for an academic report typically is interested in the literature review, theoretical foundation, methodological details, findings, discussion, conclusions, recommendations, and references. Though an academic report may discuss the managerial implications of the findings, this generally is not the case.

To learn how to write an academic report, study what others have done. If you are writing a thesis or dissertation, for example, ask your committee chair to identify other students' work to serve as models for you. If you are writing for a journal, choose one or two journals in which you would like to see your work published and study the articles that the journal has recently published.

Business Report

In contrast, ***business reports*** focus on reporting applied research results to internal and external stakeholders of an organization (see "Overview" chapter). Business reports emphasize how the problem was examined and provide suggestions for practice based on the findings. Unlike the academic report, several sections, namely, Theoretical Foundations, Research Question and/or Hypotheses, Literature Review, and Methods, are presented in shortened form. In a business report, the emphasis is on service provisions and/or management implications from the findings.

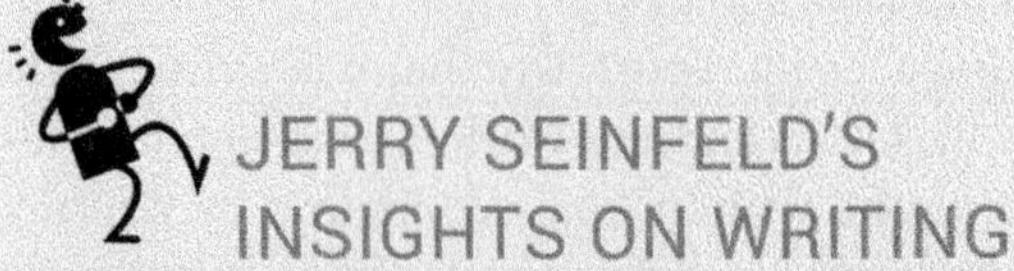

JERRY SEINFELD'S INSIGHTS ON WRITING

One of Jerry Seinfeld's memorable stand-up comedy routines is about Pop-Tarts, which you may view at http://www.youtube.com/watch?v=YmCTUBEluSE.

During an interview, Seinfeld was asked to provide advice on how to write a joke (go to http://www.youtube.com/watch?v=itWxXyCfW5s). He draws on his Pop-Tarts skit to illustrate several points, including the observation that writing takes a long time.

FINAL REPORT SECTIONS

Regardless of the type, the written final report is an extension of the written proposal. In other words, the final report contains the sections outlined in the proposal, plus additional sections. Thus, if you have done a thorough job of writing the research proposal, converting it to a final report following data collection and analysis is easier and hopefully more fun.

In general, a common format exists for writing a final report. Review the major phases (Step 1) involved in conducting research (Figure 16.1).

A comparison of the proposal and final report contents (as presented in Step 11) is reproduced in Table 16.1. This chapter focuses on the final report parts that did not appear in Step 11.

Table 16.1
Outline of What Typically Appears in a Proposal and Final Report

Heading	Contained in proposal	Contained in final report
Title Page[a]	√	√
Abstract/Executive Summary		√
Acknowledgements		√
Table of Contents	√	√
List of Figures, Tables and Appendices	√	√
Introduction	√	√
Theoretical Foundation(s)	√	√
Research Question and/or Hypothesis	√	√
Literature Review	√	√
Methods	√	√
Results		√
Discussion		√
Conclusions		√
Recommendations		√
References	√	√
Appendices	√	√

Note. The final research report contains information on all points of this table.
[a]A copyright declaration sometimes appears on the title page or the page immediately after the title page. Theses and dissertations written at American universities do not need to be registered with the U.S. Copyright Office to be protected by copyright law. Other documents, however, must be registered (for a fee) with the United States Copyright Office (http://www.copyright.gov/).

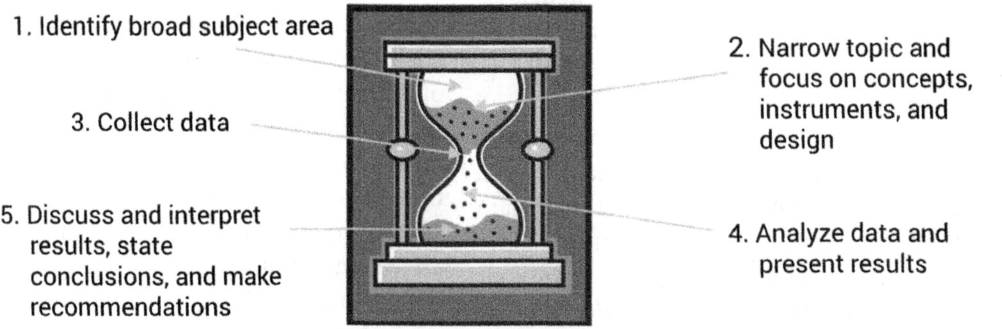
1. Identify broad subject area
2. Narrow topic and focus on concepts, instruments, and design
3. Collect data
4. Analyze data and present results
5. Discuss and interpret results, state conclusions, and make recommendations

Figure 16.1. Hourglass shape of research. Adapted from Trochim (2006).

A study that is conducted using a mixed-method foundation may deviate from the organization presented in Table 16.1. That is, the final report for a mixed-methods study may vary in how it is structured.

ORGANIZING A REPORT WRITE-UP FOR A STUDY USING MIXED METHODS

For a study using a concurrent design (see Step 7),

- present the quantitative and qualitative data results in separate sections, and
- combine the data in the Discussion section to identify convergence or similarities among the results.

For a sequential design (Step 7),

- organize the report into quantitative data collection and quantitative data analyses followed by qualitative data collection and qualitative data analyses (or vice versa, with qualitative data collection and qualitative data analyses followed by quantitative data collection and quantitative data analyses) and
- then, in the Conclusions section, comment on how the qualitative findings helped to elaborate or extend the quantitative results (or how the quantitative findings helped extend the qualitative results).

Note. Adapted from Creswell (2013).

Abstract/Executive Summary

The ***abstract*** or executive summary is a synopsis of the entire study (Case 16.1). It is arguably the most important part of the research report since its purpose is to help a reader decide whether to read the entire paper. Ultimately, more people will read an abstract than the entire report. This is why abstracts should be written to stand alone, that is, to be understandable without reading anything more about the study (Kielhofner, Fossey, & Taylor, 2006). Writing an effective abstract takes practice and many revisions.

An informative abstract will describe the following (Brown, 1996; Hocking & Wallen, 1999):

- what was studied;
- who the respondents were;
- why the study was conducted, or the importance of the research topic;
- the main results/findings; and
- the implications that the findings have for practice, theory, and/or future research.

Acknowledgements

In the final written report, you should acknowledge and thank individuals who directly supported or cooperated with you during the planning and implementation phases of the study. Additionally, you should recognize individuals and sponsors and/or organizations that provided funding for the study.

Results

Results also are often labeled as Findings. In this section of the report, regardless of whether a qualitative, quantitative, or mixed-methods study was undertaken, the analyses of the gathered information is presented.

Quantitative study. For a study that has used a quantitative approach, present the findings in the same order introduced in the Introduction, Purpose Statement, and Research Question and/or Hypotheses sections. The template for reporting quantitative findings is to (Case 16.2)

- restate the research question or hypothesis,
- name the statistical test used,
- report degrees of freedom (if pertinent),
- cite the obtained test value, and
- identify the probability level associated with the reported value.

One challenge in writing quantitative research findings is how you report numbers or percentages in your report. You may use various modes. For instance, the following illustrates the same finding expressed three ways:

- "one fourth of the respondents felt..."
- "25% of the respondents reported..."
- "1 out of 4 respondents expressed..."

SOMETHING TO REMEMBER!

To provide narrative variety, rather than always using precise numbers when writing results in the report narrative, consider adjectives that convey or relate to numbers. Possible choices include the following:

- About
- Almost
- Roughly
- Nearly
- More or less than
- Approaching
- Approximately
- Around
- Rounding up
- The modal response for
- A majority

Note. When there is a percentage > 50%, it is correct to use the word *majority*.

Qualitative study. Qualitative studies require presenting data in the report so they speak for themselves (Leedy & Ormrod, 2012). Strategies for writing qualitative results include the following (Creswell, 2013; Padgett, 2008):

- Use a ***narrative writing style*** (storytelling) to present the results so the reader feels as though he or she is embarking on a journey of discovery and interpretation.
- Adopt an ***emic/etic perspective*** or use the frame of reference of the research participant rather than the researcher.
- Use thick descriptions or long quotes as well as short passages (*Note:* To call attention, indent long quotations of 40 words or more).
- Use metaphors and analogies.
- Use wording from participants to form codes and theme categories (Case 16.2).
- Present text information in tabular form (e.g., comparison tables of different codes, matrices).

Mixed-methods study. Consider presenting the results in several parts. Alert the reader to this organization by writing a paragraph similar to the following passage: "The results are presented in two sections. The first section deals with descriptive findings from the qualitative part, whereas the second section presents hypotheses testing results."

When shifting from one result to another, prepare the reader to the imminent transition. To signal a shift from reporting one result to another finding, use ***transitional devices***, that is, "words or phrases that help carry a thought from one sentence to another, from one idea to another, or from one paragraph to another" (Weber & Stolley, Transitional Devices section, para. 1, 2011).

Crafting the narrative for the Results section of the report is complex. Use the present tense when examining the implications of the results. Finally, describe findings without comment or discussion. Save commentary for the Discussion section of the final report, which will be discussed next.

SOMETHING TO REMEMBER!

Emphasis needed	Transitional words and phrases	
Addition	Also Again As well as	Besides Furthermore
Consequence	Accordingly As a result For this reason	Subsequently Therefore
Comparison	In contrast By the same token Conversely	Instead Likewise
Diversion	By the way	Incidentally
Emphasis	Above all Chiefly	Particularly
Exception	Aside from Besides Except Exception	However Nevertheless Other than
Illustration	In particular For example	For instance As an illustration
Generalizing	For the most part In general	Usually
Shift Topic	Concerning Examining Looking at	Regarding Turning to
Summarizing	Finally In conclusion In short	In summary On the whole

Note. Adapted from "Transitional Words & Phrases" (n.d.).

PRACTICE TRANSITIONAL DEVICES IN WRITING

First, review a quick tutorial on transitional devices by going to Purdue University's Online Writing Lab at http://owl.english.purdue.edu/owl/resource/574/02/.

Now, go to and complete an exercise designed by Andrew Tucker, San Jose State University Writing Center, at http://www.sjsu.edu/writingcenter/docs/Transition_Words_Handout_FINAL.pdf.

Note. Answers are provided at the end of the chapter.

Discussion

The Discussion section is about interpreting your findings, discussing what the study results suggest or represent (for a checklist of information for the Discussion section, see Table 16.2). Begin the Discussion section by summarizing the purpose, methods, and major findings. Resist, however, the temptation to restate the Results section. Instead, focus on presenting a concise interpretation that systematically answers the questions originally proposed in the Introduction section.

Next, compare and contrast the results with previous studies on the same topic. Do the findings agree with or contradict previously published research on the topic? If your findings are inconsistent with what you reported earlier, discuss possible explanations for this.

Next, relate the results to the theoretical basis of the study. How can you explain findings in terms of theoretical models? If you used a quantitative approach, do the data support or not support the theory used in the study? If you adopted a qualitative approach, discuss the utility of your findings for developing theoretical understanding.

End the Discussion section by offering alternative explanations for the findings. Highlight plausible competing explanations to what was found. Identify another theory or theoretical approach that may have provided better insights. Point out how some of the acknowledged limitations could have skewed reported results.

Conclusions

In this section of the written final report, begin by making concise finishing remarks about each research question and/or hypothesis examined (see Table 16.2 for a checklist of points relevant to the Conclusions section). Remember, each of the concluding statements must be backed by the data results presented earlier in the report.

Furthermore, talk about the meaning and importance of the results in terms of what was learned from the study and within the confines of the limitations of the study (Step 11, Case 16.3). Limitations may stem from several sources (e.g., the theoretical approach, sampling, research design, instrumentation, data collection, and/or data analysis).

Also, make sure concluding remarks identify how study results tie in to theory testing and theory building. The challenge is writing a report that not only is true to the data but also finds meaning in those data (Leedy & Ormrod, 2012).

Write the concluding remarks carefully. One common mistake is to overstate or understate the importance of the findings. Use carefully chosen expressions that indicate the degree of certainty with which you reached the conclusions (Pan, 2008). The rigor of how the study was conducted coupled with the attained results will temper the amount of certainty you should express (see Table 16.3). As well, do not be too shy about the importance of your findings; stating them accurately is sometimes a difficult balance.

Table 16.2

Checklist for Rating the Discussion, Conclusions, and Recommendations Sections of a Report

Part I: Use the following checklist to rate the drafted Discussion section.

Discussion	Excellent	Fair	Poor	Suggestions for improvement
Study purpose and methods have been summarized.				
Major results are systematically summarized and discussed in the order found in the Introduction.				
Major results are integrated with previous research.				
Plausible explanations for inconsistent results from previous studies have been stated.				
Statement and brief narrative regarding support or nonsupport of theoretical approach was included.				
Alternative explanations to findings were discussed.				

Table 16.2 (cont.)

Part II: As you have done above, use the following checklist to assess the quality of the drafted Conclusions section.				
Conclusions	**Excellent**	**Fair**	**Poor**	**Suggestions for improvement**
A conclusion for each research question and/or hypothesis has been clearly stated.				
Conclusions are based on attained results.				
Meanings and importance of results were explained and framed within the limitations of the study.				
Implications for theory testing or theory building have been mentioned.				
Avoided making extravagant claims or inferences.				
Part III: Now review and judge the Recommendations section.				
Recommendations	**Excellent**	**Fair**	**Poor**	**Suggestions for improvement**
Suggestions on how to improve service operations and/or management.				
Ideas for future studies that address some of the limitations of the present study.				
Thoughts on how to extend the present study.				

Note. Adapted from Mauch and Park (2003).

Table 16.3
Degrees of Certainty Expressed in Conclusions Reached

Degree of certainty	Example of how to state a conclusion with an implied degree of certainty
Very certain	"The results strongly indicate the following conclusions..."
Somewhat certain	"Given the limitations of the study, the results indicate support of theory X or suggest that ..."
Rather uncertain	"The preliminary evidence of this pilot/exploratory study suggests the tentative conclusion that..."

Note. Adapted from Pan (2008).

Recommendations

A major component of the report should consist of recommendations. The Recommendations section is the all-important action link from the present to the future. If you have conducted applied research, make recommendations that link study findings to changes needed in professional practice and policy. Moreover, if you are reporting basic research, make recommendations for future research (Table 16.2 summarizes information that should appear in the Recommendations section).

Recommendations for professional practice and policy. The research process should ultimately lead to providing useful information by making recommendations for professional practice (see Figure 16.2). This means recommendations stemming from an applied research project should provide specific guidance for organizational actions (Case 16.4).

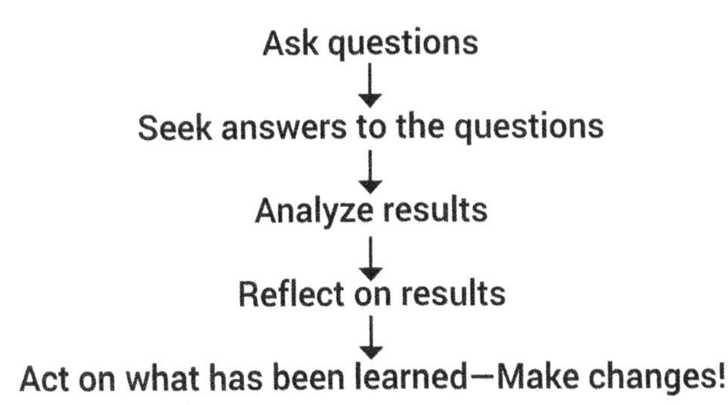

Figure 16.2. A model for linking research results to professional practice changes. Adapted from Patton (2008).

Be reflective and thoughtful when crafting professional practice and policy recommendations from research conclusions so they are not only useful but also accepted by those in positions to implement them. For instance, you may call for new directions for a program, modifications in program operations, changes in personnel policies, or shifts in resource allocation. You may need to advocate that changes occur over a certain time and consider adopting the following strategies for the recommendations:

- Be practical in what you are recommending. The advice should be feasible given the organization's available resources.
- Recommendations should be compatible with each other. For example, if you advocate for increasing services, do not propose budget cuts.
- Share preliminary recommendations with stakeholders. Do not assume that your version of the solution is the only way. You may need to modify recommendations after collaborating with the original study stakeholders (Fullan, 2007).

WRITING RECOMMENDATIONS FOR PROFESSIONAL PRACTICE AND POLICY

Practice and policy recommendations must be understandable. To foster clarity, consider addressing the following points:

What	Clearly state the recommendation. In other words, make a statement regarding a course of action.
Why	Provide a rationale for the recommendation, drawing on relevant information (e.g., research results, previous studies, theoretical suppositions).
Where	Specify what programs, facilities, personnel, and departmental functions (e.g., marketing) should be involved in carrying out the recommendation.
When	Identify the desired time frame for carrying out the recommendation. If recommendations need to be phased in, identify a timetable and ultimate completion deadline.
Who	Earmark the roles of individuals or entities who should be involved in carrying out the recommendation.

Recommendations for future research. Completed basic and applied research should inform future research (Case 16.5). You may do this by writing recommendations that fall into two areas of emphases.

First, outline your ideas for how additional research may improve what you have reported. That is, develop recommendations for future research that address the shortcomings of your study. Start by acknowledging limitations of the study. Every study has limitations that have possible effects on the outcomes of the study. Be proactive by recognizing and admitting these criticisms rather than ignoring or trying to hide them. Remember, a perfect study does not exist! Every research project has inherent weaknesses. Identify how future researchers may build upon your work by addressing the shortcomings of your study, including weaknesses related to the research design, sample selection, instrumentation, and statistical analyses.

Second, recommendations for future research should identify ways to extend the reported study. One possibility is to identify additional research questions and hypotheses suggested by the results of your study. Another way is to call for replication and extension studies (covered in Step 1). You also could advocate that other researchers examine alternative theoretical frameworks and conceptual maps (reviewed in Step 3).

CONSTRUCTIVE CRITICISM ON THE DRAFT FINAL REPORT

When you have carefully finished proofreading and editing your written research report, ask someone you trust to read it. After a while, it becomes increasingly difficult to read objectively what you have written. Additionally, do not rely solely on computer spell and grammar checks to catch your errors. They do not catch all mistakes.

Next, you should share your draft with those who have a stake in your research report. If you are a student, this initially will be your thesis or dissertation committee chair. If you are completing a program evaluation report for a service or facility, you should share your draft with the staff program manager and other important stakeholders (see Step 1). Request a one-on-one meeting with these individuals after allowing a week or two for reading the report. Ask for constructive criticism and insights that may enhance the readability and acceptability of the report. Then, revise the report according to what you learned from these "sneak previews." This adaptive step is similar to what you did in planning the study (see Overview chapter).

FINAL REPORT DISTRIBUTION

Finally, you need to disseminate the final report. Research that is not publicly shared is incomplete. ***Dissemination*** is the processes by which researchers inform others about the study. Dissemination mechanisms ensure that your findings are effectively communicated and used (Patton, 2008).

Dissemination mechanisms that you may adopt inside and outside your organization include the following:

- Conduct an "in response" campaign by implementing simple and quick ways to provide feedback to program participants (e.g., highlight the conclusions of the study and changes the organization is making accordingly in "Survey Says" flyers located at the facility's front desk, on bulletin boards, and on the organization's website).
- Prepare a popularized version of the report for a pamphlet, brochure, or booklet.
- Issue a press release to local newspapers.
- Post the report on the organization's home page.
- Present findings at a professional meeting (see Step 17).
- Write an article about the study and submit the manuscript for publication consideration by a professional journal.

Dissemination of the results of research may take many forms. Notice in this photo how effectively the message is disseminated through art. Museum of Contemporary Art, Chicago, Illinois. Copyright © 2015 Ruth V. Russell.

COMMUNICATING RESULTS OF A STUDY

See whether you understand ways evaluation studies may be used or distributed by reviewing Robert Wood Johnson Foundation's report *An Ecological Understanding of Evaluation Use: A Case Study of the Active for Living Evaluation*, which is available at http://www.innonet.org/resources/files/casestudy.ottoson.final.pdf.

Read (beginning on page 5) about the Active for Living Program, a program designed to promote physical activity among adults aged 50 years and older. Then, review major findings of the evaluation (found on pages 7 to 9 of the report).

Now outline ways or outlets for sharing or communicating study findings to different entities and stakeholders. Compare your answers to the six ways identified on page 12 of the report. What did you overlook in how study results could be used?

Note. Answers are provided at the end of the chapter.

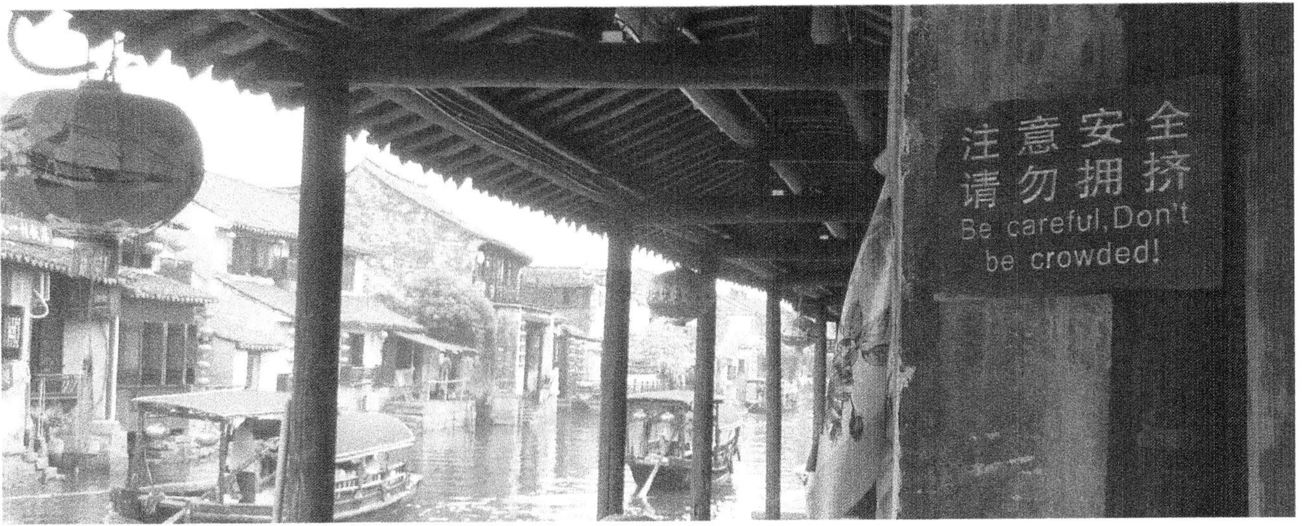

Take care in organizing and stating your thoughts, whether it is the context of a final written research report or everyday living. For instance, the English translation rendered in the sign captured in this photograph has a glitch. Erected at a popular and often crowded tourist attraction, this sign should read, "When crowded, take care and don't push others." Xitang Water Town, China. Copyright © 2015 Blake Cutler Riddick.

REVIEW AND DISCUSSION QUESTIONS

1. Distinguish between an academic report and a business report.
2. What major points are covered in the abstract?
3. Who should be recognized in the acknowledgements?
4. What should be covered in the Discussion section?
5. What goes into the Conclusion section?
6. When crafting policy and practice recommendations for an applied research project, what five points should you address?
7. Identify two emphases for future research recommendations. What role do the limitations of a study have in future research recommendations?
8. Sketch out ideas for how to gather constructive feedback to a preliminary draft of the final research report.
9. Identify ways to disseminate the final research report.

YOUR RESEARCH

1. Identify the target audience for the report.
2. Draft a report of your research project.
3. Review the drafted Results, Discussion, Conclusions, and Recommendations sections by using the checklist in Table 16.2 to rate content quality. You may also consider asking your research supervisor or someone knowledgeable about research to rate you.
4. Review the draft making sure you have not violated the writing rules reviewed in this chapter.
5. What ideas do you have for disseminating your study outcomes?

PRACTICE EXERCISES

1. Practice drafting Discussion, Conclusions, and Recommendations sections for a study. Acquire a copy of the following article (or your instructor may substitute another article):

   Dowling, S., McConkey, R., Hassan, D., & Menke, S. (August 2010). *Evaluation of the Special Olympics Youth Unified Sports® program in Europe/Eurasia*. Ulster, Ireland: University of Ulster. You may access this article at http://www.specialolympics.org/uploadedFiles/LandingPage/WhatWeDo/Final%20Report%20Unified%20Sports10%20Sept%202010.pdf.

   Before reviewing the report, tape a piece of paper over the report's Discussion and Conclusions sections. Unless otherwise instructed, prepare written responses to these questions:

   a. Read the article carefully up to the covered Discussion and Conclusions section.
   b. Write your own discussion of the results. That is, interpret the results in terms of the research questions and/or hypotheses examined in the study. Do findings agree or contradict previously published research? How can findings be explained or contextualized using theoretical frameworks identified for the study?
   c. What conclusions could be stated regarding each research question and/or hypothesis examined in the study? How do study results tie in to theory testing and/or theory building?
   d. What recommendations flow from the study for professional practice and/or policy changes needed?
   e. Given the limitations of the study, what recommendations could be made for future research on the topic? What replication or extension studies may emanate from the study?
   f. Remove the paper from the article and compare your discussion with that of the original report. Did you hit the main points? Do not be concerned at this time with the polish of your writing or differences in writing style.
   h. Compare your answers with those of your classmates.

2. Read and rate the Discussion, Conclusions, and Recommendations sections of a research report or an article that reports on applied research findings from a leisure-related program or an applied research service. You could use the report cited in Practice Exercise 1, one of articles from Web Exercise 1, or a research report or research article your instructor provides. Use Table 16.2 in this chapter to record your ratings.

WEB EXERCISES

1. Explore content and style differences that exist between business/organization reports and articles appearing in professional journals by acquiring a copy of the following references (or your instructor may substitute other reports):

   Dowling, S., Hassan, D., & McConkey, R. (2012). *The 2011 Summer World Games experiences for Special Olympics athletes and coaches: A longitudinal study in four countries*. Ulster, Ireland: University of Ulster. You may access this article at http://www.specialolympics.org/uploadedFiles/Ulster_Coaching%20Final%20Report.pdf.

   Beam, M., Ehrlich, G., Black, J., Block, A., & Leviton, L. (2012). Evaluation of the healthy schools program: Part I. Interim progress. *Preventing Chronic Diseases, 9*. You may access this article at http://www.cdc.gov/pcd/issues/2012/11_0106.htm.

   Read these references, and answer the following questions:

   a. What language and writing style differences exist between them? List three main differences.
   b. Based on Table 16.1, how do the reports differ in their adopted outlines? What similar and dissimilar topic and subtopic headings are used in the reports?

2. Review the following and identify three insights or pointers you learn from each:
   a. Watch *How to Write a Great Research Paper* presentation by Professor Jones (Cambridge University) at http://www.youtube.com/watch?v= g3dkRsTqdDA.
   b. Access the U.S. Department of Health and Human Services' Office of Planning, Research, and Evaluation's publication *Program Manager's Guide to Evaluation* (2010, 2nd ed.) available at http://www.acf.hhs.gov/programs/opre/resource/the-program-managers-guide-to-evaluation-second-edition. Read Chapter 9, "How Can You Report What You Have Learned."
   c. Daryl Beam's (Cornell University) article "Writing the Empirical Journal Article" is available at http:/dbem.ws/WritingArticle.pdf.
3. Examine the variation of how research studies may be written. Review research that has been conducted about the Playworks program (learn more about the program by going to http://www.youtube.com/watch?v-=vQM__vOjqc4), an organized play during recess initiative funded by the Robert Wood Johnson Foundation, by visiting http://www.playworks.org/welcome?_q=news/playworks-recess-much-more-than-breakin-the-day. What did you like and dislike about the style and content?

SERVICE LEARNING PROJECT

1. Draft the following parts of the final report:
   a. Abstract/executive summary
   b. Acknowledgements
   c. Results (if appropriate, use the subsections Quantitative Study, Qualitative Study, and Mixed-Methods Study)
   d. Discussion
   e. Conclusions
   f. Recommendations (use the subheadings Recommendations for Future for Professional Practice and Recommendations for Future Research).
2. Review your draft to see whether you used the following:
   a. Alternative word choices in place of exact numbers in the Results section
   b. Transitional words
3. Ask someone to review and comment on the draft. It may be useful to attach Table 16.2 and ask the reviewer to use the checklist to rate the Discussion, Conclusions, and Recommendations sections of the drafted report.

TEST YOURSELF ANSWERS

Practice Transitional Devices in Writing

Answers are provided at http://www.sjsu.edu/writingcenter/docs/Transition_Words_Handout_FINAL.pdf.

Communicating Results of a Study

Answers are provided on page 12 of the report:

- Advocacy (which encompasses educating stakeholders)
- Professional dissemination (communicating study results at conferences, via journal articles, or in written reports)
- Distributing via interagency networks, community events (including sharing findings with participants and the community, using mechanisms such as success stories, and noting in recruitment materials), websites, and the media/press.

SUPPORTING CASES FOR THIS CHAPTER

CASE 16.1. ABSTRACT/EXECUTIVE SUMMARY

Kunstler, R., Thompson, A., & Croke, E. (2012). Inclusive recreation for transition-age youth: Promoting self-sufficiency, community inclusion, and experiential learning. *Therapeutic Recreation Journal, 47,* 122–136.

Despite recent advances, youth with disabilities still face barriers to developing self-sufficiency for successful work outcomes and inclusive opportunities for participation in recreation, fitness, and sports. Developing replicable models to promote skill development for inclusive life settings is crucial. A successful program paired college students with teenagers with severe disabilities in a recreation program in a community setting. Positive outcomes related to employment, self-esteem, and social skills were reported for the youth, as well as valuable learning opportunities for the college students and the fostering of a successful inclusive environment in the community.

Keywords

Transition-age youth; self-sufficiency; therapeutic recreation; inclusion; fitness; experiential learning

Note. Reprinted with permission of the authors.

CASE 16.2. RESULTS SECTION OF A MIXED-METHODS STUDY

Duerden, M., Witt, P., & Taniguchi, S. (2012). The impact of postprogram reflection on recreation program outcomes. *Journal of Park and Recreation Administration, 30,* 36–50.

Forty-six youth (M_{age} = 13 years) participated in a program run by Global Explorers. The program consisted of a preparatory after-school program (nine to 12 sessions ranging from 1 to 3 hours), an international field workshop (held in Peru), and a posttrip service project.

The following passage exemplifies how the results from hypothesis testing were described in the Findings section:

> Results...partially supported the study's hypothesis that higher rates of post-program reflection would be associated with increases in targeted participant outcomes on follow-up assessments. Results indicated... one significant reflection correlation coefficient and that was with teamwork ($r = .18, p = .03$). (p. 45)

Based on observational field notes, interviews, and focus groups, the following themes emerged from postprogram reflection:

- Difficult to explain experience to nonparticipants.
- Return to regular life makes it hard to remember the experience.
- Contact with fellow participants facilitated reflection.
- Mementos helped participants reflect on the experience.

CASE 16.3. CONCLUSIONS IN A QUALITATIVE STUDY

Langseth, T. (2012). Liquid ice surfers—The construction of surfer identities in Norway. *Journal of Adventure Education & Outdoor Learning, 12,* 3–23.

The theoretical framework for the study relied on a combination of Donnelly and Young's (1988) understanding of identity construction in sport subcultures and Bourdieu's concepts of symbolic capital. Paraphrasing the study, the concluding remarks included the following points:

- Supporting Donnelly and Young's views, to become a full member of the surf subculture in Norway, the beginner had to go through a socialization process that consists of adopting the embodiment of surfer values.
- Integration into the surfer community (i.e., to be perceived as an "insider") was dependent on the amount of symbolic capital the individual surfer possessed.
- Flowing from Bourdieu's writings, symbolic capital was garnered by the ability of the new surfer to demonstrate skills, subculture knowledge (e.g., rules, types of boards, surf spots), commitment (e.g., surfing in cold winter conditions), and local affiliation.
- Surfing went from being a hobby toward an all-embracing lifestyle (or identification of the subculture's values).

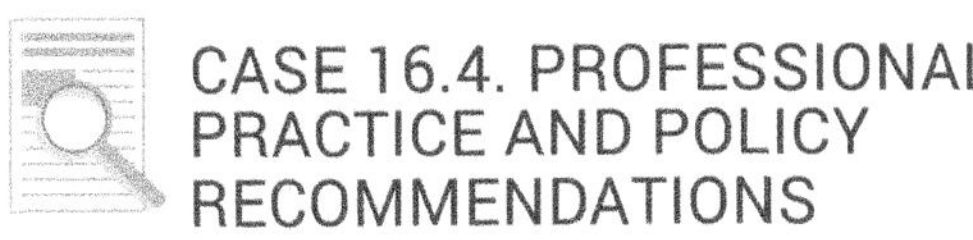

CASE 16.4. PROFESSIONAL PRACTICE AND POLICY RECOMMENDATIONS

Shrestha, S., Burns, R., Deng, J., Confer, J., Graefe, A., & Covelli, E. (2012). The role of elements of theory of planned behavior in mediating the effects of constraints on intentions: A study of Oregon big game hunters. *Journal of Park and Recreation Administration, 30*, 41–62.

During the span of a decade, the sale of hunting licenses in Oregon declined by one third, whereas the population in the state increased. The purpose of the study was to test the degree to which the elements of the theory of planned behavior acted as mediators in the relationship between constraints and intention to participate in deer hunting. The study outlined the following management steps to increase hunting participation:

- Enhance the confidence of hunters through methods such as skill enhancement training.
- Increase harvesting success through game population management.
- Extend hunting opportunities in public and private lands.
- Develop hunting promotional programs by targeting women, minorities, young hunters, and families of current hunters.

CASE 16.5. RECOMMENDATIONS FOR FUTURE RESEARCH

Langseth, T. (2012). Liquid ice surfers—The construction of surfer identities in Norway. *Journal of Adventure Education & Outdoor Learning, 12*, 3–23.

The study recommended the following:

- Carry out cross-cultural comparisons on how surfing's cultural scripts emerge in different locations.
- Compare Norwegian newly developed surf culture to other locales where surfing has emerged as a new sport (e.g., Nova Scotia).
- Compare values of surfers to other adventure or risk sports.

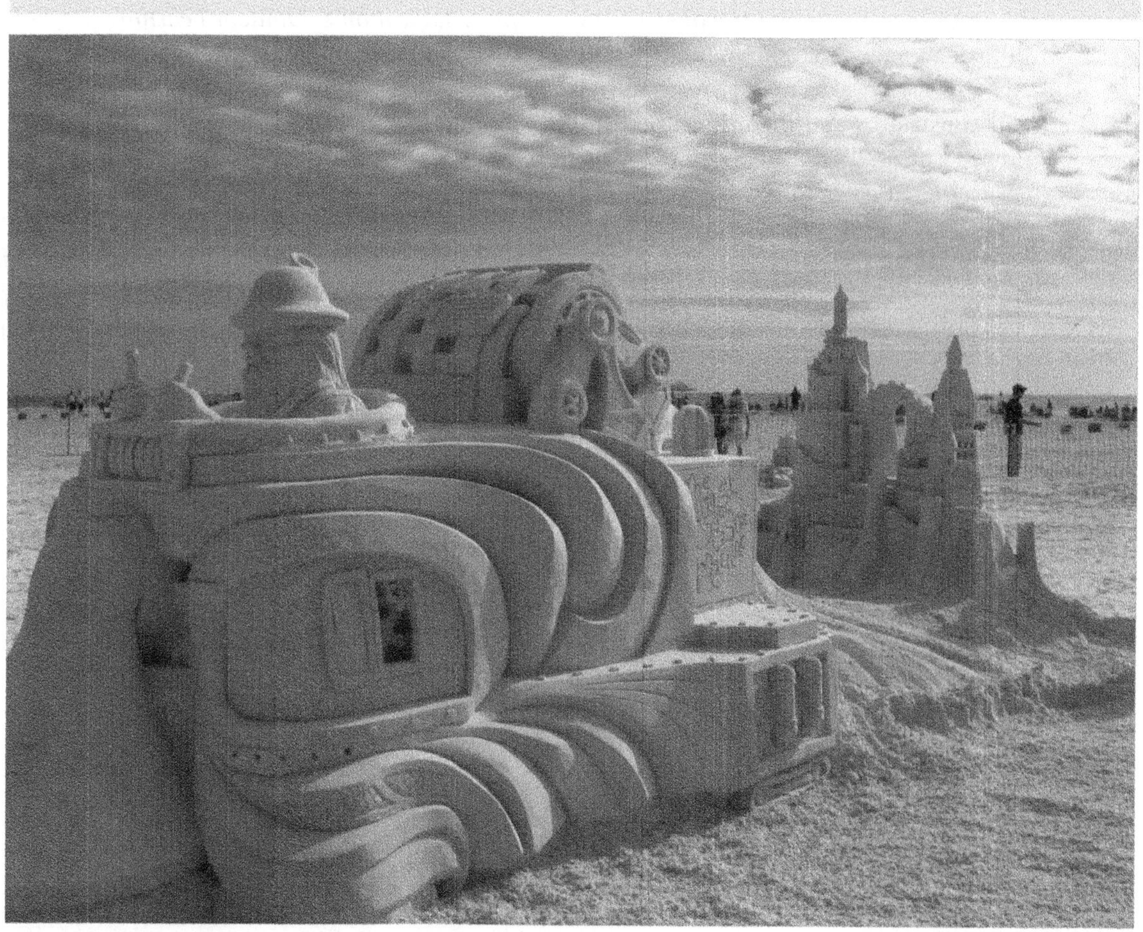

You may communicate information to an audience in many ways. Titled "The Sand Castle Machine," this entry in the Master Sand Sculpture Contest communicates through the medium of sand. Siesta Key, Florida. Copyright © 2015 Ruth V. Russell.

STEP 15 STEP 16 STEP 17

DELIVER A PRESENTATION

WHAT WILL I LEARN IN THIS CHAPTER?

I'll be able to...

1. List the audiences for a public research presentation.
2. Describe the thesis or dissertation defense form of a public research presentation.
3. In planning a presentation, list the steps recommended for determining its focus.
4. Portray a professional meeting poster session.
5. Offer advice in preparing and using PowerPoint slides, transparencies, and/or handouts in presentations.
6. Identify presentation rehearsal pointers.
7. Discuss specific strategies for reducing stage fright, beginning the presentation, and handling questions.

"Good communication is as stimulating as black coffee and just as hard to sleep after."

Anne Morrow Lindbergh
(Pioneering American aviator, author, and spouse of fellow aviator Charles Lindbergh, 1906–2001)

The culmination of a research venture is its communication. Typically, this includes a publicly delivered report. A research presentation given in public to an ***audience*** provides you an opportunity to inform the stakeholders of the study what you did and learned in the research project. Many presentation outlets exist, such as an informal briefing at an agency staff assembly, a plea for increased funding at a board meeting, a death-defying defense of a thesis or dissertation before a university faculty committee, and a peer-reviewed presentation at a national or international professional meeting.

SOMETHING TO REMEMBER!

No matter the form a public presentation takes—a toast at your friend's wedding or a formal research report given at a professional conference—the worst mistakes you may make are

- not preparing and practicing,
- forgetting who is your audience,
- not answering posed questions,
- not knowing when to stop, and
- not having fun.

Although you have many innovative outlets for publicly communicating study findings and conclusions (e.g., readers' theatre and interpretive art), the orally delivered report is the most common. According to public speaking consultant Lilyan Wilder (1999), the greatest myths about giving presentations are that you are better off "winging it" and that good speakers are "naturals." Nothing could be further from the truth! The purpose of this chapter is to help you thrive in delivering a research presentation in terms of

- analyzing the audience and venue,
- planning the presentation,
- practicing the presentation, and
- developing success strategies.

IDENTIFY THE AUDIENCE AND VENUE

The first step to preparing a public research presentation is to size up the situation. For example, knowing beforehand who is the audience is vital because the audience will define not only the content and coverage of the material but also the presentation style.

Generally, audiences for research reports are stakeholders or scientific/academicians (Kielhofner, 2006). According to the Overview chapter, ***stakeholders*** include participants in the study, funding authorities, and agency staff members who will be expected to carry out the recommendations of the study. Other stakeholders could be advocacy and lobbying groups who represent the interests of the people studied. For these stakeholders, you should include information about decisions and next step actions needed based on the outcomes of the study in the presentation.

On the other hand, the scientific/academic audience is usually more intrigued by the methods used in the study and the conclusions. Thus, presentations made to college classes, at professional conferences, and thesis or dissertation defenses are more focused on the research process used. These audiences also are interested in information from your study that could benefit future research.

In scientific research presentations, another layer of audience applies as well. In most situations, you must submit your proposed presentation (including posters) for ***peer review***. This preliminary review process is used to ensure the quality of the information to be presented and its suitability for the particular audience of the meeting or conference. Typically, experts on the subject and/or method of your study read a short synopsis (***abstract***) of your intended presentation and judge whether it is acceptable. Sometimes the reviewers conduct a ***blind review***, meaning they do not know the name of the author of the abstract.

A ***thesis or dissertation defense*** is another presentation. This defense is typically required for advanced degrees, and the student is typically required to complete a presentation and answer questions posed by an examining committee or jury (Table 17.1). This examination normally occurs after the research is finished and before it is submitted for final university approval. (Although the words are often used interchangeably, in the United States, a thesis is written for a master's degree and a dissertation for a doctoral degree; however, in Australia a thesis refers to a doctoral requirement and a dissertation applies to an honors degree.)

PLAN THE PRESENTATION

Once you understand the situation for the presentation, organize it. Seek ways for your talk to address what the audience wants and needs to know. Therefore, devote thorough preparation to focusing the presentation and developing visual aids.

Table 17.1
Anatomy of a Thesis or Dissertation Oral Defense

- Once the faculty chair of the thesis or dissertation considers the written research report the student prepared to be adequate, a final oral defense is scheduled. About 2 to 3 weeks prior to the scheduled defense, the written thesis or dissertation is distributed to the remaining committee members.
- Sometimes the defense is limited to committee members; however, many universities require the defense to be announced to the entire campus community and invite anyone in the university community to attend. Many times these guests (including other students) are asked to leave the meeting after the student provides his or her overview, or at least prior to the committee's deliberations.
- At the beginning of the defense, the faculty chair asks the degree candidate to provide a brief overview (approximately 20 minutes) of his or her study.
- During the next 2 to 3 hours, committee members ask the candidate questions. Other people in attendance may be permitted to ask questions as well.
- Once the committee members have exhausted their questions, the candidate and noncommittee members are asked to leave the room. The committee then discusses whether to pass the candidate's thesis or dissertation. Four vote outcomes are possible: (1) the research is approved, (2) the research is approved but minor modifications are required, (3) a vote on the merit of the research is withheld until major revisions are made, or (4) the research project is failed. Most of the time, if the student has followed the advice of the committee chair, approved with minor modifications is the most common vote.
- The candidate is then ushered back into the room and informed of the committee's vote and any imposed revision conditions.

USING HUMOR IN A PRESENTATION

Often in research presentations, you focus on plowing through data and forget to engage the audience. Relevant humor may help; however, the humor should be cautious, considerate, low key, and natural. To use humor effectively in a public research presentation,

- stay clear of humor that may come across as sexist or racist, convey stereotypes, or relate to religion or politically controversial topics;
- avoid telling jokes—you are not giving a stand-up comedy routine;
- plan and rehearse humor, as improvising it is dangerous; and
- do not deliver humor through insult or sarcasm.

FLESHING OUT THE PRESENTATION OUTLINE

- Begin on a genuine note (refer to a local or recent event, tell a personal story, read a quote, ask a question, offer a humorous anecdote, etc.).
- Tell how the talk is organized.
- Provide an overview or introductory remarks about the study topic.
- Review the methods used.
- Reveal and discuss major results.
- State conclusions.
- Make recommendations.
- Summarize what you told the audience.
- Invite questions from the audience.

Focus

Even though you already know the content of the presentation, you must still plan how best to focus the content. The following steps will help you plan:

1. Determine your general goal.
2. Identify specific objectives.
3. Draft a talking point outline.
4. Develop a one-sentence summary.

In determining your general goal for the presentation, consider whether you want to interest, inform, persuade, or motivate your audience. Also, identify no more than three objectives. (Case 17.1 demonstrates how this approach could be used for presenting an analysis of program for youth.)

Next, develop the talking outline. Think of it as a story you have to tell. What are the beginning, middle, and end? The beginning consists of introductory remarks related to the background of the study, the research purpose, and research questions and/or hypotheses. The middle is the body of the report addressing main points related to methods, results, and discussion of results. The end is focused on conclusions and recommendations (Torres, Preskill, & Pionteck, 2005). Telling the beginning, middle, and end of the story will require planning because in public presentations you typically have only 10 to 20 minutes to complete it.

Ultimately, your general goal, specific objectives, and talking point outline culminate with developing a one-sentence summary. These techniques go a long way to producing a successful presentation.

Concise presentation goals, objectives, and an outline are also important when developing a poster. The ***poster***, a popular peer-reviewed presentation at a professional meeting, is a large-format visual exposition of a research study or theoretical paper. Usually posted on a multiple-paneled display board measuring 4 feet × 6 feet, the poster summarizes information about the study.

In creating a poster, minimize the amount of text yet ensure the information presented is easy to comprehend. During the presentation session, many posters are displayed simultaneously. Authors stand by their respective poster boards, and the audience walks around reading posters that catch their interest. Sometimes people ask questions and/or make comments to authors about the information presented in the poster.

To assist with developing a poster, Figure 17.1 presents the layout used for this medium. Table 17.2 provides tips on preparing and presenting a poster.

Visual Aids

Visual aids supplement written or spoken information so it may be easily understood. Visual aids are useful tools in written and oral communication, particularly when presenting results. Using visual aids may enhance the audience's comprehension of what you are saying and increase the likelihood that they will remember what you shared.

The care you take to make your visual aids relevant and readable is paramount to your success. This requires breaking complex ideas into simpler visual parts. Furthermore, figures and graphs in a stand-up presentation are more effective than tables (see Step 15). This is because tables used in a written report are typically

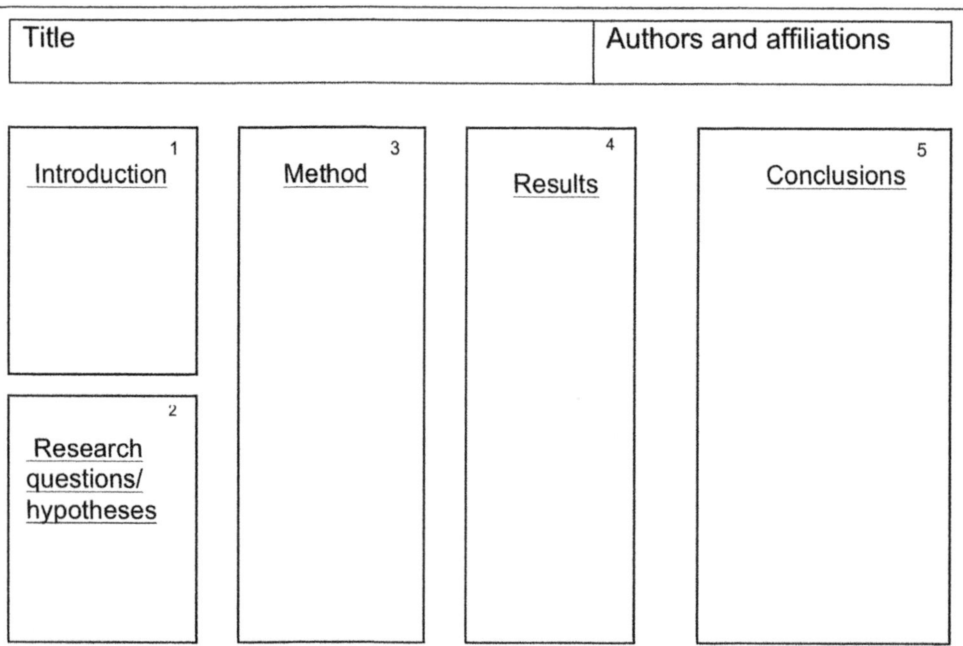

Figure 17.1. Template for a poster layout. Adapted from Nicol and Pexman (2010a) and Rosnow and Rosnow (2011).

Table 17.2

Guidelines for Preparing a Poster

- Know the space size allocated for the poster. Typically, the assigned space is 4 feet high × 6 to 8 feet wide.
- Decide whether to print the poster presentation in a series of small panels (multiple-panel format) or on one large panel (or single-panel format). Multiple sheets are easier to transport yet require care in aligning before pinning down. A single-panel format requires a large-format printer and a poster tube to transport, yet is easier to post.
- Use 48-point font for the title and at least 20-point type for the remaining sections, in either Arial or Helvetica sans serif font. If enough room is available to include the References and Acknowledgements sections, you may use a smaller font for them.
- Use colored ink to highlight keywords; otherwise, use black ink for the text.
- After the first two panels (i.e., title and author identification) number the panels. This helps readers follow the correct order.
- Limit each panel to 16 or fewer lines, use single text sparingly, and whenever possible, present bulleted or numbered lists.
- Focus on the main points. For example, present a few key findings and highlight conclusions supported by the data.
- Bring pushpins, thumbtacks, or Velcro to mount your poster.
- Arrive on time. Allow enough time to set up, especially if you have not been assigned to a specific area to set up your poster.
- Have ready a 3- to 5-minute spiel, or overview, about the contents of your poster. As visitors approach, ask whether they would like to be walked through the study.
- Consider bringing a handout version of the poster to the session. Print a double-sided, reduced version of the actual poster on letter-sized paper or post a reprint request list so a copy may be mailed or e-mailed to interested persons.
- At the end of the session, promptly remove your poster board.

Note. Adapted from Nicol and Pexman (2011) and Rosnow and Rosnow (2011).

too long and tables used in an oral presentation are too small in appearance to show on a screen. Do not show information on a visual aid that you do not plan to discuss. Explain the information in each graphic. Do not talk at your visual aid; instead, direct your oral presentation toward the audience.

Examples of visual aids are PowerPoint slides, transparencies, paper handouts, poster boards, flip charts, physical objects, whiteboards or blackboards, and video and/or audio presentations. The most commonly used visual aid is PowerPoint presentations followed by handouts (University of Leicester, 2009).

You may produce professional-looking presentations with PowerPoint presentation software or similar ***slide show software***. You may use these programs to display text and graphic images in a slideshow format. You may insert sounds and video as well as other graphical special effects. You may store your presentation on portable hard drive and carry it with you, which makes changing your presentation easy. However, using such software forces you to depend on computer technology, and if technological problems arise, you will not have your visual aid. Table 17.3 presents additional points to consider for PowerPoint presentations.

On the other hand, overhead ***transparencies*** (i.e., a thin sheet of viewfoil, usually cellulose acetate) are placed on an overhead projector. Transparencies are simple and clear, and you do not have to depend on a computer. However, they may get out of order and have poor print quality. Table 17.4 offers suggestions for using transparencies.

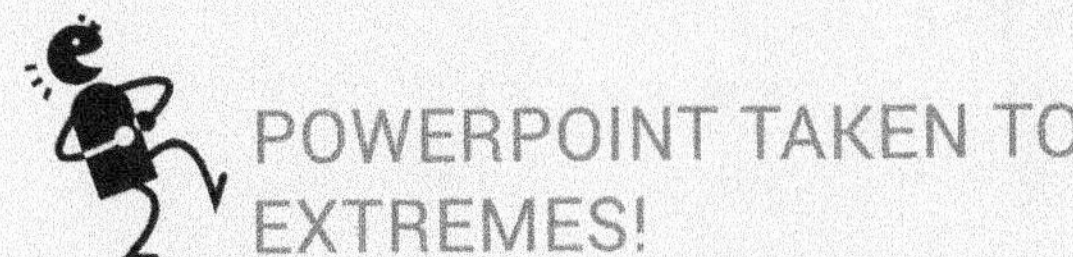

POWERPOINT TAKEN TO EXTREMES!

PowerPoint presentation software can make any presentation a first-class enterprise. However, this does not happen automatically when you click the buttons on your computer. View *Life After Death by PowerPoint* video at http://www.youtube.com/watch?v=KbSPPFYxx3o.

Table 17.3
Guidelines for Developing a PowerPoint Presentation

- Make sure you know what equipment will be available. Are a computer and projector provided, or are you expected to bring these? If a computer is provided, find out which PowerPoint version has been installed. You will have to save your file in this version.
- Deliver the presentation using a laser pointer. The pointer is a handheld device that can unleash you from having to stand next to the computer to advance the slides.
- Choose a template design that supports your message, and use the same design across slides. If using color, make sure the print and background colors are contrasting. Use only black font and a light background color if the audience is large.
- Use font styles and sizes that are readable, and be consistent across slides. Arial font is better than Times Roman font for a PowerPoint presentation. Use a minimum font size of 24. Use uppercase and lowercase letters. Before the presentation, check the font sizes on the projected screen by standing the same distance away as the audience.
- Follow the 6 × 7 rule. No more than 6 lines of text per slide and no more than 7 words per line. Use short sentences, phrases, or bulleted keywords.
- Number your slides. This will help during the question–answer period.
- If using animation, drop slides from above or from the left. Once you choose, do not change the direction of entering images, as this will cause confusion.
- Plan on one slide for each minute of your presentation. Do not make the mistake of trying to cover too many slides in a short time.
- Arrive early to set up and make sure everything is working. Find out if an extension cord or a cable between the computer and projection system is needed. If using your own laptop or tablet, have a backup copy of your presentation on a thumb drive or in an e-mail attachment to which you have access. Always have alternative visuals (e.g., handouts of the slides) available if all else fails!

Note. Adapted from Gratton and Jones (2010) and Torres, Preskill, and Piontek (2005).

Table 17.4
Tips for Using Transparencies

- Mount the transparencies into frames. This prevents them from sliding off the projector.
- Arrive early. Make sure a second workable bulb is on hand in case the first bulb burns out. Also, beforehand, take the time to focus the projector.
- Place the transparency as high on the screen of the projector as possible. This makes the transparency more readable to more audience members.
- If possible, have someone else change your overheads during your presentation. That way, you may concentrate on speaking and directing the overall presentation.

Note. Adapted from Torres, Preskill, and Piontek (2005).

Handouts, or printed information provided free of charge to accompany a presentation, may be excellent accompaniments to other visual aid options, but they also pose problems, such as cost of reproducing if the audience is large. You may use handouts to present an abstract or executive summary, PowerPoint slides, or the final research report. You also may take a shortcut and only distribute tables and figures or a list of references used for the research report.

The philosophies about when and how to distribute handouts to an audience include distribute handouts prior to the presentation, distribute them immediately after the oral presentation, or mail them only to people who express interest. For example, you may distribute handouts prior to your session by placing them on audience member seats or by making them available to people as they enter the presentation room. Prior distribution may make it easier for the audience to follow complicated material in your presentation (e.g., the contents of tables). However, handouts may be distracting because the audience may read the handout and not listen to the prepared talk.

You also have the option of not making handouts available to the audience until after the formal presentation, as you do not want to distract the audience from listening. Additionally, you may ask audience members to sign up to receive handouts later (e.g., via e-mail) so you do not have to transport paper copies to the meeting or conference.

REHEARSE THE PRESENTATION

Ultimately, the quality and effectiveness of a research presentation are determined not only by the content of the study and your preparation but also by your public speaking skills. Delivering a good presentation requires rehearsal. You should practice several times and focus on substance, delivery, and timing.

The goal is to perfect your presentation so it has a spontaneous and comfortable feel. You may accomplish this through several strategies. For example, do not memorize the talk. You may want to memorize opening lines and section transitions, but the goal is to sound natural. Reading lines does not sound spontaneous unless you are a really good actor!

Practice pausing naturally as you would in conversation. You may want to add directions on your notes such as "slow down" or "look at the audience." Practicing your speech out loud may help you clarify your thoughts. For example, record yourself and listen to the tone, pitch, and speed of your voice or enlist friends or family members to listen to a dress rehearsal of your presentation. Then, use Figure 17.2 to solicit feedback from your listeners.

In addition, practice staying within the allocated time limit; otherwise, you may lose the audience's interest and be perceived as boring. Furthermore, you could selfishly be taking time away from other presenters. Moreover, knowing how to operate audio-visual pro-

QUIZ ON VISUAL AIDS

Directions: Read the following questions and decide whether the statement is *true* or *false*.

____ 1. Effective visual aids require breaking complex ideas into simpler parts.
____ 2. In planning the visual aids for a presentation, always choose PowerPoint slides.
____ 3. Tables from the written report should be presented as handouts.
____ 4. Too much reliance on visual aids may detract from the success of a presentation made before a group.

Note. Answers are provided at the end of the chapter.

Did the presenter...	Yes	No
1. Stand erect?	_____	_____
2. Avoid reading word for word from visual aids or a paper?	_____	_____
3. Hold 5- to 6-second gazes at different audience members?	_____	_____
4. Keep hands away from mouth?	_____	_____
5. Keep hands from playing with things (e.g., paper clips?)?	_____	_____
6. Speak clearly, enthusiastically, and at the right pace?	_____	_____
7. Change pitch and volume as well as body language and position?	_____	_____
8. Use subtle pauses between key points?	_____	_____
9. Attend to the audience's body language and adjust content and/ or delivery speed as necessary?	_____	_____
10. Appropriately respond to the audience's questions?	_____	_____
11. Act relaxed and appear natural?	_____	_____
12. Dress professionally?	_____	_____
13. Avoid chewing gum or sucking on candy?	_____	_____

Figure 17.2. Judging a dress rehearsal of a research presentation. Adapted from Polonsky and Waller (2010) and Torres, Preskill, and Piontek (2005).

jection equipment will help you deliver a smooth and timely presentation.

If you are giving your presentation in an unfamiliar location, check out the space the day before so you know how big the room is and what technical options are available. For example, will you need a microphone? How do the lights work for dimming? Practice "working the room" and become familiar with the audience's perspective. In addition, specific tips for a thesis or dissertation final oral defense are presented in Table 17.5.

With the self-confidence that comes from thorough preparation and practice, your presentation will never go as you think. Fortunately, it will usually go better than you expect.

Table 17.5

Tips for a Successful Thesis or Dissertation Final Oral Defense

If you have worked closely with your committee chair and committee members, the final defense should come off without a glitch. The following are additional tips for success:

- Be prepared. Your responsibility is to convince the committee that you understood the research process. Remember, you are the expert on this particular study, so do not hesitate to speak with authority.
- Rehearse by setting up a simulation defense. Ask fellow students to act the roles of committee members. Provide these stand-ins with copies of the thesis or dissertation.
- Discuss concerns about the final defense with your advisor ahead of time. You want to feel confident explaining every aspect of your research.
- Be open and honest during the defense. Admit the limitations of the study. Be responsible for what was and was not done in the study and what was written. Do not be defensive, and do not be afraid to say, "I don't know."
- Take or record notes. One option is to use, during the defense, a voice-activated tape recorder. The committee chair sometimes takes on the role of notetaker.
- Bring to the defense multiple copies of the signature page to the thesis or dissertation. Check with your chair as to how many signature pages are needed (e.g., most universities require a student to supply copies of their completed thesis or dissertation to the school's library and graduate school). Also, you may need to gently remind your chair to bring any university forms that require signatures of committee members.

Note. Adapted from Mauch and Park (2003).

DEVELOP SUCCESS STRATEGIES

You are all set! You have analyzed the audience situation, planned, and practiced for the presentation. In some cases, however, additional preparation is necessary. To conclude the discussion of this research step, special strategies for conquering stage fright, beginning the presentation, and handling questions will be discussed.

Conquering Stage Fright

You may think that stage fright is caused mostly by what happens during a presentation, but it is what happens before your presentation that affects your state of mind. This confirms again that preparing and practicing are the best ways to eliminate, or at least reduce, stage fright.

Also, you may find it helpful to watch and listen to other presentations beforehand. Take notes on what works and what does not. Another strategy for averting stage fright is to practice in a place or situation similar to where you will be giving your talk (including in front of people). Consider performing voice and breathing exercises before your presentation to warm up your vocal cords. In addition, consider using mental imagery to picture yourself in front of an audience to consciously become comfortable with the idea.

Beginning the Presentation

Another success strategy concerns the presentation. In addition to common sense tips, such as getting a good night's sleep the night before and eating breakfast, consider these helpful ideas:

- Take a deep breath before walking to the front of the room.
- Walk slowly to the front, pause, and look at the audience before speaking.
- If your hands shake during the presentation, hold on to something such as a small object, a pointer, the lectern, or a glass of water.
- Breathe normally and take pauses.
- Focus on the audience, not your notes or visual aids. Establishing a dialogue with the audience will help you feel more comfortable in the situation.

When it is over, ask for feedback, and remember that this is a learning experience. You will continue to become a better public speaker the more times you complete the process.

Handling Questions

At some point in the presentation, encourage the audience to ask questions. Typically, at staff and board meetings, listeners often pose questions as the presentation progresses. At professional meetings, however, a 10- to 20-minute question–answer period is usually held after the conclusion of prepared remarks.

Either way, one challenge for presenters is dealing with a difficult question. Do not become defensive, answer a question that was not asked, or waffle. Admitting to not knowing the answer to a question is endearing. If a typographic error is identified, acknowledge it. If a fundamental problem is pointed out, admit the fault rather than trying to rationalize or make an off-the-cuff argument that attempts to defend the mistake. Answer questions concisely and clearly. You want to appear confident and competent.

SOMETHING TO REMEMBER!

Consider asking your audience to hold questions until the end. Although questions are an indicator that people are engaged in your presentation, saving them until the end will enable you to get through your material uninterrupted. Also, early questions are often answered later by the presentation.

Tourists riding this dragon boat were treated to a multimedia show, complete with changing patterns of water sprays that were choreographed to piped music. Delivering a presentation about a research report is also a multifaceted, multimedia show. It is imperative you consider the audience that will be attending your presentation; then, you may move forward and plan your presentation, rehearse, and develop and practice strategies for delivering a successful presentation. West Lake, Hangzhou, China. Copyright © 2015 Carol Cutler Riddick.

BE PREPARED!

The following are common questions asked at final defenses of theses and dissertations:

- Why did you choose the topic?
- If you could do it over again, what would you do differently in designing, implementing, or reporting the research?
- How has your research contributed to professional practice? Theoretical understanding?
- How should your line of research be continued?
- What have you personally learned from doing the research?

Note. Adapted from Mauch and Park (2003).

REVIEW AND DISCUSSION QUESTIONS

1. Identify general audiences for a presentation.
2. Describe the thesis or dissertation defense form of a public research presentation.
3. Distinguish between peer and blind reviews.
4. List the four steps associated with determining the focus of a presentation.
5. Briefly describe what is involved with a poster session. If you have attended one, describe your experience with classmates.
6. Recall advice for preparing and using PowerPoint slides, transparencies, and/or handouts.
7. Identify at least four behaviors to practice when rehearsing an oral research report.
8. Give examples from presentations you have attended of ways visual aids have detracted from the success of the oral presentation.
9. Discuss strategies for reducing stage fright, beginning a presentation, and handling questions.

YOUR RESEARCH

1. Using the principles outlined in this chapter, draft a PowerPoint presentation of your research.
2. Rehearse your PowerPoint presentation in front of colleagues or classmates. Provide the assembled group a paper copy of your PowerPoint presentation.
3. Identify, with feedback from your rehearsal audience, the most and least successful aspects of your presentation in terms of preparation and/or delivery. Accept the compliments and fix the problems, and rehearse again. Did you improve?

PRACTICE EXERCISES

1. Attend a research presentation. Your instructor may provide you with a list of options for sessions available at your university and/or regional, state, or national meetings. In a brief paper, critique the presenter on the following:
   a. Structure or content
   b. Delivery
   c. Use of visual aids
   d. Dealing with audience questions
2. For an effective way to practice your own public presentation skills, pair up with a classmate and video each other giving a 5-minute talk. For example, you could deliver material from this or any previous chapter in the text. After the filming, watch the videos and offer helpful advice to each other and/or ask the class instructor or other groups of classmates to provide critique.

WEB EXERCISES

1. Watch a 30-minute keynote speech by Jeremy Gutsche, *Trend Hunter.* You may access this speech at http://www.youtube.com/watch?v=P4gAkM72ah4&feature=pyv&ad=6519114391&kw=motivational%20speech. While watching, take notes on the ways Jeremy's presentation is interesting and keeps you listening and watching. What strategies have you learned? After the video, discuss your notes with classmates.
2. Learn more about effective presentations by going to the University of Kansas website: http://www.kumc.edu/SAH/OTEd/jradel/effective.html. Read the online tutorials *Developing an Effective Oral Presentation, Designing Effective Visual Aids for Presentations* and *Creating an Effective Poster Presentation.* Which of the tutorials did you like most, and why? Share with classmates at least three points you learned from the tutorials that were not covered in the chapter.
3. You may easily practice your own oral presentation skills by watching others. A good source for these is the TED Conference, where world-renowned speakers make short presentations on interesting ideas. Go to the TED website at http://www.ted.com/. Down the left side of the home page are options for watching and listening to talks according to type.
   - First, select the "Persuasive" category and choose a talk that interests you.
   - Then, select the "Informative" category and choose a talk that interests you.

   Watch and listen to both talks (they range in length from about 3 to 20 minutes). The instructor may ask you type answers to the following questions or be ready to discuss them during class.
   - Compare the two talks by identifying aspects that made them particularly persuasive or informative.
   - What strategies did each speaker use to get across the persuasive and informative focus?
   - What else did you learn about successful oral presentations from this website?
4. Type into your browser "free stock art." From the list of options provided, select at least three websites where you may obtain free visuals, including photographs, clip art, and illustrations. Which was your favorite site, and why?

SERVICE LEARNING

Prepare, practice, and deliver a public presentation about the completed research study on the campus recreation, sport program, or service selected as the focus of the project for this semester. Ideally, this presentation involves every member of your service learning group as presenters. You may also prepare an evaluation/feedback form and distribute it to those in attendance.

TEST YOURSELF ANSWERS

Quiz on Visual Aids

1. True, 2. False, 3. False, 4. True

SUPPORTING CASE FOR THIS CHAPTER

CASE 17.1. RECASTING A WRITTEN RESEARCH STUDY INTO A PRESENTATION

Pinckney, H., Outley, C., Blake, J., & Kelly, B. (2011). Promoting positive youth development of black youth: A rites of passage framework. *Journal of Park and Recreation Administration, 29*, 98–112.

Written summary:	Talking points that you could use in a public presentation about the research:
Adolescence is viewed widely as a critical stage in the development of youth as they transition to adulthood, which may be further complicated for youth of color who are additionally confronted with the meanings, expectations, and attitudes associated with their race and/or ethnicity. Experts have suggested that "rites of passage" programs are one way to accomplish the goal of promoting healthy development through this life phase. Rites of passage programs are a systematic series of lessons, workshops, and discussions that provide youth a better understanding of who they are by educating them about their ancestry. This paper suggested that rites of passage programs may be implemented in recreation settings where African American youth are served as means to effectively address adolescent racial identity, pride, and self-efficacy.	• General goal of study: To present evidence regarding the merits and values of recreation agencies providing rites of passage programming. • Study Objective 1: Identify key components of successful rites of passage programs. • Study Objective 2: Outline initial steps required to start rites of passage programming. • One-sentence summary: This presentation shares ideas on how recreation agencies may promote and implement rites of passage programs for African American youth. • Title: Rites of Passage Programming: A Vital Recreation and Park Mandate

Note. Reprinted with permission of the authors.

PART VI
MISE-EN-SCÈNE

In the theatre, *mise-en-scène* is a French term meaning placing on stage. When applied to the cinema, mise-en-scène is the arrangement of objects viewed by the camera, namely, the sets, props, lighting, and the positioning and movement of actors. By controlling the mise-en-scène, the stage and film directors guide the events (Bordwell & Thompson, 2012).

This chapter concludes the discussion on research and evaluation of recreation, parks, sport, and tourism topics by applying this analogy. Thus, the finale of the book will pull together everything that appears in a research scene. The notion that research is the discovery of knowledge according to a process that resembles an hourglass (Figure 18.1) will be reviewed. Second, a checklist summarizing the steps involved in research will be provided.

Recall that conducting research involves an hourglass process. That is, start broadly, narrow in on the particulars, and then broaden again. More specifically, the initial stage of determining your topic is a wide open enterprise. After determining the topic, narrow in by deciding what information you need to collect and open your perspective again so your conclusions and recommendations are useful to others. Taken together, this is the scene of the research process.

The research scene also may be summarized in a step-by-step checklist that details specifically what happens in this hourglass process (see Table 18.1).

1. Identify broad subject area
2. Narrow topic and focus on concepts, instruments, and design
3. Collect data
4. Analyze data and present results
5. Discuss and interpret results, state conclusions, and make recommendations

Figure 18.1. Hourglass shape of research. Adapted from Trochim (2006).

Table 18.1
Checklist for Starting, Developing, Implementing, and Reporting Research

GETTING STARTED

Step 1: Decide on Topic

- ☐ Consider all sources for research topic ideas.
- ☐ Determine the utility of concepts related to identifying an idea (i.e., reductionism, gold reference, replication study, extension study, the paradox behind science, and the scientific revolution).
- ☐ Determine whether your topic interest is applied and thus may be developed using the hierarchy for program analysis model.

Table 18.1 (cont.)

- ☐ Determine whether your topic interest is basic research, that is, refers to recreation, parks, sport, and tourism in general.
- ☐ Sort through ideas according to whether they are interesting, plausible, ethical, manageable, and/or valuable.

Step 2: Review Literature

- ☐ Think about how a literature review helps you to select a topic, conceptualize an approach, develop a rationale for the study, determine the methods of the study, and interpret the results.
- ☐ Conduct a literature search by using keywords to find secondary sources, general references, and primary sources of research literature.
- ☐ Review and analyze primary sources.
- ☐ Write the literature review.

Step 3: Identify Theoretical Roots

- ☐ Consider the appropriateness of adopting a quantitative theoretical approach.
- ☐ Consider the appropriateness of using a qualitative theoretical approach.
- ☐ Consider the appropriateness of relying on a mixed-methods theoretical approach.

Step 4: Determine Scope

- ☐ Determine unit of analysis.
- ☐ Determine variables.
- ☐ Develop purpose statement.
- ☐ Write research questions.
- ☐ If appropriate, identify hypotheses.

Step 5: Explain Significance

- ☐ Make the case for the significance of the study to professional practice, social problems, and/or contributions to scientific knowledge.
- ☐ Write a significance statement.

DEVELOP A PLAN

Step 6: Select Sample

- ☐ Identify the population if appropriate.
- ☐ Choose a method of probability sampling and/or
- ☐ Choose a method of nonprobability sampling.

Step 7: Choose Design

- ☐ Select a quantitative design and determine its validity, generalizability, and necessary sample size, or
- ☐ Select a qualitative design and determine its rigor, or
- ☐ Determine a mixed-methods design.

Step 8: Consider Measurement

- ☐ Determine the measurement to adopt.
- ☐ Decide on multiple-variable measures.
- ☐ Choose between single- and multiple-item measures.
- ☐ Consider instrument validity.
- ☐ Think about instrument reliability.
- ☐ Consider using normative data measures.
- ☐ Decide between developing your own instrument and/or adopting instruments used previously in research studies.

Step 9: Specify Data Collection Methods

- ☐ Deliberate on the use of triangulation.
- ☐ Select a quantitative data collection method and/or

Table 18.1 (cont.)

- ☐ Select a qualitative data collection method.

Step 10: Address Ethical Responsibilities

- ☐ Nonmaleficence.
- ☐ Beneficence.
- ☐ Respect.
- ☐ Honesty.
- ☐ Justice.
- ☐ Competence.

Step 11: Seek Proposal Approval

- ☐ Write a study proposal.
- ☐ Seek approval for the proposal from relevant authorities.

IMPLEMENTATION

Step 12: Conduct Pilot

- ☐ Determine the purposes for a pilot test.
- ☐ Conduct the pilot test.
- ☐ Revise the study procedures and/or data collection tools according to the results of the pilot study.

Step 13: Prepare for Data Collection

- ☐ Inventory and gather data collection materials, supplies, and equipment.
- ☐ Recruit, hire, and train data collection and analysis staff if necessary.
- ☐ Manage and supervise the research team.

Step 14: Analyze Data

- ☐ Analyze quantitative data by calculating descriptions, relationships, and differences.
- ☐ Analyze qualitative data by managing data, drawing tentative conclusions, and verifying conclusions.

REPORTING

Step 15: Create Visual Aids

- ☐ Prepare tables.
- ☐ Prepare figures.

Step 16: Write Report

- ☐ Write a draft of the research report.
- ☐ Solicit constructive feedback on the draft report.
- ☐ Prepare the final version of the research report.
- ☐ Disseminate the research report.

Step 17: Deliver Presentation

- ☐ Identify the audience.
- ☐ Plan the presentation.
- ☐ Practice the presentation.
- ☐ Develop strategies for handling questions.
- ☐ Start thinking about what you learned from this study that may be useful for the next study.

In closing, after reading and studying this text, you should have the foundation to be able to read with comprehension and understanding about research and possess fundamental skills to design and conduct a small-scale study. You are ready...lights, camera, action!

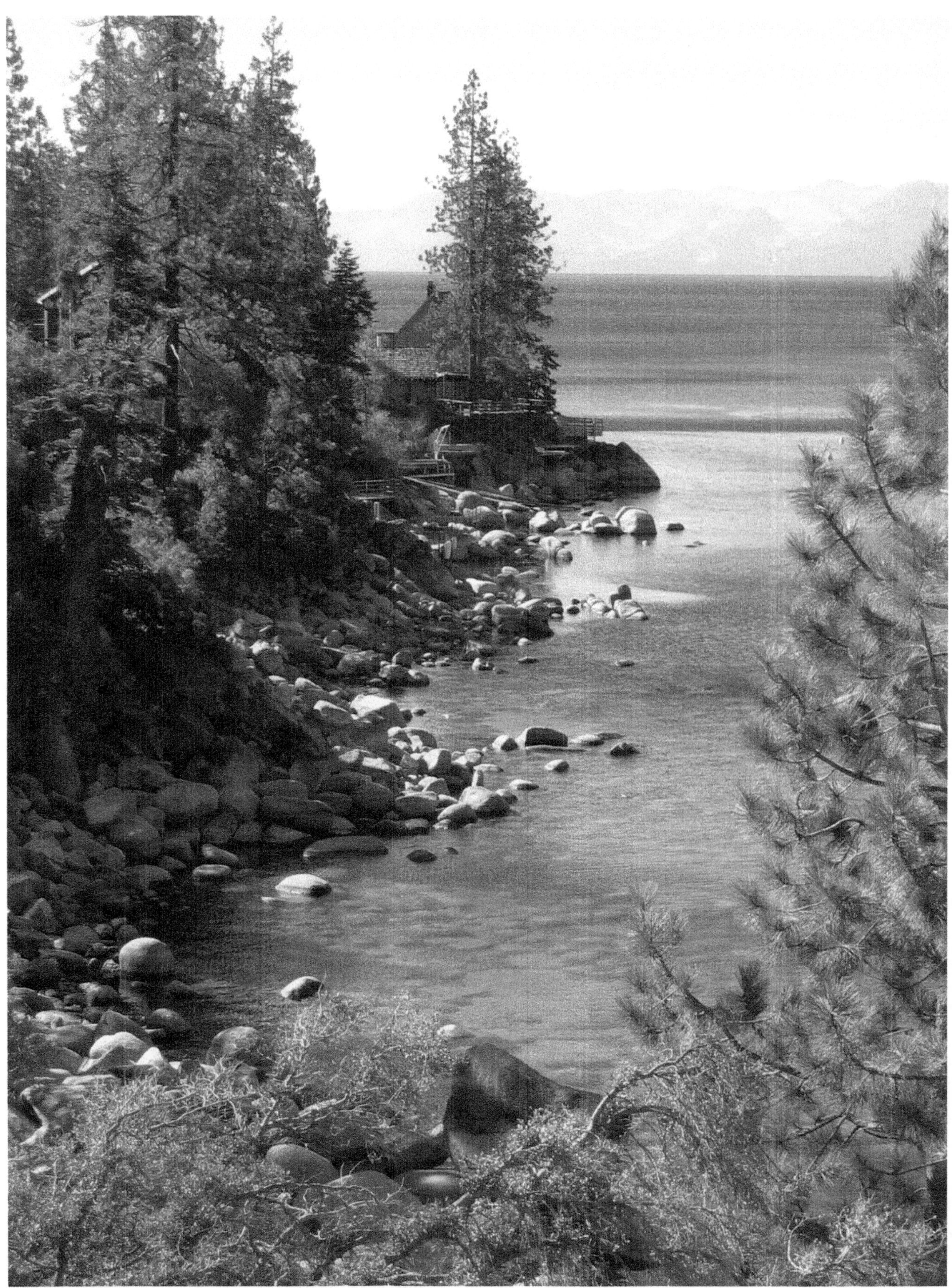

Hopefully by following the steps involved in the research process, you will be empowered to craft and deliver an informative and picturesque study. North Lake Tahoe, California. Copyright © 2015 Carol Cutler Riddick.

GLOSSARY

A

Abstract (or ***executive summary):*** found at the beginning of the research article, a synopsis of the study that includes purposes of the study, methods, findings, and conclusions

Abstract concept: an intrinsic trait or characteristic, such as a feeling or attitude, that is not visible to the naked eye

Academic report: used to present research to leisure scholars and professionals at a managerial level

Accretion physical traces: the deposit or accumulation of material that researchers may study

Achievement test: used to measure information learned, such as facts, principles, and skills

Action research: a study in which researchers tackles a social problem by identifying ways to improve conditions and practices for a particular context or situation

Active listening: when a person puts aside his or her presuppositions and listens carefully for the meanings another person is expressing

Active reading: when reading photocopies of articles, dissertations, or short chapters (not books checked out of the library), highlighting and making marginal notations and/or bracketing (in colored ink) the important information

Adaptive cycle for planning a study: the interactions between researcher and primary stakeholders

Adjective checklist: asks respondents to rate or judge something using adjectives

Anonymous: in research ethics, no information (e.g., name, phone number, address, social security number) is asked or recorded that could be used to identify an individual study participant

Applied research (or ***program evaluation*** or ***evaluative research):*** studies that are focused on practical topics such as appraising programs or social interventions

A priori theory testing: prior to; gathering observable and measurable evidence to support or reject a theory

Aptitude test: used to measure the potential for knowing, rather than what is known

Article influence score: the average influence of a journal article over the first five years after publication in terms of how often it is cited by other researchers in other journals

Associate editors: members of an editorial board of a refereed journal

At-risk: a group of individuals in a specified geographic area that are in jeopardy of experiencing a condition or problem of concern

Attitude or interest scale: a measure of respondents' self-reported disposition about a particular topic or issue

Attribute list: the row list in a matrix display; a list of the characteristics of each type in the domain list

Audience: the consumers of a research study; two audiences are stakeholders and scientific/academicians

Audit trail: notes and materials left by the researcher that enable the person conducting the external audit to trace how the researcher arrived at the conclusions

Authorship credit: the designation of whose name goes on the final research report or article

B

Bar graph (or ***column graph***): use of nontouching columns to show the response categories for a variable, compare variables, or emphasize changes in groups over time

Basic research: studies conducted to understand phenomena or behaviors at an abstract or theoretical level, "acquiring knowledge for knowledge sake"

Behavior rating scales: used to quantify observations of behaviors, often to assist in diagnosing problems

Beneficence: a concept in research ethics that refers to promoting the welfare or benefits individuals involved in research

Bibliography: a general reference with lists of books and articles relevant to a specific topic

Bivariate statistics: examines the relationship between two variables

Blind review: peer reviewer(s) do not know the name of the author(s) whose manuscript/submission they are reviewing

Boolean operator: when doing information searches on a database, a system of connecting words between keywords are used to broaden (e.g., AND) or narrow the search

Bracketing interview: discussion in which researchers identify their biases on a topic

Branching questions: questions that provide filters that determine whether succeeding questions apply

Business reports: used to report applied research results to internal and external stakeholders of an organization

C

Case study: an extensive, descriptive study of a specific unit of analysis to explain why events happened as they did; a qualitative design

Census: a study of a large-numbered population

Chair: a mentor or study advisor to the student researcher; head of a thesis or dissertation committee

Chart: used to present either a theoretical or conceptual model or to present multivariate statistical model results

Checking for data quality: in qualitative data analysis, determining whether the information upon which tentative conclusions are based is good

Classic experimental design: has six distinguishing qualities: random selection, experimental group, control group, random assignment, pretest, and posttest

Closed body posture: body language that does not convey warmth or desire to interact with the other person (e.g., arms folded in front of you)

Closed-ended questions: in a questionnaire, fixed-choice questions with an array of possible answers from which respondents may choose

Clustering: in qualitative data analysis, combining the matrices or networks into a more integrative diagram; clumping information that goes together and giving it a common label

Clusters: mutually exclusive subareas, which are sampled in cluster sampling

Cluster sampling (or ***area sampling):*** a sampling technique where the population is divided into groups, or clusters, and a random sample of these clusters is selected

Code book: in qualitative data analysis, a list of the codes assigned to transcript material

Coding: in qualitative data analysis, classifying text data or images into themes

Coefficient of determination: calculated as a percentage, which describes the amount of change in one variable that is accounted for by the change in the other variable

Collaborative research: Research through which the process and conlusions from a study are used as a change strategy

Collapsing data: to compress, condense, or group data into categories

Combination closed-ended question: in a questionnaire, fixed-choice questions and responses as well as an option for respondents to provide their own answer

Communicative ethics: entail professionally appropriate listening and conversational skills

Competency assessment: used to determine the knowledge, skills, and characteristics needed to successfully perform a job

Complete participant: the observer becomes a full member of the group being studied

Concept (or ***construct):*** a label attached to a phenomenon

Conceptual mapping: a diagram used to organize and represent speculated relationships among concepts

Concrete concept: an object, trait, or behavior that may be observed in the physical environment

Concurrent (or ***parallel) mixed-methods design:*** simultaneously and independently collecting qualitative and quantitative data to provide a comprehensive analysis of the research problem

Concurrent validity: a form of criterion validity; determining whether two or more groups of people score differently on a concept in expected ways

Condensed account: qualitative raw data in the form of phrases, single words, and unconnected sentences

Confidence interval: a margin of error for the value of a variable, emerges from a sample and is likely to be an accurate value that holds for the population; the norm is adopting a 95% or higher confidence level

Confidentiality: in research ethics, occurs when the researcher can identify a response or observation as belonging to a particular person/entity but promises not to do so

Constant comparison: each new piece of information (attitude, behavior, opinion, etc.) is compared to each other piece of data as it is gathered; used in designs such as grounded theory

Construct validity: makes a subjective judgment regarding the adequacy of an instrument

Content analysis: the study of recorded human communications, such as books, websites, paintings, photographs, meeting minutes, newspaper and magazine content, and laws

Content validity: a form of construct validity; a jury or group of knowledgeable experts have determined that the instrument contains a representation of content, elements, or instances of what is being measured

Continuous observation: watching for behaviors during a lengthy time (e.g., every evening for 7 days)

Control group: the group not participating in the treatment, intervention, program, or activity but is part of the research design

Control group interrupted time-series: quasi-experimental design featuring an experimental and a control group; members of both groups have neither been randomly chosen nor assigned to a group; multiple pretests and posttests over time

Convergent validity: a form of criterion validity; occurs when a new measure is found to be related to another previously validated instrument that was designed to measure the same concept

Correlation coefficient: a numerical index that reflects the degree of relationship between the scores of variables

Correlational statistics: a statistic that basically compares test scores

Cost-benefit study (or economic impact study): used to examine the cost of a program and its benefits in dollars (including money generated directly and indirectly by the program)

Cost effectiveness: program costs are compared to program outcomes

Covert complete participant: the complete participant observer's intentions are not disclosed to the people being observed

Criterion validity: comparisons are made between the newly developed instrument and objective evidence (or preselected standard)

Critical theory: incorporates a subjective view of social reality through meanings and interpretations provided by the self-reflections of research participants; a qualitative design

Cronbach's alpha coefficient: the statistic commonly used to measure interitem reliability; the extent to which each item used in the instrument measures the same concept; should be > .80

Cross-sectional survey: intended to determine how different age groups differ, at one point in time, in terms of the dependent variables under examination

D

Data: information collected for a study

Database: an organized collection of information

Data conversion: in qualitative data analysis, converting field notes, expanded accounts, memos, and data displays into digital form for computer software to perform data management tasks

Data display: a visual chart that is used to systematically present qualitative information that has been collected; a narrowed view of the data

Data sharing: making data from a study available under certain conditions to other investigators

Data verification: contacting a proportion of those reported as completing interviews or questionnaires to confirm study involvement

Deception: in research, the misrepresentation of information

Deductive reasoning/thinking: developing specific predictions based on general principles, observations, experiences stemming from a formal theory; patterns and relationships are established before the study is executed and collected data are then analyzed to determine whether these hunches can be supported

Dependent variable: used to measure the concept of interest in the study; the reacting, outcome, or response unit of analysis or concept being examined

Descriptive information interview: an unstructured in-depth interview used to seek information about attributes, preferences, beliefs, experiences, and/or reactions to hypothetical situations from the informant

Descriptive research: used to describe (what, where, when) the characteristics about a phenomenon, rather than provide causal explanations

Descriptive research question: seeks answers to queries such as "What is...?," "How do...?," "Do or does...?," or "Is...?" statements

Descriptive (or ***univariate) statistics:*** one variable at a time is summarized

Deviation scores: the difference between the mean value and each score in a frequency distribution

Dichotomous question: question with two response options

Diminishing returns: the statistical principle that sample size does not need to proportionally increase as the population size increases

Direct costs: personnel and nonpersonnel expenses that appear in a budget

Directional hypothesis (H_1 or ***alternative hypothesis):*** states the direction of a relationship or difference between or among two or more variables

Discovery interview: an unstructured in-depth interview used to identify impressions, concerns, suggestions, and/or ideas with respondents

Discriminant validity: a form of criterion validity; established when the new measure is found not to be related to another instrument that has been documented as validly measuring a different concept

Dissemination: the processes by which researchers inform others about study results

Document/record review (or ***content analysis):*** used to deduce people's feelings and behaviors by observing artifacts they make, including written records, art expressions, photographs, or videotapes

Documents/records (or ***archival data):*** information that is contained in public records or personal documents

Domain list: the column list in a matrix display; list of types of some quality

E

Ecological fallacy: to study one unit of analysis and then conclude the findings hold true for a different unit of analysis

Effect size: a comparison estimating the effect of an intervention or a program or activity; used in meta-analysis

Emic/etic perspective: researcher uses the frame of reference of the research participant

End results: what happens as a result of offering a treatment, intervention, program, or activity, at the community level in terms of reducing or alleviating a social problem

Erosion physical traces: degree of selective physical wear on objects or the environment that may be studied

Ethics: moral duty and obligation; what is proper and improper behavior

Ethnographic study: a qualitative design that requires an in-depth study of a group, culture, situation, or institution by a researcher who is immersed in its natural setting for an extended time

Expanded account: in qualitative data analysis, the details are filled in from the condensed account

Expedited review: IRB approval that happens when the proposed study does not present more than minimal risk to human subjects and does not involve vulnerable populations or novel or controversial interventions or data collection techniques

Experience sampling method: a method in which participants stop at certain times during the "natural" day to make notes on what they are doing and their feelings about what they are doing

Experimental group (X): the group offered or exposed to the treatment, intervention, program, or activity

Experimental mortality (or ***attrition*** or ***dropout):*** people do not complete a posttest for many reasons, including exerting their right to quit the study, they have moved away and cannot be located, and they have become ill or died

Explanatory research: relationships or linkages between or among social phenomena are scrutinized

Ex post facto: qualitative approach with a theory or explanation emerging at the end of the study

Ex post facto design (or ***correlational design):*** a variation of the survey design; used to determine whether one or more independent variables are linked to a dependent variable

Expressive skills (or ***conversational language):*** ability to communicate a message to others; may encompass nonverbal language, such as body language

Extension study: a study in which the researcher repeats an earlier investigation by adding one or more factors to the mix of variables examined to explain or understand a topic of interest or to reconceptualize how a phenomenon is viewed

External audit: a competent "outside" person examines the process used to collect data and cross-checks the results of the qualitative study to confirm the interpretations the researcher made

External validity: the ability to generalize study findings beyond the study sample to the population that the sample represents

F

Face-to-face structured interview: an interviewer must be physically present as he or she poses questions to a respondent

Face validity: a form of construct validity; an individual subjectively decides the measurement is adequate

Feminist ethics: create environments for clients that are inclusive and incorporate the experiences of individuals whose concerns have been marginalized in the past (e.g., women)

Feminist theory: a subset of critical theory and a qualitative design; the theory originally asserted that women occupy an inferior status in capitalist and patriarchal societies, thus women's experiences are shaped by social, economic, and political inequities rather than individual choices

Fidelity: a concept in research ethics dealing with honesty; establishing a relationship of trust between the researcher and study participants

Field notes (or ***observation recording sheets):*** used during participant observation sessions for recording a running description of the setting, events, people, things heard, and interactions observed

Field staff: research assistants who collect data (conduct interviews, distribute questionnaires, make observations, etc.), enter data, and/or transcribe interview transcripts for a study

Figure: Any graphic illustration (e.g, pie graph, bar graph, histogram, line graph, chart) other than a table

Figure caption: the title or label for a graphic figure

Fixed designs: the design of the study is fixed before data collection occurs (e.g., in quantitative studies); quantitative designs

Flexible designs: sometimes used as an alternative reference to qualitative designs; designs that are used in real-world studies that allow for more flexibility in data collection

Flow theory: assertion about a subjective state that is triggered by intense engagement in an activity and is characterized loss of self-consciousness, a sense of self-control, and an altered sense of time

Focus groups: an unstructured interview conducted with two or more people who are asked about their beliefs, attitudes, perceptions, and/or opinions

Forced ranking: the respondent is asked to place options in a designated order

Formal theory: an explicit statement used to understand, explain, or make a prediction about a given phenomenon or concept

Frequency distribution: a statistical procedure used to describes how data are distributed; tallying and presenting how often scores occur

Fringe benefits: the collection of benefits other than wages or a salary provided by an employer, such as health insurance, social security, workers' compensation, disability insurance, group term life insurance, and retirement or pension fund

Full-time equivalency (FTE): the percentage of time or effort that an individual will devote to a task (e.g., research project)

G

Gantt chart: a time management tool, in illustration format, used to present the calendar time projected for each task and the timing interface among the project activities

General references: indices, abstracts, bibliographies, and the like used to identify primary sources

Ghost author: an individual who has made significant contributions to the research but has been omitted from the list of authors

Gift author: a person who did not contribute to the research but has been listed as one of the authors

Gold reference: article containing invaluable ideas (e.g., insights or a synthesis of research on a topic) that may be used for a study being planned

Grand theory: broad or macro theoretical formulation that is focused on societies or social institutions; used to explain behaviors or situations

Grand tour question: used in qualitative studies, an interview question that is broad and stated in general terms; takes the form, "Tell me about..."; used in unstructured in-depth interviews when interviewee is asked to share information about themselves or their situation

Grounded theory: a qualitative design used to construct theory from the words and actions of individuals being studied; context specific with repeated data collection and analyses

Grouped data: adjacent values are combined into a category and the number of responses in each category is reported or displayed in a frequency distribution

H

Halo effect: occurs when a respondent feels pressure to provide answers that are socially acceptable, especially if their anonymity has been lost

Handouts: printed information provided free of charge to accompany a presentation

Hawthorne effect (or guinea pig effect): people consciously or subconsciously react to being tested

Hierarchy for program analysis: a program may be examined one of seven ways (inputs; activities; participation; reactions; knowledge, attitude, skills/functional abilities, and/or aspiration change; practice change; end results), with each tier in the hierarchy requiring unique evidence or data

Histogram: a bar-type graph used to illustrate a frequency distribution of interval and/or ratio data; adjacent columns in the histogram (unlike a bar graph) touch

Holistic understanding: in qualitative data analysis, the findings of the study are tied to overarching explanations

Hypothesis: a conjecture or guess about relationships between or among two or more variables; tentative statement that is waiting for evidence to support or refute it

Hypothesis testing: speculating relationships between or among variables

I

Impact factor: a standardized measure of how often articles from a particular journal have been cited in the same as well as other journals

Incidence: the number of new cases of a particular problem in a specified geographic area and during a specified time

Independent variable: the variable introduced into the situation, be it a treatment, program, intervention, demographic characteristic, or another causal factor

Index: when a number of questions are used to measure a variable and then the responses are tallied together to get a sum or average

Indices: references with lists of primary sources by subject categories, author, title, and journal publication

Indigenous field staff: persons who share similar social characteristics (age, gender, ethnicity, etc.) to the group being interviewed

Indirect costs: overhead expenses such as building maintenance (e.g., custodial services), utilities, and miscellaneous supplies purchased in bulk (e.g., paper, pencils, pens); costs that may appear in a research proposal budget

Inductive reasoning/thinking: involves developing multiple meanings based on observations of a limited number of related events or experiences; patterns and relationships emerge from the data

Inferential statistics: analysis tools researchers use to determine how much confidence they have when generalizing from a sample to a population

Informal theory: set of personal beliefs or presuppositions that a person holds regarding a description, explanation, or prediction of a phenomenon

Informed consent: an ethical commitment to ensure that a potential study participant has enough information about the study to make a sound decision about participating

Institutional review board (IRB): an ethics committee formally designated to approve and monitor biomedical and behavioral research involving humans

Instrument reliability: repeatability, constancy, and/or stability of responses of or within an instrument

Instrument validity: the accuracy of a measuring instrument

Integrity of a design: addressing the internal validity of the study, the external validity of the study, or sampling generalization

Interitem reliability: internal consistency; verifies that items used in an index belong or fit together

Interlibrary loan service: a university service wherein students may obtain copies of journal articles, books, and other resources from other libraries

Intermittent observation: observing at specific and set times and/or days (e.g., the hour before and the hour after a facility opens, on a Friday and then on a Tuesday)

Internal consistency reliability: statistic used to determine whether the questions comprising the index are "holding together" to measure the same variable

Internal validity (or ***causal validity*** or ***causal effect):*** determining whether a specific treatment, intervention, program, or activity works or has had a positive impact on the participants

Interpretivism: has a long intellectual history in which human activity is seen as "text"—as a collection of symbols expressing layers of meaning

Interrater reliability (or ***interobserver reliability):*** involves two or more observers independently rating a phenomenon at the same time

Interrater reliability coefficient: one way to determine reliability among raters; coefficient should be at least > .60 to consider the instrument reliable

Interval level of measurement: measures a variable in rank order with the distance between the numbers as equal units

Intervening variable: when an independent variable operates indirectly on a dependent variable

Inverse (or ***negative) correlation***: variables that change in opposite directions

Items: Questions used to gather data directly needed to answer research questions

J

Jury opinion: a way of establishing content validity; asking a group of knowledgeable experts to review and verify that the selected items in an instrument do indeed measure the concept

Justice: a concept in research ethics about fairness in receiving the benefits and the risks of research

K

Keywords: words or phrases used to retrieve information on a chosen topic; used in online literature search of databases

L

Latchkey children: Children who at the end of the school day must reenter their home with a key since no adult is present; typically considered a population-in-need

Latent content: in document review, the underlying meaning about the document content

Legend: a guide for a graphic figure

Levels of measurement: hierarchies for measuring a variable: nominal, ordinal, interval, and ratio

Likert scale: Respondent is asked to indicate the amount of agreement or disagreement with a statement

Limitations: occurrences that may adversely affect the conclusions of a study; may stem from several sources such as the theoretical approach, sampling, research design, instrumentation, data collection, and/or data analysis

Line graph: a continuous line used to connect data points over time; commonly used to examine rates of change and how fluctuations in an independent variable affect a dependent variable

Line-item budget: in a research proposal, a list of the expenditures according to type and cost

Logic of measurement: specifying the concepts examined, the nominal and operational definitions of the concept, and the measurement units

Longitudinal survey (or ***panel study):*** a survey wherein the same age group is surveyed at different times; used to examine how people change as they age

M

Manifest content: in document review, the visible surface content in the document

Marginal participant: the observer adopts the role of a peripheral yet completely accepted participant

Marketing and promotion analysis: used to determine what does and does not motivate a person to participate in or use a service

Matching: pairing persons in the experiment and control groups on the basis of age, gender, or another relevant characteristic

Matrix display: a qualitative data analysis tool that is helpful for understanding the connections among bits of information by offering a "thumbnail sketch"

Maturation: a major threat to internal validity; natural changes or processes that occur over time with study participants

Mean: the arithmetic average of the scores in a data set

Measures of central tendency: a frequency distribution's center described with a single number

Measures of variability: used to summarize with one number the dispersion or spread of the individual responses in a frequency distribution

Median: the score that divides a set of scores in half

Member checks: conducting follow-up interviews with study participants, asking them to identify errors the researcher may have made in understanding what was initially shared by them and/or to comment on findings and conclusions the investigator reached

Memos: in qualitative data analysis, notes written by a researcher to himself or herself suggesting explanations for the expanded account content

Mentor: an experienced and trusted advisor

Meta-analysis: using a standard metric, researcher searches multiple databases to identify, summarize, and compare relevant studies on a topic; also applies to qualitative data analysis or organizing the words and images of raw data

Meta-data: organized words and images of raw data; new words or graphics are created to represent key themes and relationships emerging from the raw data

Metaphors: literary devices that involve comparing two aspects via their similarities and ignoring their differences

Missing data: incomplete data set due to, for example, some people not answering one or more questions

Mixed-methods approach: a theoretical framework and research design that is a blend of quantitative and qualitative approaches

Mixed-methods sampling strategy: using probability and nonprobability sampling in the same study, thus increasing the likelihood of gaining more insights about the topic

Mode: the most frequently occurring response category in a data set

Model development and testing (or **conceptual mapping**)**:** testing theory by way of proposing conceptual model to describe, explain, or predict a phenomenon being studied

Multidimensional index: an index containing questions that may be broken down into clusters that measure different aspects of the variable

Multiple-choice question: question with more than two response options

Multistage approach: used in cluster sampling, consists of identifying a series of sampless

Multitrait–multimethod study: a study that requires identifying two variables and two tests intended to measure each variable

N

Naïve hypotheses: hypotheses that come from educated guesswork

Narrative analysis: use of interviews (and sometimes documents and observations) to put together stories about events and experiences as participants understand them; a qualitative design

Narrative budget: describes how the funds requested for each line item will be spent and how the amount was determined

Narrative writing style: storytelling

Needs assessment: used to determine the preferences of clients or service providers

Negative relationship (or **inverse relationship**)**:** the direction of the relationship between the variables is opposite; that is, as the value of one variable changes (increases or decreases), the value of the second variable heads in the opposite direction

Network data display: in qualitative data analysis, a collection of points connected by lines used to display streams of participant actions, events, and processes

Nominal definition: a variable that reflects the working definition of a concept

Nominal level of measurement: used to measure a variable using labels or categories that are mutually exclusive

Nondirectional hypothesis (H): speculates a relationship or difference exists among variables, but it does not provide further details about the nature of the relationship or difference

Nonequivalent control group pretest–posttest: a quasi-experimental design in which participants are neither randomly selected nor assigned to an experimental or control group; both groups are administered a pretest and a posttest

Nonexpedited review: type of IRB approval required when vulnerable subjects or controversial interventions or data collection techniques are proposed

Nonexperimental design: a treatment, intervention, program, or activity is not the focus of the study; individuals or groups are studied as they are

Nonmaleficence: an ethical principle about the doctrine of "do no harm"

Nonnumerical data: information presented in text form

Nonprobability sampling: entities selected purposively due to convenience or accidentally

Nonreactive measures: instruments used to examine "naturally" occurring information

Nonrepresentative (or **biased**) **sample:** the outcome of nonprobability sampling

Normative data (or **standardization**)**:** data produced from a study that characterize what is usual in a defined population at a specific time

Normative research questions: what is studied is compared to a standard

Null hypothesis (H_o): states no relationship or difference exists between two or more variables

Numerical data: information presented as numbers

Numerical table: used to display data in a frequency distribution

O

Observation: gathering firsthand information by watching people or events

Observational guide: prestructured and printed forms that provide specific ways to record what is to be seen or heard

One-group posttest-only: a preexperimental design that features an experimental group who are posttested

One-group pretest–posttest: preexperimental design that has involves a pretest and posttest of an experimental group

Online panels: a group of selected research participants who have agreed beforehand to participate in a study by completing an online questionnaire

Online self-administered structured questionnaires: a questionnaire administered using Web survey software

Open body posture: body language that is considered receptive and welcoming

Open-ended questions: in a questionnaire, questions without possible answer choices (respondents provide an answer in their own words)

Operational definition (or ***operationalization):*** the meaning of a concept expressed in terms of how it is measured; a measurement instrument

Ordinal level of measurement: used to measure a variable by categorizing information by size or magnitude

Outcomes: identified in program or activity objective; the desired impact of the program or activity on participants

Overt complete participant: the complete participant observer's identity as a researcher is fully disclosed

P

Paradox behind science: knowledge evolves; what the researchers thinks is true at one time is later rejected or shown to be false

Parsimonious theory: a concise and simple explanation of reality

Participant observation: an unstructured yet systematic way of recording information by meaningfully interacting with the individuals being observed

Passive participant: an observer who is present at the scene of the action but does not participate or interact with other people to a great extent

Pattern: when information has been noted a number of times

Pearson product–moment correlation coefficient (or ***Pearson's r):*** a measure of relationship between two interval or ratio measured variables; its calculation produces an index that ranges between −1 and +1

Peer debriefing: while the study is in process, obtaining an objective assessment by sharing information about procedures, findings, and tentative conclusions with a disinterested, professional peer

Peer review: the process of self-regulation by professionals to maintain standards and improve performance and provide credibility; in research, the review and critique of a manuscript or presentation; often conducted anonymously (*see* blind review)

Percentage: a relative comparison in which a proportion is multiplied by 100

Performance appraisals: examination of a person's (full-time, part-time, and seasonal employees and volunteers) work performance in terms of skills, abilities, traits, and/or behaviors

Performance-based program budgeting: itemizing expenditures related to a program

Personal documents: archival data of first-person accounts of events or personal experiences

Personality tests: used to measure self-perception or personal characteristics

Person-loading chart: a time management tool researchers use to itemize the individual/position assigned to each task and the estimated number of hours or clock time needed to complete the task

Phenomenology: a qualitative design that is focused on the everyday life that people experience and express; requires reflection of conscious experience

Photovoice: study participants are given a camera and asked to take pictures of their surroundings or activities; the idea is to experience the world through the viewpoint of a group of people

Physical tracing: a nonreactive measure of finding and recording visible evidence or traces of behavior that are not specifically produced for the research project, but are nonetheless available to measure

Pie graph (or ***pie chart):*** a circle or pie divided into sections that represent relative percentages in a frequency distribution

Pilot testing: a small-scale preliminary study to test the methods tentatively planned to be used in a full-fledged research study

Plagiarism: the act of intentionally or accidentally stealing another person's ideas or work and passing them off as your own

Plausibility: in qualitative data analysis, making tentative conclusions based on "it feels right" (makes sense or intuitively emerges)

Population: the entire set of entities (e.g., individuals, objects) being studied

Positive (or ***direct) correlation:*** the direction of the two variables is the same; that is, as the value of the independent variable increases, the value of the dependent variable increases accordingly (and vice versa)

Poster: a large, formatted visual presentation of a research study or theoretical paper; usually displayed in a public place at a professional meeting

Posttest (XO): used to collect data on a group(s) after the experimental group completes the treatment, intervention, program, or activity

Posttest-only control group: an experimental design in which research participants are randomly assigned to experimental or control groups and both groups are measured and compared after implementation of a treatment, intervention, program, or activity

Practice change: behavior changes that happen to the individual as the result of participating in a treatment, intervention, program, or activity

Predictive research: used to determine how specific factors affect future behaviors, sentiments, or events; used to provide estimates of population values

Predictive validity: a form of criterion validity; the ability of a measure to predict or foretell

Preexperimental designs: do not feature random selection, random assignment, pretest, and/or a control group

Pretest (OX): baseline data collected on a group before participants are introduced to or experience the intervention, treatment, program, or activity

Pretest–posttest control group: an experimental design in which research participants are randomly assigned to experimental or control groups; both groups are pretested and then posttested after the experimental intervention, treatment, program, or activity has been administered to the experimental group

Prevalence: the number of existing cases in a particular geographic area at a specified time

Primary data: information collected directly from firsthand sources by means of surveys, observation, and so forth; data not previously published and derived from new or original research

Primary literature sources: research appearing in refereed journals, theses, dissertations, and reports published by governments or private organizations

Principal investigator (or ***PI***)***:*** the individual who leads a research team on a project

Probability sampling: sampling method wherein every entity or unit of a population has the same chance of being chosen for the sample

Probing: follow-up question that is asked to clarify a response; to seek elaboration or more detail from a respondent

Problem-solving interview: an unstructured in-depth interview that is focused on a specific problem to be solved or goal to be set

Professional code of ethics: the norms, values, and principles that govern professional conduct and relationships with clients, colleagues, and society

Professional practice: professionals providing a high and responsible standard of service by using their knowledge and formal training and education

Program design: program organization (or components, content, elements, activities, or educational methods/techniques used)

Program economics: comparison of program costs to program effects

Program need (or ***needs assessment***)***:*** the gap between the real and the ideal in a program service; may be focus on staff qualifications, standards compliance, and/or resource amounts

Programs: formally organized events, activities, or interventions

Projective methods: used to collect responses to ambiguous or unstructured stimuli, such as a series of cartoons, abstract patterns, or incomplete sentences

Prolonged engagement: lengthy and intensive contact with respondents or phenomena in the field, or real-world settings

Proportion: a relative comparison that is a ratio of the total

Proportionate stratified sampling: sampling method wherein the subgroups are represented in the sample in the same proportion they are found in the population

Proposal: a preliminary plan that contains information on what will be studied, why the selected topic is important to study, and how the study will be conducted

Proposal meeting: a formal session between a student and his or her thesis or dissertation chair and committee to discuss the merits of the proposed research and to seek permission to execute the study in the manner outlined in the proposal

Prospectus: a preproposal, usually no more than three pages, that provides a preliminary overview of the proposed study

Protection of human subjects: there should be minimal risk, preferably no risk, of physical harm or social psychological discomfort to people involved in the research

Provenance grid: a graphic tool for tracking the disciplinary source of a theory

Pseudoscience (or ***junk science***)***:*** result of one or more of the characteristics of scientific inquiry (i.e., logical, objective, systematic) being violated

Psychophysiological measures: used to assess the physiological functioning of the central nervous system and autonomic and somatic nervous systems

Public records: archival data created to provide unrestricted information or accounting

Purpose statement (or ***problem statement***)***:*** statement about the overall intent of the study

Purposive sample (or ***judgmental, expert,*** or ***key informant sample***)***:*** nonprobability sampling method wherein researchers uses their judgment to choose for the sample individuals who best serve the purposes of the study

Q

Qualitative approach (or ***social constructivism, interpretative theory,*** or ***ideological theory***)***:*** a theoretical framework that relies on inductive reasoning to understand the multiple meanings that exist to describe, interpret, or contextualize a phenomenon; taken up to develop or generate theory; relies on unstructured or semistructured inquiry that results in analyzing text or image data

Qualitative data analysis: making sense of nonnumerical data collected in a study (e.g., text ... documents); a four-step cyclical process is used to identify patterns and relationships that emerge from the data

Quantitative approach (or ***post-positivist theory, empirical science,*** or ***normative theory***)***:*** a theoretical framework that relies on deductive reasoning to describe, explain, or predict phenomena; tests or verifies theory; relies on close-ended structured inquiry that results in analyzing numerical data

Quantitative data analysis: making sense of numerical data collected in a study; relies on deductive thinking where patterns and relationships are established before the study is executed

Quasi-experimental designs: study participants are not randomly selected to be involved in the study; if a control group is featured, individuals are not randomly assigned to one group or the other (i.e., the experimental group or the control group)

Questionnaire (or ***survey***)***:*** a set of questions used for collecting information; may be structured, unstructured, or semistructured inquiry

Quota sampling: the nonprobability equivalent of stratified sampling in which the subgroups of interest are identified, a target is set for the number of individuals needed for each subgroup, and the requisite number of entities for each subgroup is found

R

Random assignment (RA): once the sample has been selected, each person/unit is randomly assigned to an experimental or control group; probability is used to make the assignment

Random observation: observing at different times and different days

Random selection (RS): probability sampling used to identify, from a population a unit of analysis (usually an individual) to be included in the sample

Range: a measure of variability that is focused on the variation between the highest and lowest scores in a frequency distribution

Rate: a relative comparison that provides the frequency of occurrence of an outcome

Ratio: a relative comparison that compares the frequency of one response with another

Ratio level of measurement: used to measure a variable with rank order, equal units of measurement, and an absolute zero

Raw data: originally collected words or images; information collected directly from the source

Reactive measures: instruments that create and measure responses

Receptive skills: the ability to understand or comprehend language heard, read, or being expressed

Reductionism: the discipline or lens with which a person views the world; influences research topic choice and how a study is planned, implemented, and reported

Refereed journals: primary sources that print original research after the manuscript has been reviewed and critiqued by peer researchers/academics and deemed noteworthy to print

Reference librarian: a person who has received specialized training on how to identify and locate information materials on a specific topic

References: alphabetized list of citations documented in the body of a research proposal and final report

Reflectivity: in a qualitative study, acknowledgement of how the investigator's biases may affect the study

Regression to the mean: individuals with extreme high or low scores on the pretest will tend to have scores closer to the mean on the second testing

Relative comparison: descriptive statistics, including rates, ratios, proportions, and percentages

Reliability: a measurement instrument that has repeatability, constancy, and/or stability of responses

Reliability coefficient: a numerical value used to measure the accuracy of a measuring instrument; ranges from 0.0 to 1.0

Repeated testing: the first pretest may educate or sensitize people; the act of testing itself becomes the change agent; a threat to internal and external validity

Replication: in qualitative data analysis, duplication or confirmation of results

Replication study: a study to confirm or disconfirm results from an earlier study

Representativeness: in qualitative data analysis, determining whether the gathered information is typical of the people, organization, or events that are being studied

Representative sample (or ***unbiased sample):*** a sample selected using probability sampling; a representative sample that looks like the population from which it was selected in all aspects that are relevant to the study

Requests for proposals (RFP): research funding opportunities typically issued by government agencies or private organizations

Research: following a logical, objective, and systematic process to gain knowledge about a topic

Research competence: an individual is qualified by training, qualifications, and experience to conduct the research study

Research design: theoretical framework to guide a study

Researcher effects: in qualitative data analysis, determining whether the researcher influenced the data collected and/or analyzed for a study

Research ethics: the ethical principles expected when designing, conducting, and reporting research

Research process: an approach that consists Stage 1: getting started, Stage 2: developing a plan, Stage 3: implementation, and Stage 4: reporting, as well as many subcomponents.

Research question: makes the theoretical assumptions in a study more explicit as it indicates exactly what the researcher wants to know foremost; narrows the purpose statement

Research review: a focused and detailed synthesis of the research studies on a particular topic

Resource amounts: the kinds and quantities of resources used to support the program; one way to focus on resource amounts as inputs is to examine total program cost or itemize expenditures related to a program

Response rate: the percentage of people who, when solicited to participate in a study, agree to do so

Review of literature: finding, examining, and summarizing relevant information and research studies previously done by others

Rigor (or ***trustworthiness):*** the descriptions and interpretations of the findings from a qualitative design are defensible and not so subjective that they cannot be trusted

Rival explanations: in qualitative data analysis, conclusions that are opposite or different from the ones that have that have been tentatively determined from the study

Running text: the body of the text

S

Sabbatical: a paid leave for a tenured faculty member to pursue research or some other approved academic endeavor; traditionally every seventh year

Sample: a subset of the population

Sample generalizability: in survey or ex post facto design, generalizing from the sample to its population

Sample size (n): number of entities or units selected for a sample

Sampling bias: a nonrepresentative sample is drawn

Sampling error: the difference between the sample and population values; relates to the quality of the sample

Sampling frame: a list of units of analysis in a population

Sampling interval: total number of entities in the population divided by the number of entities required for the sample

Scale: an index measurement in which the answers to questions are weighted

Scientific fraud: the deliberate falsification, misrepresentation, or plagiarizing of data, findings, or ideas of others

Scientific inquiry (or ***research process):*** the structured and planned thinking process followed in discovering knowledge; characterized as being logical, objective, and systematic

Scientific research: when research has been logically, objectively, and systematically planned and implemented

Scientific revolution: radical change that overturns prevailing wisdom in a scientific field

Secondary data: information previously collected at an earlier point in time by a different person than the present researcher, or data that have been "left behind" and then used by another person

Secondary literature source: a publication that provides introductory background information about a topic

Selection bias: intact groups or volunteers possess unique attributes and/or characteristics that may be responsible for noted changes (rather than participation in a treatment, intervention, program, or activity) between pretest and posttest

Self-administered structured questionnaire: a questionnaire administered via the mail, over the Internet, or in person

Semantic differential: a continuum is set up between bipolar words and the respondent selects the point that represents the direction and intensity of his or her feelings

Semistructured inquiry: a way of gathering information in an interview or survey in which formally structured questions and response options and open-ended conversational questions are used

Semistructured interviews: an interview including formally structured questions and response options as well as open-ended conversational questions

Sequential mixed-methods design: study design wherein the study is conducted in two waves using quantitative and qualitative designs to elaborate or expand upon initial findings

Set responses: the tendency for study respondents to answer questions from a particular perspective, usually due to social desirability

Sight editing: a standard procedure to check for completion of questionnaires, usually done by someone other than the person who conducted the interview or survey

Significance: making a case for the importance or necessity of a study or the findings of a study

Significance statement: written sentence that establishes the rationale for why the study is important and necessary

Simple random sampling: each member or unit of the population has an equal chance of being selected for the sample

Single-group interrupted time-series: quasi-experimental design in which individuals are not randomly selected and only an experimental group is used; the participants are pretested several times and then posttested several times after exposure to the treatment, intervention, program, or activity

Slide show software: used to display text and graphic images in a slide show format; typically includes a feature that allows text and sound to be inserted

Smiley face contiuum: individual is asked to choose one emotion from a range provided

Snowball sampling: sampling method wherein nonprobability sampling is used to find one person who meets the study criteria, and then that person is relied on to identify another person meeting the same criteria

Solomon four-group: a design wherein four randomly assigned groups are used, two experimental and two control, with only the experimental groups receiving the treatment; the dependent variable is measured before and after treatment for one experimental and one control group, but only after treatment for the other two groups

Split-half reliability (or ***alternate-forms reliability):*** two equivalent versions of the same instrument are developed and compared

Split-half reliability coefficient: a measure of instrument reliability; should be > .80 to consider the equivalent forms as consistent

Stakeholders: individuals or groups who have an interest in a program or activity that is being scrutinized by a research study

Standard deviation: a measure of variability that uses the mean of the distribution as a reference point and is used to measure the spread between each score and the mean point

Standardization: data produced from a study that characterize what is usual in a defined population

Standards compliance: comparing how a program, facility, or organization operates against norms

Static group comparison: a preexperimental design featuring an experimental and control group, with both groups receiving only a posttest

Statistics: procedures for describing, synthesizing, analyzing, and interpreting numerical data

Strata: subgroups (*stratum* for singular)

Stratified random sample: randomly sampled subgroups or categories (known as strata) of persons or units represented in a population

Strength of the relationship: The larger the correlation coefficient value is, the stronger the relationship; that is, the closer the value is to 1.00 (considered a perfect relationship), the stronger the association between the variables

Structured inquiry (e.g., ***an interview):*** a way of gathering information that involves asking specific questions or observing specific behaviors using predetermined categories to record the answers

Structured observation: a data collection method in which the actions and events to be observed are planned in advance

Structured questionnaire: a questionnaire in which the questions and response options are chosen beforehand

Subsuming: in qualitative data analysis, the process of drawing a conclusion by moving up a step in the abstraction ladder

Survey design: typically implemented by using probability sampling and a questionnaire about individuals' self-reported attitudes, beliefs, preferences, and/or behaviors

Systematic random sampling: sampling method wherein a particular "system" is chosen by the researcher and applied to simple random sampling to select a requisite number of entities from the population

T

Table-of-contents service: a service that provides access to the tables of contents to thousands of periodicals; the title and author of articles are listed

Tailored design strategy: an approach using at least three follow-up reminder phases in a mailed or Internet questionnaire

Telephone structured interview: a questionnaire conducted by an interviewer over the telephone

Tentative conclusions: in qualitative data analysis, the first and provisional meaning statements about information learned in a study

Test-retest reliability: a phenomenon is measured with the same instrument at two times, and then these results are compared

Test-retest reliability coefficient: a measure of stability of an instrument over time; should be > .80 to be considered reliable

Theory (or ***paradigm, model,*** or ***epistemology):*** tentative explanation or assertion of why or how something works in the social world; identifies the relationship between or among concepts; may guide a researcher when choosing a research topic and/or framing the research

Theory testing: the process of identifying a formal theory that sheds light on how certain concepts are related and then collecting information to see whether these relationships hold true

Thesis or dissertation defense: a requirement for certain advanced degrees is an oral examination, normally occurring after the thesis or dissertation is finished but before it is submitted to the university; may comprise a presentation by the student and questions posed by an examining committee or jury

Thick descriptions: the context and descriptions in a written report (including quotes) that are thoroughly presented so judgments about the transferability of the findings to another situation may be judged; used in qualitative data analysis

Threats to external validity: factors that stand in the way of being able to extend study results to other individuals in the population

Threats to internal validity (or ***alternative explanations):*** a mislabeling of the cause of an effect; aspects other than the treatment, intervention, program, or activity could be responsible for the noted effect

Time budget: projects clock and calendar time needed to complete specified tasks for conducting a study

Time-lag survey: several age groups are studied over time but with different persons being used to represent each age group at the different data collection points; used to investigate age differences and age changes

Transcripts: written or printed versions of material originally presented in another medium

Transformative research: brings about change in a situation to improve people's lives; radically advances knowledge about a topic or concept

Transitional devices: in writing, words or phrases that help carry a thought from one sentence to another, from one idea to another, or from one paragraph to another

Transparencies: a thin sheet of viewfoil (usually cellulose acetate) that is viewed by light by placing it on an overhead projector for viewing

Triangulation: the views of complementary data; the use of multiple methods, data collection tools, and data sources in the same study to obtain a more complete picture of the topic being studied; to cross-check information

U

Ungrouped data: a frequency distribution used to report every score for the variable

Unit of analysis: who or what is analyzed in a study

Units of measurement: a system for categorizing collected data or responses for a variable

Unit of observation: the unit or object on which information is collected

Unstructured inquiry (or ***unstructured in-depth interview):*** a way of gathering information that does not rely on predetermined categories of answers, but instead asks respondents to describe their experiences in their own words; may require a lot of time to conduct

V

Variable: elaboration or operational definition of a concept; identifies a characteristic or property that describes a unit of analysis that must have a minimum of two values that are mutually exclusive

Virtue ethics: strive toward ideals related to humanity and moral character and thus include character traits such as courage, compassion, generosity, and self-control

Visual aids: resources audiences look at (e.g., film, slide, videotape) to supplement written or spoken information so it may be more easily understood

Volunteer sampling (or ***convenience, accidental, availability,*** or ***haphazard sampling):*** sampling method wherein nonprobability sampling is used and an entity is chosen to be in the sample because of expediency; that is, the individual is readily available or accessible at a certain time or place to help out in terms of agreeing to be in the study

W

Wait-list control group: a comparison group is offered the treatment, intervention, program, or activity experienced by the experimental group once the experiment is completed

Weighting: in sampling, drawing appropriate percentages for strata

Word tables: summarize and present descriptive text or qualitative information

REFERENCES

After School Alliance Organization. (2011). *Evaluations backgrounder: A summary of formal evaluations of afterschool programs' impact on academics, behavior, safety and family life.* Retrieved August 2, 2013, from http://www.afterschoolalliance.org/documents/EvaluationsBackgrounder2011.pdf

Alreck, P., & Settle, R. (2004). *The survey research handbook* (3rd ed.). New York, NY: McGraw-Hill.

American Psychological Association. (2010). *Publication manual of the American Psychological Association* (6th ed.). Washington, DC: Author.

Anderson, D., & Bedini, L. (2002). Perceptions of workplace equity of therapeutic recreation professionals. *Therapeutic Recreation Journal, 36,* 260–281.

Apsler, R. (2009). After-school programs for adolescents: A review of evaluation research. *Adolescence, 44,* 1–19.

Arai, S., & Kivel, D. (2009). Critical race theory and social justice perspectives on whiteness, difference(s) and (anti) racism: A fourth wave of race research in leisure studies. *Journal of Leisure Research, 41,* 459–472.

Attarian, A. (2005). *The research and literature on challenge courses: An annotated bibliography* (2nd ed.). Raleigh: North Carolina State University, Department of Parks, Recreation and Tourism Management and Alpine Towers International.

Babbie, E. (2012). *The practice of social research* (13th ed.). Belmont, CA: Wadsworth.

Bailey, K. (1994). *Methods of social research* (4th ed.). New York, NY: The Free Press.

Baker, S. (1981). *Basic attending and responding skills for human service helpers.* Unpublished manuscript, Pennsylvania State University, University Park.

Baldwin, C., Hutchinson, S., & Magnuson, D. (2004). Program theory: A framework for theory-driven programming and evaluation. *Therapeutic Recreation Journal, 38,* 16–31.

Baron-Leonard, R. (2004). *Effects of animal-assisted therapy on individuals who are deaf and mentally ill.* Unpublished master's thesis, Gallaudet University, Washington, DC.

Basit, T. (2010). *Conducting research in educational contexts.* New York, NY: Continuum International.

Bedini, L., & Wu, Y. (1994). A methodological review of research in Therapeutic *Recreation Journal from 1986 to 1990. Therapeutic Recreation Journal, 28,* 87–98.

Beeco, J., Hallo, J., Baldwin, E., & McGuire, F. (2011). An examination of the guided night hiking experiences in parks and protected areas. *Journal of Park and Recreation Administration, 29,* 72–88.

Bennett, C. (1979). *Analyzing impacts of Extension programs.* Washington, DC: U.S. Department of Agriculture.

Berg, K., & Latin, R. (2008). *Essentials of modern research methods in health, physical education, exercise science, and recreation* (3rd ed.). Philadelphia, PA: Lippincott Williams and Wilkins.

Bickman, L., & Rog, D. (2009). *The SAGE handbook of applied social research methods* (2nd ed.). Thousand Oaks, CA: Sage.

Black, T. (1994). *Evaluating social science research: An introduction.* Thousand Oaks, CA: Sage.

Bocarro, J., Greenwood, P., & Henderson, K. (2008). An integrative review of youth development research in selected United States recreation journals. *Journal of Park and Recreation Administration, 26,* 4–27.

Bocarro, J., & Wells, M. (2009). Making a difference through parks and recreation: Reflections on physical activity, health, and wellness research. *Journal of Parks and Recreation Administration, 27,* 1–7.

Bogdan, R., & Biklen, S. (2006). *Qualitative research in education: An introduction to theories and methods* (5th ed.). Upper Saddle River, NJ: Pearson Education.

Bordwell, D., & Thompson, K. (2112). *Film art: An introduction* (10th ed.). New York, NY: McGraw-Hill Humanities.

Borenstein, M., Hedges, L., Higgins, J., & Rothstein, H. (2009). *Introduction to meta-analysis.* Hoboken, NJ: John Wiley and Sons.

Borich, G. (2013). *Effective teaching methods: Research-based practice* (8th ed.). Upper Saddle River, NJ: Pearson Education.

Bouma, G., & Atkinson, G. (1996). *A handbook of social science research: A comprehensive and practical guide for students* (2nd ed.). New York, NY: Oxford University Press.

Breunig, M., O'Connell, T., Todd, S., Anderson, L., & Young, A. (2010). The impact of outdoor pursuits on college students' perceived sense of community. *Journal of Leisure Research, 42,* 551–572.

Brown, E. (2011, March 20). Father of chemical ecology loved bugs. *Washington Post,* p. B6.

Brown, R. (1996). *Key skills for writing and publishing research* (3rd ed.). Brisbane, Australia: Write Way Consulting.

Buckley, R. (2012). Risk as a key motivation in skilled adventure tourism: Resolving the risk recreation paradox. *Tourism Management, 33,* 961–970.

Burdge, R. (1985). The coming separation of leisure studies from parks and recreation education. *Journal of Leisure Research, 17,* 133–141.

Burns, J. (2007). *Meanings deaf collegians attribute to Gallaudet University's Discovery Through Nature course: A photo elicitation study.* Unpublished master's thesis, Gallaudet University, Washington, DC.

Cacioppo, J., Tassinary, L., & Berntson, G. (Eds.). (2013). *Handbook of psychophysiology* (3rd ed.). Cambridge, England: Cambridge University Press.

Campbell, D., & Stanley, J. (1963). *Experimental and quasi-experimental designs for research.* Chicago, IL: Rand McNally.

Carruthers, C., & Hood, C. (2011). Mindfulness and well-being: Implications for TR practice. *Therapeutic Recreation Journal, 45,* 171–189.

Charmaz, K. (2011). Grounded theory methods in social justice studies. In N. K. Denzin & Y. S. Lincoln (Eds.), *The Sage handbook of qualitative research* (4th ed.). Thousand Oaks, CA: Sage.

Charmaz, K. (2014). *Constructing grounded theory: A practical guide through qualitative analysis.* Thousand Oaks, CA: Sage.

Christensen, J. (1980). A second look at the informal interview. *Journal of Leisure Research, 12,* 183–186.

Clandinin, D., & Connelly, E. (2004). *Narrative inquiry: Experience and story in qualitative research* (2nd ed.). San Francisco, CA: Jossey-Bass.

Cohen, E. (1993). The study of touristic images of native people: Mitigating the stereotype of a stereotype. In D. Pearce & R. Butler (Eds.), *Tourism research: Critiques and challenges* (pp. 33–69). London, England: Routledge.

Cook, T., & Campbell, D. (1979). *Quasi-experimentation: Design and analysis issues for field settings.* Boston, MA: Houghton Mifflin.

Cooper, H., Hedges, L., & Valentine, J. (Eds.). (2009). *Handbook of research synthesis and meta-analyses* (2nd ed.). New York, NY: Russell Sage Foundation.

Corbin, J., & Strauss, A. (2008a). Basics of qualitative research: *Grounded theory procedures and techniques* (3rd ed.). Thousand Oaks, CA: Sage.

Corbin, J., & Strauss, A. (2008b). *Qualitative research* (3rd ed.). Thousand Oaks, CA: Sage.

Couper, M. (2004). Web surveys: A review of issues and approaches. *Public Opinion Quarterly, 64,* 464–494.

Couper, M., Traugott, M., & Lamias, M. (2001). Web survey design and administration. *Public Opinion Quarterly, 65,* 230–253.

Coyle, C., Kinney, W., Riley, B., & Shank, J. (Eds.). (1991). *Benefits of therapeutic recreation: A consensus view.* Ravensdale, WA: Idyll Arbor.

Cozby, P. (2009). *Methods in behavioral research* (10th ed.). Boston, MA: McGraw-Hill Higher Education.

Cozby, P., & Bates, S. (2011). *Methods in behavioral research* (11th ed.). Boston, MA: McGraw-Hill Higher Education.

Crawford, D., Jackson, E., & Godbey, G. (1991). A hierarchical model of leisure constraints. *Leisure Sciences, 13,* 309–320.

Crawford, F. (2000). Researcher in consumer behavior looks at attitudes of gratitude that affect gratuities. *Cornell Chronicle.* Retrieved June 17, 2012, from http://www.news.cornell.edu/chronicle/00/8.17.00/Lynn-tipping.html

Creswell, J. (2005). *Educational research: Planning, conducting and evaluating quantitative and qualitative research* (2nd ed.). Upper Saddle Creek, NJ: Pearson Merrill Prentice Hall.

Creswell, J. (2012). *Qualitative inquiry and research design: Choosing among five approaches* (3rd ed.). Thousand Oaks, CA: Sage.

Creswell, J. (2013). *Research design: Qualitative, quantitative, and mixed methods approaches* (4th ed.). Thousand Oaks, CA: Sage.

Cronbach, L. (1989). *Designing evaluations of educational and social programs* (2nd ed.). San Francisco, CA: Jossey-Bass.

Csikszentmihalyi, M. (2008). *Flow: The psychology of optimal experience.* New York, NY: HarperCollins.

Csikszentmihalyi, M., Larson, R., & Prescott, S. (1977). Ecology of adolescent activity and experience. *Journal of Youth and Adolescence, 6,* 281–294.

Cunningham, J. (1993). *Action research and organizational development.* Westport, CT: Praeger.

Czaga, R., & Blair, J. (2005). *Designing surveys: A guide to decisions and procedures* (2nd ed.). Thousand Oaks, CA: Pine Forge Press.

Daud, R., & Carruthers, C. (2008). Outcome study of an after-school program for youth in a high-risk environment. *Journal of Park and Recreation Administration, 26,* 95–114.

Dawson, S., Knapp, D., & Farmer, J. (2012). Camp war buddies: Exploring the therapeutic benefits of social comparison in a pediatric oncology camp. *Therapeutic Recreation Journal, 46,* 313–325.

Day, R., & Gastel, B. (2012). *How to write and publish a scientific paper* (7th ed.). Cambridge, England: Cambridge University Press.

Denzin, N., & Lincoln, Y. (Eds.). (2011). *The Sage handbook of qualitative research* (4th ed.). Thousand Oaks, CA: Sage.

DeSchriver, M., & Riddick, C. (1990). Effects of watching aquariums on elders' stress. *Anthrozoos, 4,* 44–48.

DeVellis, R. (2012). *Scale development: Theory and applications* (3rd ed.). Los Angeles, CA: Sage.

Dieser, R. (2011). A follow-up investigation of the fundamental attribution error in leisure education research. *Therapeutic Recreation Journal, 45,* 190–213.

Dill, K., & Thill, K. (2007). Videogame characters and the socialization of gender roles: Young people's perceptions mirror sexist media depictions. *Sex Roles, 57,* 851–864.

Dillman, D., Smyth, J., & Christian, L. (2008). *Internet, mail, & mixed-mode surveys: The tailored design method* (3rd ed.). New York, NY: Wiley.

Doyle, A. (1891). *The scandal in Bohemia.* New York, NY: Penguin.

Dunn, A. (1996). Getting started: A review of physical activity adoption strategies. *British Journal of Sports Medicine, 30,* 193–199.

Eichelberger, R. (1989). *Disciplined inquiry: Understanding and doing educational research.* New York, NY: Longman.

Elias, N., & Dunning, E. (1986). *Quest for excitement: Sport and leisure in the civilizing process.* Oxford, United Kingdom: Basil Blackwell.

Erikson, E. (1968). *Identity: Youth and crisis.* New York, NY: W.W. Norton.

Farhney, S., Kelley, C., Dattilo, J., & Rusch, F. (2010). Effects of goal setting on activity levels of senior exercises with osteoarthritis residing in the community. *Therapeutic Recreation Journal, 44,* 87–102.

Fetterman, D. (2009). *Ethnography: Step by step* (3rd ed.). Newbury Park, CA: Sage.

Fisher, C. (2005). *Impacts of discovery through nature course on deaf and hard of hearing students.* Unpublished master's thesis, Gallaudet University, Washington, DC.

Fisher, J., & Corcoran, K. (2007). *Measures of clinical practice: A sourcebook* (Vol. 1; 4th ed.). New York, NY: Oxford University Press.

Fishwick, L., & Leach, K. (1998). Game, set and match: Gender bias in television coverage of Wimbledon 1994. In S. Scranton & R. Watson (Eds.), *Sport, leisure identities and gendered spaces* (pp. 31–44). Eastbourne, United Kingdom: Leisure Studies Association.

Flick, U. (2006). *An introduction to qualitative research* (4th ed.). London, England: Sage.

Folkins, C., & Sime, W. (1981). Physical fitness training and mental health. *American Psychologist, 26*, 373–389.

Forsyth, K., & Kviz, F. (2006). Survey research design. In G. Kielhofner (Ed.), *Research in occupational therapy: Methods of inquiry for enhancing practice* (pp. 91–109). Philadelphia, PA: F.A. Davis.

Fowler, F. (2009). Design and evaluation of survey questions. In L. Bickman & D. Rog (Eds.), *Handbook of applied social research methods* (pp. 343–374, 2nd ed.). Thousand Oaks, CA: Sage.

Fowler, F. (2014). *Survey research methods* (5th ed.). Thousand Oaks, CA: Sage.

Fraenkel, J., Wallen, N., & Hyun, H. (2011). *How to design and evaluate research in education* (8th ed.). New York, NY: McGraw-Hill.

Fullan, M. (2007). *The new meaning of educational change* (4th ed.). New York, NY: Columbia Teachers College Press.

Furneaux, K. (2006). *Determinants of successful canoe and kayak coaches* (Master's thesis). Retrieved from ProQuest Dissertations and Theses database. (No. MR16535)

Gay, L., Mills, G., & Airasian, P. (2012). *Educational research: Competencies for analysis and applications* (10th ed.). Upper Saddle River, NJ: Pearson Education.

Geller, E., Russ, N., & Altomari, M. (1986). Naturalistic observations of beer drinking among college students. *Journal of Applied Behavior Analysis, 19*, 391–396.

Given, L. (2008). *The SAGE encyclopedia of qualitative research methods*. Thousand Oaks, CA: Sage.

Glaser, B. (1978). *Theoretical sensitivity: Advances in methodology of grounded theory*. Mill Valley, CA: Sociology Press.

Glaser, B., & Strauss, A. (1967). *Discovery of grounded theory: Strategies for qualitative research*. Chicago, IL: Aldine Transaction.

Golder, S., & Macy, M. (2011). Diurnal and seasonal mood vary with work, sleep, and day length across diverse cultures. *Science, 333*, 1878–1881.

Goulding, C. (2000). The museum environment and visitor experience. *Journal of Marketing Management, 15*, 647–672.

Goulding, C., Shankar, A., & Elliott, R. (2002). Working weeks, rave weekends: Identity fragmentation and the emergence of new communities. *Consumption Markets and Culture, 5*, 261–284.

Gratton, C., & Jones, I. (2010). *Research methods for sport studies* (2nd ed.). New York, NY: Routledge.

Green, L. (1976). *Research methods for evaluation of health education under adverse scientific conditions*. Paper presented at Extension Seminar in Health Education and Rural Health Care Research Forum, Phoenix, AZ.

Greene, J., Caracelli, V., & Graham, W. (1989). Toward a conceptual framework for mixed-method evaluation designs. *Educational Evaluation & Policy Analysis, 11*, 255–274.

Grinyer, A. (2009). The ethics of the secondary analysis and further use of qualitative data. *Social Research Update*. Retrieved from http://sru.soc.surrey.ac.uk/SRU56.pdf

Grosof, M., & Sardy, H. (1985). *A research primer for the social and behavioral sciences*. Orlando, FL: Academic Press.

Guba, E. (1990). The alternative paradigm dialog. In E. Guba (Ed.), *The paradigm dialog* (pp. 17–30). Newbury Park, CA: Sage.

Hall, J. (1984). *Instructor's manual to accompany Rosenthal/Rosnow: Essentials of behavioral research*. New York, NY: McGraw-Hill.

Hattie, J., Marsh, H., Neil, J., & Richards, G. (1997). Adventure education and Outward Bound: Out-of-class experiences that make a lasting difference. *Review of Education Research, 67*, 43–87.

Hebblethwaite, S., & Norris, J. (2010). "You don't want to hurt his feelings...": Family leisure as a context for intergenerational ambivalence. *Journal of Leisure Research, 42*, 489–508.

Hedrick, T., Bickman, L., & Rog, D. (1993). *Applied research design: A practical guide*. Newbury Park, CA: Sage.

Henderson, K. (1994). Theory application and development in recreation, park, and leisure research. *Journal of Park and Recreation Administration, 212*, 51–64.

Henderson, K., Presley, J., & Bialeschki, D. (2004). Theory in recreation and leisure research: Reflections from editors. *Leisure Sciences, 26*, 411–425.

Henry, G. (1990). *Practical sampling*. Newbury Park, CA: Sage.

Hocking, C., & Wallen, M. (1999). *Australian Occupational Therapy Journal manual for referees: Guidelines to assist referees and authors review manuscripts*. Melbourne, Australia: OT Australia.

Hopkins, D. (2008). *A teacher's guide to classroom research* (4th ed.). Maidenhead, England: Open University.

Hopkins, W. (1999). How to write a literature review. *Sportscience, 3*(1). Retrieved March 21, 2014, from http://www.sportsci.org/

Hopkins, W. (2004). An introduction to meta-analysis. *Sportscience, 8*, 20–24. Retrieved February 10, 2014, fromhttp://www.sportsci.org/

Hooyman, N., & Kiyak, A. (2011). *Social gerontology: A multidisciplinary perspective* (9th ed.). Upper Saddle River, NJ: Pearson Education.

How to write a dissertation or bedtime reading for people who do not have time to sleep. (n.d.). Retrieved March 17, 2014, from Purdue University Computer Science Department's website: http://www.cs.purdue.edu/homes/dec/essay.dissertation.html

Hoyle, R., Harris, M., & Judd, C. (2001). *Research methods in social relations* (7th ed.). New York, NY: Harcourt Brace.

Hurd, A. (2004). Competency development for board members in public park and recreation agencies. *Journal of Park and Recreation Administration, 22*, 43–61.

Institute of Medicine National Research Council. (2002). *Integrity in scientific research: Creating an environment that promotes responsible conduct*. Washington, DC: National Academic Press.

Inventor of the week: Roy Plunkett. (2000, July). Retrieved September 13, 2012, from Lemelson-MIT Program website: http://web.mit.edu/invent/iow/plunkett.html

Jacobsen, S., Carlton, J., & Monroe, M. (2012). Motivation and satisfaction of volunteers at a Florida natural resource agency. *Journal of Park and Recreation Administration, 30*, 51–67.

Janesick, V. (2003). *Stretching exercises for qualitative researchers* (2nd ed.). Thousand Oaks, CA: Sage.

Jankowicz, A. (2004). *Business research projects* (4th ed.). Independence, KY: Cengage Learning.

Jasso, G. (2001). Formal theory. In J. Turner (Ed.), *Handbook of sociological theory* (pp. 37–68). New York, NY: Springer.

Johnson, B., Dunlap, E., & Benoit, E. (2010). Organizing "mountains of words" for data analysis, both qualitative and quantitative. *Informa Health Care, 45*, 648–670.

Joiner, B. (1972). *How to read with a skeptical yet sympathetic eye.* Unpublished manuscript, Department of Statistics, Pennsylvania State University, State College.

Jones, C. (2004). Evaluating visual impacts of near-view rock climbing scenes. *Journal of Park and Recreation Administration, 22*, 39–49.

Jun, J., Kyle, G., & O'Leary, J. (2008). Constraints to art museum attendance. *Journal of Park and Recreation Administration, 26*, 40–61.

Kemeny, E., & Arnhold, R. (2012). "I can do it, you can do it": Collaborative practices for enhancing physical activity. *Therapeutic Recreation Journal, 46*, 268–283.

Kerlinger, F., & Lee, H. (1999). *Foundations of behavioral research* (4th ed.). Independence, KY: Cengage.

Kidder, L., & Judd, C. (2001). *Research methods in social relations* (7th ed.). New York, NY: Cengage Learning.

Kielhofner, G. (2006). Developing and evaluating quantitative data-collection instruments. In G. Kielhofner (Ed.), *Research in occupational therapy: Methods of inquiry for enhancing practice* (pp. 155–176). Philadelphia, PA: F.A. Davis.

Kielhofner, G., & Fossey, E. (2006). The range of research. In G. Kielhofner (Ed.), *Research in occupational therapy: Methods of inquiry for enhancing practice* (pp. 20–35). Philadelphia, PA: F.A. Davis.

Kielhofner, G., Fossey, E., & Taylor, R. (2006). Writing a research report. In G. Kielhofner (Ed.), *Research in occupational therapy: Methods of inquiry for enhancing practice* (pp. 578–590). Philadelphia, PA: F.A. Davis.

Kielhofner, G., & Takata, N. (1980). A study of mentally retarded persons: Applied research in occupational therapy. *American Journal of Occupational Therapy, 34*, 252–258.

Kinloch, G. (1977). *Sociological theory: Its development and major paradigms.* New York, NY: McGraw-Hill.

Kolcun, J. (2005). *Perceived constraints associated with participation in Gallaudet University's intramural sports program.* Unpublished master's thesis, Gallaudet University, Washington, DC.

Kornblau, B., & Burkhardt, N. (2012). *Ethics in rehabilitation: A clinical perspective* (2nd ed.). Thorofare, NJ: Slack.

Korstanje, M. (2010). The power of projective drawings: A new method for researching tourist experiences. *E-Review of Tourism Research, 8*, 85–101.

Krejcie, R., & Morgan, D. (1970). Determining the sample size for research activities. *Educational and Psychological Measurement, 30*, 607–610.

Kuhn, T. (2012). *The structure of scientific revolutions* (4th ed.). Chicago, IL: University of Chicago Press.

Kundey, S., De Los Reyes, A., Taglang, C., Allen, R., Molina, S., Royer, E., & German, R. (2010). Domesticated dogs (canis familiaris) react to what others can and cannot hear. *Applied Animal Behavior Science, 126*, 45–50.

Larson, R. (1978). Thirty years of research on the subjective well-being of older Americans. *The Journal of Gerontology, 33*, 109–125.

Lashua, B. (2010). 'Crossing the line': Addressing youth leisure, violence and socio-geographic exclusion through documentary film-making. *Leisure Studies, 29*, 193–206.

Lastrucci, C. (1963). *The scientific approach: Basic principles of the scientific method.* Cambridge, MA: Schenkman.

Le Compte, M., & Schensul, J. (2010). *Designing and conducting ethnographic research: An introduction* (2nd ed.). Lanham, MD: AltaMira Press.

Leedy, P., & Ormrod, J. (2012). *Practical research: Planning and design* (10th ed.). Upper Saddle, NJ: Pearson Merrill Prentice Hall.

Lewin, K. (1946). Action research and minority problems. *Social Issues, 2*, 34–46.

Lincoln, Y., Lynham, S., & Guba, E. (2011). Paradigmatic controversies, contradictions, and emerging confluences, revisited. In N. Denzin & Y. Lincoln (Eds.), *Handbook of qualitative research* (4th ed., pp. 97–128). Thousand Oaks, CA: Sage.

Linzey, G. (1959). On the classification of projective techniques. *Psychological Bulletin, 56*, 158–168.

Lipsey, M., & Wilson, D. (2001). *Practical meta-analysis.* Thousand Oaks, CA: Sage.

Lodico, M., Spaulding, D., & Voegtle, K. H. (2010). *Methods in educational research: From theory to practice* (2nd ed.). San Francisco, CA: Jossey-Bass.

Lofland, J., Snow, D., Anderson, L., & Lofland, L. (2006). *Analyzing social settings: A guide to qualitative observation and analysis* (4th ed.). Independence, KY: Cengage Learning.

Luborsky, M., & Lysack, C. (2006). Overview of qualitative research. In G. Kielhofner (Ed.), *Research in occupational therapy: Methods of inquiry for enhancing practice* (pp. 341–357). Philadelphia, PA: F.A. Davis.

Mactavish, J., & Schleien, S. (2000). Beyond qualitative and quantitative data linking: An example from a mixed method study of family recreation. *Therapeutic Recreation Journal, 34*, 154–163.

Mair, H. (2009). Club life: Third place and shared leisure in rural Canada. *Leisure Sciences, 31*, 450–465.

Martens, R., Vealey, R., & Burton, D. (1990). *Competitive anxiety in sport.* Champaign, IL: Human Kinetics.

Maslow, A. (1968). *Toward a psychology of being* (2nd ed.). New York, NY: Van Nostrand Reinhold.

Matchua, D. (1996). *The sociology of aging: An international perspective.* Needham Heights, MA: Allyn & Bacon.

Mauch, J., & Park, N. (2003). *Guide to the successful thesis and dissertation: A handbook for students and faculty* (5th ed.). New York, NY: Marcel Dekker.

Maugh, T. (2010, September 9). Demonstrated cancer benefit of vitamin D. *Washington Post*, p. B7.

McCrone, W. (2002). Law and ethics in mental health and deafness. In V. Guttman (Ed.), *Ethics in mental health and deafness* (pp. 38–51). Washington, DC: Gallaudet University Press.

McMillan, J., & Schumacker, S. (2009). *Research in education: Evidence-based inquiry* (7th ed.). Upper Saddle, NJ: Pearson Merrill Prentice Hall.

Melcher, S. (1999). *Introduction to writing goals and objectives: A manual for recreation therapy students and entry-level professionals.* State College, PA: Venture.

Merriam, S. (2009). *Qualitative research: A guide to design and implementation.* San Francisco, CA: Jossey-Bass.

Miles, M., & Huberman, A. (1994). *Qualitative data analysis: A sourcebook of new methods.* Beverly Hills, CA: Sage.

Miles, M., Huberman, A., & Saldana, J. (2013). *Qualitative data analysis: A methods sourcebook* (3rd ed.). Thousand Oaks, CA: Sage.

Milkovich, G., Newman, J., & Gerhart, B. (2013). *Compensation* (12th ed.). Boston, MA: McGraw-Hill Irwin.

Miller, J., & Glassner, B. (1997). The "inside" and the "outside": Finding realities in interviews. In D. Silverman (Ed.), *Qualitative research: Theory, method and practice* (2nd ed., pp. 125–139). London, England: Sage.

Miller, K., Schleien, S., & Lausier, J. (2009). Search for best practices in inclusive recreation: Programmatic findings. *Therapeutic Recreation Journal, 43,* 27–41.

Mills, C. (1959). *The sociological imagination.* New York, NY: Oxford University Press.

Moe, A. (2012). Beyond the belly: An appraisal of Middle Eastern dance (aka belly dance) as leisure. *Journal of Leisure Research, 44,* 201–233.

Moeller, G., Mescher, M., More, T., & Shafer, E. (1980a). The informal interview as a technique for recreation research. *Journal of Leisure Research, 12,* 174–182.

Moeller, G., Mescher, M., More, T., & Shafer, E. (1980b). A response to 'a second look at the informal interview'. *Journal of Leisure Research, 12,* 187–188.

Monette, D., Sullivan, T., & DeJong, C. (2008). *Applied social research: Tool for human services* (7th ed.). Belmont, CA: Thompson Wadsworth.

Moustakas, C. (1994). *Phenomological research methods.* Thousand Oaks, CA: Sage.

Neuendorf, K. (2001). *The content analysis guidebook.* Thousand Oaks, CA: Sage.

Neuman, W. (2009). *Social research methods: Qualitative and quantitative approaches* (4th ed.). Upper Saddle River, NJ: Pearson Education.

Neutens, J., & Rubinson, L. (2013). *Research techniques for the health sciences* (5th ed.). San Francisco, CA: Benjamin Cummings.

Nicol, A., & Pexman, P. (2010a). *Displaying your findings: A practical guide for creating figures, posters, and presentations* (6th ed.). Washington, DC: American Psychological Association.

Nicol, A., & Pexman, P. (2010b). *Presenting your findings: A practical guide for creating tables* (6th ed.). Washington, DC: American Psychological Association.

O'Guinn, R., & Faber, R. (1989). Compulsive buying: A phenomenological exploration. *Journal of Consumer Research, 16,* 147–157.

O'Toole, J., & Beckett, D. (2014). *Educational research: Creative thinking & doing* (2nd ed.). South Melbourne, Australia: Oxford University Press.

Padgett, D. (2008). *Qualitative methods in social work research* (2nd ed.). Thousand Oaks, CA: Sage.

Pan, L. (2008). *Preparing literature reviews: Qualitative and quantitative approaches* (3rd ed.). Glendale, CA: Pyrczak.

Palen, L., Caldwell, L., Smith, E., Gleeson, S., & Patrick, M. (2011). A mixed-method analysis of free-time involvement and motivation among adolescents in Cape Town, South Africa. *Loisir, 35,* 227–252.

Patten, M. (2012). *Understanding research methods: An overview of the essentials* (8th ed.). Los Angeles, CA: Pyrczak.

Patton, M. (1987). *Creative evaluation* (2nd ed.). Newbury Park, CA: Sage.

Patton, M. (2008). *Utilization-focused evaluation* (4th ed.). Thousand Oaks, CA: Sage.

Peacock, N., & Paul-Ward, A. (2006). Contemporary tools for managing and analyzing qualitative data. In G. Kielhoner (Ed.), *Research in occupational therapy: Methods of inquiry for enhancing practice* (pp. 358–371). Philadelphia, PA: F.A. Davis.

Peat, J., Mellis, C., Williams, K., & Xuan, W. (2002). *Health science research: A handbook of quantitative methods.* London, England: Sage.

Petrick, J., Backman, S., Bixler, R., & Norman, W. (2001). Analysis of golfer motivations and constraints by experience use history. *Journal of Leisure Research, 33,* 56–70.

Pettengill, P., Manning, R., Anderson, L., Valliere, W., & Reigner, N. (2012). Measuring and managing the quality of transportation at Acadia National Park. *Journal of Park and Recreation Administration, 30,* 68–84.

Polonsky, M., & Waller, D. (2010). *Designing and managing a research project: A business student's guide* (2nd ed.). Thousand Oaks, CA: Sage.

Prescott, P., & Soeken, K. (1989). The potential uses of pilot work. *Nursing Research, 38,* 60–62.

Pringle, P. (2012). *Experiment eleven: Dark secrets behind the discovery of a wonder drug.* New York, NY: Bloomsbury.

Protection of Human Subjects, 45 C.F.R. § 46 (2009).

Pyrczak, F. (2009). *Success at statistics: A workbook with humor* (4th ed.). Glendale, CA: Pyrczak.

Range, F., Horn, L., Viranyi, Z., & Huber, L. (2009). The absence of reward induces inequity aversion in dogs. *Proceedings of the National Academy of Sciences in the United States of America, 106,* 340–345.

Rappaport, J. (2000). Community narratives: Tales of terror and joy. *American Journal of Community Psychology, 28,* 1–24.

Rea, L., & Parker, R. (2005). *Designing and conducting survey research: A comprehensive guide* (3rd ed.). San Francisco, CA: Jossey-Bass.

Reese, H., & Fremouw, W. (1984). Normal and normative ethics in behavioral science. *American Psychologist, 39,* 863–876.

Reichardt, C., & Mark, M. (1998). Quasi-experimentation. In L. Bickman & D. Rog (Eds.), *Handbook of applied social research methods* (pp. 193–228). Thousand Oaks, CA: Sage.

Reifman, A., Larick, R., & Fein, S. (1991). Temper and temperature on the diamond: The heat-aggression relationship in Major League Baseball. *Personality and Social Psychology Bulletin, 17,* 580–585.

Reissman, C. (1993). *Narrative analysis.* Newbury Park, CA: Sage.

Richards, L., & Morse, J. (2013). *Read me first for a user's guide to qualitative methods* (2nd ed.). Thousand Oaks, CA: Sage.

Richardson, L. (1990). Narrative and sociology. *Journal of Contemporary Ethnography, 19,* 116–135.

Riddick, C. (1985a). Health, aquariums, and the non-institutionalized elderly. *Marriage and Family Review, 8,* 163–173.

Riddick, C. (1985b). Life satisfaction determinants of older males and females. *Leisure Sciences, 7,* 47–64.

Riddick, C. (2010). Gerontology-leisure research: The past and the future. In B. Humberstone (Ed.), *Third age and leisure research: Principles and practice* (LSA Publication No. 108, pp. 1–20). Great Britain: Leisure Studies Association.

Riddick, C., DeSchriver, M., & Weissinger, E. (1991). *A methodological review of research in Journal of Leisure Research from 1983 through 1987.* Paper presented at the National Recreation & Park Association's Leisure Research Symposium, Baltimore, MD.

Riddick, C., Drogin, E., & Spector, S. (1987). The impact of videogame play in the emotional wellbeing of senior center participants. *The Gerontologist, 27,* 425–427.

Riddick, C., & Gonder, D. (1994). An examination of the life satisfaction and importance of leisure in the lives of older female retirees: A comparison of Blacks to Caucasians. *Journal of Leisure Research, 26,* 75–87.

Riddick, C., & Keller, J. (1991). The benefits of therapeutic recreation in gerontology. In C. Coyle, W. Kinney, B. Riley, & J. Shank (Eds.), *Benefits of therapeutic recreation: A consensus view* (pp. 151–204). Ravensdale, CA: Idyll Arbor.

Roberts, N. (2003). *Ethnic minority visitors and non-visitors: An examination of constraints regarding outdoor recreation participation in Rocky Mountain National Park* (Unpublished doctoral dissertation). Colorado State University, Fort Collins, CO. Retrieved from Dissertation Abstracts International. (No. 3114692)

Robins, D., Sanders, C., & Cahill, S. (1991). Dogs and their people: Pet-facilitated interaction in a public setting. *Journal of Contemporary Ethnography, 20,* 3–25.

Robson, C. (2011). *Real-world research: A resource for social scientists and practitioner-researchers* (3rd ed.). West Sussex, United Kingdom: John Wiley and Sons.

Rojek, C. (1993). Disney culture. *Leisure Studies, 12,* 121–135.

Rosenthal, R., & Rosnow, R. (2007). *Essentials of behavioral research: Methods and data analysis* (3rd ed.). New York, NY: McGraw-Hill.

Rosnow, R., & Rosnow, M. (2011). *Writing papers in psychology* (9th ed.). Independence, KY: Cengage Learning.

Rossi, P., Lipsey, M., & Freeman, H. (2004). *Evaluation: A systematic approach* (7th ed.). Thousand Oaks, CA: Sage.

Rowe, D., & Brown, P. (1994). Promoting women's sport: Theory, policy, and practice. *Leisure Studies, 13,* 97–110.

Rubin, H., & Rubin, I. (2011). *Qualitative interviewing: The art of hearing data* (3rd ed.). Thousand Oaks, CA: Sage.

Russell, M. (2012). *Travel time use on public transport: What passengers do and how it affects their wellbeing* (Doctoral thesis, University of Otago, New Zealand).

Russell, R. (1991). Observation of a hotel lobby. Unpublished personal field notes.

Russell, R. (2004). Observation of a hotel lobby. Unpublished personal field notes.

Russell, R. (2012). *Pastimes: The context of contemporary leisure* (5th ed.). Champaign, IL: Sagamore.

Sale, J., Lohfeld, L., & Brazil, K. (2002). Revisiting the quantitative–qualitative debate: Implications for mixed-methods research. *Quality & Quantity, 36,* 43–53.

Salkind, N. (2013). *Statistics for people who (think they) hate statistics* (5th ed.). Thousand Oaks, CA: Sage.

Schouten, J., & Alexander, T. (1995). Subcultures of consumption: An ethnography of new bikers. *Journal of Consumer Research, 22,* 43–62.

Schutt, R. (2006). *Investigating the social world: The process and practice of research* (5th ed.). Thousand Oaks, CA: Pine Forge Press.

Schutt, R. (2011). *Investigating the social world: The process and practice of research* (7th ed.). Thousand Oaks, CA: Pine Forge Press.

Schwab, D. (2005). *Research methods for organizational studies* (2nd ed.). Mahwah, NJ: Lawrence Erlbaum.

Scitovsky, T. (1992). *The joyless economy: The psychology of human satisfaction* (Rev. ed.). New York, NY: Oxford University Press.

Shannon, D., & Davenport, M. (2001). *Using SPSS to solve statistical problems: A self-instructional guide.* Upper Saddle River, NJ: Prentice Hall.

Siderelis, C., Naber, M., & Leung, Y. (2010). The influence of site design and resource conditions on outdoor recreation demand: A mountain biking case study. *Journal of Leisure Research, 42,* 573–590.

Slavin, R. (2011). *Educational psychology: Theory and practice* (10th ed.). Upper Saddle River, NJ: Prentice Hall.

Smith, C., Santucci, D., Xu, S., Cox, A., & Henderson, K. (2012). "I love my job, but...": A narrative analysis of women's perceptions of their careers in parks and recreation. *Journal of Leisure Research, 44,* 52–69.

Snow, D., Robinson, C., & McCall, P. (1991). "Cooling out": Men in singles bars and nightclubs: Observations on the interpersonal survival strategies of women in public places. *Journal of Contemporary Ethnography, 19,* 423–449.

Soley, L., & Smith, A. (2008). *Projective techniques for social science and business research.* Milwaukee, WI: Southshore Press.

Solomon, D. (2001). Conducting web-based surveys. *Practical Assessment, Research, & Evaluation, 7*(19). Retrieved January 27, 2014, from http://Pareonline.net/getvn.asp?v=7&n=19

Spradley, J. (1979). *The ethnographic interview.* New York, NY: Holt, Rinehart, and Winston.

Spradley, J. (1980). *Participant observation.* Chicago, IL: Holt, Rinehart, and Winston.

Springer, K. (2010). *Educational research: A contextual approach.* Hoboken, NJ: John Wiley and Sons.

Stangor, C. (2011). *Research methods for the behavioral sciences* (4th ed.). Boston, MA: Houghton Mifflin.

Stewart, D., & Shamdasani, P. (2014). *Focus groups: Theory and practice* (3rd ed.). Thousand Oaks, CA: Sage.

Straw, W. (1999). Characterizing rock music culture: The case of heavy metal. In S. During (Ed.), *The cultural studies reader* (2nd ed., pp. 451–461). New York, NY: Routledge.

Strike, K., & Ternasky, P. (1993). Introduction: Ethics in educational settings. In K. Strike & P. Ternasky (Eds.), *Ethics for professionals in education: Perspectives for preparation and practice* (pp. 1-9). New York, NY: Teachers College Press.

Stumbo, N. (1985). Knowledge of professional and ethical behavior in therapeutic recreation services. *Therapeutic Recreation Journal, 19,* 59–67.

Sturges, J., & Hanrahan, K. (2004). Comparing telephone and face-to-face qualitative interviewing: A research note. *Qualitative Research, 4,* 107–118.

Suter, W. (2011). *Introduction to educational research: A critical thinking approach* (2nd ed.). Thousand Oaks, CA: Sage.

Swigonski, M. (1994). Ethics and the quest for professionalization. *Therapeutic Recreation Journal, 36,* 314–334.

Sylvester, C. (2002). Ethics and the quest for professionalization. *Therapeutic Recreation Journal, 36,* 314–334.

Sylvester, C., Voelkl, J., & Ellis, G. (2001). *Therapeutic recreation programming: Theory and practice.* State College, PA: Venture.

Szabo, A. (2003). The acute effects of humor and exercise on mood and anxiety. *Journal of Leisure Research, 35,* 152–167.

Tainsky, S., Salag, S., & Santos, C. (2012). Estimating attendance for the Ultimate Fighting Championship: A demand theory approach. *International Journal of Sport Management & Marketing, 11,* 206–224.

Taniguchi, S., Widmer, M., Duerden, M., & Draper, C. (2009). The attributes of effective field staff in wilderness programs: Changing youths' perspectives of being "cool." *Therapeutic Recreation Journal, 43,* 11–26.

Taylor, R., & Kielhofner, G. (2006). Collecting data. In G. Kielhofner (Ed.), *Research in occupational therapy: Methods of inquiry for enhancing practice* (pp. 530–547). Philadelphia, PA: F.A. Davis.

Tenenbaum, G., & Eklund, R. (2007). *Handbook of sport psychology* (3rd ed.). New York, NY: John Wiley and Sons.

Thomas, A. (2004). *Research skills for management studies.* New York, NY: Routledge.

Thomas, J., & French, K. (1986). The use of meta-analysis in exercise and sport: A tutorial. *Research Quarterly for Exercise and Sport, 57,* 196–204.

Thomas, J., Nelson, J., & Silverman, S. (2011). *Research methods in physical activity* (6th ed.). Champaign, IL: Human Kinetics.

Tirone, S., & Goodberry, A. (2011). Leisure, biculturalism, and second-generation Canadians. *Journal of Leisure Research, 43,* 427–444.

Torres, R., Preskill, H., & Piontek, M. (2005). *Evaluation strategies for communicating and reporting: Enhancing learning in organizations* (2nd ed.). Thousand Oaks, CA: Sage.

Transitional words & phrases. (n.d.). Retrieved April 16, 2014, from Study Guides and Strategies website: http://www.studygs.net/wrtstr6.htm

Trochim, W. (2006). Structure of research. Retrieved June 17, 2012, from Research Methods Knowledge Base website: http://www.socialresearchmethods.net/kb/strucres.php

Trochim, W. (2005). *Research methods: The concise knowledge base.* Marion, OH: Atomic Dog.

Turner, V. (2001). *From ritual to theatre: The human seriousness of play.* New York, NY: Performing Arts Journal Publications.

Tyson, L. (2006). *Critical theory today: A user-friendly guide* (2nd ed.). London, England: Routledge.

University of Chicago Press. (2010). *The Chicago manual of style: The essential guide for writers, editors, and publishers* (6th ed.). Chicago, IL: Author.

University of Leicester. (2009). Using visual aids. Retrieved April 6, 2014, from http://www2.le.ac.uk/offices/ld/resources/presentation/visual-aids

Van Dalen, D. (1979). *Understanding educational research* (4th ed.). New York, NY: McGraw-Hill.

Van Teijlingen, E., & Hundley, V. (2001). The importance of pilot studies. *Social Research Update, 35,* 1–4.

Veal, A. (2011). *Research methods for leisure and tourism: A practical guide* (4th ed.). Upper Saddle River, NJ: Prentice Hall.

Velasquez, C., Shanks, T., & Meyer, M. (2013). Thinking ethically: A framework for moral decision making. Retrieved September 1, 2013, from Santa Clara University website: http://www.scu.edu/ethics/publications/iie/v7n1/thinking.html

Verdnell, S., & Scagnoli, N. (2013). Data displays in qualitative research. *International Journal of Qualitative Methods, 12,* 213–234.

Walizer, M., & Wienir, P. (2000). *Research methods and analysis: Searching for relationships.* Boston, MA: Addison-Wesley.

Walker, A., & Rosalind, K. (1989). Photo albums: Images of time and reflections of self. *Qualitative Sociology, 12,* 183–214.

Walton, G., Schleien, S., Brake, L., Trovato, C., & Oates, T. (2012). Photovoice: A collaborative methodology giving voice to underserved populations seeking community inclusion. *Therapeutic Recreation Journal, 46,* 168–178.

Wann, D. (1997). *Sport psychology.* Upper Saddle River, NJ: Prentice Hall.

Webb, E., Campbell, D., Schwartz, R., & Sechrest, L. (1981). *Nonreactive measures in the social sciences* (2nd ed.). New York, NY: Houghton Mifflin.

Weber, R., & Stolley, K. (2011). Transitional devices. Retrieved September 7, 2013, from Purdue Online Writing Lab website: http://owl.english.purdue.edu/owl/resource/574/02/

Weisberg, J., Krosnick, J., & Bowen, B. (1996). *An introduction to survey research, polling, and data analysis.* Thousand Oaks, CA: Sage.

Weiss, C. (1972). *Evaluation research: Methods of assessing program effectiveness.* Englewood Cliffs, NJ: Prentice Hall.

Weybright, E., Dattillo, J., & Rusch, F. (2010). Effects of an interactive video game (Nintendo Wii™) on older women with mild cognitive impairment. *Therapeutic Recreation Journal, 44,* 271–287.

Wheatley, K., & Flexner, W. (1988). Dimensions that make focus groups work. *Marketing News, 22,* 16–17.

White, D., Aquino, J., Budruk, M., & Golub, A. (2011). Visitors' experiences of traditional and alternative transportation in Yosemite National Park. *Journal of Park and Recreation Administration, 29,* 38–57.

Wilder, L. (1999). *Seven steps to fearless speaking.* New York, NY: John Wiley and Sons.

Witt, P., & Ellis, G. (1985). *Leisure diagnostic battery.* State College, PA: Venture.

Wolcott, H. (1999). *Ethnography: A way of seeing* (2nd ed.). Lanham, MD: AltraMira.

Yang, H. (2004). Establishing the reliability of the smiley face assessment scale: Test–retest. *LARNet: The Cyber Journal of Applied Leisure and Recreation Research.* Retrieved July 23, 2013, from http://larnet.org/2002-10.html

Yates, B. (1996). *Analyzing costs, procedures, processes, and outcomes in human services: An introduction.* Thousand Oaks, CA: Sage.

Yin, R. (2014). *Case study research: Design and methods* (5th ed.). Thousand Oaks, CA: Sage.

Zabriskie, R. (2003). Measurement basics: A must for TR professionals today. *Therapeutic Recreation Journal, 37,* 330–338.

Zajonc, R. (1965). Social facilitation. *Science, 249,* 269–274.

Zuckerman, M. (1980). *Sensation seeking: Beyond the optimal level of arousal.* Mahwah, NJ: Lawrence Erlbaum.

APPENDIX 1: SELECTED REFEREED JOURNALS

RELATED TO RECREATION, PARKS, SPORT, AND TOURISM

Adapted Physical Activity Quarterly
American Journal of Medicine and Sports
American Journal of Sports Medicine
Annals of Leisure Research
Annals of Tourism Research
Asian Journal of Exercise and Sports Science
Asian Journal of Physical Education & Recreation
Asian Journal of Sports Medicine
Athletic Insight: The Online Journal of Sport Psychology
Australian Council for Health, Physical Education, & Recreation Healthy Lifestyles Journal
Australian Journal of Outdoor Education
Australian Leisure Management
Australian Parks and Leisure
British Journal of Physical Education
British Journal of Sports Medicine
California Association for Physical Education, Recreation, and Dance
Camping Magazine
Case Studies in Sport Management
China Tourism Journal
Culture, Sport, and Society
Current Therapeutic Research
Cyber Journal of Sports Marketing
Dance Research Journal
European Journal of Sport Science
European Physical Education Review
European Sport Management Quarterly
European Sports History Review
Gaming Research & Review Journal
Hospitality Education & Research Journal
Hospitality Research Journal
Illuminare: A Student Journal in Recreation, Parks, and Tourism Studies
International Journal of Aquatic Research and Education
International Journal of Computer Science in Sport
International Journal of Contemporary Hospitality Management
International Journal of Culture, Tourism, and Hospitality Research
International Journal of Event and Festival Management
International Journal of Event Management Research
The International Journal of the History of Sport
International Journal of Hospitality Management
International Journal of Hospitality and Tourism Administration
International Journal of Sport Finance
International Journal of Sport Psychology
International Journal of Sport Sociology
International Journal of Sports Marketing & Sponsorship
International Journal of Sports Science & Coaching
International Journal of Tourism & Hospitality Research
International Journal of Tourism Perspectives
International Journal of Tourism Research
International Leisure Review
International Quarterly of Sport Science
International Review for the Sociology of Sport
Japanese Journal of Physical Fitness and Sport
Journal of Adventure Education and Outdoor Learning
Journal of Aging and Physical Activity
Journal of Applied Biomechanics
Journal of Applied Hospitality Management
Journal of Applied Recreation Research
Journal of Applied Sport Management: Research That Matters
Journal of Applied Sport Psychology
Journal of Canadian Association for Leisure Studies
Journal of China Tourism Research
Journal of Clinical Sport Psychology
Journal of Combat Sports and Martial Arts
Journal of Comparative Physical Education & Sport
Journal of Convention & Event Tourism
Journal of Convention & Exhibition Management
Journal of Ecotourism
Journal of Environmental Education
Journal of Experiential Education
Journal of Facility Planning, Design, and Management
Journal of Gambling Studies
Journal of Health, Physical Education, Recreation, and Dance
Journal of Heritage Tourism
Journal of Hospitality and Leisure for the Elderly
Journal of Hospitality & Leisure Marketing
Journal of Hospitality Financial Management
Journal of Hospitality, Leisure, Sport, & Tourism Education
Journal of Hospitality Marketing, & Management
Journal of Hospitality & Tourism Education
Journal of Human Movement Studies
Journal of Human Resources in Hospitality & Tourism
Journal of Human Sport and Exercise
Journal of Intercollegiate Sport
Journal of the International Academy of Hospitality Research
Journal of International Hospitality, Leisure, & Tourism Management
Journal of Interpretation
Journal of Leisurability
Journal of Leisure Property
Journal of Leisure Research
Journal of Leisure Sciences
Journal of Outdoor Recreation, Education, and Leadership
Journal of Park and Recreation Administration
Journal of the Philosophy of Sport
Journal of Physical Activity and Health
Journal of Physical Education and Recreation (Hong Kong)
Journal of Physical Education, Recreation, and Dance

Journal of Quantitative Analysis in Sports
Journal of Sport Behavior
Journal of Sport Economics
Journal of Sport and Exercise Psychology
Journal of Sport History
Journal of Sport Management
Journal of Sport Psychology
Journal of Sport Rehabilitation
Journal of Sport Sciences
Journal of Sport and Social Issues
Journal of Sport & Society
Journal of Sport Tourism
Journal of Sports Medicine and Physical Fitness
Journal of Sports Science and Medicine: An On-Line Journal Alternative
Journal of Sports Sciences
Journal of Strength and Conditioning Research
Journal of Sustainable Tourism
Journal of Swimming Research
Journal of Teaching in Physical Education
Journal of Teaching in Travel & Tourism
Journal of Tourism and Cultural Change
Journal of Tourism Studies
Journal of Travel Research
Journal of Travel & Tourism Marketing
Journal of Travel & Tourism Research
LARNet: The Cyber Journal of Applied Leisure and Recreation Research
Leisure/Loisir: Journal of the Canadian Association for Leisure Studies
Leisure Options: Australian Journal of Leisure and Recreation
Leisure & Recreation Management
Leisure Sciences
Leisure Studies
Loisir et Societe/Society and Leisure
Managing Environments for Leisure & Recreation
Medicine & Science in Sports & Exercise
New Zealand Journal of Outdoor Education
Olympic Review/Revue Olympique
Palaestra: Forum of Sport, Physical Education, and Recreation for Those With Disabilities
Park World
Parks and Recreation
Physical Activity and Health
Play and Cultural Studies
Psychology of Sport and Exercise
Recreation and Park Law Reporter
Recreation Research Review
Recreational Sports Journal
Research in Outdoor Education
Research Quarterly for Exercise and Sport
Scandinavian Journal of Hospitality and Tourism
Schole: A Journal of Leisure Studies and Recreation Education
Soccer and Society
Society & Leisure
Sociology of Sport Journal
Sociology of Sport Online (http://physed.otago.ac.nz/sosol/home.html)
Sport, Education, and Society
Sport, Exercise, and Performance Psychology
Sport History Review
Sport Management Education Journal
Sport Marketing
Sport and Place
The Sport Psychologist
Sport Science Review
Sporting Traditions
Sports Law Bulletin
Sports, Parks, and Recreation Law Reporter
Sportscience
Therapeutic Recreation Journal
Tourism and Hospitality Research
Tourism: An International Interdisciplinary Journal
Tourism Management
Tourism Recreation Research
Tourism Research Journal
Tourism Review International
Visitor Studies
Women in Sport & Physical Activity Journal
World Leisure Journal
World Leisure & Recreation Association Journal

OTHER PROFESSIONAL JOURNALS

Adapted Physical Activity Quarterly
Age & Ageing
Ageing International
Ageing Research Reviews
Ageing & Society
Aging
Aging & Mental Health
American College of Sports Medicine Health and Fitness Journal
American Educational Research Journal
American Journal of Art Therapy
American Journal of Sociology
American Sociological Review
Anthropology and Education Journal
Applied Behavioral Measurement
Assessment
Basic and Applied Social Psychology
Behavior Assessment
Behavior Research and Therapy
Behavior Therapy
Biology of Sport
British Journal of Educational Studies
British Journal of Psychology
British Journal of Social and Clinical Psychology
British Journal of Sociology
Canadian Education and Research Digest
Canadian Journal of Aging
Canadian Journal of Behavioural Science
Canadian Journal of Experimental Psychology
Canadian Journal of Forest Research
Canadian Review of Sociology and Anthropology
Child and Adolescent Social Work Journal
Child Development
Clinical Journal of Sport Medicine
Clinical Sociology Review
Cross-Cultural Research
Cultural Anthropology

Cultural Diversity and Ethnic Minority Psychology
Current Aging Science
Current Sociology
Disability, Handicap, & Society
Disability & Rehabilitation
Disability & Society
Educational Administration Quarterly
Educational and Psychological Measurement
Educational Gerontology
European Journal of Physical Education
European Review of Aging and Physical Activity
Evaluation Family Practice
Experimental Aging Research
The Gerontologist
Global Journal of Health Education and Promotion
The Global Journal of Health and Physical Education Pedagogy
Health Psychology
Hispanic Journal of Behavioral Sciences
Hospitality & Society
Human Dimensions of Wildlife
International Journal of Aging and Human Development
International Journal of Behavioral Development
International Journal of Coaching Science
International Journal of Heritage Studies
International Journal of Mental Health
International Journal of Performance Analysis in Sport
International Journal of Rehabilitation Research
International Journal of Sociology and Social Policy
International Journal of Sports Medicine
International Journal of Therapy & Rehabilitation
International Journal of Yoga
International Review of Education
International Social Work
Journal of Active Aging
Journal of Adolescence
Journal of Adolescent Research
Journal of Aging & Health
Journal of Aging and Physical Activity
Journal of Aging & Social Policy
Journal of Aging Studies
Journal of the American School Health Association
Journal of Applied Behavior Analysis
Journal of Applied Behavioral Science
Journal of Applied Gerontology
Journal of Applied Psychology
Journal of Applied Social Psychology: Asian
Journal of Applied Social Psychology: British
Journal of Applied Social Psychology: European
Journal of Applied Sport Psychology
Journal of Asian and African Studies
Journal of Behavioral Assessment and Psychopathology
Journal of Biomechanics
Journal of Black Psychology
Journal of Black Studies
Journal of Clinical Psychology
Journal of Comparative Psychology
Journal of Consulting and Clinical Psychology
Journal of Consumer Research
Journal of Contemporary Ethnography
Journal of Counseling and Development
Journal of Cross-Cultural Psychology
Journal of Disability Policy Studies
Journal of Educational Measurement
Journal of Educational Psychology
Journal of Educational Research
Journal of Environmental Psychology
Journal of Experiential Learning
Journal of Experimental Analysis of Behavior
Journal of Experimental Education
Journal of Experimental Psychology: Applied
Journal of Experimental Psychology: General
Journal of Experimental Social Psychology
Journal of Facility Planning, Design, and Management
Journal of Gender Studies
Journal of Gerontological Social Work
Journal of Gerontology: Series B Psychological Sciences and Social Sciences
Journal of Happiness Studies
Journal of Health Education
Journal of Health Education Teaching Techniques
Journal of Health Promotion
Journal of Interdisciplinary Studies
Journal of Marketing Research
Journal of Marriage and the Family
Journal of Motor Behavior
Journal of Music Teacher Education
Journal of Nonprofit Education and Leadership
Journal of Nonverbal Behavior
Journal of Personal and Social Relations
Journal of Personality Assessment
Journal of Personality and Social Psychology
Journal of Psychology
Journal of Rehabilitation
Journal of Research on Crime and Delinquency
Journal of Research and Development in Education
Journal of Research in Science Teaching
Journal of Social and Clinical Psychology
Journal of Social Issues
Journal of Social Psychology
Journal of Social Service Research
Journal of Sport Rehabilitation
Journal of Sports Medicine and Physical Fitness
Journal of Sports Science and Medicine
Journal of Strength and Conditioning Research
Journal of Swimming Research
Journal of Teaching in Physical Education
Journal of Therapeutic Horticulture
Journal of Wildlife Management
Journal of Women & Aging
Measurement and Evaluation in Counseling and Development
Measurement in Physical Education and Exercise
Measurement in Physical Education & Exercise Science
Media, Culture, & Society
Medicine & Science in Sports & Exercise
Pediatric Exercise Science
Perceptual and Motor Skills
Perspectives in Public Health
Physical Education and Sport Pedagogy
The Physical Educator
Physical Therapy in Sport
Psychological Assessment
Psychological Bulletin
Psychological Review

Psychology and Aging
Psychology of Women Quarterly
Public Library of Science (PLOS) Medicine
Qualitative Health Journal
Qualitative Inquiries in Music Therapy
Qualitative Inquiry
Qualitative Research
Qualitative Sociology
Research in Sports Medicine
Research on Aging
Research Quarterly for Exercise and Sport
Review of Educational Research
Scandinavian Journal of Medicine & Science in Sports
Science and Sports
Sex Roles
Social Forces
Social Problems
Social Psychology Quarterly
Sociological Perspectives
Sociological Quarterly
Sociology of Education
Sports Medicine
Strength and Conditioning Journal
Theory and Research in Social Education
Wellness Perspectives
Women Studies Quarterly
Youth and Society

PROGRAM EVALUATION

American Journal of Evaluation (formerly Evaluation Practice)
Canadian Journal of Program Evaluation
Evaluation: The International Journal of Theory, Research, and Practice
Evaluation and Program Planning
Evaluation Review: A Journal of Applied Social Research
Journal of Policy Analysis and Management
New Directions for Evaluation
Practical Assessment Research and Evaluation
The Qualitative Report

APPENDIX 2: REFERENCES FOR QUANTITATIVE, QUALITATIVE, AND MIXED-METHODS APPROACHES AND RESEARCH METHODS

QUANTITATIVE APPROACHES

Recreation and Leisure

Burnett-Wolle, S., & Godbey, G. (2007). Refining research on older adults' leisure: Implications of selection, optimization, and compensation and socioemotional selectivity theories. *Journal of Leisure Research, 39*, 498–513.

Gomez, E., Freidt, B., Hill, E., Goldenberg, M., & Hill, L. (2010). Appalachian Trail hiking motivations and means-end theory: Theory, management, and practice. *Journal of Outdoor Recreation, Education, and Leadership, 2*, 260–284.

Roberts, K. (2011). Leisure: The importance of being inconsequential. *Leisure Studies, 30*, 5–20.

Rojek, C. (2005). *Leisure theory: Principles and practice.* New York, NY: Palgrave Macmillan.

Rojek, C. (2010). *The labour of leisure: The culture of free time.* Thousand Oaks, CA: Sage.

Stenseng, F., Rise, J., & Kraft, P. (2011). The dark side of leisure: Obsessive passion and its covariates and outcomes. *Leisure Studies, 30*, 49–62.

Thomson, P., & Sefton-Green, J. (Eds.). (2011). *Researching creative learning: Methods and issues.* London, United Kingdom: Routledge.

White, D. (2008). A structural model of leisure constraints negotiation in outdoor recreation. *Leisure Sciences: An Interdisciplinary Journal, 30*, 342–359.

Sport and Physical Activity

Beaton, A., & Funk, D. (2008). An evaluation of theoretical frameworks for studying physically active leisure. *Leisure Sciences: An Interdisciplinary Journal, 30*, 53–70.

Beaton, A., Funk, D., & Alexandris, K. (2009). Operationalizing a theory of participation in physically active leisure. *Journal of Leisure Research, 41*, 177–203.

Palacios-Huerta, I. (2014). *Beautiful game theory: How soccer can help economics.* Princeton, NJ: Princeton University Press.

Tavares, L., Plotnikoff, R., & Loucaides, C. (2009). Social-cognitive theories for predicting physical activity behaviours of employed women with and without young children. *Psychology, Health & Medicine, 14*, 129–142.

Tourism

Zhang, H., Fu, X., Cai, L., & Lu, L. (2014). Destination image and tourist loyalty: A meta-analysis. *Tourism Management, 40*, 213–223.

QUALITATIVE APPROACHES

General

Birks, M., & Mills, J. (2011). *Grounded theory: A practical guide.* Thousand Oaks, CA: Sage.

Calhoun, C., Gertis, J., Moody, J., Pfaff, S., & Virk, I. (Eds.). (2012). *Contemporary sociological theory* (3rd ed.). Malden, MA: Wiley-Blackwell.

Charmaz, K. (2014). *Constructing grounded theory: A practical guide through qualitative analysis* (2nd ed.). Thousand Oaks, CA: Sage.

Corbin, J., & Strauss, A. (2008). *Basics of qualitative research: Techniques and procedures for developing grounded theory* (3rd ed.). Thousand Oaks, CA: Sage.

Denzin, N., & Lincoln, Y. (Eds.). (2011). *The SAGE handbook of qualitative research* (4th ed.). Thousand Oaks, CA: Sage.

Smith, J., Flowers, P., & Larkin, M. (2009). *Interpretative phenomenological analysis: Theory, method and research.* Thousand Oaks, CA: Sage.

Recreation and Leisure

Lockstone-Binney, L., Holmes, K., Smith, K., & Baum, T. (2010). Volunteers and volunteering in leisure: Social science perspectives. *Leisure Studies, 29*, 435–455.

Mann, M., & Leahy, J. (2010). Social capital in an outdoor recreation context. *Environmental Management, 45*, 363–376.

Milner, M. (2011). *An experiment in leisure.* London, United Kingdom: Routledge.

Nicholson, G. (2008). *The lost art of walking: The history, science, philosophy, literature, theory and practice of pedestrianism.* New York, NY: Riverhead Books.

Terry, L. (2010). Interpersonal theories and applications to therapeutic recreation. *Therapeutic Recreation Journal, 44*, 121–137.

Sport and Physical Activity

Craig, P., & Beedie, P. (Eds.). (2012). *Sport sociology* (2nd ed.). Poole, England: Learning Matters.

Thorpe, H. (2011). *Snowboarding bodies in theory and practice.* London, United Kingdom: Palgrave Macmillan.

Tourism

Macannell, D. (2013). *The tourist: A new theory of the leisure class.* Berkeley: University of California Press.

McCabe, S., Minnaert, L., & Diekmann, A. (Eds.). (2012). *Social tourism in Europe: Theory and practice.* Bristol, United Kingdom: Channel View Publications.

Sedgley, D., Pritchard, A., & Morgan, N. (2011). Tourism and ageing: A transformative research agenda. *Annals of Tourism Research, 38*, 422–436.

Urry, J., & Larsen, J. (2011). *The tourist gaze* (3rd ed.). Thousand Oaks, CA: Pine Forge Press.

MIXED-METHODS APPROACHES

General

Barak, A. (Ed.). (2008). *Psychological aspects of cyberspace: Theory, research, applications.* Cambridge, United Kingdom: Cambridge University Press.

Burke, P. (Ed.). (2006). *Contemporary social psychological theories.* Menlo Park, CA: Stanford University Press.

Calhoun, C., Gerteis, J., Moody, J., Pfaff, S., & Virk, I. (Eds.). (2012). *Classical sociology theory* (3rd ed.). Malden, MA: Wiley-Blackwell.

Creswell, J., & Clark, V. (2011). *Designing and conducting mixed methods research* (2nd ed.). Thousand Oaks, CA: Sage.

Dillon, M. (2014). *Introduction to sociological theory: Theorists, concepts and their applicability to twenty-first century.* Malden, MA: Wiley-Blackwell.

Gratton, C., & Jones, I. (2010). *Research methods for sports studies* (2nd ed.). London, United Kingdom: Routledge.

Inglis, D., & Thorpe, C. (2012). *An invitation to social theory.* Cambridge, United Kingdom: Polity Press.

Johnson, A., McKenna, K., Postmes, T., & Reips, U. (2009). *Oxford handbook of internet psychology.* Oxford, United Kingdom: Oxford University Press.

Lemert, C. (Ed.). (2009). *Social theory: The multicultural and classic readings* (4th ed.). Boulder, CO: Westview Press.

Rieber, R. (Ed.). (2012). *Encyclopedia of the history of psychological theories.* New York, NY: Springer.

Ritzer, G., & Stepnisky, S. (2012). *Contemporary sociological theory and its classical roots: The basics* (4th ed.). New York, NY: McGraw-Hill.

Ritzer, G., & Stepnisky, S. (2013). *Sociological theory* (9th ed.). New York, NY: McGraw-Hill.

Slavin, R. (2014). *Educational psychology: Theory and practice* (10th ed.). Boston, MA: Allyn & Bacon.

Tashakkori, A., & Teddlie, C. (Eds.). (2010). *SAGE handbook of mixed methods in social and behavioral research* (2nd ed.). Thousand Oaks, CA: Sage.

Recreation and Leisure

Elkington, S., & Gammon, S. (Eds.). (2014). *Contemporary perspectives in leisure: Meanings, motives and lifelong learning.* London, United Kingdom: Routledge.

Peters, K., Elands, B., & Buijs, A. (2010). Social interactions in urban parks: Stimulating social cohesion? *Urban Forestry and Urban Greening, 9*, 93–100.

Pike, E., & Beames, S. (Eds.). (2013). *Outdoor adventure and social theory.* London, United Kingdom: Routledge.

Plummer, R. (2008). *Outdoor recreation: An introduction.* London, United Kingdom: Routledge.

Rojek, C. (2010). *Leisure studies* (*Vol. 1*). Thousand Oaks, CA: Sage.

Sport and Physical Activity

Anshel, M. (2012). *Sport psychology: From theory to practice* (5th ed.). San Francisco, CA: Pearson Education.

Beauchamp, M., & Eys, M. (Eds.). (2014). *Group dynamics in exercise and sport psychology* (2nd ed.). New York, NY: Routledge.

Farrow, D., Baker, J., & MacMahon, C. (Eds.). (2013). *Developing sport expertise: Researchers and coaches put theory into practice* (2nd ed.). London, United Kingdom: Routledge.

Giulianotti, R. (Ed.). (2011). *Sociology of sport (Vol. 1).* Thousand Oaks, CA: Sage.

Hylton, K. (Ed.). (2014). *Sport development: Policy, process, practice* (3rd ed.). London, United Kingdom: Routledge.

Jones, R., Potrac, P., Cushion, C., & Ronglan, L. (Eds.). (2011). *The sociology of sports coaching.* London, United Kingdom: Routledge.

Karageorghis, C., & Terry, P. (2011). *Inside sport psychology.* Champaign, IL: Human Kinetics.

Molnar, G., & Kelly, J. (2013). *Sport, exercise and social theory: An introduction.* London, United Kingdom: Routledge.

Shmanske, S., & Kahane, C. (Eds.). (2012). *The Oxford handbook of sports economics (Vols. 1–2).* Oxford, United Kingdom: Oxford University Press.

Smith, E. (Ed.). (2010). *Sociology of sport and social theory.* Champaign, IL: Human Kinetics.

Todd, D., Thatcher, J., & Rahman, R. (2010). *Sport psychology: Palgrave insights into psychology.* London, United Kingdom: Palgrave Macmillan.

Weinberg, R., & Gould, D. (2011). *Foundations of sport and exercise psychology* (5th ed.). Champaign, IL: Human Kinetics.

Tourism

Hall, C., & Page, S. (2014). *The geography of tourism and recreation: Environment, place and space* (4th ed.). London, United Kingdom: Routledge.

Prideaux, B., Moscardo, G., & Laws, E. (2006). *Managing tourism and hospitality services: Theory and international applications.* Oxford, United Kingdom: Oxford University Press.

Richards, G., & Munsters, W. (Eds.). (2012). *Cultural tourism research methods.* Cambridge, MA: CAB International.

Sharpley, R., Stone, P., & Stone, P. (Eds.). (2009). *The darker side of travel: The theory and practice of dark tourism.* Bristol, United Kingdom: Channel View Publications.

RESEARCH METHODS

General

Alvesson, M., & Skoldberg, K. (2009). *Reflexive methodology: New vistas for qualitative research.* Thousand Oaks, CA: Pine Forge Press.

Alvesson, M., & Skoldberg, K. (2010). *New vistas for qualitative research* (2nd ed.). Thousand Oaks, CA: Sage.

Boellstorff, T., Nardi, B., Pearce, C., & Taylor, T. (2012). *Ethnography and virtual worlds: A handbook of method.* Princeton, NJ: Princeton University Press.

Braun, V., & Clarke, V. (2013). *Successful qualitative research: A practical guide for beginners.* Thousand Oaks, CA: Sage.

Bryman, A. (2012). *Social research methods* (4th ed.). Oxford, United Kingdom: Oxford University Press.

Creswell, J. (2012). *Qualitative inquiry and research design: Choosing among five approaches* (3rd ed.). Thousand Oaks, CA: Sage.

Creswell, J. (2013). *Research design: Qualitative, quantitative, and mixed methods approaches* (4th ed.). Thousand Oaks, CA: Sage.

Edwards, A., & Skinner, J. (2009). *Qualitative research in sport management.* Oxford, United Kingdom: Butterworth-Heinemann.

Flick, U. (2014). *An introduction to qualitative research* (5th ed.). Thousand Oaks, CA: Sage.

Fowler, F. (2014). *Survey research methods* (5th ed.). Thousand Oaks, CA: Sage.

King, N., & Horrocks, L. (2010). *Interviews in qualitative research.* Thousand Oaks, CA: Sage.

Kozinets, R. (2009). *Netnography: Doing ethnographic research online.* Thousand Oaks, CA: Sage.

Kvale, S., & Brinkmann, S. (2009). *Interviews: Learning the craft of qualitative research interviewing* (2nd ed.). Thousand Oaks, CA: Sage.

Marshall, C., & Rossman, G. (2011). *Designing qualitative research* (5th ed.). Thousand Oaks, CA: Sage.

Merriam, S. (2009). *Qualitative research: A guide to design and implementation.* San Francisco, CA: Jossey-Bass.

O'Leary, Z. (2013). *The essential guide to doing your research project* (2nd ed.). Thousand Oaks, CA: Sage.

Osborne, J. (Ed.). (2008). *Best practices in quantitative methods.* Thousand Oaks, CA: Sage.

Rose, G. (2011). *Visual methodologies: An introduction to researching and visual materials* (3rd ed.). Thousand Oaks, CA: Sage.

Saldana, J. (2011). *Fundamentals of qualitative research.* Oxford, United Kingdom: Oxford University Press.

Schensul, J., & LeCompte, M. (2010). *Designing and conducting ethnographic research: An introduction.* Lanham, MD: AltaMira Press.

Schreier, M. (2012). *Qualitative content analysis.* Thousand Oaks, CA: Sage.

Silverman, D. (Ed.). (2010). *Qualitative research* (3rd ed.). Thousand Oaks, CA: Sage.

Silverman, D. (2013). *Doing qualitative research* (4th ed.). Thousand Oaks, CA: Sage.

Sparkes, A., & Smith, B. (2014). *Qualitative research methods in sport and exercise: From process to product.* London, United Kingdom: Routledge.

Teddlie, C., & Tashakkori, A. (2009). *Foundations of mixed methods research: Integrating quantitative and qualitative approaches in the social and behavior sciences.* Thousand Oaks, CA: Sage.

Thomas, G. (2011). *How to do your case study: A guide for students and researchers.* Thousand Oaks, CA: Sage.

Tracy, S. (2014). *Qualitative research methods: Collecting evidence, crafting analysis, communicating impact.* Malden, MA: Wiley-Blackwell.

Vogt, W. (Ed.). (2010). *Data collection (Vols. 1-4).* Thousand Oaks, CA: Pine Forge Press. *Note:* Includes topics such as surveys, interviews, ethnography, and archival and public sources of data.

Walliman, N. (2011). *Your research project: Designing and planning your work* (3rd ed.). Thousand Oaks, CA: Pine Forge Press.

Yin, R. (2009). *Case study research: Design and methods* (4th ed.). Thousand Oaks, CA: Sage.

Recreation and Leisure

Blackshaw, T., & Crawford, G. (2009). *The SAGE dictionary of leisure studies.* Thousand Oaks, CA: Sage.

Sport and Physical Activity

Atkinson, M. (2012). *Key concepts in sport and exercise research methods.* Thousand Oaks, CA: Sage. *Note:* Chapters cover critical theory, media analysis, and meta-analysis.

Kremer, J., Moran, A., Walker, G., & Craig, C. (2012). *Key concepts in sport psychology.* Thousand Oaks, CA: Sage.

Tourism

Botterill, D., & Platenkamp, V. (2012). *Key concepts in tourism research.* Thousand Oaks, CA: Sage.

Brotherton, B. (2008). *Researching hospitality and tourism.* Thousand Oaks, CA: Sage.

Dwyer, L., Gill, A., & Seetaram, N. (2012). *Handbook of research methods in tourism: Quantitative and qualitative approaches.* Northampton, MA: Edgar Elgar.

Hannanm, K., & Knox, D. (2010). *Understanding tourism: A critical introduction.* Thousand Oaks, CA: Sage.

Jamal, T., & Robinson, M. (Eds.). (2011). *The SAGE handbook of tourism studies.* Thousand Oaks, CA: Sage.

Morgan, M., Ritchie, J., & Lugosi, P. (Eds.). (2010). *The tourism and leisure experience: Consumer and managerial perspective.* Clevedon, United Kingdom: Channel View Publications.

Smith, M., MacLeod, N., & Robertson, M. (2010). *Key concepts in tourist studies.* Thousand Oaks, CA: Sage.

Wearing, S., Stevenson, D., & Young, D. (2010). *Tourist cultures: Identity, place and the traveler.* Thousand Oaks, CA: Sage.

APPENDIX 3: SECONDARY SOURCES FOR INSTRUMENTS

Aadahl, M., & Jorgensen, T. (2003). Validation of a new self-report instrument for measuring physical activity. *Medicine & Science in Sports & Exercise, 35*, 1196–1202.

Beardon, W., Netemeyer, R., & Haws, K. (2010). *Handbook of marketing scales: Multi-item measures for marketing and consumer behavior research* (3rd ed.). Thousand Oaks, CA: Sage.

Blaschko, T., & burlingame, j. (2009). *Assessment tools for recreational therapy and related fields* (4th ed.). Ravensdale, WA: Idyll Arbor.

Bolton, B. (2004). *Handbook of measurement and evaluation in rehabilitation* (3rd ed.). Austin, TX: Pro-Ed.

Bonjean, C., Hill, R., & McLemore, S. (2000). *Sociological measurement: An inventory of scales and measurement.* San Francisco, CA: Chandler.

Brannon, S., Fullerton, A., Arick, J., Robb, G., & Bender, M. (2003). *Including youth with disabilities in outdoor programs: Best practices, outcomes, and resources.* Champaign, IL: Sagamore. *Note:* Contains Outdoor Program Evaluation Battery.

Bruner, G. (2013). *Marketing scales handbook: The top 20 multi-item measures used in consumer research.* Fort Worth, TX: CreateSpace.

burlingame, j., & Blaschko, T. (2006). *Assessment tools for recreational therapy: Red book #1* (3rd ed.). Ravensdale, WA: Idyll Arbor.

Carlson, J., Geisinger, K., & Jonson, J. (2014). *The 19th mental measurements book.* Lincoln, NE: Buros Center for Testing.

Corcoran, K., & Fisher, J. (2013). *Measures for clinical practice: A sourcebook* (Vols. 1–2, 5th ed.). New York, NY: Oxford University Press.

DeVellis, R. (2011). *Scale development: Theory and applications* (3rd ed.). Thousand Oaks, CA: Sage.

Dwyer, L., Gill, A., & Seetaram, N. (2012). *Handbook of research methods in tourism: Quantitative and qualitative approaches.* Northhampton, MA: Edward Elgar.

Faulkner, S. (2009). *Poetry as method: Reporting research through verse.* Walnut Creek, CA: Left Coast Press.

Gitlin-Weiner, K., Sandgrund, A., & Schaefer, C. (Eds.). (2000). *Play diagnosis and assessment.* New York, NY: Wiley.

Goldman, B., & Mitchell, D. (Eds.). (2007). *Directory of unpublished experimental mental measures* (Vol. 9). Washington, DC: American Psychological Association.

Greenstein, L. (2012). *Assessing 21st century skills: A guide to evaluating mastery and authentic learning.* Thousand Oaks, CA: Corwin.

Groth-Marnat, G. (2003). *Handbook of psychological assessment* (4th ed.). New York, NY: Wiley.

Hemmasi, M., Strong, K., & Taylor, S. (2011). Measuring service quality for strategic planning and analysis in service firms. *Journal of Applied Business Research, 10*, 24–34.

Jamal, T., & Robinson, M. (Eds.). (2009). *The SAGE handbook of tourism studies.* Thousand Oaks, CA: Sage.

Kane, R., & Kane, R. (2000). *Assessing older persons: Measures, meaning, and practical applications.* New York, NY: Oxford University Press.

Kaplan, R., & Saccuzzo, D. (2013). *Psychological testing: Principles, applications, and issues* (8th ed.). Balmont, CA: Wadsworth Cengage Learning.

King, G., Law, M., King, S., Hurley, P., Hanna, S., Kertoy, M., & Rosenbaum, P. (2007). Measuring children's participation in recreation and leisure activities: Construct validation of the CAPE and PAC. *Child: Care, Health, and Development, 33*, 28–39.

Knowles, J., & Cole, A. (2008). *Handbook of the arts in qualitative research: Perspectives, methodologies, examples, and issues.* Thousand Oaks, CA: Sage.

Leavy, P. (2009). *Method meets art: Arts-based research practice.* New York, NY: The Guilford Press.

Manning, R., & Freimund, W. (2004). Use of visual research methods to measure standards of quality for parks and outdoor recreation. *Journal of Leisure Research, 36*, 557–579.

Maruish, M. (Ed.). (2004). *The use of psychological testing for treatment planning and outcomes assessment* (Vol. 3). Mahwah, NJ: Lawrence Erlbaum Associates.

McDowell, I. (2006). *Measuring health: A guide to rating scales and questionnaires* (3rd ed.). New York, NY: Oxford University Press.

Miller, C., & Salkind, N. (2002). *Handbook of research design and social measurement* (6th ed.). Thousand Oaks, CA: Sage.

Morrow, J., Jackson, A., Disch, J., & Mood, D. (2010). *Measurement and evaluation in human performance* (4th ed.). Champaign, IL: Human Kinetics.

Murphy, L., Geisinger, K., Carlson, J., & Spies, R. (2011). *Tests in print VIII.* Lincoln: University of Nebraska Press.

Ostrow, A. (Ed.). (2002). *Directory of psychological tests in the sport and exercise sciences* (2nd ed.). Morgantown, WV: Fitness Information Technology.

Petrick, J. (2002). Development of a multi-dimensional scale for measuring the perceived value of a service. *Journal of Leisure Research, 34*, 119–134.

Safrit, M., & Wood, T. (Eds.). (2001). *Introduction to measurement concepts in physical education and exercise science* (3rd ed.). Boston, MA: McGraw-Hill.

Stumbo, N. (2003). *Client outcomes in therapeutic recreation services.* State College, PA: Venture.

Thomas, J., Nelson, J., & Silverman, S. (Eds.). (2010). *Research methods in physical activity* (6th ed.). Champaign, IL: Human Kinetics.

Tritschler, K. (2000). *Barrow & McGee's practical measurement and assessment* (5th ed.). Philadelphia, PA: Lippincott Williams and Wilkins.

Webb, E., Campbell, D., Schwartz, R., & Sechrest, L. (2000). *Unobtrusive measures.* Thousand Oaks, CA: Sage.

Williams, D., & Vaske, J. (2003). The measurement of place attachment: Validity and generalizability of a psychometric approach. *Forest Science, 49*, 830–840.

World Health Organization. (2011). *International classification of functioning, disability and health.* Retrieved from www.who.int/classifications/icf/en/

APPENDIX 4: SUPPLEMENTAL READINGS ON DATA COLLECTION TOOLS

Altheide, D., & Schneider, D. (2013). *Qualitative media analysis* (2nd ed.). Los Angeles, CA: Sage.

Creswell, J. (2013). *Qualitative inquiry and research design* (3rd ed.). Thousand Oaks, CA: Sage.

DeWalt, K., & DeWalt, B. (2010). *Participant observation: A guide for fieldworkers* (2nd ed.). Walnut Creek, CA: Altamira Press.

Emerson, R., Fretz, R., & Shaw, L. (2011). *Writing ethnographic fieldnotes* (2nd ed.). Chicago, IL: University of Chicago Press.

Fink, A. (2013). *How to conduct surveys: A step-by-step guide* (5th ed.). Thousand Oaks, CA: Sage.

Krippendorff, K. (2012). *Content analysis: An introduction to its methodology.* Thousand Oaks, CA: Sage.

Krueger, R., & Casey, M. (2009). *Focus groups: A practical guide for applied research* (4th ed.). Thousand Oaks, CA: Sage.

Merriam, S. (2009). *Qualitative research: A guide to design and implementation.* San Francisco, CA: John Wiley & Sons.

Oster, G. (2004). *Using drawing assessment and therapy: A guide for mental health professionals* (2nd ed.). New York, NY: Brunner-Routledge.

Riffe, D., Lacy, S., & Fico, F. (2014). *Analyzing media messages: Using quantitative content analysis in research* (3rd ed.). New York, NY: Routledge.

Rubin, H., & Rubin, I. (2012). *Qualitative interviewing: The art of hearing data* (3rd ed.). Thousand Oaks, CA: Sage.

Saldana, J. (2013). *The coding manual for qualitative researchers* (2nd ed.). Thousand Oaks, CA: Sage.

Schreier, M. (2012). *Qualitative content analysis in practice.* Los Angeles, CA: Sage.

Seidman, I. (2013). *Interviewing as qualitative research: A guide for researchers in education and social sciences* (4th ed.). New York, NY: Teachers College Press.

Van Maanen, J. (2011). *Tales of the field: Writing ethnography* (2nd ed.). Chicago, IL: University of Chicago Press.

Yin, R. (2014). *Case study research: Design and methods* (5th ed.). Thousand Oaks, CA: Sage.

INDEX

A

B

C

D

E

F

G

H

I

J

K

L

M

N

O

P

Q

R

S

T

U

V

W

Y

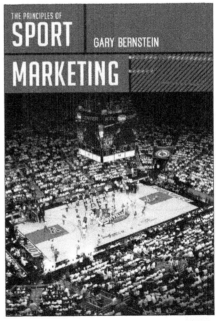

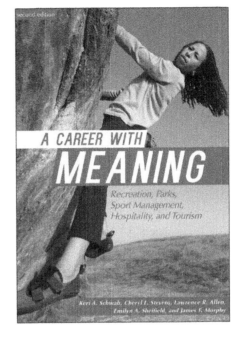